New Towns

Their Origins, Achievements and Progress

New Towns

Their Origins, Achievements and Progress

FREDERIC J. OSBORN

and

ARNOLD WHITTICK

introduction by

LEWIS MUMFORD

LEONARD HILL · LONDON
ROUTLEDGE & KEGAN PAUL · BOSTON

Published in Great Britain by
Leonard Hill
(a division of International Textbook Company Limited)
450 Edgware Road, London W2 1EG
a member of the Blackie Group

and in the U.S.A. by
Routledge & Kegan Paul of America Ltd.
9 Park Street, Boston, Mass 02108

First published 1963
Second Edition 1969
This edition 1977, being the third edition of *The New Towns: The Answer to Megalopolis*

British Library Cataloguing in Publication Data

Osborn, *Sir* Frederic James
  New towns. – 3rd ed.
  1. New towns – Great Britain – History
  I. Title   II. Whittick, Arnold
  309.2′62′0941   HT169.G7

ISBN 0–249–44140–3

Phototypeset in VIP Palatino by Western Printing Services Ltd, Bristol
Printed in Great Britain by Butler & Tanner Limited, Frome

Authors' Note

This book is concerned primarily with the foundation and development of British new towns inspired by the Garden City idea originated at the end of the 19th century. Since the Second World War many new towns, influenced by the British lead, have been founded in other countries and a list of some of these is given in Appendix 2.

In 1977 an International New Towns Association was established with substantial initial grants from the American, British and French governments and a permanent office at 7 Grafton Street, London W1. This will act as a world centre for the exchange of experience and information between bodies interested in new towns. Membership is open to governments, local authorities, private and public corporations, professional persons and other individuals.

Our purpose in this work is to give a broad account of the new towns of Great Britain, of the circumstances and lines of thought from which they arose, and an evaluation of their significance for the future of urban development. Short descriptions follow of the twenty-eight designated under the New Towns Acts up to 1977, with a selection of plans and photographs sufficient to indicate their form and character.

We make no claim to have produced either a full study of the individual towns or a definitive history of the movement that led to them; such a programme would be impossible in a single volume. Some of the towns have already found, and others will find, their own historians, for whom a wealth of data exists in the official reports of the development corporations, local records, newspaper files and the memories of inhabitants. And before long, we hope, the history of the new towns movement will be written by a scholar with time and endowments adequate to the task.

Our contribution is that of contemporary observers who have taken part in the advocacy of the new towns concept and have been caught up in the controversies that have raged around it—one of us for over half a century. That should absolve us from any charge of inhuman detachment. We are more likely to be accused of lack of objectivity by critics who have a bias differing from ours. Certainly we make value-judgements, as anyone must in discussing social affairs, but when we do so we try to be conscious of the fact. In taking sides on some contentious issues we make every effort to be fair to opposing views. Our promise, to ourselves and the reader, is 'to be candid but not impartial'.

Though the subject matter, arrangement and illustration of this book are our joint choice, its parts have been separately written. Chapters 1 to 13 are the work of F. J. Osborn, and Chapters 14 to 43 of Arnold Whittick. Each has considered comments by the other, but no complete assimilation of views has been attempted. The divergences we have discovered are few, and none is important, except perhaps in our aesthetic appraisals, and even there we find different theoretical reasons for liking the same things.

For this third edition the text has been further revised. A new chapter (13) records recent developments in British planning thought and practice and the world-wide rise of interest in the quality of the human environment. It discusses also the alarm expressed by the authorities of London and other big cities about the decline in their industries and employment, due, in fact, much more to spontaneous than planned dispersal, which remains necessary and needs to be accompanied by city renewal on standards of housing, work-places and open space comparable with those of the new towns.

As we remind the authorities in Chapter 13, central city renewal and planned dispersal are not antagonistic but complementary. Satisfactory renewal on human standards necessitates adequate space in relation to population. The continued congestion of inner-city areas makes this impossible without a further measure of dispersal.

In Part II chapters have been added on new towns started in Britain since 1968, and descriptions of the earlier towns extended to include later developments. The material available has been so voluminous that it has been necessary to make a restrictive selection. Preference has been given to the more outstanding, such as very original planning of residential areas and of town centres. The order of the sections is the same in each chapter: reasons for designation; description and assessment of the outline plan; progress of planning and building; descriptions of residential areas; neighbourhood and town centres; industrial zones and appraisal of social aspects.

New plans and photographs have been introduced, but again it has been necessary with so much material to be rigidly selective, and preference has been given to plans rather than to photographs. Many that appeared in the earlier editions have been omitted from this third edition and preference given to developments from 1969 to 1977.

The statistical tables have been updated to the end of 1976, and additions made to the bibliography of a few of the innumerable recent publications of informative value or controversial interest, but the list is inevitably selective.

The information we give is as up to date as possible, but since the book went to press in mid-1977 there have inevitably been changes of which we have been unable to take account.

July 1977

Frederic J. Osborn
Arnold Whittick

Acknowledgements

The authors express their thanks to many persons, authorities and organizations for generous assistance and information. It is not possible to name them all, but we are specially grateful to the new town development corporations and the Commission for the New Towns and their managers and other officers, all of whom have given us a great deal of help and cooperation without which this work would not have been possible.

For help with the selection and preparation of plans, illustrations and statistics thanks are due to the development corporations, the Commission for the new Towns, and the Town and Country Planning Association. Most of the photographs and plans have been supplied by the development corporations and the Commission for the New Towns and many were taken by Arnold Whittick. For Figures 15.8 and 16.4 acknowledgement is made to Aerofilms Limited. For the illustrations on the jacket our thanks are due to Milton Keynes Development Corporation. Finally a special word of thanks is due to David Hall and David Lock and other staff of the Town and Country Planning Association and to Wyndham Thomas, General Manager of Peterborough Development Corporation, for their valuable advice and support.

Contents

Introduction

The growth of cities during the last two centuries went on more rapidly than it had done since the twelfth or thirteenth century, when the historic towns of medieval Europe were taking form. But until the new towns came into existence hardly a single city was conceived as a whole, with public provision for all the physical and social components needed for a well-balanced environment. Meanwhile, in the very act of growth the older cities, which had once met many of the requirements for a high urban culture, became steadily more crowded, more insanitary, more confused, more inefficient, and more unlovable; indeed often positively repellent.

In retrospect, one can easily understand how this happened. For the most part the growth of towns was fostered by forces that had no concern for city life as such: the city was the creation of the land speculator, the estate agent, the banker, of the railroad, the tramway, and the motor car, of the factory system and of bureaucratic business organization. Even those who as architects, planners, or utopian dreamers conceived new forms for the city thought mainly in terms of new materials and mechanical processes: they dreamed of towns covered with steel and glass, of towns proliferating underground. Even now they dream of towns dominated by 60-storey office buildings and flats, stalking over the landscape in slabs and towers, or they imagine linear towns, continuous urban ribbons for rapid transportation, forming a new pattern in which motorized rapid locomotion would not so much serve the city as become its main reason for existence.

Today these dusty stereotypes still often dominate, openly or secretly, fresh proposals for modernizing the city; for it is perhaps natural for our contemporaries who are still old-fashioned enough to overvalue mechanical invention, mass production, and applied science to conceive the new forms of the city solely in terms favourable to the machine, and to an ever larger exploitation of the machine's capability. In the development of the actual town, fortunately, some attention to biological and social needs, some acknowledgement of public concern, played a part from the middle of the nineteenth century on: parks were laid out, minimal standards were fixed for street widths, for open spaces, for waste disposal and sanitation and eventually, particularly since 1920, for housing itself. But no new norms of standards were erected for the overgrown city itself; its overcrowding, its disorganization, its long dismal journeys to work, above all the continued extension of its area and the growth of its population were looked upon as marks of urban success.

Even those who sought to escape the liabilities of congestion and overgrowth, by moving to distant suburbs still surrounded by open country, were in the long run only bolstering the very process that caused them to move away. The notion that there were natural limits to urban growth, inherent in the very nature of city life, and that beyond these limits malformatiom, disorganization, and deterioration would result, was absent. Just as the smoking factory chimney was regarded, not as a biological menace, but as a happy symptom of prosperity, so the uncontrolled growth of the city was looked upon as a proof of its value for civilization. That the mechanical and financial agents of our civilization might be managed in the public interest, that it might be wiser to build new towns, of limited extent, than to overcrowd and over-extend old ones was not treated even as a theoretic possibility before the end of the nineteenth century.

Until Ebenezer Howard came forth with his proposals in *Tomorrow* no one had the audacity to conceive a new form of the city, which would utilize the facilities of modern technology without sacrificing the social advantages of the historic city. All the goods of city life were embedded, like scattered crystals, in an urban matrix that was steadily becoming more formless and more recalcitrant to human design. The shrewd eye of the novelist, Henry James, appraised this situation far better than most of his contemporaries when he wrote in his Journal, in 1881: 'It is difficult to speak adequately or justly of London. It is not a pleasant place; it is not agreeable or cheerful or easy, or exempt from reproach. . . . The fogs, the smoke, the dirt, the darkness, the wet, the distances, the ugliness, the brutal size of the place, the horrible numerosity of society, the manner in which this senseless bigness is fatal to amenity, to convenience, to conversation, to good manners—this and much more you may expatiate upon.'

Many sporadic attempts had been made to improve this or that aspect of the growing city: but no one had attempted to improve it as a whole, and above all, to alter the very method of its growth, so that it might form a new urban pattern, based on well-defined wholes. That contribution was the work of Ebenezer Howard; and its leading ideas were so simple, yet so contrary to the usual assumptions and procedures of our society even now, that their full implications have not been fully understood and assessed, much less carried out. Both here and in many other places, Sir Frederic Osborn has gone into the debt that the new towns movement, originally called the garden city movement, owes to the genius of Howard; and I do not purpose to trespass on the field the authors have so thoroughly covered in this book. What I would like to do is to emphasize certain more general features of Howard's conception, which have sometimes been overlaid, if not forgotten, in the natural preoccupation with more immediate tasks.

Howard's first great contribution to the new towns movement was his conception that the parts of a city were in organic relation to each other, and that there was accordingly a functional limit to the growth of any one element, as to the growth of the whole. Using London as the classic example of disorganized overgrowth, he sought to relieve the pressure of congestion by colonizing its excess of population in new centres, limited in area and population. This form of growth had been followed by the Greek cities, notably by Miletus, that thriving commercial centre, from the sixth to the fourth century B.C. While it lasted, it not merely prevented congestion, but maintained a balance between town and country that may have been one of the conditions that fostered the extraordinary creativity of Hellenic culture up to the Hellenistic age.

Aristotle's conception, that there was a right size for the city, big enough to encompass all its functions, but not too big to interfere with them, was re-stated in modern terms by Howard. He empirically fixed the right number as 30,000, with another 2,000 in the agricultural belt: the same number that Leonardo da Vinci had already hit upon in his proposals for breaking up the clotted disorder of sixteenth-century Milan and distributing its citizens into 10 cities of 30,000 each. There is nothing sacred about the number itself: Letchworth existed for a generation with less than half this number, and some of the new towns will eventually hold between 60 and 100 thousand people. But the principle of limits, both lower and upper, is vital: a town of less than 15,000 people lacks many of the facilities of a city, above all its variety of occupations; while a town above 100 thousand does not gain enough in variety to compensate for a loss in accessibility and in the vivid sense of a concrete, visible whole, where the activities of urban life come to a focus.

No one who has grasped Howard's realistic understanding of the function of the city could possibly confuse the garden city or the new town with a suburb. Unfortunately, this confusion is still rampant even in town planning circles, where it is nothing less than a mark of inadequate professional preparation. It is true that by an accident of history and taste, all the existing new towns in Britain, beginning with Letchworth Garden City, have been built on the open pattern, with ample private gardens: a pattern that was evolved during the nineteenth century for a much smaller community, the upper middle-class suburb, holding usually from 2 to 6 thousand people. Some of us believe that this change in scale, area, and numbers, without a co-ordinate change in design, has been one of the chief oversights of the new town planners, which needs serious reconsideration. But the suburb is, by definition, almost exclusively a residential area, occupied by people whose business takes them to a distant city. Such a specialized fragment must not be confused with a new town; for the latter must be big enough to accommodate all the daily functions of a city, industry, business, education, government, and promote all manner of other social activities.

Four fundamental principles governed Howard's concept of the new town: limitation of numbers and area, growth by colonization, variety and sufficiency of economic opportunities and social advantages, and control of the land in the public interest. Out of this a new kind of city would emerge, in a balanced, many-sided, inter-related, organic unit. Good urban design would relieve the citizen of the need for travelling long distances to obtain access either to economic opportunities or to the recreations and relaxations of the countryside. The identifying symbol of this new kind of city was not the private garden or the public park, but the permanent green belt that surrounded the urban area and defined its limits of settlement. The translation of these principles into the realities of the new towns movement is one of the most encouraging manifestations of our age. In a period when automatic and irrational forces are driving mankind close to its self-annihilation, the new towns are a victory for the rational, the human, the disciplined, and the purposeful: a proof that sound ideas are not condemned by massive human folly or institutional inertia to remain inoperative.

Howard's views, contrary to the usual impression, were not limited to decentralizing the over-congested facilities of London and building up small, self-sufficient towns: people who imagine he stopped there forget that Howard himself was a Londoner by birth, and too much of a Victorian to despise the special technological and cultural facilities of his age. On the contrary, Howard realized that there were advantages in large numbers that no small city of limited size could hope to achieve by itself. The chapter in which Howard considered these facts, that on 'Social Cities', is perhaps the most neglected chapter in his still neglected book; but it happens to suggest a further stage in the new towns movement—and in urban development everywhere—that should long ago have been claiming attention.

In discussing social cities, Howard recognized that no small city, no matter how well-balanced, could be wholly self-contained: there were many specialized functions, easily performed in a big city because of its immense reservoir of varied occupations, its diversity of human interests, and the accumulation of capital resources that no smaller unit could encompass. So, too, there were many activities, such as those of a symphony orchestra or a technical college, that required a pooling of population if they were to be maintained. If he had analysed the problem a little further, he would have reached the conclusion, I have no doubt, that the full social heritage of modern culture could no longer be encompassed by a single unit, with the limited numbers of the historic city: it required, rather, a much larger population, inter-communicating and accessible; and this need for a larger container was responsible for the continued growth of metropolitan areas, despite all the patent disadvantages traceable to the fact that the change of scale and of technical facilities for transportation and communication had not been accompanied by a change in the pattern of growth and political organization.

Howard did not suppose that a single garden city, or even a scattering of such cities, would be able to handle this problem. He called, rather, for the creation of a regional unit that would bring into a single organized system at least 10 cities with a total population of 300,000, bound together by a rapid transportation system that would unify the cities and make them operate, for any purpose that involved all of them, as a single unit. Howard did not elaborate this idea, either in *Garden Cities of Tomorrow* or his later writings; for he was too preoccupied with the problem of getting the first two experimental cities into existence to go on to the next step of creating the larger unit in which they could function, with an even higher degree of autonomy, as no longer dependent upon the facilities uniquely offered by a London. But Howard had in fact outlined a new type of municipality, called later by Clarence Stein and his colleagues the Regional City: a city whose articulated spatial organization, whose direct union of urban and rural facilities, whose social and economic balance would be the rational equivalent of the sprawl and clutter and needless confusion of the existing metropolitan areas and conurbations.

Howard called this new grouping of cities, each limited in size, the town-cluster; and he foresaw that once his model new town was built and validated by experience, the further organization of such cities should lead to the creation of a new municipal structure, whose parts, though spread over an area larger than the County of London, might with our modern facilities bring together a million people, much more closely than they were at the beginning of the nineteenth century, when that number was confined to the City of London and its contiguous boroughs. As with Howard's notion of the proper norm of population for a single city, there is nothing inviolable about his estimate of the number of cities or the total population needed to perform the functions of a metropolis. The proper size for 'town clusters' or 'regional cities' must be established by practical experiment. But even if sufficient land were available to establish green belts around every borough, I would suspect that the seven million inhabitants of Greater London are too large to function as a single municipality; and that a considerably smaller group, of the order of a million, would be adequate to reproduce, and often improve, every metropolitan function.

The creation of a new kind of metropolitan area, based on a union of greenbelt towns, and the establishment of a system of local government, federal in structure but thoroughly integrated, is perhaps one of the principal tasks opened·up by the very success of the new towns movement to date. But these are not matters in which political action alone is called for. The wider success of the new towns movement, as an alternative to functionless congestion and formless sprawl, depends upon the readiness of all the other institutions of a going city to re-establish themselves on this new principle, of controlled and normalized growth. Each growing institution, be it a factory, a hospital, a library, a university, or a department store, must handle the problems of quantitative growth, and seek to establish a dynamic equilibrium and a controlled method of growth. Only on such terms will it further its own development and harmonize it with the larger regional pattern necessary for the orderly growth of urban communities. What I would term 'Howard's principle'—the principle of controlled growth by limitation, colonization, redistribution, and integration within a larger spatial and functional unit—applies to every human institution.

The successful founding of Letchworth Garden City was the first step in establishing a better system of urban growth; and the success of its younger sister, Welwyn Garden City, showed that the new stock was viable and hardy, capable of wider reproduction. With the institution of the new towns policy on a large scale the way has been opened to carry Howard's bold vision to a fuller, if not its final, consummation, by a systematic application of his principles to all the components of the city, and by the deliberate union of many related cities into a new kind of urban unit. With the kind of integrity and stability that begins at the level of the neighbourhood unit, and with the variety and diversity that furthers interplay of larger forces, often arising outside the local area and transcending its limitations, the new urban constellation will have all the dynamism of a great metropolis. Toward this further development the new towns movement has already gone far; but even greater possibilities now loom before it.

LEWIS MUMFORD

Part One

1 New Towns in Modern Times

'I am of opinion that if, instead of one, we had twelve great cities, so many centres of men, riches and power would be more advantageous than one. For this vast city(1.1) is like the head of a rickety child.'

—Fletcher of Saltoun (1703)

All towns, of course, were once 'new'. Of many the origin pre-dates recorded or hearsay history. And not a few that appeared at various times, adventitiously or by deliberate foundation, carry to this day the labels of their former novelty; such place-names as Newton, Neustadt, Villeneuve, Novgorod, Novigrad, are found everywhere, in all sorts of combinations, and are now so sedately elderly and so woven into their backcloth that the significance of their names passes unnoticed. Much interesting history has been written of them, but they are not the subject here.

The 'new towns' with which this book is concerned are those that in the twentieth century have been purposefully founded, planned and developed, first in Great Britain and subsequently in other countries, as an alternative and corrective to city overgrowth and congestion on the one hand and unduly scattered human settlement on the other hand.

The original (and still most weighty) reason for building new towns, in the minds of their advocates and pioneering experimenters, was the necessity of reducing the concentration of people and workplaces in very large towns, which otherwise cannot be relieved of congestion, disorder and squalor and rebuilt on a fully healthy, socially satisfactory or efficient pattern. A complementary motive was that new towns based on modern industry, in agricultural regions declining in population owing to mechanization and other technical changes in farming, would bring fresh vitality and better services into such regions. This double intention should be kept in mind. Too often the new towns are discussed as if they were meant only to be ends in themselves, almost irrelevant to the redemption or renewal of the existing cities, and ruthlessly indifferent to rural interests. They were never thus dissociated in the minds of their proponents.

During the 80 years since the movement was initiated further, related but slightly different, motives have emerged: the desire to gather into more satisfactory communities people in scattered and ill-equipped coal-mining or small-industry villages, or to knit into better shape and endow with fuller facilities poorly-planned urban developments. Thus while the new towns were first conceived as instruments for decentralization or dispersal from towns demonstrably too large and crowded, they can also function as means of producing a reasonable degree of concentration for quasi-urban units demonstrably too small.

In the first British new towns (the two garden cities) a significant departure was also made in the conception of town and country planning—that of continuous intelligent control of development. Very many towns have been founded with premeditation and laid out with good original plans: for example, by military rulers like Alexander of Macedon, his successor Seleucus Nicator, St Louis of France and Edward I of England, by the Roman Empire and other colonizing nations, by great landowners, and by industrial companies(1.2). But seldom, if ever, has future development been considered, or provision made for maintaining the intentions of the original plans, ensuring their adaptation to economic and social changes, or controlling or limiting their growth in extent or density. Here and there the patterns of their original plans can be discerned in geometrical arrangements of existing streets, but in the main they have been overlaid by later developments of a more chaotic character, as for instance in Edward I's Kingston upon Hull, and often the systematic layout is only discoverable by the labours of archaeologists.

What further distinguishes today's new towns is that they attempt to apply *scale* to urban development: to define limits of town size and population; to create and retain a measure of relationship between the functional zones within towns and between town and country; to provide some degree of balance of local occupations and residence; and so to arrange and maintain the plan that services and facilities in frequent use are easily accessible to the inhabitants. In the absence of a fairly definite idea of the intended ultimate size of a town it is clearly impossible to plan it in advance. What acreage, for example, should be reserved for the shopping and civic centre? How wide should the main roads be? A planner who has to assume that his town may never cease to grow cannot arrive at even approximate formulations for such dimensions: the best he can do is to think of a number and, to be on the safe side, double or treble it. The present state of towns carefully laid out in ancient and medieval times shows what happens when the scale of a plan is overwhelmed by unanticipated growth. No matter how orderly the original design, in the absence of continuing control of development, confusion of uses must arise. No matter how generous the space allowed in the layout, central constriction inevitably emerges if expansion is unlimited. (It may be doubted whether modern city planning has yet fully absorbed this historical lesson.)

The Garden City Concept

The modern new towns movement was started by (Sir) Ebenezer Howard (1850–1928), who published his book *To-morrow: A Peaceful Path to Real Reform*(1.3) in 1898 and formed the Garden City Association(1.4) in 1899. His 'unique combination of proposals' was really new: a cardinal invention in the sphere of urban technology.

There were, as Lewis Mumford says in his introduction, foreshadowings of elements of Howard's invention in ancient and renaissance writings. Most of these however were statements of ideal or theoretical principles rather than prescriptions for immediate action in town founding or social control. Perhaps the closest approach to the pattern of town and country that Howard had in mind is the *Utopia* of Sir Thomas More (1516) in which a very attractive ideal of towns of limited size and open internal layout, spaced out at considered distances over the countryside, is presented. The *Utopia* is important as evidence of the character and arrangement of towns that seemed desirable to a man of culture, aware of the functional role of towns in his time while fully sympathetic to common human aspirations. More's capital city, Amaurote, with its terrace houses and long gardens, its grouping of social buildings, and its contact with the countryside, is much more like a modern new town than today's London or New York or Paris. He was also more definite about the provision for population growth by colonization or new foundations rather than by simple expansions. But it cannot be seen that this ideal much influenced urban development in his time or later. Nor did he foresee the complexity of future civilization that would necessitate or result from much larger regional groupings of population.

With the Industrial Revolution and its enormous disruption of the older order, the flow of population to towns, and the phenomena of great individual wealth alongside mass poverty and instability of employment, there were among movements of compunction and reform many projects for the creation of small organized communities in which powered factory industry (then emerging) might be combined with agriculture, together with social and educational facilities selected to foster the kinds of human behaviour that the promoters thought would make for happiness—or for goodness. These, unlike the formulations of Plato, Aristotle, More and others, were proposals for group or individual action. As a rule they had little permanent practical outcome within the countries of their origin, though they influenced colonial developments in the New World. The most remembered projects were those of Robert Owen (1771–1858) and his French contemporary F. M. C. Fourier (1772–1837) and their followers, by whom several experiments were made in England and America. These did not survive as closed or self-contained economic communities, probably because they were too rigid and paternalistic in conception and did not allow for individual enterprise. The only organic industrial–agricultural units of this 'communal' type that lasted for more than a few years were those founded overseas by religious bodies like the Jesuits and the Rappites, which had a quasi-monastic discipline under a hierarchy and a common creed conditioning social conduct.

These projects and experiments, and the prescriptions for systematic town-founding in overseas colonies made by Granville Sharp (1794), Edward Gibbon Wakefield (1829) and others, are of interest to students of town planning history and of modern social reform movements. So also are the proposals for home colonization, usually seeking to resettle poverty-stricken or unemployed workers in industrial-agricultural villages or small town communities as a corrective to the crowded and debased conditions in the industrial cities, put forward by John Bellers (1696), Count Rumford (Sir Benjamin Thomson) in Germany (*c.* 1790), James Silk Buckingham in England (1848) and many later writers.

Howard was influenced by Wakefield and Buckingham, though not as much, we think, as the generous acknowledgements in his book imply. A much stronger influence on his thought was the preoccupation of reformers of his time with the 'land question'—the worry about the private and unearned appropriation of increments of site values associated with the growth of the urban population and its economic activities. This issue has since receded in political prominence, owing to the change in the ratio of income from land to that from other forms of property, and to the evolution of graduated taxation of income from all sources. But it is by no means an extinct issue. It arises in a new shape through the conspicuous effects of public planning control in increasing values on some parcels of land while limiting it on others. We cannot discuss here the general problem of compensation and betterment(1.5). The increase of land value arising from urban development is however an important element in the finance of new towns, and we shall return to the subject.

Validity of Howard's Thesis

Howard's criticism of large towns, with London in the forefront of his mind, remains valid today, though many things have changed; in Britain some of the most dramatic squalor has been removed, but further growth has aggravated other serious evils, such as high-density tenement housing and the long and burdensome journey to work and its corollary traffic congestion. Howard's suggested town plan, which was diagrammatic, and his financial and administrative proposals, are naturally out of date. But his book is worth reading today for its easy and charming style, for its blending of benevolent idealism and basic commonsense, and for its importance in urban history. Unlike all the earlier utopian or closed-community schemes, Howard's conception of the planned and organized new town is fully adapted to the modern industrial system and the way of life the system requires and makes possible. It is briefly yet fairly completely summed up in the definition adopted in 1919 by the Garden Cities and Town Planning Association:

'A Garden City is a Town designed for healthy living and industry; of a size that makes possible a full measure of social life but not larger; surrounded by a rural belt; the whole of the land being in public ownership or held in trust for the community.'

A key factor in this definition is that the limitation of ultimate size is to be guaranteed by the reservation of a belt of rural (and mainly agricultural) land. When Howard wrote, the prospect of continued growth was accepted uncritically—by most people as inevitable, by many as desirable. Municipal pride in sheer numbers, competitive claims to be the largest town in the world or in the state, or the most rapidly growing town in some frame of reference, were regarded as natural and worthy. Londoners for long boasted of their numerical pre-eminence, and New Yorkers have gloated over taking from London this unhappy leadership.

The attitude is by no means dead, but it has lost assurance. We begin to see that it is about as ridiculous as it would be for a lady to claim the title of 'Mrs World' because she had the biggest waist measurement, or to brag that her 'vital statistics' were advancing faster than those of any other lady in her lunch club. There is a widespread popular interest in statistical peaks of any kind. The Heaviest Man on Earth may derive a speck of consolation from his supremacy; but he deserves commiseration rather than congratulation. And so do the swollen cities, when the consequences of their magnitude are understood.

Once it is realized that a town can be too big, the question arises as to what is the best or optimum size, taking into account the requirements of modern industry and commerce, residential standards, access between home and work, and facilities for recreation, entertainment and culture. There is no universal answer. But it is a question that we are beginning to see must be continuously studied in the light of current economic and social needs and local geographical considerations.

In a country like Great Britain where there are already many urban agglomerations inconveniently large, and many kinds of industry and business that can be economically run in local establishments employing 2 or 3000 persons, and many that employ smaller numbers, it is practicable to have a considerable number of towns of the order of 30 000 to 60 000. Towns of that size can be planned to have a predominance of family houses, with decent gardens, within walking or cycling distance of their civic centres and places of work as well as of the country. If they are much larger, densities or distances have to be increased, which may be a serious offset to any capacity to sustain larger industrial establishments or a more complete range of social and cultural institutions. The problem of the optimum size of towns is that of finding the best balance between these conflicting factors: we discuss this more fully in Chapters 8 and 10.

When the principle of limitation of the size of individual towns and of the preservation of green belts (or background of accessible open country) is accepted, for all time ahead changes in the amount of population and employment in each town are likely to become a subject of public and social governance. Difficult economic and social assessments and forecasts, and difficult measures of control or influence, are involved in the process, but they will have to be made. The new towns movement, and its component element, the movement for green belts and countryside preservation, have not produced a commonly-agreed formula for the best size in towns, nor is it conceivable that there will ever be a single universal formula, but they have placed the question of size once and for all on the political table.

Howard's own formula—a population of 32 000 in the initial garden city and its rural belt and 58 000 in a later town to be central to an associated group of towns—was a very useful opening draft. He was well aware that for some of the purposes of regional economic and cultural exchange the interconnected group would be necessary. Indeed, neither he nor the experienced business men who joined him in building the first two new towns conceived them as closed economies isolated from national or international trade and industry. In this respect they made a decisive departure from the typical 'Utopian' conception. Howard has been criticized for being too specific, but whatever doubts there may be about his actual figures, his definiteness was strategically shrewd. He was proposing a practical demonstration of a new product—what a designer of a mechanical appliance would call a 'bread-board model' or prototype. If he had been vague in his specification he could never have got together a company of men capable of action. The remarkable thing is that Howard's 'shot' at a convenient order of magnitude proved to be such a good approximation. Nearly 50 years later the New Towns (Reith) Committee after exhaustive consultation and deliberation, suggested as an 'optimum normal range' 30 000 to 50 000 people in the built-up area—almost exactly Howard's proposed size.

Planning and Economic Enterprise

In the beginning Howard's thought was to find some way of combining the idea of communities on the human scale with a local and exemplary solution of the land-value problem. But his real inspiration was to add to this combination two further elements. He saw that the collective or quasi-public ownership of a whole town site did not necessitate the collective conduct of industry and business; these could be left to private enterprise or voluntary co-operation provided that the increment of value was secured for the community by the retention of the freehold of the whole estate and the grant of sites on long leases. And he saw also that unified ownership made possible the prevention of development in the agricultural belt, and good planning and maintenance of good planning in the town area, including the measured allocation of zones for the various functions. For the use of the leasehold system as a means of the continuing control of land-use there were of course precedents in the practice of aristocratic landowners. But it had never before been applied to a whole town or extended to the reservation of a green belt to preclude its merging into a larger urban mass.

Much of the modern criticism of Howard and his associates arises from a misunderstanding of their basic assumptions. They were not 'Utopians' but practical men well aware of economic and social realities in a time of rapid scientific, mechanical and cultural change, which on the whole, as typical Victorians and Edwardians, they saw as 'progress'. But they were not philosophers of logical analysis. They would have chuckled at Bertrand Russell's statement: 'Hence it follows (though the proof is long) that "4" means the same as "2+2".' It seemed to them obvious that 2+2 = 4. They assumed that in new towns the industries and businesses would be part of the larger economy, drawing supplies and ideas from, and distributing products to, the world at large, and in a ceaseless state of flux. They never thought of planning from above either the individual enterprises or their infinite economic inter-relationships. They confined their attention to setting certain geographical limits to their grouping. Modern town and country planners proceed on the same principle. What they do to produce or maintain certain standards of convenience and pleasurability, may well have effects on economic (and cultural) developments. But they are not planning these developments; they are merely conditioning them spatially, because it has become demonstrably necessary to do so.

References and Notes

1.1   The population of London in 1703 was about 500 000.

1.2   See BERESFORD, M., *New Towns of the Middle Ages*, London, 1967.

1.3   Revised and reissued 1902 as *Garden Cities of Tomorrow*. Latest edition, with introductions by F. J. Osborn and Lewis Mumford, 1965.

1.4   The Garden Cities and Town Planning Association is now known as the Town and Country Planning Association.

1.5   The classic study of this problem is the (Uthwatt) *Report of the Expert Committee on Compensation and Betterment*, HMSO, London, 1942.

2 The Functions and Failings of Towns

'Among the noble cities of the world that Fame celebrates, the City of London of the Kingdom of the English, is the one seat that pours out its fame more widely, sends to farther lands its wealth and trade, lifts its head higher than the rest. It is happy in the healthiness of its air, in the Christian religion, in the strength of its defences, the nature of its site, the honour of its citizens, the modesty of its matrons; pleasant in sports; fruitful of noble men. Let us look into these things separately.'

—William Fitzstephen: *Life of Thomas Becket* (c. 1180)

Towns occupy so dominating a position in the human consciousness that it is very difficult to get them into a clear mental picture. For most people they have been the background of life from the earliest years, no more to be questioned than the fundamental facts of nature. The way of life they impose, with its infinitely complex blend of blessings and pains, is taken for granted. And if blessings weaken and pains increase, a normal commonsense person is not disposed to run his head against seemingly immovable masses of brick or concrete. Thus it is not surprising that among townspeople an attitude prevails of acceptance of towns more or less as they are: according to temperament a grumbling or cheerful acceptance, approaching complacency on the part of those not frequently brought up against the worst urban failings and those having alternative domiciles to which they can at will retreat.

Even the spectacular physical changes that occur in towns tend to be looked on as dictated by mysterious and implacable laws of evolution rather than as resulting from actions governed by human wills. The new phenomena are observed with dislike, pleasure, or a merely curious passivity. They are rarely thought of as controllable or requiring control. Impulses to complain of town management, and to demand that something be done, do occasionally arise concerning municipal services and movable or superficial features. But the fabric of towns—their buildings, arrangement, and street pattern—is commonly taken as somehow fate-given.

Acceptance and complacency have never been universal, however. Along with incalculably vast contributions to the power and wealth of society, towns, especially the larger and more successful, have brought upon mankind so much injury and distress in the last few thousand years that in almost every period there have been thinkers and moral leaders who have doubted whether towns could ever provide a good way of life for our species. Many philosophers have seriously urged mankind to return to the farm and village and to build civilization on another pattern altogether. There has often been a measure of popular response to this idea: 'Back to the Land' movements have frequently recurred among urban populations.

The majority, however, and most leaders of thought, have believed in towns and regarded their defects as temporary and remediable, and have maintained hope that through the further working-out of beneficent evolution, or by human effort based on experience, they could in time become wholly satisfactory. This hope has been repeatedly disappointed. Man being an optimistic as well as obstinate animal, it persists. Yet in our own age of unprecedented material advances, when we see almost every kind of manufactured article or organized service improving in acceptability, and in a great number of cases in real quality and efficiency, towns stand out as a strange exception.

Let us try to place this extraordinary paradox in perspective. Towns are the most powerful instruments, as well as the most conspicuous results, of man's constructive and organizing impulses and talents. If they cannot justly claim the title of 'cradles of civilization' (since that may belong to the homesteads of the earliest settled agriculturists, or even to the shifting camps of hunting or pastoral nomads), they have certainly been civilization's main nursery. Towns(2.1), in the commonly understood sense of lasting assemblages of buildings and occupants grouped fairly near to each other, have taken the major part in the activity and specialization of function that have led to the immense and still evolving complex of goods, services and gratifications characteristic of civilized societies.

Secular Urban Evils

Thus the authors of this book dutifully align themselves with the believers in towns. (Not to do so might seem as silly as to speak disrespectfully of the Equator.) But we cannot join in the enthusiasm unreservedly. Of all the expedients of man in pursuit of satisfactions and power over things, towns have been the least amenable to considered and intelligent human organization. Much of their past record has been indescribably shocking. Time and again they have produced social evils on a colossal scale: they have killed, disabled and destroyed the happiness of millions of their inhabitants; and even in their latest phases many of them are largely thwarting the possible advances in productive efficiency and culture offered by the diversification of skills and inter-relation of effort of numbers of people.

The larger and more populous the towns, and therefore on the face of things the greater their potency for beneficial interchange, the more devastating have been their periodic disasters and chronic social defects: recurrent plagues and pestilences, famines, catastrophic fires; and persistent patches of decay, poverty and human degradation, where masses of people have often been hidden away from the compunction and charity of more fortunate fellow citizens. These deplorable happenings and features have over the centuries been as characteristic of towns (especially large towns) as the splendid churches and palaces, noble avenues and parks, pleasant residential districts, and spacious suburbs, in which they rightly take pride. It is true that only a considerable concourse of people within range of communication could have made possible the great manufacturing establishments, commercial offices and exchanges, shopping centres, theatres, museums, art galleries, universities, libraries and other institutions; and that these are the seeds and fertilizers, as well as the fruits, of a high civilization. But a guide-book view of the rich accumulation of monuments and facilities, though all too common, is not enough. We have to be conscious of the violently contrasting aspects of towns if we are to rid them of their horrors while cherishing their benefits and beauties. And we have to consider whether, in view of the recent evolution of means of communication, physical and mental, close spatial grouping of large numbers is any longer necessary or conducive to the further advance of civilization and culture.

Civilization and Intercommunication

We cannot in this book discuss at length the role of towns and cities in the evolution of civilization. The variety of the towns that have appeared and disappeared in history and exist today is so vast as to outsoar the most encyclopaedic knowledge; and their individual complexity, especially that of the larger cities and conurbations, is almost beyond the grip of analysis. Moreover, the activities and relationships of groups of persons within any town are in a perpetual state of flux and change, of growth and decline. Even the modern planning surveys, which give a more complete picture of the physical structure and features of towns than has ever been available before, cannot be wholly up to date; they have to be considerably revised every few years.

Nevertheless we think one or two useful generalizations can be made with some assurance. Civilization and culture, at any stage, depend upon the interchange of products, services and thoughts between numbers of people of different or specialized occupations, talents or skills. Some of these occupations or skills (in manufacture, for example) require the assembly, in place and time, of persons working together in substantial numbers. Others are pursued by small groups, by families, or by single individuals. For the interchange of the results communication is necessary. And since nearness facilitates communication, the development of associated activity, specialization and interchange is (certainly has been historically) bound up with the development of fairly close spatial groupings of numbers of people—that is, of towns.

A second simple generalization is that as the variety of the occupations and skills interchanged increases, or the groups for particular products or services grow in size, the number of persons taking part in the interchange grows larger, and in so far as the convenience of proximity continues, the size of the whole assemblage also increases. Thus there is (or has been historically) a close connection between the development of civilization and culture and the growth of towns and cities.

This analysis is as old as Plato's dialogues, and we would apologize for its seeming obviousness or naivety were it not for the more mystical or romantic impulses to which the growth of towns is by some urban enthusiasts ascribed. That some people are drawn to towns because of a delight in the kind of physical surroundings or the social or cultural milieu they provide is not in question; nor that familiar scenes or habitude may induce love or affection for a particular town. But the emotional or cultural attraction to towns is not the fundamental *raison d'être* of their origin or growth. It is a resultant rather than a major cause of the complex of interchanges that numbers and wealth have made possible. Historically, indeed, the 'charm of the city' and much of its culture may fairly be considered a by-product of its essential function. The secular exodus of the most prosperous citizens to outlying suburbs and country villas supports this view.

Since the advance of civilization has been bound up with the increasing diversity of interchange, so long as spatial proximity is necessary for certain elements of this interchange the growth of towns is easily explicable. In modern times in industrialized countries, the main reason for that growth has been the expansion of manufacture and of industry and commercial and service businesses, many of which are not tied to sources of raw materials or power. There is a strong natural tendency for new industry to settle where population already is(2.2).

It is a common experience in countries with expanding populations that the larger cities grow faster than the medium-sized cities, and these grow faster than the small towns, many of which, based on agricultural economies, even decline in population.

The reasons for this phenomenon are not far to seek. In a free enterprise society the movements of population are simply the sum of the movements of individuals or groups associated in business activity. Other things being equal, a manufacturing or commercial entrepreneur will seek a location as near as possible either to the largest consumers' market for his goods or services or to a pool of employable workers; and both these advantages coincide in the largest local aggregations. The national network of railways and roads, which both as cause and effect focus on the larger centres, are also obvious conveniences to firms for the assembly of materials and the regional, national or wider distribution of their products—at any rate up to a point that we discuss below. To the workers, of all grades, the larger city offers many and diverse opportunities of employment, and over long periods during which a fairly high percentage of unemployment has been endemic this has been a vital factor.

Thus what we, as critics of the process of city expansion, consider a vicious circle —perhaps we should say a vicious spiral—of reciprocal attractions has come into being; business enterprises going where they can find many customers and workers, and workers flocking to the same places in the hope of jobs. The process is plain and simple. No subtle analysis of the magnetic attraction of the town, of its architectural 'urbanity' or grandeur or its higher cultural advantages, are necessary to explain it. The developmental spiral continues in operation even when the cultural by-products diminish in appeal. It is only checked when economic and physical disadvantages appear, such as high rents and travel costs or traffic congestion; or when, at long last, governmental restraints on city growth are applied.

The Consequences of Town Overgrowth

Study of any large town shows that as it grows the pressure on its internal space, especially near its centre, intensifies. Values of land rise because more persons seek access to the central area to work in it and to do business with it. Thus internal journeys multiply with size. In time this necessitates additional or wider streets and extra space for vehicles to load, unload, wait and park, the space for which has to be deducted from the building area and further intensifies the use of what remains. The dwellings, for reasons of economy in time, exertion or journey cost, come to be grouped as near to the centres of employment as the tolerated standards of residential space permit.

In a large town, as population and employment grow, business establishments in the centre (industry, commerce, retail trade, entertainment, etc.) naturally expand, and some of this expansion encroaches on the adjoining residential areas, thus forcing the inhabitants to crowd more closely together or to travel to and from a greater distance. Usually both effects occur. The families who can best afford it move to the town's outskirts, where they can obtain newer houses, cleaner air, more garden space and (for a time) access to the open country. Those who have to be, for occupational reasons, close to the centre, become packed tightly together; backyards are built over, former middle-class houses are sub-divided into apartments or one-room dwellings, and thus slums and overcrowding emerge, and often reach such a degree of squalor as to call for compulsory closing and clearance in the interest of public health.

It is a queer paradox that in highly prosperous cities old and dilapidated dwellings occupied by low-income workers are seldom commercially rebuilt for the same class. This is due partly to the fact that in conditions of population pressure such dwellings are still lettable—at rents low per unit but high per square foot of floor-space—and partly to the expectation or hope of owners that their sites can be disposed of at business land values.

Towns being infinitely complex, any brief sketch of the factors in and mechanism of their growth must be over-simplified. But governmental policies for dealing with urban problems have been delayed and misdirected by the lack of general understanding of the inter-connection between population increase, central intensification and outward spread. The suburban expansion of a town, the increase of the bulk and height of business buildings in its centre, the massing of persons in dwellings and of dwellings on sites, the lengthening of daily journeys, the congestion of rail and road traffic, and the shortage of recreation space, are the results, and at the same time the condition, of the one process—the growth of the population of the town. It is possible by local expedients—street widenings, subways, freeways, overpasses, one-way routing, robot signals, multi-storey car parks, and other costly devices—to carry some increase of traffic; but so long as a town remains a centralized unit and its population grows there will be greater pressure on space for housing and other land uses and more and longer personal journeys.

Traffic congestion is an affliction in itself, but in its acute forms it is a symptom of the deeper disease of urban hypertrophy, which has other and socially even more injurious effects, though they do not stir nearly as much political and press excitement.

The Environment for Living

The worst effects of town overgrowth are on the everyday human environment—in the home, the school, the park and playing-field, the journey to work, and the workplace itself.

We take Greater London as our main example, because as the largest city in Britain it exhibits the consequences of overgrowth observable in all large towns at an advanced stage, which in 1951 contained about 8.2 million but declined to about 7.4 million by 1971, due partly to a further exodus to the Metropolitan region part of which was due to dispersal to new and expanded towns.

First, housing. In former and far poorer times, including the Victorian and Edwardian periods, London, though it was grossly overcrowded and had vast areas of squalor, was almost wholly a town of what had originally been single-family houses with gardens or at least back-yards. In size, construction and fittings many of these dwellings were of low standard; but the prevailing type, often in a debased form derived from the country cottage, was the type that the great majority of British people, including Londoners, preferred then, and prefer today. The prevalence, almost universality, of the single-family house was a source of national pride.

When the 'housing of the working classes' became a public responsibility after the 1914–18 war, the Ministry in charge of it in an advisory manual to local authorities (1919) said:

'In spite of the rapid development of large towns and urban centres, the self-contained cottage has continued in this country to be the customary means of housing to a much greater extent than characterizes other countries which have undergone similar development, and this comparative freedom from the tenement dwelling has been regarded with envy by those countries and cities which have had the misfortune to adopt the tenement system to any great extent. This advantage should be maintained, and this will be the normal policy of the Ministry.'

Even where rehousing has to be carried out on the cleared area, and the cost of the land may have been considerable, it will be desirable to adopt the cottage dwelling. The fact that the adoption of tenements would allow a larger number of tenements to be placed on the site and reduce to some extent the cost of land per dwelling will generally not outweigh the disadvantages of the congestion of buildings on the site.

The Ministry have no wish to adopt any pedantic attitude on the question. But it must be borne in mind that such dwellings are opposed to the habits and traditions of our people, that they are condemned by the best housing experience, and that, as already stated, where tenements have generally prevailed, opinion is steadily becoming opposed to them.

The Fall in Housing Standards

No housing expert, no elected authority, no person in touch with popular feeling, would have questioned this at the time. The watchword for post-war reconstruction was Lloyd-George's 'A Land fit for Heroes to Live in'. And in the early stages of the great inter-war housing effort, the local authorities of large towns, including the London County Council, were loyal to the popular demand. But though their provision of new dwellings was numerically great, their effort to maintain the house-and-garden standard was defeated after a few years by the lack of space.

In the ten years 1920–29 the LCC built about 35 000 dwellings; of these 93.75% were houses with gardens (USA, yards) and 6.25% in blocks of flats (USA, apartments). From 1921 to 1937 the proportion in flats steadily grew; new houses fell to 35.2% while flats rose to 64.8%. In Liverpool no flats were built between 1919 and 1931, but the percentage rose by 1936 to 66%. Birmingham began its first 'experimental' block of flats in 1938.

After the second World War there was another revival of housing idealism, and in the country as a whole an admirable start was again made, which included higher standards of floor space and design and considerable improvements in fittings. But again, largely owing to the pressure on space (though there were other factors to which we shall refer later) key standards have deteriorated. It is a strange anomaly that a downward trend in standards for new housing should have occurred during a marked rise in the real income of the classes of persons housed.

In England and Wales the percentages of houses and flats built by public authorities in the first 7 years after the second war (1945–51) were: houses 87.9%, flats 12.1%; and almost all the flats were in large towns. In 1966 the percentages were: houses 47%, flats 53%. In 1975 the numbers of flats and houses were almost equal. This shows a change in trend since the early post-war years. The overall percentages of houses and flats from 1945 to 1975 are: houses 65%, flats 35%.

There is no evidence of any weakening in the British preference for the self-contained house over the flat. Many surveys and opinion polls have tested this issue. Enquiries among men and women serving in the 1939–45 war showed a 95 to 98%

preference for houses(2.3). Very few surveys have shown a preference of less than 90%.

Probably in the secret places of his heart the British family man cherishes the thought of living in a detached house or bungalow. His more realistic hope is that some day he may own a semi-detached house as a good second-best. Short of this he feels that he and his family could be reasonably happy in a terrace house. If it were truly impracticable to cater for these aspirations, we should have to dismiss them as pathetic. Advocates of new towns hold, and have demonstrated, that it is entirely practicable.

Unfortunately, the idealism of ministers and city administrators, unlike that of homeseekers able to exercise personal choice, has not withstood the impact of the insensate trend to urban compression. The resolve to maintain the self-contained family dwelling (shown in the manual of 1919 quoted above) gives place to a phase of temporary acceptance of tenements as a regretted *pis aller*, with which we have to sympathize. The third phase is the claim that multi-storey mass housing is a great aesthetic and social advance. It would seem that inordinately high density, as Pope said of Vice,

> . . . is a monster of so frightful mien,
> As to be hated, needs but to be seen,
> Yet seen too oft, familiar with her face,
> We first endure, then pity, then embrace.

We may add that we think that as many as 10% of households in an urban population, and in large cities (where the composition of households is exceptional) 15 or even 20%, would be content to live in and pay economic rents for good flats. But we cannot believe that a much greater percentage would willingly accept this way of living as a permanency. The policies of many big cities in Europe and the USA imply a belief that flat-life will be accepted as a norm by millions of their inhabitants. Yet it is the spontaneous outward flow of millions of the more prosperous families to suburban situations where the single-family home is obtainable that is the prime cause of the 'exploding metropolis'. Obviously a part of the answer to this problem is the renewal of the 'downtown' areas of cities in forms that will make them again acceptable places to live in; and this renewal is urgently necessary. But it cannot be done without substantial reductions of density and displacements of population—the part of the answer that is the subject of this book.

It should not be supposed that the preference for houses on the ground is a British peculiarity. Research study in France in the sixties showed that 85% of flat-dwellers regard a 'pavillon' with private garden space as their ideal, even though many of them saw no hope of attaining it(2.4). Our own enquiries convince us that the same is true of the great majority in all European countries, in North America, in Australia and in Japan.

The Journey to Work

The wastage of time and earnings in long daily journeys to and from work is a grievous deduction from the benefits of economic advance. By inventive and managerial skills, complemented by the pressure of organized labour, hours of work are shortened and real earnings increased. Concurrently many of the hours thus saved, and much of the income thus gained, are dissipated in lengthening journeys and rising fares.

Within the scope of his personal choice the average city-dweller is confronted with a dilemma. Either he and his family must live in close quarters and often graceless surroundings near the centre with its varied amusements and cultural facilities, or they must forgo these advantages, and the working members must suffer a loss of 10, 15 or even 20 hours a week of leisure time, in order to have a single-family home in a pleasant suburb. By the latter choice the city-dweller cuts himself off from the distinctive down-town advantages, except as things for infrequent resort. The former choice is made by the genuinely urban-minded minority, by those closely tied to down-town occupations, and by the mass of the poor and passive. But the proportion who will sacrifice time and money for the suburban solution is increasing with the advance in real earnings and aspirations.

That in a complex economy some people must travel longish distances to work need not be contested. Members of the same family may be employed in different places, and there is an inertia or 'anchorage' both of accustomed homes and existing work-places that makes it impossible for every person to be provided with employment on his doorstep(2.5). What is needless and fantastic is that hundreds of thousands should be housed in one situation and travel *en masse* to a remote situation to work.

Shortage of Play-space

The insufficiency of space for outdoor activities in great cities is notorious. There are few exceptions to the rule that the larger a town is the less recreation space it provides per head of population. To engage in outdoor games and sports is a passionate desire of many people; and the National Playing Fields Association, after careful and repeated study, considers that the provision for such recreation should not fall below 6 acres (2.4 ha) a 1000 persons, with at least another 1 acre (0.4 ha) a 1000 for other kinds of parks or open spaces. This is in fact now officially accepted in Britain as the standard to aim at in planning policy.

Some of Britain's moderate-sized towns reach or even excel this open space standard, with some having as much as 30 acres (12 ha) per 1000 population. In addition the people of the smaller towns have easier access to the surrounding open country. Many of the large industrial towns, however, are very much below standard with as little as 2 acres (0.75 ha) per 1000 population.

Constriction of Space for Schools

Educationists in Britain attach great importance to facilities for games, outdoor activities; and carefully-worked-out areas were adopted in 1945 for sites for new schools. Examples of the Ministry of Education's national standards were: for primary schools of 400 pupils, 6 acres (2.4 ha); for secondary schools of 450, 17 acres (6.8 ha). But owing to the space shortage in large towns these standards have had to be severely cut. In London the permitted areas for new schools are far smaller, and there are many existing schools without anything like this area.

Other Disadvantages of Size

It has long been realized that the death and sickness rates in crowded parts of cities exceed those in open suburbs and rural areas. In Britain and other advanced states the mortality differentials have been greatly reduced with the progress of sanitation; but it is a matter of observation that surviving people, especially children, are healthier in open than in crowded surroundings. The birth-rate (and with it the survival rate) remains higher in the country and the suburbs than in city centres.

On the aesthetic attraction and repulsion of large cities tastes differ so widely that it is strange that some writers seem to assume there is unanimity. (We deal later with 'amenity' as a subjective phenomenon.) Obviously as many types of pleasingness are to be found in towns as in persons. Some types of urban beauty are associated with compactness or enclosure, others with spaciousness; some derive from grandeur, others from simplicity; some depend on architectural harmony, others on diversity. Harmony can shade over into monotony, variety into chaos. The functional adequacy of a town does not in the least necessitate intense compression; the degree of closeness it has to have depends on the means of communication available and, as we have said, on the size of its population. Some spacious and lavishly planted towns are functionally efficient and sociable. Some very compact towns are charming in appearance and perhaps sociable, but far from functionally efficient; successful traders leave their rooms over shops in narrow streets for villas in the outskirts, and the upper floors of the shops become stock-rooms or dwellings for the under-privileged.

That the consciousness of having a share in the life of a place, of 'belonging', is diminished in a large city as compared with a small town or village is generally agreed, and considered by many observers to lower the quality of life. Pockets where there is a strong feeling of neighbourliness do exist in crowded cities, in slums as well as in pleasant quarters. They are however exceptional. The residential mobility characteristic of a prospering and changing society tends everywhere to reduce the 'community' sense, and there are many people who doubt if the loss matters; some free spirits even welcome it. But man is a social as well as a family animal, needing both the support and the criticism of neighbours, and the atomization and isolation of very large cities must be accounted one of their drawbacks.

References and Notes

2.1 The word 'town', as used in this book, includes 'city', except where the context implies a differentiation between a town of moderate population and one of very large population. In the USA the generic word is more usually 'city'; the words 'town' and 'township' are used to include a minor local government having only one or more quite small villages or even a wholly scattered population.

2.2 TOWNROE, PETER, *Planning Industrial Location*, London, 1976.

2.3 See TAYLOR, N., *The Village in the City*, London, 1973.

2.4 *Grand Ensembles*: (Centre de Recherche d'Urbanisme, Paris, 1966), *Les Pavillonaires*, 3 Vols. Paris, 1966.

2.5 THOMAS, R., *Journey to Work*, P.E.P., London, 1968.

3 The Experimental New Towns

'Behold now, this city is near to flee unto, and it is a little one: O let me escape thither, (is it not a little one?) and my soul shall live.'

—Genesis xix, 20 (Lot's appeal)

Howard's book of 1898 had as a practical outcome, surprisingly soon, the foundation in 1903–4 of the First Garden City, at Letchworth, Hertfordshire, 35 miles (56 km) north of London. The book had aroused much interest and press comment, the reactions ranging from wild enthusiasm to lofty scorn, scepticism prevailing. Even the news-sheet of the constructively revolutionary Fabian Society giggled at the naivety of a man who wanted new towns built in a country urbanized by the Romans 2000 years earlier.

The disbelievers would certainly not have been converted by the handwritten minutes (still preserved) of the tiny group of men who, with Howard, founded in 1899 the Garden City Association (now the Town and Country Planning Association). These men were neither well-known nor wealthy, but they were united in a conviction that what was generally regarded as a simple-minded idealistic scheme was practicable and could be carried out by private effort. They fixed the subscription to the Association at 1s. a year, held meetings under the auspices of all sorts of bodies all over the country at which Howard and other members lectured, and quickly recruited an appreciable following—though neither then nor at any time since did the Association become anything like a mass movement.

Through the energy of this small but devoted membership, sufficient interest was aroused to encourage the Association to hold, in 1901–2, two large conferences, at which the attendance included delegates of hundreds of local authorities. It is of historic significance that these conferences were held at Bournville in the West Midlands, and Port Sunlight on Merseyside. These new-type industrial villages, which pioneered the planned and planted layout of good family homes with gardens in close relationship to healthy and efficient modern factories, were then arousing hopeful interest, and were valuable signposts to the more comprehensive form of urban development envisaged by Howard and his followers. The choice of venue is also a reminder of the important part played by a few imaginative industrialists, among them George Cadbury and William Henry Lever (later Lord Leverhulme), the founders of these two villages, in promoting the garden city idea as a practical proposition.

Like the writings of many other far-sighted reformers, Howard's *To-morrow*, sound and practical as it was in its analysis and proposals, was tinged by a rosy hope of a better society, and a belief in the basic goodness of mankind, confession of which is distasteful to statesmen, business-men and many responsible persons, who fear that any suspicion that they entertain such sentiments may injure their reputation for toughness in this competitive world. And because the book was written in a simple and persuasive style, without the definitions, qualifications, and reservations customary in technical and scientific works, most professors and students of economics and political science disregarded it as just another idealistic Utopia. Even, however, if its proposals had been expressed in cold-blooded terms by an industrialist respected for his success or by a sociologist of academic repute, instead of by an unknown shorthand writer, the notion of building a completely new town by private enterprise in modern England would have seemed to most realistic people in 1898–1903 a romantic, fantastic dream.

For indeed the initiation of the Letchworth experiment was an almost incredibly daring venture. There was no precedent for it apart from a series of dismal failures in small-scale community founding. It could never have happened but for Howard's intense conviction and extraordinary determination, and the effect that his sincerity and talent for persuasion had on men of standing and experience. It could never have happened if Howard had not had the good fortune to enlist the support of a particular group, capable and courageous in business and conscious of social responsibility.

Programme of the Letchworth Company

In the very effective propaganda of the Garden City Association, and in its promotion of the Letchworth scheme, a leading part was taken by a Chancery barrister, (Sir) Ralph Neville, QC (later Mr Justice Neville), who became chairman of the Association and also of the company it formed in 1903 to build the town—First Garden City Limited. Neville, and the industrialists (mostly like himself Liberals in politics) who joined him and Howard on the board of this company, along with its first manager (Dr) Thomas Adams, extracted the essence from Howard's programme and propounded it in terms acceptable to possible investors without denuding it of its public-spirited aims. The original prospectus of First Garden City Ltd indeed, should be regarded as the definitive statement of the actual aims of the garden city movement rather than Howard's book, which was of immense inspirational importance, but was never treated as a Bible or an Athanasian Creed. The main objects of the company were stated as follows:

'To develop an estate of about 3800 acres, between Hitchin and Baldock, on the lines suggested by Mr Ebenezer Howard in his book *Garden Cities of To-morrow*, with any necessary modifications. It is believed the result will be not only to promote a great social improvement, but to provide for those who can afford to wait an investment that will prove a sound one.

The *root* idea of Mr Howard's book is to deal at once with the two vital questions of *overcrowding* in our towns and the *depopulation* of our rural districts, and to thereby reduce the congestion of population in the great towns, or at least arrest its progress.

The difficulty of dealing with the housing question in our overcrowded industrial centres becomes increasingly apparent with every fresh attempt at amendment. The expense is enormous, while improvement in any one direction frequently increases the evil in another. The only satisfactory way out of the difficulty is to start afresh and establish a new town to which those manufacturers whose businesses admit of such removal may go.'

There followed provisions for the 5% limit on dividends and for the application of any surplus increments of profits and land values for the benefit of the inhabitants of the town. The prospectus then alluded to the planning possibilities inherent in the scheme:

'The control of the site of a town from its commencement obviously offers an unparalleled opportunity for the provision of open spaces and allotments while land is cheap, and also for the supply of power, light and water on advantageous terms.'

It added:

'Sound physical condition is surely the foundation of all human development, and the directors submit to the public a scheme for securing it in a particular instance which they believe contains all the elements of success, and which, if carried to a successful issue, will lead to that redistribution of the people upon the land, in which alone, as they believe, is to be found a solution of the problem—How to maintain and increase industrial efficiency without impairing the national physique.'

We do not in this book describe in detail the development of Letchworth, well covered in other books(3.1). Certain aspects of it, however, relevant to the general subject of new towns, call for mention.

Though the essential principles of the first garden city were the same as those of the later new towns, the circumstances of its foundation were very different. The idea had a popular appeal, but as a private enterprise venture it was regarded by most hard-headed business-men as speculative in the highest degree. The odds were heavily loaded against an investor in the company's shares: on the one hand a serious risk of the loss of his capital, and on the other a prospect, after some years, of an annual return of 5% at the maximum. (The interest on Consols at the time was $2\frac{1}{2}$%.) The company's prospectus was perfectly frank about the proposition. None but persons willing to accept the chance of loss and the limit of gain in the hope of social benefit could be expected to invest on such terms. And in the event the company, whose authorized capital was £300 000, went to allotment on £40 000, subscribed in the main by its own public-spirited directors. At the end of the first year (1904) the total share capital subscribed was only £100 000. The company had already committed itself to the purchase of the site for £160 000 (£42 an acre [£105 per ha]), so that it had at the very outset to raise much money by means of mortgages and debentures, on which interest had to be paid before revenues could be created.

The company being thus under-capitalized from the start, development was slow. The site was wholly rural: roads, sewers, water works, gas and electricity works, and all the supply mains for these services, had to be provided *de novo*. The company had no money to finance houses, factories or shops: it had to induce industrialists, retailers and residents to come in and build their own premises on leasehold sites—without any real assurance that a town would in fact be successfully created, or, even if it were, how long it would take. In the circumstances it is amazing that lessees willing to venture their own capital in building on the estate could be attracted at all.

Anticipating a later stage in our story, we may compare the situation of First Garden City Ltd with that of a new town development corporation under the New Towns Act of 1946, with its governmental sponsorship, its millions of Treasury money available for estate works, housing and other buildings, and the precedents of Letchworth and Welwyn to show that new towns could be created and become satisfactory places to live and work in. At Harlow New Town, for example, in the first 10 years a capital of £35 million was invested by the development corporation (nearly £20 million in housing), 40 000 people had been housed, and 75 factory firms had been attracted. The Letchworth Company in its first 10 years had expended £400 000 and drawn in a population of 8000. In 1903–13 there was hardly any public housing at Letchworth; the workers' dwellings had to be provided in the main by public utility societies, for which the risk-taking capital was subscribed by philanthropic investors with interest limited to 4% per annum. Some houses were built by owner-occupiers, but Letchworth was too far from London or any other centre to attract many commuters. In the main the early residents had to find employment locally in the industries and businesses courageous enough to choose a place of such speculative promise. Among the early settlers there was also a sprinkling of families of independent means and of artists and other self-employed persons. These groups, with the few shop-keepers and builders, and the staff and workers of the estate company, made up the pioneer population.

Social Atmosphere of Letchworth

What is remarkable is the social and mental energy this small community in its earliest days developed. There was no theatre or cinema or public house; no church or chapel building; only two or three small and weak retail shops (the future civic centre was an empty windblown prairie); radio and television were undreamed of; the one public meeting place (apart from a county school) was a small hall (paid for by private subscriptions). Equipped playing fields came very slowly. Yet an extremely vigorous and enjoyable community life sprang into being from very early days. The absence of commercial entertainment threw people back on their own resources, and there was no lack of spontaneous leadership in running a wide variety of societies and clubs—for music, drama, politics, religion, sports, rambling, dancing, gardening, natural history, arts and crafts, and serious study. Meetings and performances took place in any makeshift building available, such as an old farm barn, and in the living-rooms of private houses. Everybody knew everybody, and met nearly everybody in some activity or other. Class and income barriers were at a minimum. A friendly democratic atmosphere and a prevailing tolerance of different views and degrees of formality in dress and manners therefore developed, and in later days, when social stratification and more standardized conventions began to invade, older residents looked back on the pioneering period as a golden age.

For people migrating from inner London to the first garden city more than half a century ago the change of physical and social environment was revolutionary to a degree unimaginable by those who settle in a new town today. To a typical city dweller who had not tried it, life in Letchworth must have seemed denuded of all amenities except fresh air, horizon light, and a cottage with a garden—seductive things to him, but surely insufficient compensation for the loss of the bright lights, the swarming vitality, and the kaleidoscopic attractions and opportunities of the metropolis. And such a man (we describe an actual experience), when to take up a job he moved to the garden city, was at first badly shaken to discover that the anonymity to which he had been accustomed had disappeared. He found himself in a society in which as a personality he was known in the round. Where he lived, where he worked, his political or religious views, his family connections, and (except within his private dwelling) his leisure pursuits, were more or less common knowledge. In the big cities only fragmented aspects of his goings-on were known, to different sets of associates; as a complete being he didn't exist for anybody but himself. This had given him a sense of complete personal freedom, which he had come to value highly. But now he became a personality in a society; for the freedom of a disregarded cipher he had to accept the responsibility of a citizen; what he did or said had influence in proportion to his mental or moral repute; for the first time in his life, he 'counted'—a very uncomfortable feeling for a native Londoner.

Of course a person of negative or easily intimidable character is nearly as much of a cipher in a small new community as in a big old one. There were plenty of this usefully accommodating sort in Letchworth. But the proportion of colourful personalities was above the national average. This added to the interest of life. As in the later new towns, the great majority of settlers in Letchworth went there just to get a job with the special advantage of a nice home nearby. But an appreciable minority were attracted by the principles that were to be tested—the pre-planning, the quasi-public ownership of the site with its prospect of a community share in rising land values, the return to a closer relationship of urban and rural activities, and so on. Among these was a sprinkling of people holding views then somewhat ahead of the time, though since generally or very widely accepted: on votes for women, democratic socialism, and vegetarianism, for instance. But there were a few who even in the present less conventional (or is it just differently conventional?) period would be looked on as 'cranks'.

No new town today, wherever situated, can be so insulated from commercial and professional entertainment or the prevailing mass-culture as Letchworth at first was. As we shall see, the development of many forms of communication have altered the position entirely. There may be losses as well as gains in the change. A 'do-it-yourself' community, with its amateur activities in the arts and sport, adds to the pleasures of spectatorship those of creation and participation. These enhance the understanding and appreciation of professional work if that is also accessible.

The early life of Letchworth was for many, probably most, of its citizens, immensely stimulating and enjoyable, and elicited much originality and in some aspects quite high standards. Later phases do not, we think, support a claim for Letchworth to any permanent superiority or distinction as a community. No town or nation anywhere has yet found the formula for high cultural standards both in participation and reception—amateur and professional. Good health and general popular contentment with surroundings and ways of life, however, are much, and these the first garden city can certainly claim. It is the first predominantly manufacturing and all-classes town of which this can be said.

Letchworth—the Plan

The town plan, for which Raymond Unwin and his partner, Barry Parker, were responsible, is simple and straightforward, and of the informal type with which their names are identified—a radical departure from the rigid or geometrical forms of most earlier plans. Fundamentally the main road scheme is radial, with intersecting roads at such distances as permit 'super-blocks' of fair size having a wide diversity of layout in closes and culs-de-sac, while at the same time avoiding sharp corners or inconvenient shapes of single plots. Cross-roads were not deliberately avoided, as they are in later practice, by staggered entries of minor into major roads; but corners were all kept open so that danger at junctions was minimized. Carriageways were at first rather narrow,

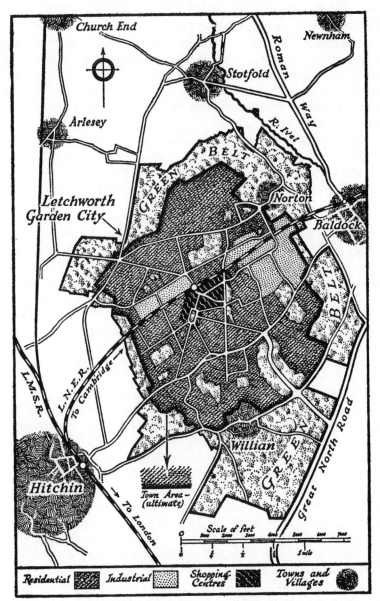

Figure 3.1 Plan of Letchworth.
(*Reproduced from* Garden Cities of Tomorrow, *Faber & Faber*)

for reasons of economy in capital cost, and often were unkerbed or had temporary kerbs of wood. Footpaths were similarly narrow, and sometimes omitted. But provision was wisely made for later widening by a general use of grass verges; no through road was less than 40 feet (12 m) wide between the frontages of plots. Thus, though Letchworth was built 'on a shoestring', its planning looked ahead, and later widenings of carriageways and footpaths have not necessitated cutting into the building plots.

Great attention was paid to landscaping and planting. Flowering and foliage trees and shrubs were introduced in an unprecedented variety of species and arrangements, and all over the town there are decorative green spaces of an infinite variety of shape and size. The positioning of roads and buildings was influenced by an almost religious care for the retention of existing fine trees or attractive spinneys. Only in the ceremonial centres of great capitals and the parades of holiday resorts had planting and landscaping on this lavish scale and with this diversity been practised before. It was a new thing for an industrial town. And the example has had enormous influence all over the world.

Letchworth, originating in a reaction against the crowded conditions in great cities, set definite limits on housing density. Zones of different maximum densities were allocated, as in many municipal ordinances under the control of new development then emerging in a number of European states. There is an element of prestige, of class distinction—one might say, of snobbery—in the prescription of zones of progressively lower density for fewer people as you go higher up the income scale; and the Letchworth company, which planned for a 'balanced' population, could no more disregard this than any other developer. But Raymond Unwin was particularly concerned to set a standard of maximum density for the lowest-income families. He was of course aware of the maximum of 7 houses an acre (17.5 per ha) (including service roads) prevailing in the first parts of Bournville. This must have seemed to him needlessly low. Under his advice Letchworth adopted the maximum of 10 houses an acre (25 per ha) including access roads, and 12 an acre (30 per ha) without roads; but this included the smaller public greens in the local layout, and a modicum of space behind the house gardens for allotments and children's playgrounds. Unwin was an extremely able and resourceful planner, who knew exactly how far the wastage of road space and frontage could be reduced by ingenious layout; but he was (unlike some later planners) equally clear about the importance of certain key dimensions inside and outside dwellings, and extremely sensitive to popular likings. After careful study and experiment he decided on a series of desirable minimum component dimensions: a light angle of 15°, just permitting sun to reach living rooms in mid-winter (in the latitude of S.E. England) over the tops of 2-storey terrace houses; a distance between rows of windows of 70 feet (23 m); a set-back of house windows of 20 or 25 feet (6.5 or 8 m) from public roads or footways; and so on. All such standards are in a sense arbitrary; why 70 feet (23 m) for example? Why not 69 feet (22.5 m)?(3.2) Therefore all can cheerfully be cut, and if the cuts are made gradually they may be little noticed. The Letchworth density maximum has been assailed; and under the changed conditions of today it can be slightly revised upward. But it is no argument against it that it was 'arbitrary', or based on a series of definite minimum component dimensions.

The standards of floor-space in the Letchworth regulations were, by those of our more affluent age, low. To keep rents within the capacity of unskilled workers—about 5*s*. a week—cottages had to be built for as little as £150 each. In the smallest 3-bedroom terrace houses, baths had to be placed in sculleries, room-heating appliances made to serve for cooking and hot water, and other fittings were few. But they were skilfully designed, and were a great advance on the by-law houses in the old cities.

Architectural Character of Letchworth

Architecturally the early Letchworth housing schemes and individual houses attained, and exhibit today, considerable charm. Their planning, grouping, landscaping and

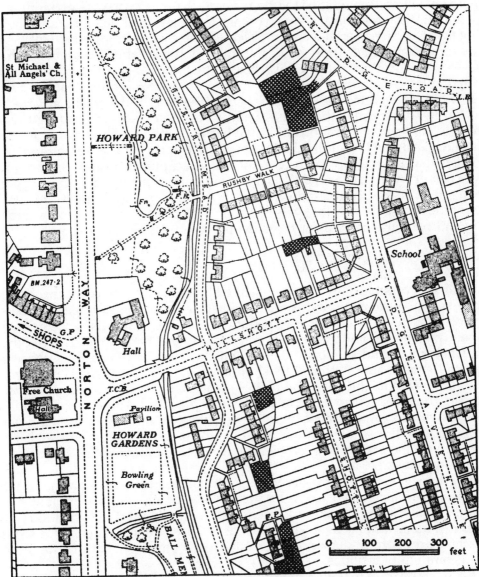

*Figure 3.2 Part of one of the earliest residential sections of
First Garden City (Letchworth), about 1904–6.*

external design have had vast influence on development throughout the world. And it was through the same school of planners' admirable later work at Hampstead Garden Suburb, where Unwin and Parker had for a longer period full control, that the types of building and layout evolved at Letchworth became so widely emulated—unfortunately mostly in 'garden suburbs' rather than in garden cities or new towns.

The architecture of Letchworth in some of its later stages cannot be said to be equally distinguished. Much of it is quietly and modestly good, but in general it is not much superior in aesthetic quality to the mass of new development in England of its time.

The company felt itself compelled for many years, in order to dispose of building sites, to give way to the prevailing tastes of owner-occupiers and builders, and the often clashing tastes of clients' architects. In its leases there were strong covenants subjecting exterior design to the approval of the town architect, and it is arguable that the control was weaker than it need have been; but that there were real difficulties in applying it must be admitted. Moreover it should not be forgotten that the aesthetic canons of trained architects are not identical with those of the public at large.

Letchworth discovered that the majority of home-seekers are not acutely architecture-conscious or desirous of visual harmony; their taste is rather for variety and as much as possible of individuality, especially in dwellings. Much more important to them than external appearance is internal accommodation and comfort, privacy from the passer-by in the road, and adequacy in garden plots. But there is a popular appreciation of trees, shrubs, flowers and grass, and near-unanimity in aesthetic judgment thereon. Letchworth, by its attention to domestic convenience and to landscaping and planting, catered for these deep human desires.

Success of the Town

Industrially and commercially it can be claimed that Letchworth has been a conspicuous success. The firms who first went there had outstanding courage in choosing a location with such uncertain prospects. But the town now has many factories, prosperous and productive, and a balance of employment that has enabled it to weather the dislocations of war and economic depressions, as well as to adapt its economy to changes in demand and methods. Its shopping arrangements exhibit no novelty of layout or organization; the now-fashionable pedestrian precinct would not have been accepted by shopkeepers when the town plan was prepared. The main centre fulfils its function adequately, and because there are only very small sub-centres it is a place of resort for almost the whole population. Like every centre, old or new, it is now embarrassed by the car-parking problem, but not to the degree that is clogging the hearts of large cities.

Letchworth will seem to the observer to have become, after more than half a century, a pleasant and well-planned town, bright and free of squalor, but no longer revolutionary. Possibly it has lost some of its early social sparkle and self-conscious enthusiasm. But inquiry among its citizens discloses no evidence of serious discontent, though there are sporadic demands, as in almost any other town or city, for improvements in community facilities.

The estate company pursued a policy of restricting itself to the functions of a good ground-landlord and leaving most of the building and social development to other agencies and the residents themselves. No one could fairly accuse it of an excess of paternalism or 'do-goodism'. Its achievement was notable. It created a town as healthy as any in the world, a well-serviced town in which every family can live in a house with a good garden within easy distance of work, the centre and open country. It demonstrated that a town based on modern industry can be economically and socially viable, even if built well out of the immediate sphere of influence of a metropolis. And it proved that a new town with a green belt can bring stimulus, alternative employment, and many services to the surrounding villages and countryside without prejudice to agriculture.

Letchworth in July 1976 had a population of about 32 700, 11 000 houses, 173 manufacturing establishments, 272 shops, 22 schools, 20 churches and chapels and many public buildings and meeting places. Its rateable value was about £6 500 000 and its commercial rates 87.6p in the £ and domestic rates 69.1p in the £.

The overall density of the present town is about 13.9 persons an acre (34 per ha). Open space (public and private but excluding the golf course) is about 6 acres (2.4 ha) a 1000 population.

The Second Experiment

We shall discuss later why Howard's first garden city, though it was regarded by town planners in Britain and abroad with admiration verging on awe, and Howard himself was internationally honoured as the symbol of a new urban idealism, did not find understanding imitators, private or public, for decades. It might indeed have enjoyed a mere *succes d'estime* and been left on the map as a vestige of an impracticable early-twentieth century ideal, had Howard not attempted a second demonstration of his concept, with the aid of a younger group of associates, in 1919–20.

The site of Welwyn Garden City was, like that of Letchworth, an open tract of land, with no existing nucleus, no public services, and only a few narrow dead-end roads. Again the creation of a new town had to be undertaken with inadequate financial resources and without governmental endorsement or encouragement. Welwyn's location (on the main railway 20 miles (30 km) from King's Cross Station) was certainly more advantageous for making a start. On the other hand Howard's second group of associates, though very able, were not nationally known as successful and dynamic industrialists. All the money available to Howard in 1919, when with almost insane daring he bought the central part (1250 acres [500 ha]) of the site at an auction sale, was a sum of £5000 borrowed from a few friends—not quite enough to pay the 10% deposit required. (The balance was advanced by his agent, the late Norman Savill of the well-known London firm of surveyors.)

The land Howard had committed himself to purchase not being nearly sufficient for a self-contained town, he and his friends had next to persuade a reluctant adjoining landowner (the fourth Marquess of Salisbury) to dispose of a large additional acreage. Obviously the prospect that the scheme would come to anything must have seemed far from certain, and it was only after much hesitation that the owner agreed to sell. There was the precedent of Letchworth to go on, but at that date First Garden City Ltd was still in arrears with its cumulative dividend of 5%, was indeed only paying 2½% p.a., and was looked on as a poor proposition in business circles. Lord Salisbury, however, did agree to sell enough land to round off a satisfactory site, and though he imposed certain powers of repurchase if the project should fail, he accepted a price that was fair, indeed generous.

Howard then selected a provisional board of directors, a company was formed, and a prospectus issued offering £250 000 in shares entitled to a maximum dividend of 7%, any surplus (as in the constitution of the Letchworth company) to be used for the benefit of the future town and its inhabitants. History repeated itself. The Welwyn flotation, which coincided with the post-war financial recession, resulted in subscriptions of only £90 000—again less than the sum the company had contracted to pay for the land purchases of 2378 acres (951 ha) (£105 000). Like First Garden City Ltd, therefore, Welwyn Garden City Ltd had to finance its early development by bank advances and mortgage loans, on which interest had to be paid before revenues could be created by development. And every urban service had to be provided—roads, water supply, sewerage, surface-water drainage, electricity and gas. No statutory undertakings for any of these purposes existed within miles of the intended town area. Small wonder that the local inhabitants, the residents in the county, and the business world, regarded the project as doomed to certain failure!

The Welwyn Policy

The intentions of the Welwyn company, as expressed in its prospectus, were in principle the same as those of its Letchworth predecessor:

'The town has been planned as a garden city with a permanent agricultural and rural belt, and with provisions for the needs of a population of 40 000 to 50 000. It will thus be seen that the scheme is entirely distinct from a garden suburb, which by providing for the housing of the people working in an adjoining district does nothing to relieve congestion and transport difficulties. . . . The method of planning proposed to be adopted by the company will not only reduce the cost of development, but will also preserve the amenities and health of the town.'

There follows an explanation of the limit of dividend on shares, the important part that the use of surplus revenues for the amenities of the town would play in attracting industrialists and residents, and the cover that the creation of urban values would provide for the shareholders' interests.

'The essence of the company's undertaking is the conversion of agricultural land having a comparatively small value into urban land ripe for building, and capable of producing good ground-rents. . . . The capital value of the land will increase *pari passu* with development. The combination of the estates which have been purchased from Lord Desborough and the Marquess of Salisbury has considerably enhanced the value of the whole.'

Then there is this interesting passage:

'The revenue-producing capacity of the company's undertaking may be gauged from the fact that the area of the proposed town and the population to be provided for will approximate to those of Cheltenham, Colchester, Eastbourne, Southport, Carlisle, Luton or Dewsbury, according to the census of 1911. Within this area the company will command, in addition to its ownership of the fee-simple of the land, a virtual monopoly in respect of a large number of enterprises of a profitable nature. The revenue consequent upon this monopoly will be employed by the company, after due provision for the shareholders' interests, on behalf of the public purposes of the new town.'

The terms of this last paragraph of the prospectus indicate a considerable change of emphasis in policy from that of the Letchworth company. This was largely due to the personalities and experiences of the four directors who were to play the most active part—Sir Theodore Chambers, Ebenezer Howard, C. B. Purdom and R. L. Reiss, all of whom took up residence in the town, spent most of their time and thought on its affairs, and entered energetically into its social and cultural life. Several members of the staff also—F. J. Osborn (Secretary and Estate Manager and for ten years Clerk of the Parish Council and UDC, who had had experience of housing in London and

Letchworth and had become an enthusiastic propagandist of the garden city concept), Captain W. E. James (Engineer and Surveyor to both the company and the Council), and Louis de Soissons, Consultant Town Planner and Architect—lived in the town from the start and were active in many aspects of its life. As citizens these men and others of the staff became in effect a powerful link between the company and the emerging community; the company never had, and never needed, public relations officers or social organizers.

The choice by Howard of Sir Theodore Chambers as chairman of the company proved most fortunate. He had great personal charm, wide connections in political, financial and technical circles, endless enthusiasm and considerable powers of persuasion. A surveyor by profession, he had become interested in town development and the idea of dispersal of industry and population from London before he had heard of the garden city movement, and it was a pamphlet that he had written on the subject that led, through another surveyor, Norman Savill (already mentioned), to his introduction to Howard. Chambers had acquired much knowledge of land values through his professional practice in London, and also through the prominent part he had taken in the Conservative Party's opposition to Lloyd George's land taxation scheme, in the course of which he had come to see the strength of the other side's case. It is curious, and indeed of importance, that another active director, R. L. Reiss, had been one of Lloyd George's chief lieutenants in the Liberal Party's side of the same struggle, and had perhaps seen the strength of the anti-land-tax case. At any rate, both had come to much the same understanding of the importance of the appreciation of land values in urban development, from radically opposed starting-points. Howard, of course, besides being the inspirer of the Welwyn scheme, had had experience of Letchworth's development as a director of First Garden City Ltd. And C. B. Purdom, who had been on the staff of the Letchworth company and a resident of the older town from its beginning, had been a critical observer of its development and finance throughout.

Conservation of Land Values

This assembly and blend of experiences accounts for the firm line that the Welwyn directors took on the conservation of land values. They were determined not to allow any leakage of increment that could be caulked. They had to grant leases to house-owners at current market values, and this was true also of sites for industrial premises, since persons and firms had, as at Letchworth, to be given strong inducements to settle in the town. But they stood out resolutely against granting long building leases for retail shops and commercial properties, though they had some offers from firms that were at fairly early dates willing to take sites at low ground rents.

Retailers were reluctant to run shops at a loss for an uncertain period before the growth of population would make them remunerative, and it seemed likely to be a long time before anything like a comprehensive shopping service could be provided by normal methods of development. The company therefore started its own departmental store, which for purposes of capitalization had to be given a temporary monopoly. This monopoly became a subject of prolonged and lively controversy within the town. It was in fact the only way in which a reasonably adequate shopping service could be provided when the population was small without giving away to retail firms or property speculators a big slice of future central land values (as had happened at Letchworth). But the fact of monopoly caused residents to exaggerate mercilessly any inefficiencies of the single shop, and to agitate vociferously for the admission of others to create normal competitive conditions. Though the issue was a useful counter for local politicians—for those of the Left who could represent the company as a capitalist exploiter and for those of the Right who could represent it as a socialistic destroyer of free enterprise—it may be doubted if there was very severe public discontent. For most residents baiting the company was an amusing and harmless game.

The directors were strong enough to stick to their guns, and the Welwyn Department Store, once the symbol of all that seemed most hated in the policy of the company, is now, by common consent, the brightest star in its main centre, and the attraction that brings shoppers from a wide area of Hertfordshire and North London, to the profit of the many other shops now established in its vicinity, as well as of the giant financial amalgamation that has taken over the Store; and, let it be added, to the creation of an unexpected car-parking problem.

The estate company, pursuing logically the policy of conserving land values, did not (with rare exceptions) grant building leases for commercial properties. It financed the shop premises, and let them on short leases at rack rents, at the expiry of which the lessees (entitled under British law to security of tenure) continue occupation at a rent fixed by agreement, or if necessary by arbitration. Thus revenues from the commercial area rise with the increase of population.

A similar policy was followed to some extent in the industrial area. While large firms took sites on 999-year leases and built their own factories, many sectional factories were built by the estate company and let on occupation leases, usually for 7, 14 or 21 years, sometimes for less. Besides making it easy for firms to start in the town, these rented factories have proved very important to the development corporation that succeeded the company, since on the renewal of leases rents can be adjusted to current market values. Changes in money values and increases of building costs have raised rents well above the original levels. On the other hand, holders of long leases of factory and house sites continue to enjoy rents much below the current market value—a leakage foreseen but considered inevitable and of far less quantitative importance than in the disposal of commercial sites.

The Welwyn company, despite the chronic shortage of equity capital in its early years, contrived, by such expedients as the issue of debentures at fixed interest and borrowing on mortgage, to finance many other developments, some of which, notably the electricity undertaking and a building company, proved profitable. Others, such as the theatre, the gravel plant and the brickworks, were less remunerative and were later disposed of or discontinued.

The company's original constitution, limiting dividends and ear-marking surplus revenues and increments of value for the benefit of the town, must have been a factor in reconciling business and residential lessees, and tenants, to the declared policy of exploiting to the full the monopoly created by single ownership of a complete town site. Another confidence-giving factor was the institution of the Civic Directors—three persons, exercising full powers, appointed by the parish council and later by the urban district council. These elements of the constitution could be, and were, cited in answer to critics within the town.

Both the dividend limit and the Civic Directors, however, disappeared in 1934, not through bad faith on the part of the shareholders, but because of a financial crisis and a reconstruction in which the debenture holders, who were not parties to the 'contract' between the shareholders and the town, took over the equity. New men were placed

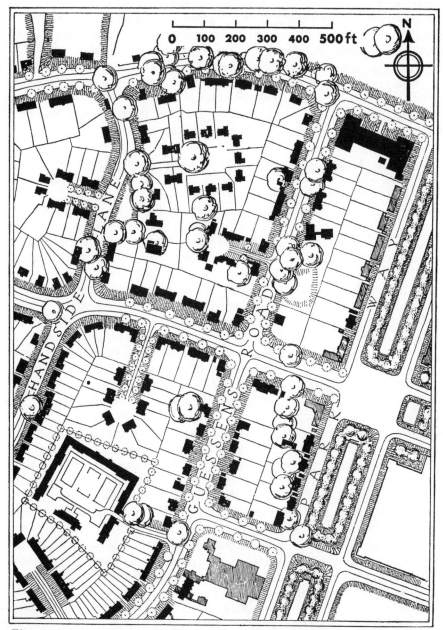

Figure 3.3 Part of the S.W. neighbourhood of Welwyn Garden City (1920–26). (Reproduced from Site Planning in Practice at Welwyn Garden City, *Ernest Benn)*

on the board, though several of the former directors remained, the capital was reorganized, the £1 ordinary shares were reduced to 2s. and various classes of debentures were converted to shares without any dividend limit. One of the major causes of this drastic change was the national economic slump of the 1920s and a heavy fall of price

levels subsequent to the company's initial capital expenditure. Another was that a
sufficiency of share capital having proved unobtainable despite immense efforts, the
large amounts of fixed-interest securities issued at a pretty high rate of interest (6%)
made the company too highly geared—which might not have mattered for a property
company in normal times, but was a serious disability on a general fall of price-levels.
The directors were in the hands of the debenture holders; whether they could have
made a better bargain with them and saved more of the future revenues or increments
of value for the town or the original shareholders is a question that may be asked, but
which it would be futile at this date to attempt to answer.

Maintenance of Planning Standards

It is to the credit of the company that it did not, after the reconstruction, in any way
lower its standards. The planning and development of Welwyn Garden City became
famous as the best example of whole-town design. The company maintained throughout the 28 years of its existence its architectural control, its insistence on good building
quality, its standard of planting and landscaping, and its policy of providing all the
social amenities it could afford.

There are some architectural lapses, due to the necessity of conciliating prospective
lessees at times when disposals of sites were specially difficult or the firms concerned
specially desirable to attract, and some patches of over-standardization of design,
especially in low-rent housing schemes. But these falls from grace are few. A general
standard of design and harmony much above that of the first garden city, and in its
time only rivalled by Hampstead Garden Suburb, was achieved. Welwyn is not a
suburb, but (like Letchworth) a self-contained industrial town in which the majority of
the population work as well as reside. In that category it must take rank as a town-
planning masterpiece.

The fashion in architecture has since changed: the Georgian style that Louis de
Soissons took from Welwyn's Hertfordshire surroundings, freshened and adapted
with great success to contemporary domestic and business requirements, no longer
seems to devotees of a later convention 'exciting' (their word); even the superb
planting and spacious landscaping of the earlier section of Welwyn are derided as
'romantic' or 'non-urban' by some fashion-obsessed critics. But to the families who live
and work in it, and to most visitors, professional or lay, Welwyn Garden City is a
supremely pleasing town visually, as well as efficient technically and human in scale.

At the time of its takeover in 1948 by a government development corporation under
the New Towns Act Welwyn Garden City had a population of 18 500. Its development
since that date is dealt with in a later chapter.

The financial history of the Letchworth and Welwyn Garden Cities is recounted in
Chapter 7.

References and Notes

3.1   See PURDOM, C. B., *The Garden City*, 1913, and *The Building of Satellite Towns*, 1949; OSBORN, F. J.,
      Green-Belt Cities, 1946, new edition, 1969.
3.2   LYNCH, KEVIN, in *Site Planning*, 1962, prescribes a minimum between facing windows of 75 feet
      (25.5 m) slightly outbidding Unwin.

4 Town Growth and Governmental Intervention

'While planning theory holds that it is never too early to begin planning, experience shows that there will be no public outcry for planning, and little, if any, effective planning done, below a certain threshold of local difficulties. In other words, the situation has to get worse before anyone will stir himself to try to make it better.'

—Dennis O'Harrow (USA 1961)

As the major instruments of civilization towns have brought to mankind gifts of incalculable magnitude, at the price of terrible deprivations. No accountant-philosopher could prepare a millennial balance sheet of their material and moral assets and liabilities. But the ratio of ills to blessings has been so high, especially in large towns, that it is lamentable that recognition of the need for control of their extent and location has come so late. In the literature of political philosophy such a recognition has been absent until the last few years. Neither the prescriptions for desirable town size by Plato and Aristotle, the protests of poets, divines and novelists, nor the projects for colonial settlements and small-scale communities, not even More's *Utopia*, seem to have extended the concept of local and voluntary limitation of urban size to that of generalized governmental regulation. So far as we know, the first academic hint of it was given by Professor Alfred Marshall in his evidence to the Royal Commission on Imperial and Local Taxation (in 1899, the year after the publication of Howard's book):

'The central government should see to it that towns and industrial districts do not continue to increase without ample provision for that fresh air and wholesome play which are required to maintain the vigour of the people and their place among nations. ... We need not only to widen our streets and increase the playgrounds in the midst of our towns. We need also to prevent one town from growing into another, or into a neighbouring village; we need to keep intermediate stretches of country in dairy farms, etc., as well as public pleasure grounds.'

Of course the municipal regulation of certain details of internal town development has existed from very early times. In all towns, whether originally planned or not, there had to be rules to maintain the width of public streets and passageways against the constant efforts of frontagers to encroach on them with building extensions or enclosures for the display of saleable goods or other uses. Building regulations have had to be imposed, as we have already noted, to reduce risks from fire or disease, to limit heights and coverages, and to prevent obstructions to light. These are in effect primitive density controls.

Such ordinances, however, did not limit growth. Nor did they amount to an attempt to ensure that a town should be or remain a good piece of apparatus for civilized living. That vital function was left to the adventitious and often clumsy interplay of a complex of separate and self-regarding forces. And up to a point and in certain respects these forces produced, if not an ideal, a workable result.

For the most part the decision as to the location and use of new buildings has rested with individual landowners and entrepreneurs, within such few rules and restrictions as have from time to time been found necessary to check acutely-felt disadvantages or difficulties. These were in their time, it should be realized, bold and imaginative governmental departures. If in the light of a wider understanding of town structure and function they now seem unskilful, and at best merely corrective of superficial symptoms to the neglect of organic causes, we have not yet earned the right to feel much superior. (Consider, for example, the attempts to palliate the urban traffic problem without attending to the matter of traffic generation.)

The reasons for this failure should be understood, because they continue to operate today. A bias against governmental interference is characteristic of any free-enterprise society; and in principle it is a healthy bias, because it is almost wholly through individual or group initiative, risk and responsibility, that the main advances in manufacture, trade and culture have been made. The process goes far back, but we can visualize it best by considering what has happened in Britain since the Industrial Revolution. In quest of profit for themselves—and, whether consciously or as a by-product, of benefit to society—inventors and men of enterprise have spent time and money in developing mechanical devices and systems of productive organization. In siting their factories and other establishments they had to take into account many technical considerations, such as water or fuel supplies, raw materials, availability of labour, and distribution to markets. They had usually some choice of landowners to bargain with. They were free to settle in any place that suited their enterprise. Their job was tough enough; they had neither the obligation nor the knowledge to consider the effects of their enterprise on the location of population or the character of towns and rural areas, or even on the interests of other businesses (an important point). They were rarely obstructed by government, and even more rarely helped, and then only in minor details.

The Mainspring of Material Progress

Whatever we may see or imagine now to be the role of government as the promoter or sponsor of economic enterprise or cultural progress, it is a fact of history that the major scientific and industrial advances originated in relatively individualistic societies. Karl Marx was as well aware of this as Adam Smith, though his religious belief in Historic Fate (coupled with a stern moral disapproval of the agents Fate manipulated) led him to different prognostications from those arising from a classical economist's analogous faith in the Invisible Hand of economic law. We need not believe wholly in either deity to understand why governments have been slow to interfere with processes that, despite their frightful incidental consequences, were demonstrably increasing overall wealth and power. The benefits were outrageously badly distributed, in the character of urban living no less than in income, hours, personal freedom, security, conditions of work, and social satisfaction generally. But in the full tide of the Industrial Revolution people of the dominant classes, and even many of the grossly underprivileged, had a profound belief in and enthusiasm for 'progress'; Macaulay's school-boy was as thrilled by scientific and industrial innovations as the schoolboy of today is by space travel and atomic physics. The inertia of governments in dealing with such appalling by-products of industrialism as child labour, starvation wages, high urban death rates, overcrowding and slums was not due entirely to lack of or defiance of conscience. Statesmen, good as well as bad, were chary of touching the mainspring of progress.

Governments and Public Opinion

It is only very recently that the planned redevelopment and renewal of towns, and the creation of new towns, have become issues of social or public policy. And we are still far from clarity of thought, true consensus of opinion, or resolute action, on the chronic or emergent problems. Democratic governments seldom enter a new field of control except to attempt to remedy some evil or inconvenience that presses strongly on some politically vocal section of society. The sections that influence policy may be of utterly different orders of numerical, economic, or social importance. They may be motivated by simple self-regarding interests, by aesthetic or religious or philosophic ideals or conceptions contagiously spread, or by human sympathy with fellow-subjects disadvantaged by things as they are or by the way they are going. In the arguments that precede and shape public policy, all these forces are mingled, and each has its own validity. Political parties, interested pressure groups, and public-spirited voluntary societies endeavour both to create public opinion and to bring it to bear on governments; and within those organizations there are often intensely convinced or persuasive individuals whose preoccupations, whether socially important or not, are reverberated in both directions.

It is idle to quarrel with the facts of political life. Some such opinion-forming and decision-making process must go on in every society, democratic or authoritarian, though very different numbers of persons in very different groupings may take part in it. If we believe in progress, in enlightenment, if we believe some things matter more and others less, we have to understand the political process. And we have to be clear in our own minds what we think society should do, and why.

Aims of Public Policy

As this book takes sides on certain issues of town development and planning, the authors' assumption as to the fundamental aim of social policy may usefully be stated, though we make no pretension to verbal precision, and are conscious that the assumption will be regarded by many as so obviously correct that it is naive to state it. We do so because experience has taught us that an assumption that almost all decent persons at once accept when it is stated in their hearing, can be ignored by such persons in discussions of social policy affecting aspects of passionate interest to themselves.

Our assumption is that the purpose of any defensible social policy is to advance, to the extent possible, human happiness, and to reduce, to the extent possible, human distress or discomfort. The improvement of public health, now so accepted a purpose as to seem an end in itself, is really a means to this end. So is the raising of the standard of living or real income, of housing, of working conditions. So also is the increase of productive efficiency in industry, agriculture, trade and administration; though there are deductions from the sum of happiness when this increase involves loss of desired leisure or the worsening of conditions of work. So again is the improvement of the look of the world: always provided that it is thought of as the look of the world to people in general, and that the improvement is to the liking of all or most of those who care about looks, and not merely a coterie with exceptional tastes.

This conception, of general or maximum enjoyment or satisfaction, comes into the assumption, though it is difficult to formulate. Many attempts have been made—'Life, liberty and the pursuit of happiness'; 'The greatest good of the greatest number' (or 'of all'); 'The optimum of human well-being'; 'Life more abundant'—and all are gallant but imperfect approximations. We will not add another. The common underlying idea is clear enough, and it is of the utmost importance in the context of town and country planning. If it is held in mind, it is corrective of many faulty emphases that have befogged discussion of and hindered agreement on a sound town development policy.

Influence of Reformers and Pressure Groups

We do not overlook the complication that human beings differ: not only in their likings, but even more in their awareness of possible satisfactions. Reformers, like salesmen and advertisers of commercial products, sometimes have to educate their prospective customers in the merits of new or little-used kinds of goods that they believe the customers will be glad to have when these merits are known and understood. And often the placing of their goods on the market has to be preceded by experiment and the distribution of samples for trial. The commercial producer may need to consider only the potential acceptability of his goods to a select clientele. The advocate of a social advance that requires governmental action has a wider responsibility—to be sincerely convinced that what he proposes will, when produced, enhance general satisfaction.

His task, moreover, differs from that of the commercial producer-salesman, in that he has to operate, not through simple advertising and distribution, but through the lengthy and complex political process to which we have referred. A democratic regime (that is, one in which all adult citizens have freely disposable votes in electing bodies that appoint governments) seems on the face of it, and in fact is, more likely to ensure that governmental actions make for the satisfaction of the many than tyrannical, feudal, or dogma-based regimes, however benevolently minded; but in the collective operations of a large society in which the desires of millions have to be transmitted to authority through a layered series of functionaries there cannot be the simple supplier–consumer relationship that exists in the free and direct selling and purchase of goods. The acceptability of the final product of governmental activity cannot be tested and revised so immediately, by sales-charts and profits and losses, as that of commercial products. Governments of populous states, confronted with a multitude of affairs, are far less well-placed, not only to find out what is most profitable to do, as business firms must, but to find out the acceptability of what they have done.

An Extreme Case of Imperfect Competition

What has been missing in the historic process of the development of towns is the direct influence of the mass-consumer on the product as a whole. There is of course competition between towns in attracting population. But the operative attractions are not those of a generally convenient, economically efficient and humanly pleasing environment. Within a town there is some competition of desirability between particular dwellings, and between residential districts or suburbs where commercial producers set standards of openness, planting and other amenities. Holiday towns and pleasure resorts compete for transient visitors by advertising environmental qualities. But the attractions that an ambitious industrial town seeking further growth stresses in its publicity are convenient sites for factories, a pool of labour, port and transport facilities, cheap electricity and so on. Pleasing surroundings or cultural endowments may be mentioned, usually unconvincingly, as a make-weight(4.1). They have not counted for much in urban competition. It has been safe for entrepreneurs to rely on the common experience that where the jobs are the workers will follow. And in general the mass of workers go for the jobs, and take a chance of what kind of housing and living conditions they will find. The executives and better-off employees can usually find decent homes for their families not too far away in a suburb where competitive production has been influenced by effective consumer choice.

The Rationalization of Congestion

In a large town to which people are drawn by opportunities of employment, the mass-consumer's preferences have relatively little effect upon his residential environment. Even when the local government is spurred by the danger to public health or by social compunction to clear slums and provide rehousing, consumer choice is so vitiated by prevailing conditions that a truly satisfactory environment is not produced. This reflects the imperfection of the governmental process now intervening of necessity, but not yet inspired by sufficient public understanding of the possibilities, or by the advice or leadership of a wise, fully-informed and socially-conscientious corps of administrators and technicians. So far, in rehousing notably, imperfect commercial competition has been partially replaced by imperfect governmental response to the mass-consumer's needs and desires. Public intervention is a real advance, of great promise for the future, but its sensitivity and skill have a long way to go before it is adequate to economic and social needs.

Unintentionally, but in effect, advantage is still taken of the unfortunate situation of the city-masses. In place of utterly detestable slum conditions they are in many cities provided with conditions certainly much more healthy and tidy but far short of those that modern art and technique could now provide.

It is perhaps easier to see the tendency to pursue the second-best, or the just tolerable, in housing by observing the processes of reconstruction in the larger cities of continental Europe, such as Paris, Lyons, Rome, Berlin or Moscow, where families who have occupied for generations the sub-divided floors and rooms of old bourgeois houses or proletarian tenements or shacks, are moved to 5-storey or 6-storey walk-up flats where the rooms are still small, but the blocks are so spaced as to receive more daylight, have modern cooking appliances, baths or showers, and other fittings, and are set among trees and grass. Relatively they feel in luxury, but what has really happened is that these people have been conditioned over the centuries to put up with a deplorable degree of congestion, decay and squalor, and then the congestion has been rationalized and modernized and the squalor cleaned up. Essentially the same thing is happening to the less privileged in British cities. Most of the better-off people, politically vocal and assertive, have long ago moved to garden-houses in the suburbs.

Viewed locally and immediately the change from dilapidated slums to new and clean multi-storey dwellings is an improvement. Often it is the best that a municipal authority within its own scope of action can do. The victims also believe it is the best, for the time being. But it is not good enough. Moreover it may well be short-sighted. Many of the multi-storey tenements now built with extravagant subsidies in old cities may cease to be acceptable long before their cost is written off(4.2).

Government Aids to Overgrowth

Unfortunate for urban man as the failure of governments to attend to the excessive growth of towns has proved, their reluctance to do so has, as we have shown, been consistent with a basically *laissez-faire* philosophy. No such justification or defence can be sustained for types of governmental intervention that positively facilitate continued overgrowth or counteract spontaneous economic checks on overgrowth. Tendencies to such economic checks certainly occur. If the disadvantages and inconveniences of a city become severe, business enterprises and residents are disposed to move out. For example, the rises of central rents and land prices, of travel fares, and of the overall cost of living, which are reflected also in higher rates of wages and salaries, coupled with cramped premises and traffic congestion, increase the costs of production, and tend to impel businesses to seek cheaper and more spacious situations. In orthodox economic theory, progressive disadvantages should in time stimulate an automatic correction. And to some extent and in a disorderly way they do. In the USA, for example, the flight of many families to suburbs has left in city cores extensive 'blighted' districts where values have fallen so low that tax-delinquency occurs, though even at minimum site costs commercial rebuilding of workers' dwellings is still unremunerative. We have referred to this economic paradox in Chapter 2.

Faced with the problem of slums and decaying or blighted residential districts, municipal governments have had to intervene with clearance and rehousing projects on a considerable and expanding scale, covering the financial losses on them out of taxes from the city as a whole. In many cities municipal governments have also had to subsidize from taxation the provision of mass-transportation systems. Such costs, and those of street widenings, new arteries and ring highways, overpasses, underpasses and tunnels, continually necessitated by town growth, become a heavy burden on business and residential tax-payers, and in theory should check growth and even produce decline. Envisaged by the steely eye of an academic economist, the climactic corrective of urban overgrowth ought to be a collapse in land values, municipal bankruptcy, and a reconstruction in altogether different shape. This has not happened—yet. And we do not want it to happen. But the crisis is being evaded, or postponed, in the wrong way.

When the burden on municipal taxpayers becomes unbearably heavy, municipal governments call for aid from their national, state or federal government, and being electorally immensely powerful, they succeed in getting substantial financial remittances. In Britain this takes the form of differential subsidies for high-density housing (to which we will refer in Chapter 10), percentage grants for street improvements, police and other purposes, interest-deferred loans for mass-transport, and block grants designed to equate tax incidence as between different towns and districts of the country. Such aids from central to local governments are no doubt in principle justifiable, and necessary, in countries where the main taxes are collected centrally. But in discussions on public finance, in Great Britain at any rate, little attention appears to have been paid to their effect on the future distribution of the population. Some of them, we believe, positively facilitate the further growth of towns now by common consent too large.

The accepted principle underlying such governmental aids is the relief of excessive local tax burdens—financial equity between places where people are relatively poor, relatively crowded, relatively few in relation to the area served. The bigger housing subsidies given to London and other congested towns are designed to enable them to rehouse their workers at rents comparable with those in smaller towns, where building costs and land prices are much lower. The intention is understandable, but such differential grants have the effect of enabling an overgrown city to retain its excess population and to grow further. Indirectly they are subsidies to the firms by which the rehoused persons are employed, who can therefore establish themselves, remain or expand where economic realities would warn them not to come or to move out.

We are not ourselves against compassionate aid from national governments to large cities. Subsidies may be necessary for their redemption from long-accumulated evils and difficulties out of which they cannot extricate themselves by their own resources. What is imperative is that government intervention, now that it has come, should be so contrived as to reduce, not to intensify, the urban difficulties that necessitate it.

References and Notes

4.1   Slough Trading Estate Ltd at one time dangled before manufacturers the nearness of Stoke Poges where they could recall Gray's *Elegy in a Country Churchyard*; but it is unlikely that the great success of the estate owes much to that attraction. For other examples see OSBORN, F. J., 'Industry and Planning', *Journal of Town Planning Institute*, July, 1932.

4.2   This sentence remains as in our first edition (1963). In 1977 many blocks of multi-storey flats built since 1920 in the USA and Britain are already being demolished.

5 Evolution of the New Towns Policy

'All reflection on the problem of a society changing itself tends to emphasize the necessity of "gradualness". The use of intelligence, even in the scientific sense, and in fields where conditions are most favourable, involves a tremendous "overhead cost", especially in the form of time.'

—Frank Hyneman Knight: *Economic Theory and Nationalism* (1934)

We have mentioned in Chapter 3 the propaganda society now known as the Town and Country Planning Association, and its activities prior to the foundation of Letchworth in 1903–4. From that time onward the history of the garden city movement is bound up with that of the town planning movement, then engaging interest in overlapping sections of opinion, of which a good account is in Gordon Cherry's book *The Evolution of British Town Planning*(5.1). We can only briefly sketch here the garden-city or new-town strand in the story. It is difficult for the present authors, ourselves active members during recent phases of the Association's campaign, to strike the right balance between objective truth and modest understatement in evaluating its share through 70 years in influencing opinion and policy. Beyond doubt its persistent advocacy, along with the visible demonstrations that it inspired at Letchworth and Welwyn, have been weighty factors in the evolution of planning thought. As members we have been particularly conscious of the obstacles the Association met in gaining public and authoritative attention for its proposals, and some account of these should be of interest—particularly as some of them still hold back the thoroughgoing adoption of an urban dispersal and new towns policy.

Sidney Webb used to say that the normal lapse of time from the first promulgation of an important reform up to its general acceptance was about 18 years, in proof of which he was in the habit of quoting impressive instances. From 1898, the date of Howard's book, to 1946, the date of the New Towns Act, the interval was 48 years. Why was the progress so slow? Some critics have placed part of the blame on the fluctuations of clarity and intensity in the campaign of the Association itself, and certainly there were such fluctuations. But small and financially weak as it was, the Association never ceased to keep the garden-city idea and the two experiments in evidence. The fact that the idea did not catch on earlier was the cause rather than the consequence of the Association's relative ineffectiveness in certain phases. No doubt if in the 1900s or 1920s the new-town idea had engaged the enthusiasm of some popular literary genius of the order of Rousseau or Tom Paine, some dynamic demagogic statesman like Lloyd-George, or even some astute as well as dedicated reformist wire-puller like Sidney Webb, things might have moved faster. Howard and his articulate followers,

Unwin, Neville, Thomas Adams and others, were themselves no mean propagandists. They stated the idea lucidly and did lodge it in many minds. Acceptance of their propositions was however delayed by two pieces of sheer historical bad luck—the coincidences in time of the suburban boom at the turn of the century and of the great national housing drive of the 1920s and 1930s.

Almost contemporaneously with Howard's book, the development of electric traction and the internal combustion engine began to revolutionize urban transportation, and it became practicable for city dwellers to obtain without a serious increase in travel time acceptable dwellings in suburbs. Nothing was there to stop the consequent exodus of prosperous families from crowded city quarters to new and more spacious environments. No governmental powers were existent or in prospect to prevent the simultaneous expansion of industrial and commercial business in city centres, drawing towards the agglomerations further populations, some of whom reoccupied the dwellings vacated by the exodus, and others of whom settled on the suburban fringes along with those who were flocking out from the centres.

The Town Planning Movement

It was the untidy fringe developments created by the haphazard outward rush that, from the 1860s on the continent of Europe and in 1909 in Great Britain, prompted the first town-planning legislation. Planning control was indeed a long-needed governmental function, and the Association had to support its introduction and application. Some of its principal members, notably Unwin, took a leading part in the advocacy and drafting of the 1909 Act. The Association was opposed in principle to the addition of further suburbs to cities too large already; but clearly suburbs were going to be built around many towns, and planning-minded people could not be indifferent to the new means of improving their character. After some heart-searchings over what seemed the questionable case of Hampstead Garden Suburb (1907), for which Unwin and Parker were appointed as planners by an independent public utility company, the Association decided that if a new suburb had to be added to London a good suburb would be better than a bad suburb, without departing from its view that garden cities (new towns) were the only solution for the fundamental problem.

This tactical decision need not in itself have caused any obscuration of principle. Unfortunately the application at Hampstead, and in other contemporary suburbs and housing schemes, of the attractive new pattern of residential design, layout and planting that Unwin and Parker had matured in the first garden city was seized upon eagerly by housing developers all over Britain and in many other countries. Commercial builders, public-utility societies, writing architects, even some town planners (but not Unwin, who was clear-minded) appropriated Howard's carefully defined term of art, 'garden city', and used it indiscriminately as a label of prestige for any kind of open residential development—suburb, industrial village, or public or co-operative housing estate. 'Garden city' and 'garden suburb' became in popular parlance interchangeable. The residential pattern that both terms were taken to stand for became the fashion and then the popular norm; and it remains the popular norm today, with variations in generosity and parsimony of space. The fundamental principle exemplified by the first garden city—that of a self-contained industrial town, for working as well as living in, and limited by a country belt—was temporarily understood by thousands of technical and political visitors, effusively praised, mentally pigeon-holed as worth consideration some day, and, in the press of practical suburb-building, dropped out of consciousness or relegated to the realm of beautiful dreams. Except in rare cases the initiation of new towns would have required governmental powers for the choice of location and the acquisition of sites; to build them was therefore beyond the scope of municipal administrators, co-operative housing groups, and technicians. And so the suburban flood went on, often, despite the expostulations of Howard's followers, under the stolen banner 'garden city'. And many able planners, who would no doubt have preferred to be designing genuine new towns, were caught in the flood and swept away from active interest in the movement. They are not to be severely blamed, save in so far as they contributed to the terminological confusion. It is difficult for a technician to earn a living in an ivory tower.

Deprived during this period of the concentrated interest of its technical personnel, and handicapped in the recruitment of lay support by the confusion of terms, the Association languished somewhat in effectiveness. Its journal, *The Garden City* (the world's first periodical in the planning field, started in 1904 and now known as *Town and Country Planning*), kept Letchworth's progress and purpose in the eye of a small public, but inevitably much of its space was occupied by information about the progress of statutory planning and about the planned suburbs and housing estates proliferating in Britain and overseas. Much journalistic ingenuity is required (as we have discovered) to put the same case over and over again in different words and with the fresh data, illustrations and anecdotes necessary to interest readers. The journal was never in a position to pay professional writers, and at times the shortage of bright copy as well as of cash compelled it to fall to quarterly instead of monthly publication. Its coverage was erratic and incomplete, but its files are indispensable to students of the history of the movement.

The New Towns Movement and Public Housing

Towards the end of the war of 1914–18 another reassertion of the true garden city principles was made by a small group consisting of Howard, F. J. Osborn, C. B. Purdom and W. G. Taylor, calling themselves the New Townsmen. Howard in letters to the press, and Purdom in a pamphlet of 1917, were the prime movers in this revival. The group issued in 1918 a little book restating the case in the light of experience at Letchworth and proposing the creation with Government support of a hundred new towns as part of the expected post-war reconstruction policy(5.2). The book aroused appreciable public interest and restimulated the Association, which welcomed its fresh accent, absorbed the New Townsmen into its ranks and appointed Purdom as full-time secretary. With the help of a generous grant from the Joseph Rowntree Village (now Memorial) Trust and with Richard L. Reiss as chairman of the executive, a vigorous campaign for new towns as an integral part of the expected national housing effort was undertaken.

But again public and authoritative attention was distracted—this time by the strength and popularity of the inter-war housing drive. New and admirable standards of accommodation and layout had been formulated by the Tudor-Walters Committee of 1918(5.3), in which Raymond Unwin was a powerful influence, and the recommendations of which were based not only on Letchworth, Earswick and Hampstead experience but also on evidence collected from all over the country as to the working people's housing desires. This was an epoch-making document, setting standards for low-rent housing that were governmentally adopted for two decades; but it was a housing report purely; it was not concerned with large-scale town planning or new towns. Lloyd-George's well-phrased slogan for reconstruction, 'A Land fit for Heroes to Live in', was soon boiled down, in practice as well as in words, to 'Home for Heroes'. The returning soldier could envisage a 'home'; he knew the sort of house and garden he and his family wanted. But he had no picture in his mind of 'a Land for Heroes'—good towns for work as well as home life in a green and pleasant land. The Association tried to enlighten him. But its still small voice was drowned by the din of hammers building 4 million houses—good houses on the whole, but, as it cried unheard, mostly in the wrong places.

Some great-city authorities made really imaginative efforts to design their major housing projects as 'quasi-satellites' with community facilities—notably Manchester at Wythenshawe and Liverpool at Speke and Knowsley, where also some provision was made for local industry—and the planning of these did represent a considerable advance. Yet they were still continuous extensions of overgrown agglomerations, not true new towns.

The Association lost the full-time services of some capable propagandists in this period by the suction of Howard, Reiss and the New Townsmen into the demanding work of building Welwyn Garden City. And once more, in order to survive, it had to combine pursuit of its main mission with an active interest in the preoccupation of the moment—housing, housing, housing. But the Welwyn group never lost sight of the wider objectives in their preoccupation with their specific project. And the Association still had single-minded enthusiasts like Dr Norman Macfadyen (of Letchworth), Sir Edgar Bonham-Carter, and the first Lord Harmsworth, who did their best to keep the garden-city concept in the public view and hearing (so far as the hammers permitted) with the aid now of two physical demonstrations of its practicability and attractiveness.

The Chamberlain and Marley Committees

Thus some impact on opinion was maintained. In these inter-war years two Government committees, to which the Association and the garden city companies gave evidence, studied the problem of urban concentration and strongly endorsed the garden city principle.

The Committee on Unhealthy Areas, with Neville Chamberlain as Chairman and R. L. Reiss as a member, made a notable advance in thought by recommending the restriction of factory industry in the London area, along with the movement of some employment and persons to garden cities (in the correct sense) where the inhabitants could live 'close to their work in the best possible conditions'(5.4). Though nothing came of this at the time, it was the first official contemplation in Britain(5.5) of the idea that control of the location of employment is the key to the redistribution of population. There is little doubt that the evidence to this committee was the origin of Chamberlain's interest in urban decentralization and the garden city idea, manifested in succeeding years by many speeches, and in 1938 (when he was Prime Minister) by the setting up of the Barlow Royal Commission.

In 1935 a Departmental Committee under Lord Marley's chairmanship, of which Sir Theodore Chambers (then Chairman of Welwyn Garden City Ltd) was a member, again recommended the governmental encouragement of the building of new towns on the garden city model. Its report also proposed the establishment of a Planning Board to promote by restrictions, facilities and inducements a better distribution of industry(5.6). No immediate action resulted, but the idea was now in the political air, and began to be discussed and even commended in responsible newspapers.

The Barlow Royal Commission

In 1936 the Report of Sir Malcolm Stewart as Commissioner for the Special Areas (regions of high unemployment) aroused political interest by a forceful reiteration of the 1920 suggestion that London should be placed 'out of bounds' for new factory construction (with certain exemptions)—for the sake of the regions suffering from industrial decline. In the same year the Association complemented Sir Malcolm Stewart's proposal with a renewal of its own campaign, arguing the necessity of dispersal from the other angle—for the sake of London and other regions suffering from plethora and thrombosis. F. J. Osborn had become honorary secretary, and the services were engaged of a young Scotsman, Gilbert McAllister (later MP), who had a great enthusiasm for the new town idea, and proved one of its most effective exponents in books and articles as well as in Parliament. New supporters of influence came in, and the decisive phase of the long struggle for a national policy began. Gilbert McAllister and his wife, Elizabeth McAllister, successively organized the activities of the Association from 1937 to 1947, and the influence of its campaign owes a great deal to their energy and devotion.

By the 1930s Welwyn Garden City had become a visible entity, and its industrial growth, social liveliness, and outstanding quality of design had made a worldwide impression, comparable with that made by the first garden city two decades earlier. Probably it was the combination of Welwyn's prestige, the pressure of the Association, and the ideas in the Marley and Malcolm Stewart reports, as well as his own report of 1920, that stirred Neville Chamberlain, on becoming Prime Minister in the Conservative Government in 1938, to appoint the Royal Commission, under the chairmanship of Sir Anderson Montague-Barlow, Bart, whose report in 1940 raised the problem of large towns for the first time to the status of a major public issue(5.7).

The published evidence to the Barlow Royal Commission, official and unofficial, contains a massive collection of facts and figures about British towns; of permanent value to students of urban history and structure and of contemporary thought (and lack of thought) about the advantages and disadvantages of large towns. The printed evidence of the Association was well documented as things went in those simple days (before 'horse-head equations' were considered indispensable in social-economic argument) and, with the supplementary verbal evidence, is known to have had much influence on the Commission. The story of the struggle within the Commission for a national policy, of which the Association had glimpses, would be of fascinating interest if it could be written. All we can say here is that supporters of the new towns policy owe a special debt to two clear-thinking and resolute members, Sir Patrick Abercrombie and Mrs Lionel Hichens, without whose efforts the recommendations in the majority report would have been less definite than they were. These two also added great force to the total effect by the minority report that they signed along with H. H. Elvin.

The majority report contained a most impressive study of the disadvantages of excessively large agglomerations, fully confirming the contentions of the Association, while, no doubt to conciliate hesitant members, making the most of the counter-vailing advantages of substantial town size. In our view it was too hopeful about the possibilities of overcoming the disadvantages of 'million cities' by better planning, but it was unequivocal about the balance of disadvantages in multi-million cities like London, and about the urgency of preventing their further growth.

Among the considerations that influenced the Commission, the social and economic drawbacks of large towns—overcrowding, ill-health, shortage of recreation space, noise and smoke, long journeys to work, traffic congestion, and so on—were prominent. The injurious effects of suburban sprawl on agriculture and countryside amenities, on which much evidence had been given, were also regarded as serious. And as the shadow of Hitler, Munich and a coming war loomed heavily over the nation, the strategic danger of having so large a proportion of Britain's population and industry massed in large agglomerations was the subject of a grave chapter in the report. All these considerations told in the same direction—towards the imperative necessity of limiting great-city congestion and further growth.

When it came to proposals for a policy, however, the Commission was badly inhibited by internal differences. The famous 'Nine Conclusions', unanimously adopted by the 13 members, agreed that 'in view of the nature and urgency of the problems' national action was necessary, and proposed the setting up of a 'central authority' whose activities should transcend those of any existing government department. The 'objectives' should include redevelopment of congested urban areas and decentralization and dispersal both of industries and population. But the Commission left open the question of whether the central authority should be executive or merely advisory, what congested urban areas should be dealt with, and whether and how far decentralization or dispersal, 'if found desirable', should be 'encouraged or developed' in garden cities, suburbs, satellite towns, trading estates, existing small towns or regional centres, or by other 'appropriate methods'.

In effect this was a promising programme for further study and research, with suggestions as to the lines that might be pursued. It was an attractive shopping list, rather than a purchasing order. Yet it was conspicuously marked 'urgent'. The Association, while pleased by the text of the report, was at first not at all sure that the conclusions had crossed the Rubicon, and hesitated whether to give it a lukewarm welcome as moral support for sound principles, or to hail it as a great historical manifesto.

The minority report, however, was much more definite, and obviously more consistent with the balance of considerations expressed in the majority report. It went straight out for a new Ministry to plan the location of industry on a national scale, and to have definite powers to impose restrictions in some areas, to provide encouragements in others, and to promote the building of 'garden cities and satellite towns' and the expansion with industry of small towns and regional centres. Starting with these powers, it concluded, the new Ministry should report urgently as to what further powers it required for the redevelopment of congested town areas and for the policy of decentralization and dispersal.

Taking together the majority and minority reports, the 'dissentient memorandum' on the defects of planning law and administration by Abercrombie, and the 'reservations' by three members of the majority, which proposed machinery for the restriction and encouragement of industrial location for other regions as well as London, the Association decided that, if the Barlow Report were interpreted as a triumphant vindication of the Association's own policy, it could be made so in fact. And this bold judgment turned out to be correct. The ex-chairman, *functus officio*, fell in with this interpretation, joined the Association, and in cordial co-operation with it took an active part in the campaign for a new Ministry with the necessary powers for central re-development, dispersal, green belts, and new towns. In effect he retrospectively endorsed the minority report. He was in due course deservedly (but sad to say posthumously) awarded the Ebenezer Howard Memorial Medal by the Association for his distinguished contribution to the garden city movement. The Barlow Report did in the event prove the historic turning point in the governmental concern with urban development.

The War and National Planning

The outbreak of war in September 1939 pushed aside propaganda and discussion on long-term issues. Building development was mostly diverted to purposes ancillary to war needs. Many planners and governmental officials were drawn into the armed forces or emergency functions. Large sections of the civilian population had to add to their work in factories, shops and offices service in the Home Guard and Civil Defence. Voluntary societies suspended or redirected their activities. The TCPA closed its London office and carried on in one room in Welwyn Garden City, with a one-person staff—Miss Elizabeth Baldwin, the business secretary—who took a part-time job in a local office.

In view of the tragic circumstances of the time—the call-up, the departure of troops to Europe, the vast evacuation of children and their mothers from cities to country towns, the fall of Britain's only co-belligerent, France, bombing from the air, losses of ships by submarine attacks, food shortages and rationing, and intense anxiety about personal and even national survival—it is not surprising that the Barlow Report, published in January 1940, went almost unnoticed on to the shelf. What is remarkable is the speed with which it came off the shelf. As a result of the great damage done to towns by the bombs, an unexpected popular interest arose as to the form their reconstruction after the war might take. Across the extensive areas of destruction and rubble, which it was the Government's policy to clear promptly and convert into melancholy vacant sites, city dwellers saw new vistas. They were astonished at the amount of sky that existed—the unaccustomed brightness of the devastated scene. Their sense of the permanence and unalterability of the built-up background dissolved; the 'urban blinkers' were dislodged from many eyes. What would replace the former crowded buildings if and when we won the war? Might we not have much better homes and work-places and retain this new sense of light and openness?

The Government saw the value of this in upholding morale: the hope of a Better Britain helped to sustain the desperate determination to fight and work for victory. They not only encouraged popular discussion of post-war reconstruction, but even devoted a modicum of ministerial and civil service attention to it. As early as October 1940 Lord Reith, then Minister of Works and Buildings, was personally charged with the responsibility of studying and reporting to the Cabinet on the methods and machinery for physical reconstruction after the war. A man of extraordinary dynamism, nationally well known as the former head of the British Broadcasting Corporation, he got to work with characteristic speed. The Barlow Commission's report was retrieved and examined, and proved to be a most opportune textbook on the sort of policy needed. Its timeliness was the first piece of historical good luck the new towns movement had had. Lord Reith, using it as his basis, called into consultation leading persons interested in physical planning, including members of the TCPA, and by February 1941 he had obtained from the Cabinet acceptance of the principle of a national authority to pursue a positive policy for agriculture, industrial development and transport, with attention to the unordered growth of congested towns and the indiscriminate sprawl over the countryside. This in itself was perhaps a safe enough decision, leaving plenty of escape holes for future choice; but it was a step in the right direction. New legislation was foreshadowed for these objectives.

Beginnings of a Government Policy

In the meantime (January 1941) an expert committee had been appointed to study the problem of compensation and betterment in planning, as had been recommended by the Barlow Commission. And in July 1941 the Cabinet accepted this committee's interim recommendations(5.8) that for purposes of public acquisition or control of land a 'ceiling' value as at March 1939 should be fixed, that the central planning authority should at once be set up to control all development, that 'reconstruction areas' should be defined, and that until proper schemes were prepared rebuilding in these areas should not be permitted except under licence.

At the same date Lord Reith was authorized to take steps to work out a national planning policy, within the framework of the general study of post-war problems then under the charge of the Minister without Portfolio, Arthur Greenwood, M.P. A Council of Ministers was set up, consisting of Lord Reith as chairman, the Secretary of State for Scotland, and the Minister of Health.

And in February 1942 came the Government's more definite decision: to establish forthwith a central planning authority—not a board or an advisory body, but a ministry. The Ministry of Works and Buildings was to become the Ministry of Works and Planning and to take over for England and Wales the town and country planning functions of the Ministry of Health. The Secretary of State for Scotland would retain the planning functions for Scotland. There were to be arrangements for co-ordination by a Committee of Ministers and a Committee of Senior Officials representing certain other departments.

This was accompanied by a highly important statement that the Government would consider the steps that should be taken towards the recommendation of the Barlow Report for the redevelopment of congested urban areas, decentralization or dispersal therefrom, and encouragement of a reasonable balance and diversification of industry throughout the regions of Great Britain. In terms this was a decision to consider setting up an authority to consider what ought to be done—not even a shopping list, but a note to consider preparing one. But the circumstances of the moment must be borne in mind. It did mean acceptance of the idea of a national planning authority of some kind: the one thing on which all schools of planners were agreed. The Government, however, added that care would be taken to avoid interference with the aim of the highest possible standard of living, the waste of existing capital equipment, and diversion of productive agricultural land to other purposes if less productive land were available. These reservations are significant as deriving from differences of accent then already apparent in planning circles, which were later to blow up into fierce controversies.

A New Ministry and the Battle of Ideas

At this stage the shape of a post-war policy was still vague, and it could not be assumed that new towns would figure in it. Lord Reith had consulted many people with views on planning, and had set up a Consultative Panel on Physical Reconstruction which had made a start on the working out of certain details of policy. He had visited bombed cities and encouraged local authorities 'to plan boldly'. The work of the advisers he had got together and the civil servants in his department—notably H. G. (later Sir Graham) Vincent—and the successive decisions he had extracted from the Cabinet, intensified the already lively public and press interest and the hope of a strong post-war policy. It is difficult to assess the weight of the various influences in the public discussion, and within the Government itself, during this period. The Conferences of the TCPA in 1941 and 1942, the debates in the House of Lords initiated by Viscount Samuel and others, the 1940 Council formed by Lord Balfour of Burleigh, the BBC talks and debates (in which TCPA members were often heard) and the publications of various specialized groups, all contributed. Inside the Government Arthur Greenwood exercised important influence; and from Lord Reith's account it is evident that Sir John Anderson (later Lord Waverley), then Lord President of the Council, was in constant touch with all the Ministers concerned. All these we have named seem to have been in favour of the 'national planning authority' proposed by the Barlow Commission. But whether any of them at that time definitely favoured the governmental creation of new towns is doubtful: some of them seem to have regarded it at most as just an interesting possibility.

To everybody's astonishment, a day or two after the Government's decision to set up a national planning ministry, Lord Reith was dismissed from office by the Prime Minister (Winston Churchill). He was replaced as Minister of Works and Planning by the late (first) Lord Portal, who in his short period of office showed no particular interest in planning policy. However, Henry G. Strauss (later Lord Conesford) who was then a member of the TCPA executive committee and keenly interested in the aesthetic aspect of planning, was appointed an additional Parliamentary Secretary to deal specially with planning functions. The work of preparing legislation on the lines of the Government's decision proceeded.

Exactly why Lord Reith was dismissed remains something of a mystery even after a study of his account of the affair in his extraordinarily candid autobiography(5.9). There were certainly tensions between him and other Ministers about the allocation of functions in the reconstruction policy: and our own view is that Lord Reith himself did not fully appreciate that town and country planning would be, if given its due status, a big enough subject to engage the full-time activity of a Minister of the highest rank. If he had shared our own estimate of the importance of planning and physical reconstruction, and had been prepared to concentrate on it as he had concentrated on the creation of the BBC, his own and national history might have taken a happier course; but admittedly this is a vain speculation. Lord Reith must be accorded credit for a remarkable contribution to the advance of planning in getting the main Barlow recommendations accepted in the short space of 14 months. Years later, as chairman of the New Towns Committee, he was to make another extremely valuable contribution.

When in 1943 the Ministry of Town and Country Planning was at last established, the first Minister was W. S. Morrison (afterwards Speaker of the House of Commons, and as Viscount Dunrossil, for a few months before his death, Governor-General of

Australia), who proceeded to build loyally on the foundations laid. Under him the important Town and Country Planning Act of 1944 was passed, giving strong new powers for the acquisition of land in bombed and obsolescent urban areas and for comprehensive redevelopment. All development was placed under interim planning control, and thus the stage was set for a national policy when the Government could find time and will to decide upon it. New towns were still not in sight. And the controversies then in full swing made their ultimate appearance seem doubtful.

War-time Conferences and Discussion

During the Reith–Morrison period (1940–45) many societies and persons entered into the discussion, and some of these were far from enthusiastic about the creation of new towns. The TCPA made many endeavours to unite the various schools of thought on a practicable and balanced policy. As early as the spring of 1941 it arranged a widely representative conference at Oxford, attended by distinguished leaders of differing views and interests and delegations of all types of local authorities(5.10). Among the speakers at this conference were Sir Patrick Abercrombie, Sir A. Montague-Barlow, Lord Brocket (Chairman of the Land Union), (Sir) Donald E. E. Gibson (then City Architect of Coventry), Sir Herbert Manzoni (City Engineer of Birmingham), F. J. Osborn, (Sir) George Pepler, Professor W. A. Robson, Viscount Samuel, Lord Justice Scott, Lewis (later Lord) Silkin, Sir George Stapledon, Lord Simon of Wythenshawe, and Dr Dudley Stamp. A stimulating discussion took place, but apart from the general acceptance of the Nine Points of the Barlow Report, it cannot be said that a common policy emerged. The published report did however prove a clarifying element in the subsequent public controversies.

In 1941 also the Association began the issue of a series of shilling booklets dealing with aspects of the national problem, and these were widely circulated(5.11).

A second conference at Cambridge in 1942 specialized on the agricultural and rural aspects of planning and industrial decentralization(5.12), and this again brought together a highly expert assembly of speakers and delegates—among whom were Professor G. M. Trevelyan, Sir Daniel Hall, L. F. Easterbrook, Sir Malcolm Stewart, Professor Sargant Florence, Professors A. W. Ashby and C. S. Orwin, and Dr Thomas Sharp. The evidence of the TCPA to the Scott Committee, a constructive effort to reconcile the urban and rural accents, was among the papers for this conference. But again general agreement on the major issues could not be attained.

A definite advance in this direction was however achieved by the TCPA in 1941 when its 'National Planning Basis' was accepted by the Royal Institute of British Architects, the National Council of Social Service, and the National Playing Fields Association. This still stands as a useful expression of the consensus of responsible opinion on which national policy was ultimately based.

The Uthwatt and Scott Reports

We need mention only briefly the reports in 1942 of the two important committees set up during Lord Reith's period. The Uthwatt Report on the relationship between land-use control and land values stands as a classic among blue-books(5.13). A brilliant analysis of the problem of equating compensation for private losses of value with the collection of part of the private gains of value is followed by a study of the possible solutions. Though the solution recommended was not adopted, the report greatly influenced opinion and led in 1947 to legislation that made possible a large scale reservation of green belts and agricultural land with compensation from national funds. The provisions in the 1947 Act for the collection of gains in value were subsequently repealed, but a further attempt was made to introduce such a collection with the Land Commission Act 1967. This measure foundered, and was repealed by the next government. This coincided with a period of extensive property speculation in Britain, and popular demand for another attempt to be made at the collection of development gains led in 1975 to the Community Land Act and its companion measure in 1976, the Development Land Tax Act. Under these measures gains in development value of 60% and more are to be collected for public benefit, but the subject remains controversial, and there may be further changes.

The Scott Report(5.14) contains a comprehensive assembly of proposals for the protection and advance of the interests of agriculture and the countryside. It accepts the Barlow thesis in principle, but its attitude to the issue of decentralization or dispersal is admonitory, emphasizing the importance of keeping any new urban developments compact and limiting them to relatively unproductive land. Certain paragraphs disquieted the TCPA by suggesting a reversion to high-density flat-building in existing towns to reduce the draft on agricultural land. When the Association expressed its alarm, Lord Justice Scott, as ex-chairman, obtained letters from all the members of the committee disclaiming any intention to thwart the new towns policy; and after a meeting between representatives of both bodies the TCPA accepted the assurances, swallowed its misgivings and publicly approved the report. The printed paragraphs, however, remain on record, and the harm done by them to countryside opinion on the new towns policy has, we regret to say, survived the effect of the personal disclaimer by members of the committee.

The First Abercrombie Plan for London

The rising public interest in planning was given a great stimulus by the publication in 1943 of the County of London Plan(5.15). This was prepared for the London County Council, at the instance of Lord Reith when Minister of Works, under the direction of J. H. Forshaw (then the county architect) and Sir Patrick Abercrombie. In many ways an advance on previous great-city plans, it is of special importance to our subject because its careful study of the numbers of persons who could be satisfactorily rehoused at given densities in reconstruction provided a realistic measure of the 'overspill' of population and employment that would have to be accommodated outside the county. Chapter Two, on 'decentralization' contains the following significant statements:

'The ideal situation for people to live in is within reasonable distance of their work but not in such close proximity that their living conditions are prejudiced by it; this ideal can be closely realized when planning a new town of limited size in which the time, money and energy spent in means of locomotion are reduced to a minimum. But an approximation of the ideal becomes increasingly difficult in existing large towns or groups of towns. This is caused by many factors such as the immobility of certain of the industries, the impossibility of obtaining satisfactory living conditions near-by, the variability of occupation within the same family or the change of work-place after a home has been purchased . . . [para. 113].

Both sides of the subject require careful handling; in the aspect of living quarters, the personal feelings and idiosyncrasies of human beings must be given the fullest consideration; in the aspect of industry the equally delicate susceptibilities of economics are involved . . . [para. 114].

To produce an ideal scheme of decentralization, the numbers of persons for living and working quarters should balance; this, of course, can never happen. . . . Nevertheless, a good deal of sorting out will gradually take place if a serious attempt is made to equate residential and industrial removal . . . [para. 117].'

Thus the authors of this Plan saw clearly that a considerable displacement of persons and employment would be necessary for any decent reconstruction:

'It is desirable to make the industrial boroughs of London so attractive that people whose work is there will not be forced out to distant suburbs for pleasant houses, gardens, open spaces, schools with playing fields and safe shopping centres: on the other hand, the people whom it is necessary to decentralize, in order to produce these satisfactory conditions, should so far as possible have a choice of work near at hand; the aim should be to avoid their being housed in distant dormitories, yet constrained to rush back to the old work-a-day haunts. The facts of the dilemma are plain, but their consequences are not always grasped. Some have been heard to ask why it is not possible for people to live in houses with large gardens, near their central work, and at the same time for the population of the borough to remain at its pre-1938 level. Others, a little more realistic, would cram everyone into lofty close-packed tenements whose high architectural qualities might mask their social deficiencies, and would also keep factories within the town, thus avoiding any further encroachment upon the countryside. Both these points of view ignore two inescapable facts: the first, that to obtain attractive living conditions a much lower density in the industrial boroughs of London must be secured, i.e. a large population must be decentralized, and so far as possible a corresponding amount of industry; the second, that the exodus of people and industry was already taking place before the war. The decentralization has been happening in an unplanned way; the boroughs see their population dwindling, as their best elements, especially the young married folk, leave the old surroundings, which are not benefited by this reduction except in strictly limited patches of new tenements. What we now propose is to anticipate this loss, to enhance it by means of a bold reduction and to produce a really satisfactory environment by wholesale rebuilding made possible by war damage. . . . The number we estimate it would be necessary to remove from the congested parts of London to secure the conditions postulated in our Plan is between five and six hundred thousand people [para. 21].'

The Greater London Plan of 1944

Bold as this planned reduction seemed, it was shown to be necessary on the standards of maximum rehousing density considered permissible in the boroughs to be decongested. These standards included 200 persons an acre (500 per ha) for extensive central areas, and a maximum of 136 persons an acre (340 per ha) in 14 of the industrial boroughs. These were certainly not generous standards. A density of 200 an acre (500 per ha) means that all persons must live in high flats, and 136 an acre (340 per ha) necessitates at least 75% and probably 80% in high flats. Such standards, as the TCPA at once pointed out, hardly seemed likely 'to make the industrial boroughs of London so attractive' as to hold people contentedly within them. Abercrombie was uneasy about them himself(5.16). He had had to compromise with strong influence in LCC circles for retaining as much population as possible. In his Greater London Plan of 1944(5.17) he suggested an alternative maximum density of 100 persons an acre (250 per ha), which would permit of 50% of terrace houses of 2 or 3 storeys, but would involve a displacement of 200 000 more persons from the county (800 000 instead of 600 000), and from the county and the inner ring boroughs together a total decentralization of nearly 1¼ millions. It is understandable that in submitting these staggering figures he should have had doubts of his own realism. Nevertheless they were imposed by the logic of the situation.

The Greater London Plan of 1944 made a further historic advance by definite proposals for the location of the 'overspill' of population and a corresponding quantum of industrial employment. Of the 1¼ millions to be displaced 125 000 were to be housed in 'satellite' suburbs on the outskirts of the conurbation, about 260 000 in additions to existing towns in the Outer Country Ring (beyond a Green Belt to be reserved), another 270 000 or so in towns at a distance of 40 or 50 miles (65 or 80 km) from the centre, and nearly ½ million in 10 new towns for which sites were suggested. This left about 100 000 persons to be rehoused outside the area of metropolitan influence.

A paragraph in Abercrombie's 'Personal Foreword' to the Plan, following his tribute to his colleagues, is worth quoting as a reminder of the mood of the time:

'The Plan thus prepared . . . is now completed, so far as it is possible to say that the stage of finality can be reached by a living organism. There is now a chance—and a similar one may not occur again—of getting the main features of this programme of redistributed population and work carried through rapidly and effectively, thereby reducing overcrowding and locating industry in conjunction. The difficulties in normal times of moving people and industry are rightly stressed; but people and industry will go where accommodation is made available; moreover, the war has made migration a familiar habit. Give a man and his wife a first-rate house, a community, and occupation of various kinds reasonably near at hand, with a regional framework which enables them to move freely and safely about, to see their friends and enjoy the advantages of London; add to these a wide freedom of choice, and they will not grumble in the years immediately following the war. The industrialist, if he is asked whether he is prepared to submit to the guidance of a Government official, will probably protest. But if he is offered a choice of sites, with every modern facility (including labour) provided, and in addition a licence to build and access to building materials and labour, he will jump at the chance to get started as quickly as possible. . . . Courage is needed to seize the moment when it arrives and to make a resolute start [pp. v, vi].'

The Greater London Plan of 1944 excelled the County Plan of 1943 as much as that Plan had excelled all its predecessors. It converted the concept of metropolitan re-development on human standards, and decentralization, green belts, new towns and country-town expansions, into a clear and concrete practical proposition. Abercrombie proved splendidly adequate to the unique opportunity afforded by the war-time circumstances and the long preceding processes of thought and advocacy.

It should not be forgotten, however, that among the prior work he and his team were able to build on was that of the Greater London Regional Planning Committee, a representative body of local authorities set up by Neville Chamberlain as Minister of Health in 1927, with Raymond Unwin as technical adviser. This Committee's second report of 1933 includes proposals for the development of new towns with governmental encouragement, and for means of dealing with the practical problems, though adequate powers were not then in sight. It is a reminder of the small importance then attached to planning that the budget of this Regional Committee was less than £4000 a year, and that in 1933 the LCC, pleading 'financial stringency', reduced its contribution to £500 a year, and Unwin accepted a reduction of his fee and undertook to carry on the whole of the work, and to provide an office, for £1700 a year. (It was in that year that Unwin, world-famous as a planner, whose advice was in great demand in the USA and elsewhere abroad, received the honour of Knighthood.)

The Party Reconstruction Committees

During the war the United Kingdom had a Coalition Government of all three democratic parties. They continued their separate organizations, and set up post-war reconstruction committees to study the problems of post-war housing and planning and formulate a party policy thereon. The TCPA, which had from its birth maintained a non-party, or all-parties composition, was called upon for advice and assistance in these studies. Some of its members in fact served on each of the party committees. All endorsed in principle the main proposals of the Barlow Report, but within each there were the same differences of accent as in the public discussion at large. However, after much argument, all three parties, with some difference of emphasis, included planned central redevelopment, dispersal, green belts, and new towns in their reconstruction programmes. Influence in this direction was exerted by members in close contact with the TCPA: on the Conservative Committee by Lord Balfour of Burleigh and John A. F. Watson, on the Liberal Committee by B. Seebohm Rowntree, and on the Labour Party Committee, of which Lewis (Lord) Silkin was chairman, by the Rev. Charles Jenkinson (of Leeds), Lady Simon (of Wythenshawe), (Sir) Richard Coppock, and others. The degree of agreement reached proved of decisive importance when in 1945 legislation for new towns was introduced. This was one of the TCPA's most successful efforts in political lobbying.

The National Planning Basis (1941)

The policy adopted in 1941 by the TCPA which emerged as prominent throughout the war years and is still applied in post-war planning includes:

1. National, regional, and local guidance of the development and redevelopment of land and building and of the grouping of people, industry and business, so as to promote the wisest use of all resources in the interests of all.

2. A policy of planned dispersal from congested cities. The new urban developments required for this dispersal, by industrial changes and by the growth of towns up to their planned limits, to be guided to new towns and existing country towns suitable for expansion: such towns to be so sited as to meet the needs of industry, agriculture and business, and designed as reasonably compact units without scattered or ribbon building. All towns, new and old, to be planned with proper facilities for a good social life, health, education, culture, and recreation. Village development to follow the same principles so far as farming requirements permit.

3. The setting of such limits to the size of towns as will avoid needlessly long journeys and protect living conditions; and such standards of residential density as will ensure adequate gardens for family houses and ample open space for recreation and amenity.

4. The preservation of wide country belts around and between towns, for the sake of agriculture and to enable townspeople to have easy access to the country; and the safeguarding from wasteful development of the best food-growing land, places of landscape beauty, national parks, and coastal areas.

5. Attention to good architecture and landscape design as well as sound construction in all development. Outdoor advertising to be restricted to approved positions and controlled in character.

6. National policy in the location of industry and business (*a*) to encourage their settlement in new towns and country towns, and (*b*) to restrict their settlement where there is over-concentration or congestion. Business firms to retain freedom of choice within the unrestricted areas.

7. The financial provisions under planning law to be so administered as to place on national rather than local funds the cost of compensation incurred in applying national standards.

8. Efficient, considerate, and speedy administration of planning at national, regional, and local levels.

9. The maximum enlistment of public interest in and understanding of planning and development, nationally, regionally, and locally, to ensure that planning is in accordance with people's desires and has behind it the driving force of public opinion.

References and Notes

5.1 CHERRY, G. E., *The Evolution of British Town Planning*, Leonard Hill, London, 1974.

5.2 OSBORN, F. J., 'New Townsmen', *New Towns after the War*, Dent, London, 1918; revised and reissued, 1942.

5.3 *Report of the Committee on the Housing of the Working Classes*, HMSO, 1918.

5.4 *Report of the Unhealthy Areas Committee*, HMSO, 1920.

5.5 It was not of course an entirely new idea. The Report of the New York Committee on Congestion (1911) proposed such an embargo. In Italy a decree of 1927 prohibited the starting of factories employing over 100 workers in any town of over 100 000 inhabitants. See OSBORN, F. J., 'Industry and Planning', *Journal of the Town Planning Institute*, July, 1932.

5.6 *Report of the Committee on Garden Cities and Satellite Towns*, HMSO, 1935.

5.7 *Royal Commission on the Geographical Distribution of Industrial Population; Report and Evidence*, HMSO, 1940.

5.8 *Expert Committee on Compensation and Betterment* (the Uthwatt Committee); *Interim Report*, Cmd. 6291, HMSO, 1941; *Final Report*, 1942.

5.9 LORD REITH, *Into the Wind*, Hodder and Stoughton, 1949.

5.10 *Replanning Britain; Report of the Oxford Conference of the TCPA*, Faber and Faber, 1941.

5.11 *Rebuilding Britain Series*, Faber and Faber, 1941–2.

5.12 *Industry and Rural Life; Report of the Cambridge Conference*, Faber and Faber, 1942.

5.13 *Expert Committee on Compensation and Betterment; Final Report*, HMSO, 1942.

5.14 *Committee on Utilization of Land in Rural Areas; Report*, HMSO, 1942.

5.15 *County of London Plan*, prepared for the LCC by J. H. Forshaw and Patrick Abercrombie, Macmillan, 1943.

5.16 Personal correspondence with F. J. Osborn, 1942–44.

5.17 ABERCROMBIE, PATRICK, *Greater London Plan*, 1944, HMSO, 1945.

6 Legislation for New Towns

'And that these things are best, if they be possible, we have sufficiently, I imagine, explained in the preceding part of our discourse.
—Sufficiently indeed.
—Now then it seems we are agreed about our legislation—that the laws we mention are best, if they could exist, but that it is difficult to get them to prevail, not, however, impossible.
—We are agreed, said he.'

—Plato: *Republic, Book VI* (trans. H. Spens, 1763)

New towns did not figure conspicuously in the competition of party programmes during the first post-war General Election of 1945. As in 1918, the major accent was on promises of maximum speed in building houses. Though the three parties had accepted the policy of planned redevelopment of bombed and obsolete urban areas, and realized that decent standards necessitated some decentralization from crowded cities, and also knew there was a wistful popular interest in the idea of new towns, their election manifestos did nothing to show the connection between planning and living conditions, only vaguely apprehended by the electorate. Stout municipal councillors still wanted more population and rateable value and held that flats and suburban housing were easier and quicker to produce than new towns; architects longed for lofty towers as more 'exciting' to design and photograph; and countryside preservationists urged high density to 'save land'. Party managers could see few votes in a strong emphasis on dispersal. The TCPA therefore felt by no means confident that the combination of central flat-building and a great suburban explosion would not be repeated, whichever party won the election.

In the event the Labour Party won it, with a substantial majority, the Liberal Party was reduced to a small fraction, and Winston Churchill's Conservative Government, which had replaced the Coalition for a few months, was succeeded by the Government of Clement (later Lord) Attlee.

Though the Labour Party had not made a feature of the dispersal policy in its election campaign, the subject had been thoroughly discussed by its reconstruction sub-committee on housing and planning under the able chairmanship of Lewis (later Lord) Silkin. A solicitor by profession, and MP for a London constituency, Silkin had been Chairman of the Town Planning Committee of the LCC from 1940 to 1945 and was well-informed on urban problems. In the sub-committee's discussions he back-pedalled the desire of nearly all the other members to give prominence in the programme to dispersal and new towns. This resistance may have been tactical. It was Silkin's habit later, as Minister receiving a deputation, to pour cold water on its ideas, to argue their complete impracticability—and then to act upon them; the exact opposite of the normal ministerial technique of listening patiently, expressing sympathy, promising careful consideration—and then doing nothing. As chairman of the Labour Party sub-committee he insisted that the emphasis must be on city rehousing, that in central districts high density would have to be accepted, and that new towns at best could only be a minor supplementary expedient. The other members wanted the emphasis the other way round. The difference of accent was so strong that the majority (while in agreement with the greater part of the chairman's draft report) submitted to the Party's main reconstruction committee a separate draft of certain key paragraphs, urging that new towns be placed in the forefront of the programme. A few members, including the Rev. Chas. Jenkinson of Leeds, were so hot about this that they wanted to override the chairman's view by a vote, but F. J. Osborn persuaded them that the gentlemanly strategy of an alternative draft was more appropriate in the circumstances.

What happened in the higher circles of the Party we do not know. At a solemn meeting with representatives of the majority of the sub-committee, Emanuel Shinwell, Harold Laski, and Morgan Phillips listened to their plaint, and, in a polite quasi-ministerial manner, assured them that their views would have due attention. The solution adopted was politically astute. The party published Silkin's report as the official policy statement, and almost simultaneously issued for mass circulation a bright illustrated pamphlet at a lower price spot-lighting new towns as a feature in future policy.

Though on this sub-committee Silkin had not been disposed to give dispersal the priority his colleagues pressed for, he had conceded that a new town or two might be built. The TCPA therefore invited him, as Chairman of the LCC Planning Committee, to join in setting up a working party with technical advice from officers of the LCC as well as from members of the Association, to study the methods by which new towns could be established. To this he at once agreed, and he and F. J. Osborn made some progress in selecting persons to serve on such a body. At this moment the General Election was called, and the study project had to be postponed.

The New Towns (Reith) Committee

Imagine the feelings of the TCPA members when, after the momentous election, the press announced that the new Minister of Town and Country Planning was Lewis Silkin! And conceive their surprise and delight when one of the Minister's first decisions was to appoint, together with the Secretary of State for Scotland, the New Towns Committee, on which a number of the persons already suggested for the unofficial working-party were to serve!

The Committee was appointed in October 1945 with the following terms of reference:

'To consider the general questions of the establishment, development, organization and administration that will arise in the promotion of New Towns in furtherance of a policy of planned decentralization from congested urban areas; and in accordance therewith to suggest guiding principles on which such Towns should be established and developed as self-contained and balanced communities for work and living.'

The personnel of the Committee was well adapted to its task. Silkin persuaded Lord Reith to be its Chairman, and the other members were:

Ivor Brown, then Editor of *The Observer*; Sir Henry Bunbury, former Comptroller and Accountant-General of the Post Office; L. J. Cadbury, Chairman of Cadbury Bros. Ltd, Director of the Bank of England, etc.; Dr Monica Felton, Member of LCC Planning Committee; W. H. Gaunt, former Estate Manager of First Garden City Ltd, Chairman of Hertfordshire County Planning Committee; W. H. Morgan, County Engineer of Middlesex; F. J. Osborn, Chairman, Executive Committee of TCPA, and former Estate Manager of Welwyn Garden City; Sir P. Malcolm Stewart, Bart, Chairman of London Brick Co. Ltd, and former Commissioner for the Special Areas; (Sir) Percy Thomas, then President of the Royal Institute of British Architects; John A. F. Watson, Member of Central Housing Advisory Committee, and Chairman of Southwark Juvenile Court.

For Scotland there were two members: Sinclair Shaw, Advocate; and Captain (Sir) J. P. Younger, Convenor of Clackmannan C.C.

The joint secretaries were L. F. Boden, of the Ministry of Town and Country Planning; and Lieut.-Colonel F. H. Budden.

Sir Hugh Beaver, and A. W. Kenyon, formerly Resident Architect-Planner, Welwyn Garden City, served as co-opted members on several sub-committees.

Under Lord Reith's energetic chairmanship, the New Towns Committee made in eight months an exhaustive study of the subject, called into consultation a great number of official and voluntary bodies, business organizations, and individual experts, and produced three lucid and decided reports with a maximum of content in a minimum of words. As these are easily obtainable, we do not discuss them at length, but they are detailed in the bibliography.

The speed and efficiency with which the New Towns Committee collected and digested a vast amount of advice and converted it into terse and practical recommendations was largely due to the skill of Lord Reith as chairman. He had at that time no knowledge of town-building. Two members (Gaunt and Osborn) had had experience in developing the garden cities of Letchworth and Welwyn, and A. W. Kenyon had been resident architect of Welwyn. But nothing that these conceivably prepossessed members advised was accepted on their say-so. Every element of policy and practice, of methods and standards, was studied *ab initio*, and examined in the light of the views of the bodies and persons concerned with the relevant aspect of urban affairs, from religion to finance, from family life to art, from drainage to landscaping, from work to leisure, from pubs to universities—in short, from A to Z. Much of the exploratory work and consultations with representative bodies was devolved to sub-committees, but tentative conclusions had always to run the gauntlet of debate in the full committee. The triumph of Lord Reith's chairmanship is that without any fluffing of issues he obtained in the end unanimous recommendations, with an admission of a difference of judgment on only one point—the ownership and administration of a new town estate after completion. We refer to this in a later chapter.

An interesting thing is the decided preference of the members of the committee, and of almost all the organizations consulted, for the governmentally-appointed development corporation as the agency for new-town building, as against the alternatives of their building by local authorities, authorized (non-profit) associations, or commercial firms. F. J. Osborn, as chairman of a sub-committee, strenuously tested this preference by putting up the case for a variety of agencies, and suggesting to witnesses from the associations of local authorities, builders and contractors, financial institutions, and building societies that they should put in a claim for bodies of the classes they represented to experiment as new-town agencies. Almost unanimously they replied firmly: 'No, thank you! This is a job for a Government corporation.' The exceptions were the Rural District Councils Association, who saw their type of authority as a suitable agency, and three individual building and contracting firms, who said they would be glad to form non-profit or limited-profit associations, to accept Government approval of plans, and to build complete towns, for the sake of a normal return on the constructional work. (One well-known building firm, Richard Costain Ltd, did in fact make a proposal for an undertaking years later, but its scheme was rejected because the site, in Kent, was said to be of high agricultural value.) While there can be no doubt that the Government corporation is in most cases the appropriate agency, we have some regret that so far other types have not had the opportunity to show what they could do. No doctrinal impulse stirs us here; no bias except against organizational rigidity. We feel that if Britain could devise some reliable form of free-enterprise limited-profit agency as an additional means for developing new towns, this might not only speed up our own progress but also give a lead to other countries more distrustful of government initiative(6.1).

The New Towns Act, 1946

Lamentably late and meagre as the first essays in guidance of the distribution of urban settlements have been in relation to the social needs, they would in our opinion have been even later and smaller but for the strong line taken by Lewis (Lord) Silkin as Minister of Town and Country Planning in 1945–47. Foundations had of course been laid for him. In all probability any Government coming into office at that time, in view of the previous official and party acceptance of the Barlow thesis, would have ventured on one or two new towns as a concession to the minority pressure-groups. But Silkin did much more than that. His New Towns Act of 1946 generalized the proposal in a more thoroughgoing way than could have been expected, and together with the great Town and Country Planning Act of 1947 created a system of land-use control and a machinery for positive town construction that was completely revolutionary. The Government of which he was a member was confronted with a welter of almost insuperable post-war problems; it could not as a whole possibly have given much thought to the complex and little understood issues of urban redevelopment and dispersal. Far more than in normal circumstances, Silkin must have been free to act or neglect to act on his own personal studies and to assume responsibility for decisions of far-reaching importance. He would be the first to agree that he had a solid basis of good thinking, the practical demonstrations of Letchworth and Welwyn, and the constructive proposals of the Abercrombie and Reith reports, to build upon.

The New Towns Act, 1946, followed closely the recommendations of the Reith Committee, with a few variations in detail. The creation of new towns was to be entrusted to *ad hoc* development corporations (normally one for each project), appointed and financed by the Ministry of Town and Country Planning (or the Secretary of State for Scotland). Subject to the approval of the Ministry, the corporations were given powers to acquire sites sufficient for complete towns, to undertake all the necessary kinds of development, including the provision of houses, factories, commercial buildings and public services, to appoint and employ full-time officers and constructional workers—in fact to have all the powers that an ordinary large-scale developing landowner would possess, plus one or two of the powers usually exercised by local authorities. They were not however to replace the local authorities; the site of each town was to be made a separate county district for which the authority would be elected in the ordinary way.

The loans advanced by the Government were to be at the ordinary rate of interest on public loans, and were to be repayable over 60 years. Subsidies on housing by the corporations were to be paid on much the same scale as to local authorities in general, though the ministries were given power to make supplementary grants.

One departure from the recommendations of the Reith report was that there was no provision for a Central Advisory Commission. This we think was unfortunate. Such a commission, if consisting of persons of relevant experience, receiving full information from all the corporations, and advising them without any power of direction or veto, would have enabled them to avoid many mistakes and some waste of money due to lack of previous experience. In its absence the advisory function had to be assumed by the Ministry, and this, being mixed up with indispensable controls, kept the corporations rather too tightly in Ministerial and Treasury leading strings. Moreover the civil servants entrusted with this function, however able, could not possess the special 'know-how' for urban development of the character and scale contemplated.

The First Government New Towns

The Government's original intention was to initiate up to 20 new towns. In fact, between 1947 and 1950 14 were started, 12 in England and Wales and 2 in Scotland. Six years later, in 1955 under the Conservative Government, a third new town (Cumbernauld) was authorized for Scotland. Then there was another long interval. The Conservative Government continued without wavering the building of the towns already started, but not until 1961, despite a growing need and much pressure from the TCPA, were any further new towns commissioned; we discuss later the reasons for this delay.

Of the first 15 new towns 8 were intended primarily to accommodate people and employment dispersed from the London conurbation: Basildon, Bracknell, Crawley, Harlow, Hatfield, Hemel Hempstead, Stevenage, and Welwyn Garden City (the last of course already well under way). Two were to serve the same purpose for the highly congested city of Glasgow: East Kilbride and Cumbernauld. Two were designed to collect into more satisfactory urban centres, with supplementary industries, populations from scattered mining villages: Peterlee and Glenrothes. The other three were to bring more and better housing and community services to industrial settlements that were socially and economically inadequate: Corby, Cwmbran and Newton Aycliffe.

Many observers regretted that Silkin decided to take over the partially built Welwyn Garden City for completion by a Government corporation. One of the reasons he gave for this was the economy and convenience of having it handled, along with the neighbouring town of Hatfield, by a single corporation. Another was that a corporation could be better relied upon to concentrate on dispersal of persons and industry from London than a private company, which might seek to attract them from anywhere. Our own opinion is that it would have been wiser to leave Welwyn Garden City to be completed by the company that had established it, on the condition of the restoration of some public participation in profits and increments of value. The company had produced the finest example of whole-town development in the world; it was still under brilliant direction, and in a position to obtain finance, and if allowed to finish its job it would probably have made the town more excellent still.

Later New Towns

After the first batch of new towns (1946–50) only one was designated in the next decade (Cumbernauld, 1955). The Government of the day, unduly influenced by the 'land-saving' pressure groups (see Chapter 10), and perhaps less enthusiastic about the need for urban dispersal, preferred the alternative method of voluntary expansions of existing small towns, described later in this chapter.

In 1961, however, a 'second generation' of new towns began, and by early 1968 8 more were in progress: 6 in England, Skelmersdale (1961), Telford (1963), Redditch (1964), Runcorn (1964), Washington (1964), and Milton Keynes (1967); and 2 in Scotland, Livingston (1962) and Irvine (1966).

Four of those in England were based on towns already of some size (20 000 to 30 000) and intended to be enlarged from 80 000 to 100 000, and two (Telford and Milton Keynes) to integrate a number of towns and villages into regional complexes of 200 000 to 250 000.

New departures in policy, coming into action in 1967–68, are the use of development corporations under the New Towns Acts to co-operate with local councils in major planned expansions of existing cities as regional or sub-regional centres; and to undertake urban development over extensive areas already containing a number of small towns and villages not suitable for simple individual expansion.

Designation orders were made in 1967–74 for four new towns in these classes: Peterborough, Northampton, Warrington and Central Lancashire, which are described in Chapters 24, 25, 31 and 32.

A Mid-Wales Development Corporation was established, first to double the population of the long-established Newtown in Montgomeryshire (now Powys) in 7 to 10 years, and then possibly to build other new towns in the region (see Chapter 37).

A number of other projects were later in various stages of gestation. In view of recent population forecasts thought was moving towards the building of 'new cities' much larger than the first new towns. There are obvious dangers in this. But if 'new cities' are conceived as cluster-towns in a green setting rather than either the clotted or sprawling blotches of the unplanned past the fundamental aims of the garden city movement can be adhered to. We discuss this and the implications for regional planning in Chapter 10.

Birth-pangs of the New Towns

We do not discuss at length the difficulties that the development corporations, and the Ministry, encountered in the acquisition of sites and the early stages of this huge enterprise. Much has been made of them in a well-documented book by Professor Lloyd Rodwin of the Massachusetts Institute of Technology(6.2). He bathed luxuriously in the subject during a stay in England, appreciated to the full the novelty, daring and danger of our attempt to tackle the colossal problem of urban overgrowth, revelled in the snags and resistances we encountered, and concluded in the end that we were blue-eyed enthusiasts who had had no inkling of what we were up against, but, being typical unscientific Britishers, had blundered into an astonishing degree of success that our lack of foresight didn't entitle us to. He is scholarly and in intention objective, and quotes experts and idiots with delightful impartiality and great entertainment value. Yet to a participant in the events he describes he seems grossly to over-dramatize the conflicts and difficulties that arose in the creation of new towns—which have not been remarkably greater or less than those which are met in any constructive enterprise of like magnitude.

No one who has himself taken part in the conduct of a great enterprise—as for example the establishment of a manufacturing business—will regard the difficulties met by the new town corporations as anything out of the ordinary. Naturally there was resentment and tough opposition on the part of owners of the land that had to be compulsorily acquired in assembling the sites, and by private residents who had settled in pleasant countrified surroundings and did not want their Arcadia invaded by what they envisaged as a horde of urban slumdwellers. On the other hand, the retail traders, and the majority of employable workers already in the designated area, generally welcomed the prospect of a new town. The elected authorities were often divided in their attitude. Some members wanted more population, higher rateable value, better services, improved community facilities. Many disliked the advent of a government-supported agency, concerning itself with housing and other big developments of a public-service character. Though usually one or two members of a development corporation were local residents and even members of the local council, the majority were not.

Thus the corporation was often regarded, as the Welwyn Company was in its early days, as 'a Hippopotamus on the Doorstep'. Tensions certainly arose from the facts of the situation. But their significance should not be exaggerated. When the leaders of both the local council and the corporation were understanding and diplomatic, the two bodies co-operated admirably, to the advantage of the old and new population. When they were undiplomatic and got across each other, a new and not uninteresting dimension was added to local controversy. Nobody shot anybody; nobody planted plastic bombs. In time the two bodies settled down either to friendly collaboration or at least to peaceful co-existence.

Compared with the difficulties encountered by the two private-enterprise garden cities, those of the development corporations must have been much less formidable. They had the government behind them, legislative as well as common-law land-owners' powers and rights, an assurance of the necessary finance for development, and co-operation from ministries and great-city authorities in encouraging the transfer of industry and population. Whereas the two garden-city companies could only offer businesses and families uncertain hopes that real towns would be successfully estab-lished, the corporations could invite them with complete confidence. Of course both the garden cities and the government towns had the problem of matching period by period the influx of employing firms and employable workers. But it made a great deal of difference that the latter always had the resources to promise the provision of factory and commercial buildings and of housing to meet the requirements of each.

There have been lapses, however. The expansion of employment in some of the towns has not invariably kept in step with the provision of houses. Several of them had difficulty in inducing industrial firms to come as rapidly as was required, and housing had to be slowed down below the intended programme. Later, the converse dispro-portion arose in a number of the towns. Industrial employment expanded in these so unexpectedly rapidly that there was a considerable waiting list for housing; a severe hardship to individuals, and quite a serious handicap to established firms. It is possible that some corporations, over-anxious to ensure diversity of employment, admitted new firms in insufficient regard for the expansion of existing firms. The matching of employment capacity to local population is an economic and planning problem of great importance and difficulty—the solution of which requires measures that no government has yet evolved, but which have to be found if the control of the size of towns and the preservation of country surroundings is to be achieved.

The Selection of Sites

Many possible sites for new towns had been suggested before 1946 in advisory and statutory plans: ten, for instance, in Abercrombie's *Greater London Plan*. Under the New Towns Act the choice has had to be made by the responsible ministries in England and Wales and in Scotland, who have found it no easy task. Obvious major necessities were water supply and drainage at reasonable cost, main road access (now more important than main rail access), and stable and level soil. Existing development had to be taken into account: in Britain it is scarcely possible to find a completely unbuilt-on site. In every case advantages and disadvantages had to be carefully weighed, and there were almost always strong resistances from farming and residential interests. The latter distorted some of the choices, but on the whole the decisions seem to have been sound in that, despite the emergence of a few unexpected difficulties, satisfactory planning and development have proved possible without ruinous cost. The main characteristics of the sites are described in our chapters on the individual towns.

The sites designated are in most cases adequate for the intended populations of the built-up areas at a tolerable overall density. But with one or two exceptions the town site acquired does not include any extensive green belt—contrary to the recommendations of the Reith report. The justification for this is that under statutory planning control country land can now be reserved against urban development, a safeguard that Howard and his free-enterprise companies could not count upon. Given a resolute national or regional policy green reservations do not now have to be in the ownership of the town-developing agency.

Whatever the planned size of a town, natural or economic forces may produce incentives to exceed its population target. Carried too far, this increase unbalances the internal plans, and brings about either an undue expansion or an undesirable increase of density.

Even when, as in contemporary Britain, the necessity of some limit is in principle accepted, town authorities and officials (including local planners) are tempted to plead for a bit more expansion before the ban is imposed. Like St Augustine in his youth they pray: 'Give me chastity and continence, but do not give it yet!' The self-restraint of institutions, as of persons, will always be subject to this weakness. It has to be conditioned by a wider social convention and in the end by law.

Expansion of Existing Small Towns

As we have seen, after the foundation of the first 15 new towns (1946–50) no more were started for some years. In the interval the Town Development Act, 1952, was passed as an alternative method of relieving urban congestion. Under this and a later Act for Scotland, agreements can be made between big cities and small towns or country districts willing to accept persons and industries from congested areas, with financial aid from the Government and the cities and in some cases from county councils. Advantage of the Acts has been taken by authorities of the London, West Midlands,

Manchester, Merseyside and Glasgow conurbations, and many expansions of country towns have resulted.

The first country-town expansion for London was at Bletchley, now part of Milton Keynes (Bucks, 45 miles [72 km] out) and the largest at Swindon (Wilts, 70 miles [110 km] out). Many others are in progress in Beds, Bucks, Herts, Kent, Hants and East Anglia. Staffordshire has been particularly successful in expanding a number of its small towns by arrangements with Birmingham and adjoining boroughs. Operations under the Acts are also in progress around the Manchester and other conurbations. The results are by no means insignificant, but the Town Development Act procedure is now regarded as a supplement, not a substitute, for the promotion of new towns, and far less efficient in its operation.

County Councils as Town-builders

There is a third procedure under which urban developments comparable with new towns may be carried out. Northumberland County Council in 1961 acquired 700 acres (280 ha) of land at North Killingworth, on the fringe of the conurbation of Tyneside, for an over-spill of 17 000 from some of its congested parts. The Ministry designated this land as a 'comprehensive development area', which gave the council power to buy it by agreement (with compulsory acquisition in reserve), to lay it out, and to provide roads and services, sites for private as well as public housing and some industry, and community facilities. After 16 years the method has proved a promising alternative for • planned co-operation between public and commercial enterprise, and with the 1976 Community Land Act all local authorities now have the power to buy land for relevant redevelopment.

And in fact the Northumberland County Council has already bettered its own lead by its project for Cramlington New Town, further out and separated from Newcastle by a green belt, which under the same procedure was planned for 48 000 with local employment. This was also approved by the Ministry, and was of special importance as it fell into the national policy of fostering new growing points in the north-east region.

References

6.1   WARD, C., 'The Do-it-yourself new town', *Town and Country Planning*, February, 1977.
6.2   RODWIN, LLOYD, *The British New Towns Policy*, Camb., Mass., 1956.

7 The Finance of New Towns

'Cash-payment is not the sole nexus of man with man.'

—Carlyle: *Past and Present* (1843)

'But it is pretty to see what money will do.'

—Samuel Pepys: *Diary* (1667)

New towns, being necessary for the salvation of existing old towns and for accommodating satisfactorily a growing population, could well be regarded as worth building at considerable public cost. No doubt many were so regarded, if for different reasons, in classical and medieval ages. Alexander and Edward I have left no audited balance sheets to justify their enterprises. Some of the capital cost of their towns, like that of castles, citadels, temples and cathedrals, came out of taxes and levies on the material and labour resources of the community(7.1). By similar means we in our own day finance highways, defence works, museums, schools, and space rockets.

Proponents of the new towns, from Howard onward, have claimed that they can be sound economic propositions. The record already shows that this is a valid claim.

Considerable sums have to be expended, of course, before any revenue is obtainable. Land has to be purchased, water and drainage works and roads constructed, service mains laid, and administrative expenses incurred, in advance of house and factory building. As in the initial stages of any other large-scale undertaking—such as a railway, an ocean liner, an oil refinery, or a tea plantation—there is a time-lag before the investment fructifies.

Investors in the two garden-city companies, originally financed by ordinary shares, had to wait years for earnings out of which dividends could be paid.

For the later new towns the capital was provided by the Government in the form of loans repayable over 60 years. Interest and repayments were chargeable from the start. During the period before revenues arose these charges were met, in small part by outright Government grants, and in the main by borrowings to meet revenue deficiencies; the latter had to be added to the balance-sheet liabilities. After a few years, however, revenues materialized, and in most of the first batch of new towns in England and Wales they have already overtaken the current loan charges on the whole of the capital invested, including the accumulated deficiencies of the earlier years.

On top of the expenditure by the corporation, further large capital sums have been spent by county councils on schools, by various authorities on public services, by business firms on factories, shops, offices and public houses, by private owner-occupiers on houses, and by other agencies on churches, institutions and social facilities.

Economy in Capital Expenditure

It would be wrong to regard this investment as a draft on the nation's capital-forming capacity that in the absence of new towns would not have been necessary. An equivalent expenditure would have been incurred somewhere in any event. In a land with an industrial economy, and an urban fabric subject to normal depreciation, a vast amount of replacement as well as new construction is continuously needed, for which capital has to be found out of the pool of general savings, either through Government loans or private investment.

As a means of replacement and expansion the new towns have undoubtedly been less costly than any conceivable alternative. If, for example, even half the number of dwellings in the first 15 new towns had been built instead as flats in cities the extra cost (wholly unremunerative) could have been of the order of £75 million.

Critics have suggested that the economy on housing in new towns may be substantially offset by the necessity of providing in them *de novo* other types of buildings already existing in old centres. But this is true only to a relatively small extent, if at all. Much of the equipment in existing cities—schools, service installations, and all sorts of buildings—is out-of-date and overdue for replacement. Modernization of dwellings carries with it many more baths, lavatories and taps, and increased consumption of water and discharge of wastes involves amplified mains, new sources of supply, sewers and outfall works. The smaller the retained population, the less costly are these expansions and renewals. Moreover, a continued over-concentration of people and their work in a great conurbation necessitates huge capital expenditures on new and wider highways, subways, overpasses, public transportation systems, parking meters and traffic signals, just to keep things going. In Britain it is the custom for the Government to contribute 75% of the cost of highway improvements, which are largely necessitated by over-centralization. And in the over-large cities there is an acute shortage of space for schools, parks and playing fields. The larger the retained population the greater is the acreage required for such open space, and the greater the local displacement of population from land taken for it.

Economy in Housing Cost and Subsidies

No doubt it is considerations of this nature, in addition to the enormous burden of subsidizing new flats, that have led the municipal statesmen of London to support a dispersal policy, and even to contribute to the cost of housing in distant towns for some of their displaced families. This is not only humane, not only imaginative; it is also financially advantageous to London rate-payers.

Recognition of the economy of new towns has been slow to come. For many years the TCPA, in its publications and statements to Ministers, showed by simple calculations that housing in new towns instead of at high density in old cities would save colossal sums(7.2). Government housing subsidies, fixed for 60 years (the same period as the loans), are so devised as roughly to equalize the rents for dwellings of different costs of construction and sites. Capitalized, the difference in the total subsidies on dwellings of various types just about equals the difference in their original capital cost. Thus in effect the Exchequer pays to the housing authority a substantial part of the loan charges on its unremunerative expenditure.

City authorities have to make up a big difference between the rents and the loan charges, but they may meet this, or part of it, out of increases of rents on their older housing projects. New multi-storey flats, though heavily subsidized by the Government, still involve a further deficiency to be met locally out of rates or the increased rents of existing dwellings.

In view of the much-canvassed concern for public economy, it seems to us strange that no section of opinion, apart from the TCPA, could be induced to take any interest in the excess cost and the distortion of development caused by differential subsidies. If government housing subsidies had been equal for dwellings in all situations (better still, if they had been proportional to floor space) a very different and better distribution of the national effort must have resulted(7.3). Local authorities would not, because financially they could not, have endeavoured to pack as many people as possible in redevelopment schemes. They would have been forced much earlier to consider the alternative of planned dispersal. There would have been, in some degree, an economic check on the expansion of employment and the increase of land values in central city areas. The differential subsidies weaken this economic check. Adam Smith and Alfred Marshall, we imagine, would have been shocked to the core at this policy. But no modern economist, no Parliamentarian, no Treasury watch-dog, paid any serious attention to it(7.4).

Studies of Alternative Costs

After many abortive attempts to raise this issue, the TCPA in 1958 challenged the then Minister of Housing and Local Government (Lord Brooke) to have its figures examined. He accepted the challenge, and the TCPA submitted calculations of the comparative public costs (in capital and subsidies) of providing 1000 dwellings of 850 sq. feet (79 m²) of floor-space: (*a*) in 12-storey city flats at 40 an acre (100 per ha); and (*b*) half in a city at 20 an acre (50 per ha), and half in new towns at 14 an acre (35 per ha).

The alternative costs in capitalized subsidies on the scales then in force were shown to be: for scheme (*a*) £1 809 000, and for scheme (*b*) £644 000. On 15 000 houses in a new town of 50 000, with 15 000 houses at low density in a city centre, as against 30 000 flats all in the centre, the saving would be £34 950 000.

Having studied the TCPA figures, the Minister's experts did not fault the arithmetic, but they disputed some of the assumptions. They argued that a flat of 750 sq. feet (70 m²) was comparable with a house of 850 sq. feet (80 m²)—a plainly ridiculous contention. They also argued that in practice a city scheme at 40 dwellings an acre (100 per ha) need not be all in 12-storey flats; it could have 42% of 11-storey flats, 35% in 4-storey maisonettes, and 23% in 2-storey houses. This seemed to the TCPA beside the point. Obviously if pressure in city centres were relieved, it would be the more costly flats that could be omitted. However, the Ministry's revisions did not reduce the estimated saving by quite half. But the Ministry commented that 'a great many considerations, both social and economic, come into the question of dispersal which could not be evaluated in figures'. What wider issues the Ministry had in mind may be surmised. We have dealt with some of them already; we shall discuss others in a later chapter.

A more elaborate study of the comparative costs of high-density central housing and partial dispersal was made by P. A. Stone of the then Building Research Station in a paper to the Royal Statistical Society in 1959(7.5). Using BRS figures Mr Stone amply confirmed the TCPA's estimate of the excess cost of high flats, but went into a wider range of costs, private as well as public, and also converted the capital costs into annual charges. His calculations were complex and involved a number of debatable assumptions. Basing his comparisons on a unit of 154 persons rehoused in various ways, and including the corollary costs (public services, workplaces, schools, other buildings and open spaces) he found that as between (*a*) housing 70 of them in 2-storey houses centrally and 84 in new towns, and (*b*) housing 122.5 of them in 5-storey flats with lifts and only 31.5 in new towns, (*a*) is somewhat cheaper than (*b*). Higher blocks than 5 storeys would, of course, show a much greater excess cost, as the TCPA figures had demonstrated. Dispersal to existing country towns, he concluded, would be cheaper than to new towns, by reason of their possession already of much community equipment; but here he seemed to ignore the financial advantage to a developing agency of owning local shopping centres and commercial buildings as part of a large-scale development. Moreover, some new towns are based on existing urban units that already have some community facilities; the distinction between a 'new town' and a 'town expansion' is one of the type of machinery used rather than of the size of the original urban unit on which it is based.

It seems to us that as the dispersal and new towns policy has been proved to be highly economical to the state, in some degree economical to the local authorities, and in many ways clearly advantageous to society, the case for it is unanswerable. Nevertheless, it is reassuring to know that, taking every calculable interest, private and public, into account, there is an overall financial gain. Seldom in the field of social policy does such a coincidence occur.

Financial Success of the Garden Cities

It is interesting to look at the financial experience of the two private-enterprise garden cities.

The Letchworth company, First Garden City Limited, started in 1903 with an issued capital of £101 000, increased over a period to a total of £250 000 in ordinary shares and £150 000 in 5% preference shares. All expenditure above this was financed by mortgage loans, debentures, bank advances, and revenues ploughed back. There was a long delay in the payment of the cumulative dividend of 5%, but all arrears were paid by 1946.

Thereafter there were surplus profits and increments of capital value that under the original constitution of the company should have benefited the town and its inhabitants. But the company abandoned its shareholders' profits limits in 1949 and 1956, and in 1960 control passed to commercial interests with no legal obligation to honour the intention that the town estate would ultimately pass into local public ownership. This obligation was restored by Parliament through the Letchworth Garden City Corporation Act 1962, but the compensation that had to be paid for the estate, over £3 million, deprived the town of the increments of value to that date, while the ordinary shareholders, for each 5*s*. originally subscribed, received 54*s*. 6*d*.—an appreciation of nearly 1000 % on their investment. The population had increased from 400 in 1903 to 25 000 in 1962.

Welwyn Garden City Ltd up to the time of the taking-over of the estate by the Government also showed a considerate appreciation. The company, started in 1920, raised in ordinary shares £119 500 (the maximum dividend in this case being 7%), and in 6% debenture bonds a further £800 000. By the reconstruction in 1934 the ordinary shares were written down from £1 to 2*s*. Debenture bonds were converted into

ordinary shares on a more favourable basis. When the company was wound up after
the Government take-over in 1948 the holders received in all £2 315 000—a surplus of
£1 395 000 over their total original investment. (The ordinary shareholders lost
£66 700.) The population had grown from 400 in 1920 to 18 000 in 1948.

We need not here discuss further the social misfortune that these increments of
value benefited the investors and not the towns and their inhabitants. What is important is that the thesis that the creation of new towns produces substantial increments is
proved.

The Letchworth appreciation is remarkable in view of the company's policy of
abstaining from the exploitation of rack-rent values in the town's commercial centre or
factory area. On the other hand the company did particularly well on its water, gas and
electricity undertakings, which proved more profitable even than its ground rents.

Welwyn Garden City retained from the start the ownership of most of the shops and
offices and smaller factory buildings, letting them at market rents which could be
raised as population grew. As in the later new towns, this policy was possible because
of the ownership of the complete town site. It is this that makes new-town building so
sound an economic proposition. But the monopoly it implies points to the desirability
of public ownership of the freehold, or at least some limit on charges or some public
share in the financial results, as is usual in the case of a gas, electricity or water
undertaking.

Housing subsidies played a very small part in the finance. Letchworth before the
1939–45 war received few subsidies. In Welwyn up to 1938 the capital value of
Exchequer subsidies under the Housing Acts amounted to about £200 000, on 2742
houses. Far larger subsidies were paid at that time for houses and flats in London and
other great cities.

The Government New Towns

There is every sign that the Government new towns are highly satisfactory national
investments. The first 12 in England and Wales, taken together, paid their way within
12 years from their start. They showed in the year to March 1967, after covering interest
during construction and repayments on the entire expenditure from the start, a
revenue surplus of £1 860 000. Their outstanding capital advances at that date were
£360 500 000. They had provided about 132 000 houses for 444 000 persons, of which
the corporations had financed about 109 400 houses, with public subsidies averaging
£32 a year a house. Far larger subsidies would have had to be paid for the alternative of
high-rise housing in large cities.

The 3 earliest towns in Scotland, on which at March 1967 the outstanding capital
advances were £94¾ million, had not yet reached profitability, but still showed a
combined loss of £654 000 in the year. They had housed about 97 200 persons in 26 400
new dwellings, of which the corporations had provided about 25 700. One reason for
the less favourable results was that house rents in Scotland were much lower than in
England and Wales, and fell far short of outgoings even with subsidies 80% greater.

All the new towns started since 1960 cannot yet be expected to pay their way. Up to
31 March 1976 the 28 towns had received net capital advances of £1 682 386 278. The
towns designated since 1947 have taken on average about 15 years to repay their capital
investment and interest to the Treasury, although in years to come the length of time
for total repayment of investment could vary.

In general the housing rents are fixed on a cost basis, so as to meet, with the aid of the subsidies, the out-goings on loan charges, repairs and maintenance. Housing is not expected to yield a surplus. For this the corporations have to look mainly to ground rents of sites leased for business purposes, and especially to the occupation rents of industrial and commercial buildings. Like the Welwyn Garden City company, the new towns have invested boldly in this class of property and have been rewarded by a return of 9 to 10% on it—a useful (indeed necessary) margin over the average of over $5\frac{1}{2}\%$ they have paid in interest and loan charges. That a new-town agency should itself build shops and offices for letting is of great financial importance, and particularly in the early days, because it is only by that means that they can obtain progressive rentals as population grows. Adequate ground rents cannot be negotiated with commercial property developers while populations are small and the rate of growth uncertain.

In many large-scale estates in the USA it is the practice to lease retail shops at rentals based on a percentage of their turnover. The British practice of periodical revision of rents as values increase with population is based, perhaps with less exactitude, on the same principle. In at least two of the British towns (Welwyn Garden City and East Kilbride) some ground rents on long leases of shop sites are assessed on a percentage of the occupation rents received by the firm owning the buildings.

In the new towns, as in any large-scale development, private or public, many sites have to be provided free or at less than cost for recreation, parks, churches, and community buildings. Contributions are also made towards sewerage, water, street works, lighting, public halls, swimming pools, sports stadiums, and youth clubs. These are included in the total expenditure already referred to.

We repeat the opening point of this chapter. The new towns have produced an immense improvement in living conditions and industrial efficiency, and a vast gain in time for leisure and useful occupation. If these benefits had cost much money they would be justified. But in fact the new towns bring the nation considerable immediate savings, as well as long-term profits.

Effect on Local Authority Finance

The rapid increases of population in the new towns have necessitated much expenditure by local authorities and county councils, but have also greatly increased rateable values and rate income. Most of the buildings being new and of modern types, the amount of rates collected per head of population is higher in the new towns but the average household income must also be considerably greater. The county councils have begun to find the provision of schools, libraries, fire, police and ambulance services an undue burden in relation to the growth of rateable value and special arrangements have now been made for the development corporations to make special contributions. The district councils, however, do find themselves unable, out of available resources, to provide as soon as required all the social facilities within their statutory powers; and it is in this field that bigger contributions from the surplus resources of the new town estates might now well be made.

Future Ownership of New Towns

All political parties in Britain have supported the new towns policy. The one issue on which there has been a conflict of views is that of their ultimate ownership. No party has questioned the principle that each town should remain in public ownership and that financial surpluses should be used in some way for public purposes. But Howard's proposal, endorsed by the original intentions of the two garden city companies, that on completion of a town the ownership should pass to the local authority or some local trust, and surpluses used 'for the benefit of the town or its inhabitants', is seriously contested.

A large majority of the New Towns (Reith) Committee doubted the wisdom of combining the functions of landowner and local authority in a single body subject to the changes of personnel 'natural to and proper in an elected body', and favoured the retention of the new town corporation as landowner. Lord Silkin's New Towns Act, 1946, went back to Howard's conception, and provided that, when substantially completed, each town estate should be handed over to the local authority.

In 1959, however, the Government decided that, in view of the scale of property management involved, the ownership should remain, 'for the time being at any rate', in the hands of a body independent of the local authority. Carried against strong Labour opposition, the New Towns Act, 1959, set up a Commission for the New Towns (in England and Wales) to take over the assets and liabilities of each development corporation as it completes its work, with the duty 'of maintaining and enhancing the value of the land' and the return from it. It was emphasized in the debate that the Commission was not to be a 'disposals body', but was to act as a 'good landlord'. And the Act requires the Commission to 'have regard to the purpose for which the town was developed and to the convenience and welfare of persons residing, working, or carrying on business there'. Powers are given to contribute towards amenities for the towns and to provide water and sewerage services, but the Commission (unlike the existing corporations) will be subject to normal planning control. It is directed to appoint local committees of management with some local members.

The Commission was duly set up in 1961 and by 1967 had taken over four of the towns—Crawley, Hemel Hempstead, Hatfield and Welwyn Garden City. The questions remain as to whether a central Commission will not be too remote from local interests and democratic influences to be permanently satisfactory; and as to what share, if any, the towns will have in the financial surpluses. The Act of 1959 requires the Commission to pay these surpluses to the Treasury. The inhabitants could claim that they should be used for their benefit, since the financial success is largely due to their activities and they need further urban amenities.

Naturally there is much argument about this. If the new towns had been conceived as speculative enterprises the 'risk-taking' investors (the nation as a whole) might be held to be entitled to the profits. But they were not so conceived and there was no real risk. The only capital sum on which interest has not been paid throughout is the bagatelle of £446 725 granted by the Ministry at the outset.

If, surely more correctly, the new towns are regarded as a public service, the first call on surpluses is for the improvement of the service. On that view the Commission for the New Towns should not act merely as the 'good landlord', charitably devoting a fraction of its gains to the tenantry, but rather as a trustee for the towns, applying its surpluses mainly to community facilities in them until they are well endowed in all respects.

As the largest landlord in the fully grown towns the Commission continues to generate controversy in local authorities and by the 1976 New Towns (Transfer of Assets) Act the housing and related assets are to be given to the local authority. The

Commission remains as landlord of industrial and commercial property and so the question remains.

In the long run it seems certain that total revenues will exceed what is necessary to maintain local amenities on a high level. At that stage taxpayers, or the nation as a whole, might stake a claim to participate. Or a fund might be set up to provide social facilities in further new towns at an earlier stage than in their forerunners.

References and Notes

7.1 But large numbers of medieval towns were in fact founded by kings and feudal lords as economic enterprises intended to yield a financial return. See BERESFORD, M., *New Towns of the Middle Ages*, 1967.

7.2 See OSBORN, F. J., *Green-Belt Cities*, 1946 and 1969, pp. 110–11.

7.3 For a brief history of the differential subsidies and a study of their effects, see OSBORN, F. J., 'How Subsidies Distort Housing Development', *Lloyds Bank Review*, April, 1955.

7.4 HALL, D., 'Inner City Sense and Nonsense', *Town and Country Planning*, November, 1976. Some useful studies have been made of the relative costs of central high-density development and low-density development in new towns. See for example STONE, P. A., *Housing, Town Development, Land and Costs*, 1963.

7.5 STONE, P. A., 'The Economics of Housing and Urban Development', *Journal of Royal Statistical Society*, **122**, Part 2, 1959. See also for an expansion of the study STONE, P. A., *Housing, Town Development, Land and Costs*, 1963.

8 The Town and Country Pattern

'The more we are together,
The merrier we shall be.'
—Popular song (*not claiming to be based on sociological research*)

Now that land-use planning and some guidance of the distribution of population are recognized as governmental functions, there is a need of public and expert discussion of the pattern of town and country. A complete and logical new layout suited to modern likings and resources is of course precluded by the vast and durable developments already located. But even if we had a virgin land to plan, there is no conceivable arrangement that would provide towns ideally satisfactory to persons of all types and temperaments.

The conception, entertained by some immature planners, that the suburban population could be re-concentrated in city cores to match an intense business and cultural concentration, must be dismissed as quantitatively absurd as well as sociologically reactionary. To the very limited extent to which suburbans could be brought back, it would involve the sacrifice of the popularly-desired type of family dwelling. There are, of course, people who genuinely prefer to live in flats close to the special set of advantages that a city centre offers; and it would be better to build for them there than to add to the present excess of centralized businesses. But these people are a small minority. And they will be among the beneficiaries if provision is made elsewhere for some of the central workplaces and people who do not share their tastes in environment.

Balance of Density and Extent

Though the disadvantages both of congestion and of excessive urban growth are now recognized, there is at present no consensus of opinion among town planners as to the optimum balance or compromise between density and diameter. Nor is it likely that a universal scientific formula will emerge. What is essential, however, for reasons already suggested, is that fairly definite upward and downward limits of ultimate size should be set for each particular unit. This is a condition of intelligent planning. As F. J. Osborn wrote in 1934: 'It would be far better if planners and their partisans were divided, like the Lilliputians, into bitterly hostile groups, of Big-Townians and Little-Townians, Fifteen-thousanders and Hundred-thousanders, than that they should remain in their present bemused state of helpful purposelessness—like gardeners hoeing and watering the plant and wondering if it is going to be a daisy or a hollyhock.'

The wish in that passage has certainly been fulfilled—almost with mathematical precision. The Reith Committee in 1946 recommended as norms for new towns a lower population limit of the order of 30 000; its Scottish and Welsh members thought 15 000 might be sufficient for some towns in their regions; and while the majority favoured an upper limit of about 50 000, with perhaps up to 80 000 within a radius of 10 miles (16 km), some felt that there might in certain localities be justification for towns consider-ably larger. The debate has continued since, and is never likely to end.

The New Towns Committee's suggested upper limit of the order of 50 000 was based on a balancing of the factors of (a) acceptable internal density and (b) convenient nearness of homes to workplaces, town centres, schools, and the open country. In the vital matter of housing density they assumed loyalty to popular preferences, and their expectation that 90 to 95% of the new-townspeople would want single-family houses with gardens has proved correct, as many reports of the development corporations (sometimes to their officers' surprise) show. The committee did not, however, lay down any precise standard of maximum or optimum housing density. The main purpose of their calculations was to ensure that the sites designated should be sufficient to permit of the lowest probable overall town density, which they estimated at 12 persons a town acre (30 per ha). They thought the density in most cases might be between 13 and 15 persons an acre (32 and 37 per ha) overall, but was not likely to exceed 15 (37 per ha).

The component factors in these calculations included the standards of net residential and neighbourhood densities prescribed for new developments by the ministerial *Housing Manual* of 1944, taking into account the desirability that the new towns should include average percentages of the national income groups, the more affluent of whom would require larger houses and larger plots than those in public housing schemes. Other factors were the areas required for industry, commercial and entertainment centres, schools, parks and playing fields, roads and footpaths. The calculations for these were based on studies of the areas found by experience to be devoted to such purposes in existing towns, and where these were deemed unsatisfactory on reliable specifications by ministries or bodies like the National Playing Fields Association. It was assumed that development would be as compact as good standards permit. But some margin over the theoretical area required should, in site acquisition, be allowed for, since there are always local topographical features that inhibit completely logical planning—and incidentally often make the plan more interesting.

The overall densities of the first batch of new towns under the Act of 1946 did in fact work out in fairly close approximation to the Reith Committee's estimates. But though they are appreciably greater than the densities of most older towns of comparable size in Britain(8.1), there is a widespread impression that these new towns are too open—that they sprawl inconveniently. The gibe of 'prairie planning' has been flung at them by some critics. There is no sign that the inhabitants share this agoraphobic reaction. The great majority of houses are built at densities not less than—in fact a litle in excess of—those customary in inter-war municipal cottage estates; gardens are somewhat smaller; roads are no wider; school sites are about as large; only the space for playing fields and parks is rather more generous. But though the total acreage per thousand persons is much the same as in the older towns, it is far less unevenly distributed. This reflects the wider distribution of purchasing power brought about by political and economic changes, taxation, and social welfare policy. Inevitably it lessens the dramatic (indeed tragic) contrast between magnificence and squalor con-spicuous in towns surviving from a former age. The new towns have no 'cosy' slum courtyards; no picturesque Tom All-Alones; no ducal palaces or estates or millionaires' rows; almost none even of the villas with several acres of garden that lower the average density of many cities. They might indeed be criticized for not having catered sufficiently for people of the higher-income groups who demand and can afford larger dwellings on larger plots.

In effect one may say that the pleasant vistas of trees, grass, flowers and harmonious design, in old towns the privilege of a few, have in the new towns been extended to everybody. If in spite of the great efforts made to produce local diversity in details of architecture and layout, the towns have some overall similarity to each other, complaint on that score is stupid. They are products of the same period and the same economic and social circumstances. Of course they cannot differ in scenic effects as widely as Venice differs from San Francisco, New York from Granada or Rothenburg from Bath. But a town is not a stage set to amuse on a single occasion a playgoer seeking a novel thrill. The perambulating aesthete who, once in a lifetime, sees a town, values it as a spectacle. He wants a change from his own town. But the resident sees the same buildings day by day for years. They ought to be pleasing to him, of course, but they cannot produce a continual sense of variation. That however can be given to him by the seasonal changes in vegetative surroundings—which is one reason why gardens and generous landscaping are not less important than architectural design.

In discussing this subject a vital distinction must be made between 'maximum' and 'average' density. Maximum residential density is the largest number of persons of dwellings an acre permitted for any part of the town. Such a maximum is often prescribed to safeguard future occupants from developers who might, for commercial reasons, crowd too many dwellings on a site; or to impose a degree of openness of development to maintain residential character or values. In any town, however, some house-plots will be at lower densities. Thus the average density will always be lower than the maximum.

Here we can discuss only briefly the subject of density standards, the assessment and formulation of which involves a study of many dimensional variables. Laymen can easily be confused by figures presented to them by experts, even when (which is not always the case) the experts understand them themselves.

Factors in a Maximum Housing Density

A maximum local density of 14 family houses a net acre (35 per ha) (including access roads), or 15 dwellings a net acre (37 per ha) if 5 or 10% of flats at 40 an acre (100 per ha) are provided, accommodates about 45 to 50 persons a net acre (110 to 125 per ha). It permits 2-storey houses of about 900–1000 sq. feet (85–95 m²) of internal floor-space, with frontages of about 20 feet (6 m), forecourts or front gardens 15 feet (4.5 m) deep (the absolute minimum for a sense of privacy from public roads or sidewalks), back gardens 60 feet (18 m) long, and road-widths of 40 feet (12 m) average (leaving, if carriageways are 20 feet (6 m) wide, only 10 feet (3 m) each side for a 6 foot (2 m) sidewalk and a grass verge). Thus the distance between facing rows of houses is 70 feet (20 m)—again the minimum for privacy. A margin of about 20% has to be allowed for cross-roads, gaps between ends of terraces, and minor set-backs to give agreeable variety. The use of narrower cul-de-sac roads will increase the possible depth of some front gardens (or forecourts) but cannot increase the density unless the 70-feet (20 m) distance between façades is reduced. That dimension can of course be reduced without destroying privacy if windows are omitted on one façade of a row of houses, but this has other obvious disadvantages.

Note that at the density of 15 2-storey dwellings an acre (37 per ha) the prevailing back garden has an area of about 1200 sq. feet (110 m²). Adding the front garden the area is 1500 sq. feet (140 m²). The garden of a detached house of double the floor area (1800 to 2000 sq. feet [170 to 190 m²]) at a third of the density (5 an acre [2.5 per ha]) is at least four times as large (6250 to 6500 sq. feet [580 to 600 m²]). The area of a normal spare-time allotment (10 rods) is 2723½ sq. feet (253 m²).

These figures (which anyone can check) destroy any illusion that a housing density of 15 dwellings (50 persons) a net acre (37 dwellings and 125 persons per ha) is lavish or lax. In relation to current popular aspirations it is in fact stern and stringent. Which is one reason why, as incomes and ambitions rise, many wage-earning families buy or rent houses on commercially built estates at much lower densities—commonly at 8 or fewer houses an acre (20 per ha). Most of the new town corporations have catered to some extent for this demand. Some, on the other hand, under ill-advised pressure from the Ministry, have built large numbers of houses at 18 or more an acre (45 per ha).

No great cleverness is required to 'achieve' a greater density. All you have to do is to reduce one or more of the component dimensions—the frontage, the distance between windows, or the area of gardens—or to add more storeys to the buildings. It is true that none of the accepted minimum dimensions can claim 'scientific' validity; they are all matters of judgment—as indeed are standards for minimum wages or holiday periods, or maximum hours. But the laws of space cannot be defied by the most brilliant ingenuity. An increase of density inexorably reduces the ground space per person. Clumsy planning, as Unwin showed in *Nothing Gained by Overcrowding* (1912), may cause an excess of road space—which is wasteful, because few take pleasure in road space—but at the density of 15 an acre (37 per ha) as now practised there is certainly no surplus for traffic and car-waiting requirements. Indeed, there is hardly room for the convenient placing of the domestic garages now required.

Overall Town Densities

The arguments for higher densities in future new towns are based on several considerations, interesting to evaluate.

First, the more compact a town is the shorter are the distances between its parts—between home and employment, home and shops, home and the green belt. And within a given area and radius, the higher the density the larger the population that can be planned for. Thus a town of 50 000 at 15 persons an acre (37 per ha) has an area of 3333 acres (1400 ha), and if roughly circular, a radius (centre to edge) of about 1⁴⁄₇ miles (2.1 km). It is a tempting fact that if the density is increased by a third, to 20 an acre (50 per ha), the population can be increased (also by a third) to 66 666, while the radius is not increased at all.

Unfortunately the consequent change in housing density is far greater than that in overall town density. The areas for industry, schools, shops, public buildings and open spaces cannot be reduced in proportion. The main reduction per 1000 persons has to fall on housing space. An increase of one third in overall density, if other uses are unaltered, will necessitate almost a doubling of the net housing density—from, say, an average of 30, to 60 persons an acre (75 to 150 per ha).

Conversely, if the population remains at 50 000, while the overall density is raised from 15 to 20 (37 to 50 per ha) and the housing density is doubled, the radius is reduced only by about 13½% (less than ⅙ mile [0.27 km]).

The following table of populations, areas and radii will enable the reader to make other calculations(8.2):

Population	Overall Town Density							
	15 *persons an acre (37 per ha)*				20 *persons an acre (50 per ha)*			
	Area		*Radius*		*Area*		*Radius*	
	(acres)	(ha)	(miles)	(km)	(acres)	(ha)	(miles)	(km)
30 000	2000	800	0.997	1.60	1500	600	0.864	1.39
50 000	3333	1333	1.287	2.07	2500	1000	1.115	2.00
60 000	4000	1600	1.410	2.27	3000	1200	1.221	1.96
100 000	6667	2669	1.821	2.93	5000	2000	1.577	2.54

Proportion of Flats and Houses

The basic dimensions in a housing layout cited above, if accepted, imply that the tolerable maximum density for 2-storey single-family houses is about 14 houses (or 45 persons) a net acre (35 houses and 112.5 persons per ha); and that at any density above this there must be cramped gardens or a proportion of higher buildings. Flats can be built, with almost every convenience except direct access to the ground and garden space, at much higher densities. In big cities tower-blocks of 10 to 20 storeys are built at up to 60 flats (200 persons) an acre (150 flats and 500 persons per ha). In general, however, for reasons of constructional cost as well as of acceptability, the density is of the order of 40 flats (about 133 persons) an acre (100 flats and 332.5 persons per ha); and it is rare that this is exceeded in the smaller towns.

The effect of combining varying proportions of flats and terrace houses is shown in the following table (flats at 120, houses at 45, persons an acre [flats at 300, houses at 112.5 persons per ha]):

Combined Density		*Houses*	*Flats*
(*persons per acre*)	(*persons per ha*)	(*45 p.p.a; 112 p.p.ha*)	(*120 p.p.a; 296 p.p.ha*)
45	112	100%	Nil
50	124	84%	16%
60	148	61%	39%
75	185	36%	64%
100	247	12%	88%
120+	296+	Nil	100%

Conclusion on Size and Density

We think we have made clear the factors pointing to an optimum or norm for a new town of a population of about 50 000 and a density of about 15 persons a town acre (37 per ha). This cannot be a universal formula, but it is useful as a sort of datum from which the gains and losses of variations upward and downward can be measured. If, for example, it were thought genuinely advantageous to have a number of large industrial establishments in one place, so advantageous in productive efficiency as to make it worthwhile for many employees to spend daily more than half an hour in travel, the town could be bigger without necessarily reducing the garden sizes. Alternatively, a number of towns could be placed (still with green belts or country reservations) near enough to each other to facilitate reasonably short exchanges of movement—which seems to us the wiser plan. But it should not be assumed that the size of industrial units is ungovernable; a minor margin of productivity does not in principle justify a major cut in the space for the home environment—the end-product of all industry. Moreover some industrialists hold that there are managerial advantages in limiting the size of local establishments. In any case, Britain has many very large towns; we ought not without compelling reasons to add to their number.

In our discussion of town size we have stressed the primacy of the home environment as an end-product of human effort, for the reason that the trends of agglomeration, and of opportunist actions to ameliorate its inconveniences, are inimical to this major interest. Re-emphasis on the home does not however imply indifference to the social and cultural aspects of living. No one questions that assemblages of population so disposed as to facilitate diverse associations and interchanges are necessary for the more highly organized institutions of society. But though a regrouping with more towns of moderate size and less intensely massed central cities might change the cultural pattern there is no reason to think it would reduce its overall richness. Certainly there are elements of culture by common consent indispensable, such as higher education, theatre, orchestral music, and market complexes, that could never have developed in villages or small towns isolated in sparsely populated regions, because they require fairly large numbers of specialized personnel with expensive buildings and equipment. The same is true of some popular institutions of culture such as dog-tracks, race-courses, and (at the moment) bingo halls.

Not everybody in a nation wants to share in the particular forms of culture characteristic of the modern metropolis, which show aspects of deterioration as well as of advance. Many find outweighing advantages in relatively small communities, and not a few in the deep country far from towns. But even for the most urban-minded 'all that life can afford' might well be provided in a regional galaxy of towns with a total population of a million or so. The embarrassments that arise by expanding a metropolitan region to 5, 10 or 15 millions are not compensated by an equivalent gain either in economic efficiency or social culture. The law of diminishing returns operates in urban size as in many other matters.

Location of Industry and Population

Once again the Town and Country Planning Association, under a new generation of enthusiasts, gave a strong lead to public and authoritative opinion. Having made careful quantitative studies of the situation in the London region(8.3), the West Midlands, the North-West and the North-East, and held a series of widely representative local conferences, the association in the 1960s formulated proposals for decentralization and redevelopment based on realistic assessments of the facts and forces. Academic experts and political study groups have taken up the subject, and along with a flood of books and pamphlets of uneven competence there has emerged a fair consensus of opinion and a new orientation of government policy.

The TCPA does not envisage a wholesale transfer of population and industry from the plethoric to the anaemic regions. It accepts that the present total population of the

South-East region, for example, cannot be positively reduced and that its further natural growth must be allowed for—not however in the central conurbation itself, but in new and expanded towns beyond its green belt. At the same time everything practicable must be done to prevent further in-migration, and to promote the transfer of industry and office business to less crowded parts of the country. To achieve this a firm restriction of the expansion of employment in and near the conurbations must be coupled with the creation elsewhere of 'urban magnets' strong enough to attract firms and workers and to be economically, socially and culturally viable.

In the late 1960s the TCPA philosophy, long dismissed by authorities and many planners as unpractical, or derided as fantastic, became the official and professional orthodoxy, with momentous consequences in legislation, administration and the emergence of new issues and problems that will be discussed in a later chapter.

First, however, we must describe some of the obstacles and resistances, interested, intellectual, or hidebound, that the TCPA philosophy encountered on its way to acceptance.

References and Notes

8.1 BEST, ROBIN, *Land for New Towns*, 1964.

8.2 For a fuller discussion of town size and density the reader is referred to KEEBLE, LEWIS, *Principles and Practice of Town Planning*, 4th Ed., 1969. In our view Mr Keeble's prescription of a theoretical overall density of $20\frac{3}{4}$ persons an acre (83 per ha) for a town of 60 000 underestimates the average areas required for playing fields and parks, for industry, for railways, for topographical pecularities or scenic interest, and for larger dwelling-house sites in a 'balanced' population. But he gives all the data for intelligent consideration.

8.3 See *The Paper Metropolis*, TCPA, 1962.

9 *Antagonisms to New Towns*

'Bring me my rows of close-packed streets!
Bring me my hopes of fewer births!
Bring me my flats, my city walls!
Bring me my maps of barren earths!'

—*Jerusalem Replanned*(9.1)

For many years after Howard propounded it, the garden-city or new-town concept was regarded by nearly everybody as an ideal, beautiful but sad to say impracticable—too good to be true. Since its practicability has been demonstrated, it has encountered opposition from sections of opinion well placed politically, well organized, skilful in advocacy, but narrow in economic and social outlook. Through their propaganda a widespread belief was produced that building new towns would involve an inordinately large sacrifice of agricultural land, endanger food supplies, and destroy the beauty of the countryside. To avoid these disasters, it was argued, the townspeople of Britain, present and future, must be housed and rehoused with a maximum of compactness—that is to say mainly in high flats at the greatest possible density.

These apprehensions and proposals, which have had a lamentable effect on housing and planning policy, are based on a grossly defective sense of scale, which it is our purpose here to correct.

The Argument about 'Saving Land'

No one would dispute that economy in the use of land, as of any of man's resources, is desirable. Nor is it to be denied that the greater the density of fresh urban development, the less the acreage that has to be subtracted from agricultural, wooded and other unbuilt-on land. Thus there is some conflict of interest between crowded townsmen who need more space for living, and countrymen (farmers and rural residents) who want to keep from building as much of the countryside as they can; and this conflict is accentuated by the growth of population.

Granted the necessity of urban expansion in some form, however, the creation of new towns, or the planned enlargement of existing country towns, especially in areas of static or sparse population, brings considerable benefits to the countryside. It is unfortunate, therefore, that new towns have drawn more fire from countryside defenders than the secular suburban sprawl, although new towns are really much more 'compact' than the run of suburbs. No doubt this is because the outward creep of suburbs has been adventitious and often absorbs land already depreciated in 'amenity' by its nearness to previous developments, whereas new towns are seen as deliberate, even wanton, incursions on land of unspoiled rural character. They are feared as the storm troops of the urban invasion.

When (Sir) Dudley Stamp's admirable Land Utilization Survey was first published it was argued that every effort should be made to avoid building on the very small area of the highest quality land (6.8% in England and Wales). But later the proposed embargo was extended to all 'good agricultural land' (44.2%), which would make the siting of new development an impossible obstacle race. And there is a tendency among 'ultra-preservationists' to press for high urban densities—'building up'—to save every possible inch of rural land. It is this extreme attitude that we deplore as inhumane and misguided.

The amount of rural land that could be saved by 'building up' has been wildly exaggerated. Estimates of the number of overcrowded people that ought to be dispersed from British cities have varied from $1\frac{1}{2}$ millions to 3 millions—the latter a maximum not likely to be achieved. But even if 3 millions were rehoused in new towns or expanded small towns, with workplaces, open spaces and all other urban facilities, they would absorb, at 15 persons a town acre (37 per ha), only 200 000 acres (80 000 ha).

Provision has also to be made for the increase of the national population, officially forecasted in 1965 as of the order of 20 million by the year 2000. There are today signs of some fall in the birth rate, but planners have to take account of the higher possibility. At 15 persons per urban acre (37 per ha) 20 million people would absorb another $1\frac{1}{3}$ million acres (530 000 ha), raising the area of town and villages (including industry, business, town services, gardens and internal open space) to just over 5 million acres (2 million ha). But there would still remain about 50 million acres (20 million ha) of non-urban land, of which nearly 45 million acres (18 million ha) would be agricultural land and rough grazing (some of it capable of improvement) and 4 million acres (1.6 million ha) forests and woodlands.

The authors of this book share the general view that a further very large growth of the population of Britain, as of the world, is not to be desired, and favour political and social efforts to restrain it. But in itself the expansion of our built-up area from about 7% to 9 or even 10% cannot be regarded as a disaster. It would still leave 90% of the land as open country, in addition to the gardens, playing fields and planted spaces inside the towns.

It is the space for housing that land-savers propose to cut. Few think it practicable to reduce the acreages for factories, shops, schools and playing fields. But if as many as $3\frac{1}{3}$ million more townsfolk (a million families) were housed in high flats at 150 (375 per ha) instead of in terrace houses (with 10% of low flats) at 50 persons an acre (20 per ha), the 'saving' would be about 44 450 acres (17 780 ha), or one-1000th of rural land. The construction cost of housing would be increased by something like £1200 million, the greater part of which, to equate rents, would have to be covered by Government subsidies. (The figure seems fantastic, but let the reader check it! It amounts to £27 000 for each acre 'saved' [9.2].)

New Towns and Food Production

The delusion that dispersal to new towns endangers Britain's food supplies was for years sedulously fostered by spokesmen for agriculture, and with especial ingenuity by the National Farmers' Union. Frightening figures were published of the quantities of potatoes, milk, loaves of bread or mutton-chops lost for ever when 1000 acres (400 ha) of farm-land were taken for housing—no offset being conceded for garden produce, and no interest taken in the huge extra capital cost of the high-density alternative. The scare thus created was relieved in thoughtful circles by the studies of the experts of Wye Agricultural College(9.4), but it continues to disturb the minds of many people.

Here again it is the popular sense of scale that is at fault. British agricultural output between 1937/38 and 1960/61 (23 years) increased by 60% (at 1945/46 prices), though the area of improved farm land declined by 730 000 acres (292 000 ha), that is by $2\frac{1}{2}$%. In the same period the area of rough grazings, as shown in the returns, increased by 1 621 000 acres (656 000 ha), and of forest land by 620 000 acres (258 000 ha).

In the ten years 1952/1962 total agricultural output grew by about $2\frac{1}{2}$% per annum, while the absorption of land for development was about 30 000 to 40 000 acres (12 000 to 16 000 ha) per annum. Not all this was taken from improved farm land, but even if it were, the subtraction is less than 0.08% per annum of the total of farm land, grazings and forests, or 1.6% in 20 years.

The common impression, due to alarmist propaganda, that Britain's agricultural land is disappearing at a calamitous rate is sharpened by casual observation over limited fields. The percentage loss is certainly greater in, for instance, South-East England and the West Midlands. Though this does not much affect the overall food-supply equation, it does point to the desirability of checking so far as practicable the trend of population and development towards these regions.

Landscape and 'Amenity'

Sensitive observers have been deeply offended in recent decades by the deterioration of the visual scene in parts of Britain; and a vigorous movement has come into being to defend the beauty of the country and lessen the ugliness of the towns. Led by the National Trust, which preserves particular places and buildings of aesthetic or historic value, extended by the zeal of the Councils for the Protection of Rural England, Wales and Scotland, and reinforced by Duncan Sandys's Civic Trust, this movement has done much to open the eyes of an easy-going nation to the injuries inflicted on its landscape. These take many forms: ill-placed buildings, bad or incompetent architecture, abandoned mineral workings, spoil-dumps, military camps, unsightly advertisements and signs, the neglect and destruction of trees, and so on. The movement has enlisted many leaders of thought, literature and politics, and is now immensely influential in its noble objective of preserving and enhancing environmental amenity.

Unfortunately the word 'amenity' is often used utterly vaguely. It is a meaningless abstraction unless related to the feeling of some person or persons. When therefore it is discussed as a subject of public interest, the numbers and classes of persons who experience the 'amenity' necessarily come into the argument. To take an example: a man's sense of solitude in a fine landscape is for him an amenity—an exalting experience, especially for a city-dweller. A throb of this feeling comes to the writer in recalling a lonely walk up Scafell Pike before the first world war. Years later, walking up Scafell Pike again, he found himself in the company of a hundred others; it was still a grand experience but not quite the same. Today he might be one of a long queue throughout the expedition, and perhaps find a snack-bar on the summit. The sense of amenity given by solitude is thereby certainly lessened. (That of the grandeur of the scene remains.) Though no-one can now at all seasons so surely find Wordsworth's 'bliss of solitude' in that place, is the totality of the subjective delight less than it was? Only a supreme egoist-exclusionist could answer 'Yes!' to that question. For him there are too many people with similar tastes in the world. He may fulminate to himself and to the order of things. But he is in a difficult position in arguing his grievance in society.

Fortunately it is possible to retain the amenity of open landscape and quietude, for permanent rural residents as well as for passing observers, in by far the greater part of the countryside. As we have shown, new urban development of decent standards need not take in 30 years more than about 2 or 3% of rural land, within which limited area the distinctive amenity enjoyed by present residents will be replaced by amenities enjoyed by millions. The amenity of the 90% of open countryside can be, and ought to be, preserved for the benefit of all. Given that the nation's creative designers retain (or recover) the skill that combined with nature produced the beauty of our landscape, there must be an enormous overall gain in personal pleasurable experience.

Green Belts and Country Background

The concept of the green belt, as a sort of protective ring, an assurance that some element of natural grace and opportunity for recreation should remain within reach of town-dwellers, seems to have persisted, or to have recurred at various periods. It was certainly present in many projects for British–American and Australasian colonies(9.5). Though it is doubtful whether the founders of colonial towns, or the theorists and projectors of ideal communities (with the exception of Sir Thomas More) envisaged any general planning pattern for the size and placing of towns in countries or regions, the implications of their ideas are of great interest in the light of modern urban developments.

The crystallization of the concept of the rural belt as a permanent element in the town-country arrangement is due to Ebenezer Howard and the garden city movement. The principle was applied at Letchworth and was expressly connected with the intention that the ultimate size of a town should be definitely limited. Howard did not conceive the agricultural belt as an exiguous ringlet beyond which further urban growth should be free for all. He thought of it as part of the countryside at large—as an area in quasi-public ownership because only by this means could other agencies be prevented from building on country land made attractive by the presence of his new town. His intention was that when the garden city reached its planned maximum population other detached towns would be founded with similar limits. The planning pattern implied was well defined by Howard's brilliant follower Sir Raymond Unwin: 'Towns on a background of open country.'

The green belt idea has become widely acceptable in Britain, and has gained acceptance in other countries. Among country-dwellers it is welcomed as promising protection for rural land against suburban sprawl and unplanned or sporadic building. Town-dwellers, for their part, are collectively desirous that the open country on their immediate fringes shall remain intact; but individually many of them passionately desire to live in pleasant places within commuting distance. Thus there is a considerable conflict between collective and personal pressures. The principle of the green belt has been officially adopted in British planning policy (through a bold decision by Duncan Sandys when Minister of Housing and Local Government) since 1953, and large areas have been proposed as green reservations in many county plans(9.6). But in the governmental policy the principle is still that of reserving protective rings around towns considered to be at or near their limits of permissible expansion. This is a sound first step; it protects the rural land most urgently threatened. It does not, however, yet amount to a clear policy of 'towns on a background of open country'. The reservation of rings of limited depth around towns in which employment and population are still increasing could lead merely to a displacement of dormitory expansion to greater distances.

The Fetish of 'Urbanity'

Attempts have been made by architectural writers to discredit the two garden cities and the new towns influenced by their design on the ground that they lack 'urbanity'. Because the buildings in them are generously spaced and interspersed with gardens, lawns and trees, they rarely produce the particular effect of absolute enclosure or packed picturesqueness not undeservedly admired by visitors to many ancient towns. It is another and more popular kind of beauty, as well as a healthier and more convenient form of layout, that the new towns exhibit. But it is none the less truly a 'town' effect. The criticism reveals in those who make it verbal confusion and aesthetic narrow-mindedness. If the word 'urbanity' is used in the accepted sense of 'good manners' or 'educated tastefulness', the charge that the new towns are without it is an affront to the architects who have taken part in their design. If it is used in the simple etymological sense of 'towniness', the users unjustly accuse themselves of crass ignorance of the infinite diversity of shape and character—openness, compactness, ugliness, beauty, healthfulness, squalor, culture, vulgarity, etc., etc.—that the world's towns display. And if it is used (illegitimately) as a synonym for high urban density or crowdedness ('cosiness' and 'snugness' are among the further synonyms) it stands for a quality most townspeople regard as a drawback and escape from if they can. This word 'urbanity' has been so maltreated that it should be eliminated from town planning discussions.

The new towns have been obedient to prevailing architectural fashions. Luckily for the profession, the average Briton, though not highly sensitive to architectural design, does not mind it, so long as the things he really cares about in a house or a town are attended to. He takes great pleasure in gardens, trees and flowers, with which the new towns are well endowed. The outlook from his windows (the 'room with a view') is more important to him than the look of his dwelling from the street. And though he would have preferred his dwelling to have some element of individuality, he accepts harmonious design and grouping without resentment. Thus, given due respect for his major interest, a pleasing ensemble is attainable.

On the whole the managers of the new towns, when living on the job and in contact with those they are housing, have held the line against the outside pressure of over-anxious land economizers and devotees of 'urbanity'.

Natural Resistances to Dispersal

The relief of congestion and over-centralization in old cities is not the only motive for the creation of new towns; they are also a means of accommodating an increase of population. It is understandable that authorities of existing large towns have not been enthusiastic for either limitation of their growth or withdrawal of some of their citizens and businesses. Historically growth has been associated with prosperity, and its absence with a dread of positive decline in rateable value leading to financial disaster. In many towns new enterprises are welcomed, and systematic efforts made to attract them. Not unnaturally, therefore, municipal authorities, even when only mildly ambitious for further growth, tend to resist positive proposals for dispersal.

This resistant attitude is slowly changing, through a wider appreciation of economic facts and social interests. It begins to be realized that increases in rateable value may be more than offset by the costs of street improvements, higher-density rehousing, and extra space for schools and recreation. This realization would have come sooner if the local burden caused by growth had not been largely transferred to the national taxpayer by Exchequer grants and the differential subsidies on high-density housing.

Another natural resistance to planned dispersal is the anchorage or rootedness of persons and businesses to their present situations. A removal is not only costly; it also disrupts existing relationships and habits. Many persons and businesses, however, will readily move from a less to a more advantageous situation, and in fact most of the new towns have had no great difficulty in attracting both residents and industries. Recently, also, some have had success in attracting office businesses.

The discovery by patient sociologists(9.7) that there are little clusters of working-class people long resident in crowded cities who are neighbourly, and that some who have moved to good suburban housing estates feel friendless and unhappy, is no news to housing managers, doctors, or parsons. Cases of distressful loneliness are to be found in any place. They are notoriously prevalent in great cities. And they occur to some extent in new towns too, though nowhere are more organized efforts made to bring people together. In our own experience social integration and neighbourliness are at a higher level in new towns than in most old towns; the very fact that many families arrive simultaneously from different places gives them a common interest in making new associations. It is often more difficult for a newcomer to an established society (for instance an old cathedral town) to gain acceptance and to feel at home. Thus it is in the pioneer stage of a new town that the community spirit is at its maximum.

Sympathy with the close ties that exist in a crowded neighbourhood—the attachment to Mum and Dad, the corner shop, and so on—is admirable. But continuous outward migration is compelled by simple biological facts. Without it a crowded precinct would, through natural increase, become ever more and more crowded. In practice the pressure causes some families or persons to hive off spontaneously. We guess that these are usually the more prosperous and ambitious people of the neighbourhood: what Abercrombie called 'the better elements'—though we would not endorse a definition implying a slur on people who like to stay put.

Slum clearance, socially necessary, involves compulsory displacement, usually with little or no choice in the future dwelling. Moving to new towns is voluntary, and the evidence is that very few families want to go back on their decision.

Political Resistances

Governmental promotion of new towns involves the compulsory purchase of rather large parcels of land, mainly rural, owned and occupied by many persons. Though a fair price has to be paid, there is inevitably disturbance of the interests and habits of owners, farmers and local residents, and the odium of this falls on the promoters. In the usual case of acquisition for public purposes, it is the initiating local authority or statutory agency that incurs the main odium; the Ministry figures as the uncommitted deity impartially weighing the arguments for and against before approving or rejecting the project. Though there is always a local public inquiry at which objections are fully heard, when the Ministry is promoter as well as final arbiter it has no one with whom to share the odium. Neither the political chiefs nor the civil service administrators enjoy being in that position, especially if there are influential and vocal supporters of the party in power in the place chosen for a new town. Moreover it is an open secret that many sites considered suitable by the Ministry of Housing had to be forgone through the intransigent opposition of the Ministry of Agriculture.

The first 14 towns were started by the Labour Government of 1945–50, which had its major electoral support in the urban industrial constituencies. It has been suspected that the later Conservative Government's disinclination to promote further new towns was due partly to dislike of the odium to which we have referred, and partly to the fear of a change of balance of voting strength in the rural counties. Conversely, Labour members for urban centres are supposed to have feared the effect on their majorities of outward migration. On balance, any party losses or gains in towns and rural counties might have been expected to cancel out; but sitting members on both sides would not be consoled for the loss of their own seats by their party's gains in other seats.

Too much should not be made of this suspicion. If some sitting members did have such anxieties, the 1959 election results did not justify them, nor the hopes of contenders for their seats. Though there was a large increase in the county electorates of the eight towns round London, and in Corby, the local swing to the Conservatives there was much the same as in the rest of the South-East. Labour majorities certainly declined in crowded urban areas, not enough however to cause serious losses; they increased in the safe Labour seats in which Glenrothes, Peterlee and Cwmbran are situated. Later general elections have shown great changes in the balance of parties, but no evidence that it is affected by new-town building.

We doubt if either party has been much influenced, in a matter so vital to good urban development, by local electoral considerations. But party managers may have been reassured to find that neither has in fact been disadvantaged.

References and Notes

9.1   OSBORN, F. J., *Can Man Plan? and Other Verses*, 1959.

9.2   See BEST, R. H. and COPPOCK, J. C., *The Changing Use of Land in Great Britain*, 1962.

9.3   Our figures do not include the much higher cost per acre of central city sites. STONE, P. A., in *Housing, Town Development, Land and Costs*, estimates the cost of land 'saved' by building 12-storey instead of 2-storey dwellings at £56 400 per acre (£138 700 per ha).

9.4   WIBBERLEY, G. P., *Agriculture and Urban Growth*, London, 1959; BEST, R. H., *The Major Land Uses of Great Britain*, London, 1959; BEST, R. H. and COPPOCK, J. C., *op. cit.*; STAMP, L. D., *Land of Britain, its Use and Misuse*, London, 1962.

9.5   See REPS, JOHN, 'The Green Belt Concept', *Town and Country Planning*, July, 1960; OSBORN, F. J., *op. cit.*

9.6   See *The Green Belts*, Ministry of Housing and Local Government, HMSO, 1962.

9.7   An excellent summary of the results of sociological research is the article 'Social Research and New Communities', WILLMOTT, PETER, *Journal of the American Institute of Planners*, November, 1967 and in YOUNG, M. and WILLMOTT, P., *Family and Kinship in East London*, London, 1957.

10 New Towns in Regional Plans

> 'Regions Caesar never knew
> Thy posterity shall sway.'
>
> —William Cowper (1731–1800): *Boadicea*

In Britain, as in many states, the concept of planning has enormously broadened in scale from the town and county to the region and even the whole country; in content from the physical and aesthetic to the economic and social; and in method from negative regulation to a combination of control, positive direction, and publicly promoted construction. Though there are differences of judgment, of accent, and indeed of political philosophy, as to the respective roles of private and public agencies in physical as in economic development, all the democratic parties now concur in practice that Britain's is a 'mixed economy'. Controversies are about particular cases rather than basic principles. Thus there is general agreement that large-scale city renewal, in many cases, can most effectively be carried out through the acquisition of land and properties by the local authorities, and the adoption of varying combinations of public and private agencies and finance for the actual work of reconstruction. There is an all-party consensus that in new housing and rehabilitation a considerable share should be entrusted to private enterprise, especially for owner-occupiers, and Parliament has provided substantial loan funds, through building societies and insurance companies, to encourage this method, with subsidized interest rates.

The utility of the development corporations as agencies for building new towns has so much impressed opinion that agencies of similar type have been proposed for redevelopment of obsolescent parts in old towns and for large-scale construction in sub-regional areas.

The Population Explosion

Consciousness of the necessity of a regional outlook has been intensified by a number of factors, among them changes in the population forecasts. Towards the end of the 1939–45 war Britain's population was expected to reach a peak by about 1970 and, unless corrective measures could be applied, thereafter to decline. The changes in trends, however, have prompted modifications in forecasts. In 1962 the official forecast, based on current trends, was that Britain would have an addition of 20 million people by the end of the century. By the mid seventies, however, the increases in population had greatly lessened and if this trend continues the additional population by the end of the century will be less than the 1962 forecast. The Greater London Plan

Figure 10.1 Map showing new towns in Great Britain and Northern Ireland. (Note: Stonehouse was designated in 1973, but it was decided not to proceed with it in 1976. It is included in the hope that better counsels will prevail.) (Reproduced by courtesy of the Town and Country Planning Association)

of 1944 could reasonably assume a fairly static population for the region and propose a dispersal of a million persons from the conurbation and the rehousing of most of them in new and expanded towns at distances of 20 to 40 miles (30–60 km), while still reserving an extensive green belt. It could also hope for some appreciable reduction of the London population by wider dispersal to distant regions suffering from industrial and population decline.

That decline, and the 'drift' of population to the congested conurbations, especially to London and the West Midlands, had been a matter of great concern since the 1930s, and successive governments had sought to attract industries to regions of high unemployment by factory estates at low rents and subsidies for housing and social facilities. These efforts have been continued and amplified; by differential taxation, financial grants and exhortations to firms to settle in specified 'development areas', and other measures. These have had some success, though they were at first piecemeal and relatively timid. But as the less prosperous regions woke up and took a hand in their own improvement and in pressing their claims, the amount of governmental aid became more and more massive. This policy rightly has the support also of the regions troubled by the antithetical disease of hypertrophy.

The growth of population, present and anticipated, national and within each region, has entirely changed the planning picture. In 1918, when a continuing but only moderate increase could be assumed, the proposal by garden city enthusiasts in *New Towns After The War* for 100 towns, distributed in a dozen regions, seemed extravagant but not absolutely ridiculous; and in 1942, when population growth was apparently slowing down, their revised programme of 50 new towns seemed almost modest; but in the 1960s the thought of building hundreds of smallish towns for an additional 20 million people seemed fantastic even to many of those who saw the necessity for urban dispersal, and atrocious to those who imagined it would obliterate the open countryside. A true sense of scale (of time as well as space) would correct both these attitudes, but the proponents of new towns have to agree that the change in the population projections complicates the simple concepts of 1898, 1918 and 1942, both as to the location of new urban developments and the machinery for their creation.

Traffic in Towns

Another new factor of profound importance is the increase in the use of motor vehicles, resulting from the growth of population and the number of cars per family. The brilliant report prepared for the Ministry of Transport by a working group led by Professor Sir Colin Buchanan(10.1) estimated that the number of motor vehicles in Britain would multiply by at least three and possibly four by the end of the century or soon after, and that the larger part of the growth would occur in the next 20 years. It demonstrated that no amount of street widening and construction, flyovers and underpasses, on the model of Los Angeles or Tokyo, could provide for free optional car-use in London or even quarter-million cities; that severe restraints on such use (by licensing or taxation) must come; and that a great amplification of public transit systems would be necessary for movements at peak hours. Even all these measures together would not suffice to permit free optional car-use. The Buchanan Report envisaged as the only solution for large cities a revolutionary reconstruction on multi-deck plans with huge central car-parks. This, with the separation of vehicles and pedestrians, it held, would enable safe and pleasant 'environmental areas' to be created for residence and social intercourse. It is a bold and imaginative picture, whether one likes it or not.

The steering group for the study confessed itself 'appalled by the magnitude of the emergency', yet at the same time 'inspired by the challenge it presents'. It admitted that the capital cost of the required constructional work would be fabulous. But the steering group declared that it was 'not frightened' by the cost, which it claimed was within the capacity of a country with rising affluence and the prospect of increasing tax revenues from the additional millions of vehicles.

The report has the merits of exhaustive analysis and a conscientious facing of a deterrent group of problems. It does not evade the issues, and cannot be dismissed as unrealistic since in one way or another extremely drastic and difficult measures are forced on society by its past neglect of control of the size and structure of towns.

Need of Radical Dispersal Policy

What the report does not seem to consider is the alternative possibility of a really large-scale deconcentration and dispersal. To reduce the amount of business activity in city cores would no doubt be politically difficult and involve immense costs in compensation. But it might well be less costly than additional tubes, flyovers and multi-decking, and it would certainly promise more efficient economic conditions and far more attractive and convenient environments for human living, working and recreation.

In any event, since the proposals for making traffic movement in cities possible do not and cannot provide for their natural increase of population, and with rising affluence popular insistence on better housing and more open space is likely to compel an overall reduction of density, there must be a vast amount, somewhere, of new urban construction, including many new towns as well as smaller-town expansions. The siting, size, density and character of these new developments remain, therefore, matters of supreme importance.

Ebenezer Howard's concept of 'social cities'—clusters of towns in which the most frequent movements, between home, work centres, and the open country, are short—remains the key to satisfactory development. Some leading adherents of our own school of thought hold that, in view of the irresistible growth impulses of existing aggregations and the importance of economic linkages, the new towns or clusters must in the main be within 30 to 50 miles (50 to 80 km) of the major points of growth. This is certainly arguable. But we would not ourselves accept the view that, with governmental initiative or encouragement, in convenient situations for economic activity, entirely new centres of industry and population could not be brought into existence tomorrow, as so often in the historic past.

The Concept of City Clusters

Now that the scope of land-use planning is extending from the town and the country to the region, intense interest has been aroused in Howard's proposal for 'social cities'—described by Lewis Mumford in his Introduction to this book. It is not widely remembered that in Howard's original (1898) edition of his book he envisaged as the next stage after the building of one garden city to demonstrate its practicability, the foundation of a cluster of garden cities separated by green belts but interconnected in such a way as to amount to 'a very great city' of about 250 000 population. This principle was illustrated by the diagram below.

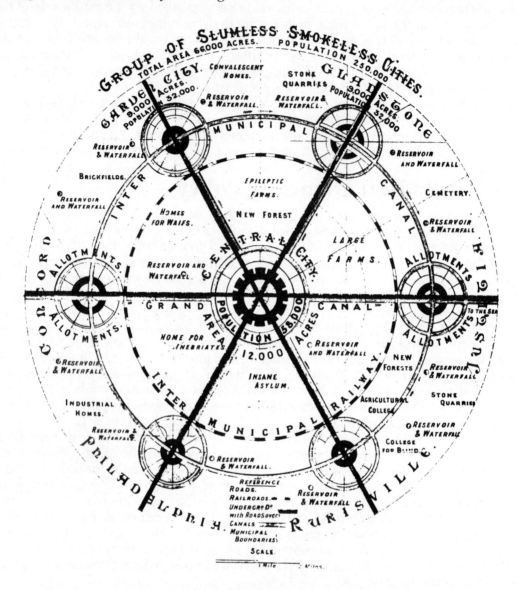

Figure 10.2 Garden city strategy. This diagram sums up much of the garden city concept: medium-sized, self-contained satellites in a functional relationship to a parent city, making the most of an agricultural hinterland and a rural setting. (Reproduced from Tomorrow: A Peaceful Path to Reform, *1898)*

But in his own finally revised edition of 1902, probably on the advice of his able and experienced supporters, he altered his text, omitted this diagram, and substituted a more modest diagram showing two additional garden cities to be budded-off from the first when it reached its intended maximum population. At later stages further offshoots could be added and the cluster thus gradually built up. No doubt this revision was tactically wise. The project for one new town of a revolutionary type was daring enough. The proposal that it should be followed as an immediate next stage by a huge cluster-city would have struck most people as altogether too fantastic.

As all later editions of *Garden Cities of To-morrow* follow Howard's own revised text of 1902, we print here the omitted paragraphs from the chapter on 'Social Cities' in the original book copies of which are not readily accessible(10.2):

'Let me here present a diagram, No. 7, representing a series or cluster of towns; though the reader is asked not to suppose that the design is put forward as one likely to be strictly carried out in the form thus presented; for any well-planned cluster of towns, must be carefully designed in relation to the site it is to occupy; though, as the science and art of engineering advances, less and less account is taken of natural obstacles, and more and more completely does mind become master of matter, and bend it and its forces to the service of man. With this understanding, however, such a diagram as I have sketched may be useful, as showing some of the broad principles which should be followed.

'It will be seen from the drawing that the idea of a carefully planned town lends itself readily to the idea of a carefully planned cluster of towns, so designed that each dweller in a town or comparatively small population is afforded, by a well-devised system of railways, waterways, and roads, the enjoyment of easy, rapid, and cheap communication with a large aggregate of the population, so that the advantages which a large city presents in the higher forms of corporate life may be within the reach of all, and yet each citizen of what is destined to be the most beautiful city in the world may dwell in a region of pure air and be within a very few minutes' walk of the country.

'The total area covered by the social cities represented in this diagram is supposed to be sixty-six thousand acres (being a little less than the area administered by the London County Council), and the total population a quarter of a million—each of the smaller municipalities having an area of nine thousand acres and a population of thirty-two thousand, while Central City has an area of twelve thousand acres and a population of fifty-eight thousand.'

Since the 1969 edition of this book there have been important changes in Britain's central and local government and in planning administration; also in population forecasts and in theories of the desirable size of towns. We discuss these briefly in Chapter 13.

References and Notes

10.1   *Traffic in Towns: A Study of the Long Term Problems of Traffic in Urban Areas*, HMSO, 1963.
10.2   Other variations between the 1898 and 1902 and later editions of Howard's book are described in an article in *Town and Country Planning*, December, 1971, by F. J. Osborn.

11 *Achievement, Challenge and Prognostic*

We claim full success for the first stages of the British experiment in creating new towns. That is not to say they meet every possible requirement of every kind of human being, every personal or associated activity in urban civilization. No town, old or new, is perfect in this sense; none ever will be. But in fundamentally important respects these towns mark an immense advance on any type of industrial towns that preceded them. They provide good homes in healthy, pleasant and well-planted surroundings, never far from the open country and in most cases near places of work. They are centres of efficient and advancing industry and commerce. They are equipped with modern urban services, schools, shops, churches and public buildings. And they are financially sound; not only more economical to construct and maintain than any alternative type of development, but positively remunerative as capital investments.

Diversities and Similarities

In their overall planning and the layout of residential and industrial sections and main and subsidiary shopping centres, the new towns, while studious of good precedents, have also made interesting innovations. Some of these are described in our chapters on the individual towns; some are experimental; not all will commend themselves for widespread acceptance; some indeed we think ill-judged. But the fact that a score of independent teams of administrators and technicians have had the chance to develop whole towns on their several conceptions and estimates of popular requirements has produced a diversity of solutions worth study by planners of future towns and redevelopers of existing towns.

Certain common problems have emerged. One is that of the adequate provision of private garages and public parking-places for automobiles, the number of which has multiplied beyond expectation since the towns were started and is now approaching an average of one car a family, with the 2-car (even 3-car) family emerging. Relatively low density has made it less difficult to adapt the older housing sections to this new need, but it is not easy. In the latest housing units many towns now allow for an average of one car a family.

Though in some towns the aberrant idealisms of 'urbanity' and 'saving land' have pushed densities too high, on the whole the popular preference for the single-family dwelling has been respected. Terrace housing of 2-storey houses at from 12 to 16 (here and there 18 [44 per ha]) an acre (30 to 40 per ha) prevail, and there are sections of free-standing or semi-detached houses at 8 down to 2 an acre (20 down to 5 per ha), mostly owner-occupied. The proportion of flats usually ranges from 5 to 10%; in a few towns it rises to 15% or more. Where high tower-blocks have been introduced the main motive has been the desire for 'vertical features' to punctuate a landscape felt to be too level, or (in reversion to an eighteenth-century taste) 'to terminate the prospect'.

Residential layouts show considerable variety, and have been much influenced by the desire to separate as far as possible the vehicular from the pedestrian access to dwellings. Many that claim the prestigious 'Radburn' label, however, fail to attain the combination of safety, privacy and pleasing outlook of Clarence Stein's New Jersey prototype, which being at a density of only about 8 houses an acre (20 per ha) permits of common green spaces accessible by footways from individual gardens—quite impossible at densities of 16 to 20 an acre (40 to 50 per ha). Safe pedestrian access is of course highly desirable, and it does not necessitate the sacrifice of other precious environmental amenities. It is to be hoped that the consciences of planners, or the reaction of consumers, will correct the tendency to excessive densities and other experimental mistakes in design.

Some critics have complained that in their domestic architecture the towns are too much alike. This is an impercipient view. Anywhere in the world, in any given period and at any given level of family incomes, the majority of houses must have a degree of similarity in scale and character, since the families occupying them differ only marginally in numbers, habits and requirements. A human observer of a football crowd or a theatre queue does not complain that hardly anyone in it is less than 4 ft 6 in (1.5 m) or more than 6 ft 6 in high (2 m); though members of another species (birds or fish for example) might think humans over-standardized. One looks for and finds variety, not in scale, but in facial expression, carriage and dress. And the hundreds of architects in the new towns have certainly striven for variety within these limits; have sometimes, indeed, overstepped into eccentricity and whimsicality. But on the whole sanity has prevailed and the known preferences of prospective occupiers have been respected. Housing in the new towns is far less monotonous than in the old industrial cities or most council housing estates, or the apartment blocks in many parts of the world. Which is not to say that the quality of design, diversity and structure cannot be improved.

Neighbourhoods and Functional Zones

For shopping centres the pedestrian precinct, anticipated as 'a possibility' by the New Towns (Reith) Committee, is now often applied; and there are some very attractive examples, with large adjoining car-parks. While it cannot be said that the car-parking problem has been fully solved, it is less intractable in new towns than in densely-built great cities.

Most of the towns have adopted the principle of neighbourhoods varying in population from 5000 to 10 000, usually with at least one junior school, a group of shops and service work-shops, and a public house and some facilities for meetings. Minor centres are indispensable for access to schools and convenience in every-day shopping. But their effectiveness in creating 'neighbourhood' consciousness seems to vary; and there are some observers who think the generous provision of social facilities in local sections of a town may weaken the development of its main cultural centre—an issue that calls for further study.

The factory zones, appropriately enough in this industrial age, yield some of their most striking architectural effects. We spend today far more capital on manufacturing and commercial structures than on cathedrals, churches, theatres, town halls and museums; so the propensity of entrepreneurs to value a touch of 'display' in their workplaces is to be welcomed. The design and grouping both of the small sectional factories for letting and of the larger ones built for individual firms reach a high standard and make them one of the towns' impressive visual features as well as their main economic base. Moreover the daily experience of working in gracious, well-appointed and attractively landscaped factories must be having a tremendous effect on the employees' standards of aesthetic appreciation, certain to be reflected in the furnishing and care of their homes.

Public and Community Buildings

Of the public buildings the most noticeable, because most numerous, are the schools—primary, secondary, and for further education. With a few temporary lapses, the provision of these has kept pace with the exceptionally high proportion of children of school age; and they are first-class in design and accommodation and have as a rule ample and well-laid-out space for recreation.

The building of churches in new communities is a heavy burden on the religious organizations, since in Britain it is not financially aided, as it is in Sweden for instance, by the state. There were initial delays that had to be mitigated by temporary makeshifts. Admirable co-operation between the denominations, however, has conduced to a careful placing of the new churches, which though mostly modest in scale now make pleasing additions to the architecture of the towns. Designs are varied and often original and ingenious. One useful expedient resorted to is the sealing-off of the consecrated part of the church building so that the main area can be used for secular community purposes.

Public houses (licensed to sell alcoholic drinks), an important element in British social equipment, have also been the subject of good co-operation between the bodies interested in their provision—brewers, licensing authorities and corporations. Here again new ideas have been introduced. Some of the pubs serve the double purpose of refreshment houses and community meeting places, with obvious advantages for both functions. In one at least (Hatfield) a welfare clinic is part of the complex.

All the towns now have their post offices, local government offices, banks, employment exchanges, insurance offices, restaurants and libraries. Some of these are buildings of distinction. Major hospitals exist in several, usually to serve wider districts of which the new towns are becoming important centres. New cinemas are few, owing to the decline in the popularity of this form of entertainment, but no town is without at least one, and some have excellent concert halls and small theatres.

Playing fields and outdoor sports facilities are well provided for, and this is having a beneficial influence on recreational habits. Despite a degree of parsimony in the provision of halls and meeting-rooms for clubs and societies, innumerable activities of the amateur or 'do-it-yourself' type have proliferated, many quite spontaneously and others on the initiative of devoted social organizers appointed by the corporations. Especially for young people there are many organizations, though much remains to be done under this heading in view of the age-composition of the towns.

Past philanthropy and bequests have endowed long-established towns with buildings and facilities that in these days can only be financed out of public funds, and for relative shortages in this respect the local authorities, suzerain ministries and the Treasury compete in apportioning blame. However, with the addition of a few facilities that it will not be too difficult to provide as populations near their target and revenue surpluses grow, towns of the new type can become as satisfactory as the laws of space allow for a large percentage of the urban people of Britain, and, we hold, of the people of the world.

Some Features of Individual Towns

Natural features of town sites, though sometimes presenting difficulties to planners, have often been turned to advantage. Welwyn, Stevenage and Harlow, for example, have retained wedges or drifts of woodlands striking right into their centres. Hemel Hempstead has converted a small stream threading through its shopping centre into a charming water-garden. Peterlee, faced with a daunting problem of underlying coal-seams and likely subsidence, has evolved special types of free-standing houses on rafted foundations, and engaged a famous painter (Victor Pasmore) to advise on an original pattern of design and layout. Cwmbran has integrated and partially harmonized a confused jumble of old industrial buildings and houses on a difficult hilly site. Cumbernauld has adventured on a multi-level shopping-residential centre on a high ridge, giving many of the houses extensive views; this is a highly controversial plan, attracting much interest as an experiment. Cumbernauld has also applied even more logically than Harlow and several of the other towns the principle of walkways and cycle tracks, and has proved that many deaths and injuries can be avoided by pedestrian segregation. Basildon has skilfully pulled together a scatter of shack dwellings miserably served by muddy grass-tracks. Welwyn has transformed a worked-out gravel pit into a first-class athletic stadium, and Cwmbran has done the same with a derelict clay-pit.

While all the towns, as their populations grow, soon acquire an assortment of facilities for social life, entertainment and culture, it is interesting to note that these vary widely in combination and accent. No town in Britain could fail to have circles and organizations devoted to outdoor sports, gardening, party politics, religion, dancing, business, trade-unionism, social welfare, and friendly forgathering in like-minded groups. But some go further than others in particular spheres of activity. Welwyn has national renown for its extremely high standards in amateur dramatic work. Harlow is acquiring a reputation as a town with a widespread popular interest in music. Both these towns, as well as Basildon and Redditch, have Arts Councils embracing professionals and amateurs. Bracknell, Crawley, Harlow and Cwmbran have already built centres for indoor sports.

Most of the towns now have community centres for a comprehensive range of activities, and others have plans for these as soon as their resources (or government consent) permit.

We have given only a few examples of the social, welfare and cultural institutions already established. Others include colleges of further education, youth clubs, hospitals, clinics, swimming pools, neighbourhood associations, hotels, hobby workshops, and societies and clubs for innumerable special interests.

If, as was inevitable, the provision of buildings for all the activities that people in a new community desire to pursue did not keep pace with the demand, there can be no question of the energy and initiative of the people themselves as they come together in new towns. Many of them in the early years are happily preoccupied with the establishment of their own homes and the beginning of their families. But the community spirit soon becomes immensely strong, and produces an irresistible demand for the necessary facilities, which the financial success of the towns make it possible to meet.

We can have no doubt that the new towns will not only look after their own internal social life and culture, but will contribute handsomely to that of the nation.

12 International Influence of the New Towns Movement

The British idea of creating new towns, both as a corrective of urban overgrowth and as a means of providing for increases of population, has engaged widespread interest and study abroad. 'Garden City Associations' were started in France (1903), Germany (1904), Holland (1905), Italy (1906), the USA (1906), and Russia (1911). Translations of *Garden Cities of To-morrow* were early published in four languages, and summaries and commentaries in others. Before the 1914–18 war a world-wide movement for new towns seemed to be emerging. There were in fact a few practical essays in emulation of the Letchworth experiment. And in 1913 the International Garden Cities and Town Planning Association (now the International Federation for Housing and Planning) was founded, with members from many countries and with Sir Ebenezer Howard as its honoured President for its first 15 years.

Reports of the early congresses of the Federation show that at first Howard's concept of city limitation, green belts, and new towns with local employment was well understood and enthusiastically approved by the leading planners. They produced eloquent speeches and able papers, but did not succeed in inducing their nations to initiate new towns or to facilitate their promotion by commercial or co-operative agencies.

Approaches and Deviations

The 1939–45 War interrupted urban development, and after it in many European countries, as in Britain, governments undertook or encouraged large-scale house-building, often on the open, landscaped and economical pattern that Raymond Unwin and Barry Parker had evolved at Letchworth Garden City (1903) and Hampstead Garden Suburb (1907)—which had, and has, an almost universal popular appeal.

Unfortunately the term 'garden city'—which meant a planned new town with local employment and a considerable degree of social and cultural self-containment—came to be confusingly used to describe the 'garden suburb'—which was no more than a pleasantly planned assemblage of homes for commuters to the city. New means of public transport and the private car made dormitory suburbs seductively easy and profitable to produce. Thus arose the suburban explosion over what might have been green belts. Good planners, who had to live, were inevitably drawn into designing them. And some, regrettably, forgot the true conception of the 'garden city' and even concurred in the use of that name for the substitute product(12.1).

Though the innumerable so-called 'garden cities' of the 1905–39 period were mostly open and well-planned suburbs, there were a few intermediate types of interest. Some industrial companies built housing estates or 'garden villages' for their employees on the model of Bournville or Port Sunlight, a great advance in humanity and design on the grim nineteenth-century 'company town'. There were a few 'satellite towns' which local industry that legitimately claimed garden city parentage, the first of which was Hellerau, near Dresden (1908). Canberra, the federal capital of Australia (1909), planned by W. B. Griffin of Chicago, follows, indeed amplifies, the verdancy and spaciousness of Unwin's plan for Letchworth (1903). In the USA Radburn, New Jersey (1928), was originally planned as a garden city(12.2) to have local employment, and attained fame for pioneering the modern concept of pedestrian segregation from the car. But along with the three Green Belt towns of Roosevelt's New Deal (1935–38), Radburn was overtaken by the metropolitan flood and turned into a commuters' dormitory.

The small towns of the famous Tennessee Valley Authority (1933–42) are exceptional in that they have a local economic base (hydro-electric plants), as also have the 'atomic cities', Los Alamos, Richland and Oak Ridge (1942–47).

During the same period, in countries with rapid population growth, many new towns came into existence for reasons apart from metropolitan decongestion. In the USSR, for example, hundreds of towns were founded in the course of the state programme of industrialization, many of them built with great urgency before any general control of growth or regional arrangement had emerged. In newly developing countries, especially near sources of power or raw materials, new urban settlements arose, as often in history, more or less adventitiously and without specific pre-planning of scale or structure. But in all countries, advanced or otherwise, far and away the greater part of development occurred in places where population was already most concentrated—that is, in existing cities and towns, to which people from the country-side flocked in quest of jobs, and business firms in quest of markets and labour—with the results we all know.

The New Towns Concept Catches On

Since the 1939–45 War and the adoption of the policy of decongestion and dispersal by Great Britain, the idea of building new towns with local employment and of controlled size has been widely discussed, seriously entertained in many countries, and acted upon by some, more or less logically. Indeed the number of 'new towns' designed with a definite regard for scale and structure is already so great that we can allude only to a few examples.

Almost all states in the world now have some powers of control over development and construction, but these differ greatly in scope and strength, in methods and skill of administration, and in the aims pursued. Some of the conspicuous disadvantages of existing towns, especially great cities, are universally recognized, but governments' policies, and the proposals of their expert advisers, tend to be triggered off by single starting points of troubled interest, and to attend to the solution of the single problem with insufficient regard to others with which it is interlocked.

In the nineteenth century the dominating urban problem, which aroused passionate concern and compelled governmental and philanthropic action, was that of bad housing for masses of people—slums, overcrowding, lack of garden space, low structural quality, and decay, causing high death-rates and the spread of disease, crime and social depravity. That problem remains, though for many people it has been relieved by the suburban outflow and the 'rationalization of congestion' in the form of sanitary multi-storey dwellings. Far from satisfactory solutions as these are, they have considerably appeased the sufferers and eased the consciences and fears of the better-off.

Today's dominating problem is that of traffic congestion, which has reached such a critical point that it cannot be politically ignored. Unless it is attended to, the cities, as economic and social mechanisms, will not continue to work. Long distance commuting involves a frightful loss of cash and time to millions of workers, but they do not understand the cure, and their tempers do not rise to the critical point so long as they can just get from home to work and back. So governments, being forced to do something when the machine grinds to a halt, are torn in two as to whether to forbid car-use and subsidize more public transport, or to drive more speedways and tunnels through the cities and multi-deck their centres; both highly objectionable solutions: the one restrictive of freedom, and the other immensely costly, not only to the city but to the state.

In a ruthlessly *laissez-faire* economic system the corrective would be a spontaneous movement of business concerns to less congested situations, and a catastrophic fall of values in big cities followed by radical reconstruction. But in all modern economies, collectivist, capitalist or 'mixed', governments are impelled to intervene to avoid the catastrophe and do so in ways that keep the system working, though at less than optimum efficacy and at a colossal sacrifice of financial resources and of environmental amenities. All over the world there are thinkers who see this, but the forces for the continuance of the process are enormously powerful and the difficulties of reversing it daunting. And it is not surprising that many 'practical' planners still cling to the hope of enabling great cities to continue to work and even to expand, by reconstruction on an intensive basis. At the moment that seems to be the general consensus of opinion. But the idea of limitation and decongestion is at last catching on.

In 1975 the UK government established the British Urban Development Services Unit to make the British experience of new town development available to overseas clients on a commercial basis.

Some National Policies

A comparison of the metropolitan planning policies of the countries of the world would require another book as long as this. No doubt one or more will soon appear, and up-date or out-date the following selective characterizations.

These are all too brief, incomplete, indeed perfunctory, and we have had to omit reference to many countries whose policies include the development of new urban units, either to relieve existing congestion or to accommodate growing populations and activities.

A list of 'new towns' created since 1900 will be found in the Appendices. Many of these could not claim to comply with the definition with which this book began, or to have been much influenced, directly or indirectly, by the British initiative, and opinions will differ as to their location, quality of design, or adaptability to economic requirements and human desires. But they are all, we think, in some measure planned, and that is a matter of great world interest and promise.

City Planning in America

The USA, with its fabulous rate of urbanization, is clearly one of the countries in direst need of a policy of planned limitation and dispersal for the relief of city constipation and avoidance of suburban sprawl. But though a new towns policy was brilliantly advocated there as an essential element in large-scale regional planning by Clarence Stein, Henry Wright, Lewis Mumford, F. L. Ackerman, Benton MacKaye, Alexander Bing, Catherine Bauer and their colleagues in the Regional Planning Association of America (1923–33)(12.3) and in many writings since(12.4), it was not until the 1960s that the beginnings of a governmental policy were visible. As in many other countries, the central government has since World War II made lavish and increasing grants to cities for housing, slum clearance and road construction, and in the 1950s aid was extended to 'comprehensive renewal' projects. But these grants were not specifically related to urban dispersal, the regional relocation of population and employment, or the reservation of green belts. In the main planning was exercised through zoning and sub-division ordinances, and the elaborate (and often superb) surveys, studies and advisory plans aimed at predicting economic trends and changes in social requirements, in order to lessen the inconvenience of inordinate growth; not with any hope of restraining it. Thus when the computers showed that city growth and motorization must multiply traffic movement and intensify housing pressure, the attitude of planners and authorities was to consider how to amplify the transportation network or the density of building rather than how to check the increase of population and business. Instead of appealing to the central government for national measures to relieve them of their intractable internal problems, they appealed for (and obtained) funds to sophisticate their congestion and to lubricate slightly their ever tightening traffic stricture.

Since World War II many planned communities have been initiated by commercial developers, a few of which have been intended to provide for local industrial employment. One of the best, Park Forest (1948), 30 miles (48 km) from the centre of Chicago, excellently planned with good community facilities, is already drowned in the metropolitan flood. Peachtree City (1960), 30 miles (48 km) from Atlanta, Georgia, may escape this. The imaginative projects in the Washington (DC) region, Reston, Virginia (1963) and Columbia (1964) are really new towns as defined in this book; it remains to be seen whether they will attain the desired balance of income groups and diversity of local employment. But the majority of current developments, such as the three Levittowns (New York and Philadelphia), are residential dormitories for commuters to large cities. Many, however, mark a welcome advance in design, landscaping and community facilities.

In the USA housing and planning problems are complicated by that of racial segregation. The existence of large 'ghettos' of non-whites in many great cities is a serious obstacle to a policy of decentralization to new housing elsewhere; and also to attempts to attract back into the cities the better-off suburbans, which some authorities (we think too hopefully) see as a condition of their satisfactory renewal and the continued increase of their central commercial values, now suffering from the competition of extra-urban shopping centres more easily reached by the private automobile. This business interest is, we suspect, politically a more potent force for urban renewal and the pressure for federal financial aid than the improvement of family housing and environmental conditions; but we do not pursue this highly controversial question, now at last under intelligent discussion in the USA itself.

American new towns are financed by private enterprise and owing to the recent recession in property development, many US new towns are in financial difficulty.

In Canada, city over-concentration causes similar concern but has not yet produced a positive dispersal policy. There are, however, some well-planned urban quasi-satellites, such as Don Mills, adjoining Toronto, a commercial development with an industrial zone and good social facilities. Canada has a large number of single-industry towns, of varying merit in design and social structure. Kitimat in British Columbia is a self-contained new town based on the aluminium industry, for which Clarence Stein was the consultant planner.

New Towns in the USSR

In the USSR over 800 new towns and some 2000 other urban-type settlements have been founded in the course of the systematic industrialization of the country since the 1917 Revolution. Until quite recently, however, many of these seem, like the older cities, to have been allowed to grow without specific limits, to the depreciation of their initial plans. Russian technicians of today would doubtless agree that the form of some of these towns was too stereotyped and too regardless of topographical and sociological considerations. Under the stress of a hasty pursuit of economic progress, collectivism, like capitalism, tends to *laissez-faire* in social and aesthetic matters.

The fact that all land and industrial enterprises, and all but the smallest retail and service businesses, are collectively owned and run would appear on the face of it to make physical planning politically easy. But even in a communist society, each individual 'firm' has its own immediate interest in location and growth and can put up a fight on plausible economic grounds against governmental planners and ministries concerned for wider and longer-term community interests. This may explain why Greater Moscow, which had a population of about 5 millions in 1958, and was then considered too large and due for the transfer of some excess industry and people to a number of new towns beyond a wide green belt, had by 1976 about $7\frac{3}{4}$ millions.

In the early 1960s the government severely rebuked Moscow architects for building flats of 6 or more storeys with lifts instead of the more economical (and humane?) 4-storey walk-ups. In 1968 the authorities were pointing with pride to the many new flat blocks of 12 to 17 storeys, and to the latest projects for 25 and 27 storeys. But the determination to put a stop to the growth of population, to reduce the journey to work to half an hour, to disallow any new industries, and to move out 200 factories by 1980, was manfully reiterated. All of which goes to show that the great city is an animal not easily tamed by the most authoritative keeper.

Nevertheless the USSR has a considered policy for urban and rural planning and the rational distribution of industry and population, in which the creation of new towns plays a vital part, and their growth is intended to be kept within 'optimum limits'. For new cities the optimum population now favoured by Soviet planners is between 150 000 and 200 000 and for satellite towns from 50 000 to 100 000(12.5). A good relationship between larger and smaller settlements is aimed at by considered regional arrangement. In many respects thought on structure and internal planning has been influenced by that in Britain, though there are wide differences in housing and other standards, due partly to climatic and traditional but even more to economic circumstances and technocratic fashion.

The USSR, with its huge backlog of housing, is still striving to attain a minimum floor-space standard of about 130 sq. feet (12 m²) per person housed—about half that of the British public housing standard. And though the suburban *dacha* with its garden is still the ideal of well-off citizens, it is not in sight for the masses for generations ahead—though we do not understand why the certain future demand for houses with private gardens is not anticipated in the layout of new moderate-sized towns. On the other hand, the provision of parks and public open spaces in Soviet towns is generous, and tree-planting often quite magnificent. Most of the new towns have green belt reservations: and much attention is paid to communal facilities, education, health services and the state's characteristic culture.

Policies in Eastern Europe

Poland is another communist country in which a highly advanced national plan is based upon exhaustive surveys and studies. Scientific principles are being evolved, with cost-benefit analyses, to ascertain the limits of any town's advantageous growth and the point at which the creation of new settlements is necessary. Many new towns are being built, some as satellites of large cities, and others as units in planned regional complexes. Whether the housing standards at present adopted will satisfy people of a more affluent age outsiders must not claim to judge. But it is a question that Polish planners, like all others, should ask themselves and their clients.

We have not the space to describe the policies of the other communist states. Those of Bulgaria, Czechoslovakia, Hungary, Rumania and Yugoslavia resemble Poland's in that they closely integrate economic with physical planning policies and are concerned for the distribution of population and industry throughout their states. Some still have much land in private ownership, and there are interesting variations in their planning methods and administrative systems. All seek to check excessive city growth, and are building new towns, or expanding small towns and villages.

Other European Policies

Radically as the states of Western and Eastern Europe differ in their political and economic systems, all have the same problem of urban over-concentration. And though the 'Iron Curtain' is a barrier to personal movement, it does not preclude interchanges of technical thought and fashion. Thus there tend to be within each country similar differences of opinion as to the possible solutions. But states differ again in the degree of priority they give to land-use planning. Politically, as we have noted, national planning is more readily applied in countries where land and industry are state-owned. There are other factors that influence priorities. Where for instance, average income is still low and private cars fewer, the critical stage of traffic congestion is deferred. And mass housing and subsidized transport facilities are methods more consonant with collectivist than free-enterprise philosophy.

The extreme urban housing shortages caused by war destruction and rapid industrialization have driven states of both kinds to subsidize housing on a vast scale, and their peoples have been so desperately in need of any kind of shelter that consumer choice has become minimal. In such a situation the bureaucrat is caliph and the technocrat his grand vizier, and they are the decision-makers. Neither occupiers' preference nor value for cost has anything like the influence that it has in a market (sale or rental) relationship. The epidemic of multi-storey tenements that raged through the world in the 1940s to 1960s could only have occurred in a period of housing famine, with which an unfortunate international architectural contagion coincided. And it is only with the partial relief of the famine in the 1960s that the epidemic began to subside and only in countries where consumer demand is articulate.

States' housing and planning policies are also affected by their national population densities. In most European countries there is ample space for dispersal to towns of convenient moderate size. But in some regions of economic growth, for example Holland, the population density is such as to arouse fear that separating towns by wide green belts would preclude the reservation of any really extensive stretches of open land. Ideally much of the growth of population in Holland should be diverted to less crowded parts of the Netherlands; and the national plan contemplates this to the extent practicable. But, as in Britain's south-east, the regional impetus to economic growth is formidable, and a government concerned for the mainspring of prosperity can plead excuse for concessions in standards of residential environment and of access to employment and the countryside. If economic growth really cannot be diverted from 'Conurbation Holland', or population growth checked, then the Netherlands' policy can be seen as justified. The plan is brilliantly worked out and well administered. But it is not a model for states less embarrassed by similar space considerations.

France and West Germany have had to devote immense resources and energy to the reconstruction of war-damaged towns. Both countries officially favour a wider national distribution of industry and population, and Germany has expanded many of its smaller towns and founded new ones of planning interest: for example, Sennestadt, near Bielefeld. France also has founded new towns in the Pyrenees and North Africa to house workers in the natural gas and oil industries.

Italy, again, has placed most of its new planned developments in expansions of existing cities, without local industrial or head office employment. It is not repeating the type of towns (more correctly villages) founded under the Fascist regime in the Pontine Marshes and Libya, which were very thoroughly but rigidly planned and organized. Many of its war-destroyed hill towns have been replaced by charming new towns on level land lower down. One important new town is Ivrea, a self-contained industrial satellite of Turin, the character of which was inspired by the late Adriano Olivetti's enthusiasm for planning with full respect for family and social needs.

Sweden, paradise of the architect-planner, has expanded its capital city with a masterly blending of technical and aesthetic considerations. The new suburbs of Stockholm (Vällingby, Fårsta and others) are deservedly famous as examples of a complete integration of design only possible on land owned by the developing authority. They are, however, mainly dormitories for commuters, and have more high-rise dwellings than the British (and probably the Swedes themselves) would desire. Sweden's industry is exceptionally widely distributed in towns of moderate size, and the possibilities of good planning and design in related clusters of such towns are impressively demonstrated in the Örebro region(12.6).

Finland's Tapiola Garden City, a sea-encircled satellite of Helsinki with some local industry, is widely admired as one of the world's most attractive modern urban developments. The project of its leading promoter, Heikki Von Hertzen, for 7 new towns beyond a green belt around the capital, sets a pattern for emulation by other countries.

Norway has only 3 cities over 100 000, and much of its industry is distributed in about 250 towns (*tettsteder*) of 1000 to 14 000, many with only one industry, which were not preplanned. It is an aim of national policy to stimulate economic activity in the less developed parts of the country, and the growth of regional clusters centred on bigger towns, with good plans, diversity of employment, and community facilities. The capital, Oslo (about 500 000), in its fine situation between sea and mountains, cannot be extended laterally, and the creation of 'overspill towns' is considered necessary.

Denmark, with nearly a third of its population in its chief city, has a planning system similar to that of Great Britain, and a well-advanced advisory national plan based on exhaustive surveys, which attends to all the major considerations including the location of industry. The plan for Copenhagen is of the radial 'finger' pattern of the USA's 'Washington 2000', and like that plan, is the subject of controversy. Some new towns are under construction and the foundation of others is contemplated. As in the USA, France, Sweden and other countries with uncomfortably crowded cities, the 'secondary dwelling' is popular, and is absorbing considerable areas of rural land.

Spain, where planning control was not extended to all areas until 1956, is currently in the throes of evolving a national policy. It has not yet built new towns for the decongestion of its larger cities, but the need is there. Many new agricultural villages have been built, having great architectural variety and charm but a somewhat strict authoritarian social structure. They do demonstrate however a fine sense of design that we hope may inspire the future new towns of Spain.

In almost all Western European states national policies now favour a check to the unbroken growth of major cities, and there are movements for the creation of more detached or more self-contained new towns. But most of the developments since the war have been annexes to existing towns, which though systematically planned are often at excessively high density with little or no local industrial or head office employment.

The necessity of a marriage of physical with economic planning, and of extending their scope from the town to the region, is however increasingly recognized, and many variations on the dispersal and new towns theme are in progress or contemplated.

Some of the extension plans for greater cities—notably those of Paris and Hanover—are compromises between the old form of continuously built-up expansion and the London principle of dispersal to new towns beyond a circular green belt. The intention is to define larger areas for urban development, inter-penetrated by reservations of open country, and to locate their zones for employment and residence within reasonably convenient distances and thus check the increase of commuting to the city centre. These projects are of great interest, but we hope they do not imply a belief that the expansion of a metropolis is entirely irresistible, and that they will not replace the effort to transfer economic and population growth to more sparsely populated regions, to new towns, and to existing small towns that would really benefit by enlargement. Nor should the need for a reduction of density in the old cities be neglected.

In the Other Continents

Israel, being a new state, has perhaps pursued more logically than any other the planned location of population and industry. Before the 1939–45 War too large a proportion had been massed in three cities. Later the effort was made to restrain their growth, and the national plan was for the creation of 24 regional centres of 10 000 to 60 000, with many smaller towns and villages. There is now a reaction towards somewhat larger urban units, but the principle of control of size is intelligently retained.

India and Pakistan are building many new planned towns and villages, but are faced with stupendous difficulties in view of the condition of their older cities and the prevailing low level of real incomes. The necessity of strong planning is understood by their governments, legislative powers and the administrative systems are progressing, and it is certain that new towns will play an important part in the future of these countries.

Japan, in view of its amazingly rapid industrial progress, is strangely backward in planning. Tokyo, with a population of over 10 millions, is growing at fantastic speed; the housing standards are abysmally low considering the rise in personal spending power, journeys to work insufferably long and crowded, and the costly network of speedways, rivalling that of Los Angeles, an unwise attempt to facilitate the further growth of a city long overdue for a check and reversal. The same is true of the other great cities. Advanced Japanese planners agree that the British dispersal and new towns policy is one that should be followed in principle, but national policy and legislation lag far behind the obvious necessity.

Of the great country of China we have insufficient recent information for useful comment. A special emphasis in its economic policy at the present stage is given to agricultural development and the effort to check the drift from the country to cities, and many small industries are being set up in rural villages along with the necessary housing. During the economic crisis of 1960–63 large numbers of urban workers were actually sent back to the countryside, and many have not returned. We understand that the project announced some years ago for a ring of industrial 'garden cities' of the order of 100 000 each around Shanghai (7 000 000) is being carried out. China has not recently been represented at international planning conferences. An exchange of experiences and practices would be valuable to other countries as well as to China itself.

Latin America, from Mexico down to Argentina, is a huge region, on the whole, for various understandable reasons, hesitant in its acceptance of planning. There is an enormous secular drift of population from the agricultural areas to the great cities, coupled with a spontaneous outward movement from the slums to shack suburbs in the outskirts, which surround even the new capital of Brazil—itself a monumental and political rather than a functional or social achievement, though of much interest. Few new planned towns have yet been built in these countries, but it is hardly possible that a great movement for their creation will not emerge in the near future.

Australia, where metropolitan concentration has been extreme, is now building some new industrial towns, for example, Elizabeth, near Adelaide, and Kwinana and Medina, near Perth, and others are projected. There are many villages or small towns for single industries with an element of community planning.

New Zealand also has small new towns of this type, and though there is, so far, no national policy for the distribution of industry, firms are officially encouraged to settle in provincial towns rather than in the greater centres.

Africa, with many developing countries of high potential, already has a number of new towns of different types, as well as a rising interest in both physical and economic planning. It has a wonderful opportunity to create urban patterns that will avoid the grievous mistakes of Europe, America and Asia.

*　　　*　　　*

These few examples of national policies illustrate a world-wide concern for the common problem of over-concentration, which no country can claim to have solved. Through the special agencies of the United Nations, the International Federation for Housing and Planning, professional organizations, and books and technical journals, instructed opinion has already arrived at some tentative generalizations, as for example: 'World society must learn to guide the process of urbanization', 'We must rejuvenate the city', 'We must reduce daily travel', 'We must return to city-dwellers the benefits of nature'. (*Report of U.N. Meeting of Experts*, Stockholm, 1961.)

The doctors still differ as to the prescription. Should city growth go up into the sky, out into further suburbs, down into subterranean catacombs, at large over the country-side, or into defined and planned new towns? The new towns solution requires stronger governmental powers of initiation than the alternatives, but it is not inimical to essential freedoms, and because it can provide for human satisfaction as well as for economic productivity it gains in favour as understanding and planning powers advance.

Future of Cities: the Alternatives

Planned towns, satellites, and city extension and renewal projects are appearing in so many regions of such diverse character that the influence of the British garden cities and new towns on urban patterns is becoming more and more entangled with that of later ventures. Britain has not yet exploited fully the possibilities of its own invention. But (though some writers on new towns ignore the fact) Britain has set going a movement that promises immeasurable benefit to urban man.

Not that urban man and his advisers have yet abandoned the idealism of the Great (that is, Large) City. Faiths and fetishisms outdated by science and social ethics may retain loyal priests and medicine men for generations. There are still planners who cling to the belief that by contriving road and rail networks on, below and above ground level, and multi-decking centres with subterranean car parks, pedestrian walkways, and layers of shops and offices capped by residential crows-nests, million-cities can be made agreeable containers for production, trade, personal living and a high culture, without much reduction of their population capacity. Essays in renewal on this pattern can be studied in Philadelphia, where it has a certain mechanistic and aesthetic appeal, and on another in Los Angeles, where two-thirds of the city core is given over to the automobile.

It can be argued that these are experiments that may be improved upon. But what will be the end-term of scientific compression if cities continue to grow? We envisage it as a structure resembling a stupendous transport terminal, with platforms and courts, elevators and escalators leading up and down to tiers of supermarkets, restaurants, bars and saloons for mass feeding, wherein an amorphous swarm of passengers scurry about among offers for sale of 'all that life can afford'—except quiet, repose, sociability and contact with the living earth.

Now this is a way of life that has its coterie of true lovers. There are congenital megalopolitans. And we congratulate them on their prospects, for many cities will certainly go that way. The human propensity to accept a long-set trend, and the genuine difficulty of a revolutionary reversal, forbid us, as realists, to expect a sudden wholesale conversion of authorities and technicians. We (and they) know also that the far more numerous city-dwellers who dislike this pattern of renewal can be counted on to put up with it—for a time, anyway.

Such complexes, however, cannot be created on the necessary scale, or integrated with city-wide communication systems, without decisive governmental promotion and planning and a colossal outlay of social capital. Before long it must be detected that these powers and resources could be more wisely, and indeed more profitably, employed in a systematic dispersal policy including the foundation of new centres, making possible the renewal of the old ones in a more efficient, adaptable and humanly acceptable way.

Another school of planners, more alive to the strength of the craving for the individual home, plot of land and private car, returns to the thorough-going diffusion of population forecast by H. G. Wells in *Anticipations* (1901). The idea is that the tradition of the town as a local society, having fallen to zero in mass cities, should be abandoned as obsolete. Mobility and instantaneous communications have made face to face contacts far less, and selective associations far more, dominant in our lives. Thus, argues this school, there is no longer any sense in a distinction between town and country; so long as we have pleasant homes, and places within motoring reach for work, shopping, exercise and entertainment, it is unnecessary that these facilities should be in the same town, or in towns at all. We may have to drive long distances for some purposes, but lots of people enjoy driving, and we might as well weave about in a regional criss-cross of roads as shuttle daily on 6-line speedways or crowded trains in and out of coagulated cities. Again this is an attractive way of life for some. And the outer parts of many metropolitan regions are going this way, though the planners of their inner areas strive to entice 'ex-urbans' back into super-terminals.

If these two patterns are the only alternatives offered, we think the diffusionists will easily outbid the compressionists in a free market and an affluent society. There is much truth in their view of the selectivity of association and the growing insistence on space for living.

But the town, if of moderate size, remains an institution of profound importance not only as a convenient assemblage of all sorts of services and a means of minimizing daily travel time, but a check on narrow specializations in work and leisure and the atomization of society. Just as an individual is enriched as well as constrained by the family, so he and they in turn are enriched and constrained by the unchosen associations of a local community, all the more if it is of diverse social composition. This we think is essential for the healthy working of an elective democracy, which must suffer by a total lack of acquaintance between people of different selective interests. But we need not stress these quasi-sociological dicta. The practical convenience of the moderate-sized town as against extreme diffusion is justification enough.

Towns for New Populations

The new towns concept was originally addressed to the rescue of overgrown cities from their present plight and disastrous trends. We have had to admit that at the best the rescue can be only partial; the mistakes and negligences of history cannot be completely obliterated. The existing million-cities, with slow and painful amelioration, will remain. There is a far greater question: will they, need they, be repeated in the new urban developments of the future?

According to temperament or philosophy, one may be terrified to despair or spurred to advocacy or action by the world population forecasts for the next 3 or 4 decades. Clearly there must be an end to the neglect of urban control; yet one is staggered at the thought of the number of new towns that will have to be created as control becomes effective.

In Britain education in family planning and advances in methods of control have recently slowed down the birth rate, but in many countries a major slow-down is unlikely for decades. Even in Britain, assuming a static population, the demand for space per household will continue to rise, and the obsolescence of homes and work-places gives to urban dispersal a continuing urgency.

For the whole world, current estimates show that there were 191 million-cities in 1975, and project that there may be 273 in 1985, containing 805 million inhabitants, or 37% of the world's urban population. Even in the few years 1970 to 1975 it is estimated that about 106 million individuals transferred their residence from rural to urban places. The number of new towns of moderate size needed to cope with this continuing movement is so prodigious that one must feel unrealistic in doing the sum.

Yet in one form or another, unless the human race is catastrophically curtailed by pestilence or scientific warfare (which, even if anybody wants it, is not to be assumed) urban development on something like this unimaginable scale is certain to occur.

The practical question is: How much of it will be so placed and planned as to make for a good life for the people of the world, and how much of it will be allowed to flow adventitiously into existing and new huge agglomerations, with the sorry consequences for health, convenience, productive efficiency and the pursuit of happiness with which we are now all too familiar?

References and Notes

12.1   The history of this sad decline is recounted, with quotations from early Congress proceedings, in F. J. Osborn's address, 'Bigger Cities or More Cities?', *Report of Golden Jubilee Conference of IFHP*, Arnhem, 1963.

12.2   Stein, Clarence, *Towards New Towns for America*, 1957, 1966.

12.3   See Lubove, Roy, *Community Planning in the 1920's*, 1963.

12.4   A proposal for 'Twenty new towns for America' was made by C. F. Palmer of Atlanta after a visit to Britain in 1936.

12.5   See Baranov, N. V., 'Building New Towns', 1964, in *Planning of Metropolitan Areas and New Towns*, United Nations, 1967.

12.6   See IFHP, 'Report of Orebro Conference', 1965.

13 *The Human Environment: The People's Awakening*

'All countries should establish as a matter of urgency a national policy on human settlements, embodying the distribution of population, and related economic and social activities, over their national territory.'

Recommendations for National Action No. A 1
'Habitat'
United Nations Conference, Vancouver
June 1976

We have not found it necessary to make more than minor revisions to Chapters 1–12 of this book for the third edition, as they are essentially historical and we think accurate as far as they go. Recent years have, however, brought a world awakening of interest in land-use planning and urban development which has been reflected in a vast increase of public, political and academic discussion of the subject. Hundreds of additional new towns, influenced by the British lead or prompted by parallel concern for metropolitan overgrowth or rural decline, have been founded (see Appendices).

The information and arguments about new towns, in books, journals and conference reports, have proliferated enormously, and the discussion has extended in scope beyond physical planning to embrace every aspect of the human environment, from pollution and conservation of natural resources to the possible control of the numbers and distributions of our planet's population. We cannot pretend to have assimilated more than a fraction of the facts and (often controversial) theories in recent literature. To do so would require another book longer than this. We confine ourselves here to comments on changes and developments closely related to our topic.

British Planning: Recent Changes in Method and Structure

In Great Britain there have been radical changes in the organization of the state department concerned with town and country planning, and of the whole local government system. By the Local Government Act 1972 the number of local authorities in England and Wales was reduced from about 1400 to 422 (not including the Greater

London Council and its 32 borough councils). A major reason for this change was that the pattern of urban growth had made many existing boundaries and responsibilities meaningless. All the 422 new councils are now planning authorities each with its own officials(13.1).

There is now a two-tier system of county councils each having within its area a number of district councils, some counties having been amalgamated and many boundaries changed. For the six major urban concentrations new 'metropolitan county councils' have been set up, within which there are component 'metropolitan district councils' analogous to the borough councils of London. The county councils are responsible for the administration and planning of county-wide services such as highways, education and waste disposal, while the district councils are responsible for detailed development control, housing and local planning. There is considerable overlap between the counties and districts, particularly in the planning of land-use, and there are published agreements to help resolve conflict (Development Control Schemes and Development Plan Schemes). The boundaries of the new metropolitan counties have been drawn very tightly around the urban areas they serve, and so there are some conflicts between them and their neighbouring counties, particularly over the planning of dispersed urban growth, which have to be resolved at a political level and by efforts to marry their strategic plans. While the new system is an improvement, most people agree that a further reorganization will be needed sooner or later to adapt local government to the true pattern of existing city regions.

The county strategic plans, now termed 'structure plans', result from changes in planning methods, coincident with the local government reorganization. Under the Town and Country Planning Acts of 1968, 1971 and 1972 the county councils have to prepare structure plans of far wider scope than the former development plans, since they are now concerned with interactions between the various parts of the broad area which they cover, and with surrounding areas. Structure plans attend to all the major issues of development, including the location of employment, shopping centres, education, communications and recreation, and set out the intentions for change, growth or restraint of urban areas (including new towns) and reservation of rural areas. They now take into account economic and social considerations; but they do not deal in detail with the internal planning of the areas, which falls to the district councils(13.2).

Scotland enjoyed its own reorganization in 1975, by which a two-tier system was also established, though 'regional councils' covering extensive areas replace the county councils that have lived on in England and Wales. In Scotland the structure plan is replaced by a regional report which is similar in that it looks at the broad planning picture for the area and takes into account the surrounding areas, but is very different in that it is a short written statement annually revised. There is a widely held view that the Scottish system of local government will be the model for the future in England and Wales.

In Northern Ireland the political predicament is such that all planning activity, including the new towns, has been placed in the hands of central government in the Ministry of Development, and through a system of district development officers. Even in the midst of the civil and military tensions the need to plan for urban growth and change continues.

In 1970 the central government arrangements for town and country planning in Great Britain were also reorganized. A new Department of the Environment was set up embodying the former Ministries of Housing and Local Government, of Public Building and Works, and of Transport. The new Department established planning as a broad-based activity enjoying considerable influence at a national level, and having a team of Ministers who between them were responsible for housing and construction, planning and local government, transport and the many additional responsibilities of preservation of amenities, historic towns, buildings and monuments, the protection of the coast and countryside, national parks, and the control of air and water pollution. It has powers to set up *ad hoc* regional bodies to prepare 'strategic plans' for areas that embrace several county councils; the first of these was the Strategic Plan for the South East (1970), which was reviewed in 1976. The strategic plan has proved a most useful vehicle for the discussion of solutions to urban overgrowth and forms of planned dispersal. Similar studies have followed in the North West and other regions.

The Department of the Environment has been particularly important in encouraging different professional disciplines to work together on environmental matters, and there has been some dismay at an apparently backward step in 1976. The transport interests were hived off from the Department of the Environment to a separate Department of Transport. Concern for convenience and speed in movement is important, but even more so is the location of houses, workplaces and other facilities to reduce the problems of long daily journeys.

The ministerial post of Planning and Local Government was abolished, its functions being absorbed into the Department of the Environment. At the time of writing it is uncertain how this will affect the operation of the nation's planning system. The moves have coincided with the cut-backs in public expenditure and so the pace of change is slowing down somewhat anyway—we may hope for only a short period.

Recent Changes in Attitude to Policy

All strategic and local plans to which we have referred are subject to approval by central government, though the local plans of district councils automatically take effect if they conform to an approved structure plan and if there is no objection from the inhabitants of the area who may press for a public inquiry into most planning proposals. Those with property interests at stake always have the right to appeal both against the planning proposal that affects them, and against the amount of compensation offered. The system avoids being choked by appeals and inquiries by ensuring that full public consultation takes place early in the process, before decisions are made. This tends to produce planning proposals that meet far less objection.

It can be fairly claimed that the British land-use planning system has become among the world's best in the completeness of its powers and its subjection to democratic influences, though at the time of writing (1977) it is going through a period of 'growing pains'. It is not fully appreciated by foreign observers that in Britain practically every kind of development, including any change of use of land or buildings, is subject to planning consent, without financial compensation where consent is refused. There has been some resentment at controls on the freedom to carry out minor extensions and adaptations, particularly of domestic property, and it is likely that the rules will be revised accordingly, in order that planning should retain its popular support.

Another recent change in attitude has been alluded to in Chapter 5, where we have referred to the popular revulsion against property speculation and windfall profits. This has caused all political parties to promise that they will maintain a system capturing for the community the benefit of betterment caused by planning consents. The present solution is the Community Land Scheme which seeks to endow local government with powers of 'positive planning' approaching those possessed by the new towns development corporations.

There has also been some criticism of the green-belt principle, on the ground that excessive expansion of belts could prevent the dispersal of city population and employment to a sufficient yet practicable distance, and therefore inhibit the region's natural growth as an economic, social and cultural unity. In our view it is a mistake to attack the green-belt principle, which remains popular and aids the fight against contiguous suburban sprawl. But the green belt should not be conceived as invariably a rigid geometric ring, and the land safeguarded by the policy should be put to evident good use. Dereliction and waste must be actively contested, and every opportunity taken to increase the accessibility of the countryside to the urban dweller. Some most encouraging work in this respect is being undertaken by the Countryside Commission under the title 'Recreation at the Urban Fringe', involving various experiments in land management to marry the needs of agriculture with those of recreation.

Reaction against New Town Policy

A more serious change in attitude has been a reaction against Britain's policy of decongestion and dispersal by the London and other metropolitan authorities. London, which for many centuries boasted of being the world's greatest city, has since 1946 earned a wiser (and nobler) claim to pride as the world's first big city to co-operate in and even help to finance a reduction of its own swollen population by organized transfers of people and their jobs to new towns and other towns of moderate size. Thereby London set an example that other great cities in Britain and abroad have admired and sought to follow.

During the first 20 years after the New Towns Act of 1946 the populations of the conurbations failed to fall as expected in spite of planned dispersal. Rising birth rates were accompanied by a failure to renew the cities to more human standards for living and working that were the primary purpose of the dispersal policy. In the late 1960s, the birth rate at last declined and, having been used for so long to coping with overall growth, the Greater London Council and other metropolitan authorities were panicked into alarm at their losses in rateable values, obsolete buildings and out-dated infrastructures, and contrasted their fortunes with the social and economic successes of the new towns. In recent years these authorities have called on government to reverse the national policy, to cease financing new towns, and to use the money instead for aid to the big cities in dealing with their otherwise insoluble problems. The government expressed sympathy with this demand, and though they would not promise to stop the development of the existing new towns, stated that few if any new designations would be made in the near future.

The GLC's contention that the worsening conditions in London were mainly due to the decentralization policy was certainly not justified. Other causes were far more influential in the fall of population and increase in unemployment in the inner city. Of more than 500 000 jobs lost by London since 1961, for example, only about 7% can be accounted for by planned movements to the new towns and small town expansions and about 20% by the voluntary movements of industry and people to outer suburbs or other regions, and it has been estimated that something like 70% of the loss of jobs is due to the closing down of firms. Wandsworth Borough Council in October 1976, with 8000 unemployed, blamed its own slum clearance and redevelopment actions for the displacement in the past ten years of 250 firms, only 13 of which had been relocated. Another inner London authority, Lambeth Borough Council, stated that its present housing programme could affect 300 firms and 3000 jobs(13.3).

Though some newspapers and some elements of public opinion inimical to the new towns hailed the first response of the government to the demands of the GLC and other conurbations for a radical change of policy, the Secretary of State for the Environment, Mr Peter Shore, has since reduced the population targets of the third generation new towns not as a 'reversal' of policy, but in response to reduced population forecasts. The TCPA came back with a vigorous reassertion of the case for more new towns and a counter-attack on the big cities for not having taken advantage of the reduction of their populations in order to renew their centres on acceptable standards. In this they were supported by the new towns' corporations themselves, who could claim that they had not only provided far superior environments, but had proved to be profitable public investments(13.4).

In the 30 years from 1946 the eight new towns around London had a positive surplus of more than £13 million after covering all interest and amortization charges to date on their 60-year loans. The first 12 towns in England and Wales showed a combined surplus of over £12 million after allowing for losses on three of them. Though the later new towns had not yet reached a profitable stage, it is fair to assume that in a few years there will be an overall financial surplus that will be a useful offset to the enormous national costs of grants in aid for renewal of the old cities, on standards of housing, workplaces and open space that will be accepted as permanently satisfactory to their reduced populations(13.5).

Towns Must Have a Stop

As we have said in Chapters 8 and 9, there is no scientific formula for the ideal size of a town. But we gave reasons, based on a balance between density and convenience of daily movements, for substantially self-contained urban units of 30 000 to 60 000 persons, and for clusters of such units up to a total of 250 000—which total again cannot claim scientific validity. But if a town has been designed in advance for an ultimate maximum population the intended limit cannot be much exceeded without obvious distortion of its internal zoning and either an increase of housing density or an outward expansion over its rural belt. This has happened to a number of the British new towns, and is officially proposed for others. In some, as at Stevenage and Harlow, the enlargement has been strongly opposed by their inhabitants and by neighbouring villages and towns, sometimes with success.

Since the main motive of the new towns policy is to check overgrowth and congestion of existing cities, it would be anomalous if there were no limit to their own growth. But the forces for their continued expansion are formidable. Successful industries grow and want more workers and houses for them. Retail traders would like more customers. Births exceed deaths and a new generation of school leavers want jobs, locally if possible, and later may marry and want houses. Thus in some new towns there is a waiting list for housing. Of course there are many counter-movements as some businesses fail, and some move to other places, but on balance the population of a prosperous and pleasant town tends to grow.

What is the solution? Britain needs more new towns and expansions of towns not already too large. But for civil servants in Whitehall it is much less trouble to advise their Minister to enlarge existing towns than to designate sites for more new ones—a process that always encounters opposition from some devoted countryside preservationists, farmers and residents who are themselves already happily housed in spacious surroundings.

High-rise Housing: A Return to Sanity

In the 1970s there has been a strong reaction against multi-storey housing—a form much employed in the cities of Britain, as in Europe, America and elsewhere, for several decades, despite the consistent evidence of opinion polls that 70 to 90% of families prefer houses with gardens. In Britain the official conviction that high flats could be made acceptable faded in the early 1970s, though a few projects remained under construction. Many cities have found it hard to keep their flats contentedly occupied. In Stockholm, it was reported in 1973, there were 25 000 empty flats in the famous new suburbs. In the USA crimes of violence are many times more numerous in high-rise than in low-rise dwellings(13.6).

Advocates of new towns, who have always opposed mass housing in flats as socially deplorable, were in the 1950s and 1960s derided by *avant-garde* architects as hidebound old fogies. *Avant-garde* fashion, however, has since moved towards low-rise housing, though still at what we think excessive density. In *Confessions of a Criminal* (Delos Symposium 1971) the eminent Greek architect Dr Constantine Doxiadis wrote:

'We are committing architectural crimes. . . High-rise buildings work against Nature, by spoiling the landscape; against Man, especially children; against Society . . . *'Death to the Dinosaurs'*. . . The criminal buildings are going to die some day. But it will take time. Humanity will suffer in the meantime . . . Our duty is not to wait patiently for their death, but to fight for their extermination.'

We need not agree with the late Dr Doxiadis' proposed methods to applaud the courage of his 'Confession'. And at least on a small scale the extermination has begun. In 1973 St Louis, USA, dynamited a number of its apartment blocks. And in 1976 the City of Leeds decided to demolish completely its 930 Quarry Hill flats, regarded when built in 1938 as the model for the Brave New World.

The World Awakening

We opened this chapter with a resolution of the United Nations conference in Vancouver 1976, which reflected the rising world interest in land-use planning and the problems of urban overgrowth. Much common ground having been found at the Stockholm conference of the UN in 1972, it was gratifying to us that these issues should inspire the agenda for this most prestigious international event.

British planners who took part report that Habitat is difficult to sum up. Its hundreds of simultaneous meetings proved the intensity of interest that prevails. Sessions on the problems of the exploding cities of the developing world confirmed the international need for land-use planning to control excessive urban growth and to promote policies of settlement dispersal.

Habitat enabled valuable connections to be made between officials and interested individuals, many of whom committed themselves to ensuring that their governments follow up the resolutions to which they are signatory. In describing the current position in Great Britain, our objective has been to chart some of the obstacles that await any nation that embarks on a planning policy of new and expanding towns.

New Towns and Megalopolis: Cui Bono?

New towns were not conceived by Howard and his followers solely as ends in themselves, but also as demonstrations of a healthy, pleasant and efficient form of urban environment, which could be adopted by existing cities when their congestion had been relieved by some reduction of their population. As proofs of the practicability of a better human environment, the British new towns are unquestionably a success.

Yet the old cities have not sufficiently taken advantage of the reliefs afforded by planned and spontaneous dispersal. Their traffic congestion has in fact grown to a critical point by the multiplication of car ownership, and the increase of commuting by the continuance of suburban expansion. And there are still grave housing shortages though overcrowding of some individual dwellings has been somewhat relieved by the decline in the size of the average household—an important social gain, but no consolation to those who are still homeless.

Such voluminous surveys have been made of city regions that all the facts and figures about them are known, and in many respects terrifying. The problems are complex but we are convinced that the highly trained planners of today and tomorrow will find solutions, and that the governments and authorities they advise, which in Britain have all the necessary powers, will take appropriate action. At the present stage in many cities—London for example—planning policies are subjects of controversy and decisions inconsistent. The outward movement of manufacturing industry to new and expanded towns has been encouraged with much success. But while a similar movement of office business was promoted by a governmental agency, the planning authorities still granted permits for massive new office buildings, some of which remain unoccupied for years. And there is a deep difference of opinion as to what the ultimate population of Greater London should be. In 1961 it was about 8 million, in 1971 it had fallen to a little under $7\frac{1}{2}$ million, and in 1977 it was about 7 million.

We think it should be less, because we do not believe that a city can hope to retain a balanced population of occupations and income classes unless the greater part of its residential areas are renewed at moderate densities comparable with those in the new towns. Mr John Silkin(13.7) gave as his own assessment of the optimum size of London over the next fifty years as 6 million(13.8).

The Problem of High Land Values

A major obstacle to redevelopment of a city at lower densities is the cost of sites. It is surely anomalous that land which cannot profitably be used for new housing without a government subsidy, or for new commercial buildings without planning permission for an increase of floor space, has any market value at all. We can only suppose that it is the confident expectation that such a subsidy or permission will be given that creates the market value, and that if a government announced that such subsidy or permission would be discontinued the market value would disappear, since in essence it is speculative. The fantastic 'yardstick' by which housing subsidies increase with density should be abandoned, and a uniform subsidy per square foot of housing be applied in all town and country areas. In over-centralized cities like London permits for increased commercial floor space should not be granted.

Old out-dated cities cannot be satisfactorily renewed without considerable national aid. In view of their precious heritage and functional importance that aid should be forthcoming. But as we have argued in Chapter 5, it should be granted for real improvements such as the reduction of density or de-concentration of employment; never for developments that maintain or increase their density or centralization.

The Joys of Pioneering

The British new towns have been the subjects (or victims) of many sociological surveys which point to the deficiencies of new and immature communities. Some towns are accused of being too exclusively working-class; others of not catering for a due percentage of the very poor and unskilled. What the surveys generally underplay is the immense improvement most inhabitants have gained in their immediate house-and-garden surroundings and the increase in their leisure time by nearness to jobs. It is probably true, and regrettable, that some corporations' planners, staff and architects, and the executives of some business firms, have chosen not to live in the towns themselves but in nearby old towns and villages. These classes are, by their capacity for initiative and organization, natural leaders in the foundation and running of voluntary societies. The new community loses much by their absence. They themselves miss an experience of endless interest and pleasurability. And there are many people retiring from professions and businesses, or from service abroad, and seeking attractive homes, who would find it more enjoyable to settle in new communities where they would count and make contributions to social and cultural development, than to be non-entities in a conventional resort for the aged and relatively inert. It would be sad if the descendants of the adventurous colonizers of the past, Britons and Americans for example, lost the pioneering spirit.

References and Notes

13.1 The planning context of the reorganization is fully described in CHERRY, G. E., *The Evolution of British Town Planning*, London, 1974.

13.2 A lucid up-to-date description is given in *The New Citizen's Guide to Town and Country Planning*, TCPA, London, 1974.

13.3 HILLMAN, JUDY, in *The Guardian*,12 October, 1976.

13.4 Those interested in the continuing debate will find its twists and turns adequately charted through the pages of the journal *Town and Country Planning* and its companion weekly news sheet, *The Planning Bulletin*.

13.5 The most authoritative contribution to the debate was generated by the House of Commons Expenditure Committee Environment Sub-Committee examination of new towns from 1972 to 1974. Their *Report* and *Minutes of Evidence*, HMSO, 1974, are particularly commended, especially the memorandum submitted by the TCPA.

13.6 See for example *How to Save Urban America*, New York Regional Planning Association, 1973.

13.7 Minister of Planning and Local Government, 1974–76.

13.8 SILKIN, J., 'New Towns and the Inner City', *Town and Country Planning*, September 1976, p. 302.

Part Two

14 *Stevenage*

In the first interim report of the New Towns Committee of March 1946 reference was made to Stevenage, one of the satellite towns proposed by Sir Patrick Abercrombie, and it was suggested that, as a matter of urgency, an agency should be chosen for this town in advance of legislation. A draft charter for a corporation for Stevenage was drawn up for the committee by the Treasury Solicitor. However, following the second and final reports of the committee, the New Towns Act, 1946, provided necessary powers for establishing corporations to develop new towns.

Stevenage, 'as a matter of urgency', thus became the first new town to be designated—on 11 November 1946.

During the thirties the Stevenage Urban District Council had favoured plans for permitting the development of the existing small town from its population of 6500 to about 30 000, and during the war officials of the Ministry of Town and Country Planning had been sketching plans for Stevenage as a possible prototype of future new towns. It was thus ripe for development of this kind. In the Greater London Plan Abercrombie had pointed out that the site is 'excellently located for transport', that it 'is tending to develop industrially' and that there is 'ample land for industry on the west side of the railway'. He suggested that 'expansion should take place mainly on the east of the present town, leaving an area on the west of the railway for industry, where it is undesirable to have residential development'(14.1).

The site selected, of 6100 acres (2470 ha), included the Urban District of Stevenage, and parts of the Rural Districts of Hitchin and Hertford. The town centre is about 30 miles (50 km) from the centre of London, on the North-Eastern Region main railway line from King's Cross to the north, and on the Great North Road. The country is undulating, with a general slope towards the south-west, which makes it a good site for a town. Fairlands Valley which runs across the centre of the site from north to south in the original plan was to be preserved. It is now being developed by the borough council as the town's main park and amenity area which includes a boating lake about $\frac{1}{3}$ of a mile (0.5 km) long.

With the reorganization of Local Government in 1974 the Stevenage District Council corresponds in area to that of the new town.

Outline Plan

As early as 1946 a draft Master Plan was prepared by the Ministry of Town and Country Planning, which provided the basis for subsequent plans. Revisions were made up to its final adoption in 1950, and they continue to be made, but in broad principle the

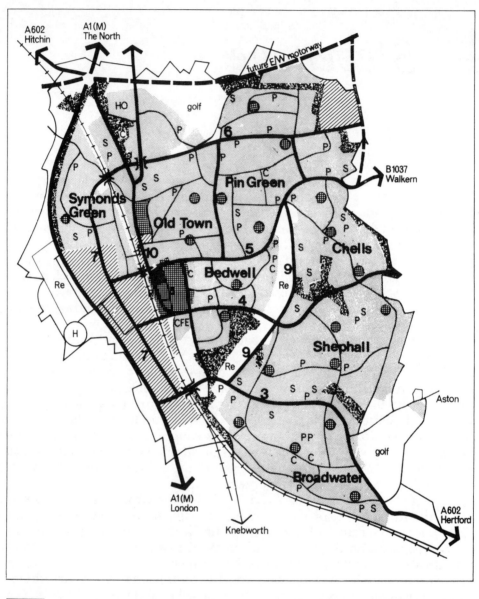

Figure 14.1 Stevenage – outline plan

adopted plan has been the guide in building the town. As an example of the planning of a satellite town, Abercrombie prepared, in accordance with the general principles he advocated, an outline plan for Ongar (Essex)(14.2) with a population of 60 000, divided into 6 neighbourhoods of about 10 000 each, and in the plan for Stevenage this approximate size of the town and of the neighbourhoods is adopted. The town centre is placed south of old Stevenage and the neighbourhoods are grouped in a semi-circle round this centre, old Stevenage (1) with extensions to the east forming one neighbourhood to the north, then Bedwell (2) immediately to the east of the centre, Pin Green to the north east (6), with Chells (5) further to the east and Shephall (4) and Broadwater (3) to the south-east. (The numbers indicate the order of building.) Fairlands Valley separates Bedwell and Pin Green to the west from Chells, Shephall and Broadwater to the east (see plan). Each neighbourhood was originally planned with 2 primary schools, 8 secondary schools being conveniently spaced throughout the town. Owing to the increase in maximum population most neighbourhoods will require 3 primary schools while the number of secondary schools has been increased to 12. A County College of Further Education is situated near the town centre. Each neighbourhood has a shopping centre, where in many cases sites are provided for a church and a public house; and there are a few additional groups of shops in parts of the neighbourhoods away from the centres. Community centres are also provided in some of the neighbourhoods. All the principal town roads run between the neighbourhoods so that young children attending primary schools need not cross these roads. The plan shows a diversion of the Great North Road (the A1 Motorway) to the west of the industrial area.

Part of the green belt is included within the boundary of the designated area, on the north, south-east and west; and it is hoped and expected that open country areas beyond the boundary will be preserved as such so that the town will enjoy a green belt of at least 3 miles (5 km) wide.

The plan prompts certain criticisms, and it is doubtful whether it can be considered as good as some of the other plans for new towns. In one widely accepted theory the size of a neighbourhood should be governed by the capacity of a primary school, but in Stevenage each neighbourhood has 2 or 3 primary schools. If the neighbourhoods had been half the size, each would support 1 school, while it would have obviated the necessity of having the small groups of shops in addition to those in the neighbourhood centres as these would have been adequate for smaller neighbourhoods as at Crawley. Another point of criticism is the placing of the town centre. This criticism was made by the Stevenage Urban District Council at the master plan inquiry in October 1949. The objection to the location of the centre, an objection which the explanations of the original draft plan do not meet, is that it is too far from the outlying parts of the town. It is, for example, 2 miles (3.25 km) from the eastern areas of Broadwater, Shephall and Chells, which may be thought too far for a town of 60 000. As the District Council Surveyor said at the inquiry, 33 000 persons would live beyond $1\frac{1}{4}$ miles (2 km), 10 000 beyond $1\frac{3}{4}$ miles (2.8 km). The council suggested a site further east on higher ground, more in the geographical centre. If the centre had been where the neighbourhood centre of Bedwell is located it would have reduced by more than a $\frac{1}{2}$ mile (0.8 km) the distance to the outskirts. On the other hand, the situation of the town centre places it near the railway where a new station has been built, and it is easily accessible from the industrial area, but these considerations are surely less important than the convenience of the majority for whom the town is built.

One criticism frequently made which, we think, has not the same validity, is that it lacks compactness—that there is too much sprawl. This is accentuated by Fairlands Valley running through the town. But this generous use of land and mixing of trees and grass with houses helps to make life pleasant, and Fairlands Valley brings a stretch of very pleasant country right into the town. The opposition of many residents to the later proposal to build on it is significant. It confirms that there is a popular liking for the sense of constant contact with the natural world.

If the placing of the town centre can be criticized, there is little to criticize in the plan for the centre itself, which is excellent in every way. Here the desirable ideal of grouping shops in a pedestrian precinct with bus station and car parks close by has been realized. It is one of the finest of modern town centres and will be described in some detail later.

The location of the main industrial area west of the railway (with railway sidings for many factories) and east of the new Great North Road met with some opposition, chiefly because, as originally planned, it meant the demolition of over 100 houses at the northern end of the site. The Urban District Council suggested that the industrial area should stop south of the residential development in Fairview Road, and proposed an alternative site north-east of the town. The disadvantage of such a site was mainly of poor transport access: no railway and no main roads. Although there is natural sympathy with people having to be turned out of their homes—not, however, without being offered other and often better accommodation—it would have been unwise to allow this to spoil what is a very good location for an industrial area, having the advantages of proximity to the railway and the Great North Road, and easy access to the town centre, while being admirably suited for the purpose. However, a compromise was later reached by which Fairview Road remains a residential area on the eastern outskirts of the industrial area and the extensive demolition of houses was thus avoided, while some new residential development has actually taken place there.

In June 1958 the development corporation was asked to prepare a new master plan for an increase of population to 80 000. In July 1962, just before this plan was ready for submission, the Minister asked the corporation to examine the feasibility of a larger expansion to about 150 000. In January 1963 the corporation submitted a report by its Chief Architect and Planner, Leonard G. Vincent, dealing with the technical practicability of such an expansion. In this report it was stated that 'an ultimate population of 130 000 to 140 000 is thought to be more desirable than 150 000 so as to keep all parts of the town within a 2-mile (3 km) radius of the centre, to use the A600 as the westward boundary, and to preserve the green belt between Hitchin and Stevenage'.

In October 1964 a Draft Designation Order was made for a further area of some 1500 acres (650 ha), mostly west of the A1 Motorway. A public inquiry followed at which there was much opposition to the proposed expansion. In April 1965 the Minister decided not to proceed with the proposed expansion, but to extend the designated area by 100 acres (40 ha) on the north-east. The corporation then continued with its preparation of the new master plan. This was duly submitted and approved in June 1967 for a population by intake up to 80 000 with a further increase by natural growth.

The extensions are in 12 areas, mostly on the periphery. The largest are two new neighbourhoods: St Nicholas in the north-east, Simons Green in the north-west, between the railway and the motorway and north of the principal industrial area. Other fairly large extensions are south of Broadwater and east of Shephall. An additional industrial area is sited on the 100 acre (40 ha) extension in the north-east.

The implementation of the 1966 plan was well advanced in 1972. The Secretary of State for the Environment then asked the corporation to consider an extension of the designated area by as much as 3000–4000 acres (1200–1600 ha). In January 1973 the corporation published a preliminary report in which five alternative ways of expanding the town were given, and invited the people of Stevenage to express their views—a useful exercise in public participation. Following this the corporation submitted its proposals to the Secretary of State in April 1973, which involved an extension of 3600 acres (1460 ha), about half of the existing area, mainly to the west, but also a little to the north and east. This major expansion to the west would have meant that nearly a third of the town would be divided from the rest by the A1 Motorway and the railway, a most unsatisfactory example of planning.

In this exercise in public participation it was found that the great majority who responded to the questionnaire on the subject were against expansion: 1593 living in Stevenage and 1068 living in surrounding areas. Those who supported expansion numbered 212 inside and 41 outside. Those who expressed no view either way were 1823 inside and 422 outside. If this expansion had been agreed it would have meant a maximum population of 150 000 instead of the 105 000 in the 1966 plan.

Fortunately the Secretary of State decided in January 1974 not to proceed with this big extension, but to extend on a smaller scale, and this was confirmed after a change of Government when the request was made to the corporation for proposals for an additional 1000 acres (405 ha) to serve local needs until about 1990. In September 1974 the corporation published a preliminary report and invited public comment, and in January 1975 the full report of recommendations was published. The proposals were for an additional 1079 acres (437 ha) but 385 acres (156 ha) of undeveloped land to the west could be released within the boundary meaning an addition of 695 acres (281 ha).

Following further discussions with public authorities, local organizations and individuals and officers of government departments, the corporation submitted to the Secretary of State, in April 1975, lower minimum option growth proposals for an expansion which showed a gross land requirement of 1154 acres (481 ha) (made up of 865 acres (360 ha) of additional land and 289 acres (121 ha) of land within the present designated are). It was still prepared to release the 385 acres (160 ha) of undeveloped land to the west from the designated area, giving a net additional land requirement of 480 acres (200 ha) in the north and east.

A public inquiry into the proposals was held in April 1976, and the corporation was supported by the Stevenage Borough Council and the Stevenage and District Industrial Employees Group. Those opposing the proposals included the Hertfordshire County Council, North Herts District Council, East Herts District Council, Hertfordshire Society, National Farriers Union and several adjacent parish councils and local amenity groups. In his statement on new towns in the House of Commons on 28 April 1977, Peter Shore, Secretary of State for the Environment, said that he had decided not to make an extension order for Stevenage.

Building the Town

In the early years, progress in building was very slow; the first houses were not begun until September 1949, nearly 3 years after designation. The main reason for this was the local opposition to the new town. Similar opposition occurred at Crawley and

Hemel Hempstead, designated a few months later, but it was particularly strong at Stevenage, and delayed the start of construction.

A public inquiry was, of course, held before the designation order was made. Although the Urban District Council voted in favour of supporting the enterprise, three residents representing the Residents' Protection Association and the local branch of the National Farmers' Union brought a High Court action to have the designation order annulled on the grounds that the objections at the public inquiry had not been fairly considered. Heard in February 1947, the action was successful, but the decision was reversed in the Court of Appeal in March, and this was upheld in the House of Lords in July. The litigation meant delay in the preparation of detailed plans, because not a great deal could be done in the atmosphere of uncertainty occasioned by the first successful opposition in the High Court. Looking back on a case where the interests of the few were opposed to those of the many, it may be questioned whether the opposition could not have been handled with more persuasiveness and diplomacy by the Minister of Town and Country Planning. Nobody likes to be told that they are going to have the town whether they like it or not.

The civil engineering works—roads, water supply and other public services—are among the first things to be provided in building a new town, and some progress had been made with these in 1948 to 1950, and by 1952 the first new neighbourhood, together with the additions to old Stevenage, were well under way. By the end of 1956 Bedwell was nearing completion, Broadwater was about two-thirds completed, Shephall about a third, a start had been made on the town centre, and many factories had been built. By the end of 1962 these neighbourhoods and much of the town centre had been completed, and about a half of Chells had been built.

Being designed to receive industry and population from London in conformity with the policy of dispersal, while the housing is for those working in the town, it was necessary to synchronize factory building as closely as possible with housing, and keep the former a little ahead of the latter. This was for the most part accomplished, except for one period when industry lagged a little behind, and it was necessary to allow one or two firms to come from other parts of the country to maintain the balance.

After the slow start in house building satisfactory progress was made. The first houses were completed in 1950, and by the end of 1952 some 1070 had been built; 806 in 1953, and for several years at least 1000 houses were completed annually. Later, due to uncertainty regarding the maximum size, the number dropped to about 600 in 1963 and 1964, to rise to about 850 in 1965, 1100 in 1966, and 750 in 1967.

In 1968 there was a drop to about 500, to rise again to about 900 in 1969. This high level was maintained in 1970 and 1971 when over 1000 were built each year. About 870 were completed in 1972 to drop in 1973 to 300 and 375 in 1974. In 1975 563 were completed and in 1976 500. Altogether a total of 22 700 houses had been completed since designation up to the end of 1976 of which 19 768 have been provided by the development corporation, 1277 by the local authority and 1725 by private enterprise.

Housing and Residential Areas

The majority of houses provided at Stevenage have been of the 2-storey type, although there is a conspicuous minority of other types. The 2-storey unit has been built to many different designs so as to give variety, but they may be classified broadly as having mainly 3 or 2 bedrooms, and of 3 basic types, largely determined by orientation; that with north aspect in which the kitchen and bathroom are in the front with the living rooms and main bedrooms facing south towards the garden; that with the south aspect in which living rooms and main bedrooms are in the front and the kitchen and bathroom at the back; and that in which the houses face east and west and are provided with a through living room with windows front and back. There are many plan variations on these basic types and a considerable variation in elevational treatment where different materials are juxtaposed. Bricks of various hues are related to cement rendering of different colours and to panels of painted boards and sometimes of natural timber. Variety is also secured in the designs of the entrances.

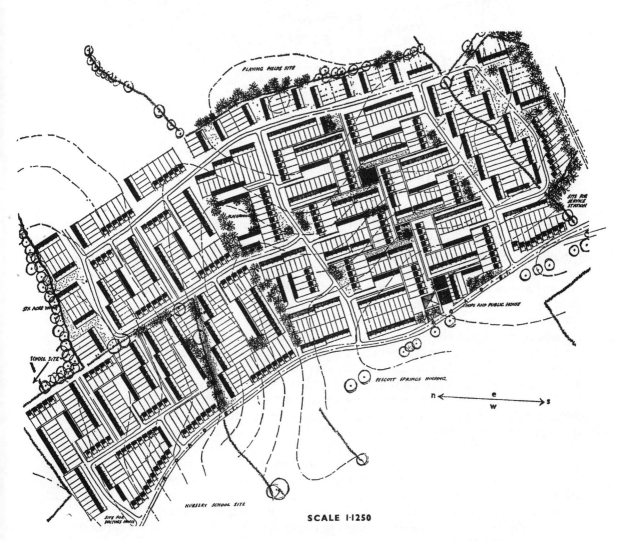

Figure 14.2 Elm Green residential area in the Chells neighbourhood. Culs-de-sac run into the areas at the backs of houses many of which face onto pedestrian ways, a partial adaptation of the Radburn layout.

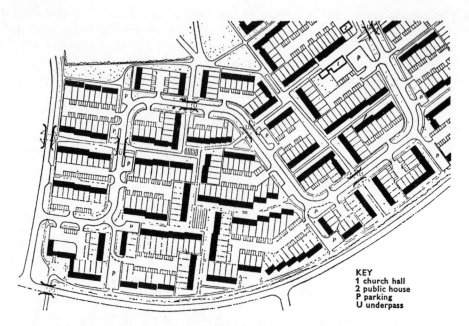

Figure 14.3 Part of the Pin Green residential area. A feature of this layout, like that at Elm Green, is the cul-de-sac with garages at the rear of houses which in many cases face onto pedestrian ways.

One of the first parts to be built was Stony Hall immediately south of old Stevenage and a little north-east of the town centre. It represents an experiment in high density development and includes blocks of 3- and 4-storey flats, and one 7-storey block of 54 flats, making a total of 103 flats. The building of the tall block, especially at so early a stage, has since been recognized as a mistake. Probably the motive was to have a small proportion of flats near the town centre. Designed for middle-class tenants, they did not prove very acceptable to the workers who first came to the new town, whose natural reaction was that there are plenty of tall blocks of flats in London in the midst of all the recreations of life the metropolis provides. If they were merely to get the same thing at Stevenage they might as well stay in London. That also was the reaction of people going to East Kilbride when confronted with the prospect of living in flats there. In its report for 1952 the Stevenage Development Corporation admitted 'that this project has been undertaken too early in the general development plan in relation to the demand for accommodation by middle-class tenants, and that the flats are perhaps of too urban a character for a town such as Stevenage surrounded by open country', although it was anticipated that they would be let as fast as they were completed. It actually took over 3 years for all the flats to be let. And it is interesting that, as late as 1961, some newcomers on the waiting list had to qualify for family houses by consenting temporarily to live in flats that the corporation found it difficult to let.

In a booklet on building Stevenage published by the development corporation in 1954 it is stated that:

'Almost every person coming to live in a new house at Stevenage, which is after all a country town, wants at least a small patch of garden to make the country seem yet a

Figure 14.4 View of footpath and houses at Sishes End in Pin Green neighbourhood, showing open spaces and variety of architectural design.

little closer. Discussion with representatives of the Stevenage Residents' Federation has shown that few wish to have a flat as a home and still fewer to live in a high building in spite of concentrated design and luxury amenities. They have expressed their desire to get away from communal staircases, balconies or landings, and to have a house with its own front door.'

Stony Hall is perhaps the least satisfactory housing development in Stevenage; it does not escape a touch of the dreariness of much industrial and municipal housing. A far pleasanter area is that of Whomerley in Bedwell which was the first neighbourhood to be completed. Here the layout is of an irregular character consisting of curved roads with the spaces at the backs of the houses formed into common gardens like village greens, linked with each other by footpaths. The estate merges into the woodland area from which it derives its name, and many of the trees are retained among the houses. Some of the road patterns may be likened to tree branches from a main stem, and the value of this is that there is no through-traffic. One of the simpler examples is the pattern of branches in Shephall, south of Hydean Way. There is a centre stem with 4 branches, one of which connects with a short road linked with the main one. Another arrangement is a series of culs-de-sac running off a curved road like Peartree Way, some of the culs-de-sac being secondary branches. The contours of the undulating site contribute to the character of the layouts. The houses are rarely sited parallel with the roadway, there is generally considerable variation in alignment, and the space between the roadway and the houses widens and narrows in a variety of shapes.

In Elm Green in the Chells neighbourhood and in Fairlands in the Pin Green neighbourhood, completed in 1966, a modified form of the Radburn layout has been followed. Its principles are described more fully in the chapter on Basildon which was the first new town to adopt this form of layout. The idea is roughly that houses are arranged on three or four sides of a rectangle; three of these face outwards to pedestrian ways and squares and a road runs into the centre of the area at the rear of the houses where garages are provided. The Elm Green estate is a long rectangular site between two roads linked by transverse roads, and from these roads the culs-de-sac run into the central areas at the backs of the houses, the majority of which face on pedestrian ways between the fronts of houses. It can be appreciated that such layouts conduce to quiet, privacy and safety, while being aesthetically very pleasant.

In Sishes End, a residential district of Pin Green, a series of greens or squares are partially enclosed by attractively designed houses, some terraced, some in an echelon sequence. Footpaths run through the greens and continue in a network between the houses. Mature trees that have been preserved and sizeable planted trees enhance the general effect.

Neighbourhood Centres

With neighbourhoods as large as about 10 000 one shopping centre would mean insufficient ease of access to the food shop for many residents, so at Stevenage, in addition to the principal neighbourhood centres, there are a few sub-centres. In Bedwell there is a large centre due east of the town centre and midway between two major roads running east-west, while there is a small sub-centre to the south of the neighbourhood at Monkswood. At Broadwater, in the extreme south-east, the next

Figure 14.5 Fairlands sub-centre with six shops and the 'King Pin'
public house.

Figure 14.6 Plan of Pin Green neighbourhood in the north-east, the last and largest to be developed.

neighbourhood to be completed, the principal centre is in the south at Marymead, the part farthest from the town centre, while others are east of the neighbourhood at Longmeadow, and west of it at Roebuck. This principle of placing the chief neighbourhood centre in the more remote area is also followed at Shephall, which is in the eastern part of the neighbourhood at Half Hyde, with 2 smaller groups of shops, of 6 at Hydean Way, to the west, and 4 at Bandley Hill, to the north.

These neighbourhood centres generally follow a pattern similar to that found at Crawley and other new towns, of keeping the shops on one side of the thoroughfare, often arranged on two sides of a triangle, or three sides of a square, with a spacious area for pedestrians, and a church at one end and a public house at the other. That at Bedwell North has a row of 4 shops and a public house, 'The Gamekeeper', on the east side of the square, 7 shops on the north side, with an extensive paved forecourt, several trees, and a telephone exchange further to the west beyond the road, while a church occupies a site south of the road. The shops have service areas and garages at the back, and flats over making 3-storey buildings, tall enough to give a pleasant scale and sense of enclosure. In the Marymead centre at Broadwater the shops are similarly arranged, with the public house, 'The Man in the Moon', in the same position as at the Bedwell centre, while a church occupies the west side of the area. The paved forecourt is not so extensive as at Bedwell, the traffic comes closer to the shops, and the general aspect is not quite so agreeable.

One of the largest neighbourhood centres is that at Half Hyde in Shephall, which has as many as 33 shops. On three sides of the central square, which is half for vehicles and half for pedestrians, there are rows of shops. This square faces east, and off to the south is a pedestrian way flanked by shops, and at the rear of the long line of shops on the west side is a service way which swings round on the north side, where there is another row of shops. Most of the shops have flats above in 3-storey buildings and opposite the square on the further side of the road is a tall 5-storey block. Height, which is complained of as being difficult to obtain in new town architecture, is here secured, and again a sense of enclosure is obtained. It is ingeniously planned.

Pin Green, in the north-east, is the last and largest neighbourhood, with an eventual population of over 20 000. The district centre to serve this population, called 'The Oval' largely completed by 1975 is the largest in the town outside the main centre. It consists of pedestrian ways faced by shops, offices, old people's home, a public house and social complex, included in which is a community centre and an ecumenical church shared by Anglicans, Methodists and Catholics. There are car parks at the rear of shops and under offices. A library and another office block are planned additions.

The Fairlands sub-centre, completed in 1965, consists of 6 shops, with the 'King Pin' public house at one end and a community hall at the other, enclosing on three sides a paved pedestrian area connected with the footpath system of the neighbourhood. There is, of course, rear vehicular access to the shops.

The Town Centre

The town centre at Stevenage is internationally famous mainly because it is the first centre of a modern town with a completely pedestrian precinct. A foreign architect has remarked that if you have seen Coventry and Stevenage you have seen the best contributions to urban planning that England has made since the war. The precinctual area at Coventry is probably about the same size as that at Stevenage, but being only part of the centre of a much larger city it is obviously not so complete.

By the end of 1967 much of the centre was finished, including the middle portion with the shops. It is a rectangular area bounded by roads consisting of a long central pedestrian way, named Queensway, running north–south, from which two other pedestrian ways branch eastward, and a small town square opens westward and connects with a bus station. All the ways are lined with shops, in 2-storey and 3-storey buildings, and a continuous canopy above the shops not only affords protection to pedestrians in bad weather, but is a unifying motif in the ensemble which permits individuality in shop fronts without destroying the general architectural harmony. In the centre of the town square there is a pool with an insignificant fountain and a very ugly clock tower rising from it. The square is not large and a desirable sense of space is

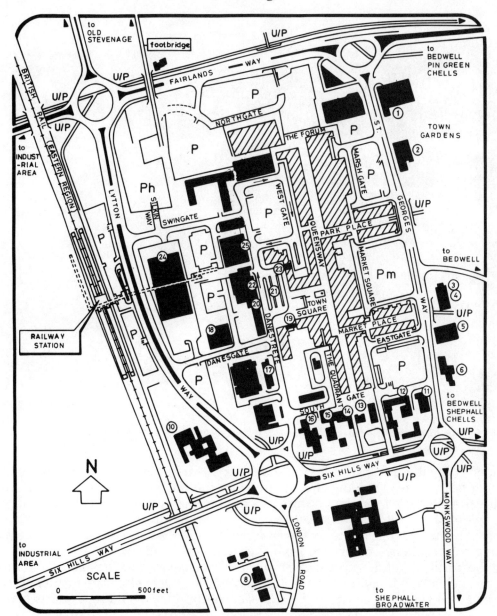

Figure 14.7 Town centre plan.

1. Swimming Pool; 2. Bowes Lyon House; 3. St. Georges Church; 4. Manulife (S.B.C.); 5. Fire and Ambulance Brigade; 6. College of Further Education; 8. Women's Royal Voluntary Services; 9. Police; 10. Southgate House (S.B.C.); 11. Health Centre; 12. Central Library; 13. Health Centre; 14. Museum; 15. Bus Enquiries; 16. Law Courts; 17. Post Office; 18. Daneshill House (S.D.C.); 19. Bus Station; 20. Family Centre; 21. Arts and Sports Centre (this is a little further west on Lytton Way); 22. Swingate House (S.D.C. Head Office); 23. Brickdale House; 24. Hotel; 25. Cinema.

P Car Park; Pm Multi-Storey Car Park/Market: Ph Heavy Vehicle & Car Park; U/p Underpass; Cross-hatching: Pedestrian Shopping Centre.

Figure 14.8 Main square in town centre with pool and clock tower.

diminished by these features. It would have been far better if the clock tower at least had not been there. Dividing the square from the bus station is a raised terrace, a feature of which is a bronze sculpture of a mother playing with her child, a vigorous and rhythmical work by Franta Belsky. Such are differences of taste, however, that there are some who like the clock tower and care little for the sculpture. Service roads coming behind the shops branch from the periphery road.

At the north end of the square, central with Queensway, is a site allocated for town hall, municipal buildings and offices. To the west, near Danestrete are further offices, a dance hall and bowling centre. A Leisure Centre complex including a sports hall and a theatre, has been built off Lytton Way. On the east side beyond St George's Way there is the very interesting Parish Church of St George, completed in 1960 to the designs of Lord Mottistone, which has an interesting construction of concrete parabolic arches, and a tall campanile of original design. Also on the east side are sites for further offices, a park area and swimming pool. South of this is a youth centre completed in 1965 which is briefly described under social aspect. To the south beyond Six Hills Way is the College of Further Education. A new railway station has been built west of the centre, which is linked with the bus station in Danestrete by an overhead walkway which passes through the new Leisure Centre.

If there is one regret about so excellent a centre it is that the town square is not more spacious. It is good to have some sense of enclosure, but that should be combined with a sense of space. These two qualities are obtained in the centres at Crawley and Harlow, but not at Stevenage. Still, it is good to see the idea of the pedestrian precinct so completely realized in the face of much opposition.

The Industrial Area

In addition to the main industrial area of Grunnels Wood to the west of the town, there is the smaller industrial estate in the north-east. The flow of industry to Stevenage has been generally satisfactory so that the building of factories has been a little ahead of houses, although there have been times when the development corporation wished that the flow was a little quicker. As in other new towns, the balance of industry is constantly being adjusted with a view to future stability.

In 1966 there began a planned slowdown of industrial intake, to avoid the danger of an excess of employment in relation to the planned population.

The first factory built by the development corporation was that for the Bay Tree Press in Caxton Way, completed in 1952. Some firms for which factories were built, or who built their own in this new industrial estate, were already established in Stevenage, among them being George W. King Ltd and W. H. Sanders (Electronics) Ltd.

Many firms representing a variety of industries have come to Stevenage, among the larger being Amoco International Laboratories Ltd; Associated Bowater Industries Ltd; British Aircraft Corporation Ltd; British Visqueen Ltd; Ether Ltd; Flexile Metal Co. Ltd; the Furniture Industries Research Association; Hawker Siddley Dynamics Ltd; Hilmor Ltd; International Computers & Tabulators Ltd; International Exhibition Co-operative Wince Society Ltd; John Lewis & Co. Ltd; Kodak Ltd; Mentmore Manufacturing Co. Ltd; Shunic Ltd; and Taylor Instrument Companies (Europe) Ltd.

Many factories have been built with a view to later expansion, and in several cases extensions have already been made. The area gives the impression of a spacious layout, while the undulating ground, the variety in the design of factories, and their different heights, give an agreeable feeling of diversity. The diversity is apparent also in the kinds of industry, offering a good variety of employment. Since designation to the end of 1974, 36 new factories had been built in the Grunnels Wood area, 14 firms occupied unit factories built by the development corporation, while there were 27 service industry premises, 4 research laboratories and a training centre. In the Pin Green industrial estate to the north-east 5 new factories have been built and 15 firms have occupied unit factories. About 21 500 are employed in the two industrial areas.

A Transport Experiment

The projected increase of population to 105 000 provided in the 1966 master plan, means more people travelling to work from the residential areas to the workplaces involving an increasing number of private cars. It was calculated therefore, that at several main road intersections traffic would become overloaded in the mornings and evenings during work/home journeys.

It was estimated that to meet the resulting need grade-separated roadworks would be required which would cost £4⅓ millions at 1966 prices. It was decided to investigate saving part or all the cost of such work by encouraging a transfer of workers from cars to buses, and Nathaniel Lichfield and Associates were commissioned by the corporation to make a cost-benefit analysis. They reported that an improved bus service might be a means of effecting the change and suggested experiment. It was, therefore, agreed with London Country Buses that a suitable bus service should be provided to the Chells neighbourhood, and this was started in May 1971 and introduced in stages. At first a 7½ minute service by superbus, as it was called, was introduced, which was later improved to a 5 minute service.

The response of the public exceeded all expectations. Weekly ridership in May 1971 was 17 300. After 3½ years, in the month of October, the average weekly ridership was 48 152. A survey was conducted in June/July 1974 covering 1851 of the 3000 households in Chells, and the changed mode of travel to work was:

	Working in Town Centre or Ind. Area		Working elsewhere		All Workers	
Driver	32%	(42)	51%	(46)	40%	(43)
Car passenger	14%	(24)	12%	(15)	13%	(20)
Superbus	48%	(20)	13%	(6)	33%	(14)
Other	6%	(14)	24%	(33)	14%	(23)

(the percentages for 1971 are shown in brackets)

The Social Aspect

The majority of people coming to the new towns are young married couples, sometimes with small children, who have acquired a house because their employment has been moved to the industrial area. There is also a proportion of single persons who have moved with their jobs and who live in flats or lodgings. One of the chief tasks in the social building of a new town is to provide opportunities for the full life. Many of the young couples are busy creating a home, and this itself is an absorbing occupation.

Many have been uprooted from a congested environment in the inner suburbs of London where they have occupied a few rooms in an old house or tenement block. They are generally quick to realize that the change to a house with a garden all their own, spaciously situated, with trees and the rolling country not far away, is an exhilarating change for the better. But in their old home they were in the midst of friends and acquaintances, and were, in a sense, members of a clan from which they have been taken, and with all the advantages of the change they often at first have a feeling of isolation and of loneliness.

From available evidence provided by competent observers it is fair to conclude that the inhabitants of the new towns have settled down remarkably well. It is in part due to the prosperity that the country enjoyed during the period of building. The people have had well-paid regular jobs in the factories and this was conducive to producing a feeling of contentment. It has enabled them to furnish their homes well, to acquire television, cars, and domestic gadgets, so that many who came as habitual grousers were transformed into contented citizens in a few years. Another expression of this change is an increased interest in family life, and parents seem particularly anxious that their children should be well educated. One headmaster at Stevenage has commented that children stay at school longer than in most industrial towns, and that the number who remain beyond 15 is four times the national average.

The homes, jobs and schools have contributed to what may be regarded as a satisfactory social state, but what of recreation and cultural interests outside the home?—for sometimes a man and his wife want to get out and mix with other people in the town, a desire present with single persons from the start.

As in all the new towns there are numerous clubs and societies representing a wide variety of interests, some of which are organized by the various churches, and some by interested groups of individuals. There are dramatic societies, art clubs, horticultural and gardening societies, political groups, sports clubs for almost every sport, numerous women's and youth organizations: in fact several such organizations for those wishing to join. There is, however, a deficiency of premises for such activities; there are, it is true, community centre buildings at Old Town, Pin Green, Broadwater, Bedwell, Chells and Shephall, but the provision of adequate premises both in the centre and in the neighbourhoods has been slow.

There are many, however, who do not wish to find their recreation always with clubs and societies, and look rather to the chat in the pub or coffee bar, or for dance halls, concerts, cinemas or theatres such as are easily found in London. These have gradually been provided. In the town centre the 'Locarno' dance hall for 2200 was completed in 1961, and an American-style bowling hall in 1962. County buildings occupy the south of the town centre of which the Library, Health Centre, Police Station and Geriatric Out-patient Clinic have been completed. There is a twin-auditoria cinema above a large Tesco supermarket in the town centre, while there is a pub and café in each neighbourhood. A good multi-purpose hall which could be used as a theatre, concert hall and for large meetings was needed. However, in 1976 the Borough Council completed an arts/sports centre complex including a theatre. A hall in the College of Further Education is also widely used by the dramatic, musical and cultural associations. A hall is also provided when the Borough Council builds its offices. A youth centre was built in 1965. Situated, as previously mentioned, in St George's Way, it was provided by the Stevenage Youth Trust with grants from the Ministry of Education, the County and UD Councils, and the development corporation. It is named 'Bowes Lyon House' in memory of Sir David Bowes Lyon who was the first chairman of the Stevenage Youth Trust.

The building for 2000 young people consists of a large open plan area for a variety of uses, which can be sub-divided by movable partitions as needs arise. A lecture room, small theatre, lounges, coffee bar, and club rooms are on the first floor which is surrounded by an open gallery for promenading, sitting and talking. The centre attracts a large number of young people from the town and surrounding districts, and is generally admired by visitors.

References and Notes

14.1 PATRICK ABERCROMBIE, *Greater London Plan* 1944 (London 1945) para. 420.
14.2 *Greater London Plan op. cit.*, pp. 169, 171—plan and perspectives.

15　Crawley

The New Town of Crawley was designated on 9 January 1947. The designated area of 6047 acres (2449 ha) is situated at the conjunction of Surrey, West Sussex and East Sussex, about 30 miles (48 km) south of the centre of London and about 22 miles (35 km) north of Brighton. It includes the small town of Crawley and the villages of Three Bridges and Ifield, and had originally a population of about 9500(15.1). The main London to Brighton railway line runs through the eastern part with a junction at Three Bridges from which a line goes west to Horsham and the West Sussex coast, with stations at Crawley and Ifield; and eastward to East Grinstead and Tunbridge Wells (regrettably closed in 1967). The main London to Brighton road runs through the centre, with a by-pass west of the old town of Crawley while the M23 passes east of the town with a spur to a point near the industrial area. The site is generally flat to the north, but gently undulating to the south, with a general slope from south to north. It varies between open and wooded country, and is bordered to the south-east by the beautiful forests of Worth and Tilgate. The land is of moderate agricultural quality with top soil varying between stiff weald clay and Upper Tunbridge Wells sand.

With the reorganization of local government it became in 1974 the southern part of the Crawley District Council area which also includes Gatwick airport.

In April 1962, as mentioned in Chapter 7, the assets of Crawley Development Corporation were transferred to the Commission for the New Towns and the corporation was dissolved in the following August. This transfer was premature as further neighbourhoods were planned.

Outline-Plan

Dr Thomas Sharp had been appointed to make a survey and prepare an outline plan for Crawley in August 1946, but resigned in the following summer, and Mr Anthony Minoprio was appointed to continue the work. The plan was approved by the Ministry of Town and Country Planning in February 1950. This main outline has formed the basis of development, but details have been changed and modified as development proceeded.

The town was originally planned for a population of 50 000, with some provision for extension. Of the 6047 acres (2447 ha) the plan covers 4000 acres (1620 ha). The remainder of the designated area is farmland, mainly to the south-east, south and north, reserved in part for future housing and industry to allow an increase to 56 000 and beyond, probably to 70 000 by 1981 which would result partly from natural

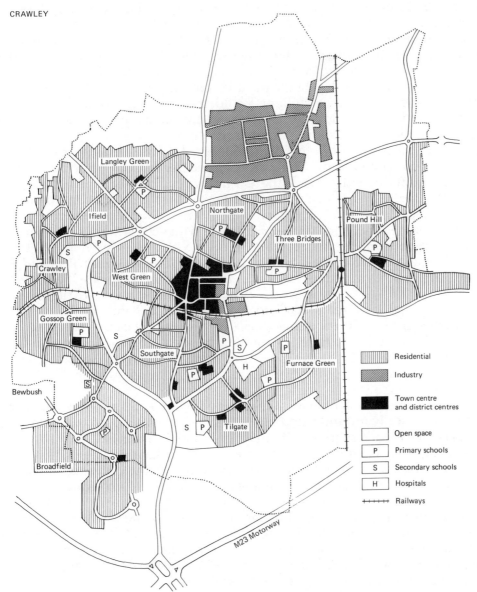

CRAWLEY

Langley Green

Ifield

Northgate

Pound Hill

Three Bridges

Crawley

West Green

Gossop Green

Southgate

Furnace Green

Bewbush

Tilgate

Broadfield

M23 Motorway

	Residential
	Industry
	Town centre and district centres
	Open space
P	Primary schools
S	Secondary schools
H	Hospitals
+++++	Railways

Figure 15.1 Crawley – Outline plan.

growth. Nine neighbourhoods were provided, grouped round the town centre which adjoins the high street of old Crawley. The centre is thus well situated geographically in relation to the rest of the town, no part being more than $1\frac{1}{2}$ miles (2.4 km) away with the exception of a small area at the eastern extremity. The industrial zone is to the north of the town; thus goods transport between it and London will not have to pass through the town, while the area allocated mainly to heavy industry adjoins the railway, which is not likely, however, to be used. Three parks are situated about $\frac{1}{2}$ mile (0.8 km) from the centre in different directions, while sports grounds and playing fields are conveniently placed in the various districts.

Nine neighbourhoods for a population of 50 000 means that 1 primary school and 1 shopping centre are provided for each neighbourhood, a much simpler and more satisfactory arrangement than at Stevenage. Referring to the decision to make comparatively small neighbourhoods when the recommended size was about 10 000, the Crawley Development Corporation stated in its 1957 report 'that these smaller neighbourhoods could more readily build up a community life, could be more closely integrated, would ensure that children could travel to the primary schools more readily, and that people could more easily reach the shops, public houses, churches and the other buildings in the neighbourhood centres'.

Each primary school, apart from 3 denominational schools, is as near as possible to the centre of the neighbourhood. They are all placed between the principal town roads which radiate from the centre, while there is a ring road between the inner and outer neighbourhoods, the by-pass being utilized for the western part. On this ring road secondary schools are grouped, all of which have now become comprehensive schools, and a large college for further education with 4000 students is in the centre. The neighbourhoods in the first plan are: 4 inner within the ring road: West Green (pop. 5000 including town centre), Northgate (5900), Three Bridges (7000) and Southgate (5000), their names indicating their positions; and the 5 outer are Ifield (6900) and Langley Green (9000) to the north-west, Pound Hill (7000) to the east, Tilgate (9300) to the south and Gossops Green (6000) to the south-west. Later, in the early sixties another neighbourhood, Furnace Green (3800) to the south-east was added, and in the late sixties and seventies two further neighbourhoods were added in the south-west, Broadfield and Bewbush(15.2). The inner neighbourhoods all had substantial existing populations, while outer neighbourhoods all had small existing populations, which made their planning a simpler matter.

The original plan is excellent in most respects with inner and outer neighbourhoods grouped concentrically around the centre. It is perhaps a little unfortunate that the railway east of the town rather cuts off a neighbourhood, Pound Hill, and that there are not more pedestrian links through the railway embankment. The existence of the by-pass constructed in the late thirties, to relieve traffic through the high street of Old Crawley, presented a problem in the original plan. With the town nearing completion, it tends to separate five neighbourhoods in the west and south-west from the rest of the town, a separation accentuated at the beginning by the absence of pedestrian crossings. Only one existed when the new town was designated—a subway from the cemetery westward. In the original plan of the town there were, we believe, provisions for pedestrian crossings, but twenty years passed before the first one appeared. There are five major intersections along its route, and it was not until the late sixties that pedestrian bridges were placed across two of these, at Ifield Avenue and Gossops Drive, and an underpass at the southern end of Southgate Drive. By 1977 there was still no bridge or underpass at the intersection with Horsham Road, nor where it joins the London Road at the northern end. This represents a serious case of transport or planning negligence. In planning the later new towns, pedestrian over or underpasses across main roads within the town have become automatic. In procrastinating the provision of these at Crawley the authorities usually said that the motorway (M23) east of the town which was opened in 1974 would reduce traffic through the town. This is doubtful, partly because the volume of traffic tends to increase everywhere.

In 1961 West Sussex County prepared a development plan for Crawley for the period 1961 to 1981, the first development plan to be prepared for a new town. In this plan it was proposed to provide for an increase in the population of 54 000 at the beginning of 1961 to 70 000 by 1981. Nearly all of this addition, some 15 000, is made up by natural increase, and only 1000 by inward migration. The migration into the town in the first 5 years of the plan is anticipated as more than 1000, but in the remaining 15 years it is intended that most of the development corporation houses which become available for re-letting shall be occupied by people already in Crawley. The additional houses will thus be mainly for the younger people who at present live in Crawley and who marry and start new households. As the average age increases there will also be the vacation of a number of houses.

The position changed, however, in 1966. In response to the demands of Crawley industry the MHLG set a programme for the town of 4600 houses. Completed much later than the planned date of 1970, these were built mainly in the existing neighbour-hoods, particularly Furnace Green, and in Southgate West (commenced in 1967) and the new southern neighbourhood of Broadfield.

The population at the beginning of 1966 was 62 000. If another 4600 houses had been completed as intended in the 5-year plan this would have meant an increase by early 1971 to a population of about 77 500(15.3). This is on the assumption, however, that nearly a thousand houses would have been built each year. The rate up to 1977 was slower than anticipated. The population then was about 75 000.

The further neighbourhood of Broadfield in the south-west extends well beyond the boundary of the designated area, taking in parts of Cuckfield and Horsham rural district (changed to mi-Sussex and Horsham Districts since April 1974). The site of this neighbourhood is about $1\frac{1}{2}$ miles (2 km) north to south and the same distance east to west, and is for a population of 14 000 with a centre for about 30 shops initially. This is a regrettable development as it does not conform to the principles on which Crawley was planned—as a town of small neighbourhoods grouped round a centre within a green belt. Instead of a new neighbourhood to take its place with the others, Broadfield, as proposed, is more like a small town joined on to Crawley; it is on the other side of the by-pass and it sprawls across the green belt as originally conceived.

Yet another neighbourhood, Bewbush, planned by West Sussex County Council in collaboration with Crawley Borough Council is also being built in the south-west. It consists of 456 acres (185 ha), 347 acres (141 ha) of which is between the railway and Horsham Road (A264) and 109 acres (44 ha) north of the railway. The whole neigh-bourhood is planned for a population of 9207. Like the southern part of Broadfield it sprawls across the originally conceived green belt and is a regrettable development. As planned the neighbourhood cannot be seen as a whole as the northern part is cut off from the remainder and is linked only by a pedestrian underpass. The northern part is thus rather an extension south of Ifield neighbourhood.

Building the Town

As with Stevenage, progress was slow in the early years of building. Delay was caused at the start because of opposition which resulted in action being taken in the High Court against the designation order. Unlike the Stevenage case, the action, heard in July 1947, was not successful, nor was the appeal, heard in the following December. The national economic difficulties of that year were also a brake on progress, so that it was not until early 1950 that the first houses were started. Nearly 1500 had been built by the end of 1952, and the rate of building from that year until 1957 was between 1000 and 2500 houses a year, in 1957 about 2484 having been built. In 1958, however, there was a considerable drop to 465. Output kept at about this level in 1959 (692) and 1960 (540), but dropped in 1961 to 252 and in 1962 to 227. There was a rise to 520 in 1963 then a fall to 222 in 1964 and output continued at about that level in 1965 (247) and 1966 (246) and then rose to 419 in 1967. The reason for the decline after 1957 was that the town was nearing its originally planned maximum, and decisions had not then been reached regarding a larger population.

From 1968 onwards output increased a little with a greater proportion of houses built by the local authority and private enterprise. The completions for the successive years from 1968 to 1976 were 643, 621, 764, 873, 559, 567, 434 , 503 and 550. By the end of 1976 since designation 21 773 houses had been built of which 13 258 were by the development corporation and the Commission, 3455 by the local authority and 5060 by private enterprise.

Factory building has generally been ahead of house building and employment in factories, shops and at Gatwick has absorbed all newcomers. Crawley industry had several times pointed out to the Minister of Housing and Local Government that the provision of houses was not keeping pace with the industrial development, and that there were several hundred notified vacancies which could not be filled because houses were not available. The Minister agreed to extensions of the housing programme. If such a demand from the industry of Crawley were to occur often the question would arise whether the town could meet it and yet adhere to the principles on which it is planned.

The neighbourhood shopping centres have kept pace fairly well with housing, having been completed for the most part a little before completion of the residential areas. Most of the shops section of the town centre was completed by the end of 1957.

The first neighbourhoods built were the three inner residential districts of West Green, Northgate and Three Bridges, all nearly completed by the end of 1954. Meanwhile progress had been made with Langley Green to the north-west and Pound Hill to the east, both of which were mainly completed at the end of 1955, while Ifield was completed about a year later. Southgate was about half completed at the end of 1957, the building of the westerly part being deferred. This was commenced in 1967. Tilgate was completed at the end of 1958, most of Gossops Green was built by 1962 and most of Furnace Green by 1968. Thus a new town of about 55 000 had been built in little more than 10 years, to rise to 65 000 in another 5 years. It was no mean achievement.

In 1966 the large neighbourhood of Broadfield in the south-west was planned and by 1977 most of the northern part—about half—was completed. In 1973 Bewbush was planned, site preparation began in 1974 and several houses were completed by 1977.

Water supply has been derived from a new source. None of the existing supplies when the town was designated were capable of being developed, and a scheme was put into operation by the Weir Wood Water Board on behalf of the corporation, whereby a reservoir was built on the River Medway near Forest Row. An impounding dam 1680 feet (512 m) long and 40 feet (12 m) high was constructed and 300 acres (122 ha) of land were flooded. This supplies Crawley with about 2 million gallons (9 million litres) a day, and also supplies 116 sq. miles (300 km²) in East Sussex. While this reservoir was under construction a temporary supply was obtained from Ardingly. As the ultimate needs of Crawley may be in the region of $4\frac{1}{2}$ million gallons (20.5 million litres) a day, additional supplies will be obtained from the River Rother at Hardham.

Housing and Residential Areas

How has the plan, in its widest sense, worked out? It is best to consider first the housing and the residential areas; then the town centre; then, after glancing at the industrial area, to ask whether a good setting has been provided for a full and happy life. A new town cannot be more than a good stage set which can contribute much to the success of the play; although some would go further and say that with bad theatre design and acoustics the play has not a good chance, in which there is much truth.

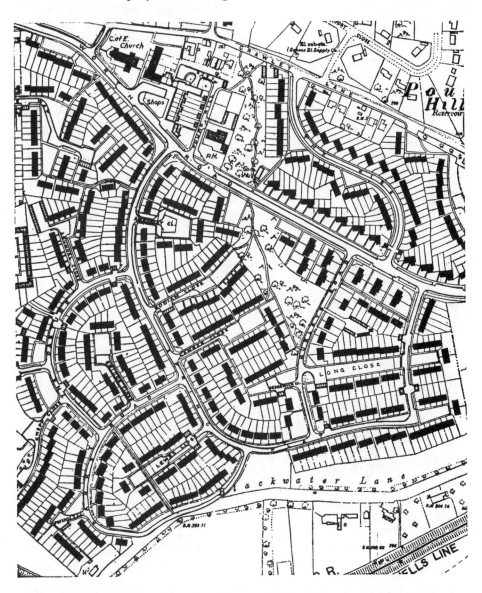

Figure 15.2 Part of the Pound Hill neighbourhood completed in 1955.
The centre with church and public house can be seen at the top of the plan.
Much of the housing layout consists of closes and culs-de-sac.

As a general policy, the development corporation concentrated on providing family houses with gardens, because it found that this is in accordance with the wishes of the majority. In the early stages a proportion of flats was provided, and of the first 622 dwellings to be built in the first neighbourhood of West Green, 96 were 3-storey flats, and 50 were 2-storey flats; in Northgate, of the first 758 dwellings 66 were 3-storey flats and 36 2-storey flats. In the neighbourhoods built later a smaller proportion of flats was

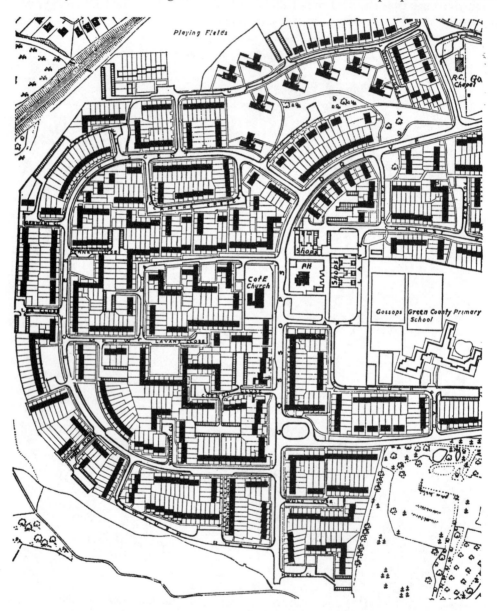

Figure 15.3 Part of Gossops Green neighbourhood completed in 1961. The shops form two sides of the centre square with a public house in the middle. In part of the housing layout a cul-de-sac ends in a small square at the rear of the houses where garages are provided.

provided. The corporation stated in its report for 1952: 'Flats have been erected in a decreasing proportion as it is abundantly clear that once tenants decide to come into the country to live they almost universally prefer a house with a garden.' The corporation also stated that it had 'closely examined the cost of constructing high flats' and that 'in every case . . . they cost substantially more per square foot of created space than do houses, and they cost a great deal more to administer. The corporation has not, therefore, considered that in the circumstances of a country town high flats can be justified, either socially or economically.' The corporation also remarked in its 1957 report that 'by careful research, the corporation learnt that not more than $2\frac{1}{2}\%$ of tenants wanted to live in flats, and that there was a universal desire for a garden, and this therefore dictated the general pattern of housing'.

The corporation originally based its programme on 64% 3-bedroom houses, 25% 2-bedroom, 5% each 1-bedroom and 4-bedroom, and 1% 5-bedroom (see 1952 report). A year later (1953 report) this was amended to 75% of 3-bedroom houses, and a reduction of the 2-bedroom type to 15%, as the corporation found this more in accordance with demand. Some of the 1-bedroom and 2-bedroom houses are bungalows for old people. Many larger houses with garages, detached and semi-detached, have been built in the neighbourhoods for letting and for sale, while land has been made available for private development to build houses for sale. Generally the family houses have been built at densities between 10 and 16 to the acre (25 and 40 per ha). A wide variety of types, as many as 249, has been provided, some of them ingeniously planned, compactness and a full utilization of available space being noteworthy features. One plan incorporates a covered passage between houses which serves as store and utility space and as a valuable sound barrier.

Layout of Houses

One of the most striking features of the residential area of Crawley, as of most of the new towns, is the grouping and layout of the houses. Unity and variety, quietness and safety from traffic have been guiding principles. There has been a general avoidance of the long straight street, and the long unbroken terraces of houses which spell dreariness and monotony. Instead the roads curve and wind, while other roads are culs-de-sac round which houses are grouped; or the roads change to lawns or pedestrian ways, which often pass under arches formed by the houses. Sometimes houses form three sides of a square set back from the road.

A favourite method of planning has been the familiar one of arranging houses round a plot of irregular shape, with the houses facing outwards, and gardens inwards, with a cul-de-sac or close running into the centre. This cul-de-sac often terminates in a square or irregular rectangular plot of grass round which the houses are grouped, and the effect is exceedingly pleasant, especially as existing trees are often preserved or new trees planted. Several good examples of this kind of planning can be seen in the southern area of Pound Hill, where each cul-de-sac is given the name of a close derived from a Sussex castle such as Amberley, Bodiam, Camber, Eridge, Lewes and Sedgewick Closes. Some of the other neighbourhoods also offer good varied examples of this kind, such as Butts, Lodge, Kites and Deerswood Closes in West Green, and Lancing and Treyford Closes and Patching Place, in Ifield. The three last-mentioned culs-de-sac terminate in generous areas forming quiet attractive precincts. Other arrangements are the grouping of houses round greens of various shapes—squares,

*Figure 15.4 Houses built by the Commission for sale in Broadfield in 1973.
Broadfield is the latest of the neighbourhoods and in 1976 was about half built.*

triangles, segments—set back from the roadway. Where houses line the curved roads, bends are such that there is a pleasing sense of partial enclosure with glimpses beyond at intervals, effects that are also present in the culs-de-sac. An example of the former is in Forester Road, Southgate, where the road bends a little before the neighbourhood centre is reached, and the space is enclosed by the church and centre at one end and by the bend at the other, yet there are glimpses here and there on either side through pedestrian ways to places beyond. Another grouping in Southgate which is note-worthy has houses facing on the playground of the primary school with just a strip of green and pedestrian way between, and a road at intervals stopping at the school fence.

Although houses are sited along curved roads and around squares and various shaped greens, much thought is given to orientation. Many of the roads in Northgate and Three Bridges run roughly north–south so that the houses are of approximately east–west orientation. Where the rows of houses run east–west the plans of the houses are arranged accordingly. Thus in the roads running east–west in the Southgate neighbourhood houses on the south side have the kitchen facing the road with the living room and bedrooms facing the south, while those on the north side have the living room facing the road, with the kitchen towards the garden. One of the pleasantest neighbourhoods is Gossops Green situated on a hill which was formerly well wooded. It has been possible to retain a proportion of trees which can be seen in some profusion in Dower Walk that runs north–south on the summit of the hill and which once formed the avenue to Woodhurstlea House.

Furnace Green is a neighbourhood built largely without subsidy for the slightly higher income groups. Many houses are detached and semi-detached with garages and there are also some very attractive 3-storey terrace blocks with garages on the ground floor. An interesting development by a co-partnership association group has a formal layout of footpaths and cul-de-sac roads and a central garden with a nursery school. The houses are of 2 and 3 storeys with mono-pitched roofs and built with artificial stone blocks. The development belongs to the type of close building essayed by many architects that sometimes prompts a sigh for a little more space.

The planning of the northern part of the latest neighbourhood of Broadfield is on similar lines to much of the planning of the other neighbourhoods with a generous use of culs-de-sac, branching from the minor roads, with houses grouped round them. Houses are also grouped round green spaces adjacent to the roads, and many fine trees, some mature, have been preserved and form central clusters in the green spaces. Broadfield was formerly largely a forest area. Houses are of a wide variety, terrace, semi-detached, a few detached, and one- and 3-storey blocks of flats. The mono-pitched roof is used extensively.

In the middle of the northern part of the neighbourhood is a first and middle school. Another will be built in the eastern part. The district centre, which is larger than the others in the town, is centrally placed and consists of 19 shops, a large supermarket, a large pub, a garage and service station and a multi-storey car park. A church/community centre, health centre and library are still to be built and completion of the district centre is expected by 1980.

Along the northern stretch of the neighbourhood, bordering Crawley Avenue (the by-pass) are playing fields and a small park with an attractively landscaped lake which serves the purpose of a sump to prevent flooding in the area.

Neighbourhood Centres

In most towns of England we are accustomed to local shops being grouped on either side of a main road. During busy shopping times cars and vans are usually parked on either side of the road, making it dangerous to cross. In most of the new towns, such an arrangement is avoided in the neighbourhood centres, and the shops are grouped only on one side of the road.

A common pattern seen in the Crawley centres is a row of shops, or shops on two or three sides of a square, with a public house at one end and a church at the other, and the primary school either opposite or nearby. The Three Bridges centre is a simple example: a row of 15 shops, with St Richard's Church at the west end and a public house, 'The Maid of Sussex' at the east end, forming one side of a triangle, so that in front of the shops is a triangular green. The primary school is opposite.

The centres of Langley Green with its 19 shops and Pound Hill with its 12 shops, each form two sides of a square with a public house ('Dr Johnson' and 'The White Knight') and a church at either end (St Leonard's and St Barnabas'). The space in front of the shops at Pound Hill is a triangular green in which some of the existing trees have been preserved to contribute to the pleasant effect. Langley Green is a little more formal, with large rectangles of grass and rows of planted trees, although some

Figure 15.5 The shopping centre of Gossops Green has shops, a pub and other facilities for 6000 residents.

existing trees are preserved. In West Green and Northgate the shops are in a row, the former with only 7 as it is the nearest to the town centre and old Crawley, and the latter with 13. Opposite the shops at West Green is a public house 'The Apple Tree', and a little way up the hill of West Green Drive is a community centre which forms one end of the primary school. At Northgate in front of the shops is a square parking area with a public house 'The Black Dog' on the west side; and opposite the shops across the road is a community centre and nearby (west) is St Elizabeth's Church and across the road on the east side is the Methodist church of St Paul's which is architecturally innovatory. Ifield is another straight row of 13 shops, again with a public house, the 'Pelham Buckle', at one end, while Tilgate is a fine curved terrace of 21 shops. Southgate has 10 shops, 8 in a straight row and 2 round the corner, with a public house 'The Downsman' at one end, and, opposite, St Mary's Church, the largest new church in Crawley, combined with a hall making an original and handsome building. Gossops Green, the last to be built by the development corporation, has shops on two sides of a square in which is a public house, 'The Windmill', with a garden between it and the pedestrian ways. It is the most secluded of the centres.

The latest neighbourhood centre of Furnace Green follows the pattern of the earlier examples, with a row of shops facing the road, the wide paving for pedestrians being raised from the level of the road. It is a little strange that the exceptionally good secluded centre at Gossops Green should have been followed by a reversion to an inferior layout. The provisions for the centre of Broadfield are indicated in the previous section.

The Town Centre

East of old Crawley High Street and north-east of Old Crawley Railway Station is the new Town Centre, bounded on the north by a straight east–west Boulevard and on the south by Haslett Avenue and the railway. Queens Square formerly had a road—Queensway—running through on the north side, but this was experimentally closed in 1967 on Fridays and Saturdays, then completely closed in 1971. The road was paved over in 1974–75 and the resulting effect is one of agreeable spaciousness.

A pedestrian way, the Martlets, links the square with Haslett Avenue, and another—Broad Walk—connects from the old High Street to Broadway(15.4) a north–south road which intersects the centre. An opportunity was missed at the beginning in not creating a complete pedestrian precinct like that at Stevenage. Hopefully, perhaps inevitably, it will become one, and the complete transformation would be a great improvement.

The architecture in the Square, if not very distinctive, has a general effect of unity, with a calculated relation of horizontals and verticals with slight variations in building heights, while the façades have a bright effect with varied colour and texture. Groups of trees and flower tubs occupy two corners of the Square; there is plenty of seating, a bandstand, a kiosk and an attractive decorated fountain designed by Bainbridge Copnall. In 1966 a clock tower, given by the Commission, was added to the Square. It was removed in 1973 as the people of Crawley disliked it.

The Boulevard is a handsome straight thoroughfare with the terminal feature of the tall block of the College of Further Education at the east end. Between the buildings and road on the north side are lawns and flower beds. The buildings are of varied architectural merit yet compose a good ensemble, helped by a few trees. At the west end is a picturesque old building separated from the tall attractive mass of the Government building by a group of trees. It is an example of the old blending with the new in a particularly felicitous way. Next is the well designed Post Office, and beyond is a large office building of Woodall-Duckham, of a rather heavy aspect, and next the town hall heavier still with some unfortunate crudities of design. Then at the end is the very attractive group of Court and Library buildings by the County Architect and the three blocks of the large College of Further Education, the most recent tall block with a lecture theatre at its base being particularly pleasing. With the exception of the large office block and the town hall, all the buildings have a lightness of effect and well proportioned massing, which makes them distinctive examples of modern architecture. Other distinctive examples are the Crawley Hospital in West Green, designed by Yorke, Rosenberg and Mardall, and the swimming pool designed by H. S. Howgrave-Graham where good advantage was taken of a pleasant natural setting.

Between the shopping area and the College is the Memorial Garden, which is a very pleasant grouping of trees, shrubs and flower beds among spreading lawns. Unfortunately it is closed by a wire fence and a tall hedge. It would be a more integral part of the centre if the hedge were removed and it was open for shoppers and others to see.

South of the centre is the bus station and beyond this the new railway station completed in 1968. It has a large office block above, which may be financially rewarding for British Railways but is hardly good planning, for it means a high concentration of car parking for the station and for the offices. A railway station is, or should be, a transport centre, and it would have been better to build a multi-storey car park over or adjacent to the station.

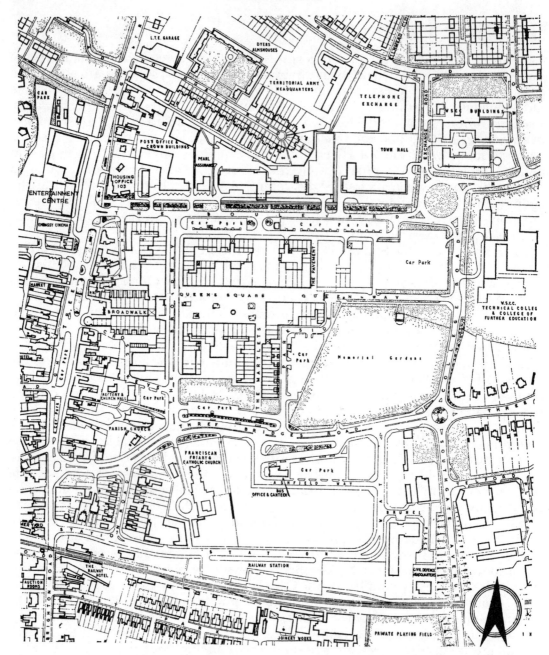

Figure 15.6 Town Centre plan.

Between the railway and bus stations is an extensive area scheduled for commercial development. It would be an ideal site for an arts centre building, better than the site for this purpose at the Hawth on the other side of the railway and too far from the centre. If Crawley is to become a regional centre its main cultural building should be easily accessible by public transport.

Near the town centre is the old Crawley parish church and churchyard which

Figure 15.7 View of Queens Square (Crawley Town Centre) since its conversion to a pedestrian precinct.

integrate exceedingly well with the new development. Haslett Avenue that passes between the parish church and a Franciscan friary affords some very pleasing views of these in relation to the new buildings of the centre.

In most good plans of new town centres, as at Harlow, the shopping centre and the civic centres are often compactly grouped and closely related. In the civic centre are generally comprehended cultural and recreational facilities other than sport. Crawley Centre has been criticized as not fulfilling these requirements. The shopping areas are satisfactorily planned, except for the through roads, but the civic buildings: town hall, library, health centre, college, are rather widely spread with a large car park in the middle, surely the ugliest feature of the urban scene. The spread is made worse by the remoteness of the arts centre and theatre site on the other side of the railway.

Industrial Area

Diversification of industry has been one of the principles in planning the industrial area, a diversification which is necessary, as previously stated, to maintain employment so that the population shall be less at the mercy of a depression in one industry. It is also important to provide a variety of employment so that men and women are free to change their jobs. Thus the corporation encouraged industries of several kinds. There were 95 factories in 1976 in the industrial area, representing a variety of industries which include engineering; electrical and electronics; metal working; wood working; printing; food and pharmaceutical; plastics; and others (which includes clothing); a total employment of over 19 300 in 1976.

Some of the factories have been built by the development corporation for letting, while others have been built by the firms themselves, on 99-year leases.

Visitors to the industrial area have been impressed by the attractive layout and the

*Figure 15.8 Crawley industrial area from the south-west. The London–
Brighton road runs diagonally across the front of the picture and the
industrial area lies to the west.*

pleasing effect of the factories. Many of them are grouped on either side of a main
avenue—Manor Royal—running east from the London–Brighton road, with lawns
spread in front of the factories giving a fine spacious effect. Manor Royal widely forks
at the eastern end where further factories are grouped. Some of the buildings are
excellent examples of industrial architecture.

The Social Aspect

The population of Crawley, as of the other new towns round London, migrated mainly
from the inner and outer London suburbs, the industrial firms moving out took a large
proportion of their workpeople with them. Thus the population consists largely of
young married couples between 20 and 40 with young children. They have exchanged
a flat, lodgings or a small house in the suburbs for a house with a garden in a new town.
From the standpoint of physical environment they have made a change for the better.
For many it is the first time that they have had a house and garden of their own, and
there is no longer a feeling of congestion of living conditions. Making a home of the
house and cultivating the garden provides opportunities for leisure occupation, and
there is plenty of evidence of enthusiastic gardeners. Some of the inhabitants may sigh
for the old days in the inner London suburbs, but it is doubtful if the feeling is very
deep because people rarely go back: over a 15 year period only 0.2% per annum have

done so. The preoccupations of a house, the making of new friends, the convenience of the shops, the feeling that the country air of Crawley is healthy especially for their children, are important factors. Rather than go back, some of the people are wanting their old folk to come out; thus there was some demand for homes for old people which the corporation and later the Commission were anxious to provide as making a contribution to a balanced population.

A criticism that might be made is that there is insufficient mixing of different types of dwellings in the various neighbourhoods. Whole areas consist too much of small houses for similar income groups. A more generous sprinkling of houses for the slightly higher income groups would introduce a greater variety in the social and architectural aspects of the neighbourhood. Often it is found that people in the factories live in Crawley, but the executives, managers and directors tend to live in the villages and small towns of the surrounding country. It is true that the development corporation built larger houses, such as those at West Green, and land has been made available to private enterprise which has built estates of houses for owner-occupiers, but this means some degree of segregation. It may be that this works better, for when houses of this kind have been built by private builders in separate locations more of the directors and managers live in Crawley. This has already happened in some degree at the estates built by Wates at Ifield and Gossops Green.

Also, the last neighbourhood of unsubsidized houses in Furnace Green for the slightly higher income groups means some degree of segregation, and the class feeling that inevitably arises in a new town has classified Furnace Green and some of the privately built estates as snob districts. This, of course, may be an assessment by a few for in Furnace Green there is a fair mixture of income groups. The urban district council built 440 dwellings here, some of which are for the lower income groups. At the same time it should be noted that if classless societies are not fully possible, the nearest approach to them is found in the new towns, including Crawley.

The success of any town or community depends in a large measure on how people spend their leisure, and it must be asked whether in Crawley there are adequate facilities for recreation and leisure pursuits? Much has been done but is it enough? There are a fair number of clubs and societies for various activities in Crawley as a whole and in each neighbourhood. A community association was already in existence before the town was built, and this helped to lead the way to the provision by the development corporation of a community centre building in each neighbourhood except that in West Green which was provided by the county council. These community centres are used for various activities, like those of drama groups, political, naturalist and other societies, art clubs and youth organizations. The huts were a little primitive and resembled army huts of the First World War. The Commission for the New Towns had, however, replaced all of them by 1973 and each of the 10 neighbourhoods has its well equipped community centre building. There was already a cinema in the old town of Crawley which continues to be well attended. A project in the early sixties for a new one was abandoned.

A comment has been made that social, recreational and cultural activities tend to take place too exclusively within each neighbourhood, which are thus becoming socially self-centred, and that there is not very much combined activity of the neighbourhoods. One of the factors that determines a desirable size for a town is that it shall be large enough to support the cultural, social and recreational activities that many people ask of urban life. If these activities are to be confined to neighbourhoods of about 6000 then this is largely defeated, for it will be found that such a small population would not be large enough to support some rather specialist societies. As a sociologist resident of Crawley, Mrs Gillian Pitt, remarked in an article on Neighbourhood Planning in the New Town(15.5):

'The specialist organizations draw on a small minority of a population for membership, and whereas in a town of fifty or sixty thousand this minority of interested people is enough to maintain a club, in a community of five to eight thousand, there are not enough to keep the specialist group in existence. In Crawley a club will be started by a group of enthusiasts in the belief that there will be enough interested people to maintain it, but they will be disappointed after a few months to find that people are unwilling to travel to another neighbourhood for a meeting. In many instances "unwilling" becomes "unable", unless you have your own means of transport, or enjoy long evening walks, as public transport facilities do not encourage travel between neighbourhoods. Bus services are provided to take people to and from the town centre, or the industrial estate at certain times, but there is no circular route round the town.'

One of the criticisms of Crawley as of some of the other new towns round London, like Stevenage and Harlow, is that the public transport system is inadequate. This has meant inconvenience, frustration and even hardship to many people. It has checked the development of communal activities between neighbourhoods and in the town as a whole. Some of the planners of later new towns such as Runcorn have realized this and planned with better provision for public transport and the integration of the town, but it remains to be seen if these can be maintained without subsidies.

With regard to the provision of cultural and specialist interests adequate facilities should be provided in the town centre, so that people from each neighbourhood interested in certain pursuits, can come together and form societies large enough to ensure a vigorous and successful life. The town as a whole could ensure the success of much that a neighbourhood could not. For example, a drama group in one neighbourhood might have a very weak and precarious existence, but if membership is recruited from several other neighbourhoods it might become a very successful group, and the place where its work should be done is obviously in the town centre to which journeys can easily be made. Unfortunately adequate facilities in the town centre, such as a good multi-purpose hall, rooms for meetings and exhibitions, are late in coming. Many social activities and voluntary associations would have a far better chance of developing if there were good meeting facilities in the centre of the town.

Much exploratory work was done on the provision of an arts centre which will possibly include a theatre, multi-purpose hall, and functions room, and architects engaged by the UDC in 1968 made a feasibility study. The site first selected, at the rear of the town hall, was far too restricted for the purpose, and it was subsequently decided to build it at The Hawth, a site on the further side of the railway about $\frac{1}{2}$ mile (0.8 km) from the centre where work of clearance and preparation began in 1974 but this was abandoned on economical grounds in 1975. Most people and societies interested in the project considered that the ideal site was the large area between the rail and bus stations which had been used as a car park.

Crawley is well endowed with parks and playing fields, but is deficient in children's playgrounds.

In 1964 the Crawley UDC acquired 207 acres (84 ha) of the Tilgate estate, partly from the Commission and partly from a private owner, for a public open space near the southern boundary of the town. It was opened as Tilgate Park in the summer of 1967. It is a beautiful stretch of undulating woodland country that was formerly the grounds of a large country house. It has numerous magnificent trees, many imported, and extensive areas of rhododendron, while there are 3 artificial lakes, one of 17 acres (7 ha) that is being used for boating. The UDC built a restaurant on the site of the country mansion now demolished.

Crawley is situated near some of the most beautiful undulating woodland country in England, for in addition to Tilgate Forest to the south, there is St Leonards Forest to the south-west and Worth Forest to the south-east. Numerous streams and small lakes spread throughout the woodland scenery.

References and Notes

15.1 In the First Annual Report of the Crawley Development Corporation 1948 the population was given as 8000, but it is now accepted that this was too low.

15.2 These were the approximate populations in the summer of 1967. The populations given in the original plan of 1950 were West Green 5200, Northgate 4300, Three Bridges 4500, Southgate 4400, Ifield 6600, Langley Green 5400, Pound Hill 5300, Tilgate 4700 and Gossops Green 4600.

15.3 The statistics of the MHLG gave a population of 80 000 by 1976, but both figures were excessive, as the population in 1976 was about 74 000.

15.4 At present public transport uses Broadway. If it were closed to traffic public transport could be re-routed along the Boulevard and along College Road and on to the bus station. This would have advantages over the present route as it would serve the Town Hall, the health centre and library and the college (with appropriate stops).

15.5 *Town and Country Planning*, July–August 1959, pp. 263–65.

16 *Hemel Hempstead*

Among the proposed sites for satellite towns in Abercrombie's Greater London Plan was one a little south-west of the village of Redbourn, between the towns of Harpenden, St Albans and Hemel Hempstead. This site was not adopted because, in the opinion of various government departments and the Advisory Committee for London Regional Planning, it would have brought the built-up area too near to the three neighbouring towns, with the risk of ultimate coalescence and of the loss to agriculture of an unnecessarily large area. The alternative of expanding the town of Hemel Hempstead from a population of about 21 000 to 60 000 was adopted, and the new town was designated on 4 February 1947. The site of 5910 acres (2392 ha) is about 26 miles (42 km) from the centre of London. Along the valley of the Bulbourne, which runs west–north-westerly from Watford to Aylesbury, is the main railway line from Euston, the A41 trunk road, and the Grand Union Canal. The old town of Hemel Hempstead, situated to the north of this valley about 7 miles (11 km) beyond Watford, was of roughly triangular shape with the main shopping street along the valley of the Gade. The designated area of the new town lies north of the Bulbourne valley and the new residential areas surround the old town to the north, east and west but not south.

The assets and liabilities of Hemel Hempstead were transferred from the development corporation to the Commission for the New Towns in April 1962 and the corporation was dissolved in the following August.

With the reorganization of local government in 1974, Hemel Hempstead became part of the Dacorum District Council which also included the former urban districts of Berkhamsted and Tring.

Outline Plan

The task of planning and welding in a satisfactory manner new urban areas to a very substantial old town is necessarily different from planning new towns like Stevenage, Crawley and Harlow, where the existing urban development is not so large as to preclude the complete application of the principles of new-town-planning. In Hemel Hempstead modifications and compromises have been inevitable especially as the new neighbourhoods are built round the existing town occupying the central area.

G. A. Jellicoe was appointed to prepare an outline plan, and his scheme was exhibited at the town hall in the autumn of 1947. Jellicoe acted as advisor for a further year and then his official connection with the work of planning terminated. Details of the outline plan were continued by the staff, and it was submitted to the

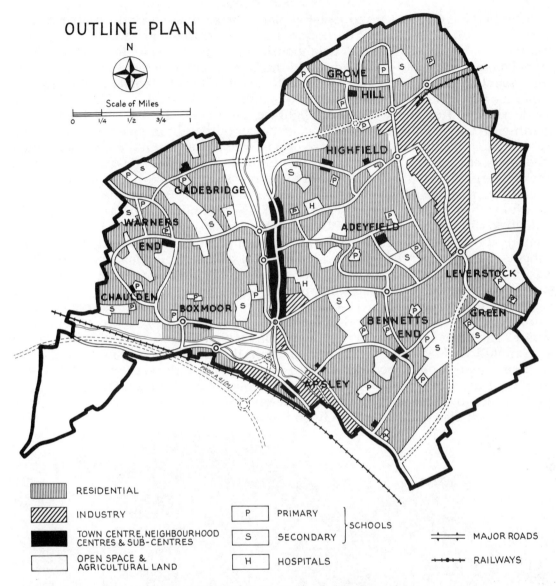

OUTLINE PLAN

N

Scale of Miles

0   1/4   1/2   3/4   1

GROVE HILL

HIGHFIELD

GADEBRIDGE

WARNERS END

CHAULDEN

BOXMOOR

ADEYFIELD

LEVERSTOCK

BENNETTS END

GREEN

APSLEY

	RESIDENTIAL
	INDUSTRY
	TOWN CENTRE, NEIGHBOURHOOD CENTRES & SUB-CENTRES
	OPEN SPACE & AGRICULTURAL LAND

P	PRIMARY
S	SECONDARY
H	HOSPITALS

} SCHOOLS

MAJOR ROADS

RAILWAYS

Figure 16.1 Hemel Hempstead – outline plan.

Minister in August 1949, modified at his request, and published in September 1951, but was not finally approved until June 1952, nearly 5½ years after the designation and more than 2 years after the approval of the plans of the other three new towns designated about the same time. The development corporation stated in its report for 1949 that two matters caused delay in submitting the plan: the planning of the town centre and the siting of schools. It was pointed out that the former 'is a complicated and controversial issue in a town with already 21 000 inhabitants'; while with regard to the latter the corporation felt that 'greater flexibility in meeting possible changes in educational fashion might be achieved by grouped siting of secondary schools rather than separate siting adopted by most authorities'.

Including the revisions up to 1960 the plan consists of a new industrial area to the north-east and 8 new neighbourhoods, but the old town in the plan constitutes another 2, while some of the new neighbourhoods include parts of the old town. Their populations vary from that of Adeyfield the largest, immediately east of the centre, with about 12 000, to Leverstock Green with about 3000 on the eastern extremity. The other neighbourhoods are Bennetts End (south-east), Chaulden, Warners End and Gadebridge, all on the west side, Highfield on the north-east, and then further north-east, Grove Hill which was the last neighbourhood for development and was reserved to accommodate the increase of population from natural growth after planned intake ceased. The districts or neighbourhoods of Apsley and Boxmoor shown in the outline plan are mainly parts of the old town. Part of Leverstock Green with houses round a central village green existed previously and is being retained. Each neighbourhood has primary schools and there are secondary schools in Highfield, Adeyfield, Boxmore, Chaulden, Warners End, Gadebridge and Grove Hill, and in a campus at Bennetts End there are 3 schools: a comprehensive school and two primary schools. Shopping centres are provided for all of the new neighbourhoods, but these vary in character according to needs, because parts of the old town incorporated in the new already had several small shopping areas.

The main thoroughfare of the old town, known as Marlowes, runs from south to north, and at the northern end is the High Street, previously the main shopping centre. The River Gade winds roughly parallel with and west of Marlowes, and the area around Marlowes and east of the river forms the site of the new town centre which includes a market place, pedestrian ways, service roads at the back of the shops, new municipal and Government offices, a library, police courts and an assembly hall. The plan for the town centre involved considerable demolition of the property in Marlowes, which was somewhat loosely built up.

Figure 16.2 Sun Square, east of the old High Street where a number of Tudor cottages have been rehabilitated.

Unlike the plans for Stevenage, Crawley and Harlow, where a start could be made on an almost clean slate, or where the existing built-up areas were so small as to be conveniently absorbed into the new plan, that for Hemel Hempstead has had to take into account the comparatively large existing population. As the 1957 report says 'the Corporation is expanding and reconstructing an old town rather than building a new one'. The difficulties in pursuing the plan were considerable and it was necessary to keep it flexible to admit of adjustments. This raises the question discussed in the Final Report of the Reith Committee (10–15): the relative advantages of enlarging a town of substantial size, or of selecting for new towns sites with much smaller existing developments, and leaving towns of the size of Hemel Hempstead to grow more slowly, with governmental encouragement if need be. The rapid expansion of such a town involves much grafting, and is necessarily a more difficult process.

On the other hand the expansion serves the purpose of bringing the town up-to-date and of infusing new life into it. This appears to have happened, for the development has revivified Hemel Hempstead.

Building the Town

There was much opposition to the new town at the time of designation and, as in the cases of Stevenage and Crawley, the validity of the designation order was challenged, in this case on the ground that there had not been adequate consultation with local authorities as required by the New Towns Act. The case was heard in July 1947, about a fortnight before the Crawley case, and the opposition was unsuccessful.

Building the town was slow in starting because of the uncertainty created by the litigation, the restrictions in building caused by the economic crisis of 1947–48, and the delays in finalizing the outline plan. When, however, house building did start in April 1949 progress was rapid, so that by the end of 1953 some 3861 houses had been built, more than in any other new town. From 1953 onwards progress was steady at a little over 1000 houses a year—about 1268 in 1954, 1075 in 1955, 1482 in 1956 and 1195 in 1957. In 1958 there was a drop, owing to the slight economic recession of that and the previous year, to 815, to recover to about the thousand mark from 1959 to 1962. Then as the town was nearing completion there was a gradual fall in housing output, 680 in 1963, about 630 in 1964, about 450 in 1965, 284 in 1966 and 400 in 1967, and in the nine years from 1968 to 1976 the totals were successively 685, 648, 325, 591, 546, 475, 511, 409 and 711 with a decreasing proportion built by the Commission. By the end of 1976 20 413 houses had been built, the greater proportion, some 12 310, by the development corporation and the Commission, 4115 by the local authority and 3988 privately.

The first neighbourhood to be built was the largest, Adeyfield in the east. There was already a population of about 1500 and the neighbourhood was nearing completion by the end of 1953. Bennetts End was started shortly after Adeyfield, and was followed by Chaulden and Warners End, and in 1959 these four neighbourhoods were mainly complete. Gadebridge was half completed, and building had commenced in Highfield.

By 1962, when the town was transferred to the Commission for the New Towns, these six neighbourhoods were all completed leaving Leverstock Green and Grove Hill to be built(16.1). The former was almost completed by 1965 and in that year a start was made with Grove Hill neighbourhood for a population of 10 000, to accommodate the increase from natural growth. Its first group of houses was completed in 1967, and it was nearing completion in 1977.

The shopping area on the west side of Marlowes in the town centre had been built by the end of 1958, and considerable progress had been made on the east side. The building of the industrial area has kept pace with the housing and has been more than sufficient to provide employment for those living in the town. Such has been the progress in building the town that the development corporation was able to say in its report of 1959 that 'When the corporation was set up in 1947 it was estimated that the town would be built in 15 to 20 years. It now seems certain, apart from some quite unforeseen contingency, that another 3 years, or 15 in all, will see the completion of the work, this despite the fact that no construction was possible in the first 2 years owing to national economic restrictions.' This has proved to be substantially true and after 1962 the main work of building has been the provision for increase from natural growth.

Housing and Residential Areas

A wide variety of houses has been provided in Hemel Hempstead, something like 200 different types having been designed, about two-thirds by the corporation's architects' staff and a third by independent architects working for the corporation. The smaller houses, from 750 to 1000 sq. feet (70 to 93 m²), which form the majority, are built mainly in terraces, at about 12 to the acre (5 per ha) in Adeyfield, to about 15 to the acre (6 per ha) in later neighbourhoods. These terrace blocks are mixed with a few 3-storey flats and some one-storey houses for old people. The accommodation is roughly in the proportion of 33% of 2-bedroom, 47% of 3-bedroom, 10% of 4-bedroom and 10% of flats and old people's bungalows. In addition there is a proportion—between a fifth and quarter of the whole—of semi-detached houses of about 1000 sq. feet (93 m²), with garages, and a small proportion of larger detached houses some of which were built for sale.

Many of the houses are attractively designed. The different types, layouts and different facing materials have all contributed to variety. Brick is often used in contrast with pale cement rendering, painted weather-boarding, and tiles. When, however, brick is unrelieved for a considerable number of houses of a similar design, especially if they have small windows, the effect is apt to be monotonous. It is better where the lines are broken by hilly ground, or by echelon treatment or irregular siting. As in all the new towns, with units of a similar size, a difficulty has been to avoid sameness. Variety is generally achieved most successfully by differences of layouts. If groups of brick houses sometimes appear monotonous, they will appear much less so in a few years' time when trees have grown to give natural, decorative patterns against the plain walls.

The winding road, the close, the cul-de-sac, the irregular alignment of houses, grouped round differently shaped spaces adjacent to the roads, have all been employed to give variety to the residential areas. This has often been assisted by different contours, particularly in the north-western areas. An example at Adeyfield is the layout along Windmill Road and Homefield Road. On the side of the former the close has been a motif and 3 are arranged along the north side, each differently planned, with terrace blocks facing them with space for allotments at the rear. On an island site north of Homefield Road, terrace blocks face outwards, and the inner areas are devoted to allotments at one end and children's play spaces at the other, with 2 rows of garages. A little further to the south-east are some blocks of flats facing a garden served by a loop road.

Figure 16.3 Plan of part of Grove Hill neighbourhood, the most recent neighbourhood to be built.

Another example of irregular layout is the effective grouping in the area bounded by Warners End Road, Spring Lane and Boxted Road in the Warners End neighbourhood. Here a small cul-de-sac terminating in a small close, called Winding Shot, runs off Spring Lane. This close is connected by a footpath with another cul-de-sac called Peartree Close. In addition to existing trees, others have been planted, and the whole creates the impression of a delightful irregular mixing of houses, trees and grass patches. It is one of the effects of which there are many in Hemel Hempstead that give the impression of happy accidents, but which we know are the results of careful artistry.

More formal, by contrast, is Goosecroft which runs off Micklem Drive, in Warners

End. Here smaller terrace houses are arranged on either side of regular rectangular greens, further from the road and closed by a short terrace block. Another attractive formal arrangement is the curve of a terrace block of 3-storey houses at the end of Long John in Bennetts End. This suggests that it is easier to obtain a good effect with a long curved block of 3-storeys than of 2. Indeed some of the most successful housing in Hemel Hempstead from the standpoint of appearance is in the 3-storey terrace blocks, either of houses or of 2-storey maisonettes over old people's flats as in Warners End and Chaulden. In parts of Warners End, Gadebridge and Highfield neighbourhoods there are some adaptations of the Radburn layout, in some cases attractively employed. In the new neighbourhood of Grove Hill, a further adaptation of the Radburn layout is introduced. In the first development—Precinct A—branches from the periphery road terminate in courts with rows of garages, while the houses face footpaths and lawns. In one layout the branch road forms a square with an inner square formed by 3 rows of terrace houses. In precincts B and C the Radburn principle has been applied with some pleasant variations such as at Tamar Green and Tresilian Square.

   Grove Hill was planned mainly to accomodate the increase of population from natural growth and is designed for about 10 000. The first precinct (A), begun in 1966, consisted of 594 dwellings built by the Commission and completed by the end of 1968. A large part of the second precinct (B) was built by the local authority—some 673 dwellings, while this precinct also includes some groups by a housing society. A substantial part of the third precinct (C) was built by private enterprise. The remaining western part of the neighbourhood consisting of 1100 houses is in 1977 in course of building.

Neighbourhood Centres

Adeyfield being the largest neighbourhood logically has the largest local centre. It was the first to be completed and consists of a square through which a road runs diagonally. On two sides of it are 28 shops and a branch library with continuous canopies and flats over, making 3-storey buildings of a height that gives a satisfactory scale. On the opposite corner of the square is 'The New Venture' public house, and nearby is a community-centre comprising a public hall and maternity clinic, while in the opposite corner is the architecturally interesting church of St Barnabas. At the rear of the shops is a group of buildings for service industry. For a neighbourhood centre the square is large; the road through its centre and the triangular car parks rather preclude that feeling of intimacy so desirable in such a centre. One can imagine the total elimination of vehicular traffic and the square made into a pedestrian precinct with trees and flower beds, and a corner for children. A delightful place might become even more so.

   The Bennetts End centre is similar with 23 shops in 3-storey buildings on two sides of a square. In the middle is a grass area, on sloping ground, encircled by the roadway. Opposite, across Peascroft Road, is St Benedict's church and across Leys Road is 'The Golden Cockerel' public house. The shop buildings are arcaded, with the upper part coming forward, which is more satisfactory architecturally than the projecting canopy while more space is available above. It might have been better if the green had spread from the footway in front of the shops and the car park kept to the further side. But these town centres were built fairly early before the present awareness of the destructive intrusion of the motor vehicle.

The centre at Warners End provides a degree of seclusion for the shopper, as a pedestrian way runs off the recessed space on the south side of Long Chaulden road. On the west side of this way maisonettes are built over the shops and on the east side along the front facing the car park are one-storey shops, making a total of 26. At one end is 'The Top o' the World' public house, while opposite on a corner site is the church of St Alban. The centre at Chaulden is different again with a row of 9 shops in a 3-storey building with maisonettes above, and with a projecting canopy. A church and public house, 'The Tudor Rose', completes the centre. Gadebridge centre is situated on a corner with a car park recessed from each road, forming a square. Part of the centre is a pedestrian shopping way.

The Town Centre

In all the larger new towns with the exception of Hemel Hempstead the town centres have been planned and built on new land, and thus from scratch. Such freedom has not been possible at Hemel Hempstead. Here the new centre has been based on a built-up area in the old town consisting of mixed housing, industry and shops. Its

Figure 16.4 Aerial view of the town centre.

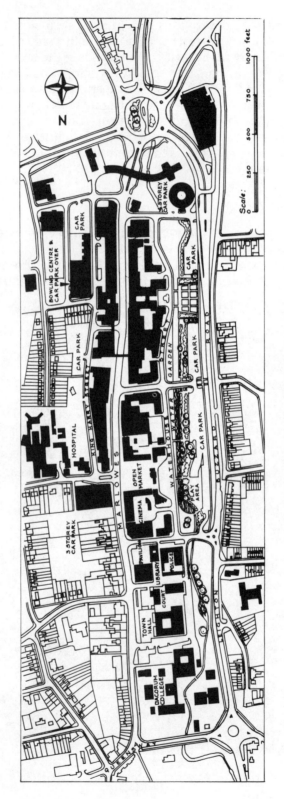

Figure 16.5 Plan of town centre.

creation has thus involved a good deal of demolition of existing property and the re-accommodation of a number of traders and owners. Considering these difficulties it has been built very quickly.

The old town shopping centre, which is being preserved, is mainly round the High Street, in which are the old Town Hall and St Mary's Church. The new centre is placed south of this, stretching the whole length of Marlowes from Queensway southwards to the roundabout where 6 roads meet, a distance of about $\frac{3}{4}$ mile (1.2 km). Parallel with Marlowes on the west is the new Leighton Buzzard Road, planned as one of the major town roads to connect northwards with Leighton Buzzard. Between Marlowes and Cotterells, some $\frac{1}{4}$ mile (0.4 km), is the River Gade, while new roads have been provided, several transverse east–west roads, and one following the course of the river for about half the distance. The major part of the centre, most of which had been completed by the end of 1962, is between the River Gade on the west and higher ground on the east, with Marlowes as its centre.

At the north end of Marlowes between the new centre and the old is the group of civic buildings consisting of the town hall, the 'Pavilion' multi-purpose hall, Crown offices, public library, and health centre, police station and magistrates' court, while beyond is the College of Further Education. The whole group is spaciously planned and the buildings are well designed and convey the appropriate impression of civic dignity. Particularly notable is the town hall designed by Clifford Culpin and Partners. It is a well-proportioned square building with a very spacious forecourt underneath which is a car park. The building is planned round a garden court, and in the entrance hall the pleasing sense of spaciousness is maintained. The council chamber on the first floor with its horse-shoe of desks, has on one side a glass wall looking on to the garden court. This is one of the best designed modern town halls in England. It was completed in 1966.

On the south side of Combe Street are a new cinema and a block of offices, and then the shops, occupying the long area between Marlowes and the new Waterhouse Street. At the northern end of the latter is the bus terminal adjoined by the market square.

As a shopping centre it has much of the character of the long village street, except that there are also shops arranged transversely in depth, thus giving a series of short pedestrian shopping ways. The long central shopping street resembles more the old haphazard development than the precinct conception as realized in Stevenage and partly realized in Crawley and Harlow. Also it has the disadvantage of an important through road in the centre of the shopping area, for although Leighton Buzzard Road is the main through road, there is no certainty that Marlowes is not sometimes used as such. It would be a considerable improvement if the central stretch of Marlowes could be changed to a pedestrian way or at least a bus-only route. Still there is much in the Hemel Hempstead centre that is aesthetically very good. Many trees have been preserved which add to the attractiveness, enhancing especially the pleasant character of the market square—a colourful sight on market days with its varied stall canopies.

The stretch of country immediately west of the town centre, through which runs the River Gade, has been made into very attractive water gardens, designed by G. A. Jellicoe, well known as a landscape architect. Hemel Hempstead is fortunate in having a new town with a river near its centre, and full and effective use has been made of this natural amenity. Lawns spread to the river which is crossed by several small pedestrian bridges, and on its further side are footpaths among trees, while at the southern

*Figure 16.6 Kodak House and Hempstead House (offices) from across
the River Gade and Moor End gardens.*

end the river broadens to a lake. There is nothing formal about the layout; everything
has been done to give it the semblance of an entirely natural feature, and the result is
wholly delightful. These water gardens received a Civic Trust Award in 1965.

In addition to the shops and the various recreational facilities that are provided in the
centre several large blocks of offices have been built; two 7-storey blocks on the east
side of Marlowes, two near the water gardens, while Hempstead House, a large block
of offices, spans Marlowes at its southern end and extends to near the lake and a
circular multi-storey car park producing an impressive effect. At the southern end of
Leighton Buzzard Road overlooking the garden the tall 20 storeys Kodak office block
was completed in 1974. Thus the town is contributing to commercial and administrative decentralization as well as industrial, providing office employment for several
thousands.

Industrial Area

The industrial area to the north-east beyond Adeyfield is 256 acres (104 ha) spaciously
planned, the factories being placed on either side of a principal avenue and along

adjacent roads. They vary considerably in size from the largest, those of Lucas Aerospace, Kodak and Addressograph-Multigraph, to some quite small. Seventy-seven firms have factories here, denoting a fair diversification of industry, with a preponderance of light engineering. In some cases firms have built their own factories, in others the development corporation has built them to the firm's requirements. Some standard factories have also been built, and have proved an attraction to many firms.

As in many of the new town industrial areas the general architectural effect of the factories is pleasing. Most of them are fronted with offices which face the roads, but the factory sections which in many cases are partly apparent from the road generally integrate well with the office blocks—an architectural advance on many factories built between the two world wars, where often a handsome symmetrical pseudo-Renaissance office block is backed by a series of sheds.

Where factory buildings are fairly low, either 1 or 2 storeys, it is difficult to avoid sameness, but this has been partially avoided by varying the heights of the different parts of the buildings so as to break continuous horizontal lines from one building to another. The different treatments of the factory front gardens with their lawns and flower beds and low ornamental walls all give notes of variety.

Social Aspect

The first question that inevitably presents itself when a new town is grafted on to an existing old town, with long history and many traditions, is: how did the newcomers mix with the old inhabitants? The question has more point in Hemel Hempstead than in any other of the first generation of new towns, because no other had so large an existing population with such deep roots. Welwyn Garden City, although it had almost as big a population as Hemel Hempstead at the time of designation, is in a different category, because it began as a new town in 1921, and its designation as such nearly 30 years later meant a continuation of its planned growth. Hemel Hempstead, on the other hand, has been a town since the middle ages with an imposing twelfth-century church(16.2). Here, therefore, is the impact of the old and new.

All the available evidence shows that the mixing has been very successful. Indeed, in the 1957 report the corporation was able to quote the Mayor of Hemel Hempstead as saying, 'There is a far greater sense of unity between the various communities of the borough than there ever was before the new town started'.

There were a fair number of recreational, cultural, women's and youth organizations active in the old town; several more came into being as the neighbourhoods were completed and these have coalesced in various ways. In Adeyfield, the earliest of the new neighbourhoods, some 30 organizations had grown up and temporary accommodation had been provided before the permanent community hall was built. A neighbourhood council was formed on which the various social and other organizations were represented. The same occurred in Bennetts End, and later the neighbourhood councils were represented on the Hemel Hempstead Council of Social Service. This is obviously an attempt to integrate the activities of the various neighbourhoods and to avoid the neighbourhood isolation in danger of occurring at Crawley.

Permanent community halls were provided at Adeyfield and Chaulden by the development corporation. A third at Bennetts End was provided jointly by the corporation, the Ministry of Education and the borough council. The last mentioned also provided community halls at Warners End, Gadebridge, Highfield and Leverstock

Green with contributions from the Commission and County. These halls are well used by the numerous voluntary associations.

The large new hall called 'The Pavilion' offers a coalescing centre for various neighbourhood activities and professional entertainment. An Arts Trust was formed in 1958 which has conducted several successful festivals of the arts which have attracted the co-operation and interest of many people in the town.

On the whole the development of social and recreational life in Hemel Hempstead is such as to make it a subject for emulation rather than criticism.

References and Notes

16.1   In the final report of the development corporation in 1962 four maps are given of the stages reached by the years 1952, 1955, 1959 and 1962.

16.2   Hemel Hempstead was originally a Roman settlement and there are remains of a Roman villa. Excavations uncovered a large Roman swimming bath, part of which runs underneath the by-pass to Leighton Buzzard. There is also a round barrow dating back to 1700 BC.

17   *Harlow*

Harlow was one of the 10 satellite towns which Sir Patrick Abercrombie proposed in his Greater London Plan. Among the reasons that he gave for this choice was that it has fine potential features, with good access from the proposed new London to Cambridge arterial road and from the existing London–Epping–Bishop's Stortford road; 'it is relatively near to the overcrowded East End industrial areas and should prove for that reason an attractive one to develop'.

The site of 6395 acres (2590 ha) was designated on 25 March 1947. It is about 23 miles (37 km) north-east of London and lies to the south of the Stort valley and the railway line from Liverpool Street to Cambridge. Roughly square in shape, it includes the old small town of Harlow to the north-east, and the hamlets of Netteswell Cross, Great Parndon and Potter Street, having then a total population of about 4500. The land is gently undulating and in parts well wooded. Beyond the Stort valley to the north are the Hertfordshire hills, to the west a tributary of the Stort Canons Brook flows north into the Stort, while another tributary runs east–west across the site parallel with Stort valley. This very pleasant country was described by the development corporation in its first report as exceptionally beautiful. With the reorganization of local government in 1974 the Harlow District Council area corresponds to that of the new town.

Outline Plan

Early in 1947 Sir Frederick Gibberd was appointed by the Minister of Town and Country Planning to prepare a master plan. This was published in August of that year, and submitted to the Minister for approval in January 1948.

In making this plan Gibberd appears to have been fully conscious of the beauty of the district and in his plan he has preserved several stretches of country in their natural state. 'Whereas it is proposed that a rural environment is to be turned into an urban one,' he says, 'the design seeks to preserve and develop the natural features which give the area its particular character; the valleys, brooks, woods, clumps of trees, are all therefore retained as "pegs" on which the design is hung.' Thus 'the valley and hills on the north of the River Stort are to be left in their natural state', as are Canons Brook valley and Todd Brook valley, while Netteswell Cross valley on the north side will form a town park. The beauty of the site and the desire to preserve parts of its rural character obviously influenced the plan, so that the natural landscape becomes a part of the town. This has meant a generous interspersion of open space, broad green bands being preserved between the main residential groupings.

HARLOW

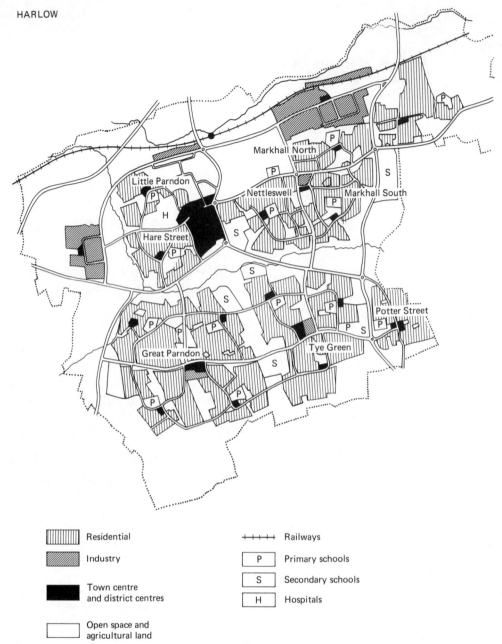

▥ Residential	┼┼┼┼┼	Railways
▨ Industry	P	Primary schools
■ Town centre and district centres	S	Secondary schools
	H	Hospitals
☐ Open space and agricultural land		

Figure 17.1 Harlow—Outline plan.

This has prompted the same criticism that has been made against Stevenage, with its broad valley: that the town is too much of a sprawl with a lack of general compactness; but the advantages of this close juxtaposition of the natural countryside with housing areas in these conceptions greatly outweigh the disadvantages, while in Harlow, because of this introduction of green wedges into the town, the residential areas have been very compactly planned. The aim in the plan for Harlow has clearly been to mingle town and country, the urban with the natural environment—to make, in fact, a garden city. Gibberd said that 'this broad flow of landscape in between the groups of buildings gives people a chance to drive and walk about the town in natural surroundings; it stops the town closing up into one vast mass of buildings and it gives a fine contrast between the work of man and the work of God'.

The town was originally planned for a maximum population of 60 000, but because of the compact planning at the comparatively high net density of 50 persons (about 15 houses) an acre, with 20% of flats included for sociological and architectural reasons, it was found that that number could be accommodated in a smaller area than was designated, making it unnecessary to develop parts of some of the neighbourhoods. As the scale of services required for a town of 60 000 would serve a larger population, it was considered more economical to increase the maximum to 80 000; the target population was further raised to 90 000 in 1972 following a review of additional land available for residential development.

There are four main groupings in the plan, occupying roughly the four main quarters of the square, like the four quarters of a shield, divided by broad green bands. These groupings include 14 residential areas with populations from 4000 to 7000. Each main grouping has a major neighbourhood centre with the exception of the group of two to the north-west where the town centre is situated, while each residential area has a sub-shopping centre, and a primary school nearby, and 8 secondary schools are provided in the dividing green spaces. There are 2 main industrial areas, the larger to the north-east just south of the railway and on either side of a road that runs parallel with it, and a smaller area to the west of the town. In addition there are 4 service industrial areas, one near the town centre, and one each adjacent to the major centres in the north-east at the Stow, in the south-east at Bush Fair and in the south-west at Staple Tyre. The major town roads are largely parkways, radiating from the town centre and factory areas, while cycle ways and footpaths introduced independently of the roads, follow a similar system of radiation, take more direct routes through neighbourhoods.

One question that occurs regarding this generally admirable outline plan is whether the town centre is in the best place. In a town covering a considerable area, as this does, it is an advantage, as has been previously emphasized, to have the centre geographically so; otherwise dwellers on the periphery will find it too far away. The centre at Harlow is situated well to the north-west, so that residents in old Harlow to the north-east, and those at Potter Street to the south-east, are 2 to 3 miles (4 km) away, which is too far. In this respect Harlow suffers from the same fault as Stevenage, although not to the same extent, while neither has the same convenient plan in this respect as Crawley.

In July 1962 the Minister asked the corporation to make an assessment of 'the maximum population which Harlow could accommodate, disregarding the designated area, but having regard to sewerage, water supply, the planning of the town and its relation to other towns'. The corporation made the necessary survey and concluded 'that Harlow could be expanded from its present target population of 80 000 to meet the needs of a population of between 120 000 and 130 000 and that many advantages to the town would result from its increased size'. It was stated that 'the additional 50/60 000 population would be housed mainly by extending the designated area approximately 990 acres (400 ha) in the west and 460 (186 ha) in the east' and that 'two neighbourhood clusters would be added to the original four and would be planned on a similar pattern'.

In 1973 the Secretary of State for the Environment suggested that to meet the housing needs of London an even larger expansion would be necessary, and that 1000 acres (405 ha) should be made available for private house building in an enlarged Harlow, and the corporation, in response, prepared a scheme to include this requirement and also for additional public rented housing and ancillary facilities. The corporation's proposals were published in May 1973 and provided for an ultimate population of 150 000. Public participation, however, resulted in adverse comments on so large an expansion, with the result that a revised plan was prepared for an ultimate population of 120 000/125 000 and this was submitted to the Secretary of State in August 1973.

In January 1974, however, the Secretary of State decided not to proceed with this major expansion, and decided instead to consider expansion on a smaller scale to meet local needs, as in the case of Stevenage. This was largely confirmed in April 1974, after the change of Government, and Sir Frederick Gibberd prepared a plan for this more modest expansion which was published in September 1974.

The proposed expansion was to be by means of two new neighbourhood groupings, one to the south-east and one to the south-west, each with three residential areas with their sub-centres grouped round a major neighbourhood centre. There is also a small extension of one industrial area. This addition would have increased the designated area by 764 acres (309 ha) from 6395 to 7159 acres (2590 to 2899 ha), and would have provided for a population by 1990 of 98 000/102 000. They would have invaded the originally conceived green belt, both in the south-east and south-west.

In this Harlow Expansion Plan, four alternative methods of expansion are discussed: to the north, south, east and west, and the advantages and disadvantages of each alternative are assessed, leading to the advised conclusion that the one proposed is the best. The plans showing the extensions to the north and west, however, have the advantage over that proposed, as securing a more equal distance of the outer residential areas to the centre, thus having it more geographically so. Further, the criticism of the plan with major extension to the east that 'one large area tacked on to one side of the town would make it lopsided' could apply to the extension to the south-east in the preferred plan. However, a public inquiry was held into these proposals in July 1976, and in April 1977 the Secretary of State announced in Parliament that, as part of his appraisal of the new towns' programme, he had decided not to proceed with the making of an Order to extend the designated area. He considered that the normal growth of the town, especially for second generation families, should be the concern of the Local Authority—including the possibility of any necessary extensions to the new town.

Building the Town

Little opposition was encountered to the proposal to build the new town of Harlow; it was much more fortunate in this respect than Stevenage, Crawley and Hemel Hempstead. The master plan was submitted to the Ministry of Town and Country Planning in January 1948, and at the public inquiry held in July of that year there was no opposition and the proceedings were merely formal. The proposed sequence of building was from the north-east westward; and then from the south-east westward. The first neighbourhoods to be built were therefore the group in the north-east, Mark Hall North and South, and Netteswell, while several factories in the area north were built at the same time. By 1956 this north-east group was completed, by 1959 the north-west group, and by 1963 the third group to the south-east. By 1968 a considerable part of the south-west group had been built. The rate of house building seems to have been as rapid as that of any of the new towns. The approximate figures for these years 1954 to 1957, including a small proportion by the local authority, were 2130 in 1954, 1704 in 1955, 1523 in 1956, and 1994 in 1957. There was a drop in 1958 to about 1112, and in 1959 to about 940 owing to restrictions in capital expenditure. In 1960 the total rose to 1093 and in 1961 to 1074. There was a lower rate in the following few years of 809 in 1962, 573 in 1963, 719 in 1964, 699 in 1965, and 784 in 1966, to rise again in 1967 to 1220 and in 1968 to 1220. From 1969 to 1973 there was a marked decline being 662, 542, 428, 310 and 248 in the successive years. In 1974 completions increased to 654 and in 1975 to 717, to fall to 321 in 1976. By the end of 1976 a total of 25 051 houses had been built since designation of the town of which 22 400 were by the development corporation, 1348 by the local authority and 1361 by private enterprise. Much of the shopping area in the northern part of the town centre had also been completed, and factory building had kept slightly ahead of housing.

Water supply from existing sources proving insufficient, wells were sunk at Hadham Mill, Sacombe and Thundridge in Hertfordshire while a 4 million gallon (18 million litre) storage reservoir was constructed at Rye Hill within the town boundary. The three sources of supply are regarded as adequate for the future needs of Harlow.

Housing and Residential Areas

As previously indicated the residential areas are built at an approximate net density of 50 persons per acre (123 per ha). To obtain this with reasonably sized gardens for the single-family houses it is necessary to provide for about 20% of flats, but owing to lower demand for small accommodation this proportion is generally somewhat less, while a large proportion of the family houses are in terraces at 14 to 15 to the acre. The flats are mainly in 3-storey and 4-storey blocks with the exception of 9 point blocks: 2 9-storey, one 10-storey, one 11-storey, 2 12-storey and 3 15-storey blocks.

There is a sense too of segregation of the neighbourhoods from the main town roads which run between them. For example, Netteswell lies to the south of First Avenue, one of the main roads of the town, and the rows of houses abut on this road endwise or diagonally; the areas between are masked from the road by walls, a separation that continues with a varied layout either by means of the walls or by belts of trees. Many of the blocks of flats are designed with an open colonnade on the ground floor which gives glimpses of the scene beyond, often an attractive effect; a design and construction first developed in modern architecture by the influential Le Corbusier. An example is to the north of Mowbray Road where the flats are situated at the top of rising ground, and the glimpse through the open colonnade is of groups of houses on descending ground with the wooded landscape beyond.

The pattern of long straight blocks involving the repetition of a very simple unit, although generally well proportioned, is apt to result in sameness: a little more variety here and there would have been welcome. It may be that when the trees, which have been generously planted, spread their foliage some further notes of variety will be introduced. The terraces at Pittman's Field in Netteswell that surround the rectangular grass area, with Willi Soukops bronze Donkey make a pleasant arrangement, but rows of simple houses with the frieze of windows are a little monotonous. Front gardens with divisions are rare, most being open stretches of lawn which look well in a general

KEY
1. electric sub-station

Figure 17.2 Residential area in which culs-de-sac are at the rear of houses with garages, with footpaths between the fronts of houses—an adaptation of the Radburn system.

effect. The back gardens are rather small as is inevitable with a density of 15 to the acre, and it may be wondered whether the majority of tenants would not have preferred larger gardens at some sacrifice of the generous green spaces that traverse the town.

Two later housing schemes at Great Parndon of a totally different character merit attention. The Charters Cross/Bishopsfield scheme was the subject of an international competition won by Michael Neylan. In this plan flats and maisonettes on a hill encircle a central podium from which radiate descending pedestrian ways, flanked by rows of patio houses with small enclosed gardens. A feature of the scheme is the segregation of vehicular traffic from pedestrians. It is an unusual conception which has attracted much interest from architects. Standing on the balcony above the podium and looking round one may be a little oppressed by the unrelieved brick and concrete, and one person remarked that it would make a wonderful film set for a prison. Some trees have been planted in the central space; it could do with a few more, and when these have grown the effect may be a little more inviting.

Another development in the same district is Clarkhill by the architects Bickerdyke, Allen & Partners. This is a fairly high density scheme of one-storey houses flanked by 3-storey terrace blocks of maisonettes and flats. The area is completely pedestrian with roads and garages on the periphery, while running across the middle of the site is a

Figure 17.3 Housing at Clarkhill, Great Parndon, 1964–67.

Figure 17.4 Longbanks—mixed development July 1974.

green strip with trees. The ways between the houses occasionally broaden and the spaces are used for odd bits of children's play furniture. The one-storey houses are in pairs each L-shaped with a small square garden entirely enclosed by the adjoining houses. The outer walls of each house are completely blank, all the windows being concentrated on the square garden orientated towards the south. Each house enjoys complete privacy. There is much that is attractive in this layout; it would be very suitable for old people and those who like seclusion. It is good that a town should have some houses of this kind, although it is doubtful whether they would be widely acceptable.

Generally, a good deal of variety in house design and layout has been achieved in Harlow. This has been helped by many different architects designing the various housing groups.

The Neighbourhood Centres and Sub-Centres

Three neighbourhood centres have been built, one, The Stow, for the north-eastern group, Bush Fair, for the south-eastern group, and Staple Tye, for the south-western group, while the 14 sub-centres have been completed. These sub-centres follow the pattern found in other new towns, and often consist of a row of shops, a public house and a church with a primary school not far away. Thus at Ward Hatch in Mark Hall North there is a row of shops on the south side of Mowbray Road, with a public house,

Figure 17.5 The Stow shopping centre which was converted to a pedestrian precinct in 1965.

'The White Admiral', at the west end and a church at the east end with a primary school opposite; and at Fisher's Hatch sub-centre at Netteswell, a row of shops with a public house, 'The Garden Tiger', at the north end, and a church at either end with a primary school nearby. Prentice Place, the shopping centre of Potter Street, is an attractive layout forming three sides of a square with a tree in the centre, maisonettes over the shops, and a clinic. All these sub-centres are conveniently grouped on one side of the road.

The main centre for the north-eastern neighbourhood, The Stow, is in the north-west corner of Mark Hall South. It originally consisted of a narrow principal shopping street curved somewhat like an S, with shops on either side, a group of service industries to the west, a church, library, health and community centre, public house, and a dance hall. The unsatisfactory feature of this centre was the road running through with nothing in the nature of a pedestrian area in which all shops are accessible without crossing a road. The development corporation rightly wished this to be a pedestrian way but apparently the opposition in the early days was too strong. In 1966, however, it was all changed to a pedestrian precinct and the road paved over. The shopping blocks are of 3 storeys with the first and second storeys projecting beyond the ground floor, thus providing an arcaded shelter for the shoppers, but the architecture of the façades is a little dull.

Bush Fair, the centre in Tye Green, which provides shopping for the south-eastern neighbourhood, came later and is more satisfactorily planned. Here the shops face a

Figure 17.6 Old Harlow shopping precinct.

fairly large pedestrian precinct with service roads on the circumference serving the rear of the shops. At one end is a public house, and grouped on either side of the centre are car parks and garages, while to the east is a group of service industries.

The Staple Tye centre in the south-west has an elevated pedestrian shopping area with 33 shops reached by ramps and stairs, with the service ways for the shops below at ground level. Above the shopping space are rows of flats. The centre has most of the amenities found at The Stow and Bush Fair.

At the time of designation the old town of Harlow in the north-east had much of the traditional village character with a narrow high street with several old buildings. With the development of the neighbourhood and increased population the High Street could not adequately accommodate shoppers and traffic. In 1970, therefore, it was converted into a pedestrian way, and the transformation was effected so as to combine the traditional village character with the facilities of a modern shopping centre. A few less distinctive buildings were taken down and some new buildings were erected and although in the modern idiom they are in scale with those existing. The whole conversion received Civic Trust Awards in 1971 and in 1975.

In effecting the transformation it was necessary to re-plan the network of roads. A by-pass was constructed to accommodate through traffic, and a new road parallel to the old high street, while service roads were provided to give rear access to shops.

Town Centre

The town centre called 'The High', is spaciously planned. It consists of several rectangular plots on which buildings are formally grouped with periphery roads.

At the north end is the Market Square, surrounded by shops, those on the west side being on 2 levels. On the south side of the square is East Gate road which originally ran east–west through the centre, but which is now wholly converted to a pedestrian area to link with the wide Broad Walk running south between shops. Branching off this in both directions are narrower pedestrian ways. At the south end of Broad Walk was another east–west road across the centre, but this has also been converted into a pedestrian area with culs-de-sac on either side. South of this are further shops, a library and offices, and beyond is the civic square round which are grouped the town hall and municipal offices, a tall 11-storey building to mark the centre like the medieval bell tower, with a group of buildings on the east side comprising the court house, police station and Crown offices. To the west of Civic Square are St Paul's Church and the Harlow Technical College, and nearby is the 'Playhouse' theatre and arts centre, completed in 1971.

A cinema has been built west of East Gate and 'The Painted Lady', a public house and restaurant, occupies a north-west corner of Market Square. The bus station is on the east side, parallel with Broad Walk. Car parks are provided on the periphery, and because of the increase in the use of the private car and the growth of Harlow as a regional centre, this parking provision has been augmented by the conversion of some of these to multi-storey car parks, one on the east side and one in the north-west.

Most of the buildings in the centre are, like the general plan, square and formal, perhaps a little cold with large areas of curtain walling, and are very much of the fifties and sixties. Some observers have wondered whether a little more variety in the architecture, less formality and a touch of gaiety might have been more appealing to the people of the town, but when some of the trees have grown more the general effect

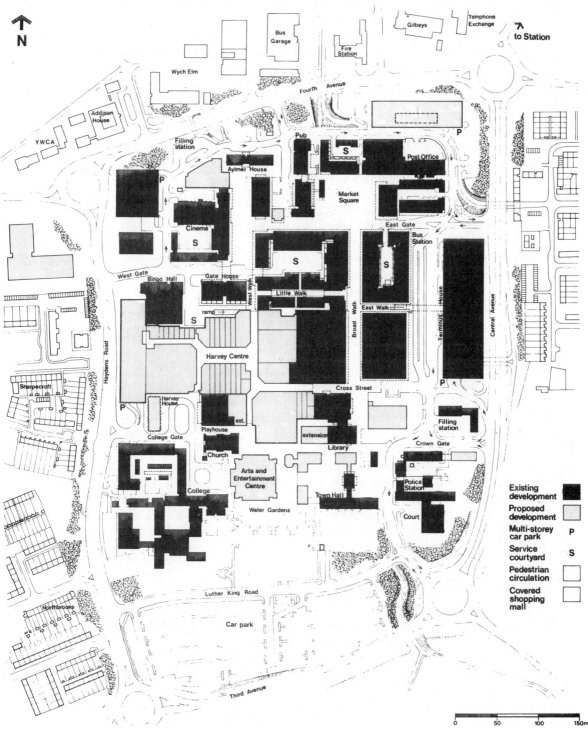

Figure 17.7 Town centre plan 1975.

may be more attractive. Some think that the Market Square looks best on market days with the colourful canopies of the stalls and the bustle of life.

Formal rectangular treatment is entirely successful in the garden adjacent to the town hall. It is laid out with long straight paved ways, flower beds and 2 long rectangular pools, one flanked by a blue mosaic wall with decorative panels both attractively reflected in the water, while the other is graced with a terminal sculpture. There is something Greek-like in the general massing and it is very happily related to the tall Town Hall building.

North of the centre is Gilbey's large office and warehouse, which is a dominant feature in the scene with its white vertical panels alternating with darker masses between the windows, a distinctive example of modern architecture which adds a visually attractive note to the central area.

By 1974 Harlow had become very much a central place serving surrounding districts as well as the town itself with a population in all of some 350 000. To meet the needs of this population a considerable extension of the town centre was planned by Sir Frederick Gibberd in collaboration with the chief architect of the development corporation Alex McCowan. Construction is due to start in 1977 and completion is scheduled for the end of 1979.

This new development is mainly on the west side and is called the Harvey Centre after B. Hyde Harvey who was General Manager of Harlow Development Corporation for 25 years. The extension is on two levels; a first floor service area, ground and first floor shopping levels with a long main central mall at right angles to Broad Walk, with minor malls off. Work is due to begin in 1977.

The whole enclosed shopping area is air conditioned. The mall is a triangular tent-like structure with galleries along the sides. This treatment gives a pleasant impression of spaciousness.

Between the town centre and the new well-designed railway station are the sports centre and the town park. The former includes a large hall which provides facilities for a wide variety of indoor sports and games (it has also been used for large choral concerts), while the outdoor facilities include a running track and athletics arena of international standard, cricket and football pitches, a floodlit training area and an artificial ski slope. In the town park full advantage is taken of a beautiful site through which the River Stort flows. Facilities provided include water gardens, an open air bandstand, paddling pools, roller skating rink, playgrounds to suit all ages, a children's 'Pets Corner', and a riverside café/boathouse called the 'Moorhen'.

The Industrial Areas

As previously indicated there are 2 principal industrial areas, one to the north-east called Temple Fields between the railway on the north and Mark Hall North and one to the west of Hare Street called the Pinnacles. There are several small areas for light and service industry in the centres of The Stow, Bush Fair and Staple Tye, and warehouse strips north of the railway and north of Little Parndon.

Temple Fields, the largest and chief industrial area, was near completion by the early seventies while several factories had been built in the Pinnacles. Edinburgh Way which runs parallel with the railway is a wide grass-verged road forming the spine of the Temple Fields industrial area with factories to the north and south. To the south of Edinburgh Way the general plan consists of a series of rectangular island sites with several factories facing the roads and the back land left open for possible expansion. On the north the factories are arranged along Edinburgh Way and round a series of culs-de-sac. In the middle of the industrial area, set back a little from Edinburgh Way, is a row of shops with a clinic nearby as part of the Harlow industrial health service.

Most of the factory buildings are one-storey or 2-storey structures and the designs generally are not of marked architectural distinction. The whole effect of Temple Fields is a little stark and monotonous; the prospect is lacking in trees; and this industrial area is generally less pleasing than those of many of the other new towns. The factories have not the variety and architectural interest of those at Stevenage or Hemel Hempstead nor the fine general effect of those at Crawley or Bracknell.

One good social and economic quality of the industrial estate, however, is that considerable diversity of industry is represented in the 90 or more firms that have come there. The industries represented include plastics, radio and television cabinets, engineering tools, electrical equipment and devices, glass, clothing, photographic apparatus, printing, various forms of light engineering, and 5 major research establishments.

Near the Pinnacles is a particularly distinctive large office building for the British Petroleum Co. Ltd in which some of the idioms of modern concrete architecture are used with marked success. It is spaciously laid out and partly encloses some attractive gardens. There is also an impressive office building for Longmans Green at the Town Centre.

Social Aspect

Most of the inhabitants of Harlow have migrated from various parts of London, largely with the firms of which they are employees. When such firms decided to go to Harlow, often with the purpose of expansion, the question was usually put to the employees whether they would like to go too. Generally a majority agreed to go, partly because they wanted to keep their jobs in the firms, but also because they could get houses (for which many had been waiting), and a change from crowded to more spacious living conditions. From the evidence it has been possible to collect, few who went to Harlow have regretted their decisions, and only a very few, around 5% per annum, leave the town. These go to other parts of Great Britain, to other new towns, and overseas, and a small proportion only return to London.

Some of the social problems that are inevitably encountered in a new town have been considered in the chapter on Stevenage, and many of these apply equally to Harlow which enjoys a very vigorous social and cultural life. There are over 400 societies, clubs and organizations of various kinds in the town. Interest in drama and music seems to be particularly strong. There are 13 amateur dramatic societies, a very active Harlow Music Association and many other music groups, a ballet club and school, 5 youth centres and many smaller clubs. Facilities for sport include the Sports Centre and a central swimming pool, while the extensive playing fields provide a home for the largest recreational league in the country.

From the early days of the town a group of enthusiasts has been active urging that a theatre should be built, and a working committee was set up. In 1963 the Harlow Arts Council was formed and one of its objects was the establishment of a Theatre/Arts Centre. The urban district council gave its wholehearted support and arranged for the preparation of plans. The stage reached by October 1967 was that contributions

Figure 17.8 The Playhouse Theatre and Arts Centre.

towards the cost had been made by the development corporation, the Arts Council, and the British Film Institute, while the remainder was provided by a sanctioned loan for the purpose to the UDC making a total of about £350 000. The plans were completed and in 1967 the go-ahead was given, but due to cuts in capital expenditure the project was postponed for a time.

Later, constructional work started and the Harlow Playhouse and Arts Centre was completed and opened in November 1971. It consists of two theatres, the main one being so designed as to be adaptable to five forms for different purposes, and a studio theatre on the top floor which can similarly be adapted to various forms of production including those in the round. The building also contains an exhibition gallery, club rooms, restaurant and bars.

Harlow possesses a collection of sculptures, quite unique amongst new towns and for more than 20 years the Harlow Art Trust has been placing in the town works by such sculptors as Henry Moore, Elizabeth Finck and Rodin.

Not far from the town centre along Third Avenue is Passmores House in a park of five acres (2 ha), which was acquired for a Harlow museum in 1972. It is devoted to local history and contains space for changing exhibitions, library and lecture room, while a walled garden near the house includes an ornamental garden.

The health service in Harlow deserves especial mention as it is one of the most notable in the country, and is probably in advance of that in any other of the new towns. Lord Taylor, MD, writing in *Town and Country Planning* (January 1959) of this health service refers to 'the remarkable degree of co-operation achieved between local representatives of the three branches of the National Health Service', and he believes that in Harlow they 'are building a possible pattern for the future health services of Britain, up to, but excluding, in-patient hospital care'. Opportunity for experiment in the health service was made possible because Harlow, alone of the new towns, was without a pre-determined pattern of health services. Buildings for the purpose have been provided in the town centre, in the neighbourhood centres and sub-centres. The premises have been provided from funds made available by the Nuffield Provincial Hospitals Trust, for whom the development corporation acted as agent. An aim in developing them has been to provide a pleasant, homely and 'non-clinic' atmosphere in which the patient could feel at home, an aim partly secured by furnishing the visiting rooms rather like a modern home, with accents on colour and interesting pictures(17.1). In addition, Harlow has an Industrial Health Service, with clinics at each of the major industrial estates. This experiment in co-operative medical care is run by a non-profitmaking association and over 21 000 workers are covered by the scheme.

One thing that seems to be widely appreciated in Harlow, which has some relation to health, is the opportunity of getting so quickly into very pleasant country, into the stretches between the neighbourhood groups and into the green belt beyond. That appreciation is one justification for the plan of the town.

References and Notes

17.1   In the annual reports of the Harlow Development Corporation from 1966 to 1975 in addition to the brief factual record for the year a specific theme is taken for fuller treatment as follows:

1966   Health services
1967   Industrial and commercial development
1968   Housing (on the occasion of the 20 000 dwelling built by the Corporation)
1969   The landscaping of the town
1970   Education and leisure
1971   The people of Harlow
1972   Moving around in Harlow—road traffic and transportation
1973   Harlow and its environment
1974   The changing face of Harlow
1975   Conservation and preservation

A special theme does not appear in the 1976 report.

18 _Welwyn Garden City_

An account has been given earlier in this book of the origin and planning of the second garden city of Welwyn in 1919–20. It was then designed, in accordance with Sir Ebenezer Howard's intention, to have a maximum population of 50 000. By 1938 it had reached a population of about 13 500, and ten years later about 18 500. In that year, 1948, it was decided to develop it further as one of the new towns. It was designated as such on 20 May, and a single development corporation was appointed for Welwyn and the neighbouring new town of Hatfield, which was one of the towns proposed for expansion in Abercrombie's Greater London Plan.

The question is raised in Chapter 7 whether it was necessary for the Government to take over the development of Welwyn Garden City. The reasons were given by the Minister of Town and Country Planning in an explanatory memorandum to the Draft Designation Order. It was argued that the expansion of Welwyn Garden City was an integral part of the Greater London Plan, that the creation of new towns and decentralization from London were complementary aspects of the same policy, and that a 'private company concerned only with expansion, and having no responsibilities for decentralization could hardly be expected to ensure the complete co-ordination of these two aspects in the same way as they would be ensured by a public corporation created by the Minister and acting in accordance with his general directions'. The Minister thought it 'undesirable that a private company, however public-spirited, should by virtue of its ownership of most of the land and buildings, be in a position to determine the character of a whole town and the living conditions of the majority of its inhabitants'; such power should be vested not in a private concern but in a body representing the people. The argument was not very convincing because the whole policy of dispersal by means of new towns sprang from the ideas on which Welwyn had been founded. It is possible that the decision was influenced by political considerations of a rather doctrinal or academic character. But the subsequent history of Letchworth gives colour to the Minister's doubts, and it is also true that the Urban District Council requested Silkin to designate Welwyn Garden City as a new town.

Another reason adduced for taking over Welwyn was that its development could be integrated by a single corporation with that of the neighbouring town of Hatfield. Again this is not very convincing, because there is no reason to suppose that the Welwyn Garden City Company would not have co-operated to the full on plans approved by the Ministry.

Welwyn Garden City is about 20 miles (32 km) north of King's Cross on the main line to Peterborough, the Great North Road forming its western boundary. The whole site of 4317 acres (1747 ha) was in the area of the Welwyn Garden City Urban District Council and since April 1974, the Welwyn Hatfield District Council. The land is gently undulating with a general gradual decline to the south-east and is somewhat hilly in the north-west. There is a good deal of woodland. A maximum population of 36 500 was at first proposed, but this was increased to 50 000 in 1954 in accordance with the original intention as the land in the north-east originally allocated for gravel extraction would not be used for that purpose, and would thus be available for housing. Intake would stop when the population reached 42 000, and the remaining expansion would occur from natural growth.

Outline Plan

The original plan had been prepared by Louis de Soissons, RA, and in 1948 the corporation decided to continue his appointment as planning consultant, to ensure continuity on the established lines.

The designated area is divided into quarters by railways, the main line to the north and the branches west to Luton and east to Hertford, and this has controlled the plan which consists of 4 principal sections. The south-west section was almost fully developed at the time of the designation when it had a population of 7300, which it was proposed to increase to about 8300. This included the spacious town centre. Part of the north-west section had already been completed with a population of 1088, and this has been increased to 7710 by an extension northwards. The industrial area lies to the east of the main railway, and on both sides of the branch line to Hertford. The north-east section was an almost entirely new development: its population, only 77 in 1948, was enlarged to about 13 465. The largest of the four sections is the south-eastern, which had a population in 1948 of 9800 and which had increased to over 20 500 by 1977.

These four main divisions are served by principal centres and minor centres. The revised plan (1957) provides for 3 of the former: one in the north-east (Halden), one in Panshanger, and an extension of Woodhall centre. There are 7 minor centres: 1 in the north-west, Shoplands, 4 in the south-east, 2 entirely new, Ludwick and Hatfield Hyde, and 2 existing, Peartree and Knella; Handside in the south-west; and a sub-centre at Panshanger. Some of these centres include a public house, a church, community and health centre. In each of the centres the shops are on one side of the road only, and are often provided with a generous footway in front of them. Each of the areas has junior and primary schools, and originally had secondary modern and secondary grammar schools which have since been changed to the comprehensive system. There is also a private school catering for all ages from 4–18, and a college of further education.

Open spaces are provided generously in the plan. Within the designated area there is agricultural land to the south and east, amounting to about 500 acres (200 ha), playing fields of about 250 acres (100 ha), a golf course along the western boundary of about 80 acres (32 ha), while adjoining this and stretching northwards in the north-west area is Sherrards Wood, which includes Brocks Wood, Temple Wood and Reddings Plantation. Sherrards Wood with the tree belts, the handsome parkways in the town centre, the Stanborough Lakes and the smaller open spaces intermingled with the residential areas, make a total of about 600 acres (240 ha).

Of the total area of 4317 acres (1747 ha), about 1507 acres (610 ha) are open space much of which is of a woodland character. There is reason to believe that a green belt will be

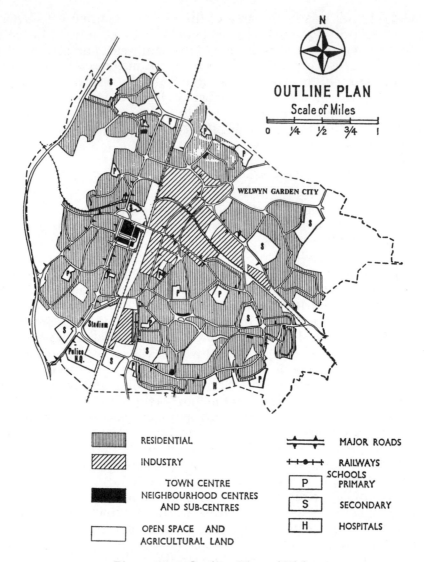

RESIDENTIAL

INDUSTRY

TOWN CENTRE
NEIGHBOURHOOD CENTRES
AND SUB-CENTRES

OPEN SPACE AND
AGRICULTURAL LAND

MAJOR ROADS

RAILWAYS

SCHOOLS
P   PRIMARY

S   SECONDARY

H   HOSPITALS

Figure 18.1 Outline Plan of Welwyn.

maintained to the west, north and east but the southern boundary of Welwyn is the northern boundary of Hatfield, and between the two towns the green belt is only 1000 yards in depth. This green belt should be regarded as inviolable. A second, council golf course has been provided at Panshanger.

Building the Additions to the Original Town

The town was continued under the development corporation in 1949 firstly by the completion of Parkway and the south-west followed by an extension of the south-eastern area, with the new neighbourhood centres of Ludwick and Hatfield Hyde, and an extension of that of Woodhall which was completed by 1958. Work on the north-west section began in 1956 and was completed in 1964. A start on the north-eastern section was postponed by delay in determining the line of the north-east industrial road which, originally to run east of the section, now runs through its western part; but by the end of 1967 the Haldens area was completed and by the end of 1973 three stages in the western part of Panshanger had been developed. In the Spring of 1974 a working party gave a report on the development of the eastern remaining part, south of Panshanger airfield. A planning application had been made by a private owner for the residential development of the airfield, but this was rejected on the grounds that it is a site in which green belt policy applies and its use for housing would be contrary to the concept of the town.

The complete plan for Panshanger includes a neighbourhood centre, now under construction, with shops and a supermarket, health centre, combined community and pastoral centre and a library. The Sir Frederic Osborn Comprehensive School already occupies the southern area of Panshanger and a site for a further comprehensive school adjoining Springfield Primary School is already allocated. A further primary school has been completed and another is under construction.

The number of houses built up to the end of 1952 from the time of designation was about 420, after that the rate was much higher, an average of about 500 a year up to 1962; then, as the town was nearing completion, there was a fall to about 300 a year up to 1967, then a further drop to less than 100 a year. By the end of 1976 about 8698 had been completed of which 6406 had been built by the corporation and the commission, 1606 by the local authority and the rest privately. In the same period 23 new schools were built and more are under construction.

Industrial employment was ahead of housing in Welwyn Garden City. At the time of designation 8300 persons were employed in the manufacturing industry, and another 3600 in retail trade, building and other service industries, professional work and various forms of agricultural work. 11 900 employed persons in a town with a population of 18 000 meant that a considerable number, probably some 3000 to 4000 came into Welwyn each day to work. Thus there was considerable housing leeway to make up, and it was important that house building should be at a faster rate than industrial building. Steady progress was made with the building of new factories of various kinds for a diversity of industry, but a satisfactory balance of industrial building and housing had not yet been achieved, and in 1963 industrial development was restricted to the expansion of existing industrial firms so as to enable the demand for housing, from those already working in the town, to be met.

In 1963 the new general Queen Elizabeth II hospital with 400 beds was completed on a site in the south-east of the town. It serves not only Welwyn, but Hatfield and the surrounding areas.

As the town was nearing completion in 1966, it was transferred to the Commission for the New Towns in April of that year, and the development corporation was dissolved in the following August. This transfer might be thought premature because the work of the corporation was not entirely finished. In its final report in 1966 the corporation expresses regret 'that it was not able to see the completion of its large scale projects of reasonably priced houses for sale at Panshanger, the new town centre and the new road systems with car parking facilities sufficient to meet for some years ahead the ever growing demand of the motor car'.

Residential Areas and Housing

One criticism that has been made of some of the residential areas of the new towns is that the houses are predominantly for one stratum of society and although they may have much variety of layout and architectural treatment there is for this reason still a consciousness of sameness. A greater mixing of income groups as symbolized by the houses would have been welcomed. This is not easy to achieve in a new town; but social variety has been a constant aim in building Welwyn Garden City, and by 1948 considerable success was achieved in this respect. But even here the criticism was sometimes made that there was too much separation of the housing for the different social strata and that in the north-west neighbourhood and in a large part of the south-west there was too high a proportion of middle and upper-middle income groups, whereas in the south-east there were in proportion too many houses for the lower income groups. The development corporation aimed to rectify this. In endeavouring to obtain a more balanced development houses are grouped into the categories of weekly rented, monthly rented and privately owned which roughly represent the three strata. The first are generally the smallest houses and are built at the highest density, and contain a large proportion of terrace houses; the second are built at a somewhat lower density, and include fewer terrace houses and a fair proportion of semi-detached, while the privately owned are built at a still lower density and include a large proportion of detached houses. It was felt by the development corporation that there were too many of the weekly rented houses in the south-east in relation to the other types, and not enough of these in the north-west area, and the aim in the completion plan was to rectify this and secure a good balance throughout the town. The aim was to provide in the south-west for 37.5% of the population in weekly rented houses, 22% in monthly rented and 40.5% privately owned. The corresponding proportions in the other neighbourhoods are: in the north-west 46.4% (w.r.), 26.7% (m.r.) and 26.9% (p.o.); in the north-east 77.8%(w.r.), 20.8% (m.r.) and 1.4% (p.o.); and in the south-east 87.1% (w.r.), 9.8% (m.r.) and 3.1% (p.o.). This has been largely realized with some minor variations. It is doubtful, judging from these figures, whether there is here a sufficient balance of types for it will be seen that the higher income groups are still in a majority west of the town and in a minority on the industrial side east of the town. A little more mixing would have social and aesthetic advantages, but no town in England is free of this kind of segregation.

The layout of the houses in the new areas follows very much that of the former development. The residential roads are, for the most part, a series of curves forming a pattern of islands or 'super-blocks' into which run culs-de-sac. Sometimes these form loops with grass areas in the centre, sometimes the terminations of the culs-de-sac are connected by footpaths. In many cases, following some of the attractive features in the earlier north-west and south-west sections, the conventional front gardens separated by hedges or fences are eliminated, and instead lawns stretch in front of the houses which gives a spacious open effect. The first housing groups, as early as the nineteen twenties, had this open layout, but it was found that most occupiers prefer front gardens for their own cultivation, and both methods have been employed since. Trees either line the roadways or are grouped in particular spots, and wherever possible existing trees are preserved. The landscaping of the residential areas of the earlier Welwyn was brilliantly effective in producing a setting of trees and shrubs and lawns for houses of all kinds, as near to a natural grouping as possible. Its aim was to bring the country, with much that makes it delightful—the sense of peace, the seasonal changes, the sound of the wind in the trees and the song of birds—into the residential area. The older parts of Welwyn planned on these lines constitute some of the most felicitous residential areas in England.

A special nursery—Digswell Nurseries Ltd—was started at the time of the foundation of the town in 1921 to supply it with trees and shrubs for landscaping, and the firm was taken over and extended by the development corporation and is continuing the work both in Welwyn Garden City and Hatfield. In the early stages when small trees and shrubs have just been planted the roads are apt to look a little bare, but after a few years the new districts begin to have something of the charm of the older.

The houses vary with the architects and with the types and sizes, but there seems to be a pervading spirit which gives them unity. It might be described as a liking for plain walls with careful attention to the placing of the windows on the wall space; and as design actuated by a taste for simplicity and good proportion, very much in the spirit of the Georgian tradition. Much has been due to the influence of Louis de Soissons who was responsible for the design of many of the earlier houses, and whose work has much of Georgian character. It must be admitted that some of the terrace houses for the lower income groups hardly live up to these standards, but the majority certainly do. Among the best of the groups from an aesthetic standpoint that belong to the early sixties are 4 terraces of 3-storey houses (a flat on the ground floor and maisonette above) on a hill in the north-west area which occupy the four corners at the crossing of Knightsfield with Digswell Road. The proportions are excellent, the detailing is of a refined character while some delightful stylistic balconies are introduced. In these four short terraces much of the grace of Georgian domestic architecture at its best is revived. That they are designed by the firm of architects, Louis de Soissons, Peacock, Hodges and Robertson, which has been responsible for a large amount of the housing in the new town, is testimony that the spirit that actuated the architecture of the original town still prevails.

The latest residential areas to be built to accommodate natural growth from 42 000 to 50 000 are at Panshanger. The western part completed by 1974 consists of traditional residential layout with a mixture of culs-de-sac and through roads. A criticism of Panshanger 1 and 2 is that there are perhaps too many through roads for a residential area. The greater profusion of culs-de-sac in the planned later developments of the eastern part of this neighbourhood with greater provision for footpaths and cycle tracks is more satisfactory.

In this neighbourhood considerable provision is made for elderly persons' dwellings in the form of 2- and 4-storey flats and one-storey houses sited within walking distance of the neighbourhood centre or near a bus route.

Neighbourhood Centres

As most of the building in the early period of the development of the new town was in the south-east area, it is here that the chief completed examples of major and minor neighbourhood centres are found. Woodhall, which had been partially built before the war with 10 shops, has nearly trebled its size, while the new minor centres of Ludwick and Hatfield Hyde in the south-east, Shoplands in the north-west and Haldens in the north-east were built in that sequence.

Woodhall consists of a considerable number of buildings grouped round an oval

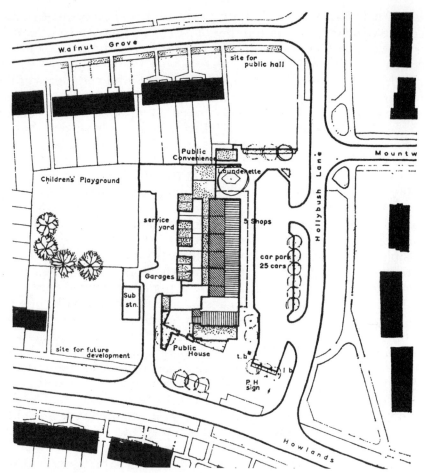

Figure 18.2 Hatfield Hyde Centre plan.

open space which makes it a large and fully equipped neighbourhood centre. To the north of the green is a curved convex 3-storey block with 26 shops and banks with bachelor flats over and a service way at the rear. On plots to the north-east is a Methodist church and Hall, and beyond in the same direction is a public house. To the east of the central green is a Pentecostal church, a health centre, a branch library, old people's home and flats, a day nursery and a nursery school. Curved along the south of the centre are semi-detached and terrace houses, terminating in the southern curve with another public house. To the west is a community centre, and Old Folks' Club, a Roman Catholic church and a Congregational church and hall. One might say what more could one wish, for the centre of a large neighbourhood, unless it be a cinema, and even that in the days of television is problematical. Halls for dancing, amateur drama and music exist in the various church halls and the community centre. If there is one criticism it is that the buildings are a little scattered; a more compact arrangement around a more exclusively pedestrian area might have had advantages.

Ludwick with 7 shops, Hatfield Hyde with 5, Haldens with 11 and Shoplands with 8 are on similar lines. Each consists of a row of shops with a service yard at the back, a wide footway in front, and a space for car parking. At the end of the row of shops in the first mentioned is the Ludwick family club and a public house together with a church (C of E) and a petrol filling station. There is also a public house at the end of the row of shops at Hatfield Hyde, with the Hyde club and a church on the opposite side of the road. Haldens centre includes 'The Mayflower' public house with associated community rooms, and a church (C of E). Shoplands includes a community hall over the shops with a Roman Catholic church and 'The Hedgehog' public house on the opposite side of the road.

Town Centre

The plan of Welwyn Garden City is an interesting combination of irregular layout of roads and spaces—a system of varied curves, culs-de-sac and closes—and the classical formal planning of its centre. An almost straight broad thoroughfare runs parallel with the railway from the southern extremity of the town to the northern. From South Parkway it broadens out to Parkway—a broad green between two roads. The road rises very gently and this middle green terminates in a semi-circle, flanked by parklands. The road continues however up the hill over the railway, becomes Digswell Road and traverses the hills and valleys of the north-west neighbourhood and separates it into two. It is a traffic thoroughfare, but it is segregated with hedges and grass verges almost as completely as a railway track. There are two pedestrian underpasses for shoppers and school children.

At right angles to the broad central Parkway is another, Howardsgate, named in memory of the town's founder, which stretches for about 400 yards (365 m) to the railway station. On either side of this between Parkway and the station is the town centre. It consists for the most part of shops in rectangular blocks surrounded by straight roads, the descendant of the Greek chess-board plan. Additions of several shops and offices have been made south of Howardsgate, some of which flank a

Figure 18.3 Campus West—cultural centre.

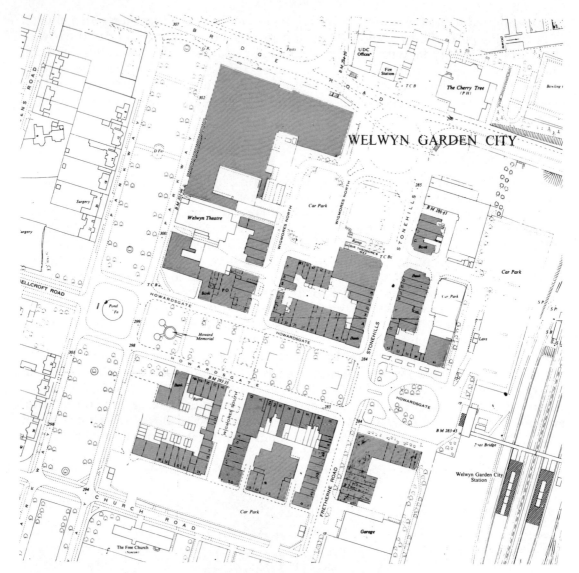

Figure 18.4 Town centre plan.
O Offices; S Shopping; R Residential; P Car Park; MP Multi-Storey Car Park.

pedestrian way; and in the semi-circular area north of the shopping centre there are the College of Further Education, the council office, and the police station. A theatre, library and exhibition hall have been built at Campus West, thus forming a valuable cultural centre. Town centre shopping and commercial developments are proceeding in accordance with local planning strategy. A perimeter road is proposed to take through traffic out of the centre.

Since Welwyn Garden City was originally planned, ideas have changed of what a centre for a town of medium size should be. In 1921 the motor vehicle did not occupy so prominent a place in the urban scene as it does in the late seventies when the necessity of segregating the motor vehicle and the pedestrian in urban centres is felt more

Figure 18.5 Multi-storey car park in town centre.

strongly; in 1921 it was mooted but strongly opposed by retail traders. Thus with the examples of Stevenage and Harlow a problem may be how to make the centre of Welwyn Garden City more of a pedestrian precinct, for it must be insisted that this is desirable in any modern shopping centre. It is important that people should be able to go shopping with that relaxed feeling that freedom from the thought of road traffic can give. Equally important is provision for waiting cars. Welwyn Garden City has (unexpectedly) become a shopping centre for a wider region, and at peak periods many hundreds of cars are parked in the town centre. To meet this need parking for 2000 cars has been provided around the town centre and the first multi-storey car park for 470 cars, on 5 floors, was completed at the end of 1973.

Whatever is done with the centre of Welwyn Garden City it is important that the central avenues of Parkway and Howardsgate, with the circular campus to the north should remain as they are because they represent one of the most beautiful examples of formal landscape planning in Europe. As one comes down Digswell road over the railway bridge the view along the lawns of Parkway to the central fountain spreading its spray against the trees that diminish in the long perspective to the blue distance beyond, is one of the unforgettable sights of England.

Industrial Area

The main railway running south–north cuts the town in half, with a little under two-thirds of the population on the east side and a little over one-third on the west side. The industrial area is fairly central immediately to the east of the railway, with a small additional industrial section to the south. By the end of 1976 there were 94 factories employing about 19 000 persons. Many of the larger factories representing over 80% of the industrial area have been built by the firms for their own requirements while others have been built by the original Garden City company and the development corporation for letting to smaller firms. The two largest factories are those for the Plastics Division of ICI, situated at the northern end of the industrial area and employing nearly 3000, and the factory for Murphy Radio, now Rank Xerox Ltd, which employs about 1200. The central situation of the industrial area makes it within easy reach of any part of the town, the greatest distance being little more than a mile.

If the industrial area has not the attractive general effect of the industrial area of Crawley, it yet has an interesting variety of buildings many of which are of a distinctive architectural character as well as being well and spaciously sited with a view to possible future extensions. In this area the monotony of the 1-storey industrial estate is avoided. Among the more distinctive buildings are the two already mentioned, the Roche Products factory, built shortly before the war and later extended, and those of Nabisco Ltd, Smith and Nephew Ltd, Smith, Kline and French Ltd, and G.K.N. Lincoln Electric. The sectional factories for letting usually have a 2-storey administration building in front with a one-storey section in the rear.

The Social Aspect

In the emergence of a social life the new town of Welwyn Garden City had certain advantages over the new towns where previously there had been only small scattered populations because many social activities were already in existence at the time of designation, and a great number of societies catered for a variety of interests. These were able, in some cases, to provide a nucleus for extension into other areas of the town. Yet there was no community association, which had proved so valuable at Crawley, and it was necessary to help to provide some general social and recreational life for the newcomers to the town. Married couples and single men and women had come to work in the factories of the new town, the former to set up home, the single to live in lodgings or flats. Some had been accustomed to an urban type of life and had enjoyed recreational pursuits of various kinds and they naturally wished to find these at Welwyn. It is inevitable that some at first experienced a feeling of disappointment at the lack of choice of several cinemas, dance halls and cafés and opportunities for recreational pursuits, and Welwyn has with other new towns been criticized for a shortage of these. Yet more active inquiries on the part of newcomers to a town would often result in an awareness of manifold social activities that were initially unsuspected. There is the Barn Theatre, which is an important centre for three or four dramatic groups, there is no lack of societies of all kinds, there are playing fields and many rugger, soccer, cricket and tennis clubs, churches of many denominations are active in providing for recreational and social needs and many small halls and meeting rooms are available.

Two enterprises of a less usual character deserve special comment. To the north-west of the town is Digswell House which was for some time a school, but has been discontinued as such. It was too fine a building, the development corporation felt, not to be put to some valuable use. In 1957 an Arts Trust was established in Welwyn Garden City with a number of eminent persons in the art world as trustees and Digswell House became the arts centre. The purpose was to provide residence, studios and workshops for artists of all kinds, not only painters and sculptors but designers and makers of stained glass and furniture, pottery, metal work, fabrics; indeed for practitioners in all the visual arts. Seventeen artists were in residence by 1967 and they included several well-known sculptors and painters who have held one-man shows in London, and one of the designers of the stained glass windows in the new Coventry Cathedral. The Digswell Arts Centre is becoming one of the most important artists' communities in the country. In 1965 the Trust acquired an exhibition gallery on the ground floor of a large house in Parkway which it rents from the Commission.

Not far from this arts centre is Digswell Lake, some 17 acres (7 ha) in extent. In 1956 a society was formed with the object of preserving it for its natural beauty and as a sanctuary for certain fauna and flora and aquatic birds. The corporation granted a lease to the society and the area was fenced off and enjoyment of this lovely sanctuary is secured by becoming a member of the society, a membership which includes the family.

Another somewhat unusual but valuable enterprise is the establishment by the corporation of a well equipped workshop under the supervision of a committee and a skilled manager, where anyone on payment of a small fee may do constructional or repair work. In this workshop furniture is re-made and upholstered, models of various kinds are made, canoes are built, photographic studios are set up and many other craft activities are pursued.

A YMCA hostel was completed in 1968 at Peartree providing accommodation for about 80 young persons of both sexes. In the north-west of the town the Old Barn and Cowman's Cottage, originally known as Digswell Lodge Farm and situated in the Vineyard Barn, was converted by the development corporation who owned it, into a building for social purposes and opened in May 1959. In 1967 another such building was opened in Shoplands also in the north-west. Both are administered by the Vineyard Barn Association formed for the purpose. A further one was opened in 1967 in Hollybush Lane in the south-east of the town, which together with that at Shoplands receives grants from the Department of Education and Science, the Hertfordshire County Council, the Hatfield District Council and the Commission for the New Towns. The two administering associations are responsible for 25% of the total cost. They provide an example of the useful work performed by voluntary associations. The Gosling Stadium, named after the first chairman of the WGC development corporation, is of international standard with a fine cycle track and a training ski-slope.

The original conception of a diversified layout round a formally planned centre has been maintained throughout although adjustments in planning have been made from time to time in answer to changing needs. It has been accomplished with consummate skill, and one of the results is that Welwyn Garden City is certainly among the most beautiful modern towns in Europe, is deservedly famous, and is justly a place of pilgrimage for planners throughout the world.

In 1977 it is substantially complete, and reached a population of approximately 40 000. Further intake of industry and population is unlikely, and future building will be for the increase from natural growth. It is the second town to be inspired by the ideas of Ebenezer Howard. Planning is team work, and Welwyn had an exceptionally strong team of directors and executives and from the beginning almost to completion the design was under the direction of Louis de Soissons, RA, FRIBA. He was the original consultant, planner and architect in 1920, and when the town was taken over by a development corporation in 1948 he continued as chief planner and architect until his death in 1962. Thus, as the corporation remarks in its final report in 1966, it is probably true 'that few other towns have been started and evolved for 40 years under the planning control of a single man'.

19 *Hatfield*

Sir Patrick Abercrombie in the *Greater London Plan* proposed that Hatfield should be enlarged from its 1938 population of about 9000 to 22 000. This proposal was supported by the Advisory Committee on the Greater London Plan that reported in 1946. The proximity of Hatfield to Welwyn Garden City, which had been similarly recommended for expansion, prompted Lord Silkin, the Minister of Town and Country Planning, as previously noted, to designate the two at the same time. The explanatory memorandum on the draft designation orders stated that although the two towns are to be kept separate, their close proximity means that 'the development of one cannot be carried through without the closest regard to, and some integration with, the development of the other'. Although two development corporations were appointed, they had the same personnel. This would 'ensure the closest co-ordination and the greatest economy in the development of the two towns'. With Welwyn Garden City, Hatfield was transferred to the Commission for the New Towns in April 1966 and the corporation was dissolved in the following August.

The designated area is 2340 acres (948 ha) originally for a population of 25 000, which was reached in 1968. Natural growth and small scale development increased the population to about 26 000 by 1976. Situated in the former Hatfield Rural District, now part of the Welwyn Hatfield District, it is approximately 18 miles (29 km) from London on the main line from King's Cross to Peterborough and $2\frac{1}{2}$ miles (4 km) on the London side of Welwyn Garden City station. The site extends for about $3\frac{1}{2}$ miles (5.5 km) in the south–north direction and is only about a mile (1.6 km) wide east–west, enclosed by the main line railway and the Great North road on the east, and the Barnet bypass to the west. The area broadens out in the north where it adjoins the boundary of Welwyn Garden City, but this part, through which flows the river Lee, forms the green belt between the towns, the northern boundary of the Hatfield built-up area being approximately the North Orbital Road. A green belt on the south separates Hatfield from the village of Welham Green. The country is undulating with some attractive woodland scenery in the southern part.

Although Hatfield is a close neighbour of Welwyn Garden City, too close some would say, it presented at the time of its designation completely different material for the planner. The latter was a town gradually growing on preconceived lines to the maximum ultimately determined, it represented some of the best residential planning in the world and was a subject of international admiration. Modern Hatfield, on the other hand, was an ill-conceived growth resulting from the impact of the introduction of a large aircraft works on an ancient semi-urban settlement. The old town of Hatfield is pleasant enough; it had grown in proximity to Hatfield House, the ancestral home of the Cecil family, and had spread from being a stage on the road-route northwards from London on either side of the Great North Road, and later round the railway station. The aircraft factory of the De Havilland Company (now Hawker Siddley Aviation) moved from Edgware to Hatfield in 1934 and was situated west of the Barnet bypass about a mile west of Hatfield railway station. The modern industrial town had grown up in the area between, mainly in the years 1934 to 1939. The number of employees had increased from about 1000 in 1934 to over 4000 in 1939, and reached over 10 000 in 1959. Although Hatfield grew quickly in pre-war years, it was impossible to accommodate all the workers and they mostly lived in St Albans, Welwyn Garden City, Edgware and London. Other factories were also built in the vicinity mainly in a triangular area north of the town, and these include the engineering firm of Jack Olding Ltd, employing about 1000.

The chaotic growth of the six pre-war years was adversely criticized by Abercrombie in the Greater London Plan. In that book he gave examples of more detailed planning as illustrations of pursuing the aims of the general plan. He chose the example of Ongar (Essex) for a new town, and Hatfield for an expanded town, entitling it the 'Integration and Extension of a Rural Industrial Town', and his suggestions were obviously of value to the planner appointed by the development corporation. Abercrombie criticized the pre-war siting of the factories at Hatfield, 'scattered', as he said, 'in open fields with no attempt to form a single industrial area, and congesting the bypass with their workpeople and traffic (at the very point where it carries the orbital as well as the Great North Road)'.

He felt that 'the confused medley of housing' was hardly less serious. He spoke of the general tendency to keep all new development as far as possible from the old town and Hatfield House; and this, he suggested, 'may be one of the reasons why the land immediately adjoining the bypass and the aerodrome, which should at all costs have been left open, has been built up'. Abercrombie also remarked that 'the opportunity to establish a centre for the new town and to plan the housing in well defined units has not been realized'.

Outline Plan

The task of the Hon. Lionel Brett (now Lord Esher), who was appointed to prepare a master plan for Hatfield, was, therefore, very different from that of Louis de Soissons, who merely had to continue in more detail his original plan of Welwyn. It must be admitted that Lionel Brett performed his difficult task well. This was a totally different problem from the planning of Crawley or Harlow where the proportionately small existing development could be absorbed fairly simply into a new plan; instead there was much unrelated scattered development which amounted to nearly two-fifths of the calculated maximum.

In Lionel Brett's plan the town is divided into 7 units or neighbourhoods of varying shapes and sizes. There is Old Hatfield east of the railway, planned to have a slight reduction of population to about 1000 with a small extension northward. The Great North Road runs through the centre of this, but through traffic has now been diverted to the southern link road at the southern end of the town so that there shall be no major road barrier between the new town and Hatfield Park now open for the enjoyment of the public.

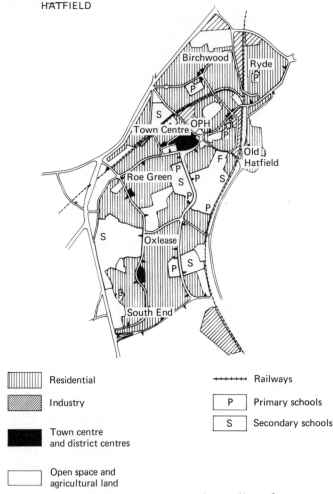

HATFIELD

Figure 19.1 Hatfield—outline plan.

Ryde is a small neighbourhood of 1200 to the east of the railway and north of Old Hatfield, planned for a fair proportion of private housing for owner occupiers. Birchwood, which was already built mainly before and after the Second World War by the Hatfield Rural District Council, is a larger neighbourhood with a population of some 4000 in the northern part, bounded by the railway that runs to St Albans on the south, the Barnet bypass to the west and a strip of industrial development along the railway on the east. Newtown, in the central area, includes some of the existing western extensions of Old Hatfield, and the town centre, and was planned for a population of 7000. To the south-west is Roe Green with a population of 5000 with an open space—the town's park—to the east; to the south-east is Oxlease with a population of 3500, and the large technical college and school with extensive grounds to the west; and then in the southern extremity is South Hatfield with a population of 5000. A generous and well-distributed provision of schools, infant, junior and secondary, is made in the plan.

Industry presented difficulties. There was the De Havilland Aircraft factory on the west of the Barnet bypass with 10 000 employees, while other factories to the north represented another 1500 workers, which alone means a town of 25 000 to 30 000 if all these workers lived in it. It was also very much a one-industry town which is unsatisfactory for stability of employment. Desirable diversification of industry could thus only be secured by overloading the town with industry, and a dependence on a considerable proportion of the workers living elsewhere. Nevertheless some attempt was made in the plan to provide this diversification, including a greater provision for female labour. Space for additional industry was provided near the town centre and near the neighbourhood centre of South Hatfield together with the Birchwood industrial area in the north. The plan was approved in principle by the Minister of Town and Country Planning in August 1950.

It was stated in the memorandum on the draft designation order that the industry and population which will provide the expansion for Hatfield are to be drawn from London. But it is obvious that there was already more than enough industry in Hatfield for its planned maximum population of 29 000. Hatfield, therefore, is hardly an example of a new town to accommodate dispersed industry from London, but rather a new town to house mainly an existing working population, of which, however, many are being dispersed from home in London and thereby saved from daily travel.

In 1962 Lionel Brett was succeeded by Walter Chapman as consultant planner. Chapman began plans for a new town centre and for the redevelopment of Old Hatfield, but he died in 1964 before they were completed. He was succeeded by Maxwell Fry who completed these plans. The plan for Old Hatfield involved redevelopment of residential and commercial zones in the area south of the station, the introduction of a pedestrian shopping centre and the provision of a bypass so that through traffic can avoid Old Hatfield.

Building the Town

Of the seven neighbourhoods, Old Hatfield, Birchwood, and a proportion of Newtown already existed, although subject to some replanning and rebuilding; the remaining four had to be built from scratch. Shortly after the master plan was approved a start was made on Roe Green in the centre which was completed in 1957. In 1954 a start was made with South Hatfield at the southern extremity of the town of which the districts of Hazelgrove and Angerland were completed in 1959. Oxlease was commenced in 1956, and completed in 1961. Factories in the Birchwood industrial estate to provide mainly female employment had nearly all been built by 1962.

Housing did not progress as fast as in many of the new towns which was perhaps regrettable in view of the needs of factory workers in the area. Delay was caused by the Colne Valley Trunk Sewer not being completed until the end of 1954, and building could not commence in South Hatfield until connections into it could be made. A similar delay was caused at Oxlease served by the Batterdale sewer which was not completed until 1957. Up to the end of 1954 a little over 1000 houses had been completed; the rate of production improved considerably up to 1956, declining in 1957–59 due, no doubt, to the restrictions on capital expenditure during those years. A rough idea can be obtained from the approximate figures, which were nearly 400 in 1955, about 850 in 1956, a little over 400 in 1957, about 100 in 1958, about 150 in 1959, 390 in 1960, 405 in 1961, 198 in 1962, 129 in 1963, 354 in 1964, 322 in 1965, 101 in 1966, 315 in 1967 and 160 in 1968. From that year until 1976 an average of about a hundred were

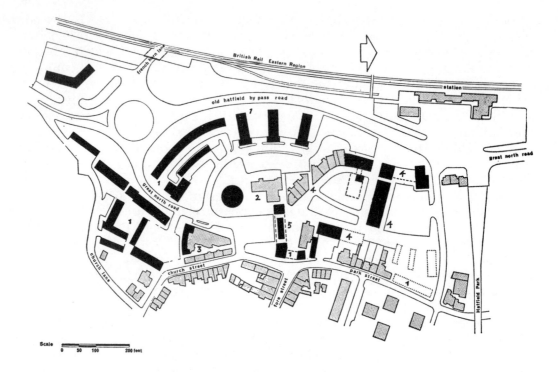

1 . 2- and 3-storey terraced houses and 3-storey flats
2. New Roman Catholic Church of St. Teresa
3. Salisbury Arms Hotel and extension
4. Shops, some with maisonettes over
5. 2-storey office building

Figure 19.2 Plan of Old Hatfield.

completed each year. Since designation to the end of 1976, about 6964 houses have been provided of which 4293 were built by the corporation and the Commission, 2137 by the local authority and about 534 by private enterprise.

By 1968 the town as originally planned in 1950 was practically completed. Further work was concerned mainly with implementing the new plan for the centre and the redevelopment of Old Hatfield.

Housing and Residential Areas

As with Welwyn Garden City the housing is grouped under the three headings of weekly rented, monthly rented and those for sale, and the proportions are fairly evenly distributed in each of the new neighbourhoods, the greater majority being weekly rented. However over 600 former rented houses have been sold, mainly freehold, to sitting tenants.

The hilly character of the southern end of the new town provides opportunities for some interesting housing layouts in the three neighbourhoods situated there, namely Roe Green, Oxlease and South Hatfield, and the architects have used their opportunities well. Much of the housing has an architectural distinction which it is not easy

Figure 19.3 Part of Roe Green neighbourhood showing centre and housing layout.

to give to small units and which makes it particularly noteworthy. In Roe Green, with the more conventional brick houses, are several where a low-pitched gable end appears on the front of the house with the upper storey faced with cedar boarding and the effect is distinctive. Several houses in all the three neighbourhoods are arranged in echelon fashion either singly or in rows of 2, 3 or 4, thus providing varied shaped lawns in front of the houses.

In the Hazelgrove area of South Hatfield, which lies mainly to the west of the neighbourhood centre of Hilltop, the layout and design of the houses are original. Culs-de-sac are freely used, and these are mixed with footpaths through lawns between rows of houses. In many of these, by Kenneth Boyd, one senses the application of Georgian character to long terraces of small units in an effective manner. Broad eaves of flat or slightly tilted roofs overhang plain brick or rendered walls, with windows strongly framed in white, with simple canopied entrances. The long terraces run in curves which give a pleasant effect and certainly avoid the monotony sometimes characterizing terrace blocks.

In Oxlease there is an attractive group of houses by Sir Basil Spence. Some are designed in short rows of 4, grouped at different angles to give variety and to provide spacious lawns in front. There is a refinement in the design of these houses which puts them among the most distinctive examples of domestic architecture in the new towns. They are mainly of brick, and in a row of 4 houses, 3 have pale straw-coloured bricks, and the fourth—one of the middle ones—dull purple bricks. In one row the upper storey is faced with red tiles with semi-circles downwards. All have first floor balconies, with elegant curved railings, while the introduction of timber boarding near the entrances provides another effective touch.

In South Hatfield are several detached houses faced with dark timber boarding, and linked with their neighbours by garages, and these provide a further example of refined design applied to the small units. Some of the best domestic architecture of the smaller kind during the 1950s is to be found at Hatfield. In some cases, however, the density is too high, gardens too small and forecourts too shallow for privacy; reservations which must be made in assessing the architectural achievement.

Figure 19.4 Hilltop, neighbourhood centre of South Hatfield.

Neighbourhood Centres

The first two neighbourhood centres to be completed were those at Roe Green, and South Hatfield. The former, being fairly near to the town centre and to the shops in St Albans Road, is small, but it is a well arranged, compact centre on the slope of a hill. It lies on an island site and consists of a row of 5 shops with a paved area in front and a service way with garages behind. To the south, up the hill, one mounts to another paved area on one side of which is a meeting hall and assembly rooms, while on the other side, shut off a bit, is the 'Cavendish' public house. In the space at one end of this hall is a sculpture in bronze of boys wrestling.

Hilltop, the neighbourhood centre on top of the hill at South Hatfield, is a particularly felicitous design. On the east side is a concave row of 19 shops facing a broad paved pedestrian area. Opposite is a large building combining a public house, community centre and health centre, an experiment in this kind of combination. It includes an assembly hall with stage, committee rooms and facilities for the health service. At the north end of this neighbourhood centre is a 4-storey block of flats with a car park between the two. At the south end is a church of modern and arresting design, and beyond is the parsonage and youth centre; while between the church and Bishops Rise is a lawn with trees, altogether an excellent centre.

Town Centre

In the report of the Hatfield Development Corporation on the progress and position of the plan prepared by Lionel Brett, it is stated in the note on the town centre that 'Hatfield started its life as a new town with the advantage of having, albeit a small one, an established shopping centre. The gain is economic, social and aesthetic. The centre can grow naturally out of what exists, and will avoid the suggestion of a "model community"'. It is difficult to appreciate the advantage, and it is difficult also to appreciate the social and aesthetic gain, while it may be asked why should one be afraid of a model community. On the contrary a disadvantage of the town centre is that it is part of an older shopping district where shops have grown haphazardly on either side of the road. The new plan consists of two squares, one north of St Albans road with shops on three sides, and one south reached by a pedestrian way. The latter forms the market which is adjacent to Queensway, a main road running south of the centre. The market square has an attractive setting partly enclosed on the north and west sides by 2-level shops. Immediately behind the shops on the west side is a massive 14-storey block of flats which gives a somewhat heavy note to the architectural composition.

That the centre was not more of a pedestrian precinct denied the advantages which have been indicated in the chapters on some of the other new towns. The circumstance that the old shopping centre is combined in the plan necessarily makes this more difficult, but it would have been much better if St Albans road had been eliminated through the centre and had made a cul-de-sac to the west(19.1). The traffic road round White Lion Square on the north side should also have been eliminated. Shoppers, especially mothers with young children, could then have done their shopping with the relaxed feeling that traffic roads render impossible.

However in the summer of 1967 changes towards segregation of pedestrian and vehicular traffic were made in conformity with a new plan for the town centre. They include the conversion of St Albans Road and White Lion Square into pedestrian

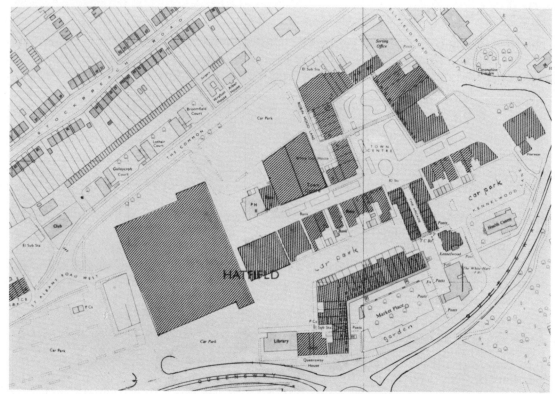

Figure 19.5 Hatfield Town Centre.

areas, begun in September 1968, the introduction of several car parks, the completion of a circular road round the centre, a departmental store over part of St Albans road, and a block of flats and civic entertainment centre.

In its final report in 1966 the development corporation expressed regret 'that it could not see the completion of the new town centre, with its pedestrian shopping areas and residential provision nearby for many more people, and that it could not make a start on the redevelopment of the old town'. It added, however, that it 'carried these projects to a stage from which they could go ahead rapidly'.

However, Hatfield town centre is now wholly pedestrianized with substantial car parking facilities around it. The main shopping attraction is a 100 000 sq. foot Woolco hypermarket which is linked by shop lined malls with protective canopies to more shops in White Lion Square and Market Square. A particular feature of the centre is Kennelwood House, a black and white building now used by the Commission for New Towns as its local office. There is also a sculpture and a fountain in each of the two squares. Dominating the sky line is the 14-storey Queensway House with offices on the ground floor and flats above.

Industrial Areas

As has been pointed out there was adequate industry in Hatfield at the time of designation to support the planned population, yet there was not a satisfactory

Figure 19.6 Town Centre shopping precinct.

diversification of industry, and it was considered by the development corporation that there was a need to provide additional industry in part to give employment to women. Since designation to 1977, over 20 new factories have been built ranging in size from 2500 sq. feet (225 m²) to 3700 sq. feet (333 m²). This industrial development has taken place mainly in the Birchwood area to the north of the town. In the last few years very little building of this kind has taken place, and any future industrial development is reserved for the extension of existing factories, apart from new factories in the Beaconsfield road area to accommodate firms affected by the old Hatfield redevelopment scheme.

Social Aspect

Much that has been written of the social activities and problems of the other new towns has some application to Hatfield. Like the other new towns, it possesses its various clubs, societies and associations for cultural and recreational pursuits and its women's and youth organizations. The last named deserves special mention. In 1950 a large house called 'The Breaks' with 8 acres of ground near the town centre was acquired by the development corporation, and was allocated for a youth centre formed in co-operation with the de Havilland Aircraft Co. and now run by a public committee. A full time warden was appointed, whose salary is paid by de Havilland's. By the early part of 1952 the centre was full to capacity and consisted of 160 boys and girls. Among the activities at the centre were drama, music, arts and crafts, various sports and indoor residents (a task later taken over by the Cavendish Club), for a day-time old folks' club games. 'The Breaks' was also used by the corporation for welcoming parties for new and for the 20–35 club. Later welcoming parties have been held at Cavendish Hall and 'Hilltop' as they are usually held as near as possible to the latest new residents.

It was inevitable that with the success of the youth centre the premises should prove to be inadequate for its activities. Early in 1954 there was a waiting list of 75 young people, and it is interesting to note that according to the 1954 report of the development corporation 'the adolescents of every single family housed have joined or attempted to join this club'. The de Havilland Aircraft Company had already provided additional accommodation, but even with this the provisions were inadequate, and later the centre received the gift of a prefabricated building from the company which, according to the 1956 report, 'was being erected for the corporation by a firm of builders, which unfortunately went bankrupt'. The foundations were completed, however, and the boys and girls themselves undertook to continue the erection under supervision, and the appropriately named 'Enterprise Hall' with its 3500 sq. feet (325 m²) was completed late in 1957. This very successful youth centre should itself be an inspiration to other new towns, and it is perhaps a pity that the Gulbenkian Committee, in studying the need for a youth centre at Stevenage, did not give some attention to this highly successful example at Hatfield. It prompted plans for another youth centre in South Hatfield where some old buildings of Downs Farm were converted and a new hall built in the same way by voluntary labour. Imperial Chemical Industries of Welwyn Garden City assisted by giving a large sectional wooden building.

This community feeling of youth in Hatfield expressed in its highly successful youth centres is itself a reflection of the very strong community feeling that exists among the residents in the different neighbourhoods. The success may be due partly to the large industrial population that was already there when the new town began to be built, but it is also in no small measure due to the work of the development corporation in collaboration with industry.

Reference

19.1   This plan of the centre is the seventh that has been made. In earlier plans St Albans Road was
        changed to a pedestrian precinct, but local interests forced the revision of the plan.

20 *Basildon*

The region north of the Thames estuary between London and Southend was, until the late nineteenth century, of a pleasant rural character. Then in consequence of the depression in agriculture at that time much of the land was sold by farmers to land development companies who resold in small plots for building, and many rather mean houses and shacks were built there. This process was much accelerated after the First World War by the popular movement towards the country. Along with dwellings for commuters to London and for retired people, houses and shacks were built as weekend cottages, and plots were taken for poultry farming. It became in many parts a scattered, unplanned bungaloid growth without proper services, drainage and roads. Among the regions where this was particularly apparent were those round Laindon and Pitsea and the district between(20.1). Laindon is about 24 miles (39 km) from the centre of London and Pitsea about 28 miles (45 km). These had become centres for the scattered development, and by 1939 each had a population of about 8000.

Sir Patrick Abercrombie had proposed in the Greater London Plan that Laindon should be increased in size to 17 500 and Pitsea to 17 000. Following this the Essex County Council and the South Essex Joint Planning Committee proposed a new town with a maximum population of 50 000. The proposal received support from the Billericay Urban District Council in whose area the two small 'towns' were situated, and from the County Boroughs of East and West Ham who were interested in a reception area for some of their overcrowded populations. As a result, in January 1949 the Minister designated an area of 7818 acres (3166 ha) for the new town. This large tract, is about 6 miles (10 km) from east to west and 3 miles (5 km) north to south. It comprises the small town of Laindon and the villages of Langdon Hills and Lee Chapel to the west, the small town of Pitsea, and the villages of Vange and Basildon in the east, the last giving its name to the new town. In all the population in 1949 was about 25 000. The country is gently undulating, fairly low in the south-east at Pitsea and Vange where, in some places, it is little above sea level, while to the south-west in the Langdon Hills district, there is a range of low hills rising to over 350 feet (105 m).

Before progress could be made with the outline plan it was necessary to determine a maximum population for the town. The Advisory Committee on Greater London Planning had suggested 50 000. As the development corporation pointed out in its second annual report, this could have been achieved by increasing to urban density the scattered development of the two principal cores of population, Laindon and Pitsea, but this would have made 2 towns not 1, with a thin line of development linking them, while it would have involved considerable lengths of major roads and services, excessive and uneconomic for a town of the proposed size. It was, therefore, decided to plan for a larger town with a population of about 80 000, and later it was decided that this maximum should be of the order of 106 000. Then in 1967 in accordance with a suggestion in the South-East Study of 1964, a plan for about 140 000 was agreed.

Outline Plan

In the first outline plan, approved in August 1951, the town centre, well placed geographically, is intended to serve not only the town but surrounding districts with a population of about 150 000 within an 8 mile (13 km) radius. The proposed built-up area was originally divided into 9 neighbourhoods: Pitsea to the extreme east with a population that, under revised proposals, may reach 14 200; Fryerns to the north-east with 15 600; Barstable east of the town centre (11 700); Vange in the south-east (12 650); Kingswood south of the centre (4900); Lee Chapel, North and South, immediately west of the centre (8300 and 4900); and lastly the two neighbourhoods in the west end,

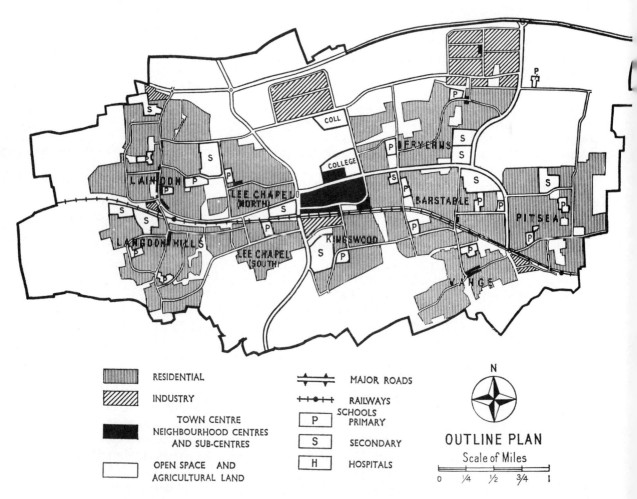

Figure 20.1 Basildon Outline Plan I.

Laindon (19 700) and Langdon Hills (19 500). In 1954 a tenth neighbourhood, Ghyllgrove immediately north of the town centre was added in response to Government pressure to increase the target population. Each neighbourhood, besides its chief shopping centre, has smaller ones suitably placed. In the plan large pockets of agricultural land on the urban outskirts, but within the designated area, forms a partial green belt extending to about 40% of the designated area. Primary and secondary schools are similarly distributed throughout the area. Industry occupies two large rectangular areas to the north separated from each other by about 1 mile (1.6 km). Since the original plan, however, the central part of this intervening area has been occupied by Ford's tractor plant. An industrial site, a good proportion of which is already let, has been established at Burnt Mills and to the north-east a 17 acre (6.9 ha) warehouse site, to be called the Nore, is proposed. In addition, a fifth industrial area is proposed for the north-west corner of the town, called Smithfields. The railway runs east–west through the centre of the designated area, with Pitsea station at the east end and Laindon at the west end, and another station has been built with offices adjacent in the town centre. The station was opened in November 1974. There are small areas of service industry near the town centre and at each station; ample open spaces and playing fields are spread fairly evenly throughout the town, and a large park to include a

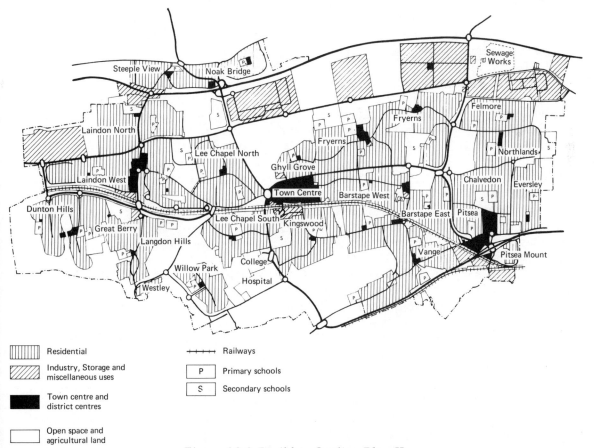

Figure 20.2 Basildon Outline Plan II.

multi-sports centre is sited between the town centre and the western industrial area.
The long shape of the town from east to west places some of the residential districts
rather a long way from the centre. For example, the eastern areas of Pitsea are $2\frac{1}{2}$ miles
(4 km) away, and the western areas of Laindon are a similar distance, due to the
pre-existence of these small towns. Whether it would have been better to have kept
them as such with a separation of about 1 mile (1.6 km) of green belt between the two,
on the pattern of the twin towns of Welwyn Garden City and Hatfield is a matter on
which there are good reasons on both sides.

In response to the suggestion in the South-East Study for the further expansion of
Basildon, the development corporation was asked by the MHLG to examine the
possibilities, and in reply the corporation concluded that 140 000 people could be
accommodated in the existing designated area. A new master plan was submitted to
the MHLG in August 1966, and after an inquiry it was finally approved with certain
amendments in December 1967.

In this new master plan extensions were made on the periphery of the existing
development. The whole area was divided into fairly small neighbourhoods, some of
them sub-divisions of those in the first plan. This preference for the small neighbourhood derives from the advantages mentioned in the chapter on Crawley, and the
disadvantages of the large mentioned in the chapter on Stevenage. There are now 23
neighbourhoods in Basildon either existing or proposed, and starting from Fryerns just
north-east of the centre, which is one of those in the original plan, they are, moving
clockwise, Fryerns (15 100), Felmore, further east (5900), Northlands (5900); then the
division into four of Pitsea to become Eversley (4500), Chalvedon (5700), Pitsea (3600)
and Pitsea Mount (1000); then the division of Barstable into Barstable East (3800) and
West (6800). Vange (13 300) remains as in the original plan, as also does Kingswood
(5200) immediately south of the town centre, Lee Chapel North (8600) and South (4900)
immediately west of the town centre are the same as in the original plan. The former
neighbourhood of Langdon Hills becomes four smaller ones south of the railway and
extending well to the west: Langdon Hills (3300), Westley (1200), Great Berry (5400)
and Dunton Hills (4900). Laindon is divided into three: Laindon East (7900), West
(4200) and North (7300). Lastly in the north-west on the further side of the A127 are two
additional neighbourhoods, Steeple View (3000) and Noak Bridge (4000). In this new
master plan as first prepared, there were two further neighbourhoods on the south,
Kingston Ridge (4000) and Hawkesbury (2600), but these were deleted as the result of
objections at the inquiry and on the recommendations of the inspector. The main
grounds of objection were that the development would have spoilt the area, by
reducing it as a regional open space, and by the separation of the town from Westley
Heights and Langdon Hills.

The deletions of the neighbourhoods of Kingston Ridge and Hawkesbury fundamentally affected the plan for the whole of the south-west area. In consequence the
development corporation revised it for the south-west. A draft was published in 1970,
the plan was exhibited and public meetings were held. The Basildon Urban District
Council opposed the plan on the grounds that the open space aspect had dictated the
proposals and that more land should be allocated for residential development with a
reduction of open space. The plan was consequently revised and submitted to the
Secretary of State for the Environment in July 1973. An exhibition of this further plan
and more public meetings were held. Fifty-nine representations regarding the proposals were received by the Secretary of State, which meant some public opposition based

primarily on the introduction of Lower Dunton neighbourhood into the plan and on the evaluation by the Nature Conservancy Council of parts of the south-west area being of special ecological interest. To some extent the objections meant a reversal of the opposition of the Basildon Urban District Council's attitude over the first draft. The opposition on the grounds of too much invasion of open space is, we think, justified. Basildon is a very large new town and the preservation of its green belt in accordance with the conception of new towns is important, and if as large as Basildon the penetration of open spaces from the periphery into the residential areas is an advantage, especially if the country is of scenic value as is the undulating, partly wooded, character of south-west Basildon. Consequently, the corporation introduced a revised plan for the south-west area in 1974 which proposed the deletion of Lower Dunton neighbourhood. Nevertheless public opposition continued and in November 1975 a public inquiry was held. In his decision of July 1976 the Secretary of State requested that in addition Willow Park neighbourhood be deleted from the plan, the boundary of Dunton Hills neighbourhood be slightly amended to avoid its possible intrusion into the landscape when viewed from the west, and that greater consideration be given to proposed Road 35. The effect of these amendments was to reduce the target population to 130 000.

Most of the small neighbourhoods have their shopping centre and primary school, while the larger neighbourhoods like Fryerns and Vange have a few of each.

Because of the size of the town, especially its length from east to west, there has been some replanning of centres. In addition to the main town centre there are 2 other major overspill centres in the east and west, both of which are partially complete, the former in Pitsea and the latter between Laindon West and East. There are also 5 neighbourhood group centres. With all these sub-divisions over a considerable area for a population of 140 000 the question must arise whether the town will not get too big for a sense of community.

A further industrial area is being developed in the north-west and another in the north-east, with a smaller one in the south-east, and one to the north of Laindon Centre adjacent to the Southend Arterial Road (A127).

Building the Town

There was little local opposition (as at Stevenage and Crawley) to the building of the new town of Basildon; instead, as previously indicated, the idea was sponsored and supported by the local authorities in the region. Being designated about 2 years after the first new towns, Basildon was unable to enjoy for the same number of years the benefit of low interest rates of the period following 1945, which enabled the first new towns to carry out large schemes of capital development financed at these low interest rates. Basildon was early caught in the rising tide of interest rates. Also the restrictions on capital expenditure in 1955 came when Basildon was in need of amenities for its growing population. There were other difficulties which served to delay progress, the principal of which has been perhaps the acquisition of land from so many different separate owners of small plots, each with its small house, or shack. This necessitated about 13 000 negotiations up to the end of 1976. For the most part the property was acquired by agreement, but in some cases powers of compulsory purchase had to be exercised, while in a few hundred cases it was not possible to trace the owners, and twenty-eight per cent of the land parcel acquisitions were from unknown owners.

Where compulsory purchase orders were used, it was in the majority of cases to overcome the difficulties of proceeding against unknown owners. It is to the credit of the corporation that under 1% of all land purchases resulted in objections being received to compulsory purchase orders, and only one in four of these objections were maintained to public inquiry. The acquisition of property is regarded as a social problem and not merely an administrative necessity. The development corporation took the wise precaution of acquiring the land well before it would be needed for development, sometimes as long as three years ahead. This was not, of course, possible in the early years. Another cause of delay in the early stages, both in housing and in the development of the industrial areas, was the work necessary to provide adequate sewerage which was begun in 1952 and largely completed by 1955. This was so well advanced by 1954 that progress was made with the eastern industrial area, and housing began on a much bigger scale. The first house had been completed in June 1951, and up to the end of 1952 about 600 had been built. About 860 were completed in 1953, about 880 in 1954 and then from 1955 onwards well over 1000 were built each year, 1480 in 1955, about 1350 in 1956, about the same number in 1957, 1440 in 1958, about 1070 in 1959, 1428 in 1960, 1243 in 1961, 1158 in 1962, 574 in 1963, 1252 in 1964, 1412 in 1965, 1023 in 1966, 1246 in 1967, 913 in 1968, 569 in 1969, 1590 in 1970 and 1274 in 1971. From 1972 there was some reduction in output: 508 in that year, 665 in 1973, 855 in 1974, 1238 in 1975 and 1322 in 1976. Altogether, from designation to the end of 1976, 27 369 houses have been built of which 21 600 were by the development corporation, 3618 by the local authority and 2151 by private enterprise.

Building has proceeded mainly from east to west; first in Fryerns to the north-east, Barstable to the east, and Vange to the south-east, and these were the principal scenes of operation in the early fifties. In 1956 building began in Kingswood immediately south of the town centre, while a start on a smaller scale was made in Lee Chapel South, and in 1958 Ghyllgrove, to the north of the town centre, was begun. By the end of 1967 Fryerns, Barstable, Kingswood, Lee Chapel South, Lee Chapel North, and Ghyllgrove were all completed and by 1974 the neighbourhoods of Pitsea, Vange, Laindon were also largely completed with Chalvedon and Langdon Hills well advanced. In 1956 a start was made on the first phase of the town centre, which was mainly completed by 1971. In 1967 a hospital with 906 beds was begun on a site $\frac{3}{4}$ mile (1 km) south of the town centre. This was sufficiently finished for part occupation by 1973 together with a postgraduate medical centre and staff building. The College of Further Education immediately north of the hospital was completed and opened in 1971.

Housing and Residential Areas

As in other new towns a wide variety of house types has been provided. The majority are 3-bedroom and 2-bedroom, 2-storey houses in terraces, but a small proportion of 4-bedroom houses, 2-bedroom maisonettes and one-bedroom flats and bungalows have been included. The proportion of flats is low. The 2-storey flats and maisonettes have in some cases been built as corner or end houses of terrace blocks, while a tall block of flats has been built in the town centre.

When in 1960 the planned maximum population of the town was increased to 106 000, density of development was increased to 19.5 houses per acre (48 per ha). It was found that with a predominantly 2-storey development with more garaging provision and play area facilities it was difficult to achieve a satisfactory environment with this higher density. Consequently in the new plan opportunity was taken to lower the density to 16 houses per acre (40 per ha) although the maximum population was increased to possibly about 130 000 in the same designated area.

One of the aims in housing is to secure architectural variety. This cannot be done only by differences in layout; it requires also diversity in the design of the houses, especially of their elevations. The type most in demand, which constitutes the majority, is the 2-storey house with garden, and if the monotony is to be avoided it must be handled skilfully and imaginatively. Help is afforded by undulating rather than flat ground. Monotony has not been entirely avoided. It has been aggravated perhaps by the considerable length of some of the terrace blocks, as at Clopton Green. A unit according to its character can be repeated a certain number of times but a limit must be imposed to avoid monotony.

To achieve variety some 3-storey houses and flats have been built, while several different materials have been used in the elevations. One of the really successful rows of 3-storey houses is the curved block of about 20 houses, with a block of flats at either end, in Long Riding in the Barstable neighbourhood. The elevations are made interesting by the projecting balconies on the first floor and the trellis and reeded timber panels of the entrances. The balconies, however, give no privacy, and a design of balcony with a degree of seclusion from neighbours, as is secured in many flat designs, would, we feel, have been an improvement.

Variety has also been obtained by the use of colour and texture in the elevations. A particularly good example is a row of 4 houses in 'Tangham Walk' in the Fryerns neighbourhood. Here the first floor is faced with timber boarding, and on either side of the window on the ground floor are vertical panels of cobblestones, with a plain cement-rendered dado beneath the window. The end and party walls project as brick piers. The whole effect is dependent on the artistic disposition of materials.

Earlier layouts such as those in the Fryerns neighbourhood follow very much the irregular patterns seen in most of the new towns, only here the cul-de-sac is not very much used. There is the irregular-shaped island round which the houses are arranged, and the alignment of the houses often departs from that of the road so that lawns of varied shapes appear between. Sometimes a square, or a parking space, is taken into the island between the houses. The varied spacing between roads and houses and differently shaped lawns is very apparent if one takes a walk along the principal winding road of Fryerns neighbourhood. Here the green spaces sometimes narrow and sometimes broaden out almost to the size of a village green; and in this road one is not disturbed by the monotony of 2-storey dwellings because the land is gently undulating and the course of the road is never flat.

In Basildon there has been a serious attempt to plan for the increasing use of motor vehicles. In the early stages about one garage to 6 houses was provided, but with the more widespread ownership of cars extending to the lower income groups this, in common with the other new towns, proved to be inadequate, and plans for residential areas since 1957 have provided one garage for every two houses. More recently, however, the government have imposed temporary cutbacks on expenditure for garaging or car parking in excess of that likely to be utilized within the early years of a scheme. For dwellings, apart from those for old people, 100% parking spaces will be provided initially but reservations would also be made on the basis of 30% garages and 20% parking spaces. Ultimately, therefore, schemes will have 150% provision, 120% in the form of parking spaces and 30% garages.

More frequent traffic in residential areas has prompted the attempt in Basildon at some degree of segregation of pedestrians and motor vehicles, because, although the motor vehicle brings several benefits to its user, its presence in residential areas is attended with disadvantages. It brings an element of danger to pedestrians, especially children, while it is often noisy. Attempts at segregation have often been made during this century, and probably the best known plan for this so far evolved is that at Radburn(20.2). In some cases the Radburn principles have been adapted for housing schemes in Basildon.

These partial adaptations of the Radburn plan have been made in the areas nearer the centre where the densities have been as high as 14 to 16 to the acre (35 to 40 per ha), whereas at Radburn the densities are not more than 6 to 9 to the acre (15 to 22 per ha). This higher density is clearly the reason for the partial adaptation; for the segregation of pedestrians and motor traffic is nowhere in Basildon so complete as at Radburn, and where it has occurred it has been in comparatively small developments. It is seen in some degree at Barstable, designed by the development corporation's architect Anthony B. Davies, and at Vange, designed by Sir Basil Spence. In the former the cul-de-sac service roads branch into the spaces at the rear of the encircling terrace houses, with lines of garages at the ends of the gardens at an approximate ratio of one garage to 2 houses. In a few places pedestrian ways are between the fronts of the houses, but as often the houses face the roads. In Sir Basil Spence's scheme at Vange the pedestrian areas are more extensive, and in parts there is the impression of houses situated among lawns untroubled by roads and traffic; but even here segregation is only partial. In Ghyllgrove a small-scale segregation has been made, and just south of Fryerns shopping centre is another example with a block of flats bridging the entrance to a courtyard of 2-storey houses called Orsett End.

A further example in which the principle of houses backing on to an area served by a service road is adopted, is that in Kingswood, designed by William Crabtree, but here in only one small section do the houses face a pedestrian way; they mainly face the roads. It is, however, a layout with a good deal of variety, and includes a very pleasant arrangement of semi-detached houses with garages placed diagonally on to the road (Sparrows Herne) forming a series of triangular lawns. Partial as these segregations are compared with that at Radburn they must be welcomed as a move in the right direction, for they achieve some degree of seclusion from the motor vehicle.

The housing density of Radburn is only about half that at Basildon, a factor which contributes much to the agreeable character of the former. At Radburn the backs of the houses face on the service lanes, so that cars can be driven directly into the garage built into the house; and the gardens are in front of the houses; whereas in the earlier schemes of this kind at Basildon the backs of the houses are separated from the service lane and garages by the length of the gardens. The Basildon arrangement is not really so convenient either for the occupants or deliverers of goods.

At Laindon East neighbourhood, built later, there is a more complete and comprehensive separation of pedestrian and vehicular traffic ways. Footpaths traverse the whole neighbourhood and interspersed among the houses are lawns and broad paved areas.

Following one footpath in an easterly direction one comes on an extensive lawn sprinkled with trees and containing in one part the various odd objects of a children's playground. Some of the houses front on to this open space, others have their small walled or white-fenced gardens adjoining it. Continuing along the path which is for

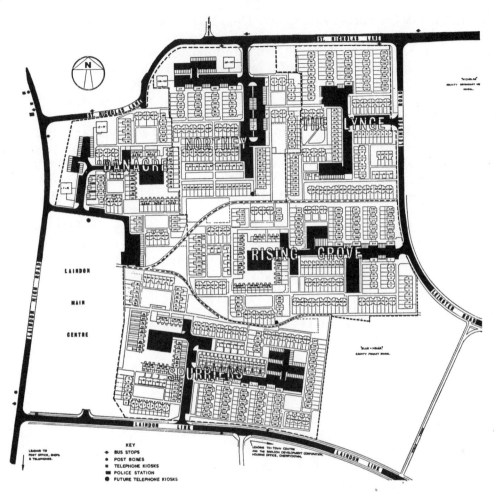

Figure 20.3 Laindon neighbourhood. Plan of housing layout.

part of the way enclosed on both sides by houses, it again opens to a broad paved area at the end of which is an attractively built school. The houses are flat roofed 2-storey structures built mainly on the Siporex gas concrete system employed partly for speed although the corporation expressed disappointment in 1966 at the rate of progress.

Another interesting development in Laindon East, near the west centre, is a 2-level segregation with pedestrian level above. The plan is mainly in squares of terrace houses open at the corners and facing on to an extensive balcony, which surrounds the lower level, the centre of which is used as a car park, the connecting road coming in at one of the corners of the square. The ground level of the houses forms the garage, then above the upper pedestrian level are the 2-storey houses surmounted by flats with balcony access. It is an ingenious scheme and the houses, with light and dark square patterning, like geometric abstract paintings, are architecturally effective, but to make a car park a central feature for a residential square is surely a regrettable arrangement. A central fountain in a garden with a few suitable trees and shrubs and ramps or steps to descend to it would have made a more attractive scheme, and a better environment for living. The car parking should be far less obtrusive and tucked more completely under the balconies. To do this may have meant more space and lower densities, but that would have been an improvement. The densities in both schemes mentioned are too high (about 18 to the acre [45 per ha] in Laindon East). More spacious disposition of the houses with larger gardens would have been better.

Other recent developments at Vange are chiefly notable for the variation in house designs, all mainly flat-roofed. A few terrace blocks of 2-storey houses have well designed canopies on slender supports with translucent roofs as car ports, a more economical provision than garages. It is an ingenious attempt to make the car port attached to the house architecturally pleasant. In this neighbourhood are some good compact designs of 2-storey terrace houses by William Crabtree and W. T. Jarosz where the garage is an integral part on the ground floor with balcony above, while an excellent effect is achieved with the warm brown rendering of the walls, the black painted timber panels and white window frames.

Residential areas built later with interesting layouts and house designs are those at Laindon and Langdon Hills. The former built in the late sixties and designed by Clive Plumb and his team at the development corporation consists largely of a series of square paved pedestrian courtyards linked by ways that are roofed by the first floors of houses which enhances the effect of seclusion and intimacy (see illustration). There is a rear vehicle access to the houses.

The development at Langdon Hills was in the early seventies and also designed by

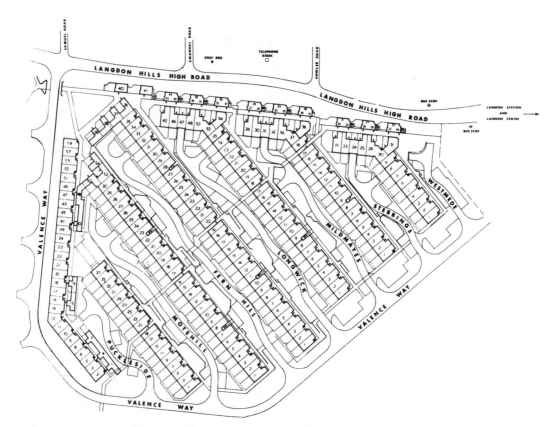

Figure 20.4 Langdon Hills Housing Area I plan.

Figure 20.5 Langdon Hills Housing Area I.

Clive Plumb and his team. The site is 33 acres (13.37 ha) on which 556 houses are provided thus a fairly high density of about 17 houses to the acre (42 per ha). This is an ingeniously designed scheme with good pedestrian and vehicular segregation. The site is situated east of the High Road which has near and parallel with it a double row of terrace houses with a straight elevated footpath between them. The houses intermittently arch the footpath. Running diagonally north-east are six rows of various lengths of wedge-shaped terrace houses with the first storey side containing the kitchen facing a footpath on the north-west side, and the 2-storey side with living-room on the first floor and bedrooms below facing south-east and the garden. Between the rows of houses are slightly winding service roads, fingers from the site circumference road, and these continue under the High Road houses to garages and car parks. Also under these houses are service ducts including provision for district heating. The footpaths provide direct pedestrian links with the neighbourhood shops and primary schools. This is an admirable and well thought out housing scheme.

District and Neighbourhood Centres

In the original plan of Basildon, to which it was being built from 1951 to 1967, the neighbourhoods were large, many with populations of 10 000 or more, with fairly big centres with 1 or 2 sub-centres. That at Fryerns is of a good size while there is a sub-centre towards the north-east of the neighbourhood. Barstable has a centre to the east of the neighbourhood, with a sub-centre between it and the town centre, while Kingswood has a somewhat smaller one as it is not far from the town centre. Many of these neighbourhood centres have, in addition to shops either in a row or on two sides of a rectangle, a public house, church, and community centre, while a school either primary or secondary is nearby. One of the largest and most attractive is that at Fryerns which has some 18 shops the majority arranged on two sides of a square with a canopy linking the shops and giving protection from rain. The building on the east side is of 2 storeys, and that on the north side of 5 storeys, with balconied flats above the shops. The architectural composition of one low and one tall block is very successful. It is perhaps unfortunate that the public house and garage, which also forms part of this centre, are sited on the other—south—side of Whitmore Way, which is the main neighbourhood road.

The shops at both the Barstable and Kingswood centres are arranged in a row, the former one of 16, elevated a little from the level of the road, and approached from the lower footway by steps and ramps. This upper footway is walled round, and is sheltered by a long canopy supported by slender columns. The walling changes at intervals from brick to slender iron railings, which also border the steps and ramps, giving a pleasing light effect. Above the shops 2 abutting blocks for dwellings rise to 3 and 4 storeys, and again the architectural ensemble is effective. The 9 shops at the Kingswood centre are similarly canopied with one floor above, while at one end is a community hall lifted to the first floor on columns, and a covered space in front of the shops is thus formed.

The Lee Chapel North Centre completed at the end of 1965 is segregated from the road, with a row of shops set transversely to it and facing a pedestrian paved area and car park, while adjacent is a community building. To the rear of the shops and community hall are some one-storey houses for old people, while trees and shrubs are introduced as a contrast to the paving—altogether a pleasant and peaceful precinct.

With the revised plan of 1967 increasing the maximum population to 140 000, two district or overspill centres in the east and west, as previously mentioned, are provided. These are intermediate in size between the neighbourhood centre and the town centre. That in the west between Laindon West and East was mainly completed in 1971. It is notable as being a 2-level centre with the pedestrian area and shops above and a roadway with service access to shops below. In the principal shopping way are a series of massive concrete free standing ventilating shafts along the centre. They are ugly and give a starkness to this shopping precinct. To the question why could there not be tubs of flowers, or birdcages or sculpture along the centre as in the delightful Lijnbaan in Rotterdam, apprehensiveness of vandalism appeared to be the answer. This raises the further question of whether this apprehension should deter authorities from doing what is good. It is, after all, regrettable defeatism.

The other district centre in the east at Pitsea was completed by 1977. Among the provisions in this centre is an open market, significant in view of contemporary discussions on whether these are anachronisms. There are, of course, arguments on both sides. The building of a department store of about 130 000 sq. feet (11 700 m²) floor area was commenced early in 1977 on a 10 acre (4 ha) site within the district centre.

Town Centre

Situated almost exactly in the middle of the town immediately north of the railway, the town centre is, like that at Stevenage, distinguished by the arrangement of a considerable part as a pedestrian precinct. There is a large pedestrian square about 620 feet (189 m) long by about 130 feet (39 m) wide, approached by footways. Surrounding this are shops with offices over, while at the east end a tall block of flats provides a vertical mass. At the east end is a smaller square on a lower level, approached by a ramp and steps. This block of flats is partly supported on diagonal stilts and nearby is a pool and a fountain with bronze sculpture by Maurice Lambert of a mother playing with her child. This arrangement of sculpture, pool, stilts and descending ramp to the lower square, where the enclosing buildings are so well in scale, is one of the most dramatic architectural compositions that has appeared in Britain in the sixties. To the south-east another small square, reached by a short pedestrian way, is flanked on the east side by a 4-storey departmental store.

The central area is encircled by a road, and within this road and branching off from it and situated behind the buildings that face the town square and the pedestrian ways are a series of car parks and service ways to the shops. It is thus similar in principle to some of the rear-access ways in the housing areas, with houses facing pedestrian ways.

East Walk is a long wide pedestrian shopping way running east from the main town square. The shops have canopies on one side formed by a cantilevered projection, the storey above being in line with the shop façade; while on the other side is an entirely different treatment with the projecting floor above forming the canopy with bays divided by tapering concrete fins. There does not seem to be schematic connection between the two sides and there is thus a lack of architectural cohesion.

Within the northern boundary of the encircling road, Broadmayne, is a group of

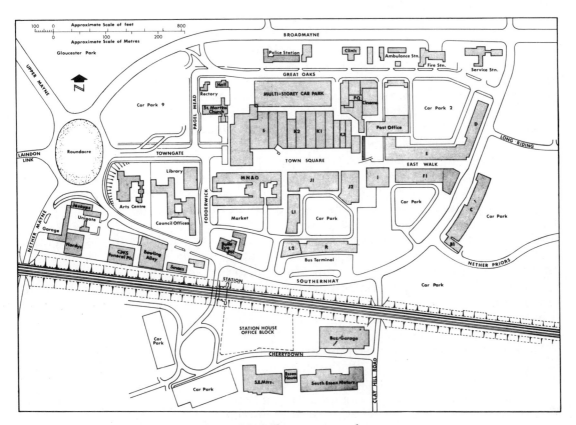

Figure 20.6 Town centre plan.

county buildings—fire station, ambulance station, health clinic and police station with a site for a courthouse; while in the south-west is both an open market and a site for a market hall. In the centre on the south side is a bus station, almost opposite the new railway station opened in November 1974, for which the town had to wait 20 years, although public opinion strongly pressed for it. To the west is the town church, and on the south-west island temporary civic buildings and an arts centre have been built here by the district council. These will be replaced by permanent buildings designed in 1975 for a site to the north. A plot in the south-west adjoining the railway is used for service industry. A multi-storey car park for 1100 cars was built behind the shops on the north side of the town square in 1971–72. Later 2-level development with entertainment buildings and a public house was introduced on the north side of the town square with escalator approach.

By 1977 this centre was about two-thirds built. When it is completed it promises to be one of the finest of all the town centres. The handsome main square, with its fine spatial composition and the discreet use of furniture, and the two smaller subordinate squares make a notable example of urban planning. Construction is due to commence in 1978 on a proposed 520,000 square ft (46 800 m^2) expansion programme incorporating additional shops and offices.

Industrial Areas

In the first outline plan described there are 2 industrial areas on the north side of the town, and separated by about a mile. The eastern of these, the Cranes industrial estate, was almost fully developed by the end of 1974, 90 factories having been built, representing a diversity of industries. Among the larger factories which align the London–Southend arterial road, are Ilford Ltd, Ford Motor Co. Ltd, Teleflex Products Ltd, Carreras Ltd, and Marconi's Wireless and Telegraph Co. Ltd occupying a large corner site. Other large factories on the south side of the site are York Shipley Ltd, and Carsons Ltd. On the east side of the southern half of Honywood Road is a group of medium-sized factories, many of which are for light engineering; while on the west side is a group of nursery factories formally sited round a broad court or cul-de-sac called Bowlers Croft. North of this is a small commercial centre which includes 7 shops, garages, public house, canteen, 2 banks and a petrol-filling station: this is a valuable amenity for those working on the estate.

Although in this industrial estate there may not be any outstanding examples of industrial architecture the buildings generally reach a good standard. Some of the office blocks, chiefly 2-storey, in front of the factories facing the London–Southend road have a handsome appearance enhanced by the spacious layout in front, but more integration between these facing blocks and the factories behind would have contributed to the general architectural ensemble. Perhaps the chief visual impression is of a rather formal and spacious grouping of buildings.

The Pipps Hill industrial area immediately north of the town centre and town park began to be laid out much later. By the end of 1960 the roads and sewers had been laid, and by the end of 1976, 58 factories were completed including 24 nursery units.

A little later large factories were built for the Standard Telephone Co. Ltd, and for Yardley & Co. Ltd, both excellent modern examples of industrial architecture. In the former, pyramidal skylights are used with good external effect, while in the Yardley

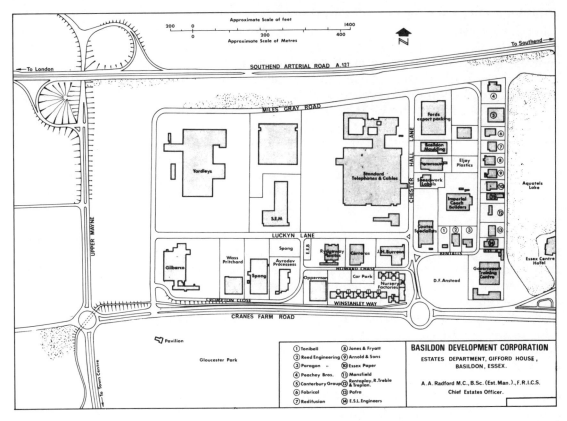

Figure 20.7 Plan of Pipps Hill Industrial Estate.

factory a large block has a façade of narrow concrete verticles with window slits between, and the general effect from a little distance is distinctive.

A third industrial zone between these two is a 100 acre (41 ha) site occupied by the Ford Motor Company Ltd, which was completed in 1964. The whole of the tractor producing plant which formerly operated at Dagenham, with 3500 employees, has moved into this factory. A fourth industrial area, Burnt Mills to the north-east, is in course of development primarily for the accommodation of untidy industries, relocation cases, hauliers and contractors' depots. At the end of 1976, 50 factories were occupied.

Social Aspect

In the early days of Basildon there was, as in many other new towns, a serious lack of premises for social activities. In 1953–54 2 small, temporary community halls were built, but that was all Basildon had for a population of about 30 000. The development corporation deplored the circumstances in its 1954 report. It was viewed as a matter of concern 'that in the five years of its existence it has not been able to secure more public meeting space for community centres than two halls, each of about 1000 sq.feet (90 m²). In fact, there is no building at all in the designated area (except schools) of 5000 sq. feet, (450 m²), which is the minimum required for such social purposes as dances and other entertainments. The need for community halls is perhaps greater in Basildon than in other new towns, for the designated area contained an existing population, proportionate to the area, larger than that of any other. The demand for communal centres for recreation has therefore been insistent from the beginning.

Progress in the provision of community halls continued to be slow. A third temporary structure, the Vange Community Hall, was built in 1955, and the circumstance that these first three halls were built largely by voluntary labour was testimony that they were very much wanted. Over 160 clubs and societies of all kinds were active, and it was obvious that the provision of premises was a matter of some urgency. The schools helped a little, but these were no substitute for an adequately sized fully equipped community centre. As the corporation remarked in its 1957 report, virile organizations were 'making do' with unsatisfactory accommodation. It is incidentally evidence of some success in the social life of Basildon that it contained these virile social organizations.

In 1956 a permanent community centre was planned for Fryerns, the largest and first to be built of the neighbourhoods, but work did not begin until late in 1958, and it was completed only in 1960. A community centre in Laindon was opened early in 1959, a small community hall in the Kingswood neighbourhood centre was opened at about the same time, while work on another such hall in the Lee Chapel South neighbourhood centre was started early in 1961. In 1964 a community centre was completed at Lee Chapel North which proved to be a great asset for the social activities of the neighbourhood. In other districts, Ghyllgrove and Barstable, there are also tenants' meeting rooms which serve similar purposes, but not so comprehensively. A large hall in the town centre has been adapted by Tiffany's as a dance hall. Later a major community centre was provided in Blue House farm in the Laindon neighbourhood centre for 1000 persons, and is now making a valuable contribution to the social life of the town. A bowling alley was provided at the town centre which was useful while enthusiasm for the game lasted, but has since presented the problem of conversion to other uses, and is now used partly for bingo.

Where there is so wide a gap between supply and demand discontent is bound to arise. There was overwhelming evidence of a desire for social facilities in the voluntary labour devoted to building temporary premises, and the existence of so many active clubs and societies. In commenting on the provision of community centres in its 1966 report the corporation says 'the pressure for use of these buildings is very great indeed, and comes from every generation. The cost of providing and maintaining the buildings is a small price to pay for the social benefits derived.'

Still, by 1968 some progress had been made in providing sports' and cultural facilities. In the Spring of that year swimming pools were completed for the Basildon UDC in Gloucester Park; a large pool, a small teaching pool, accommodation for spectators and a café, at a cost of about £435 000. A further swimming pool was provided at the Pitsea district centre in 1976.

In 1955 the Basildon Civic Arts Society was formed, sponsored by the development corporation and the district council. This has held successful festivals of the arts, which have given scope and stimulus to many of the societies of the town, but it has long been felt that the accommodation for the pursuit of the arts has been inadequate. The district council realize that a town of the size that Basildon will ultimately become will need an adequate permanent building for an arts centre, yet in view of its other commitments it is unlikely that this could be provided for some years to come. To meet the more urgent needs, a temporary building was completed in September 1968 in the town centre at a cost of about £82 000. It consists of a multi-purpose hall to seat 500, with a stage and apron, 6 studios for the practice of the visual arts, lounge, restaurant and committee rooms. The hall, however, is wholly inadequate for a town of 100 000 with an equal number at least in surrounding districts which look to Basildon as a central place. The seating and furnishing of the theatre has, however, greatly improved since it was first opened and by 1976 it had an attractive interior. When a permanent arts centre is built it is hoped that it will include a good sized theatre/concert hall and an exhibition gallery.

In 1971 a twin cinema was opened in the town centre in premises above a supermarket and public house which met a long felt need.

North of the town between the Pipps Hill industrial area and the Ford tractor plant is the Aquatels Family Recreation Centre occupying a 104 acre (42 ha) site. This is a venture by private enterprise which was partly completed for use in 1972 and wholly completed in 1974. It provides facilities for a variety of outdoor and indoor sport and includes a fishing and boating lake, tennis courts, indoor swimming pool, squash courts, an ecology centre, hotel, restaurant and bars.

In the south-west of the town an equestrian centre was opened in 1974. This has one of the largest indoor riding schools in the country. It will be seen, therefore, that there is a generous provision for sporting interests in Basildon.

References and Notes

20.1   Sir Patrick Abercrombie in writing of outdoor recreation in Chapter 7 of *Greater London Plan*, 1944 says, 'It is possible to point with horror to the jumble of shacks and bungalows on the Langdon Hills and Pitsea. This is a narrow-minded appreciation of what was as genuine a desire as created the group of lovely gardens and houses at Frensham and Bramshott.'

20.2   An account of the Radburn plan is given in Clarence Stein's *Towards New Towns for America*, Liverpool 1951 and Cambridge, Mass. 1966.

21 *Bracknell*

Among the 10 sites for new towns suggested by Abercrombie in the Greater London Plan was White Waltham about 3 miles (5 km) south-west of Maidenhead, on the main-line railway from Paddington to Reading. Abercrombie suggested that 'it would form a good centre for decanted population from the overcrowded areas of West London, such as Acton and Southall'.

The Minister of Town and Country Planning agreed that there should be a new town west of London for this dispersal, but a site was chosen about 5 miles (8 km) south of White Waltham, at Bracknell on either side of the railway line from Waterloo to Reading. The reasons given in the explanatory memorandum on the draft designation order of 1948 for not adopting the site suggested by Abercrombie were that it 'consisted of high quality agricultural land, and partly because it would have interfered with the full use of the White Waltham airfield'.

In the draft designation order an area of 2623 acres (1062 ha) was proposed for a town with a maximum population of 25 000, but as the result of objections at the public inquiry 763 acres (309 ha) of agricultural land were deducted, and it was therefore decided to build a town of the same population on the reduced area of 1860 acres (753 ha), which was designated on 17 June 1949. The report of the development corporation for 1951 stated that the Minister might need to ask for some of the excluded land to be reinstated in the designated area. Uncertainty attended this for a few years. A more detailed examination of the site by the development corporation confirmed that more land would be required for the industrial areas, to the extent of 140 acres (57 ha). This, however, was not agreed to by the Minister, though a draft designation order for an additional 59 acres (24 ha) of Farley Copse was made on 20 June 1952, and was the subject of a public inquiry in August and December of that year. As this was not confirmed, the development corporation had the task of satisfying industrial requirements within the originally designated area.

In September 1961 it was decided to increase the maximum population of Bracknell from 25 000 to 60 000 and extend the area by some 1230 acres (498 ha) on the western and southern sides. Some sacrifice, of about 150 acres (61 ha), from the south-western salient was agreed after the inquiry because of its value as agricultural land, thus making the addition 1080 acres (437 ha). In October 1962 a further 346 acres (140 ha) were added to the area, bringing the total to 3286 acres (1331 ha).

The site is about 30 miles (48 km) west of London and 10 miles (16 km) east of Reading. The small rural town of Bracknell, lying roughly in the centre of the designated area, had a population in 1949 of between 5 and 6 thousand. It is a very pleasant undulating wooded region between 200 and 300 feet (60 and 90 m) above sea level, sloping gently from the south-east to the north-west. The east–west A329 Woking-ham road passed through its centre, and the railway from London, already mentioned, runs about ½ mile (0.8 km) to the south of the road.

Outline Plan

Preparation of the master plan was subjected to many delays, the principal of which was the procrastination in determining the size of the designated area. However, the plan was finally lodged with the Ministry of Housing in September 1954.

The town in this plan has 4 neighbourhoods: Priestwood in the north-west with a population of 8500(21.1), Bullbrook in the north-east, 6800, both north of the railway, Easthampstead in the south-west, 6100, and Harmans Water, 5100, both south of the railway. A large part of Harmans Water is occupied by the Ramslade RAF Staff College with extensive grounds. In addition there is a small district north of the centre called Wick Hill in which there are houses of a larger type, and it is proposed in the plan to continue the development here on similar lines.

Each neighbourhood has a shopping centre, and Priestwood, Bullbrook and East-hampstead also have sub-centres. Each has a new primary school. There are 2 campus sites for secondary schools, one in the north and one in the south part of the town and a small C of E Grammar school.

There are 2 industrial areas, the larger in the west between the railway to the south and Priestwood to the north, and the eastern area in the south-west part of Bullbrook. There is a generous provision of open space for playing fields, and in the east in Bullbrook is Lily Hill a considerable area of parkland which is to become a public park. The town is surrounded by farms and undulating woodland country which makes the green belt particularly pleasant.

When the extension was made in October 1962 of 1426 acres (578 ha) to the west and south a new master plan was prepared by May 1964 for this additional area. Five new neighbourhoods were added: Wildridings for an ultimate population of 4850; Great Hollands, 7630; Hanworth, 7630; Birch Hill, 7640; and Crown Wood, 5850, each with its neighbourhood centre. With a population of 1000 in the town centre, the total includ-ing the 4 neighbourhoods already built was estimated at 60 000 which was expected to be reached by 1978.

An extension of the industrial area is planned south of the railway about the same size as the existing area. The segregation of pedestrians and vehicles, in line with modern planning practice, is worked out in an original manner exemplified in detail in the plan for Wildridings the first to be built. Each neighbourhood, with its centre, is surrounded by a distributor boundary road which sends in branches to the neighbour-hood with sub-branches round which are grouped rows of garages conveniently related to the houses. Within each neighbourhood is a main spine footpath between the periphery roads, with branch footpaths among the houses. The same pattern is repeated on a smaller scale with the branch footpaths and sub-branches, sometimes opening to squares and courts, situated centrally between the branch roads. This ingenious planning can be seen in the illustration which shows groups of houses round the Wildridings centre. The main spine footpath is continuous throughout the neighbourhoods passing under the peripheral and main roads, while it connects with the shopping centres, primary schools, social buildings and junior playing fields. It

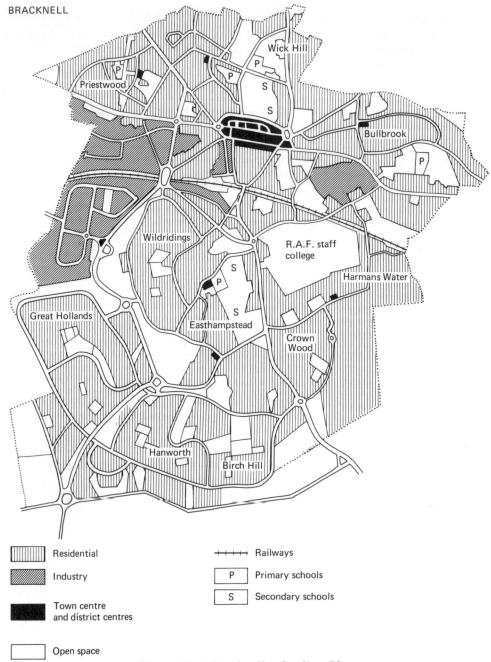

BRACKNELL

Figure 21.1 Bracknell—Outline Plan.

will be possible to walk on the spine footpath from one end of the extension area to the other.

As in the case of Stevenage and Harlow the development corporation was asked in April 1973 to examine the feasibility of a further expansion of Bracknell, to provide 1000 acres (405 ha) of land for houses for sale and some additional land for houses to rent. Sir

Hugh Wilson and Lewis Womersley were commissioned in the following June to investigate the feasibility of so large an expansion. It was calculated that the additional land required to meet the stated requirement, and to include provision for schools, amenities and open spaces would be about 2500 acres (1012 ha).

This proposed expansion prompted an exercise in public participation by the development corporation. Questionnaires were posted to the 45 000 electors of the town and surrounding districts, with a parallel sample survey. The individual response of 18.45% and the sample response of 56.06 showed that 60% of those who had replied were against further expansion. (Annual Report to 31 March 1974.) A large variety of suggestions and comments were received especially on what it was considered the town should provide and these were studied both by the development corporation and consultants. In January 1974 the Secretary of State for the Environment decided not to proceed with this major expansion and requested the development corporation to prepare a scheme for expansion on a smaller scale to meet local needs. The work of the consultants was therefore adjusted accordingly and an interim report entitled *Progress Report on Local Needs* was published in July 1974. This was largely a survey of existing conditions and of the potentials for expansion.

The development corporation was requested in February 1975 to proceed with the study for a limited expansion of Bracknell to accommodate a population of between 69 000 and 77 500 plus natural increase. The final report of the consultants in September 1975 confirmed that the town should be expanded but in April 1977 the Secretary of State decided against any expansion.

Building the Town

Very slow progress was made with building in the first few years, and up to the end of 1953, about 4½ years after the new town was designated, only about 300 houses had been built. From 1954 progress was much more rapid, and a rate of over 500 houses a year was thereafter secured: a little over 500 in 1954 and 1955; about 650 in 1956 and 1957; a few over 800 in 1958; and about 730 in 1959 which is exceedingly good progress. There was, however, a decline in output in 1960 to about 350, while that in 1961 was about 520, then 227 in 1962, 497 in 1963 and 563 in 1964. By that year the original target population of 25 000 had been reached and altogether a total of 6150 houses had been provided of which 5706 were built by the development corporation and the few others by the local authority and private builders. After 1964 house building was mainly in the extension area, but its designation came too late for the previous output to be maintained. Only a comparatively few houses were built in 1965 and 1966 but by 1967 output was on a bigger scale, when 735 were completed, and by the end of that year a substantial proportion of the houses of the first neighbourhood of Wildridings was built. Then in 1968 output reached its highest level for Bracknell with 1226 houses built. A fairly high level continued of 434 in 1969, 805 in 1970, 775 in 1971, 530 in 1972, 671 in 1973, 501 in 1974, 602 in 1975 and 1012 in 1976. By the end of that year 13 457 houses had been built since designation, of which 10 943 were built by the development corporation, 391 by the local authority and 2123 by private enterprise.

The reasons for the early delays were the subject of comment by the development corporation in its annual report of 1953. After mentioning that in the absence of a master plan a 3-year programme prepared by the officers was approved in November 1952, the report says that 'there were three limitations to the speed of development.

Firstly, after the completion of the building in the Priestwood area, it would be impossible, due to overloading, to connect any houses to the sewerage system until the new sewage treatment works were constructed' which would not be before November 1954; 'thus the planned rate of house-building had to be reduced'. The second reason was that the development of the industrial zone was dependent on the decision whether Farley Copse Farm should be included in the designated area, because if it were not, the zone would have to be replanned. A third reason was concerned with the town centre, and the decision whether the centre should be north or south of the High Street.

The first work in all the new towns is the site preparation, levelling, building of roads and trenching for services. In Bracknell work began in the Priestwood neighbourhood, and later, while the first houses were being built there, engineering works started in the other neighbourhoods of Easthampstead and Bullbrook. Priestwood was completed by the end of 1958, and by the end of 1959 considerable progress had been made with Easthampstead when it was more than three parts finished, while Bullbrook was a little over half built. A start was made in 1959 with Harmans Water, the last neighbourhood of the originally planned town, and by 1964 this was mainly completed. The building of factories in the industrial areas had kept a little in front of the housing, as it should do, while by the end of 1959 about half the shops' section of the town centre, in accordance with the original plan, had been completed. Since then, however, because of the increased population and because of the changing conceptions of shopping areas, the centre has been extended and replanned as a pedestrian precinct.

Of the five new neighbourhoods included in the extension plan of 1964, Wildridings to the south was largely completed in 1968. By 1973 Great Hollands in the south-west was substantially complete. By 1976 the neighbourhood centre of Hanworth to the south was built and the rest of the neighbourhood was about half-way towards completion. In April 1974 a start was made on the first housing contract in Birch Hill, also in the south. In 1975 site works for the development of Crown Wood in the south-east were begun, there having been some delay because of consultations with residents in the adjacent Harmans Water neighbourhood.

Housing and Residential Areas

Housing in Bracknell was originally divided into three categories plus flats. The majority, called 'standard one' and representing about 69% of the total, are houses with floor areas complying with Parker Morris requirements built at a density of about 13 to the acre (32 per ha). They are let on weekly tenancies, and are built mostly in terraces. 'Standard two' houses, representing about $13\frac{1}{2}\%$, are slightly larger, between 1200 and 1300 sq. feet (110 to 120 m²), are mainly semi-detached units, each with a garage, and are built at about 7 to the acre (17 per ha). These are let on monthly tenancies. The third standard, representing about 2%, are detached houses at about 4 to the acre (10 per ha) for the managerial classes. These and some standard two houses were built for direct sale. Flats are built within both standard one and two categories and represent some 15% of the total provision.

The houses built according to standards two and three were not mixed throughout the town with the smaller houses of the first group but were mainly segregated in various districts. The standard three types were concentrated in Wick Hill and to the east of Bullbrook. During the 1970s private developers built houses for sale throughout the town.

All the earlier house building was of the first two standard types, and began in Priestwood. The first houses were a group of 72 with 19 garages designed by Louis de Soissons and Partners similar to those built at Welwyn Garden City, and these were erected in the central part of the neighbourhood. The first house was occupied in August 1951. Priestwood was continued from this central area firstly to the west, then to the east to the designs of the corporation architects. For the most part the housing is simple and pleasing, predominantly of brick, and some variety is obtained by colour washing. Occasionally there is a variation in the facing material, as in the long terrace block facing south on Priestwood Avenue where the upper storey for part of its length is faced with timber boarding. The initial slightly monotonous effect of some of the housing is less apparent now that the planted trees have grown sufficiently to introduce a further note of variety.

A greater degree of variety is found in the southern neighbourhood of Easthampstead which won a Civic Trust award in 1959. Here there are several pleasant groups of houses. Among them are the semi-detached houses arranged on three sides of a square on the opposite side of the green in front of the neighbourhood shopping centre. A little north of the centre is a delightful and excellently proportioned curved terrace block of 11 3-storey houses with curved bay windows on the first floor, somewhat reminiscent of Georgian terraces. The effect is enhanced by the generous lawn in front.

The layout of the residential areas is similar to that found in many of the other new towns. The roads are mostly curved and form islands, and the houses face outwards on to these roads. Culs-de-sac run into these islands in a variety of ways. Sometimes a road stops and is continued by a footpath, two examples being Spencer Road and Fane's Close just north of the Wokingham Road in the Priestwood neighbourhood. Although the houses for the most part face outwards on to the roads they are not aligned in the conventional parallel fashion; instead there is a varying width of green between the houses and roads, while many of the shorter blocks are arranged in echelon fashion. There is also a very generous sprinkling of trees in Priestwood, and a plan of part of this neighbourhood was reproduced in the Ministry of Housing and Local Government's book on *Trees in Town and City* as an example of tree preservation and planting.

A good example of varied and effective cul-de-sac treatment is provided in the centre of Easthampstead neighbourhood. In one layout the terminations of two culs-de-sac—Clive Green and Herbert Close—are linked by pedestrian ways and a broad rectangular green, and in others the pedestrian ways link with the culs-de-sac to give access to other roads. The houses in this area are in varying lengths of terrace blocks mainly from 3 to 6 houses with a few semi-detached types. When the terrace blocks are longer than 6 houses the alignment is usually broken by a set-back to avoid the monotony that otherwise might result.

Harmans Water was the last of the original neighbourhoods to be completed and in many ways it is the most delightful. Much of it gives the feeling of an estate in a wood, with trees removed only to make sufficient room for the houses, paths and roads. The irregular grouping round the neighbourhood centre is particularly pleasing. In one part the 2-storey terraced housing surrounds extensive lawns in which there is a sprinkling of tall firs mingled with a few silver birches, while there are glimpses

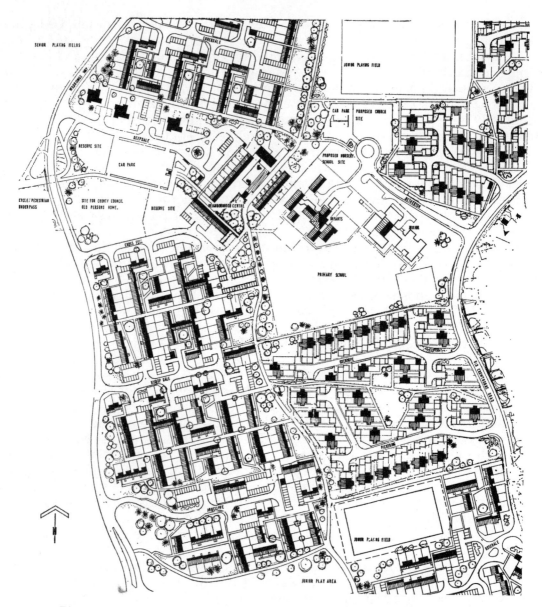

Figure 21.2 Plan of Wildridings, the first neighbourhood of the town extension (1967–69).

beyond of a background of more trees. One is a little reminded of Tapiola—that beautiful satellite of Helsinki in a pine forest near the sea. Another grouping of houses is round a paved square with flower beds, at the end of a cul-de-sac road. Across the road from the neighbourhood centre is a 2-storey car park set amongst tall trees, and surrounded by some 3-storey dwellings. Its unobtrusive presence provides a good example of siting.

Some indication has already been given of the layout of Wildridings, the first neighbourhood to be built in the 1964 plan extension. This layout has a central spine

Figure 21.3 Harmans Water near the neighbourhood centre. 2-storey garage surrounded by tall conifers, and 3-storey blocks of flats.

footpath with branches in each direction among the houses, and between these branches are cul-de-sac roads running from the road encircling the neighbourhood. The same principle of planning of a central spine footpath with branches among the houses, and the periphery road from which culs-de-sac branch inward between the footpaths and to serve the houses is followed in Great Hollands and Hanworth. One notable feature of parts of Great Hollands is the arrangement of houses round small squares which have a secluded intimate character so suitable for a residential atmosphere.

Hanworth, like Harmans Water, is built on a site where there was a profusion of tall conifers, and as many of these as possible have been preserved among the houses. The foliage of these tall trees is generally above the roofs and does not therefore obscure the houses which are seen in the distance behind the pattern of tree trunks, an attractive effect characteristic of many residential districts in Bracknell.

Neighbourhood Centres

Priestwood Square, the first neighbourhood centre to be completed, is an excellent shopping precinct. It lies to the east of Windlesham Road and consists of 10 shops on three sides of a pedestrian area, partly open on the east side. The shops on the north and south sides are 3-storey structures with flats over. Several trees that have been preserved greatly add to its attractiveness. A church forms part of the centre and nearby an existing large house has been converted into a hotel, 'The Admiral Cunningham'. The small sub-centre of Priestwood at the corner of Shepherds Lane and Horsneile Lane includes a Methodist Church and 'The Prince of Wales' public house.

The neighbourhood centre of Easthampstead, set well back from the road, consists of 14 shops and a library arranged in an L-shape in 3-storey buildings with flats.

The last neighbourhood centre of the originally planned town is that of Harmans Water which consists of a 4-storey block of maisonettes over a row of 9 shops with covered way. The block being set well back from the road allows a generous parking area in front. At one end is a group of trees, and a public library and a church, and at the other a community building over a further 4 shops with a first floor supported on columns and projecting well out towards the road. On the further side of this building is an attractively designed public house called 'The Newtown Pippin' the exterior of which forms an excellent pattern of plain brick walls, weather-boarding painted white and large windows.

The community building provides facilities for the meetings of various local societies and includes a separate youth club room. The provision of a shopping centre and social facilities at a fairly early stage was important in the case of Harmans Water as there was nothing of the kind existing in the area or nearby as there was in the other neighbourhoods. The provision of centres at a similarly early stage was also necessary in the neighbourhoods of the extension area. The first of these, Wildridings, was built in 1967–70. The site is hilly. The main square along two sides of which the shops are built has been suitably levelled. The spine footpath along the east side of the square rises at the south end well above the shops, and on this higher ground to the east of the footpath are infant and junior schools. Access roads on either side of the centre are on different levels, the variation of which gives the whole composition a scenic interest.

Great Hollands is the largest of the neighbourhood centres so far provided. It is a pedestrian precinct with road access both to the north and south with appropriate car parks. A pedestrian shopping way runs into a square where there is an unusual but attractive barn-like public house called 'William Twigg'. On the east side of this square is a community centre and library, and integrated with the centre is the Primary School. A health centre was opened there in 1976.

A little way to the north is an old people's home consisting of 41 flatlets. It is a long 2-storey building of distinctive design in which large windows and soft, grey roofs and brick walls are all well proportioned and related. This distinctive design is by Clayton and Ellis, architects in Brighton.

The Town Centre

The town centre of Bracknell was originally planned not only for a town of 25 000 population but as a centre and market for about another 15 000 living in the surrounding agricultural districts. It was partially an extension northwards of the shopping centre of old Bracknell with its 63 shops on either side of the High Street. The area was terminated east and west by roundabouts, while facing the northern boundary is a by-pass road. Provision was made for about double the number of shops that existed in the old town.

As the centre existed at the beginning of 1969 a spine road called Broadway ran east–west parallel with the High Street and linking the two roundabouts. Shops with offices above face the central section of Broadway and a pedestrian way similarly faced with shops and offices linked Broadway with the High Street. At the rear of the shops on the north side of Broadway was a service road. At the eastern end on the north side there was to be a paved square surrounded by local government offices, a central library and a civic hall, and south of this was a police station, magistrates' court and central post office, while in the south-east was a college for further education. To the

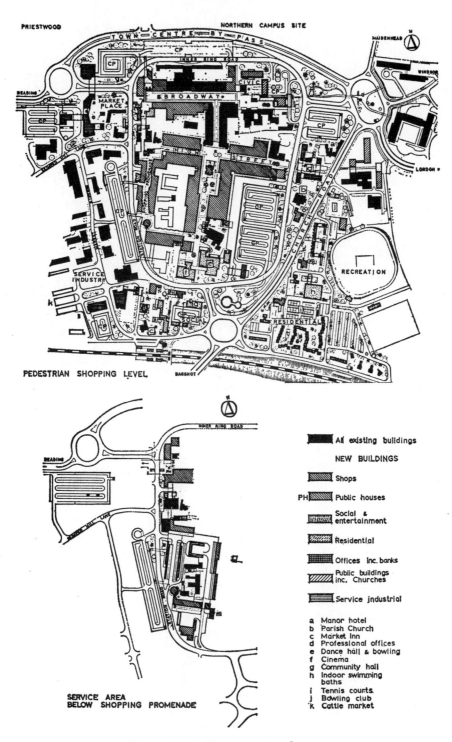

Figure 21.4 Town centre plan.

Figure 21.5 A view of Charles Square showing, left, the Honeywell building and, beneath it, the mural depicting scenes from the history of Bracknell, by William Mitchell. On the right is an earlier Honeywell building.

west on the south side was an open market. To the south-west was an area for service industry, and a new cattle market which replaced the old one.

This plan could not be regarded as good and fortunately it has been entirely superseded by one published in 1963. In the first plan a new spine road is taken through the centre, and there is nothing to stop its being used as a through road. It means that there are three routes from London to Reading through the town; the High Street, Broadway and the by-pass. It may have been hoped that the through traffic would use the northern road, but there was no guarantee of this. In the plan of 1963, the whole central area was changed to a pedestrian precinct encircled by a ring road. The reasons for this change were that the town centre would have to serve a larger population because of its increased size, and because of the desirability, in accordance with contemporary planning trends, of segregating pedestrians and vehicular traffic in shopping areas if both were to exist happily together without getting in each other's way, with the great benefit of the increased security of the pedestrian.

The ring road is a one-way-three-lane-no-waiting road with four points of entry and with several underpasses to provide access for pedestrians and to the open market. Plans allow for 7 multi-storey car parks and one surface car park adjacent to the ring road. There is provision round the centre for parking 5000 vehicles with direct access to the pedestrian precinct.

In making the whole area inside the ring road a pedestrian precinct, the High Street and Broadway, formerly busy streets, were closed to traffic and have become pedestrian ways. In the centre of the area, running south from the High Street, is another spacious pedestrian shopping way. A good impression of this very interesting and notable plan can be obtained from the plan. Although it involves the demolition of much old property, the buildings of historical and aesthetic interest are being preserved. It has become among the best of new town centres.

Industrial Areas

As previously implied the establishment of industry in Bracknell has been a little in advance of housing and it may be said that the town seems to have proved attractive to industrialists. By 1962 27 firms were established and by 1967 this rose to 33, and by 1977 it rose to over 54. As an indication of the success of industry here 30 extensions to factories have been built since they opened. Several firms are concerned with some form of engineering, including the manufacture of aircraft components and equipment, jigs and tools, ball bearings and electronic equipment, while other firms are concerned with building mastics and blocks, civil engineering, soil and foundation engineers, men's tailoring, furniture and artists' materials. In some cases the factories were built for the firms by the development corporation; in others the firms built their own premises. The result is certainly satisfactory. The western industrial area must rank as one of the pleasantest in the country. Grouped mainly on either side of Western Road which is gently undulating, the factory buildings are set well back, which allows for stretches of lawn interspersed with flower beds, or edged with troughs of plants in front of the buildings, which show varied and generally pleasing industrial architecture. Its setting among wooded rural surroundings, still very much apparent to the west, greatly enhances its pleasantness. In addition the considerable premises of the principal Meteorological Office and of the Computer Centre are located at Bracknell.

Social Aspect

The original new town of Bracknell was built round a small existing town, so the nucleus of many social activities was already there; but a question that inevitably arises in new town development is whether the existing population mixes well with the newcomers, and whether the extension of social and community activities is shared by the old and new population. As far as the development corporation has been able to observe there has been a satisfactory mixing, and the corporation was able to state in its report for 1954 that 'the "Old inhabitants" are welcoming the newcomers and that up to date there has not been any move to form separate clubs for the incoming residents'.

As in the other new towns there are the usual societies and associations concerned with drama, art, music, horticulture, women's organizations and sport and youth clubs, many of which had existed in the old town, but which with the newcomers greatly expanded. In March 1953 the Bracknell Community Association was formed to which the majority of the then 40 existing associations of various kinds became affiliated.

Adequate premises for the expanding activities of these associations have been gradually provided. Three small halls already existed in Bracknell which served the needs of many associations. The premises of the Youth Centre in the High Street were, however, inadequate, and in 1955 new premises at Coopers Hill near the railway station were acquired. A little later, early in 1956, a new youth club was opened in Priestwood.

As the town grew so more associations catering for additional interests were formed and demands for suitable premises became more urgent. This was met to some extent by the acquisition by the development corporation of a large house which was let in June 1957 to the Community Association as a centre on a 7-year lease. It proved to be a great success as one of the principal centres of social activities in Bracknell. During 1958 over 800 meetings of various kinds were held there, and by 1959 the centre was being used by about 2000 persons a month. Another community centre, a converted rectory, was opened in Easthampstead during 1959. This had to be demolished in 1961, and a new hall was completed in 1962. In 1959 a small community hall was built and occupied in Bullbrook in the same year and this proved so popular that it was enlarged in 1961. In that year a Bracknell Civic Society was formed which we understand was the first of its kind in a new town. Further community centres were opened at Harmans Water in 1965, and at Priestwood in 1966, at Great Hollands in 1972, Hanworth in 1975 and Birch Hill in 1976.

The provision of the Bracknell Sports Centre by the Easthampstead Rural District Council, assisted by the development corporation and other public bodies, with its large multi-purpose sports hall offers excellent recreational facilities well used by people of all ages.

The development corporation is very much alive to the growing needs of youth, as there is a very high proportion of teenagers, and thus the provision of youth centres has been given much consideration. The various churches are giving assistance and new centres are being formed in the neighbourhoods.

The mansion of South Hill Park to the south of the town was acquired by the development corporation and has been converted into an Arts Centre. It is a large eighteenth-century house, considerably renovated in the late nineteenth century, standing in about 40 acres (16 ha) of beautiful parkland. The adaptation was sufficiently advanced for use by October 1973. The Centre consists of a studio theatre, a small cinema, a delightful music recital room, craft rooms, exhibition rooms, restaurant, cafe and bar with lounge which opens to a terrace with a view of the extensive lawn spreading to the lake beyond with its tall fountain. This lawn is utilized for exhibitions of sculpture. Later it is proposed to build a theatre adjacent to the mansion. South Hill Park Trust Ltd has been formed to administer the centre.

One of the notable social circumstances of Bracknell, which has been confirmed by later experience, is the satisfactory mingling of the new population with the old, and their joining together in the activities of the numerous voluntary associations.

Aesthetically Bracknell is one of the most attractive of the new towns partly because of its natural setting. As previously indicated the whole area is undulating and well wooded with a great variety of trees, due to parts having once been forestry commission land with tall conifers and the other parts having been the parks of country houses where many different trees were planted. It is a tribute to the planners that with the residential development this woodland character has so often been preserved.

Reference

21.1   These populations of the four neighbourhoods are later revisions. They were originally 9020, 8310, 5740 and 2280

22 Introductory–three later "South-East" Towns

In the White Paper on 'London—Employment: Housing: Land' of February 1963, a principal theme was the need for a regional plan for London and the South-East and a study was made of 'the growth and movement of population in the South-East, including overspill from London, and related employment and transport questions'. 'The need for a second generation of new and expanded towns' was examined, 'which would provide both houses and work for Londoners, well away from London itself, and draw off some of the pressure on the capital'. The South-East Study 1961–1981 which followed the White Paper was completed in February 1964. The proposals made in the Study were based on birth-rate trends from 1855 to 1962 which showed an unexpected rise and a change from previous trends. These led the authors of the South-East Study to base their calculations and proposals on the current rise in population and also on the expected inward migrations. In consequence it was expected that there would be an increase of population in the South-East from 1961 to 1981 of $3\frac{1}{2}$ millions, of which $2\frac{1}{2}$ millions would be due to natural increase and one million to inward migration. The increases since 1962, however, have not been as expected, and seen in the light of trends in 1977, the increase in population in the South-East from 1961 to 1981 is more likely to be $1\frac{3}{4}$ millions than $3\frac{1}{2}$ millions. In 1961 the population of the area of the South-East Study was 17 747 000 and by 1971 this had risen by only about a million.

Judging by the returns of the Registrar General, the trends since 1971 show a tendency towards a further lessening of the rate of increase. Also the population of Greater London decreasing more rapidly than had been anticipated when the South-East Study was prepared, prompted the Secretary of State for the Environment to ask, early in 1974, for more provision for housing within the Greater London area, and not to proceed with the proposed expansions of Stevenage and Harlow. In April 1977 the Secretary of State limited the further expansion of new towns generally thus discouraging the movement of population envisaged in the South East Study, a decision prompted by the concern for the decline in the population of inner city areas.

In Chapter 13 of the South-East Study, proposals of places for expansion were made in three categories, A—3 new cities, B—6 big new expansions and C—12 other (smaller) expansions by about 30 000 each. The 3 new cities proposed were in the Southampton/Portsmouth area, the Bletchley area and the Newbury area. The 6 big new expansions proposed were of Ipswich, Northampton, Peterborough, Swindon, Ashford (Kent) and Stansted (Essex).

Following the South-East Study an assessment of the interrelated growth of North-ampton, Bedford and North Bucks was made in a study by a design team led by Sir Hugh Wilson and Lewis Womersley and published in 1965. In this Study it was considered that 'Northampton is a suitable town for major expansion', and that, 'there should be no difficulty in increasing the population by about 50 000 by 1981 rising to about 100 000 by the end of the century', and sites were suggested to the south-east and south-west of the town for the major part of the expansion.

With regard to development in the Bletchley area, two sites were considered as possible for a new city of about 200 000, one just north of Wolverton, which was, however, considered too close to Northampton, and the other about 3 miles (5 km) north of Bletchley which was recommended. It was pointed out that 'there is merit in a scheme which combines the advantages of town expansion in the early stages with those of a new city in the later stages'. At the time the South-East Study was being prepared Sir Henry Wells was engaged on an expansion study of Peterborough of which more details are given in Chapter 24. Of the other subjects of 'big new expan-sions', Ashford and Swindon are being expanded under the Town Development Act. A draft designation order for the expansion of Ipswich was made in February 1968, but the Minister of Housing and Local Government decided not to proceed with its designation. Stansted, the sixth of the proposed large extensions, was dependent on a third international airport for London being located there, but this site was then rejected in favour of Maplin, which in turn was rejected. Thus the 3 new towns which are largely the outcome of the South-East Study are Milton Keynes, Peterborough and Northampton: the subjects of the three following chapters.

In the second edition of this book (1969) brief notes were given (Chapter 37) of the proposed expansions of 5 towns of considerable size: Peterborough, Northampton, Warrington, Ipswich and Preston–Leyland–Chorley, the first three of which had by then been designated. It was stated that they are not strictly new towns, but rather town expansions. The differentiation made was 'that if the existing town is small and the addition is much larger so that an overall plan treats what exists as a subordinate part then it is 'a new town', but if the town is already of considerable size and the addition is smaller than that which exists then it is a town expansion by whichever Act it is developed'. Thus Harlow, increased from 4500 to 80 000, and Redditch from 29 000 to 90 000, are new towns: but Peterborough and Northampton with increases from about 120 000 to 200 000 are town expansions. Also, when the essential character of the existing town continues and influences development and the new centre is an evolu-tion of the old then it is hardly a new town. On the other hand if the expansion is considerable and is being done under the machinery of the New Towns Acts, and its planning contributes something valuable to the subject, this justifies inclusion of a description in this book. Also they come within the White Paper typification of 'a second generation of new towns'.

23 Milton Keynes

In conformity with the recommendations in the South East Study, the new city of Milton Keynes was designated on 23 January 1967, as the new city of 'Milton Keynes', with an area of 21 900 acres (8870 ha), an existing population of about 40 000, mainly in Bletchley in the south with 25 000, Wolverton and Bradwell in the north with 10 000, Stony Stratford nearby with 3750, and the remaining few hundred in the villages of Milton Keynes, Willen and Woughton-on-the-Green. The planned intake is 150 000 and the total population, with the addition from natural growth, is expected to rise to a maximum of 250 000 by the end of the century.

The site is an irregular square tilted north–west, south–east, with a protrusion in the south around Bletchley and another in the north-west embracing the villages of Wolverton and Stony Stratford. The small village of Milton Keynes, which gives the new town its name, is near the eastern boundary. Other small villages include Woughton-on-the-Green, Simpson, Fenny Stratford, Shenley Church End, Shenley Brook End, Loughton and Bradwell. Most of the area is undulating agricultural land and there are over 100 separate farms on the site.

From its centre to the heart of London is about 45 miles (72 km), its southern boundary being about 25 miles (40 km) from the edge of the London conurbation. Northampton, is about 18 miles (29 km) north of the centre, Bedford with 65 000 is about 15 miles (24 km) north-east, and Luton with 133 000 is 18 miles (29 km) south-east. The main line railway from Euston to the north-west runs through the middle of the site, with stations at Wolverton and Bletchley where a line crosses which links with Oxford to the west and Bedford to the north. The famous Roman road, Watling Street, passes near Bletchley and continues north-west through Stony Stratford. The M1 forms part of the north-east boundary. The Great Ouse runs near the northern boundary of the site and its tributary the River Ouzel flows through the eastern part, with the Grand Union Canal a little to its west.

In the draft designation order the proposed site was larger, being 25 200 acres (10 210 ha). Following objections at the inquiry the inspector suggested a reduction to 18 600 acres (7530 ha), which excluded the considerable area of 5100 acres (2070 ha) on the east side and 1600 acres (650 ha) on the west side. The main reasons were the retention of more land for agriculture, including the fertile land in the valley of the Ouzel and that in the vicinity of Calverton; and because the area proposed was considered unnecessarily large for the intended population, as a slightly higher density could reasonably be accepted. The size he suggested would accommodate 279 000 people at 15 to the acre (37 per ha), or 223 000 at 12 to the acre (30 per ha), which compared favourably with the overall densities of other new towns. The Minister not only accepted the suggested exclusion in the west, but increased it by another 1300 acres (530 ha), but could not agree to excluding more than 400 acres (160 ha) on the east side. It was essential, he said, to include in the designated area the land in the north-eastern corner to provide relatively flat sites suitable for large scale industry. Of the remainder at least 1000 acres (405 ha) would be needed to be worked for gravel (and it would be desirable for the completed workings to be used constructively in the later stages of the town's development). Thus the overall density would be about 12 to the acre (30 per ha).

Both the situation and the proposed size of the town prompted criticisms which were expressed by many of the objectors at the inquiry. The National Farmers' Union and the National Union of Agricultural Workers claimed that the area was one of the most important corn growing regions in the country, and that it could be an area of exceptionally high production if drainage were improved. They conceded, however, that if major development is necessary in the area, it should take the form of a major expansion of Bletchley which had produced plans to house a population on the scale envisaged in less than 10 000 acres (4050 ha). The North Bucks Association, which was formed for the purpose of opposing the proposal and which represented the parish councils of the area, made some telling points in its objections. It stressed the need for a national physical planning policy for Britain which should aim at securing a more even distribution of population throughout the country, to relieve areas now congested and over-populated and to relocate population in the relatively empty parts of the country where space, water supply and sewage disposal would not present such serious problems. Within the broad framework of such a policy towns should be spaced well apart.

The main criticisms at the inquiry were (1) that the new town should not be built so near London, (2) that the proposed population is too high for this area, (3) that the area selected is too large for the purpose and is wasteful of land, and (4) that the engineering problems would be difficult to overcome.

Although these objections merit serious consideration, they do not fully reflect the regional planning efforts which led to the designation of Milton Keynes. Thus Buckinghamshire County Council first proposed that this area should be developed as the North Bucks New City. The site was thought to be sufficiently far away from London, and the proposed city would be sufficiently large to enable it to be a 'countermagnet' to London. This analysis was confirmed by the South East Study (1964), the 'Strategy for the South East' (1967) and the 'Strategic Plan for the South East' (1970). We, however, believe the city is too large and it would have been better to accommodate the population in three new towns. Milton Keynes is being planned and developed in such a way as to have large open spaces of parkland and traversing the urban areas and in some degree separating them, which mitigates a little the objections to size.

Outline Plan

The plan for Milton Keynes was prepared by the consultants Llewelyn-Davies, Weeks, Forestier-Walker and Bor. An interim report was presented to the development corporation in December, 1968, followed by the final report which was submitted to the Minister of Housing and Local Government in March 1970. Concurrently with the

MILTON KEYNES

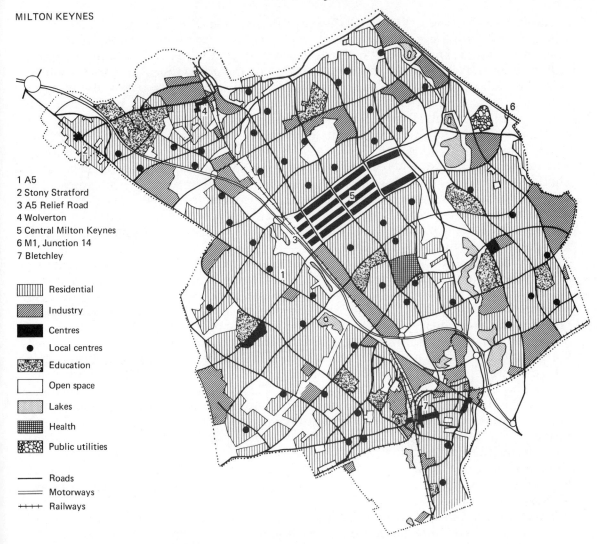

1 A5
2 Stony Stratford
3 A5 Relief Road
4 Wolverton
5 Central Milton Keynes
6 M1, Junction 14
7 Bletchley

|||||| Residential

///// Industry

■■■ Centres

● Local centres

Education

Open space

Lakes

Health

Public utilities

——— Roads

≡≡≡ Motorways

++++ Railways

Figure 23.1 Milton Keynes Outline Plan.

public exhibition of the plan, public meetings were held to discuss it and answer questions. 127 objections to the plan were received and a public inquiry was held. The plan was accepted by the Minister in May 1971.

The final, or strategic, plan as it is called, follows the interim report in essentials, and the concept of the latter was, after further investigations in several details, fully confirmed, and as a result of these further studies the corporation is firmly convinced of the soundness of the plan. The proposals in the interim report were concerned with principles illustrated by diagrams, and in the subsequent strategic plan these principles and diagrams were applied to the existing landscape, villages and towns.

The broad concept promises a very good plan for the new city. The aim is spacious development with good landscaping and a generous provision of open spaces and is largely a return to the garden city concept. The intention is to try to give people what they want, to encourage participation at every level, and to interpret people's wishes as carefully as possible. 'What', ask the consultants, 'does this mean in practice? How will a city offering these freedoms look? A city with room for change will look more open; homes that can grow will have more space around them; trees and landscaping will establish the visual character of much of the city including the primary roads which could be built as parkways.' And instead of the high densities and close building in some of the second generation new town development there is a return to more spacious siting with an all-over average net density, for the majority of dwellings, of 8 to the acre (20 per ha), with variations of from 6 to 10 to the acre (15 to 25 per ha).

The proposal is to build half the houses for owner occupation and half for renting. The former may not be fully realized until completion and there will probably be some change later from renting to ownership. In the plan, therefore, care is to be exercised to design and build the houses to similar standards irrespective of whether they are for sale or rent. This is a wise precaution. In other new towns where families wish to change from renting to owner occupation, it is not their present house that they wish to buy but another more spacious one.

The plan consists of a grid of primary roads of approximately one kilometre squares. Within these squares are residential areas, called environmental areas, of about 250 to 300 acres (100 to 120 ha) each for about 5000 people. Estate roads branch from the grid to serve the residential areas, while a system of pedestrian routes traverses the whole city crossing the primary roads roughly in the middle of the sides of the squares and at the corners by over or underpasses. At the former points are the 'activity centres' with major bus stops, and a concentration of residential facilities like shops, first schools, pubs, places of worship and other requirements. There will be about 60 of these centres with different groupings at each. Thus one centre may provide just one shop and a first school, another a group of shops and a pub, another a church and a library, another a youth and/or a community centre and so on. A person could comfortably walk to his nearest centre, none of which is more than 550 yards (500 m) away from dwellings; or if he is wanting a service provided in another centre, like evening classes or a library, he can either use the frequent bus service or go by car, or if it is in the next environmental area (as they are called) it would not be more than a walk of one mile (1.6 km).

It will be seen that the residential areas are not planned as inward looking neighbourhoods, as in the first generation of new towns, but rather as outward looking to a transport route that links rapidly with other parts of the city. Following the principle of giving the maximum possible freedom of choice to future residents, the plan aims to give scope for 'the free use of the car unrestrained by congestion' while at the same time providing 'a high quality public transport system from the beginning, not only for those who need it but for those who might choose to use it instead of private transport'.

Central Milton Keynes is approximately the geographical centre on a virgin site midway between the railway and the Grand Union Canal. It will provide a regional shopping centre, leisure and cultural facilities, civic offices, a new inter-city railway station, and offices for new firms locating in Milton Keynes. As planned, the shopping areas in Bletchley, Stony Stratford and Wolverton have been expanded to provide district scale facilities. Local shopping needs are met by the activity centres.

An aim of the plan is to preserve, as much as possible, the attractive character of some of the historically and architecturally interesting small towns and villages in the area. For example, the High Street of Stony Stratford, a coaching town on the old Roman Watling Street. It is to be hoped that the many very pleasant old churchyards in the designated area will remain as they are, and that incumbents will resist the temptation of removing the memorials to the wall of the church or churchyard or using them as paving stones. If they do this the churchyards will lose their historic distinction and become open spaces like any other. Also, kept as they are, they sometimes become bird sanctuaries, because the memorials evoke that necessary sense of peace.

Nursery, first and middle schools will be at the activity centres, in some cases combined in the same building. Schools for the 12 to 18 age group will be grouped throughout the city. Four colleges of further education are proposed, and a higher education centre between Stony Stratford and Wolverton. In 1969 the headquarters of the Open University was established near Walton in the south-east of the designated area. A site for a large hospital and health centre is allocated about a mile (1.6 km) south of the city centre while local health centres are distributed throughout the city.

Industry is located in several areas throughout the city, the larger sites towards the periphery and the smaller within the city. Two fairly large areas are near the M1, several near the railway lines, and a few near the western boundary. Those industries that employ a large proportion of women and part-time labour are located in or near residential areas.

The site of the city presents opportunities for some very attractive open spaces. A large linear park traversing the city from north to south is proposed along the courses of the Grand Union Canal and the River Ouzel and is being developed. Another linear park along the course of Loughton Brook, a small tributary of the Ouse, is proposed in the western area of the city. The consultants were impressed with the visual attractiveness of the Grand Union Canal. They remarked that 'its route is extremely picturesque, running through delightful countryside, formed by the landscape, woodland and old villages. At its northern extremity, at Great Linford, it runs through a particularly beautiful eighteenth-century park, with views of the seventeenth-century almshouses and the parish churches.' Two golf courses are in use and more are planned.

The proposals constitute generally a very good conception, for the city is planned with the recognition that improved standards of living and giving people, as far as is practicable, what they want, means spacious development with reasonably sized gardens. It is also recognized that a good residential environment means a liberal infusion of open spaces with lawns and trees and other pleasing features and is a refreshing return to the garden city concept. A fundamental of the overall plan is flexibility, allowing for change in the light of experience as implementation proceeds. Thus, a few modifications of the original plan have been made, and these will obviously continue, but the essential principles by which the plan is made are likely to remain.

Building the City

Even allowing for the time necessary to prepare plans for so large an area and the extensive preparatory civil engineering works, progress has been slow. This has been due partly to the planning procedures in a democracy, when it was necessary to consider the 127 objections to the master plan and to hold an inquiry, and partly to the uncertainty regarding the siting of the third London airport and the protracted deliberations of the Roskill Commission, which was appointed in May 1968 and reported in December 1970. Two of the sites that were considered are near the designated area: Cublington, only 6 miles (10 km) from the boundary, and Thurleigh, 15 miles (24 km) away. The development corporation was opposed to the siting of the airport so close to the new town and Lord Campbell of Eskan, the chairman of the corporation, stated in his evidence to the Commission that if either site were chosen the plan of Milton Keynes would need complete review, and development would be disrupted. Noise from either site would bedevil large areas of the city's environment; and, in the case of Cublington, would stop development of 15% of the designated area. Other objections were that Milton Keynes as planned could not be regarded as an airport city—it was not big enough; while in the case of Thurleigh its building and the associated urbanization simultaneously would strain the resources of labour, materials and transport, and jeopardize the success of Milton Keynes.

The Roskill Commission in its report gave first preference for Cublington ('that in the overall national interest Cublington should be the site of the third London airport'). Sir Colin Buchanan in his dissenting minority report favoured Foulness. Four months later in April 1971, the Government announced its choice of Foulness, and significantly a month later the plan for Milton Keynes was accepted by the Minister of Housing and Local Government. Although this decision gave much satisfaction to those concerned with planning and building Milton Keynes, about 3 years had elapsed between the appointment of the Roskill Commission and the Government's decision, which for the development corporation was a period of uncertainty inhibiting progress.

Considerable progress has been made in the existing towns in the designated area. The Brunel Centre at Bletchley, a combined shopping and office development is already complete and with the Leisure Centre, has brought a new vitality to an otherwise modest and mundane townscape. In Stony Stratford, the offices and shops provided in Cofferidge Close are a first-class example of how the old and new in Milton Keynes are being carefully blended together. In Wolverton, the Agora is under construction. When completed, this multi-purpose development will accommodate the city's weekly market, a range of sports and community activities, a café, offices and shops.

Notwithstanding the uncertainty stemming from the Roskill Commission, and the efforts directed towards the existing towns, by 1977 the development of the new city was well underway. During the first ten years after the designation of the city, new development is concentrated in a crescent converging on Central Milton Keynes and linking the existing towns together.

By December 1976, 13 948 houses had been completed since 1967 of which 6764 have been provided by the corporation, 3078 by local authorities and 4106 by private enterprise. By autumn 1979, about 100 000 people are expected to be living in Milton Keynes. To date 152 firms are in industrial premises on land made available by the development corporation, of which 116 are advance factory units built by the corporation.

Housing and Residential Areas

Between 2400 and 3000 dwellings are now being completed each year in Milton Keynes. It is a primary goal of the corporation to provide a wide variety of the housing types and to cater for a diversity of tastes. There is no question that this goal is being achieved with over 53 housing for rent estates and 32 housing for sale estates already completed or under construction.

Many of the early estates were built in the north of the designated area on the fringes

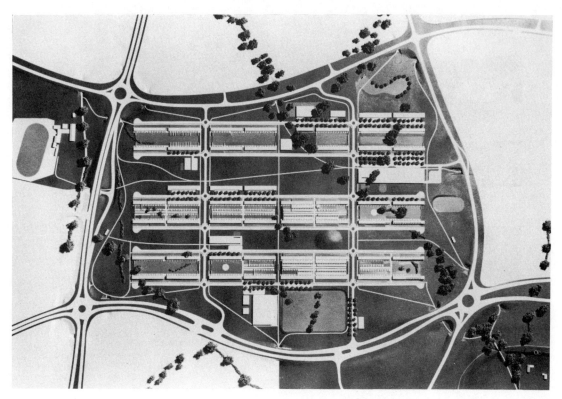

Figure 23.2 Plan of Netherfield housing estate.

of Stony Stratford, Wolverton, and New Bradwell. They reflect the corporation's efforts to experiment with materials and are dominated by mono-pitch roof lines. Thus, for example, the homes at Fullers Slade are 3-storey, narrow frontage dwellings in long terraces with car ports in front. They are architecturally attractive, with long bands of fenestration mono-pitched roofs and walls faced with diagonal cedar boarding. While the estate is large (453 dwellings) all living-rooms overlook private gardens and public open space beyond, not another dwelling. Some of the other early schemes include: Galley Hill where the semi-detached dwellings are located around informal courtyards; Greenleys with 2-storey terraced dwellings arranged around square, enclosed landscaped courtyards with parking provided in adjacent courts, and Bradville, where the woodframe dwellings feature ½-storey lounge-diners, and are clad in plastic coated panels.

The Woughton Area of the city, midway between Central Milton Keynes and Bletchley includes the Netherfield estate with 1043 dwellings planned in long terrace rows facing long straight roads running north–south. The estate is divided into a grid of 20 rectangular blocks, 5 widths east–west, 2 of which form long gardens between the blocks. Another scheme for 652 dwellings, at Coffee Hall is planned on a similar principle. Both of these grid squares are almost exclusively housing for rent.

In marked contrast to the uniformity of these developments are the homes being built at Eaglestone. Designed by the famous Swedish domiciled English architect,

Figure 23.3 Shops and housing at Fishermead.

Ralph Erskine, this mixed rent–sale estate, features an informal layout of detached, semi-detached, and terraced homes with car parking provided in garage courts.

In many parts of Milton Keynes, the residential areas are planned so as to integrate housing for rent and housing for sale. This objective is being achieved with the greatest success in Great Linford. Based on the existing village, 20 different housing schemes are being developed in a single grid square, albeit a large one. The diversity of style, materials and form, the sensitive interweaving of the old parts of the village and the new estates, and the relatively small size of each housing scheme will make Great Linford one of the most outstanding residential areas in Milton Keynes.

In the past few years the development of the central housing grid squares around Central Milton Keynes has gained momentum. Planned at the higher densities—up to 200 persons per acre (494 per ha)—appropriate to an area adjacent to the city centre, houses are completed in Springfield, Conniburrow and Fishermead. Even within the constraints of these higher densities, all dwellings (except for a small number of flats) are being provided with gardens. A wide variety of designs are being used ranging from 3-storey dwellings with flat roofs in light colour brick at Fishermead to the 2-storey duo pitched dwellings in red brick at Springfield.

The designers of the residential areas in Milton Keynes devote considerable efforts to the landscaping of all of the public open spaces. While in many of the recently completed estates, it is still too early to evaluate the results, in the first estates to be completed, like Galley Hill, there are clear indications that the planting of trees and shrubs will bring an early maturity and softness to many of the residential communities.

Figure 23.4 Housing for sale at Calverton End.

Figure 23.5 Cofferidge Close—Stony Stratford's new centre.

City Centre

The site for Central Milton Keynes, approximately in the geographical centre, extends from the railway in the west where a new station is planned, to the promontory on Willen Lake and the adjacent parkland. The site occupies three and one quarter city grid squares. The whole eastern square is reserved for parkland and housing so the main part of the centre will occupy two and a quarter squares—a total of about 500 acres (200 ha).

The plan shows how each grid square is divided into eight 'blocks' of land and these are further divided into four 'blocklets', each of one hectare. Thus boulevards, lined with trees traverse the area in an east–west direction. All car parking is at ground level. An unusual feature of CMK will be a network of covered pedestrian routes. Most of the buildings are designed in such a way that the first floors extend over part of the pavement to shelter people from the weather. Covered walkways, called porte cocheres, will extend from the buildings over the car parking roads, to the edge of the boulevards.

The heart of CMK is one of the largest covered shopping areas in Europe. With over one million square feet of space under construction, over 150 units will be provided accommodating a department store, four large stores, two supermarkets, a variety of smaller stores, catering and entertainment facilities and small service trades. The entire

Figure 23.6 Drawing of open square in the shopping building.

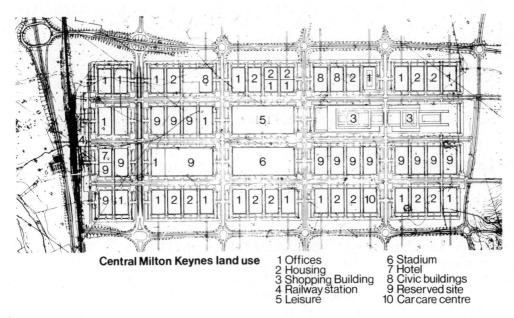

Central Milton Keynes land use

1 Offices	6 Stadium
2 Housing	7 Hotel
3 Shopping Building	8 Civic buildings
4 Railway station	9 Reserved site
5 Leisure	10 Car care centre

Figure 23.7 Plan of city centre.

ground floor is a pedestrian area, including two arcades. These arcades, like the old Crystal Palace, will be naturally lit, and extensively landscaped with trees, plants, and shrubs. Both arcades will lead to the two public squares—the garden courts, open and landscaped, and the covered square, which will form a natural focus for promotional events during the day and for a wide variety of activities outside shopping areas.

Lloyds Court, an office complex including a range of shops, a pub, and a bank is already open adjacent to the shopping building. In addition, several housing schemes will shortly be under construction along with the civic offices. Additional schemes currently in the advanced stages of planning and design include further office and housing developments, the city club entertainment/leisure complex, a car care centre, a hotel, and a stadium to accommodate a first division football team.

Industry and Industrial Areas

Experience in most of the former towns indicates that the speculative provision of good factory premises is one way of attracting industry and of contributing therefore to the rapid growth of the town. This is realized by the Milton Keynes Development Corporation which has embarked on methods of system building of industrial premises, some examples of which can be seen in the first industrial estate of Kiln Farm in the north-west. This is a system based on standardized frame construction and standardized cladding units which permit adaptations to various requirements. Some of the advance factories built at Kiln Farm with panels of plastic coated steel repeated over large areas of walls without break or variation may for some have a monotonous appearance and invite the derisive comment of packing-case architecture. Variations and the introduction of trees will doubtless overcome these slightly unsatisfactory effects.

In addition to the provision of advanced factory units, the corporation also develops offices on a speculative basis. The Sherwood Drive offices and Stephenson House in Bletchley and the offices in the Cofferidge Close complex in Stony Stratford are all sound examples of modern office developments.

Firms also have the opportunity to build their own premises (with or without the assistance of the corporation as architects) on land provided by the corporation. Firms such as Rank Xerox, Telephone Rentals, Hoechst, Scicon, Tesco, and Steinberg and Sons have built their own factories and/or offices in Milton Keynes.

Social Aspects

Health centres have been built at Water Eaton in Bletchley, Stony Stratford, Wolverton, and Eaglestone. The temporary health centre in Stantonbury will be replaced with a permanent facility in the next few years. The Community Hospital is scheduled to open in 1978 and construction will start on the District Hospital in 1979.

As a result of close co-operation among the development corporation, Milton Keynes Borough Council, and the Buckinghamshire County Council, the Stantonbury Leisure Centre was opened in May 1976. Part of the Stantonbury Campus, which also includes three secondary schools, a theatre, and a youth club, the leisure centre provides sporting and swimming facilities which are used by both the school children and residents in the north of the city. The Bletchley Leisure Centre includes several sports halls, an indoor bowls court, and a swimming pool, covered by a clear perspex pyramid and complete with indoor palm trees, sauna and solarium. Additional commercial leisure facilities, and a sports stadium are planned for Central Milton Keynes.

24 *Peterborough*

Peterborough was designated on 1 August 1967, and it is the first of the new towns with a very large central nucleus (24.1). It is a very old city with a famous Romanesque cathedral of the twelfth century, which formed the Abbey of the Benedictine monastery established in Peterborough in the seventh century. The later west front of the cathedral built in the thirteenth century is one of the finest examples of Early Gothic façades in Europe. The cathedral and its beautiful precincts, the west gate and the area beyond inevitably form the centre of the city and the new town, and the maintenance of its traditional character is fortunately one of the objects of the planning proposals.

A main purpose of the expansion of Peterborough, as with other urban expansions in the south–east, is to contribute to the provision of housing for the people in the Greater London area. In 1966 it was estimated that there was in London a deficit of 330 000 houses, accommodation for about a million people, which it was the aim to provide by 1981. Because of the difficulties and restrictions within the Greater London area most of this provision would have to be found in the areas outside London, and it was proposed that Peterborough's contribution could be an intake of population from London of 70 000. At the same time provision for employment by industrial and commercial intake would be secured.

The Expansion Study of Peterborough by Sir Henry Wells was published in 1963. His report stated that Peterborough was a suitable city to expand to the extent of 50% or 100% or even more, and he suggested how it might best be done. His suggestion included a linear urban growth extending 5 miles (8 km) north-west of the city.

Subsequently a planning consultant, Tom Hancock, was appointed to propose an area for designation and to indicate an outline plan; and his report was published in March 1966. He suggested a total area of about 18 640 acres (7550 ha) which included the whole of the City of Peterborough, part of Old Fletton in the south and parts of the rural districts of Peterborough, Norman Cross and Thorney. The consultant rejected the suggestion of Sir Henry Wells of an extension north-west, and considered 'that a satellite town south-west of Peterborough would be feasible if it were self-contained and far enough from Peterborough not to compete with it; but this', he considered, 'would not constitute expansion and would bring few benefits and improvements to the existing city'. The proposals of the consultant were submitted to several local authorities in the region for their comments before designating an area, and it is interesting to note that the County Council of Huntingdon and Peterborough, while not objecting to expansion, objected to the consultant's proposals for development to the west, involving the villages of Sutton, Castor and Ailsworth in the Peterborough rural district, and added that it would have preferred a satellite town to the south-west of Peterborough. There is much to be said for such a satellite instead of the continuous spread of Peterborough in spite of the consultant's implication that it would be feasible only apparently if it were self-contained and far enough from Peterborough not to compete with it. Surely it is hardly a question of competing but of towns of a limited size being complementary to each other, and of one sometimes providing facilities of various kinds for both.

After the publication of the consultant's proposals a public local inquiry was held. Most of the objections were on the grounds of the good quality of the agricultural land in the proposed areas of extension. The Inspector considered, however, that he could not recommended that the area should not be so designated in the national interest as other considerations weighed more heavily. Yet he agreed with the representation made by nearly all parties that the area was too large for the proposed population, and recommend that the area of about 2 000 acres (810 ha) of the village of Marholm and its surroundings in the north-west should be excluded. The Minister accepted this and in addition excluded 4 other small areas on the periphery with the result that the whole area was reduced from 18 640 acres (7550 ha) to 15 940 acres (6455 ha) and this was designated, as previously mentioned, on 1 August 1967.

Peterborough is about 78 miles (125 km) due north of the centre of London, being on the main railway line from King's Cross to the principal Yorkshire towns and Newcastle and Edinburgh beyond. Lines also go to Leicester and Northampton in the west and Norwich in the east, so that it is an important railway junction. The A15 branches from the A1 about 5 miles (8 km) south of Peterborough and passes through the centre of the city northwards to Lincoln. The A605 links Peterborough with Northampton and the A47 from Leicester in the west passes through Peterborough and on to King's Lynn, while the road from Peterborough to the Port of Harwich is being improved. Communications therefore are good. The River Nene flows west–east between Peterborough and Old Fletton and on through the Fens to The Wash. The population at the time of designation in 1967 was about 78 000, of which about 63 000 were in the City of Peterborough, about 12 000 in Old Fletton and the remainder in the rural districts.

Master Plan

Subsequent to designation a draft basic plan for Greater Peterborough was prepared by the consultant (operating as the partnership Hancock–Hawkes) and published in September 1968. Earlier in the year the development corporation had been appointed, and it was the intention that the corporation in developing the town should work in partnership with the County Council of Huntingdon and Peterborough and the City Council of Peterborough.

Comments, questions and criticisms on the draft basic plan were invited, and as a result of these it was revised, an interim report was published with an exhibition of plans, further comments were considered and finally a master plan was produced, submitted to the Minister in September 1970, and approved by him in May 1971.

The designated area, whose shape might be likened to a battered butterfly with its head pointing south-east and its tattered wings spread north and west, is divided into 4 townships, involving developments mainly to the north and west of the existing city. Paston is to the north, Bretton to the immediate west, Castor further out to the west

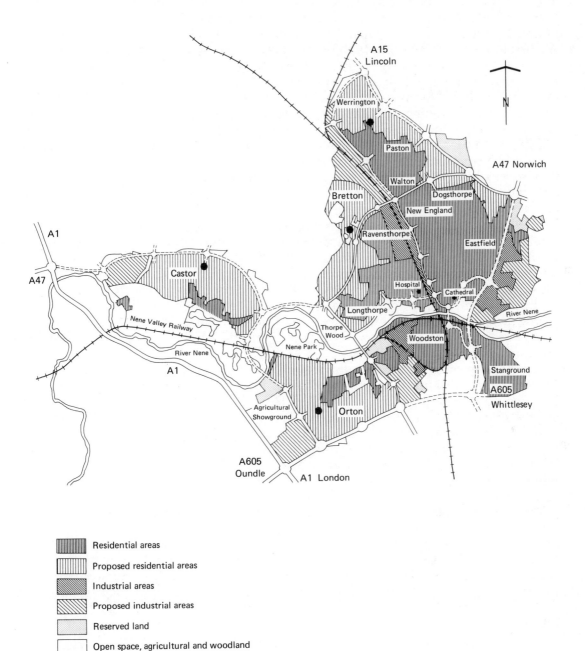

Figure 24.1 Greater Peterborough Structure Map.

and Orton to the south-west. Each township is being developed for a population of between 20 000 and 30 000, each will have its centre, and will be divided into residential neighbourhoods, many of which will also have a local centre (see later description of the first township of Bretton). In the centre between these townships, stretching along the River Nene for its entire length of nearly 10 miles (16 km) through the town, is a linear park varying in width from $\frac{1}{4}$ to 1 mile (0.4 to 1.6 km). The largest area of the park is central to the adjoining townships of Castor, Ortons and Bretton, and includes a northerly belt of existing woodland and a sizeable lake. It is claimed in the master plan of the development corporation that this plan is 'the first attempt to create what Ebenezer Howard, the original advocate of new towns, conceived as their ultimate form—the Social City, consisting of a cluster of separate townships or "garden cities" in a green setting, each largely self-sufficient but all closely linked with one another and with a somewhat larger "central city", the whole sustaining a regional centre of big-city calibre'.

It is difficult to appreciate the parallel. Howard's garden city cluster results from establishing new cities in the region as the existing cities approach their maxima. Each new city is located 'some little distance beyond its own zone of "country" so that the new town may have a zone of country of its own'. 'This principle of growth,' he asserts, 'this principle of always preserving a belt of country round our cities' (24.2) means groups of towns in open country, a very different conception from the Peterborough plan which consists of 3 or 4 townships abutting a central garden. This is not meant as an adverse criticism of the Peterborough plan, but rather as questioning the parallel to Howard's conception, which may be misleading.

The existing manufacturing industry is located to the east of the existing city at Eastfield along the railway running north and south-west of the centre at Woodston. It is proposed to extend these industrial estates a little and to develop 2 entirely new estates, one in the west part of Orton and one in the extreme west at Castor. It will be seen, therefore, that there are 5 main industrial areas spread throughout the town so that the journey to work is in many directions. This is probably an advantage over the location of industry mainly in one area, as occurred in several of the first new towns, where the movement in one direction in the morning and evening is apt to result in congestion.

The very irregular shape of the designated area has obviously made planning difficult. The division into townships abutting on a central park is a good and ingenious plan, and the ambition of the development corporation and its partners is a laudable one. That ambition or determination as given in the publication of the master plan is 'to make Greater Peterborough a pre-eminently good place in which to be born, to grow up, to make friends, to have fun, to learn, to work, to play, to bring up children, to lead a full adult life at any cultural level and to spend a contented retirement'.

Building the Town

As it would mean considerable delay to wait until the approval of the master plan by the Minister it was necessary for the development corporation to propose, and receive approval of, building in advance of this at Ravensthorpe, Woodston and Bretton.

The Master Plan was approved in 1971. Corporation and private building accelerated. Building began at Paston and Orton. By the end of 1976 (6 years after the start

Figure 24.2 North Westwood industrial area.

of building) 10 362 houses had been completed—4302 by the development corporation, 2784 by local authorities and 3276 by private enterprise.

As in other new towns, industry is encouraged to come to Peterborough in a variety of ways, and one of them is the provision by the corporation of unit factories. By 1977 it had built 133 of these at North Westwood in Orton, (south-west of the centre) which assisted greatly in attracting industry to the town. Another 34 factories are under construction at Orton. Some firms build their own factories, while the corporation sometimes builds to a firm's specifications. The secret of rapid progress now that trade with the European continent has reached a greater volume, will be convenience of access from ports and airports and in this respect Peterborough is well placed.

Housing and Residential Areas

The first township, Bretton, is west of the existing city and of the north–south railway and next to the western primary road Soke Parkway. In the area thus formed between the Parkway and the new town boundary is a linear sequence of residential neighbourhoods with a spine road (with dual carriageway) linking them. Each neighbourhood has a local centre on this spine road while about halfway is the township centre linked across the primary road and railway, with the city centre. There is a system of footpaths independent of, but related to, the roads, so that on these footpaths one could traverse the whole of the township and ultimately, it is intended, the whole of Greater Peterborough on these footpaths without being bothered by vehicular traffic; it's a happy thought.

Figure 24.3 Development corporation rented housing in Bretton, the first full scale township. This shows care in landscaping.

City Centre

The two dominating factors in the plan of the city centre are the preservation of its distinctive character and its conversion to a pedestrian precinct, which are really very closely related. The city centre has not changed in essential character and layout of streets since the sixteenth century. The cathedral square, formerly the market, west of the cathedral precinct, the roads running north (Long Causeway) and south to the river (Bridge Street) and some of the adjacent roads round the square (Westgate,

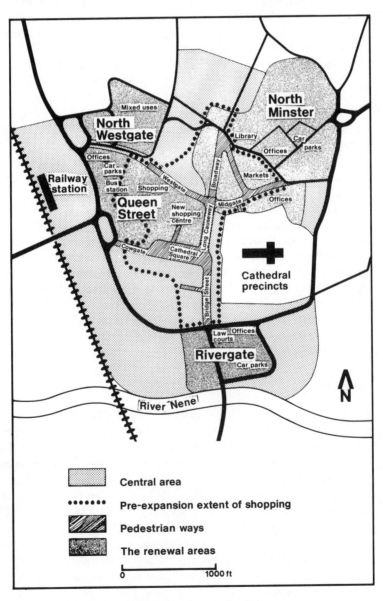

Figure 24.4 Peterborough city centre.

Cowgate and Priestgate) are very much as they were in the reign of Elizabeth I. This central part round the cathedral square has been designated a conservation area, and its character and future enjoyment can best be secured by its complete pedestrianization which is the aim of the plan. This includes the north–east street with its extension to The Market in the north, the square and Cowgate to the west, Westgate and several small linking streets. It is, of course, much more difficult to convert an existing centre, where people are habitually accustomed to vehicular traffic, to a pedestrian precinct, than to start from scratch as with several of the new town centres.

One of the difficulties experienced in many continental cities is the delivery of goods to shops, a difficulty experienced at Cologne when the old High Street was converted into a pedestrian way, and access by vehicles carrying goods to the shops is done by allowing vehicles to use the pedestrian way before and after certain hours, in the early morning and night—not an entirely satisfactory arrangement. It will not be necessary to introduce this in the city centre at Peterborough, and rear access to shops is planned. It is stated, however, that 'complete pedestrianization must await rear access to all the shops' and this will be possible when the first and second carriageways of the inner relief road (Bourges Boulevard) are completed. Most of the area west and north-west of the cathedral precinct is devoted to shopping, and this will continue as such with some needed replacements, and the whole central area will be surrounded by car parks, several of them fortunately multi-storey, because an open car park generally provides the ugliest feature in the urban scene. The process of pedestrianization involves the conversion of roads to large flat paved areas, and it is the intention, as stated in the plan, to plant trees and shrubs, to install seats, and flower tubs and kiosks disposed, 'for the shopper's comfort, pleasure and convenience'. 'The scope', it is stated, 'for imaginative design in street flooring and furnishing opened up by the expulsion of motor traffic is immense, and the benefit to shoppers in terms of safety and amenity will be duly reflected in the growth of trade and the enhancement of property values.'

Thus the plan of the centre which was approved by the Secretary of State for the Environment in September 1972, is very much the pedestrianization and conservation of a historic city centre and is interesting as a study in this context together with many continental cities like Cologne. When it is completed, Peterborough should be a very pleasant place to visit.

Social Aspect

There is evidence that a large number of families living in crowded conditions in London welcome the opportunity of moving to more congenial conditions and surroundings, even if it means going as far as nearly 80 miles (129 km) to Peterborough. This certainly was the experience of the development corporation in working with the GLC and London Borough Councils, among them Lambeth, Islington and Haringey, in interesting and helping the people of these boroughs in moving to and settling in Peterborough. In Lambeth in 1970 a Peterborough week was held and met with an enthusiastic response. During that week alone about 500 families registered a wish to come to work and live in Peterborough. The development corporation has little doubt that it will be able to attract a considerable migration from London. The actual process of transition has, however, to be effected with care and understanding, a task that is fully appreciated by the corporation.

As with all new towns, one of the chief social tasks is the happy transition of a large number of people from old and familiar surroundings among friends, to totally new surroundings among strangers, even if it means, as it often does, the change from poor and congested living conditions with squalid surroundings to a newly built house with a garden in a comparatively spacious and verdant setting. Still, however much better the physical setting is, people naturally look for substitutes for some of the pleasantly remembered interests and friendships of the old place, and it is one of the tasks of the development corporation to help in creating a new life of interests and friendships in this infinitely better environment and to demonstrate that the move has been worthwhile. The Peterborough planning and building partnership seems to be particularly alive to these factors, and there is every prospect that it is building not only a very pleasant Greater City, but a happy community. The foundations are being well laid, but it is a little early in 1977 to say whether the superstructure is realizing the ambitions.

References and Notes

24.1 Telford has a large nucleus but it is not like Peterborough. At Telford an entirely new centre is being built, at Peterborough it is an evolution from the old centre.

24.2 *Garden Cities of Tomorrow* 1946 edition, edited by Sir Frederic Osborn, p. 142.

25 *Northampton*

The new town of Northampton was designated on 14 February 1968. The designated area of 19 952 acres (8081 ha) consisted of the existing County Borough of Northampton, about 10 241 acres (4148 ha), and several villages to the east, and south. The population of the area at the time of designation was 130 000; the master plan provided for an intake of population of about 70 000 mainly from London, so that, with natural increase the population was expected to rise to about 230 000 by 1981, and possibly to about 260 000 by 1991.

Northampton is about 67 miles (108 km) north-north-west of the centre of London, on a loop of the main railway line from London to Crewe. The M1 runs along the south-west boundary and the River Nene and Grand Union Canal flow west–east a little south of the town centre. The site is gently undulating.

Northampton has ancient origins. There was a Roman settlement at Dunston in the western part of the town, and the medieval village of Hamtune was built on the banks of the River Nene. There are Roman and Medieval remains in the area and a few survive, among them some interesting churches, but much was destroyed in the fire of 1675. The town was quickly rebuilt with an extensive central market square. From the middle of the nineteenth century it became the famous centre of the boot and shoe industry, and reached a population in 1961 of 118 000.

Outline Plan

The planning consultants, Sir Hugh Wilson and Leonard Womersley, prepared an outline plan for the designated area and it was published for public comment and discussion in December 1968. The development corporation had been appointed on 30 August 1968, to work in partnership with the Northampton County Borough Council. On the basis of the consultants' proposals the development corporation and the County Borough Council submitted the master plan to the Minister of Housing and Local Government in December 1969. A subsequent public inquiry was held and the many objections heard, a substantial number concerned with the effects of the road plan on various properties. The plan was approved by the Secretary of State for the Environment in September 1970.

The bases of the plan were 2 roughly parallel high speed roads running mainly in a north-easterly direction from the M1, north and south of the existing town. Much of the existing radial network of roads from the centre would be retained, but in the eastern and southern extensions there would be transverse distributor roads between

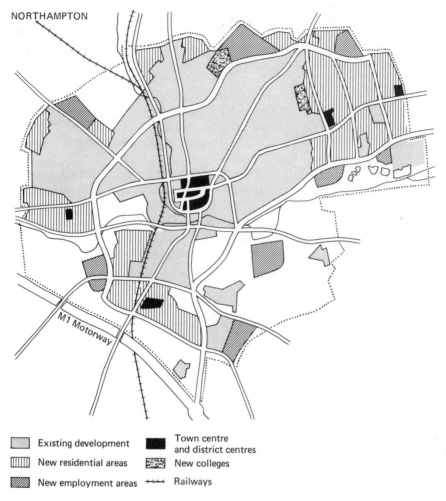

NORTHAMPTON

M1 Motorway

Existing development		Town centre and district centres	
New residential areas		New colleges	
New employment areas	++++	Railways	

Figure 25.1 Master Plan.

the northern and southern high speed roads. Residential areas between the main roads would have a local centre, while there would be 4 district centres. Eight industrial areas were proposed to the north-west and south-east areas beyond the high speed roads. The development of the town centre would be mainly the responsibility of the county borough council now the Northampton District Council, who will arrange for it to be partly pedestrianized.

Plan for the Eastern District

A plan for the eastern extension was prepared and published in January 1971 and submitted to the public for comment, consistent with a full degree of public participation, which earned from the Secretary of State for the Environment when giving approval to the plan in June 1972, commendation in the manner in which the proposals had been publicized.

This is a fairly detailed plan and provides for a population of about 44 400 in its 3034 acres (1228 ha). It was hoped to complete the development in 1977. The population already living in the area was concentrated mainly in Weston Favell, an eastern suburb of Northampton, and near the west boundary of the extension, and the two villages of Great Billing and Little Billing, the former on the Wellingborough Road (A45) which runs east–west through the middle of the district, and the latter towards the south of the district. Three distributor roads would link the northern and southern high speed roads. Twelve residential communities were planned each for populations of between 3000 and 5000. There were to be 9 local centres and 2 district centres, the larger on the A45 near to existing development and the smaller near the east side. The housing densities were to be planned at about 12 to 15 per acre (30 to 37 per ha), and the layout of the residential areas would follow a similar pattern to much new town planning of cul-de-sac roads branching from the transverse and local distributor roads, to convenient places in the midst of the houses. An independent system of footpaths would traverse the whole area. Towards the centre of the district would be 3 areas of parkland and/or woodland and a site for a hospital on the eastern boundary. Land for employment was reserved in one area in the north of the district, and 2 others were proposed south of the southern high speed road.

Plan for the Southern District

The planning proposals for the southern district in the form of a draft for consultation were published in June 1973. This was about 4 years after the preparation of the master plan and experience of trends during this period had prompted several revisions in the overall plan. For example, it appeared that the average size of households of 3.6 persons assumed in the master plan was too high and that 3.2 persons is a more realistic figure. Also it was unlikely that the amount of land allowed for the estimated population in the designated area would be adequate, as experience in the eastern district showed that private development was at lower densities than had been anticipated. To accommodate the total population the development corporation would either have to increase housing densities, which it 'would find unacceptable' or would need to develop the white land in the designated area which was included in the master plan to meet the then unforeseen demands on land. The corporation decided on the second alternative. There is a third alternative which is in the long run likely to prove the most realistic, and that is to reduce the intake of population. This may be inevitable because of the very marked slow-down of population increase in the south-east. As mentioned in Chapter 22 the designation of Milton Keynes, Northampton and Peterborough which results largely from the South-East Study was instigated on the assumption of an increase of $3\frac{1}{2}$ million in the region in the period 1961–81, whereas the increase is likely to be nearer 2 million. In view of this we consider that the population of the new town of Northampton will probably be nearer 190 000 than 230 000 in 1981. It would, therefore, be wise to keep the 'white' land still in its virgin state for some years.

The southern district of 5327 acres (2157 ha) was planned for about 13 000 new houses for a population of 40 000. With the inhabitants of 3 existing villages and parts of the existing town the population will be about 55 000. The 3 villages are in a south–north sequence near the A508, Collingtree near the M1 in the extreme south, Wootton next and then Hardingstone, and it is the intention that the character of these interesting villages should be preserved.

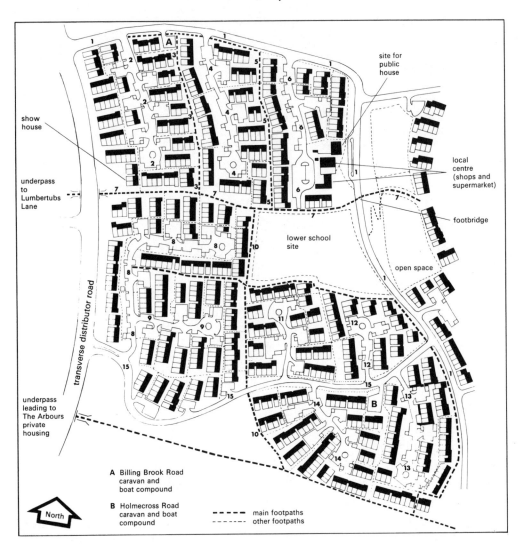

show
house

underpass
to
Lumbertubs
Lane

transverse distributor road

underpass
leading to
The Arbours
private
housing

site for
public
house

local
centre
(shops and
supermarket)

footbridge

lower school
site

open space

A Billing Brook Road
caravan and
boat compound

B Holmecross Road
caravan and boat
compound

North

- - - - - main footpaths
- - - - - other footpaths

Figure 25.2 Plan for the Southern District.

In the plan 4 main residential districts were proposed. Hunsbury in the centre between the northern and southern high speed roads, Upton to the west and Wootton Fields east of the existing village, and Brackmills. These 4 housing areas were subdivided into smaller residential units each with its local centre of which there were 9, while a district was located in the middle of Hunsbury. The whole southern district was planned on similar principles to those for the eastern district. Parkland was to be along the River Nene and Grand Union Canal and at Hunsbury Hill. In the south-west corner, just east of Kislingbury, a large industrial area on the M1 was proposed. It is questionable whether it would not have been better to have moved or extended this industrial area a little east to border the railway, because there is every prospect that the railways will be much more used for freight in the future.

The Secretary of State's decision on the proposals for the southern district was given

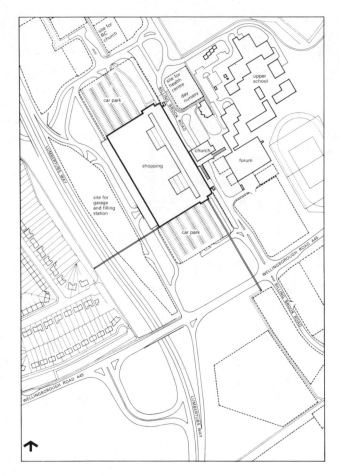

Figure 25.3 Thorplands site plan.

in September 1974. He accepted them as a general indication of the future pattern for the area, and gave formal approval for the development of the Hunsbury residential area which forms the central part of the district.

Developments

Much of the town centre is being redeveloped to meet the needs of a larger population. Forming a focal point in the heart of the town are the new Grosvenor Shopping Centre and the Greyfriars bus station. There is a direct pedestrian link between the two which sits astride a five acre (2 ha) site between Abingdon Street and the historic Market Square. It provides 300 000 sq. feet (27 000 m²) air-conditioned shopping area and a 1000 space car park. Also completed in Northampton's commercial centre are new offices which include Barclaycard House, Greyfriars House over the bus station, and Belgrave House forming part of the Grosvenor Centre. Close by is the town's newest hotel—the Saxon Inn.

To accommodate the town's rising population well over 11 600 new homes have been

Figure 25.4 Weston Favel district centre.

built, some for sale and other for letting. Since 1970 over 20 000 newcomers have been housed. By December 1976, since designation, 5193 houses have been completed by the development corporation, 3062 by the local authority and 5901 by private enterprise. One of the advantages that Northampton can offer to firms moving to the town is the immediate availability of rented homes for employees. Much of the success of the town's expansion depends on industrial development and more than 1000 of land have been allocated for employment.

Much of the eastern district is now complete and work has started on the construction of roads to open up the southern district. Here it is proposed to build about 13 000 new homes for 40 000 people, as well as all the attendant facilities. The residential areas of Lumbertubs, Thorplands, Standens Barn and Lings are already complete; new schools and local centres are in use, and a community spirit is rapidly developing.

26   Newton Aycliffe

In 1940 a large Royal Ordnance factory was built at Aycliffe in South Durham to which the work people came from surrounding districts and nearby towns, principally Darlington, Middlesborough, Stockton and Bishop Auckland. By the end of the war 15 000 persons were employed in the factory. After relinquishment of war purposes, the buildings were handed over to the North Eastern Trading Estates Ltd (now the English Industrial Estates Management Corporation part of the Department of Industry), and by 1947 approximately 50 firms employing about 3000 persons occupied these factories which by 1976 had increased to over 75 firms employing over 9000 persons of whom three quarters were male. A wide variety of industries are represented, including engineering products, electronics, office machinery, building materials, chemicals, paints and varnish, plastic materials and many others.

It was to provide housing accommodation for the people working in the Aycliffe Industrial Estate that the new town of Aycliffe was designated on 19 April 1947, on a site of 865 acres (350 ha), and it was agreed with local authorities in the area that the maximum population should not exceed 10 000. In 1957 this was increased to 20 000.

This first designated area was formerly within the urban district of Shildon and the rural districts of Darlington and Sedgefield. Later it was all within the Darlington Rural district and since the reorganization of local government it became in 1974 part of the Sedgefield District. It is about 6 miles (10 km) north of Darlington and 9 miles (14 km) south of Durham. The site varies from gently undulating to flat land, mainly agricultural with a few farmhouses and small cottages. At the time of designation the population was about 60.

Extension of the Town

On 13 April 1966 a large extension of 1643 acres (665 ha) was designated for another 25 000 population thus making a town of 45 000 in 2508 acres (1015 ha). This extension emanated from proposals for the development of the north-east made in the White Paper of November 1963. The Department for Industry, Trade and Regional Development selected as the principal growth zone of the region that which extends a little beyond Tyneside in the north and Teesside in the south, the western limit a little to the west of the Great North Road and the eastern limit the coast. 'Within this zone', it was stated, 'the biggest concentration of factors favourable to rapid growth are to be found in the conurbations of Tyneside and Teesside and the Darlington/Aycliffe area. These are accordingly envisaged as the main centres of expansion, and for the time being priority will be given to them in the public investment programme.' Some of the advantages of further development of Aycliffe Industrial Estate were enumerated, and it was mentioned that its potentialities are to some extent shared with nearby Darlington, which is well endowed with housing land and good communications, and is in need of new jobs. The Government therefore 'concluded that there is a good case for increasing the planned population of Aycliffe from 20 000 to about 45 000'. The Minister of Housing and Local Government consequently asked the Aycliffe Development Corporation to recommend a suitable area for the necessary expansion. The report defining a suitable expansion area, with an outline plan, was prepared by C. Edmund Wilford and Son, planning consultants, with advice on traffic from Professor Sir Colin Buchanan and Professor Thomas Williams.

In April 1973 the administration of the Aycliffe Industrial Estates was transferred from the English Industrial Estate Corporation to the development corporation, and in January 1974 the area of this estate of 578 acres (233 ha) was added to the designated area, thus making an overall size of 3083 acres (1248 ha).

The Outline Plan for the First Designated Area

The outline plan was prepared by the Grenfell Baines group, but it has been continually modified as the work proceeded. The industrial area was outside the designated site to the south of the railway that ran east–west from Stockton to Bishop Auckland, and the new town is situated immediately north of this line and west of the old A1 trunk road, now the A167, which forms the height and base of the triangular area of the

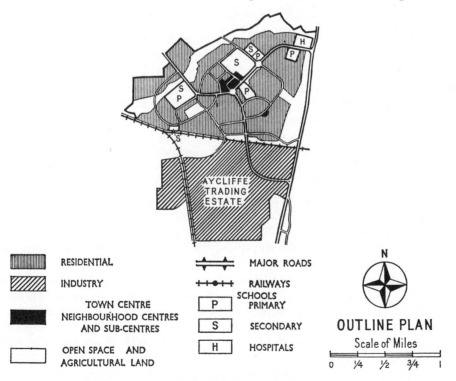

Figure 26.1 Newton Aycliffe—Outline Plan.

town. The outline plan consisted of 6 wards or neighbourhoods grouped round a town centre, with strips of open space to the east, joining the diagonal along the north-west boundary. Each ward was divided into 3 or more precincts. There were 4 ward centres, the 2 wards without them both abutting the town centre. Four primary schools are included, one near the town centre and 3 on the outskirts, north, east and west. Three secondary modern schools and a grammar–technical school were envisaged on a campus near the town centre. The principal road system of the town took the form of a loop from the A1 integrating the residential parts with the industrial estates and intersected by a ring road linking the ward centres with the town centre. The minor roads within wards mostly curve like the traditional English country lane. An important characteristic of the plan is a system of 'village greens', generally one for each precinct, round which the houses are grouped. The town centre was as nearly as possible in the geographical centre of the triangle.

A population of 10 000 in 865 acres (350 ha) represents a fairly low density, but in 1951 the plan was revised and it was proposed to house the 10 000 in a smaller area, but even then it meant a density of no more than 9.7 dwellings per acre (24 per ha). One of the reasons for this change was that it would reduce the costs per dwelling, while under this revised plan land was made available for an increase in the maximum population. This anticipation was realized in 1957 when, as previously noted, the maximum population was raised to 20 000. It was regrettable that an even larger size more in the region of 50 000 was not adopted at the beginning, for a new town of 10 000 is not adequate to support the amenities and recreational facilities that most people require.

Outline Plan for Extension

When C. Edmund Wilford and Son's team prepared the 1966 Master Plan for Expansion, they said in their introduction: 'It should be borne in mind that a master plan is a guide to future development. All the answers cannot be known in advance and should new conditions arise or experience suggest different solutions the "guide" must be modified. Accordingly we hope that our present proposals will not be considered immutable because society cannot and will not live in an inflexible strait-jacket.' Since the acceptance of this new master plan, Aycliffe Development Corporation has followed the principles of the plan while simultaneously reflecting the planning team's views as outlined above. Changing situations have of necessity brought changes in the detailed implementation of the plan, particularly in the timing of some of the development, especially that by the private agencies. In broad terms of land use, however, the corporation has remained faithful to the expansion master plan.

Along the north-west boundary of the original site is Woodham Burn Valley—a small stream with wooded banks. Beyond this boundary is the extension, roughly rectangular in shape.

In the expansion plan residential areas of varying densities are grouped round a wide spine road, and a square pattern or roads on either side. At the north-east of the rectangle is a large golf course with a well-wooded space and a lake to the south. At this end the woodland penetrates the residential area and half encloses a large site for a secondary school. At the south-west corner of the rectangle there are extensive areas for playing fields.

The division into neighbourhoods that characterizes the first part of the town is not followed in the area of the extension. Thirteen shopping points, each consisting

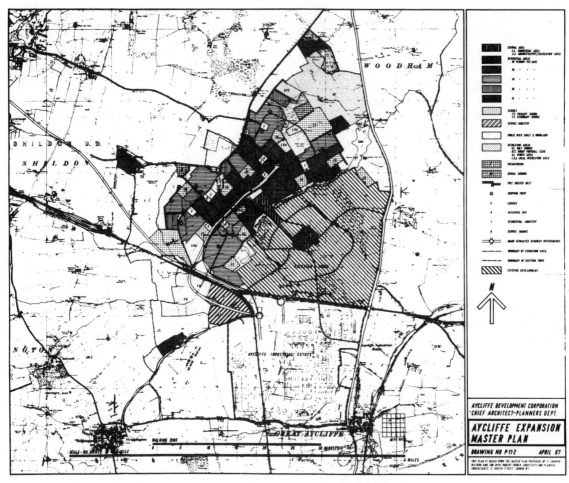

Figure 26.2 Newton Aycliffe extension, Master Plan.

possibly of one general shop, or at most 2 or 3, are scattered at convenient places in the residential areas. Also located at various points are 9 sites for primary schools. Six small sites of about 2 acres (0.8 ha) each were allocated for what is termed residential industry in various localities through the expansion area, to give part-time employment to married women and retired persons in certain types of manufacturing industry. It was subsequently decided not to implement the plan for these 'residential industry' sites.

Five main housing densities are proposed:

80 persons (23.0 houses) per acre (198 persons [56.8 houses] per ha)
65 persons (18.6 houses) per acre (161 persons [46 houses] per ha)
50 persons (14.3 houses) per acre (123 persons [35.2 houses] per ha)
35 persons (10.0 houses) per acre (86 persons [24.6 houses] per ha)
15 persons (4.3 houses) per acre (37 persons [10.6 houses] per ha)

The higher densities would be near the main spine road and the town centre and along Woodham Burn Valley, and the lower densities on the outer fringes and towards both ends of the rectangle. In the higher densities there would be a proportion of flats but these would not generally exceed 4 storeys. There appears to be a fair amount of the residential area—about half—at 23 and 18.6 houses to the acre (56.8 and 46 per ha), which seems to be unnecessarily close building. The people themselves would probably prefer a more spacious development. The low density of 4.3 houses to the acre (10.6 per ha) is in small pockets north and south of the golf course, and in apparently isolated spots in the extreme west and south-west. Spaces for cars are provided in the residential areas on the basis that by the year 2010 car ownership will probably be $1\frac{1}{2}$ cars per family.

With the existing town centre near the geographical centre of the triangle, its location to suit the much enlarged town presented a problem. To enlarge it to serve the whole of the future town would mean its being rather towards the south-east corner. A new one further to the north-west within fairly equal distance of all parts of the town might have been geographically satisfactory, but it would possibly have meant two centres in competition with each other. The plan proposed to enlarge the existing centre as the commercial part with additional shops, and to locate that for administrative and recreational purposes a little distance away and partly in the expansion area, the two being linked by a pedestrian way.

The commercial centre would include, in addition to shopping, the chief post office, a library, a public house and hotel, a health centre, and entertainment buildings, while the administrative–recreational centre would include civic and community buildings and a hall, offices, magistrates' court and a police station, a church and both indoor and outdoor sports facilities. Both centres would be pedestrian precincts with road access to buildings at convenient points and to the rear of shops, and car parks close by including two fairly large multi-storey constructions.

Since the Expansion Plan was accepted in 1968 Aycliffe's planners have continued the process of monitoring changing needs and have undertaken studies of transportation patterns and requirements. In the light of changing circumstances some detailed amendments have been made to the Plan and it seems likely that further modifications will be made.

The whole centre is well over half a mile long (0.8 km), which for a town of this size is rather much. It is not a comfortable or convenient walking distance for everybody. It would have been an advantage if it had been more compact and the arrangement originally proposed must inevitably be seen as one of the disadvantages of planning a town in pieces consequent upon initial inadequacy followed by large-scale extension.

One of the main considerations in the road system is to provide efficient communication between all parts of the town, but particularly between the residential and industrial areas. Between the new residential region and the centre provision is made for one-way traffic. Emphasis is on the use of the private car, and the movement of vehicles to places of work from the new residential areas can be visualized as a feeding from the loops to the main spine road and the procession to the industrial area along wide roads. Efforts are made to avoid high traffic volumes. Throughout the town is a system of footpaths independent of the road system, with overpasses and underpasses at points of intersection, thus securing the maximum segregation of pedestrians and vehicles. Public transport, including buses, mingle with the private. This emphasis on private transport was probably based on the results of the traffic survey. Four categories are given of modes of travel to work:

| Car driver or passenger | 43.1% | Two-wheeled vehicles | 25.9% |
| Bus or train | 16.4% | On foot | 14.6% |

About half of the families in Aycliffe own a car, and it was naturally assumed that with increased car ownership more will travel to work in this way. This, however, is prodigal of land for car parking in the industrial area and it may be questioned whether this transport plan could not be improved. One can visualize a more efficient and well-disciplined system based on public transport.

When the town reaches 45 000 population, 19 500 workers are estimated, 4000 of whom will travel out. Of the remaining 15 500 about 9000 will work in manufacturing industries. Assume, then, that all these go from the residential areas to the industrial estate by car, either as drivers or passengers with an average car occupation of 2, it would mean 4500 cars each morning, with the need for large car parking spaces for a great number of them.

If, however, they all went by conveniently scheduled buses, each with a capacity of 60 and an average occupancy of 45, there would be 200 vehicles instead of 4500 with much less need for large car parking space in the industrial area. These are the two extremes, and there will probably be a proportion of both, but on the basis of the present plan it will have a marked emphasis on the private car. A marked emphasis on public transport with an exclusive route for it would mean far fewer vehicles and far less parking space, and this would secure greater all-round efficiency. Also, stronger emphasis on public transport, with perhaps exclusive routes between the residential areas and the town centre would be an advantage. Women shoppers are less likely to enjoy the availability of cars if these have all gone with their menfolk to the industrial area. The emphasis on public transport is seen in the progressive plans for Runcorn and Redditch, and it is regrettable that the transport plan for Aycliffe is not similarly progressive.

What can be done by public transport to serve workers between their homes and places of work is well illustrated by the super-bus service first provided at Stevenage in 1971 and gradually improved since.

Building the Town

Other than the short-sighted, restricting requirements of the local authorities for the small size of Newton Aycliffe, there was little opposition to the town at the beginning, and fairly good progress was made with housing. By the end of 1953 about 1250 houses had been completed, and then for the next few years until 1962 between 300 and 400 houses were built each year. Then in 1963 until 1967 there was a drop to about 200 a year to rise and fall in the succeeding years to 1976 between 360 and 120, not a big output considering the plan for extension. By the end of 1976, 7445 houses had been built, nearly all by the development corporation; 419 were built by private enterprise and 66 by the local authority.

Residential Areas and Housing

In building the first two wards, A and B, the corporation provided a proportion of flats, 109 combined with 1534 houses. The annual report for 1952 stated that 'as a result of experience gained in the letting of the first 400 dwellings in the town the corporation has found that there is as yet little demand for flats. It has, therefore, been decided not to build any further flats for the time being after those already being erected are completed.' The corporation was anxious to attract a certain number of the middle

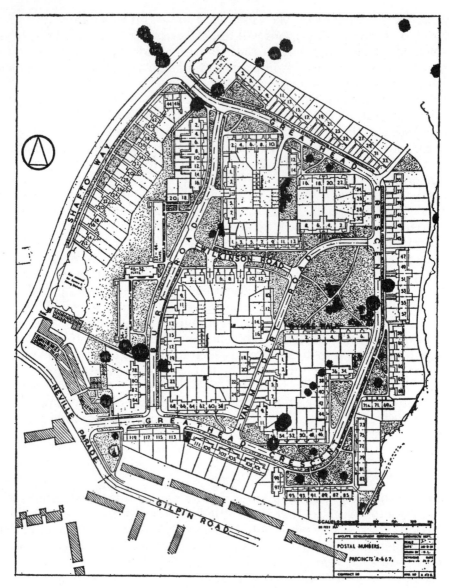

Figure 26.3 Plan of Ward A.

income groups to the town and arranged to provide in 1952 about 10% of the dwellings for them. The remaining 90% for the lower income groups were divided as 2.7% of one-bedroom houses, 48.6% of 2-bedroom houses, 36% of 3-bedroom and 2.7% of 4-bedroom houses. By 1956 these proportions were modified to 2.5% one-bedroom, 29% 2-bedroom, and 61% 3-bedroom, half of which were 4-person houses (one double and 2 single bedrooms) and half 5-person houses (2 double and one single bedrooms). The houses are mostly in 2-storey terraces in short blocks, 3 to 6 or 8 but rarely longer, grouped with considerable variety. They are built mainly of brick, with varying finishes of brick and rendering, with generally low-pitched roofs and gabled ends which gives a restrained appearance.

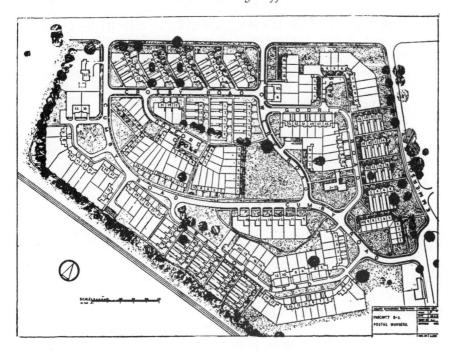

Figure 26.4 Plan of one of the precincts in Ward B.

In conformity with the village green idea which actuated the planning, and with the liberal allowance of space that a 10 000 population in 865 acres (350 ha) made possible, the houses in wards A and B are grouped round generous green areas of varying shapes.

One particularly attractive green is the triangular-shaped area in B2 precinct bounded by Cumby Road and Lowery Road. Along the former road to the south-east is an attractive row of patio houses, linked together by walls and garages, with lawns in front. Towards the point of the triangular green on the further side are trees and a shrubbery near a row of houses, which present a felicitous grouping.

Attractive as are these generous stretches of green plentifully spread in the residential areas, it may be wondered whether they are not overdone, suggesting a too liberal use of land for the purpose. If they had been a little smaller the balance of space could have been used to give slightly larger gardens. When the population was increased to 20 000, later wards were built at a somewhat higher density.

One pleasing aspect of Newton Aycliffe is the practice of naming the streets after persons of historical importance in the region. Thus Aycliffe has its Elizabeth Barrett Walk (after the poet) and Dixon Road (after Jeremiah Dixon of Cockfield, an engineer and surveyor partly responsible for the Mason–Dixon line in the Southern United States) and others. This has served to give people of the town an identity with tradition.

Ward Centres

The shopping centres of A and B wards were completed by the end of 1955. Ward centre A provides 11 shops on a slightly curved alignment on one side of the road

(Neville Parade). A Methodist church is opposite and a little further along the road on the same side as the church is 'The Oak Tree' public house, so that the centre follows a pattern familiar in the new towns. Ward B centre is smaller with 7 shops on one side of the road (Simpasture Gate) with 'The Iron Horse' public house a little away on the other side of the road. Except that the shops are on one side of the road there is little in the nature of a precinct in either, such as might be obtained by being set well back from the road with a broad footway like those found in many of the other new towns.

The Town Centre

The town centre, to the north-west of the Central Avenue at the end where it terminates with a roundabout and connects with Stephenson Way, was a long rectangular area originally with a spine road—Beveridge Way—that curved off the roundabout and became a central straight street between shops. At the north-east end it terminated at Dalton Way, on the further side of which is a group of health and community buildings, a school clinic and a child welfare centre, a library, and a youth club. At the south-east end of Beveridge Way is a short pedestrian shopping precinct. A large car park adjoins Central Avenue at the back of the shops. It did not seem to us a good layout; however, it has been radically altered, for in the 1962 report it was stated that the development corporation had agreed, in principle, to the town centre being re-designed to secure segregation of pedestrians and vehicular traffic in accordance with the need. The substantial improvement was soon effected by the complete pedestrianization similar to that which was advocated in an earlier edition of this work. Further improvement followed the 1968 master plan with the considerable expansion of commercial and recreational facilities in a central area more compact than first envisaged in the expansion master plan. In 1977, the corporation was in the process of developing the town centre further, partly through the (voluntary) transfer of certain amenities (such as the Boys Club) to residential areas more appropriate to their nature than an extended town centre.

Industry

In the first three years following the addition of Aycliffe Industrial Estate to the designated area of the new town, 31 new factories or major extensions were completed, together with a large number of smaller developments. The increase in industrial floorspace was almost 1 000 000 square ft (90 000 m^2) giving a new total of approximately 4 200 000 square ft (390 000 m^2). The corporation built seven factories (or major extensions) for specific clients, seven standard advance factories and nine small advance (workshop units) during this period. Eight factories were built by individual firms.

During this period, some 1800 new jobs were created at Aycliffe which was a considerable achievement in view of the major international recession. By the end of 1976, total employment in Aycliffe, including the industrial estate was more than 10 000 people.

Industrial development is continuing. Early in 1977 several major projects were underway for companies on the estate and the corporation was also constructing two new advance factories capable of flexible sub-division. An older vacant factory was being divided to provide six smaller units at low rents.

Social Aspect

Newton Aycliffe suffered initially in its planning and building from much too small a maximum population, and from the uncertainty whether it was to be 10 or 20 thousand. But even the latter figure was inadequate for the provision of those amenities and facilities of civilized living that most people expect. Anything under 40 000 makes the social problems of providing entertainment and cultural facilities more difficult. Often in the new towns the complaint arises that there are not the social amenities of other older places, and these can only be provided on a reasonable scale if there is the population to support them. Thus the social difficulties of this kind are rather being invited when the population is made initially as low as 10 000. With the expansion to 45 000 many of these amenities are promised.

Aycliffe Development Corporation has endeavoured to come to terms with its difficulties and there is evidence that a large measure of success has been achieved. An active social development department maintains close contact with the 150-plus social organizations in the town and also provides specialist imput at the planning stage of residential, commercial and leisure developments.

Those parts of the town developed under the original Master Plan have particularly good access to town centre facilities, plus the church and meeting halls provided at Neville Parade and Simpasture. In the newer areas, a hierarchy of community-use buildings has been created. The Greenfield Meeting Hall in Horndale is an excellent example of a simple and flexible community building. At Elmfield, an unfortunate instance of arson which destroyed a junior school afforded an opportunity for the corporation to join the Education Authority and the Great Aycliffe Town Council in providing a community-use module as an integral part of the replacement school. At Middridge, the corporation assisted the Village Association to create a new village hall with grant aid from the Department of Education and Science.

The local authorities have been active in fulfilling the social and recreational requirements of Newton Aycliffe, too. In 1974, Sedgefield District Council opened a major indoor recreation facility in the town centre, which had been started by the old Darlington Rural District Council before local government reorganization, at a cost of over £1 000 000. The corporation made a contribution of £100 000 towards this from the Major Amenity Fund. This building contains two swimming pools, two sports halls, plus squash courts, sauna suite, meeting rooms, creche, restaurant and bar. Early in 1977 Sedgefield Council were actively pursuing proposals to develop a large arts and social activities centre on an adjacent site in the town centre. This would provide for facilities for drama, music, painting, sculpture and associated activities.

In January 1977 the Great Aycliffe Town Council embarked on an ambitious new project to develop a major outdoor recreation centre at School Aycliffe. It adjoins a 9-hole golf course development under the MSC Job Creation programme.

27 *Peterlee*

The proposal for a new town in the mining area of east Durham was originally made by the Easington Rural District Council with the purpose of housing a proportion of the scattered population, amounting to some 82 000, of the Easington district. The proposal was adopted by the Minister of Town and Country Planning who stated in the Explanatory Memorandum to the Draft Easington New Town (Designation) Order of 1947 that, 'it seemed clear that the district did have a special claim in that it is situated on the richest part of the Durham coalfield and must in any case receive a high priority in housing, and also that it offered an outstanding opportunity for breaking with the unhappy tradition that miners and their families should be obliged to live in ugly, overcrowded villages clustered around the pitheads, out of contact with people in other walks of life, and even for the most part with workers in other industries. Unless an early start were made with the development of an entirely new settlement in keeping with present-day ideas there would be a serious danger of a resumption of emigration away from the district altogether—one of the most unsatisfactory features of the economic and social experience of the area before the war.'

The new town was designated on 10 March 1948, and is planned for a maximum population of 30 000. The site of 2350 acres (952 ha) is situated about 10 miles (16 km) due east of the city of Durham, a little south of the village of Easington, while the village of Horden lies just beyond the north-east border. A tongue of the designated area stretches eastward to the sea. The ground is hilly in all parts with some steep valleys of considerable beauty to the south.

The majority for whom housing was provided in the new town were employed in the coal mining industry. It is the aim, however, to introduce industry for the minority not so employed which includes a considerable amount of female labour. During the period of building the new town, however, there has been a marked decline in coal mining in the area and it has therefore been necessary to make larger provision for other industries. Thus in 1965 the designated site was increased to 2492 acres (1009 ha) to allow for larger industrial areas. 117 acres (47 ha) were added to the north-west corner on the west side of the A19, an addition of 13 acres (5 ha) to the originally planned industrial area of the north, while two further additions each of 6 acres (2.5 ha) were made in the south-west corner, following the re-alignment of the A19 trunk road. The maximum population by intake remains at 30 000.

It has been named Peterlee after one of the most famous of Durham miners' leaders—Peter Lee—who was secretary of the Durham miners and later president of the Miners' Federation of Great Britain. He was also a Chairman of the Durham

County Council. He died in 1935 and was buried at Wheatley Hill just outside the designated area.

Outline Plan

The site of the new town is over mines containing some 30 million tons of coal. Mining operations continued at the same time as the new town was being built up to 1974 and then they ceased below the town. It was, therefore, necessary to prepare two co-ordinated plans, one for the coal mining and one for the new town. This made the plan one of the most difficult to prepare, while the necessity of securing co-ordination with the National Coal Board caused delay.

Some useful preparations for a plan had been made by C. W. Clarke, the Surveyor to the Easington Rural District Council, whose enthusiasm had contributed much to furthering the idea of a new town.

An advisory committee which preceded the development corporation by a few months early in 1948, appointed Berthold Lubetkin as architect-planner who, it was hoped, would 'not only plan the town, but who would also build it'. On the instructions of the Minister an outline for a master plan was to be prepared 'on the purely

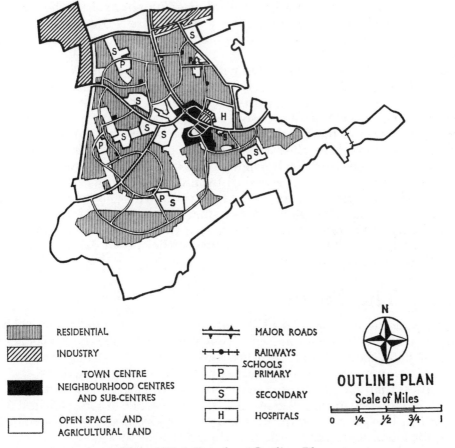

Figure 27.1 Peterlee—Outline Plan.

theoretical assumption that the problem of coal did not exist', a kind of ideal plan from which realistic plans could be made. This ideal plan was presented to both the Minister and corporation in November 1948. Later three alternative apparently realistic outline plans were produced from which the corporation selected one. In March 1950 Berthold Lubetkin resigned and was succeeded by Grenfell/Baines and Hargreaves as planning consultants. They prepared a plan which was published in September 1952; some further revisions were made and the whole scheme was submitted to the Ministry in December of that year. Agreements had been reached with the Coal Board.

Owing to the mining and the risks of subsidence and to the natural features of the site only a part of it, some 1060 acres (429 ha) of the total of 2350 acres (952 ha), is available for building. Along the south of the area is Castle Eden Dene, a wooded valley varying from 600 feet to 1250 feet (180 m to 381 m) wide and up to 150 feet (46 m) deep. This is joined by Blunts Dene which starts as a small valley in the centre of the town and broadens and deepens southwards, and is about 600 feet (180 m) wide and 150 feet (46 m) deep at the point where it joins Castle Eden Dene. These Denes account for about 540 acres (219 ha). Of the several strips of land that have had to be avoided owing to subsidence, one strip runs east–west in the south-west corner of the site, another runs north from it on the west side and joins strips forming a rectangle west of the town centre, while another runs northward from this. Parts of the area to the north-east where it adjoins the village of Horden will not be available because they are used for games and allotments, part is very steep, part is occupied by the ancient Yoden village of some historical interest, while the ground is not geologically satisfactory for building.

The plan consists of residential areas with populations of between 5000 and 7500 each sub-divided into 2 or 3 units. This plan seems to fall naturally into 5 or 6 neighbourhoods: the south-east, north-east, north-west, west and south-west; the last mentioned, being divided by an east–west subsidence strip, could also be regarded as two. Between each of the 5 main neighbourhoods are main town roads which all connect with the town centre, almost the geographical centre, and no more than a mile from houses on the outskirts. Each neighbourhood has infant, junior and secondary schools. The shopping centres are well distributed, 2 being provided in each of the neighbourhoods with the exception of the south-east where, because of its proximity to the town centre, one is adequate. An industrial area of about 80 acres (32 ha), mainly for light industry to provide alternative employment to coal mining, and to absorb a proportion of female labour, is sited along the northern boundary, while an area of service industry is placed in the town centre.

Building The Town

A start with building was made in 1950, and it was aimed to build about 500 houses a year, an aim that was achieved in 1952. Thereafter the number built was generally a little short of that—about 450 in 1953, 380 in 1954, 525 in 1955, 360 in 1956, then a further drop in 1957, as in most other new towns, owing to credit restrictions, the number being a little less than 200. Some recovery was made to 360 in 1958, about 220 were built in 1959, 330 in 1960, 360 in 1961, 225 in 1962, 310 in 1963, 366 in 1964, 480 in 1965, 378 in 1966 and 156 in 1967, so that by the end of that year 5500 houses had been built, thus providing for a population of a little over 18 000.

There was a considerable rise in output in 1968 to 620, a high level which was nearly maintained in 1969 and 1970 with 465 and 494. Then in 1971 there was a sharp drop to 175, and this low output continued in 1972 with 158 to rise a little in 1973 to 298 and to 402 in 1974 and then to fall to 274 in 1975 and 143 in 1976. Altogether since designation up to the end of 1976 about 8050 houses have been built of which 7389 were by the development corporation, 229 by the local authority and 432 by private enterprise.

Except for a group of 106 dwellings at Thorntree Gill in the eastern extremity of the town the first developments have taken place in the north-eastern and north-western neighbourhoods. The schools and the shopping centres, 2 in each, have been completed. One row of shops had been provided in the town centre by the middle of 1959. A complete re-appraisal of the fundamental structure of the centre was made in the early 1960s. As a result a 2-level pedestrian shopping centre was planned and built. By 1977, 131 shops were open, together with a large departmental store and a big office block. The technical college immediately to the west of the town centre was completed in the late sixties and a swimming pool also adjacent to the centre has been provided. The parish church of St Cuthbert to the south of the centre was dedicated at the end of 1957, and a little later the Peter Lee Memorial Methodist Church and group of buildings a little to the west were opened. Delay in building the town centre appears to have been due mainly to the difficulty of co-ordinating surface development with the information given by the National Coal Board on underground workings.

The development of the industrial zone was a little slow, some difficulty apparently being experienced in the early years in attracting industry. In spite of the slow start, however, the corporation was confident, as stated in its report for 1958, that 'from the interest which has been shown during the recent period that additional industry will be established in the near future'. This was slowly realized and by the early sixties the position greatly improved.

Housing and Residential Areas

The early housing was in accordance with the standards proposed in the Dudley Report, but in 1952 some reduction was secured in the circulation space by tight planning in accordance with a regrettable national policy, and what was known as the 'Q' type was employed at Peterlee for a considerable number of houses in the north-eastern and north-western neighbourhoods. It was the policy of the corporation to build mainly 2-bedroom and 3-bedroom houses in the proportion of 45 and 34% in terrace blocks of 4 houses, or as semi-detached houses. The area of the 'Q' type 2-bedroom house was 756 sq. ft (70 m²) and that of the 'Q' type 3-bedroom house 895 sq. ft (83 m²); the former of which is by accepted minimum standards 100 sq. ft (9 m²) too small and the latter 50 sq. ft (4.5 m²) too small. Thus, much of the housing in Peterlee during the early fifties was not of very high standard, but the later dwellings show some improvement. The proportion of flats, mainly of 2 and 3 storeys, is not more than 10%, while a few houses have been built for middle and higher income groups.

If criticisms can be made of the space standards of the dwellings there is little that is wrong with the layouts of the houses and the architectural effects, many of which are delightful. The pattern in the residential areas, like that in most of the new towns, is of an irregular character, with curved roads and culs-de-sac, sometimes with the ends connected to roads by pedestrian ways, while there are open spaces of various shapes and sizes spread throughout the neighbourhoods. Several are small, but several are of

Figure 27.2 Peterlee—Chapel Hill with the neighbourhood centre.

a considerable size, as one in the north-west neighbourhood, giving the impression of houses round a very spacious village green. Another, also in the north-west, has a triangular green bordered by 2 rows of one-storey houses for old people. Advantage has been taken of the contours of the low hills to make the roads curve with them.

Some good effects have been obtained on the east side of Essington Way. This is one of the principal town roads which runs north from the town centre between the north-western and north-eastern neighbourhoods. On the west side the neighbourhood has been partitioned off by means of fences or shrubs from this main road and the houses abut variously on to it. On the east side, on the contrary, there is a broad green sloping up from the road and on the lawns are an occasional tree, groups of shrubs and flower beds. At the top of this broad slope houses are variously grouped, some forming a partial courtyard, while at one point 3-storey blocks of flats give height and variety. The landscape effect of this east bank of Essington Way is one of the highlights of the town.

Among the earlier houses that are architecturally pleasing are those of brick with garages and low-pitched roofs for middle income groups along Essington Way, and some entirely flat-roofed houses with sand lime brick walls and weather boarding between storeys in the hilly area immediately north of the town centre.

The south-west neighbourhood immediately west of Bluntsdene was the subject of an interesting experiment. In the 300 acres (122 ha) 4 groups or communities were planned with a total of some 2000 houses for a population of about 7000.

The first two groups, completed in 1962, aroused a good deal of attention, especially in architectural circles. The whole south-west scheme emanates from a desire of the manager of the development corporation, A. V. Williams, for improved and more distinctive housing in Peterlee; and he instigated the collaboration of the famous modern painter, Victor Pasmore, with two architects of the development corporation's staff: Peter Daniel and Frank Dixon. Williams had carefully examined the structure of the town which revealed that in earlier developments sufficient emphasis had not been laid on the organic use of space. Williams had previously worked with Sir Charles Reilly whose ideas for village greens had been developed in schemes at Bilston and Dudley which Williams put into operation. He was also influenced in his ideas by Dr Otto Neurath, the Viennese sociologist. Before the team was appointed Williams and Pasmore fully discussed their ideas, and the planning, spatial and social conceptions realized in the south-west neighbourhood are largely the result of their collaborations.

There are 13 different types of houses in these groups of 388 houses, the net housing area being about 30 acres (12 ha), thus a density of about 13 to the acre (32 per ha). Because of the special precautions due to mining subsidence, building was restricted as a general rule to not more than 2 storeys with a few light 3-storey constructions. The house types include detached and semi-detached 2-storey dwellings, short rows of 3-storey terrace houses and some one-storey houses for old people.

The whole conception of this first section of the neighbourhood is of a formal geometric character. The rectangular blocks of varied houses are sited on roads laid out in a rectangular fashion, many of which terminate as culs-de-sac and branch from a road which links with the spine road of the neighbourhood. This spine road connects the town centre with the A19 road bordering the west of the town.

The layout results from a carefully conceived grouping of houses and functional spaces. One group of detached houses is arranged in echelon fashion linked by entrance units. Some have square spaces between them where children can play and cars can be parked. Some of the semi-detached blocks are cubes flanked by small gardens which are walled in on two sides and fenced on a third, thus giving a degree of privacy. In the patio type of semi-detached house the courtyard garden is enclosed on two sides by the house, and on the other sides by the front wall and a heavy dividing fence. The part of the house opposite the entrance is a one-storey structure used, it seems, as a lounge, while the kitchen and dining room are near the entrance. The patio garden is small.

In the 3-storey terrace houses a garage and drying room and a small verandah at the back are on the ground floor, living room and kitchen on the first floor, and 2 or 3 bedrooms on the second floor.

The façades of the houses are reminiscent of some of Victor Pasmore's pictures. They are rectangular patterns of black or dark grey and off-white brickwork, and timber boarding painted black, grey, white and sometimes red. The greys and blacks seem to predominate and they make a rather sombre effect which is supposed to harmonize

278

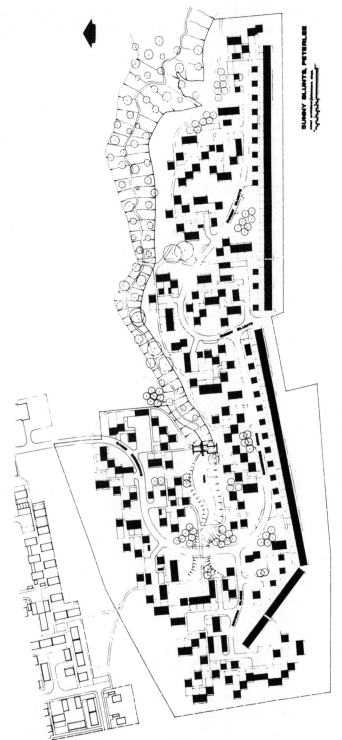

Figure 27.3 Plan of the Sunny Blunts development.

with the bleak atmosphere of the north. One would have thought that the bleak north would have welcomed a bright, warm effect.

The spaces created by the arrangement of the houses are often pleasant and are occupied by such features as a play sculpture, a paddling pool, areas of grass and an occasional flower bed, while the variety of textures in the footways, concrete slabs, dolomite, gravel and macadam, give interest. Bollards are prominent items of furniture placed to keep cars in their places, but they sometimes provide decorative notes and objects for children to climb over.

The scheme prompts some misgiving. Although thought has been given to the relation of the housing to the landscape, to some it is a formal geometric conception imposed on the site and rather alien to the landscape. Also there is the feeling of compactness at any price; the tiny gardens seem boxed in. One visitor thought of crated human beings, a very depressing feeling that is not without justification. Residents seem to be very willing to show visitors over their houses. A resident of more than average intelligence when interviewed was asked what he thought of the scheme. He remarked that he thought it probably looked very good on paper, which carried a note of critisism. He also remarked that it would be nice to have a bit of garden. (He lived in a 3-storey terrace house without a garden.)

What will we think of the scheme in 20 years' time? Its authors have been very scornful of the earlier more traditional housing, one remarking rather despotically that 'we decided that we shall not tolerate the back garden mania of the new town', but it is not improbable that in 20 years' time we shall realize that the earlier housing of Peterlee was nearer to human needs and wishes than this rather academic architectural experiment. This type of development would be more acceptable with more generous space standards, especially in the matter of gardens. It is a question whether the open space that flows between the groups would not be more appreciated if it were utilized as larger private gardens.

The third group of houses in the south-west neighbourhood was continued on similar lines, but with some significant modifications.

There are 292 houses in an area of $18\frac{1}{2}$ acres (7.5 ha) thus about 16 to the acre (40 per ha), slightly higher than the first two groups. The houses are of 7 different types, 5 of which are 2-storey. Of these the largest are detached with 4 bedrooms, small gardens and garages, others with 3 bedrooms have a single-storey wing forming a courtyard. There are rows of 3-bedroomed terrace houses, pairs of 2-bedroom houses, and a few maisonettes cantilevered over carports. A few one-bedroom single-storey houses for old people are mingled with the other houses, and there are a few 3-storey blocks of single-bedroom flats over garages. Two hundred and fourteen garages are provided, 15 carports and parking space for another 110 cars, so that there is a little more than one car space per household. The houses have dark blue-grey brickwork with window frames and timber panels painted white.

The area is largely pedestrian with squares and footpaths to which the principal rooms face, with roads that give access to garages. There is a large green around which the varied houses are grouped, and in its centre some fine mature beech and elm trees have been preserved. They partly suggested the plan.

The general effect of the third group in which Victor Pasmore also collaborated is rather more pleasing than the previous two because the whole has been done with a little more restraint, with more consistent dependence on compositions of cube and rectangle for architectural effect and a slightly softer, more subdued colouring, while the composition of the houses round the green with the large trees has a Greek-like serenity which makes it one of the finest things of its kind achieved in any of the new towns.

Other recent housing is in the fourth, fifth and sixth residential areas of the Acre-Rigg neighbourhood on a hill in the north-west. The fourth, consisting of 272 houses at a density of 13.8 to the acre (34 per ha) completed in 1966, is an adaptation of the Radburn layout with a footpath system and two forked culs-de-sac feeding into the area, thus achieving a high degree of segregation of pedestrians and wheeled traffic. Two-storey houses are in clusters, some arranged in echelon fashion and others in terraced rows, the former having low mono-pitched roofs, the others flat roofs. The walls are of 2-storey height, vertical panels of pale sand lime bricks alternating with slightly recessed fenestration areas with dark timber infill panels. The ensemble on the hill strikes a decided mid-twentieth century note making much of the earlier housing look rather cottagey by contrast. The houses in the sixth Acre-Rigg area completed in 1968 are somewhat similar in style, and were built on the Swedish Skarne concrete slab system, with various finishes.

Neighbourhood Centres

Of the neighbourhood shopping centres completed, that of Chapel Hill in the north-west neighbourhood of Edenhill Road is the most attractive. It consists of 8 shops, 5 of which are parallel with, and set well back from, the road, with buildings, one a common or community room, at each end sited obliquely from the road so that a large bay is formed with wide pavements and stretches of grass in front of the shops, which are in 2-storey buildings with flats above. The centre off York road in the north-western neighbourhood consists of 2 rows of shops forming two sides of a square with a triangular space in front. Opposite this is the attractive building of the secondary school.

Two centres are just rows of shops on one side of the road, the footway in each case being raised from the road. That of Edenhill in Yoden road in the north-eastern area consists of a row of 8 shops with flats above, and a public house, 'The Royal Arms', at one end. Opposite this is a community hall. The other at Beverley Way in the north-west area is a row of 4 shops set in a 3-storey building block of interesting design. The top storey has a recessed balcony, the 2 square windows are set in a brick wall, the middle storey is faced with timber boarding, while the shop front is framed in a strongly defined rectangle, with entrances on either side. The building is interesting architecturally, but as a small shopping centre it is a little uninviting and has not the intimate quality of the partial enclosure of the Chapel Hill centre.

Town Centre

The design for the town centre in the master plan of 1952 was not a very progressive one and was planned on stereotyped traditional lines before the value of the pedestrian precinct as exemplified at Stevenage and Coventry was fully realized. Two later plans were made, both completely different from the first plan. They incorporated several pedestrian areas and shopping ways on 2 levels. In that finally adopted, Yoden Way is changed to a pedestrian area, which broadens out to form the main town centre square. At right angles to this is another pedestrian shopping way called The Chare

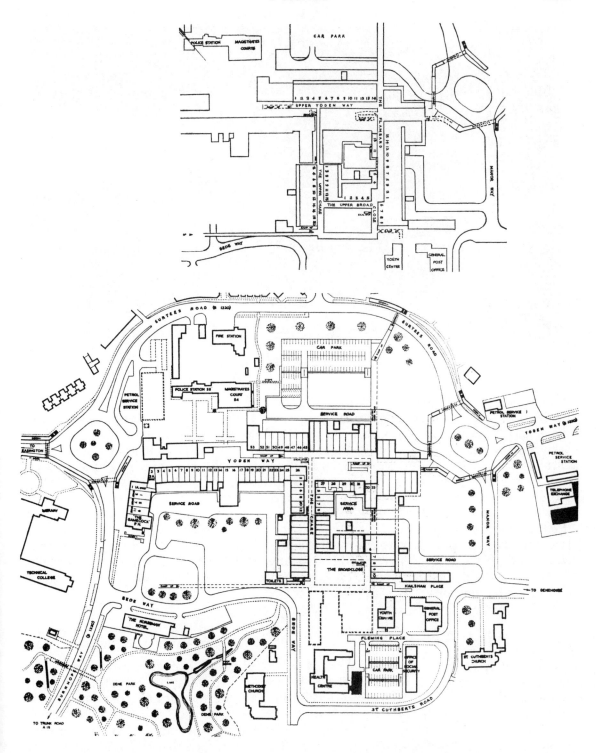

Figure 27.4 Plan of Peterlee town centre which is mainly a pedestrian area on two levels. Above: upper level. Below: lower level.

Figure 27.5 Town centre showing two level shopping.

which leads to a square called Broadclose and on to a group of buildings that includes health and youth centres. A ramp leads up from Yoden Way to the upper pedestrian ways and Upper Yoden Way, the Upper Chare and the Flambard which bridges a service area below. Both lead to the upper level of the Broadclose in which is an escalator. The 2-level development is facilitated by the contours of the site. Two multi-storey car parks are on the periphery of the centre; and on the west side is the Norseman Hotel which overlooks the wooded declivity of Dene Park with its lake, thus providing an attractive landscape near the town centre. Among other buildings round the town centre are the technical college, library, health centre, magistrates' court and two churches. A sports centre complex is currently under construction by the district council. With the large departmental store built in 1975 the centre was substantially complete. As a pedestrian centre on 2 levels adapted to a hilly site it is a design of considerable ingenuity.

Industrial Area

As previously noted the industrial situation in Peterlee has changed since the new town was designated. It was originally planned for a mining community, with coal mining as the major industry with provision for a subordinate amount of employment in manufacturing industry located in the north-east. During the fifties, however, conditions changed. In the early years of the decade not enough coal was being produced to meet the country's needs; in the late years of the decade there was excess of production; and early in 1963 undistributed stocks amounted to about 25 million tons (25 500 000 t). As a consequence uneconomic pits were being closed and employment in the mines gradually fell; and so it is important to find alternative employment for displaced miners in the coal areas of which Peterlee is one. Thus manufacturing industries in Peterlee have become more important in providing employment, which explains the addition of 142 acres (57 ha) to the area in the town for this purpose. In 1961 there were 5 factories, by 1977 there were 35 providing about 5000 jobs with the early employment ratio of two women to one man changing in the new incoming companies, which are mainly engineering, to seven men to one woman. Companies from the USA, Japan and Italy have moved in and the industrial attraction of the area in 1977 is growing.

Social Aspect

Talks with miners in Peterlee show that for the most part they like the new town; they appreciate what is being done for them in improved housing. Some are beginning to think of Peterlee as a beautiful place. Peterlee is designed partly to meet the needs of a scattered population of some 82 000 in the Easington district. In creating a town centre with recreational facilities the development corporation aims at providing for this population. Also, if the north-east is to attract employment, amenities must be provided so as to make it competitive with other parts of the country. A multi-purpose hall of the Technical College, completed in 1962, is available for public use; in 1974 a swimming pool was opened by the district council and in 1975 another neighbourhood community hall came into use while the sports centre is under construction.

There is no doubt that the community association performs a useful service, and that the community halls and common rooms such as those in the neighbourhood centres, and that at Eden Lane, are valuable, but they are usefully supplemented by the facilities provided near the town centre for those who wish to take some of their pleasures apart from community organizations and societies. It may be questioned, too, whether the various societies affiliated to the community association are satisfied with their premises, and whether, for example, the drama group would not appreciate a small theatre in the town centre partly as a stimulus to its own activities, or whether many of the other associations would not find a good hall in the centre of value for some of their larger meetings.

28 *Washington*

In the White Paper outlining the Government's policy for regional development in the north-east of England (November 1963), it was pointed out that new towns are not only an important way of helping to relieve housing needs and congestion in cities, but they can play a big part in stimulating a region's economic and social development and raising the quality of its life. Peterlee and Aycliffe were performing these functions in the north-east, and their success suggested that there was a good case for a third new town to provide a stimulus to industrial development in the north-east, and that it should be Washington. A draft designation order was therefore made on 26 March 1964 and after the usual public inquiry the new town was designated on 24 July 1964.

The comparative depression of industry in the north-east, the migration of population away from the area and the need for industrial stimulus were very strong reasons for building another new town here. Many of the urban areas on the Tyne showed stationary or declining populations in the 20 years following the Second World War. In the 10 years from 1951 to 1961 Newcastle and Gateshead together showed an actual decrease of population from 406 831 to 372 939, a reduction of nearly 40 000. The decrease continued in the 1961–71 period from 372 939 to 316 610, a reduction of about 56 000. In most other Tyneside towns the populations were mainly stationary or slightly declined, meaning a considerable migration away from the region.

The site of Washington, originally some 5300 acres (2147 ha) and extended in June 1972 by 285 acres (115 ha), is close to Tyneside conurbation. It is now part of the Tyne and Wear Metropolitan County Council. The centre of Washington is only about 6, $4\frac{1}{2}$, 3 and 5 miles (10, 7, 5 and 8 km) from the centres of Newcastle, Gateshead, Felling and Sunderland respectively, with a narrow strip of between $\frac{1}{2}$ and $1\frac{1}{2}$ miles (0.8 km and 2.4 km) of open country between the boundaries. The strip is partly proposed and partly approved green belt. A socially satisfactory way of contributing to industrial revival and stimulus of such an area as Tyneside and Wearside is by new town clusters. Departing from the concept of the first generation new towns, the town is not conceived as being self-contained and considerable travel to work across the boundaries occurs. However, the green belt should remain inviolate, otherwise Washington will just become an addition to the conurbation.

The site of the new town is fairly flat in its northern part, sloping towards the south-east where the River Wear is within the boundary. In 1964 there were 4 small communities on the site, New Washington to the north, Washington village, in the centre Washington Station, towards the south-east, and Harraton and Fatfield in the south, making a total population of about 20 000. The population depended on a modicum of industry in the area, principally mining and manufacturing located mainly near the Washington Station.

The name Washington is derived from the Manor and family who owned it. Originally called the manor of Wessyngton it was acquired by William de Hertburn in 1183 who took the name of Wessyngton as was then the custom. Gradually Wessyngton became Washington. Two members of the family, John and Lawrence Washington, emigrated to Virginia in 1656. The former, who became Colonel John Washington, was the grandfather of George Washington, the first president of the United States. The Old Hall (the Manor) of Washington had by the thirties become very derelict, but has been restored and was opened by the American Ambassador, Winthrop Aldridge, in 1955 and is now under the National Trust. The coat of arms of the old Washington family had bars and mullets which are thought to be the origin of the stars and stripes of America.

Outline Plan

The master plan for Washington prepared by Lord Llewelyn Davies, J. Weeks and Partners, with Sylvia Crowe and Associates as landscape consultants was published in January 1967. It follows the interim proposals in broad principles, but there are several changes in their application. The town is planned for a maximum population of about 80 000, reaching 60 000 to 65 000 by 1981, the remainder being by natural increase.

The plan consists of 18 neighbourhoods or villages, as they are called, each with a population of about 4500, and occupying an area of approximately $\frac{1}{2}$ sq. mile (1.30 km²). This size is determined by the population which, it is calculated, would feed a 2-form entry primary school. Each village is planned round a centre containing some shops for daily needs, the primary school, a village social centre, and a public house, similar to the neighbourhood centres of the older new towns but with more pedestrian precincts. The villages are grouped within the grid of primary roads that form approximately one-mile squares (2.6 km²). In the interim plan the road network was based on a $\frac{1}{2}$-mile (0.8 km) grid, each square enclosing one village. Such a road network consisted of one level of road only which it was hoped could carry the predicted peak traffic effectively. This was found not to be the case, so in the master plan the grid is changed to one-mile (1.6 km), squares, with 2, 3 and 4 villages in each with a system of secondary roads feeding the primary road network at specified points, called nodes in the plan. This secondary road network 'comprises two classes of road: "secondary spur" and "secondary distributor"'. The former are the short lengths of road immediately adjacent to the node points on the primary system. The more extensive and numerous 'secondary distributors' pass through industrial areas and village centres and give access to development roads serving individual buildings and sites. The primary roads link with the A1(M) the A194(M) and the A108 on the western, northern and eastern boundaries respectively.

In addition to the road system there is a comprehensive pedestrian network, mainly of straight footpaths, termed 'inter-village walkways', based on a $\frac{1}{2}$-mile (0.8 km) grid. These walkways link the residential areas with each village centre, and pass over or under the primary roads at quarter points on each square mile, by means of underpasses or bridges.

The outline plan refers to a rapid transit rail system possibly passing through Washington between Newcastle and Sunderland. Development of the rapid transit

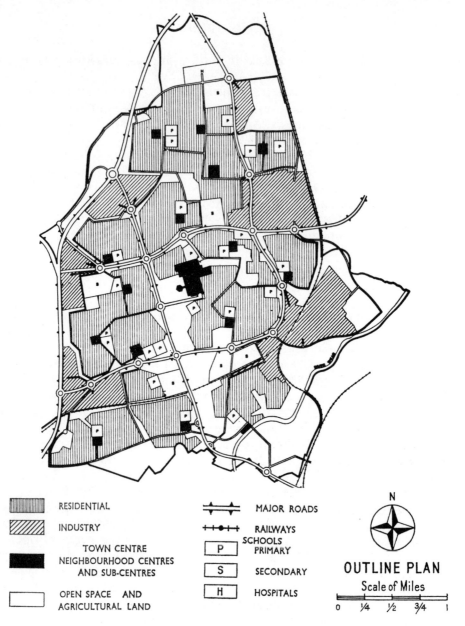

RESIDENTIAL

INDUSTRY

TOWN CENTRE
NEIGHBOURHOOD CENTRES
AND SUB-CENTRES

OPEN SPACE AND
AGRICULTURAL LAND

MAJOR ROADS

RAILWAYS

SCHOOLS
P — PRIMARY

S — SECONDARY

H — HOSPITALS

N

OUTLINE PLAN

Scale of Miles

0   ¼   ½   ¾   1

Figure 28.1 Washington Outline Plan.

system for Tyneside (METRO) is under construction and its extension to Sunderland via Washington could take place in the 1980s depending upon the preferred structure plan transport strategy.

In the interim plan the proposed location of the principal shopping centre was towards the south of the site, with the main civic centre a little away to the north. However, because the load bearing capacities of the original site were unsatisfactory, this was changed and the main shopping centre is now approximately in the geographical centre, linked by a parkway to the administrative centre. The shopping precinct is directly connected with two nodes on east–west and north–south primary roads. The main pedestrian thoroughfares have vehicle access to the rear of the shops.

Among the facilities provided are a health centre, a main library, public houses and restaurants, offices, a college of further education, and a little to the west a sports stadium. The administrative centre includes the county and local authority offices, a labour exchange and national insurance office, police station and magistrates' court.

In addition to the town and village centres 3 local ones are proposed in the plan; that in the north, which already exists as the centre of the residential area of New Washington, a second near Harraton a little to the south-west of the town centre, and a third on the River Wear at Fatfield, where the river will be developed as an amenity. With the villages adjacent to the town centre or local centres separate village centres were considered unnecessary in the plan.

Industrial sites are grouped near the east and west boundaries, on either side, and closely related to nodes on the primary road system, in order to relieve traffic loads at peak times. A further area of 194 acres (79 ha) has been added to the east, within the extension to the designated area, giving 8 industrial areas in all.

A fair variety of housing is provided with the higher densities towards the town and village centres, becoming lower towards the outskirts. Houses are grouped in relation to secondary roads. These are interspersed with public gardens and footpaths and the houses generally face onto cul-de-sac roads, footpaths and gardens. Such layouts give a pleasing degree of residential seclusion.

The original plan for high rise development at the town centre is not being implemented although there is a higher proportion of flats near the town centre which are designed for the single person and small family accommodation.

The plan is generally excellent, better than one was led to expect from the interim proposals. An especially good feature is the communication system.

Building the Town

The master plan was formerly approved, with minor alterations, by the Minister of Housing and Local Government following the public inquiry in July 1967. In this year building commenced.

Between 1968 and 1977 good progress has been made with building the residential areas of the villages and by 1977 more than half the town has been built, which is very good progress. By the end of 1975 8762 new dwellings had been completed and a further 1597 were added in 1976 giving a total of 10 359, 6682 by the development corporation, 1284 by the local authority and 2393 by private enterprise.

The first village centre to be completed was that of Donwell in 1969, followed by Barmston, Blackfell and Sulgrave built in 1973, and later Albany, Biddick, Oxclose and Glebe. Good progress was also made with the town centre the first part being completed in 1973 and phase 2 started in late 1976. The building of factories has made similarly good progress, and industrial development began shortly after the designation of the town. Before designation there were in addition to the basic coal mining industry, some 10 factories in the 2 eastern sites employing about 3600, and the corporation began building industrial premises in order to attract industry as early as 1966. By the beginning of 1977 there were over 150 new factories employing about 9000 making a total employment in manufacturing and service industry and in shops and offices of over 18 000. This is creditable progress in view of the demise of coal mining in the area; the last mine closing at the end of 1975.

Housing and Residential Areas

As mentioned in the description of the master plan, 2, 3 or 4 villages are situated within each of the one sq. mile (2.57 km²) areas formed by the grid of primary roads. Secondary roads enclose each village, and the residential precincts are fed by culs-de-sac branching from the secondary roads. The houses variously face the branch roads or pedestrian areas and ways between the houses. Thus there is no through road within a village, although buses do have access through the centres. There is a principal walkway which passes through the village centre and connects with the other villages, crossing the secondary roads by under- or over-passes. The pedestrian ways, whether the principal walkway or the subsidiary paths among the houses, occasionally open to squares with lawns and trees, as in one particular spot near Rowan Avenue, Harraton—the housing here incidentally receiving a Ministry award for good design. Along the pedestrian ways and intespersed in the residential areas are children's playgrounds of various kinds.

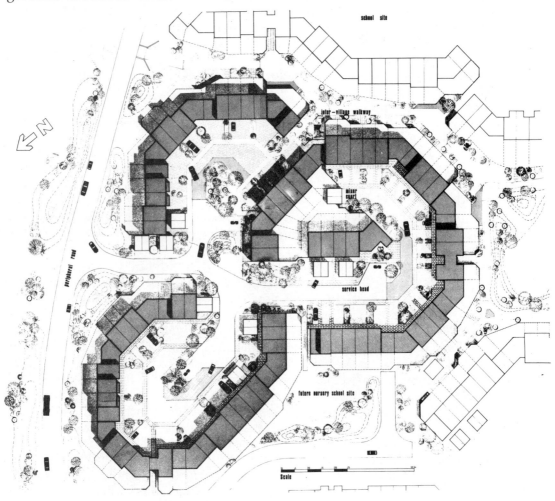

Figure 28.2 Plan of mixer courts—Glebe I and II.

Figure 28.3 A group of houses in Glebe Village Projects I and II. The houses are arranged around pedestrian /vehicular mixer courts at a density of 20.7 dwellings per acre (51 per ha).

The branch roads are often of considerable length with several subsidiary branches mostly with T-shaped terminations. Gargages are variously placed in rows, or at the ends of gardens or are provided as an integral part of the housing development, this being done with good effect in a number of cases. Some recent developments at Glebe and elsewhere are provided with 'mixer courts', which are attractively planted and paved thus serving as open space and play space for children while also giving access to private cars.

Most of the dwellings for letting are terrace houses with small gardens, while those for sale are either semi-detached or detached. The mono-pitched roof has been employed very often with good effect. One good example is a group of variously designed houses for sale at Blackfell village, yet all with the mono-pitched roofs making attractive variations on a theme. Some of the domestic architecture is distinctive, a particularly attractive group being the split level houses at Donwell. Here between 2 solid flanking walls the frontages are formed by large areas of fenestration on ground and first floors separated by horizontal bands of boarding.

The use of articulated terracing and a variety of house types within a small area is aesthetically pleasing and lends a high degree of individuality to the buildings.

Village Centres

The village centres serve populations of 4000–5000 and the 8 of those that have so far been built are small, intimate pedestrian precincts consisting of a few shops, a meeting hall, a public house, sometimes a social club, an open air sitting out place, while nearby is the primary school. Two particularly attractive ones are those at Blackfell and Donwell.

Figure 28.4 Blackfell village centre.

In the former, round the central precinct north of the main pedestrian walkway, shops are arranged diagonally with a covered way in front, while on the east side is a meeting hall, and on the west side, 'The Honest Boy' public house. In the centre of the paved area is a sculpture, and nearby is a sitting out place with a few trees, shrubs and flowers. On the south side of the walkway is the social club and primary school.

The Town Centre

As previously mentioned the town centre is in the geographical centre. The principal shopping area is mainly pedestrian, set in a square formed by a periphery road from which, north and south, there are 2 service roads. In the south-west corner of the square is the large Woolco department store, adjacent is the extensive covered shopping and commercial area known as the Galleries. Further north, within the square, work on phase 2 has started. In the south-east corner is a group comprising public library, health centre and police station. The shopping provision and facilities follow very much those of the other new towns, except that here they are more compactly planned than was usual with the earlier new towns—a compactness that makes easier fairly complete pedestrianization. In the north-west beyond the periphery road is a large government computer centre, while other office blocks are provided in the north-east and south-west of the centre. In the south beyond the periphery road is the award winning sports centre which includes a sports hall, swimming pool and stadium.

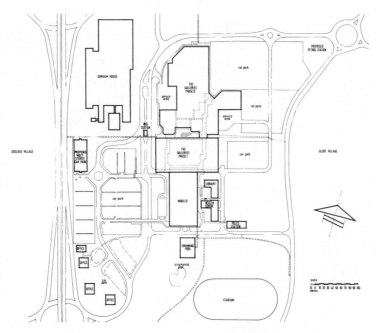

Figure 28.5 Town centre plan showing disposition of shopping, commercial and community facilities. To create a safe environment pedestrians and vehicles are vertically segregated.

Industry and Industrial Areas

As in other new towns factories for the manufacturing industries consist of those built by the firms themselves, which are generally the larger factories, and premises provided by the development corporation, often of a standard design and built in a

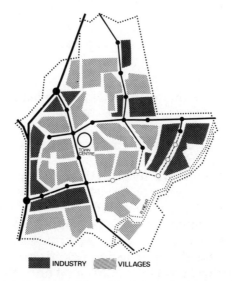

INDUSTRY   VILLAGES

Figure 28.6 Relationship of industrial areas and villages.

Figure 28.7 Crowther industrial estate—small advance nursery factory units, 3300 sq. ft. (300 m²), with 10 000–13 000 sq. ft. (900–1200 m²) standard units in the background. The layout of the nursery units is based on enclosed circular courts relating to former mine shafts which enables uninterrupted flows of vehicular movement.

variety of sizes from the large to the nursery. These, called advance factories, are built as an inducement to firms to come to Washington, and, as with some of the other new towns, the policy is meeting with success. They vary in size from 3225 sq. feet (300 m²) to 12 900 sq. feet (1200 m²). The development corporation has also built larger factories to particular firms' specific requirements.

Many of the factory buildings in the industrial estates are distinguished by architectural excellence. They are often spaciously set surrounded by car parks and at the fronts by lawns, occasionally articulated with trees, shrubs and flowers. While a number of major industrial concerns, such as Philips and Rotaprint, have come to Washington during the seventies, some of the firms already there, such as Tube Investments Ltd, have extended their existing factories.

One particularly notable development is a group of nursery units, 9 of them concentrically arranged with space for entrance to the circular court.

Social Aspect

The original population of 20 000, comprised of the 4 existing communities, had risen by the end of 1976 to nearly 46 500. There had necessarily been a good deal of mixing, therefore, of the original resident and immigrant populations. The rapid immigration of a substantial population into a fairly large existing community inevitably creates problems, as it did with some of the earlier new towns. At Washington the process of mixing seems to have gone fairly smoothly.

There is, however, a difference in the kind of immigration from that which took place in the new towns round London in the fifties. With these it was dispersal of industry and population chiefly from London, and intake was composed mainly of the employees in the migrated industries. In the allocation of houses, preference was given to these employees; in fact for most years when these towns were being built it was difficult to obtain a house if the applicant was not an employee of a migrated firm. No such controlled migration exists at Washington. On the contrary, immigration is free and its character is indicated by a sample Household Census taken in 1974, the results of which are as follows: because of jobs 29.9%; availability of houses 45.1%; social or personal reasons 15.2%; general amenities 5.6%.

Most of the families came from the Tyneside and Wearside: about 80%, with 20% from elsewhere. It will be noted that only 30% moved because of job, and that with the other 70% there was probably considerable freedom of choice. Probably a certain number, and it would be significant to know how many, moved as the result of the influence of friends who were already there. 'Looking for a house, George, you might do worse than come here, they are nice houses, pleasant surroundings and the people are pally.' When this occurs, it is helpful in developing the community spirit which leads so often to the formation of voluntary associations. Some already existed before the new towns, but a great many more have been started since, and assistance has been given by the development corporation.

Many social services are performed by the social development officer of the corporation. A very important one is to make immigrants feel at home and to give as much information as possible. The first suitable house in any new village is used as a community development office. From this office visits are made to new residents soon after they arrive and information is given about schools, shops, recreational facilities, the needs of young children and the formation of playgroups, and residents are invited to attend meetings at the development office to hear talks on the development of the village, with discussions and questions. Often from such meetings new voluntary societies are started, and with the assistance of the corporation, village associations have been formed which have as their headquarters the meeting halls in the village centres already mentioned. Recently schools in village centres have been provided with village hall facilities incorporated in the educational buildings.

The corporation has reclaimed or improved some 500 acres (1235 ha) of derelict land including colliery spoil heaps at Albany, Glebe, Insworth, Harraton and the Riverside. Work has begun on the first phase of a scheme to reclaim 110 acres (270 ha) of derelict land at Pattinson South for industry and riverside open space. A wildfowl refuge on improved land on the northern bank of the River Wear opened in 1975.

Perhaps the most notable cultural event is the arts centre at Fatfield where the old buildings of Biddick Farm are being converted into a theatre, museum, art gallery and craft workshop. The first and second phases will be completed by mid-1977.

29 Skelmersdale

At the time of the 1961 Census, Liverpool was still one of the most congested cities and outside London had the highest population density of the English conurbations. 747 490 people living in an urban area of 27 810 acres (11 255 ha) could be compared to Manchester's 661 041 in 27 255 acres (11 030 ha) or Birmingham's 1 105 651 in 51 147 acres (20 705 ha). Liverpool's congestion combined with some of the worst slums had provoked the housing and planning authorities to carry out an extensive programme of slum clearance. The unsatisfactory living conditions caused by this overcrowding were made intolerable by the presence of thousands of appalling slum houses. By 1961 an extensive slum clearance programme was under way, and the resulting rehousing coupled with planned dispersal and a voluntary drift of people away from the north-west region as a whole has enabled a relief of congestion. By the time of the 1971 Census, the population of Liverpool had fallen to 603 210, and in Manchester, where similar processes had been at work, the population had fallen to 541 468.

With the surrounding towns of Bootle, Crosby, Huyton-with-Roby, Kirkby and Litherland, the conurbation of 1 030 000 had in 1961 about 80 000 slum or obsolescent dwellings. But these were so mean and at such a high density that it was impossible to rehouse the people in the same areas consistent with the standard of accommodation decent and acceptable to the majority; and it was necessary for a large proportion, therefore, to move elsewhere. As there was little room in other parts of Liverpool or in adjacent districts, and as it was vital to preserve a green belt round so congested a city, it was the right step to provide accomodation and work in the form of a new town some miles away. The local authorities in the region had long realized this, and Skelmersdale and district about 13 miles (21 km) north-north-east of Liverpool, being considered a suitable place, was proposed in 1956 as a new town in the Lancashire development plan. Although sympathetic to the proposal, the Minister of Housing and Local Government did not then approve of this being done under the New Towns Act, and in consequence local authorities began to prepare schemes for overspill under the Town Development Act 1952.

In 1960 the Minister reverted to the proposal of the Lancashire development plan because he realized that procedure under the Town Development Act would place a strain on local authorities, and would be unlikely to ensure development on the scale and at the speed required to satisfy the urgent housing needs. After preparing a draft outlining the scheme and holding the necessary inquiry into objections, the Minister designated an area of 4029 acres (1631 ha) as the site for the new town of Skelmersdale on 9 October 1961, the first new town to be designated in England for 11 years. This together with the designation of several other new towns in the sixties represented a welcome return to a planning policy that, as we have tried to demonstrate, has shown such excellent results. The plan for Skelmersdale was for a population intake of about 50 000 with provision for growth to 80 000 but it is likely, in view of recent government statements, that this figure may be reduced. The population of the designated area in 1961 was about 8000, mostly in Old Skelmersdale (6300).

The site lies roughly midway between Ormskirk and Wigan, about 4 miles (6.5 km) to the east of the former (1971 population 27 000) and about 6 miles (10 km) west of the latter (1971, 81 000). It will be seen, therefore, that it is very close to a town at present about the size of its originally proposed maximum, and one of the objections of the Wigan County Borough Council was that the new town would be so near its western boundary as to become a continuation of its urban area. The reply of the Minister was the difficulty of finding an alternative site to take the urgent overspill from Liverpool, that was not open to even greater objections. It is to be hoped that a green belt, at least 2 miles (3 km) wide, between Wigan and Skelmersdale will be retained.

The site is on the the eastern edge of a valuable agriculture region and is gently undulating, except for Ashurst Ridge along the north-east boundary which rises to a height of about 550 feet (168 m) and which includes the beautiful Ashurst Beacon, lying just outside the designated area, affording extensive views of the surrounding country. Local authorities in the region hope that this will be preserved as an amenity, and the Minister indicated that the vicinity of Ashurst Ridge might suitably be used for playing fields and recreation.

The new town is on the western edge of the South Lancashire Coalfield, but most of the mines in the vicinity are now exhausted. In the past both deep and shallow mining have taken place. All the deep mines have since flooded and the risk of damage due to subsidence in them is not great provided appropriate structural precautions are taken. The chief problems occur where old shallow workings are within about 100 feet (30 m of the surface). Other mineral extraction is that of sand for the glass industry in the north-west of the designated area, and of brick clay in the south-east.

On 5 February 1969 the designated area was enlarged by 94 acres (38 ha) in the Pimbo Industrial estate which increased the availability of industrial sites.

Outline Plan

Sir Hugh Wilson was commissioned to prepare a plan for Skelmersdale in November 1962. Interim proposals were approved by the development corporation in November 1963 and the basic plan was then prepared, and submitted to the Ministry and approved in June 1966. In this plan the neighbourhood system, as in the case of Sir Hugh Wilson's plan for Cumbernauld, is abandoned and there is fairly close concentration of residential areas near the town centre. The River Tawd flows through the centre of the site from north to south with fairly level land on either side and a ridge along the eastern boundary. The valley of the Tawd is utilized to make a park through the town, and the town centre, approximately in the geographical centre, is sited along the east of the river. The main residential area is placed east of the town centre, covering about 1 mile (1.6 km) east to west and about $2\frac{1}{2}$ miles (4 km) from north to south. This is to accommodate about 61 000 at 'between 60 to 70 persons per acre (148 to 172 per ha) over the greater part of the area and 40 persons per acre (99 per ha) over the remainder'. A second residential area is at the existing town of Skelmersdale with

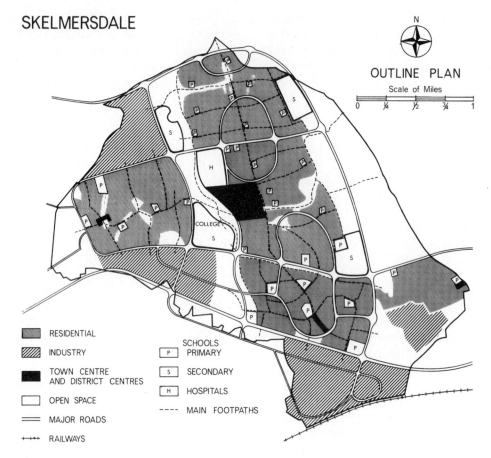

Figure 29.1 Skelmersdale Outline Plan

its population of about 6000 which lies to the west of the centre, and it was proposed to develop this for a population of about 14 000 at an average density of 45 persons per acre (111 per ha). The third area is the small town of Up Holland in the south-east corner with an existing population within the designated area of about 2000. It is proposed to accommodate 5000 persons here at a density of 50 persons to an acre (123 per ha).

Most parts of the first two areas are within a mile (1.6 km) of the town centre and about half the total population will be within $\frac{1}{2}$ mile (0.8 km) of it.

The major part was planned for the fairly high density of 60 to 70 persons to the acre (148 to 172 per ha) which at an average size of family of 3.5 (the new towns have larger households than the national average of about 3.15) means 17 to 20 houses to the acre (42 to 49 per ha). There was to have been a proportion of higher densities, possibly some blocks of flats, towards the centre, with a gradual reduction towards the outskirts, but in this the plan has changed during implementation as higher densities have become unacceptable.

Industry is sited in 3 principal areas: those to the north and south of Old Skelmersdale which forms the western residential area, providing about 340 acres (137 ha) together; while the third of 363 acres (147 ha) is at Up Holland in the south-east corner of which 270 acres (109 ha) is within the original designated area and 93 acres (38 ha) in the extended area designated in 1969.

The main town roads form roughly rectangular grids with a regional road running near the southern boundary while the M6 runs north–south about 2 miles (3 km) east of the town. Two of the town roads running east–west enclose the north and south ends of the centre; one north–south road encloses the main residential areas on the east while another runs west of the River Tawd. In addition, in accordance with the theme of 'a hierarchy of roads depending on traffic function' there is a secondary network of district distributor roads. The footpath system that transverses the town and provides access to the centre from most parts, although linked at various points with the road system, is mainly independent of it. The corner shops, schools, churches, public houses and small community buildings are sited in relation to these footpaths.

Unfortunately the area is not likely to be well-served by railways. A plea was made that if the passenger service on the Liverpool–Wigan–Manchester line that runs near the southern boundary is withdrawn in accordance with the Beeching report, 'it is essential that the route should be kept open so that services can be restored, with a new station in the future'. This has been heeded and the line is to remain open. The line to the west with Skelmersdale station was closed some years ago and the track removed. These circumstances reflect on the unwisdom of recent railway policy based on what will pay without relation to the planned development of the country as a whole.

The town centre is envisaged to secure the utmost segregation of pedestrians and vehicles, and two suggestions are made of the form that the centre should take: 'a cluster centre accepting the division of the town by gullies, and a linear deck accommodating a variety of buildings. Both types involve a measure of vertical separation of vehicles and pedestrians: in the former the car parks are arranged in low multi-storey blocks around the centre, in the latter car parking is on 2 or more levels below the centre. In each case servicing is from below.'

The plan is good and imaginative and in its tentative outline, subject to variation, it is well abreast of modern trends of living in towns.

Building the Town

Building in the residential areas has progressed broadly from south to north, although the first housing site was in Old Skelmersdale at New Church Farm, which was begun in 1964. By 1976 the first contract for 612 houses there was completed. In 1965 a start was made with housing at Little Digmoor (south-east of the centre) and these were nearly all completed by the end of 1967. By that time house building was in progress on many other sites, including those at Pennylands in Old Skelmersdale, at Digmoor and in the Hillside district of Tanhouse.

Thus by the end of 1968 the development corporation had completed 1810 since designation, with 326 by the local authority and 270 by private enterprise. From that date, progress accelerated for a number of years and in 1969 1161 houses were completed by the corporation. This was followed by 1429 in 1970, 773 in 1971, 958 in 1972, 598 in 1973 and 223 in 1974.

Housing development at Hollan Moor (south-east of the centre) and Birch Green (north-east of the centre) began in 1969. Since then development of the different phases of these schemes and those at Tanhouse, Digmoor and the later site at Ashurst (north of the town centre) have continued so that by 1975 the development corporation had provided a total of 7564 dwellings. In 1976 491 were completed by the development corporation giving a total of 8055 and in addition 455 had been provided by the local authority and 864 by private enterprise. From the date of designation until 1972 growth of industry in the town was steady, however in the later seventies industrial progress has reflected the economic situation of the country as a whole. However, by the end of 1976 the total industrial floor space was over 4 million sq. feet (380 000 m²) and the building of advance and nursery factories at the Pimbo and Gillibrands industrial sites is continuing.

Progress with the town centre has been slow. Plans were reappraised in 1968, a new plan was adopted and approved in 1969, but a start was not made on the first phase until February 1971. This first phase was completed 12 years after the designation of the town.

Housing and Residential Areas

The two residential districts completed by 1967—New Church Farm and Little Digmoor—consist of rows of terrace houses sited around pedestrian courts with culs-desac branching from a periphery road. Garges and car ports are lined along these branch

Figure 29.2 Housing for rent/sale on Ashurst 1 at a density of 53 persons per acre (130 per ha).

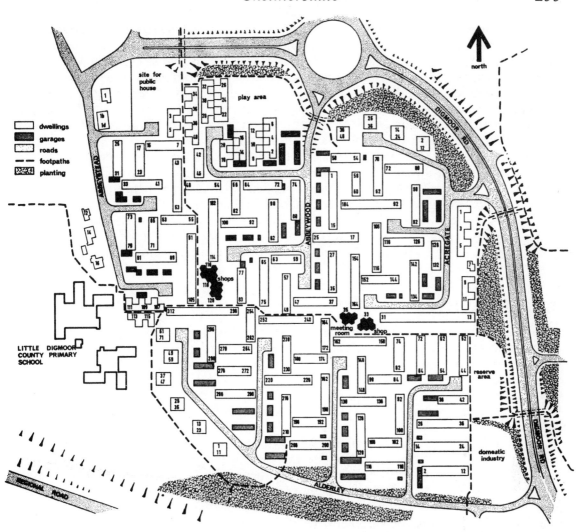

Figure 29.3 Plan of Little Digmoor residential district.

roads on the basis of one per dwelling. Ultimate provision is to be one garage plus hard-standing off the highway for each dwelling, with additional parking areas for visitors on the basis of one car space for every 2 dwellings. Initial provision within these residential areas is one garage plus hard-standing to 2 dwellings. This initial ratio of one or 2 has been reduced on later housing areas because, although accurately reflecting car ownership rates, it overestimates the demand for lock-up garages. The paved pedestrian ways broaden occasionally into squares, many of which are utilized as children's playgrounds, some furnished with groups of concrete objects for play purposes, and there are occasional trees and beds of shrubs and flowers neatly bricked round. In one of the spaces on the west side of both New Church Farm and Little Digmoor is a group of shops with a primary school nearby, and in another space a little way off is a meeting room and a shop. The houses are mainly 2- and 3-storey with low mono-pitched roofs, and all have small gardens fenced off from the paved areas. Net densities are about 18 to 20 houses to the acre (44 to 49 per ha).

The theme set in the residential districts of New Church Farm and Little Digmoor is followed in principle in the planning of the other districts with variations especially in the lengths and character of the branch roads. In the example of Holland Moor there are 2 precincts north and south of Ormskirk Road. The former has 2 long branches with subsidiary branches like those of a tree. The houses for the most part face the footways with gardens towards the roads and garages along them or at their ends. The layout south of Ormskirk Road is a little more complex and has the disadvantage of a through road (Cherry Croft) which hardly seems necessary.

Tanhouse presents further variations of the planning of the branch roads which can be seen in the plan of Tanhouse 4, and in the various districts of Birch Green the long straight branch road terminating with a square is repeated. In these layouts, as in Holland Moor, the gardens back on to the roads, while the fronts of the rows of terrace houses face the footways, which are of varying widths and which occasionally become squares, sometimes with trees, shrubs and seats, and sometimes with children's playgrounds. In these residential districts there are primary schools, public houses, and meeting rooms.

Local Centres

Skelmersdale is not planned on the neighbourhood system instead there are residential precincts of a fairly high density, and groups of shops are introduced at convenient spots. Provision is made, however, for 2 local centres, one in the western part of Pennylands, and the other in the south-east at Little Digmoor. The former called Sandy Lane Commercial Centre, consists of 2 level rows of shops on either side of a covered pedestrian way, with squares at either end and car parks on 2 sides, and a sports centre (Coronation Park) at one end. The centre at Little Digmoor is somewhat larger and consists of a fairly long covered pedestrian way, or parade, with shops on one side and houses on the other. At the north-west end is a church and C of E primary school, a clinic and group medical practice, and at the other end is a public house and meeting hall, thus the facilities provided are similar to one of the larger neighbourhood centres of the first group of new towns. A district centre has been planned for Ashurst in the Cobbs Brow housing area, the most northern in the town and the last to be developed.

Town Centre

In the outline plan 2 suggestions were made of the form the town centre should take. Both involved a measure of vertical separation of pedestrians and vehicles with no through road in the centre. In 1968 a reappraisal of plans for the centre was made by the development corporation and 3 forms of development were considered. To quote from the 1969 report of the corporation these three schemes were, 'first, a dispersed form of Town Centre with all shop servicing at ground level, designed to be representative of the type of solution normally adopted by developers when they have unlimited land at their disposal. The second, at the other extreme, was the development of the same facilities in decked form, making the structures as compact as possible and minimizing the use of land. For the third form tested, the architects and planners were given freedom to choose the site most likely to minimize development costs and to develop a mixed scheme, partly with all facilities at ground level and partly in multi-level form.'

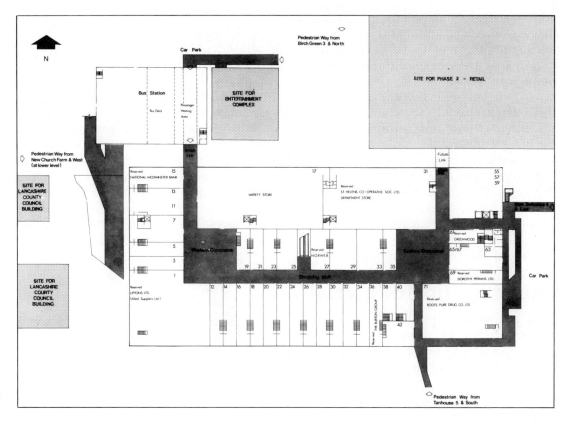

Figure 29.4 Town centre shopping area.

The merits of the three schemes were evaluated, not in conventional terms of viability at a point in time, but in terms of discounted cash flow to provide an average rate of return on capital invested by the Corporation over a period of time. In addition to those elements which could be quantified, intangible costs and benefits of the various schemes were also listed.

'In the event, no one scheme in Skelmersdale conditions emerged as being much better than any of the others. But in the process, however, a great deal was learnt by all participants and perhaps the value of the exercise lay, not so much in the exercise of the technique itself, but in the greater understanding which rubbed off on those concerned with the exercise. Aspects of this understanding were that the Commercial Centre was not to be an exercise in structural form; the convenience of the people who will actually shop and work in the Centre was to be given greater weight; the application of discounted cash flow techniques demonstrated that the timing of the provision of facilities was as crucial as the principle of their provision at all.'

On the basis of this research, a revised plan was prepared to be implemented in 3 stages, and this was approved by the Ministry in July 1969. Promise of finance for the first phase was made by the Exchequer in February 1970, but it was not until a year later, in February 1971, that work actually started on this first phase, which was completed in 1974.

The centre consists of two large buildings for shops with the principal covered air-conditioned shopping area on the first floor and servicing on the ground floor. The south building which is included in the initial phase has on the first floor a shopping mall linking two squares at either end. On the north side of this block is a shopping street with mostly service shops. At the north-west corner is the bus station at first floor level, and near this are entertainments buildings which include 2 small cinemas and a dance hall. On the west side of this shopping building are police headquarters, Magistrates Court and County Library, while a little further out occupying much of the western periphery of the centre, is the College of Further Education and offices. On the north side an ecumenical centre is being built for the use of several religious denominations. There will be ample provision for car parking, some in the form of multi-storey structures. Provision for easy access to the centre is made for both public and private transport, while the system of walkways which traverse the town links the centre with surrounding residential areas by means of underpasses and elevated ways. The first part of the shopping centre to be completed is, as mentioned, in the south building and consists of the covered shopping mall and 2 squares. It was opened in June 1973.

Industry and Industrial Areas

Although some of the bigger firms have built their own factories, the development corporation has, in common with other new towns, built advance factories of various sizes to standard designs so as to attract industry, especially the smaller and growing firms, and this has been an inducement for industry to move to Skelmersdale.

Figure 29.5 Purpose-built factory in Pimbo industrial estate. The area in front provides a recreational space.

By 1972, of the 67 manufacturing firms in Skelmersdale with about 8000 employees, 55 firms were new, occupying the 2 southern industrial estates of Gillibrands and Pimbo. Considerable diversification of industry had occurred and there were high hopes of maintaining stable employment. However, in 1976 2 major factories closed with very little warning to the employees and the community. Thorn Colour Tubes at Gillibrand closed down, causing loss of 1300 jobs, and Courtaulds at Pimbo closed soon afterwards. This has introduced to the new town the social and economic problems associated with relatively high unemployment. By mid-1977 it is still too early to unravel the complicated economics of major international employers in order to draw lessons for future industrial planning from the Thorn and Courtaulds closures. The incidents have emphasized, though, the vulnerability of a town's economic fortunes when its industrial sector is dominated by one or two major employers.

Despite these setbacks, Skelmersdale has attracted some new industries, and there are now more than 100 firms employing 8350 out of the 13 500 employed in the town. Six advance factory units were completed at Pimbo in 1976 and a further 7 are under construction. 1976 also saw the completion of the largest rented factory, 45 959 sq. feet (4136 m²), built by the corporation for BOC Ltd.

Both industrial estates are well laid out with generous space round the factories with room, in many cases, for expansion.

Social Aspect

Essential requirements of a new town are meeting places with at least one fairly large one in the centre that includes a good multi-purpose hall. This may come ultimately when the town is nearing completion, meanwhile there are 10 meeting places dispersed in the residential areas on either side of the centre. The principal of these is the meeting place at Quarry Bank, in Tanhouse, an existing house and grounds, which was acquired by the community association with the aid of grants from various sources, and extended to form a fairly large meeting place. The extension was completed in 1970 and is used by over 30 local organizations.

Another notable contribution to provide facilities for leisure was the conversion of a large temporary industrial building at Digmoor to an indoor sports centre, which can accommodate a variety of sports at one time.

The mixing of the immigrant population with the existing one is always a social matter that requires attention from a development corporation, and this need is greatest when the existing population is fairly large and scattered. In the case of Skelmersdale the existing population was not very large (8000) and it was mainly concentrated in the old town where the mixing seems to have taken place fairly well. The eastern districts of the designated area were comparatively sparsely populated so that large scale adjustments were not involved.

30 Runcorn

Designated on 10 April 1964 the new town of Runcorn is being built to accommodate a dispersed population from Liverpool and to relieve congestion generally on the north side of the Mersey. The site is about 7234 acres (2930 ha) and is an extension eastward from the existing town of Runcorn which lies on the south bank of the Mersey immediately opposite Widnes on the north bank, with which it is linked by both road and rail bridges. The east–west length of the site is about $4\frac{1}{2}$ miles (7 km). The Manchester Ship Canal continues the northern boundary eastwards, while the route of the London–Glasgow railway line forms the southern boundary. Nine miles (14 km) to the north-east is Warrington, designated as the site of another new town, and 7 miles (11 km) to the north-west are the outskirts of Liverpool with another 7 miles (11 km) to its centre. The population of the designated area in 1964 was about 28 000, of which about 27 500 were in the existing town of Runcorn. The new town is planned for a population of 90–95 000 by 2000 with an allowance for a further increase from natural growth to about 100 000. Since 1974 Runcorn is within the area of the Halton District Council.

An inevitable criticism of the location of the town is that it is too near the conurbation, and has the same defect in this respect as Redditch and Washington. If the Merseyside conurbation continues to grow the new town of Runcorn will become part of it. This growth is the more likely because of the expansion of Warrington and its surroundings, under the New Towns Act, from a population in 1961 of about 127 000 in 18 650 acres (7553 ha) to 170 000 by the late 1980s. The south-west boundary of the new town of Warrington adjoins the north-eastern boundary of Runcorn.

In the last 20 years, however, there has been a considerable drift of population away from this industrial area of the north-west and the building of a new town here and the expansion of Warrington and district, with the introduction of more industry will be some contribution to industrial revival in the region. From 1951 to 1971 there were actual declines in population in Liverpool, Warrington, St. Helens, Manchester and Salford, while in several other towns populations were stationary. A declining or stationary population when compared with the 5 million increase in population in England and Wales from 1951 to 1971 means a considerable migration from the area, as there is no evidence to indicate that natural growth in the north-west is any less than in the rest of the country.

The only town in South Lancashire that has shown a marked increase in population is the new Liverpool suburb of Kirkby, which increased from 3210 in 1951 to 59 759 in 1971.

The declines in population of the south-east Lancashire and Merseyside conurbations from 1951 to 1971 contrasts with an increase in population in England and Wales from 43 757 888 in 1951 to 48 593 658 in 1971 and with the increase in the South East from 15 127 267 to 17 133 277.

The significance of these facts for the location of Runcorn is that in spite of its closeness to the Merseyside conurbation a very good case could be maintained for building a new town here.

Outline Plan

Shortly after the site was designated Professor Arthur Ling prepared a plan, a draft of which was completed in November 1965 and published for comment in January 1966.

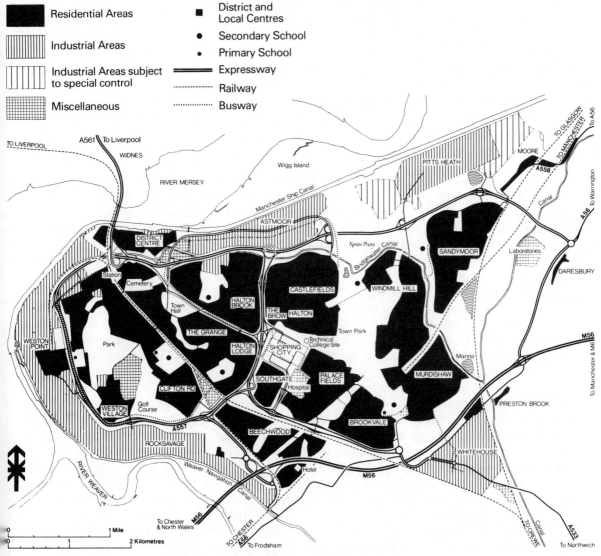

Figure 30.1 Runcorn—Outline Plan.

The master plan was completed and submitted to the Ministry early in 1967. It has many interesting and original features. As in the case of Redditch, planning has been made more difficult by the existence of a sizeable town on the site, but Professor Ling met the difficulty with skill. The principle of neighbourhood planning is followed, but with differences. The neighbourhoods, or residential communities, as they are termed in the plan, are each of about 8000 with shopping centre, schools, clinics and social facilities strung together on a spine transport route which forms the figure 8, with the town centre at the crossing. The average household size on the new town estates is about 3.2 persons per house. The range varies from 3.87 persons per house at Halton Lodge to 2.51 persons per unit on Southgate 1. If the average dwelling units per acre is taken as 16 (39.5 per ha) then an average of 51 persons per acre (126 per ha) are housed on the new town estates. The development at 150 to the acre (370 per ha) in the central areas means, of course, a majority of blocks of flats. It is very doubtful whether such close building, and such high densities, will accord with the wishes of the people who go to live there. The evidence provided by questionaires on the subject indicates that if they were asked they would express the wish for a greater proportion of 2-storey family houses with a more generous provision of gardens, even if it means some sacrifice of the public open spaces which are liberally provided.

The existing industrial area lies to the west of Runcorn, and consists mainly of the chemical industry and the premises and plant of Imperial Chemical Industries Ltd. ICI proposes to extend in a further area to the north-east of the town, and other industries are being established along the north of the town and in the south-east corner. The development corporation is conscious of the need to introduce a diversification of industry so that employment will not be wholly dependent on the state of world markets for chemicals. It will be seen that the industrial areas largely encircle the town, and they will be separated from the residential areas by the Expressway.

The spine public transport route in the figure of an 8 on which the communities are strung together forms the essential basis of the plan, and is a highly original and valuable contribution to new-town planning. It represents an effort to restore public transport to its right place as a service which has too often been sacrificed to the imagined interests of the private motorist. This transit service which links all the local centres with each other and with the town centre, is for buses only, and all private cars and commercial vehicles will be excluded from it. The local centres are at approximately ½-mile intervals (0.8 km), and all houses in the communities will be within a ¼ of a mile (0.4 km) or 5 minutes walk from the transit system. The plan includes links from the system into the new industrial areas.

Four types of monorail were investigated for this transit system but it was felt that a special type of easy-access single-deck low-floor one-man operated bus would be more practical; and these buses have been adopted with accommodation for 80 to 90 persons including standing passengers. They have multiple sets of doors to give quick access and egress and provide space for prams and push-chairs. It is estimated that most of the population (63%) will ultimately have a 5 minute off-peak service in each direction and the remainder (23%) a 7½ minute service. At peak periods the frequency of service will be much higher. Such a service makes the town centre and all the neighbourhoods easily accessible to the whole population without the use of a car.

This provision overcomes the handicap of limited public transport from which some of the first generation new towns have suffered. The inadequacy of the public transport service of Crawley, for example, has caused a lot of discontent. It is no fault of the transport undertakings who have to make a service pay. But for a new town in the course of its growth, there is a case for subsidies. It is to be hoped that in the early stages of the growth of Runcorn the bus transit system will be given financial support if necessary. Later, when the habit of using the system is established, it will probably pay its way.

An urban motor-road encircles the town in the green belt surrounding the residential areas with a crossing linking the centre, and with spurs into the residential and industrial areas. This encircling parkway has a link with the motorway on the south. The area is well served by rail. One line passes south-east to north-east and crosses the site and the Mersey with a station at Runcorn a little south of the bridge.

The alternatives of developing the existing centre or of using an entirely new site nearer the geographic centre immediately south of Halton village were considered, and the latter was decided. The disadvantages of the former are that it would be badly located in relation to the population; that scope for provision of all the central facilities would be restricted; and that being situated near the bridge over the Mersey there would be a serious risk of transport congestion. The site nearer the geographical centre south of Halton gives space for the numerous facilities proposed, which, in addition to covered shopping precincts and the usual public services, include 2 cinemas, restaurants, clubs and public houses.

The provision of open space in the plan is liberal. A large town park is located in the valley a little to the east of the centre; and this is linked with the Manchester Ship Canal by a green wedge through the industrial area.

Advantage is taken of the natural features of the undulating site with its succession of hills and valleys. Just north of the proposed town centre is Halton Rock with its ancient castle dating from 1070 some 337 feet (326 to 136m) above sea level. Extensive views can be obtained from this point. Another existing feature which is being utilized is the Bridgewater canal which runs along the north side of the area. At the point where it passes through the town park its banks will be laid out for recreational purposes. There is a marina for 350 canal craft at Preston Brook.

The plan for Runcorn is ingenious and original, especially in the matter of transport facilities. If the housing densities were a little lower it would be excellent in every way.

Building the Town

Site development began early in 1966 shortly after the master plan was completed and published for comment. The residential communities to be built first are immediately north and west of the town centre, namely Halton Brook, where the first house of the new town was completed in January 1967, followed by The Brow, 1968, Castlefields in 1970, Halton Lodge and Palace Field in 1971. In the first 2 years, 1966–67, the development corporation built 117 dwellings, the local authority 56 and private enterprise 45. Since then the development corporation has increased its output considerably and built 273 houses in 1968, 555 in 1969, 990 in 1970, 1200 in 1971, 380 in 1972, 688 in 1973, 1300 in 1974, 1198 in 1975 and 423 in 1976. By the end of that year since designation 7287 had been built by the development corporation and another 956 by the local authority and 1771 by private enterprise.

The major part of the town centre was completed by the end of 1972, and considering its size this is no mean achievement. The building of the two industrial areas, Astmoor in the north and Whitehouse in the south-east, have made excellent progress, while about a third (6¼ miles [10 km]) of the expressway and 7½ miles (12 km) of the total of 12 miles (19 km) of the exclusive busway, or rapid transit route, were completed by the end of 1972. This progress, especially of the town centre, has been remarkably rapid, and the speed of building Runcorn compares very favourably with that of any other new town. By Spring 1977 the main framework of the Busway was completed involving a total length of 11.37 miles (18.1 km) and 8.88 miles (14.2 km) of the Expressway completed.

Housing and Residential Areas

The existing town of Runcorn lies to the west of the designated area, and the new residential communities (or neighbourhoods) are sited in the eastern part of the site,

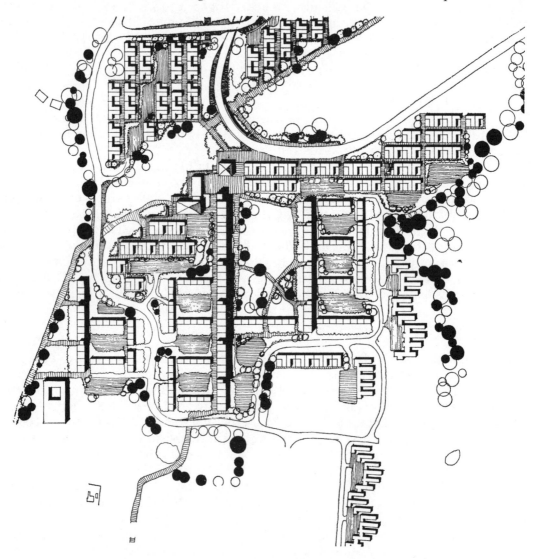

Figure 30.2 Plan of housing layout, Halton North.

Figure 30.3 Flats and houses on the Castlefields estate.

with the exception of Cavendish Farm which is planned in the south of the old town. The communities grouped round the town centre are Castlefields, The Brow and Halton Brook to the north, Halton Lodge to the west, Southgate on the south and Palace Fields to the east, and these are the first to be built. The communities of Windmill Hill, Murdishaw and Brookvale are further out to the east, with Beechwood to the south.

The planning of the first communities of Halton Brook, The Brow, Castlefields and Halton Lodge follows the principle of grouping the houses mainly in pedestrian areas, with footpaths winding among the houses and interspersed with childrens' playgrounds, and with cul-de-sac road access at various points and to groups of garages. In the layout of Halton Brook, which consists of terrace and patio houses, the arrangement is a little formal with the rows running straight north–south and east–west. In The Brow, which is situated on the western slope of Halton Hill, the siting of the houses is more informal with shorter rows sited at different angles, and the effect of the footpaths threading between these 2-storey houses, with their dark bricks and mono-pitched roofs, and among gardens and playgrounds is particularly pleasing. The dark brown bricks were chosen to harmonize with the existing village of Halton and with the cropping sandstone of Halton Rock of which several of the old houses were built, which prompts the thought that some of the new houses might be built or faced with this sandstone, if not with the cut natural stone, with blocks in which the sandstone forms the aggregate. The Brow justifiably received a Ministry of Housing award.

Castlefields is a larger community with a fair variety of housing. The site is steeply sloping in parts and this has been utilized in the layout. Blocks of 5-storey flats run approximately east–west along the south side of the bus transit route, and wings from these blocks run south on the sloping ground where the number of storeys is gradually reduced so that they terminate as 2-storey dwellings with small gardens. Access is by means of galleries or decks which at one end can be entered at ground level. These flats are principally for small families, and provision for larger families is made in other types of dwellings.

The blocks of flats form courts and in these are built rows of L-shaped, 3-bedroom, patio bungalows, with the house on 2 sides of the patio and a high fence on the third side, with the fourth side open to the south. The whole area is very attractively and informally landscaped with appropriate trees and shrubs. Other types of dwelling for larger families include rows of 2-storey, 4- and 5-bedroom houses, arranged between culs-de-sac with footpath access.

Spanning the bus route is the small shopping centre of Castlefields, and nearby are 2 churches, a youth centre, a primary school, and an old persons home, and a little to the west a children's home.

Town Centre

One of the remarkable achievements in the building of Runcorn is the town centre which has attracted attention throughout the world. The first substantial part was opened by the Queen in May 1972, and the whole was largely completed by 1975.

This centre is designed to serve not only the town of Runcorn but the region, which explains its ambitious scale. The first part to be completed is the shopping city as it is

Figure 30.4 Runcorn shopping centre.

called. The construction is of a vast concrete platform, below which is the ground level service area with headroom for the tallest vehicles. The shopping city on the concrete platform is divided into 20 squares of 108 feet (33 m), with service towers at each corner. The whole is closed-in and air-conditioned with low pyramidal roofs for each square, the central roof of the town square being a little higher (40 feet [12 m]) to allow for clerestory lighting and smoke venting. The streets or ways between the shops are paved with terrazzo, and the walls, columns and general framing of the shops, to secure a general unity of effect, are faced with polished soft veined white Carrara marble. A large part of the central square is carpeted, easy chairs are provided, and the whole is graced with large indoor plants. In addition to shops (115 were occupied at the time of the opening by the Queen) there are banks, a post office, a cinema, public houses and restaurants. The southern part, built 1974–76, will form the entertainments section.

Access by car from the expressway and town roads is by means of the 4 multi-storey car parks which flank the shopping area on the east and west sides. There is parking space for 2400 cars. Access by public transport is from the town bus station on the elevated bus route on the north side. From this bus station one descends by escalator to the shopping city. Access from regional buses is equally convenient at ground level.

On the north side are the law courts, police station and offices and this group of buildings will be similarly flanked by 2 multi-storey car parks, as also will the southern entertainments area, so that when completed there will be 8 such garages with a total accommodation for 4800 cars. To the east are the large DEP offices, and the site to the north-east is for the technical college.

The Southgate residential community adjoins the centre on the south side and the dwellings here are mainly flats or deck housing designed to give access to the shopping centre by pedestrian decks. The exterior is faced with white, easy to maintain ceramic tiles. The building at the time of opening by the Queen looked a little stark in the landscape, but there has been extensive tree planting in the vicinity, and when these have grown to break the severe lines and somewhat regular mechanical massing of the structure, the effect should be pleasing. From the standpoint of fulfilment of function the centre must be regarded as one of the most imaginative and ingenious of the mid-twentieth century.

Industrial Areas

As mentioned in the description of the outline plan, the chemical works of ICI was the major existing industry of the town occupying the western and southern areas of the old town of Runcorn. ICI owns Sandymoor, the north–eastern area of the new town, where the company proposes to extend. The development corporation has planned and is developing two industrial areas, the Astmoor estate in the north along the Manchester Ship Canal, and the Whitehouse estate in the south-east. One of the purposes in attracting industry to the town is to avoid too great a dependence of one type of industry and to secure a measure of diversification as one means of maintaining employment. Over 60 firms are now established in these 2 estates, and they include those engaged in the manufacture of goods for clothing, food, medical and surgical equipment, electrical equipment, plastic components and toys. Two of the biggest units are on the Whitehouse estate: the Guinness kegging plant, and nearby the Bass

Figure 30.5 Astmoor industrial estate.

Charrington Ltd brewery complex, which in size and scale bears comparison with ICI industries in Runcorn.

As in the other new towns the industrial premises are of two principal kinds, those provided by the development corporation for renting, which consist of standard and nursery unit factories, and the premises built by the firms themselves. The former are usually the smaller, with scope for expansion and the provision of these serve to attract industry to the area. The majority of the firms on the Astmoor estate occupy these, but there are a few purpose-built factories here erected by the firms themselves, of which Kawneer Amax was the first taking occupation early in 1969. The larger factories involving large scale organization, such as the Bass Charrington complex, are necessarily purpose-built by the firms themselves. It is very much to be hoped that Runcorn will continue to attract industry and contribute to maintaining the employment in the north-west.

Social Aspect

With the new town hardly one-third built, it is a little early to say what measure of social life and progress has been achieved. One of the factors, as in all the new towns where there was a substantial existing population, is the mixing of the old residents with the new. This generally has turned out well. What has been less satisfactory in many of the new towns of the first generation is the lack of integration of the parts of the town into a whole so as to facilitate community interests, and people following common interests together. One of the main reasons for this is the very poor public transport system in many of the new towns which has been realized as a serious defect, and has led partly to the excellently planned public transport in Runcorn. It makes for the easy accessibility of the town centre, the centres of the residential communities, industrial areas and major recreational centres. The completion of the Busway in 1977 through old residential areas will increase use of these facilities.

The social and recreational facilities so far provided at Runcorn include four permanent community centres, two county council youth centres, two joint use primary schools, a recreation centre on the edge of the town park, six churches, 10 public houses, two cinemas, squash courts and an artificial ski-slope.

Two new comprehensive schools have been built, and at one of these the community shares the use of the sports facilities. Another comprehensive school with joint use facilities is expected to be completed in 1978. Evening classes for various subjects meet in schools, community centres and church halls. Pre-school play groups and pensioners' luncheon clubs are quickly established in new areas.

As in most of the new towns during their periods of growth, a large number of voluntary associations are started – social, civic, cultural, recreational, political – and they become very actively infused, no doubt, by the pioneering spirit in which a new town is built. Runcorn and other second generation new towns have learnt from the experience of the earlier new towns, and each residential area has a centre for social activities, at first in a converted pair of bungalows and later in permanent premises. Industry is also playing its part in contributing to a sports and social centre which is shared with the community.

The distinctive outdoor recreational features of Runcorn are its Town Park with trails for walkers and horse-riders, woodland and lake, and the Bridgewater Canal with the new boating marina at Murdishaw. A site of major archaeological interest is that of the former Norton Priory now excavated and opened to the public.

31 *Warrington*

As implied in the chapters on Skelmersdale and Runcorn, there are two main purposes in building new towns in the north-west; firstly to relieve congestion in the South Lancashire conurbations, principally those in and around Liverpool and Manchester; and secondly to reverse the drift of population away from the region and attract people and industry to it. In the early sixties when Skelmersdale was designated, the first of these objectives was paramount, and it is still important, but the second objective has a greater degree of urgency if a satisfactory and more equitable distribution of population over the country is gradually to be realized. It was shown in Chapter 30 on Runcorn that in South Lancashire there was an actual decline in population from 1951 to 1971 which meant a considerable movement of population away from the region. It is, therefore, an important purpose of the four new towns of the north-west to aim at arresting this outward migration.

An expansion of Warrington, then in South Lancashire, as a contribution to the objectives indicated, had been considered in the early sixties, and in October 1965 a study was commissioned for large scale development of the town and its surroundings. An area of 21 500 acres (8700 ha) was proposed for a new town, and a draft designation order was made in May 1967. After a public inquiry a slightly reduced area of 18 612 acres (7535 ha) was designated as the new town of Warrington on 26th April 1968.

Warrington, formerly a county borough, is situated on the River Mersey with the Manchester Ship Canal passing along its southern boundary. It is roughly midway between Manchester and Liverpool being about 17 miles (27 km) west of the former and 16 miles (26 km) east of the latter. The designated area comprehends considerable extensions to the east, west and south, and takes in Woolston and Fearnhead in the east, Great Sankey and Penketh in the west, and Stockton Heath, Grappenhall and Appleton in the south. The population of the county borough of Warrington at the time of designation in 1968 was about 72 000, and that of the surrounding districts included in the designated area amounted to about 60 000. Warrington and the extensions east and west were in South Lancashire, and the area south of the canal was in Cheshire. With the reorganization of local government the whole of the new town of Warrington is in North Cheshire (District No 1) with the Metropolitan Counties of Greater Manchester and Merseyside to the east and west.

Warrington is well situated for rail and road transport. It is on the main railway line from Euston and Crewe, to Preston and Scotland, and on the east–west line from Manchester to Liverpool. The M6 passes north–south on the east side of the town, the

M62 runs east–west along its northern boundary, and the M56 passes east–west along its southern boundary. It is about halfway along the Manchester Ship Canal, while the airports of Ringway and Speke are about 13 miles (21 km) due east and west respectively. From the standpoints of communication and transport, could a town be more favourably situated?

Warrington is an ancient town. A settlement existed here on the Roman road from Chester to the north. It was an important medieval market town and in 1277 Edward I granted a charter for a Friday market and an annual fair. It grew to quite a size in the nineteenth century owing largely to several manufacturing industries being located there, among them coarse textiles of various kinds, metal goods and engineering, food manufacture, chemicals and several others. By the middle of the present century (1951 census) it had reached a population of about 80 000, but declined to 76 000 in 1961, and still further to about 68 000 in 1971. This decline was no doubt due partly to the general drift of population away from South Lancashire and partly to inadequate housing accommodation in Warrington. Much of the older pre-1914 housing is in the centre, including much obsolescent housing and overcrowding. In 1951 there were 749 more households than dwellings (22 007 dwellings compared with 22 756 households) (31.1) which probably contributed to a movement away. By 1961 this had been rectified as there were 418 more dwellings than households (24 425 compared with 24 007 households), but still much of the remaining housing would not be considered fit for human habitation. The poor and obsolete housing in the centre was probably a factor in the further decline of population to 1971. The designation of Warrington as a new town will no doubt put new life into the place and produce a much needed revival(31.2).

Outline Plan

The planning consultants Austin-Smith/Lord presented their proposals for the Draft Master Plan in October 1969. They were widely circulated for comment by the development corporation which is working in partnership with the Warrington Borough Council. The corporation is anxious that there shall be the fullest public participation in the planning and building of the new Warrington. Subsequently an outline plan was published in April 1972, and after public comment and discussion it was later approved in principle by the Secretary of State for the Environment in June 1973. The plan provides for the intake of a population of about 40 000, mainly as overspill from Manchester, and for an increase of population from 132 000 in 1969 to about 200 000 in 1991. Owing to the rapid decline of population in Manchester in the decade from 1961 to 1971 (from 661 800 to 541 500), Manchester is now better able to rehouse its population within its own area and it is probable therefore that the intake will be as much from other areas(31.3).

In the plan the designated area is divided into 5 main districts, each with a target population in 1991 indicated in brackets, the central district (71 500) approximately the area of the former county borough, two districts in the eastern extension, Padgate (26 500 since amended to 33 200) between the old town and the M6, and Birchwood (21 000 since amended to 18 000) to the north-east beyond the M6, Westbrook (44 500) occupying the western extension, and Bridgewater (38 000) south of the Manchester Ship Canal. Although the county borough area is fairly closely built up, the outer districts consist mainly of villages with considerable areas of white land, while in Birchwood, Westbrook and Padgate, there are fairly large derelict areas. Birchwood

Figure 31.1 Warrington Outline Plan.

was formerly occupied by the vast Risley Royal Ordnance Factory, which was abandoned and became derelict. Separate district plans have been prepared. That for Birchwood was published in August 1973, that for Padgate in April 1975, those for Westbrook and Bridgewater were prepared in 1976.

The main centre of the new town will be a development of the existing centre, which will be partly pedestrianized, and 5 district centres one each in Birchwood, Padgate and Westbrook, and two in Bridgewater, one situated on the Ship Canal, and one at Appleton. There will be many local centres distributed fairly evenly throughout the town. Existing industry and employment areas are concentrated mainly round the centre of old Warrington. New industrial areas are mainly on the outskirts of the designated area, five along the M62 forming the northern boundary, two to the east in the Padgate district, and another in the south-east. Open spaces and park areas are provided in linear fashion traversing the various parts of the town, and areas bordering the River Mersey will be considerably utilized as amenities. The outline plan is purposely very flexible and is a broad framework for the detailed plans of each district.

District Plans and Residential Areas

Birchwood, which has little existing population, is planned for a population of about 18 000, accommodated in about 5000 houses, with employment for about 9000. The area is 1700 acres (688 ha) of rectangular shape about $2\frac{1}{2}$ miles (4 km) long and $1\frac{1}{4}$ miles (2 km) wide, in the extreme north-east corner of the new town. The western boundary is formed by the M6, the northern by the M62 and the southern by the railway line from Liverpool to Manchester. On this line a new station will be opened in the south-west corner of Birchwood near the M6, a few hundred yards from the former Risley station which served the Ordnance Factory.

Diagonally across the rectangular site is an expressway, planned as a parkway. In the centre north of this occupying 127 acres (51 ha) of the former Royal Ordnance Factory site is the complex of the United Kingdom Atomic Energy Authority, which is developing the site as a national centre for the nuclear power industry. North of this is a research establishment owned jointly by the Universities of Manchester and Liverpool, and east and west of the UKAEA site are new industrial areas. In the south-east is Risley Moss, an area of peat moss which will probably become a nature reserve of

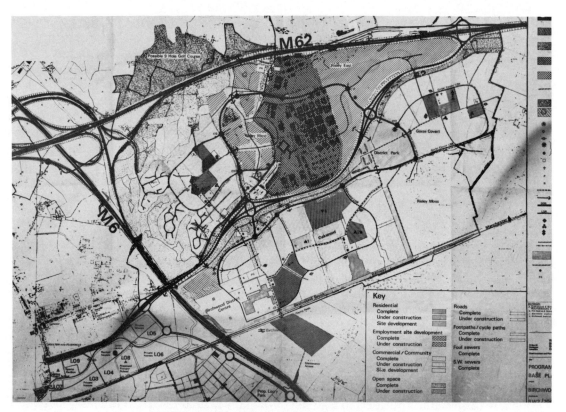

Figure 31.2 Plan of Birchwood estate.

Figure 31.3 Longbarn 4—rented housing.

scientific interest. A central open space borders the expressway, and a large golf course curves round the north-west. Three principal residential areas are Locking Stumps in the north-west, Oakwood in the south and Gorse Covert in the east, served by 4 local centres, 6 primary schools, mostly adjacent to these centres, and one secondary school. The district centre is in the south-west corner, fairly close to the industrial area in Padgate on the west side of the M6. Being in the south-west corner it is centrally placed to serve both districts, but as Padgate will have a district centre about a mile (1.6 km) to the west it is a question whether the Birchwood centre would not have been better placed more in the geographical centre of the district, in the area allocated as open space between UKAEA and Risley Moss. It is a pity that the golf course curving round in the north-west is not planned as a general open space and not mainly for the minority who play golf. The places for golf courses are not within urban areas but rather on the outskirts towards open country.

A detailed plan has been prepared for the residential area of Oakwood in the south, on the derelict site of the Royal Ordnance Factory, between Birchwood District Centre and Risley Moss, and was published in August 1974. The planning here starts with a clean slate as there is no existing population and very little else, and the action area plan describes it as 'a flat featureless area covered with poorly drained sub-soil supporting a few naturally regenerated isolated trees'. The total area of Oakwood is 299 acres (121 ha) of which 143 acres (58 ha) are assigned for housing. It is planned for a population of 5700 to 6200 by 1991. Dwellings are divided into rented (55%), private development for owner occupiers (31%), and those provided by agencies such as housing associations (14%). Rented houses are planned at a net density of 14 per acre (35 per ha) grouped to the west and round the centre; houses for owner occupiers are 11 per acre (27 per ha), grouped to the east of the area; and those by agencies at between 12 to 15 per acre (30 to 37 per ha), all of which are reasonable densities.

The premises of the United Kingdom Atomic Energy Authority in Birchwood employing some 4000, planned for expansion as a national centre for the nuclear power industry, is surrounded on three sides by the residential areas of Birchwood. These will presumably be planned to accommodate a proportion of the staff. At present a considerable number commute varying distances from surrounding areas and the provision of car parking takes therefore a great deal of space. It would obviously be a great advantage from many points of view if an increasing number became residents of Birchwood and Padgate. It is therefore of importance for such prospects that the residential areas of these districts should be such as to attract the employees at the UKAEA, with some diversity of housing, more so perhaps than is indicated by the plan for Oakwood.

Padgate district, which is situated east of the existing town of Warrington and between it and Birchwood, has as its eastern boundary the M6 motorway. In the outline plan for Warrington, Padgate district was envisaged with a population by 1991 of 26 500, but in the plan for Padgate of April 1975 this was increased to 33 200, because of a higher average density made possible by a change in the ratio of rented to owner occupied houses, and because more land is available for housing. The existing population in 1971 was 16 000, so that the planned intake by 1991 is about 17 000. Most of the new housing will be in the northern parts of the area of which 3980 are planned as rented dwellings, and 2034 for owner occupiers. The district centre of Padgate is approximately the geographical centre, about a mile west of the M6, and is a little north of the Padgate railway station with which it is linked by a pedestrian way. Industry is located mainly in the east and south-east of the area along the M6, with one smaller area in the south-west in a loop of the River Mersey.

In both the plans for Birchwood and Padgate, a system of footpaths traverses the whole of the areas with under and overpasses at intersections with roads.

District and Local Centres

Each of the four districts will have its major centre with a few local centres in each. As before noted, Birchwood has its major centre in the south-west corner with one local centre in each of the residential areas of Oakwood, Locking Stumps and Gorse Covert and one in the Risely employment area. An outline plan of the District Centre of Birchwood was approved in October 1974.

The centre is planned mainly as a pedestrian precinct encircled by a local distributor road with two branch road accesses, and footpath access from the principal directions and from the railway station to the south. The shopping facilities, including a departmental store and supermarket, are grouped round pedestrian areas, while a library, health centre, youth and community meeting rooms and old people's day centre are grouped round a pedestrian square. In the south-east of the centre is a secondary school with part planned for community use, while in the northern section of the centre an area is devoted to housing, some 280 dwellings, at a density of 13 per acre (32 per ha). A narrow green belt surrounds the centre on three sides. If built as planned it should be a good district centre with easy access serving well the needs of the community.

Two local shopping centres were completed by 1975, one at Longbarn, and one at Hood Manor, at Westbrook. Each includes a supermarket. The Forge, at Stockton Heath—an extension to an existing shopping area—was completed in 1974 and constitutes one of the two district centres which will serve Bridgewater.

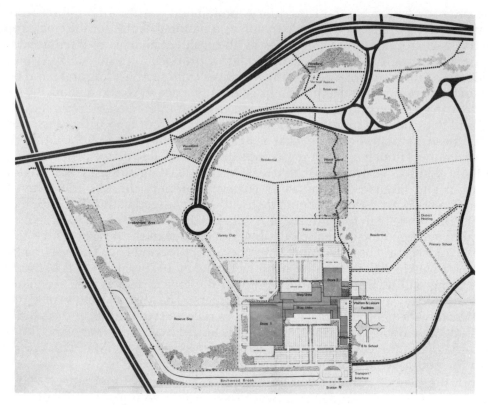

Figure 31.4 Birchwood district centre plan.

The Town Centre

Warrington being an ancient town its centre has in the course of centuries been continually renewed and more closely built up, with the retention here and there of old and valuable buildings. That it has suffered some decay with the fall in population over 30 years to 1970 is inevitable, which makes the task of revitalizing it to serve the modern needs of an expanding town a very welcome if difficult one. There are parts that merit conservation and parts that need remodelling, and it will often be a question of what to retain and what to let go.

Modern needs spell a considerable degree of pedestrianization and a restriction of the damaging effects of the motor vehicle, so that people can do their shopping, follow their business and enjoy recreation in the peace and freedom that pedestrian areas can give. In the chapter of the outline plan devoted to the town centre, the introduction of pedestrian ways and spaces and the restriction of the motor vehicle have been major aims. 'Pedestrian routes', it is stated, 'are proposed which will, in time, provide a continuous system of paths, free from major traffic, throughout the Town Centre'. It is pointed out in referring to the likely demand for car parking spaces in the centre, that if all these requirements were to be accommodated in surface parking the space would occupy an area larger than the commercial centre, and would displace many of the facilities that they were intended to serve: their very size would prevent convenient access to the remaining facilities and would seriously impede the efficient functioning

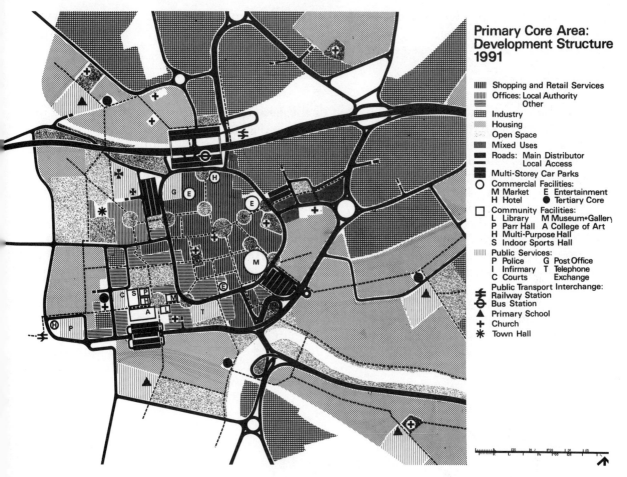

**Primary Core Area:
Development Structure
1991**

||||| Shopping and Retail Services
||||| Offices: Local Authority
═   Other
▦   Industry
▨   Housing
░   Open Space
||||| Mixed Uses
■   Roads: Main Distributor
            Local Access
■   Multi-Storey Car Parks
○   Commercial Facilities:
        M Market   E Entertainment
        H Hotel   ● Tertiary Core
□   Community Facilities:
        L Library   M Museum+Gallery
        P Parr Hall   A College of Art
        H Multi-Purpose Hall
        S Indoor Sports Hall
||||| Public Services:
        P Police   G Post Office
        I Infirmary   T Telephone
        C Courts   Exchange
        Public Transport Interchange:
⚑   Railway Station
⬒   Bus Station
▲   Primary School
✚   Church
✱   Town Hall

Figure 31.5 Town centre plan.

of the centre. On economic and operational grounds the required spaces must therefore be accommodated in multi-storey car parks. This is sensible and far-sighted thinking and it is a pity that such thoughts did not actuate some of the planning of the centres of some of the earlier new towns, where surface car parks take a large part of the centre and are an eyesore.

In the replanning of Warrington centre there are three major concentrations described as cores: a commercial core constituting the main shopping area; a municipal core (to the west) which would include the town hall, local authority offices and other civic facilities; and a cultural core which will provide a nucleus for community facilities and include public halls, the museum, library, art school, and multi-purpose sports centre. In this envisaged zoning the utilization of the existing fabric and minimization of disruption are essential purposes.

Many of the needs of shoppers in Warrington will be served by shops in the local centres, and in the district centres of Birchwood, Padgate, Bridgewater and Westbrook.

An aim is to concentrate more fully the shopping in the centre and thus make it more efficient. Access to shops will be, as far as possible, from pedestrian precincts and rear servicing to shops will be done by using existing streets or by developing new service links. Among the first buildings to be provided in the town centre renewal is the large covered market which was completed in 1974.

Industry

At the time of the designation in 1968 of the new town there was a fair diversity of existing industry, and although it suffered some decline of employment, it was not so marked as in other parts of South Lancashire that depended so much on the textile industries. The main industries of Warrington for many years have been metal goods, engineering, electrical goods, chemical manufacture, paper and printing; while a large employment has been in scientific work, research and combined office work because of the United Kingdom Atomic Energy Authority establishment in Birchwood. Most of the existing industry is in the cruciform growth in the centre of the town.

In the outline plan, as previously mentioned, new industrial areas are located towards the periphery of the new town: a fairly large one in Westbrook in the north-west corner near the M62, and other sites in the north along this motorway; areas in Padgate near the M6 and another site in the south of Bridgewater.

A major task of the development corporation is to attract industry, because on the success of this the planned growth of the town so much depends. In the early years the hoped for increase in employment did not materialize. The consultants estimated an increase of 1800 from 1966 to 1971 in the designated area, but during those years there

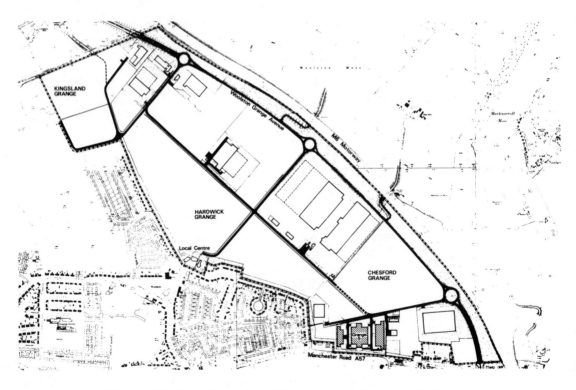

Figure 31.6 Location plan of Grange unit factories, Padgate.

was a decline of 2300. The first new industrial area to be developed is the Grange site in Padgate along the M6, where the development corporation has built several advance factories for letting. This has served to attract smaller firms who appreciate the advantage of the provision of new modern premises. Also a number of firms are building their own factories here.

Social Aspect

The social and cultural activities in a new town are very much a combined enterprise by the development corporation, the local authority and voluntary associations. In a fairly large town like Warrington many of these activities already exist, and it is a question of extending them to the new districts, and encouraging the institution of further activities prompted by modern needs. One of the very valuable provisions being made at Warrington is the planning of schools so that they can also be used for recreational and cultural purposes by adults.

The development corporation in collaboration with the local authority is fostering the establishment of community associations, and community centres are being provided in several of the new districts. By 1976 three centres were completed, one at Padgate, one at Grappenhall and one at Hood Manor in Westbrook. The corporation has also assisted in the expansion of the activities of the local sports and arts councils.

Warrington has had for many years cultural activities which have served not only its inhabitants, but people from surrounding areas. For example, the concerts of the Padgate Winter Concerts Society held in the main hall of the Padgate College of Education, are widely known and have attracted people from a wide region.

The great need of all cultural activities, particularly the drama, music and art exhibitions, is for adequate premises to serve them, which in themselves are a stimulus to progress and improvement. It is hoped that in the provision of these, especially in the renewed centre, Warrington will not have to wait too long, which unfortunately has been the fate of many new towns.

References

31.1 These statistics are derived from the Census Report.

31.2 A valuable account of the early and industrial history of Warrington is entitled, *The Archaeology of Warrington's Past*, Development Corporation and Archaeology Surveys Ltd, 1976.

31.3 Peter Shore, Secretary of State for the Environment, stated in Parliament on 5 April 1977 that 'For Warrington induced growth should continue until the population reaches 160 000, which, together with natural growth, should mean a population of about 170 000 by the late 1980s in place of the previous target of 205 000.'

32 Central Lancashire

Early in 1965 the then Minister of Housing and Local Government, Mr. Richard Crossman, stated that the Government had been considering how it could help Manchester with its housing problems, in a way that would contribute to the general prosperity and growth of the north-west, and the Government decided to designate a site in the Leyland–Chorley area for a large new town. The hope was expressed that the new town, in addition to meeting the long-term overspill needs of Manchester, would contribute to the industrial revival of the whole region and form a new focus for urban renewal. As implied in the previous chapter on Warrington, because of the rapid decline of population in Manchester its overspill needs in 1975 appeared as a little less urgent than in 1965, but the objective of an industrial revival in the north-west, and of attracting population to the region is as important as ever.

Significant in Mr. Crossman's statement was the mention of a new focus for urban renewal. This could be interpreted as an area that gives opportunities for the provision of a good urban environment in place of some of the overcrowded areas of South Lancashire with their large districts of obsolescent housing. Also in Central Lancashire there was a more stable population from 1951 to 1971 than in South Lancashire, and there has been far less movement of population away from the region than further south.

Sir Robert H. Matthew, Stirrat Johnson-Marshall and Partners were commissioned to carry out a two stage study to: (1) advise the Minister on the area to be designated for development under the New Towns Act; and (2) produce for the development corporation a draft master plan. The report on (1), the area to be designated, was completed in January 1967 and published in the following May under the title of 'Central Lancashire—Study for a City'.

The consultants realized the development possibilities of this central Lancashire region. 'The new growth', they say, 'will be based on a thriving and energetic group of communities with a population of about a quarter of a million already. It will be centred on a national communications route which was established 2000 years ago for geographical reasons which still hold good (and is now being rapidly upgraded to twenty-first century standards), and it will be in easy reach of, among other good things, four universities, an extensive seaboard with an international resort, the Lake District, wild Pennine moorlands of breathtaking beauty, and the rich and varied culture of two of the half dozen great metropolitan cities of the British Isles. The new city, given that it is built well, and above all quickly, will thus naturally attract people and industrial organisations of the highest calibre and will present them immediately with a wide range of social facilities and community life'.

The consultants recommended an area of 51 460 acres (20 825 ha) for designation with an increase of population in the area from 253 000 to 503 000 by 1991. They experimented with 10 variations of an overall plan, and for each the central places were Preston in the north, Chorley in the south and Leyland midway.·

The site actually designated on 14 April 1970, was much less, being reduced to 35 255 acres (14 268 ha). The development corporation, appointed a few months later, then prepared its planning proposals in collaboration with the consultants. The designated site is in the 3 new district council areas of Preston, South Ribble, and Chorley, established in April 1974, which together have an area of 117 077 acres (47 400 ha). If these 3 districts are seen together then the designated area of the new town occupies the central part of the combined districts.

The area is generally fairly flat with hills towards the east. The River Whittle follows a winding course south of Preston, joining the sea south of the attractive resort of Lytham St. Annes. It enabled Preston to become a port in 1843 when docks and quays were completed which have subsequently been extended. Settlements in the designated area date from Roman times and there was a Roman Station at Walton-le-Dale. A guild existed at Preston in the Middle Ages and in the seventeenth century it became one of the centres of woollen weaving and later, from the eighteenth century, of cotton spinning.

The region is well situated for communications and transport. The main railway line from London and Crewe on to Scotland passes through its centre with stations at Preston and Leyland, while lines run from Preston to Blackpool and to Manchester with a station at Chorley; other lines run to Liverpool, and eastward to the Yorkshire towns, providing a valuable network. The M6 passes south–north through its centre, while there is a radial pattern of roads at Preston.

Outline Plan

In November 1973 an outline plan was published as a consultative document for consideration by local and public authorities concerned in the Central Lancashire project. This was followed by a slightly fuller and revised edition of the plan published in the Summer of 1974 with the invitation for public comment.

The population in the designated area in 1971 was about 235 000, and in the plan an increase was proposed to about 321 500 by 1986, and to about 420 000 by the year 2001.

The essential structure of the new developments proposed consisted of villages of about 3000, combined to make districts of about 20 000, which again were combined to make 5 townships, each with ultimate populations of between 52 000 and 130 000. A net residential density of 9 to 12 houses to the acre (22 to 30 per ha) was proposed. In these groupings the authors of the plan were actuated by 3 factors which were elucidated. Housing areas, it was contended, must be developed 'in such a way that people can identify the place they live in as a recognizable physical unit as well as, to a lesser extent, a recognizable social unit. There is some evidence to suggest that at the kind of density we are proposing these criteria can be satisfied within a population unit of about 3000 people. A more tangible consideration that affects the attractiveness of housing is convenient access for the residents to shops, schools and other facilities. Our studies of the supply of facilities in relation to population size make it clear that below a population of about 3000 very few local facilities are justified, whereas with a larger population a wider range of services can be supported. In order that residents should have at least the minimum facilities to satisfy daily needs within five to ten minutes' walk, we propose that the village of at least 3000 people should, wherever possible, be the smallest unit of development. However, a much better choice of facilities begins to be viable in populations of 20 000 and above. Thus there appear to be good reasons, wherever possible, to build up three or four village units into a district of at least 20 000 people'.

For the ultimate development by 2001 it was proposed that the Grimsargh township in the north-east should consist of the two new districts of Grimsargh and Haighton of about 25 000 persons each; the township of Preston should include additions to Ingol and Fulwood, each with a target population of 20 000, the township of Walton in the centre should include additions to Penwortham, Lostock Hall, Tardy Gate, and Walton-le-Dale, Bamber Bridge, making three districts of a little over 20 000 persons each; the township of Leyland to the south-west should have two almost completely new districts of about 23 000 each; and Chorley township in the south and south-east should include additions to Whittle-le-Woods, Clayton-le-Woods and Euxton of about 53 000 together. Up to 1986 only a part of each township would be built.

At the time of designation the population of the three areas of the Preston, South Ribble and Chorley District Councils, in which the new town is situated and of which it forms the centre, was approximately 298 000 in 117 077 acres (47 381 ha). This means that the immediately surrounding areas of the new town within these district councils had a population then of 63 000 in 81 822 acres (33 113 ha) which is fairly low density with considerable agricultural land, and which thus forms a partial green belt round the new town.

As the new town area in the north extends to the boundary of Ribble Valley District on the east side and reaches near the boundary of Fylde District on the west side, it would be necessary if a green belt of not less than 2 miles (3 km) wide is envisaged, to include about 10 000 acres (4047 ha) in each of these districts, making a total of about 137 000 acres (55 444 ha). The tip of the new town area in the south reaches nearly to Greater Manchester, with only about 2 miles (3 km) separating the two boundaries.

The principal centre of the new town is Preston and it will be developed accordingly. The existing centres at Leyland and Chorley will be enlarged and become the centres of the townships. There will probably be new district centres at Grimsargh in the north-east, at Fulwood in the north, at Ingol in the north-west, at Walton and Midge Hall in the central area. There will also be local centres of the residential neighbourhoods or villages.

For the most part the townships are separated by areas of open space and tree belts, which also flow into the various districts, some of which are golf courses.

In the prologue to the plan it is pointed out that the linked townships each with its own special character and identity being separated from the others by a green wedge of open country means that the development corporation must control the use of more land than with smaller new towns on green field sites where continuous urban development can occur. If these green wedges were substantial, not less than a mile (1.6 km) wide the Central Lancashire development could be regarded as a new town cluster, but they are really too close, for nowhere is the separation of townships by open space extensive, and there is the inevitable impression that when population reaches its proposed maximum, and prosperity continues, pressure on space will mean the coalescing of the townships into one continuous urban mass, as has so often happened in the past.

designated area

existing development

new residential areas

new employment areas

expansion land for existing industry

township centres

new district centres

expansion of existing centres

open space

existing golf courses

new golf courses

motorways

motorway junctions

motorway limited access junctions

motorway junction possibly closed

north-facing slip roads possibly closed

primary corridors

other major roads

main bus priority routes

railways

existing stations

proposed stations

unallocated areas predominantly in agricultural use

400 hectares

400 acres

km 2 4 6

miles 2 4

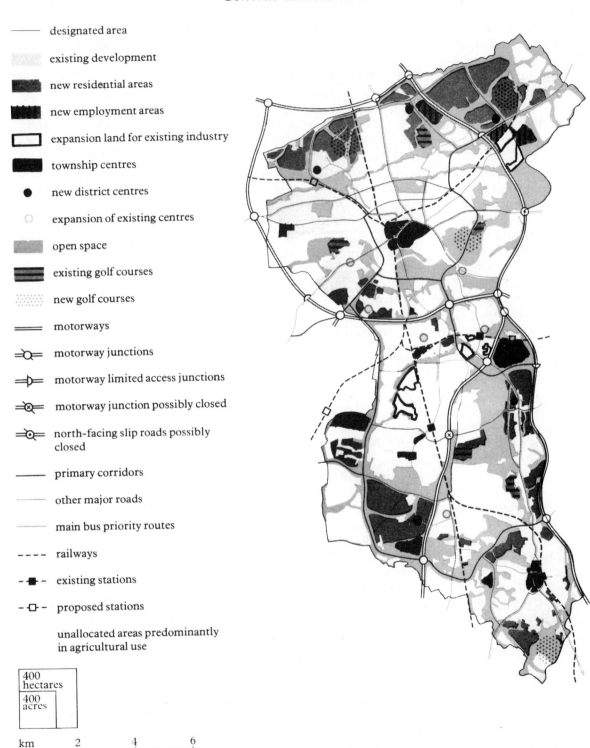

Figure 32.1 Central Lancashire Outline Plan.

As the experience with the first group of new towns demonstrates, green areas within the town and on the periphery are in danger of disappearing with industrial and commercial prosperity and consequent expansion. When those who, like the development corporations, value the original concept are superseded by local authorities who are pleased with and encourage expansion of all kinds, it may mean higher densities within the town and the urban spread into the country at the expense of the quality of life which new towns aim to provide. While it is desirable that there should be flexibility in planning a new town, there are certain principles, which are firmly based on the lives of people which should guide policy. One is the proximity of town and country. It may be argued that a close proximity of two or three miles (3 or 4 km) distant is not so necessary when most people have cars and a journey of five miles (8 km) out is only a matter of ten minutes, but this argument does not apply to children and young people, and to older people who appreciate and value the country, with its woods and fields, within walking distance. For all, fairly quick pedestrian access from homes to the country is a valuable amenity.

The green wedges between the townships that compose the new town of Central Lancashire would be more adequate if they were on a larger scale. For example, it would, we think, have been an improvement to the plan if more generous provision of open space had been introduced between the townships of Preston and Grimsargh. As proposed there is almost continuous development, with little break between Fulwood in the former and Haighton in the latter. In any case the open spaces should be regarded as inviolate, and when proposals are made, as they inevitably will be, for building in these green areas, then every effort should be made to adhere to the original concept.

At the same time it is desirable that the open spaces on the fringes of the new town area, to a depth of at least two miles (3 km), should be preserved and not built on. This bears on another aspect of building the new town. If in the region building and development is to be concentrated in the new town area, then to enable this to be done development in its fringe areas should be restricted. It will be difficult enough for the development corporation to attract industry and population to its area without the competition of surrounding areas. As stated in the plan the corporation is disturbed by 'the large number of outstanding planning consents or commitments for housing in the fringe area, amounting to as many as 16 000 sites for individual dwellings. As the population grows inside the area its fringes may well come under increasing pressure to provide space for various kinds of development and the construction of a substantial proportion of the 16 000 dwellings could make the process of growth in the designated area, particularly in the early years, much more difficult. If this happened it would take much longer for the Development Corporation to build up adequate centres for facilities of all sorts and our investment in new roads and sewers would be less economically utilised'.

This, the corporation, considers 'should be recognised as a strategic issue. Designation implies the deliberate concentration of urban development in this part of Lancashire within the boundary of the designated area and the preservation of the concept of a clear transition from urban to non-urban development'. The corporation suggests that 'in settlements within this fringe area new development should be limited to infilling and rounding off, and also that it should be phased in relation to growth within the designated area. In this way the best use will be made of investment in the designated area, it should be possible to avoid unplanned strain on the highway network, and the people living in surrounding villages will know that the character of their locality will remain substantially unchanged'.

It is important that there should be the fullest cooperation in the preparation of the structure plan for Lancashire with the development corporation, so that the dual purpose of a green belt round the town and assistance with concentrated urban development should be secured.

An indication of what may happen is the application for development of over 700 dwellings at Longton, a village only two miles (3 km) from the designated area boundary, but fortunately, after a public inquiry, at which the development corporation put its case, the application was refused.

The principal locations of existing industry are north of the central area of Preston and along the River Ribble to the west, Red Scar in the north-east, north of the Leyland centre, a large area between Leyland and Chorley, and several smaller sites scattered over the area. In the plan 8 new industrial areas are proposed: at Red Scar in Grimsargh, at Fulwood next to the M6, at Preston west of the docks, at Penwortham south of the River Ribble, three south and west of Leyland, and one at Walton Summit. Dispersing industry over the area continues to some extent the previous pattern.

The road system is inevitably related to the motorways that run through the area encircling Preston in the north, running along the east boundary in the south, and through the area between Leyland and Chorley. A system of three categories of local roads is planned, the primary, district, and local distributor roads, the last of which serves the residential areas. A balance of private and public transport is aimed at, with some bus-only routes and bus-only lanes in other routes. A system of pedestrian ways is introduced into residential areas and new districts, to be extended, as far as possible, into the older areas.

Figure 32.2 Some of the development corporation's first housing to rent at Clayton Brook which will be a development of approximately 1800 dwellings plus a village centre.

Building the Town

Approval of the outline plan was given by the Secretary of State for the Environment on 5 April 1977, and not unexpectedly he concluded that there is no longer a requirement for growth on the scale originally envisaged for the new town. He reduced the population intake from about 100 000 to about 23 000, with early consultations to take place with the development corporation and the local authorities involved about the future of the new town beyond that.

In land use terms, the Secretary of State, subject to further consultation, approved the outline plan except for the deletion of large areas in the north-east and south-west of the designated area. The effect of these changes in broad terms is to reduce the amount of developable land from 16 000 to 10 000 acres (6500 to 4000 ha).

In order to avoid an intolerable delay, the development corporation has already made progress on several village and employment area projects where newcomers are already in residence and in employment in many instances. In all, over 2000 houses are completed or under construction/contract for rent, in four separate locations, and 1800 houses for sale are completed or under construction. In the commercial field, three village centres are complete and the major commercial operation at the first district centre is under construction.

The first employment area, of approximately 250 acres (100 ha), has already over 60 advance factories completed or under construction, of which nearly half are let and in operation.

At the same time as the Secretary of State gave his approval to the outline plan, he gave the go-ahead for another village for about 2000 houses and a golf course, in the area to the north-west of Preston.

33 Corby

In the northern part of Northamptonshire ironstone has been quarried for centuries, and the resources of the mineral in the area are still considerable, and are the largest in England. Until 1931, however, extensions of the workings were slow. The village of Corby, the centre of the Northamptonshire ironfields, had a population in the middle of the nineteenth century of about 850 and by 1931 it had risen to only 1600; but in that year Stewarts and Lloyds Ltd came to the area to extract ironstone on a big scale by the most modern methods, and to build steelworks for the production of steel strips and tubes.

The old village of Corby is about 8 miles (13 km) north of Kettering on the east side of the main railway line from London to Nottingham. The steelworks of Stewarts and Lloyds Ltd were built a little north and north-east of Corby village. It was necessary to provide houses for over 4000 employees in the company, most of whom came from Scotland, and as assistance was not forthcoming from local housing authorities, Stewarts and Lloyds Ltd embarked on the task itself. In 5 years (1934–39) the company built 2200 houses on 280 acres (113 ha) to the west of the railway in the districts of Pen Green and Studfall, and also provided premises and grounds for a large social and sports club. Until 1939 the area came under the Kettering Rural District Council, but in 1939 the Corby Urban District Council was established. After the war that authority took over the task of providing houses for the workers at Stewarts and Lloyds Ltd, and it built them on an estate in Willowbrook at the southern part of Studfall forming a half-circle to the west of the earlier housing estate, thus providing a further 1500 houses by 1950. The population at that date had risen to about 16 000. The number of workers in Stewarts and Lloyds Ltd was then in the region of 6000, while proposed expansion would provide employment for an additional 4000. A proportion of the workers, well over 1000, travelled from surrounding villages and towns, principally from Kettering. It was unsatisfactory that they should have to make these long journeys to work, especially as the steelworks operate on a continuous shift process; thus it was necessary to build a considerable number of additional houses at Corby if people were to live in the vicinity of their place of employment. It was decided in 1949 that the best way of doing this, so as to provide also the educational, recreational and shopping facilities to ensure a satisfactory home environment, was to build a new town under the New Towns Act with a target population of 40 000. A draft designation order was issued for an area of 3550 acres (1437 ha), including Corby village and the existing housing estates west, south-west, south and north of these. Subsequently it was decided to exclude from the new town an area of 420 acres (170 ha) to the south-west which was regarded by the Ministry of Supply as essential for ironstone working, and another area of 630 acres (255 ha) to the west which was regarded by the Ministry of Agriculture as essential for food production. This meant a total reduction in the area by 1050 acres (425 ha), and Corby New Town was designated on 1 April 1950 on a site of about 2494 acres (1010 ha) to accommodate a population of 40 000.

In August 1950 Professors William Holford (made a life peer in 1965) and H. Myles Wright were appointed as planning consultants to prepare a report and an outline plan. In reducing the designated area while retaining the proposed maximum population it appears to have been understood that the area could be mainly housing and that this could be at a fairly high density, while land from which ironstone had been extracted could be made available later for other needs. But the consultants took the view that Corby needed a town centre and other amenities that require land at once, if it was to be a town in the full sense, while, on the matter of housing densities, the consultants pointed out 'that there was evidence that most of the people who would live in the new neighbourhoods were likely to prefer a house to a flat or maisonette', while flats cost more than 2-storey houses to build. The consultants, therefore, proposed an extension of the designated area southwards in the region of the 202 acres (82 ha) which had been taken from the original area for ironstone working, and the development corporation accordingly requested an addition to the designated area. This was finally agreed to and a designation variation order was made on 12 September 1952, for an area of 2696 acres (1092 ha).

The site of the designated area is gently undulating and consists of 4 shallow valleys draining eastwards. The general slope is from the north-west where the ground is about 440 feet (132 m) above sea level to the south-east where it falls to 300 feet (90 m). In the centre of the area are Thoroughsale and Hazel Woods, attractive open spaces comprising some 220 acres (89 ha).

In 1960 Stewarts and Lloyds Ltd received authority for a considerable enlargement of its steelworks which would involve the employment of 2500 more than had been envisaged when the plan for a town of 40 000 had been made. Consequently the development corporation was invited by the Ministry to make proposals for the extension of the town, and as a result an area of 1600 acres (648 ha) to the south of the town was designated early in 1963 for the purpose. A new master plan prepared by John H. D. Madin and Partners was submitted to the Ministry in July 1965.

The new plan was for a population of 55 000 with provision for natural growth to 80 000 by about the end of the century. According to the report of the corporation in 1967, prospects in the steel industry in 1967 indicated that it was unlikely that Stewarts and Lloyds would employ another 2500 in Corby. Developments in the mid-sixties made it clear that increased steel production did not necessarily involve greater manpower, while the future development of the steel industry may mean a different distribution of the industry with large plants situated on the coast using imported ore. It was not intended that these possibilities should modify the plan for the extension of Corby, but it would mean a greater increase of other manufacturing industries.

Outline Plan for the First Designated Area

In the plan prepared by the consultants the town is divided into neighbourhoods with considerably varying populations. Three of these existed when the plan was made in 1952, namely Corby village which, in the plan, was to have some reduction of popula-

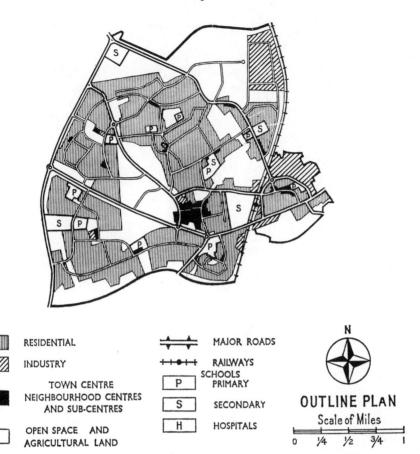

RESIDENTIAL

INDUSTRY

TOWN CENTRE
NEIGHBOURHOOD CENTRES
AND SUB-CENTRES

OPEN SPACE AND
AGRICULTURAL LAND

MAJOR ROADS

RAILWAYS

SCHOOLS
P PRIMARY

S SECONDARY

H HOSPITALS

N

OUTLINE PLAN
Scale of Miles
0   ¼   ½   ¾   1

Figure 33.1 Corby—Outline Plan.

tion from 1800 to 1500; Pen Green and Studfall which had been built mainly by Stewarts and Lloyds Ltd, and which were to have slight reductions, from 3300 to 3000 and from 7600 to 7300 respectively; while Willowbrook which had been half built by the Urban District Council was to have a population of 6300. Two completely new neighbourhoods were proposed, Lodge Park to the north-west with a population of 5750, and Beanfield to the south-west with 9000, while the south-eastern neighbourhood, comprising Wheatley, Gainsborough and Exeter, would be almost completely new with a population of 6500 (existing 500). Each of the smaller neighbourhoods was planned to have 1 primary school, while the three larger neighbourhoods, Beanfield, Willowbrook and the south-east, each would have 2. Of the secondary schools proposed, 2 were in the south-west and one in the north-east, while a grammar school and technical college were proposed near the centre. There were 5 existing shopping centres, and a few more were added in the new neighbourhoods of Lodge Park and Beanfield. It was proposed that Thoroughsale and Hazel Woods should be preserved as a large open space, with paths and roads introduced to provide walks, while a part could be devoted to playing fields and a part to a commercial timber plantation.

The town centre is on high ground, not quite geographically central, but towards the

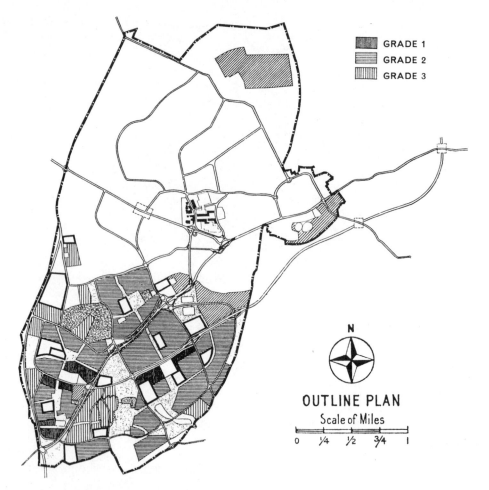

GRADE 1
GRADE 2
GRADE 3

N

OUTLINE PLAN
Scale of Miles
0   ¼   ½   ¾   1

Figure 33.2 Corby—housing densities proposed in the extension area.

south-east. The result was that it was between ½ and ¾ of a mile (0.8 and 1.2 km) from the most remote residential area in the south-east, but nearly 2 miles ((3 km) from the most remote residential areas of Lodge Park in the north-west. It would, however, have been rather difficult to place the town centre more in the geographical centre as that position immediately to the north was occupied by the Urban District Council housing. To avoid the disadvantages of an entirely one-industry town, 2 additional areas were planned for light and service industries, one fairly large at Earlstrees in the north-east and one immediately south of old Corby village.

For some years Corby will be surrounded by opencast ironstone workings, but it is hoped that these will ultimately become green belt land. This first master plan was approved by the Minister of Housing and Local Government in November 1953.

New Outline Plan Occasioned by the Extension

The extension of 1600 acres (648 ha) is a little over a third of the total area. John Madin and Partners, therefore, produced a new master plan for the whole town in 1964–65 so as to integrate the old and the new in a satisfactory way. They stated that they had gratefully grasped this opportunity to take a new look at the existing town of Corby, and had not hesitated to propose major changes where they appeared to be necessary in the light of present-day conditions and practice. In the town centre, in particular, they proposed not only a considerable expansion (against the possibility of which there had in past years been provided a reserve of land), but also a reorganization of traffic and shopping and other facilities, to ensure the separate circulation of pedestrians and vehicles, for which the existing centre (the first to be constructed in any new town) did not adequately provide.

The original new town is divided into 8 neighbourhoods. The extension has 5 neighbourhoods, determined partly by the physical features, and each neighbour-hood—or residential area, as it is called—is formed by small housing clusters each of about 300 to 400 dwellings. The principle of development is well illustrated by the neighbourhood that will be provided first, namely Kingswood, part of which lies in the original designated area. It is roughly a square divided into 4 housing groups round a primary school, with the neighbourhood centre in the south-west group. Roads are on the four sides of the area, from which culs-de-sac branch into the residential areas, but there is no through road, and the neighbourhood is planned mainly for pedestrian circulation. There are 2 main green walkways between the four housing groups, which can be used also by cyclists, and these greenways are planned to form a continuous network throughout the extension while footpaths within each housing group link with the greenways. Kingswood was planned for about 8000. The other neighbourhoods are Danesholme (5875) to the west, Oakley Hay (4725) in the south-west corner, Great Oakley (4250) on the south, and Snatchill (13 750) on the east, thus an additional population of about 36 600. Part of the area, mainly Snatchill, will continue to be worked for ironstone for the period 1963–83 and this will govern the building sequence.

Care has been taken to preserve the natural beauties of the area and enhance them as much as possible, because this southern part of the town will be surrounded for many years to come by ironstone workings. Within the extension is the Great Oakley estate which consists of the Hall and park, the village, and 5 farms—an old-world agricultural community of 231 people. This is the subject of a special study in the plan, and it is proposed to preserve as much as possible undisturbed. The park provides part of a green wedge that continues northwards to playing fields, and woodland as far as the boundary of the original new town.

Housing in the extension is planned in 3 grades, the first to include flats, maisonettes, and small dwellings; the second to be mostly 2-storey housing of the orthodox types, these together providing about 87.5% of the total, of which 20% will have the fairly high density of 20–22 dwellings per acre (49–54 per ha), and the remainder 13.25 dwellings an acre (33 per ha). It is proposed to provide one garage per house, compared with 37% in the original plan. The third grade, forming the remaining 12.5% is allocated mainly to private developers for owner occupiers, at much lower densities. Two new industrial areas are to be provided, one fairly large area to the north-east of the extension just south of the Exeter district and thus fairly near to the town centre, and a small area in the south-west neighbourhood of Oakley Hay. These are important, as it is essential that Corby should not be entirely a one industry town, and that some diversification should be secured.

The plan was especially good for the segregation of traffic, with each neighbourhood largely a pedestrian area with culs-de-sac branching into it. Such excellent planning deserves emulation. The only regret was that somewhat lower densities were not proposed.

Implementations of the New Outline Plan

The outline plan proposed by Madin for the extension to the designated area was not destined to be fully implemented. In September 1971, the Department of the Environment instructed the development corporation to cease building houses for rent after their current scheme at Danesholme for 600 houses was completed, and that from then on they should concentrate their housing efforts in providing sites for housing for sale, and encourage their rapid development. Furthermore, they should continue their strenuous campaign to sell houses from their own stock of rented housing.

Consequently, within a short space of time, apart from the corporation's current scheme for 600 rented houses, the plans for Danesholme were quickly re-drawn. Land was sold to four property developers who together would immediately commence building some 450 houses. The corporation set aside two areas comprising 80 plots especially for purchase by persons wishing to build their own homes. Finally, an area to the south-west, suitable for the development of a further 200 houses, was held in reserve. The corporation also decided to build the neighbourhood centre for both the Danesholme and Oakley Hay communities at Danesholme, as there was no possibility of further development taking place after Danesholme had been completed.

In September 1973, as a result of the corporation's representations, the Department of the Environment authorized the continuation of a limited rented housing programme, initially for about 200 units a year. This was to ensure the corporation's role in diversifying industry by enabling it to have under its control a rented house building programme to meet the needs of industry attracted to Corby and the need to provide housing for people from London.

Since that time, steady progress has been maintained. The reserved site at Danesholme for 200 units has been taken by the corporation for rented housing, and 516 units of mixed rented and private housing in Oakley Hay were nearing completion in 1977.

In October 1974 the Department of the Environment authorized the corporation to commission a firm of planning consultants to undertake a needed review of Corby's Master Plan of 1965.

The main reasons for the review were: (1) to re-define the objectives of the development corporation as the result of changed circumstances; (2) to provide for the future development of Corby in the context of the County Structure Plan; (3) to allow for the emphasis now being placed on the diversification of industry and the increasing employment prospects in the town; (4) to allow for the possibility of the area known as Snatchill (the restored land in the Great Oakley Quarry area) proving unsuitable for housing the population planned for it in the Madin Master Plan.

The corporation commissioned Sir Colin Buchanan & Partners to undertake the review, in consultation with the Northamptonshire County Council, the Corby District Council, the Department of the Environment, the British Steel Corporation and Corby Development Corporation. The consultants submitted their report in the summer of 1975. The Minister, after consideration, declined to approve the expansion recommended within the Report (33.1).

Building the Town

The corporation decided at the beginning that together with the urgently needed houses the town centre should be provided quickly, as there was already a population of 16 000 in need of such a centre and in a few years this would be much increased.

At the time of designation in April 1950, the Corby Urban District Council was building houses at the rate of between 300 and 400 a year. Housing by the development corporation began in 1952 in the south-east neighbourhood near the town centre and by the end of the year 80 were completed. Both the Urban District Council and the corporation continued to build several hundred houses a year, the latter at an increasing rate and the former at a diminishing rate.

In the years 1953 to 1956 the development corporation built 364, 365, 496 and 475, and the local authority 202, 286, 144 and 75. From 1957 the local authority in most years built few houses with the exception of 181 in 1973, 160 in 1975 and 150 in 1976. From 1957 to 1967 a fair average output was maintained by the development corporation, the totals for those years being 587, 514, 402, 462, 336, 798, 291, 425, 180, 289 and 631. From 1968 to 1976 the output was rather lower being 130, 235, 261, 264, 177, 276, 336, 315 and 428. Altogether by the end of 1976 since designation a total of 13 253 houses have been provided, of which 9038 are by the development corporation, 2551 by the local authority and 1664 by private enterprise.

It will be seen, therefore, that the corporation gradually took over the task. In addition, in 1962, the corporation purchased the 2200 houses built by Stewarts and Lloyds Ltd. The population of Corby in 1977 was about 54 000, thus nearing the population envisaged in the plan of 1965.

Rapid progress was made with the building of the town centre in the early stages to answer the needs of the existing population and by 1967 most of it had been built according to the original plans, including the shops on either side of the main thoroughfare of Corporation Street, the maret square with the shops surrounding it, the bus station and the civic centre. Good progress was made with the provision of schools, including a grammar school and a central technical college, and with the building of factories in the two industrial estates, and it can be said that generally the provision of the various types of buildings has advanced in satisfactory unison.

Housing and Residential Areas

The policy in providing dwellings was, in the first place, to redress the lack of balance in the housing by Stewarts and Lloyds Ltd and the Urban District Council. In a survey it was found that a very large proportion of the dwellings had 4 and 5 rooms, while there was a deficiency of both small dwellings of one, 2 and 3 rooms and of large dwellings of 6 rooms or more. The corporation thus planned to build more of the smaller and larger types in the first few years. Some of the former have been flats near the town and neighbourhood centres.

The principal residential areas included in the original plan were completed by the development corporation at the end of 1967 and the new neighbourhood of Kingswood forming part of the extension was well under way. The layout of the residential areas is generally attractive and compares favourably with that of the other new towns. In their variety they offer a contrast to the residential areas of the Urban District Council and of Stewarts and Lloyds Ltd, which are a little monotonous with their

Figure 33.3 Corby—a part of the south-east neighbourhood.

straight roads and straight rows of houses of similar design.

The Exeter estate of the south-east neighbourhood, a good example of housing layout (early fifties), consists of a road, looped south from Oakley Road, one of the main town roads. Off this loop are several smaller irregular loops on either side and around these the houses are grouped. There is a 'village green' near the centre of the areas, and a little to the east of this is an attractive group of 5 shops forming a concave front on a corner, adjoining another row of shops with flats over. Opposite is 'The Lantern' public house, and a degree of height in this grouping is obtained by hilly ground at the front and a few blocks of flats in the vicinity. If one criticism can be made of this generally pleasant residential district, it is that there are too many through roads, too many traffic loops; it would have been better if many of these had stopped short of the complete loop, and have become pedestrian ways for a part of it.

A little to the west in the triangle formed by the new Exeter Way and Oakley Road, these defects are overcome, and the layout consists of a series of culs-de-sac running off the principal roads with pedestrian ways connecting them. It is an excellent layout, worthy of study by planners.

Gainsborough Road is the principal road of the district running east–west. For a little way Constable Road runs roughly parallel to it on the north side. A series of culs-de-sac off Constable Road link with a footpath called Rubens Walk. A little further west a similar series of culs-de-sac off Leighton Road are connected at their terminations by a footpath called Llewellyn Walk. These examples are typical of the area. The housing is of a fair variety of terrace blocks, mostly of 4 and 6 houses with some of 8, and semi-detached and detached houses. The shopping centre is again a group of shops on a corner with a public house opposite. Incidentally all the roads in this part of the south-eastern neighbourhood are named after artists, all British, except two—Rubens and Holbein—who both spent some time painting in England. The latest residential area, Danesholme, which is within the extension area, was for 786 dwellings and 378 garages. It was completed in May 1976.

Town Centre

The town centre as built follows in principle the lay-out proposed by the consultants in the original plan. It consists of a main street—Corporation Street—running east–west and linking two of the main town roads—George Street and Elizabeth Street—running north–south. At the eastern part of Corporation Street on the north side is a market square with shops continuing on its west and south sides while on its east side next to Elizabeth Street is the bus station. On the further side of Elizabeth Street are the police station and magistrates' court which serve as an eastern terminal building to Corporation Street, while at the western end a civic centre has been built which was the subject of a competition in 1959. The winning design by Enrico de Pierro, Nigel Farrington and John Dennys consists of a civic square intended as a pedestrian precinct round which are grouped the assembly halls on the north side, municipal offices on the east side, and swimming pool in the south-west corner. The civic square is open at the point opposite Corporation Street, which thus permits a view from the street of the existing woodland beyond the square. In his report the assessor Edward Mills referred approvingly to the compactness of the layout. It is a good scheme which provides a balance to the police station and market square at the further end.

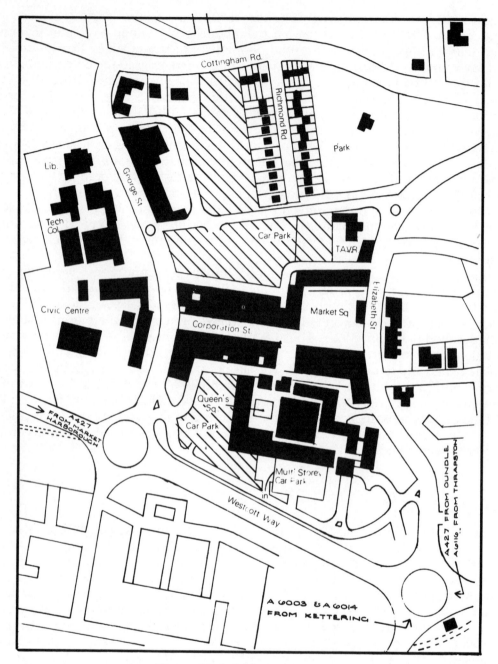

Figure 33.4 Corby town centre.

The civic centre was completed in October 1965 and was opened by Richard Crossman, then Minister of Housing and Local Government. It consists of council chamber and offices, a civic hall seating 1400 persons, a small hall for 300, a theatre for 550 and a large indoor swimming pool. Nearby is the much needed Strathclyde Hotel, also completed in 1965, with its 40 bedrooms, restaurant and private reception suite.

Figure 33.5 Aerial view of Corby town centre with Phase I extension in the foreground.

The shopping centre, with a wide street as the main feature and shops on either side, follows the traditional arrangement resulting from the haphazard grouping of shops on either side of a main traffic thoroughfare. It was, however, a bad tradition to follow for a modern shopping centre, as it perpetuated the mixture of traffic and pedestrians which is one of the serious disadvantages of modern urban life. Corby centre could not, therefore, have been regarded as a good example of a modern town or shopping centre. Traffic should only move to, and not through, a centre, and car parks are provided on the periphery for this need. One good feature in the plan, however, is that the market square is neatly tucked away on one side of the shopping highway and makes a safe precinct with close proximity to the bus station. The centre is architecturally pleasing and in many of the buildings there is canopied protection for shoppers.

The extension plan included proposals for a complete change of the town centre. John Madin and Partners had considered whether to expand the existing centre to serve the whole of the enlarged town or to provide another centre in the extension area. They wisely adopted the former course. That there is a reserve of vacant land north and south of the existing centre, and that it is situated towards the south-east of the town, and thus in easy reach of most extension areas, were governing factors.

The proposed replanning of the centre provides for the segregation of pedestrians and vehicular traffic. It was proposed to exclude vehicles from Corporation Street and change it to a pedestrian way, and to have a sequence of pedestrian 'squares and malls' extending north and south, thus forming roughly a cross plan. Two-level development was planned in parts of the centre, a development which the sloping ground on either side facilitates, and which would permit vehicles to come near the centre, while generous car parks would be provided on the periphery.

Work on the extension plan commenced in the summer of 1968, and by September 1972, Phase I had been completed on the south side, adding 41 shops with storage accommodation below. Further office accommodation has been provided in three locations. The Crown Building on the extreme eastern side had already been completed and occupied by various Government departments. Other features included in the development were the multi-storey car park for 600 cars, the new Bus Station, and the novel twin cinema offering family entertainment from two 340-seater cinemas. With the opening of the extension, the whole town centre, old and new, became a pedestrian precinct.

Industry

Most of the early factory building was in the St James Estate south of Corby village, and industrial development in the larger estate to the north at Earlstrees occurred later. By the end of 1975 over fifty manufacturing firms occupied 53 factories in both estates and a degree of diversification of industry has been secured. Most of the factories have been built by the corporation and are of either 10 000 or 20 000 sq. feet (900 or 1800 m²).

Figure 33.6 Aerial view of Earlstree industrial estate showing new factories and, in the distance, the steelworks.

These industrial estates have been carefully planned and landscaped.

In the early years of the new town an overwhelming preponderance of workers was employed by Stewarts and Lloyds (now British Steel Corporation), but in later years an increasing proportion has been employed in other industries. At 30 September 1957, 1336 persons were employed in manufacturing industries and 3785 in service industries, the total of 5121 being only about half the 10 294 employed in Stewarts and Lloyds. The increase and expansion of the manufacturing industries in the St James and Earlstree estates was such, however, that by the same date 17 years later (30 September 1974) 5880 were employed in manufacturing industries and 8073 in service industries, the total of 13 953 comparing with the 12 761 employed by the British Steel Corporation. Of the total employed in the manufacturing and service industries, about half, 6916, were women. Thus a good deal of progress has been made towards more balanced industry.

As previously mentioned it was planned to expand Corby so as to accommodate a further 2500 steel workers. This did not occur. If the new plan was to be implemented there would have to be provision for other industry to take its place 'on a scale greater than envisaged in the Master Plan' (33.2).

In June 1967 negotiations were concluded with the Greater London Council for Corby to participate in the London overspill Industrial Selection Scheme, and in the following year a further 127 acres (51 ha) of land especially suitable for industry was designated to the north of the town near Gretton Brook Road.

Social Aspects

The task of making Corby a happy and successful town depends partly on securing a greater variety of employment and of cultural and recreational interests. Up to about 1956 it was practically a one-industry town with the Scottish workers of Stewarts and Lloyds having a strong influence on the pattern of social life, but, as mentioned, by 1974 very good progress had been made towards the introduction of other industry so that a considerable proportion of the population are now employed by other firms. The probable future distribution of employment mentioned will almost certainly mean that in the years to come between a half and two-thirds will be employed in industries other than steel works.

Like other new towns Corby has a large number of societies of a cultural and recreational character, some of which are very active and successful. The Civic Centre is already acting as a stimulus to many activities and interests. This Civic Centre was provided by the local authority, and the development corporation comments that 'apart from the material advantages which it affords it is symbolical of the growing confidence, power and financial strength of the local authority'.

References and Notes

33.1 26th Annual Report of Corby Development Corporation 1976.
33.2 17th Annual Report of Corby Development Corporation 1967.

34 Telford

The West Midlands conurbation consists of Birmingham and the Metropolitan Districts of Dudley, Sandwell, Walsall and Wolverhampton, and part of the Metropolitan District of Solihull. The total population in 1961 was about 2.38 millions. (It was roughly the same in 1891 at about 2.37 millions.) This was about 4.8% more than in 1951 and the increase was slightly less than the national average of 5.3%. This was due to migration from the conurbation. While Birmingham showed a slight reduction in population, some of the residential areas on the fringes showed marked increases.

This tendency continued in the intercensal period from 1961 to 1971 with more marked changes in some areas. For example there was a dramatic decrease in the population of Birmingham from 1 110 683 in 1961 to 1 013 366 in 1971, and there was generally dispersal from the conurbations to the small country towns. The dispersal in the West Midlands is, of course, assisted in some measure by the two new towns of Telford and Redditch.

A primary task for the future was seen in the late 1950s and early 1960s as the need to rehouse those living in the slums and congested areas of the conurbation, to provide for the regional increase in population and to do this in a way that was socially and economically the most satisfactory. It was estimated that it would be necessary to provide by 1981 for at least a ½ million persons.

Existing slum areas were at such high densities that if the rehoused population was to enjoy improved standards a substantial proportion would have to be housed elsewhere. The extent of the resulting dispersal was estimated in a memorandum outlining a policy for the West Midland Region and submitted to the Minister of Housing and Local Government by the Town and Country Planning Association and the Midlands New Town Society in September 1961 (34.1).

The Association and the Society proposed that the overspill should be accommodated in 2 or 3 new towns and by the expansion of several small towns in the West Midlands region. The new towns proposed were Dawley in Shropshire, one in the Woofferton-Orleton area on the Shropshire-Herefordshire border and a possible third in the vicinity of Swynnerton in Staffordshire. It was suggested that Dawley and Woofferton should be increased in size by 50 000 each, and a list of town-expansion schemes was proposed that would take another 150 000, making an overspill total of 250 000, which leaves at least another 50 000 for which provision would have to be made.

At the time this memorandum was being prepared, Sheppard Fidler, the Birmingham City Architect, was making a survey of Dawley and its surroundings as a possible site for a new town, and Fidler's report indicated that, in spite of certain anticipated site difficulties that could be overcome with some additional expenditure, the region offered good scope for a new town. The Minister's decision to issue a draft designation order for the new town of Dawley, the predecessor of Telford, in September 1962, which was confirmed on 16 January 1963, followed Fidler's report, but was also probably encouraged by the memorandum of the Town and Country Planning Association and the Midlands New Towns Society.

The area designated was 9100 acres (3683 ha) for an ultimate population of about 90 000. The existing population was about 21 000. About 11 miles (18 km) west of Wolverhampton, 23 miles (37 km) north-west of Birmingham and 13 miles (21 km) east of Shrewsbury, the site was roughly square in shape with the existing town of Dawley slightly north-west of the geographical centre. The northern boundary ran south of Wellington and Oakengates, and the River Severn was just inside the southern boundary. This is a particularly interesting part of England. In the south-west corner of the site is the valley of Coalbrookdale which can be regarded as the cradle of modern industrial progress and the very lovely stretch of the Severn Gorge along the southern boundary of the site is being preserved unspoilt as an amenity. Many attractive old Georgian houses, some in terraces, survive in the village of Ironbridge, but several are in a poor condition.

Much of the hilly character of the western part of the site originated as spoilheaps of former mineral workings now covered with vegetation and so integrated into the landscape that it is now difficult to distinguish the natural from the artificial. These conditions, together with the soil disturbance caused by mining have created large areas of derelict land which presented problems to planning and constructional work.

The existing road communications provided a good basis for development. The A464 road from Wolverhampton to Wellington traverses the northern boundary, while the A442 north-west from Bridgnorth to Wellington runs through Dawley; the B4380 runs near the southern boundary and the B4373 along the western boundary. Until recently there was an excellent railway network in the area developed in the days of industrial prosperity a hundred years ago, but this network has been destroyed by modern policy. A main line from Wolverhampton to Wellington runs near the northern boundary, a line along the southern boundary ran south of the Severn, and these 2 lines were linked by 3 running north and south. But for passengers they have all been eliminated except the first mentioned. One of the lines is kept for goods transport. We talk much in our plans of segregating pedestrians and vehicles but here was a century-old public transport system that could be efficiently modernized with many advantages over the road system, but we prefer to scrap it in the interests of the latter. In the old railway network covering the Dawley site there was the nucleus of an exclusive public transport system comparable to that planned at Runcorn, but it requires imaginative interpretation of existing potential for this to occur.

Outline Plan

A draft master plan for the designated area of Dawley was prepared by John H. D. Madin and Partners and exhibited to the public in January 1965. Although this plan was superseded by the larger basic plan for Telford, many features of the draft Dawley plan were retained.

A prominent feature of the original draft plan for Dawley was a road of motorway

standard roughly square in the overall plan towards the northern half of the site. It had
a loop in the south encircling Madeley, which linked in the south-east with the A442 to
Bridgnorth. At the north-east and north-west corners it linked with roads running
north to industrial areas and with the A464. Within this major circular trunk road there
was a circular distributor road which passed through the centres of the residential units
and encircled the town centre towards the north of the site. There were 9 residential
units each of about 8000 population. Each residential servicing centre, as it is called,
included a group of shops, 2 primary schools, a church or church hall, public house,
community building, a doctors' group practice building and a maternity clinic.
Secondary distributor roads ran through the residential areas and fed into the centre,
while an independent footpath system traversed the whole town, the aim being to
secure segregation of vehicles and pedestrians. South of the town centre is an extensive town park taking advantage of the attractive natural features of the landscape
which include a very beautiful lake surrounded by woodlands. Industry was located in
the south-east and the west where some already existed in both areas, and in the
north-east corner which was a new industrial area.

   While the master plan for Dawley was being considered by the MHLG, a Regional
Study of the West Midlands was issued by the Ministry of Economic Affairs and
referred to the West Midland Economic Planning Council. In its proposals for the main
lines of development and planning was one for 'a series of projects on an arc round the
west of the Birmingham conurbation, each project taking at least 50 000 overspill
population from the conurbation by 1981, in or near Worcester City, Wellington–
Oakengates (the planning to be related with that of Dawley) and the area between
Stafford and Stoke-on-Trent'. A further proposal was that a study should be made of
the possibilities of building up, for the longer term, a new regional centre in Shropshire based on Shrewsbury and Dawley, designated to facilitate an eventually faster
rate of westward dispersal in the region and the development of a new axis of national
growth northwards towards the Dee and southwards towards the Severn estuary.

   Following the first of these proposals the MHLG appointed the authors of the
Dawley draft plan in December 1965 to study and define a possible site for an overspill
of 50 000 in the Wellington–Oakengates area and then to prepare a master plan for this
combined with that of the new town of Dawley. The consultants produced their
proposals for the area of development at Wellington–Oakengates in 1966 for an area of
12 015 acres (4862 ha). A draft designation order was made in January 1968. This was
followed by a public inquiry in April and May 1968. Objections were made to the
amount of land proposed for designation and the loss of good agriculture land, and in
consequence Walter E. Lane, who conducted the inquiry, recommended a reduction in the area by 2344 acres (949 ha). The Minister accepted a reduction of 1872 acres
(758 ha), and confirmed the designation on 24 October 1968. The name of Telford, after
the celebrated civil engineer Thomas Telford (1757–1834), was at the same time
adopted for the enlarged new town.

   The site proposed for the development of Wellington–Oakengates to take an overspill of 50 000 is thus 10 143 acres (4105 ha), which added to the 9100 acres (3683 ha) of
Dawley means the large area of 19 243 acres (7788 ha). The population of Wellington
and Oakengates in 1965 was about 47 500. With the 21 000 of Dawley new town this
gave an existing population of about 68 500. With an intake of overspill of 50 000 each
the result was to be a population of 168 000. Due allowance for natural growth was to
mean a population probably of about 220 000 by the late 1980s.

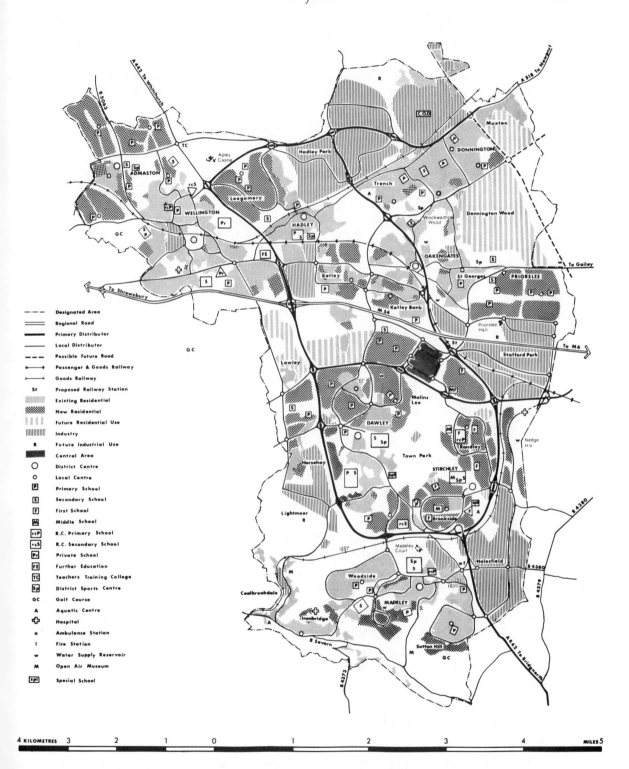

Figure 34.1 Telford outline plan.

In 1975 a reduced interim target was published and further amendment was proposed by the Secretary of State in April 1977, following revised overspill calculations announced in September 1976 when modifications to the Structure Plans for the conurbation were proposed. Induced growth will now continue until 1986 when the population is expected to reach 130 000 to 130 500 and natural growth should result in a population of 150 000 by 1990.

The basic plan for Telford prepared by the development corporation in consultation with the John Madin Design Group, which followed the draft structure plan of July 1969, was finalized in August 1970, when it was submitted to the Minister of Housing and Local Government and was approved with slight modification in December 1971.

The transformation from the plan for Dawley is occasioned mainly by the inclusion of the built-up areas of Wellington and Oakengates and presented rather different problems from Dawley, as there are at both Wellington and Oakengates fairly closely built up centres which involve replanning and demolition. Among the changes made in the overall plan are the elimination of the inner circular distributor road, but the major circular trunk road is retained in principle. Distributor roads loop off from the main circular road and through roads are avoided in the residential units. The main centre is moved a little to the north so as to be geographically central for the enlarged new town. The large park is retained becoming slightly larger. Six district centres are dispersed throughout the town, each of which serves a few residential districts. Three are south of the main centre, namely Dawley, Stirchley and Madeley in the extreme south near the River Severn, and 3 north of the centre—Oakengates, Wellington, and Admaston in the extreme north-west. Several local centres are grouped round these.

The industrial areas are located mainly towards the periphery, with Tweedale and Halesfield estates in the south-east, Stafford Park east of the centre, and Horton Wood in the north. The proposed area in the south-west is now unlikely to be developed.

Plans have been prepared for the centres of Wellington and Oakengates; the former called the 'draft Wellington Centre Policy Plan', prepared by John Madin Design Group in co-operation with the development corporation's chief architect-planner, was published in October 1969, and was ultimately approved by the Secretary of State for the Environment in December 1972. The latter called the 'Oakengates Centre Plan for the period up to 1991', by the same authors, was published in January 1971, and was submitted to the Secretary of State in 1972. Both plans are actuated by similar principles, and involve the considerable transformation to central pedestrian shopping precincts with rear servicing, and the introduction of ring roads round the centres as complimentary to this and to relieve the pressure of traffic in the centres. Both schemes involve the demolition of much old property which includes housing unfit for habitation and inevitably involves some sacrifices, but at the same time efforts are being made to preserve and improve the more attractive existing groupings as in the case of the complex of streets at Wellington, such as Church Street, Market Street, Duke Street and Crown Street, where some degree of pedestrianization would accord with their original character.

Building the Town

In the building of a new town the first activities are the civil engineering work of site preparation, the various kinds of levelling and earth works, surface water drainage, the construction of roads and provision of main services: water supply, sewerage, gas, electricity and others. This work varies considerably with the character of the terrain. In the case of the originally designated area of Dawley, this site preparation is rather more difficult than in most new towns, as nearly half the area is derelict land, and for much of it site preparation is a matter initially of reclamation. The subject is dealt with at some length in the Seventh Annual Report (1969–70) of the development corporation, where it is stated that, 'it has always been recognised that the existence of the dereliction, a legacy of the area's industrial past, would require a major commitment of resources and organisation', and that it is 'one of the main reasons why the area was selected for development as a new town'. It is proposed to reclaim nearly 3000 (1214 ha) of the 5000 acres (2024 ha) of derelict land up to 1991, and the work has been to some degree assisted by the open cast coal operations since 1966 on 2 sites of 103 acres (42 ha) and 96 acres (39 ha), with a possible third of 40 acres (16 ha). One scheme of reclamation is in the Malinslee/Dark Lane area which will form part of the town centre. To date 4 sites covering 438 acres (177 ha) have been reclaimed by the development corporation.

As it was desired that the building of the new town should commence before waiting for the completion and acceptance of the master plan for the whole Wellington–Oakengates–Dawley area of 19 243 acres (7788 ha), the development corporation decided to proceed with the building of the 3 residential units of the Madeley district: Sutton Hill, Woodside and Madeley, each with its local centre but grouped around the larger centre of Madeley. This development is in the south of the site, the area most remote from Wellington and Oakengates. These 3 residential districts provide for a population of about 27 000 and were completed in 1973.

Building started on the first residential area—Sutton Hill—south-east of Madeley early in 1966 and by the autumn of 1969 some 1233 houses had been completed here by the development corporation, while a few hundred were subsequently built by private enterprise. By 1973, 2420 houses were completed by the corporation in Woodside, and 185 near the district centre at Madeley. In 1968 a start was made on the residential areas of the Stirchley district a little to the north, and by 1976 well over 1792 houses had been completed at Brookside, 655 to the east of Stirchley centre, while several hundred were under construction there and in the Randlay area. Houses were also under construction in 1976 in the Melinslee area of the Rawley district, and in the Leegomery area of the Hadley district. The overall picture shows that by the end of 1970 the development corporation had completed 1222 houses, with 475 by local authorities and 675 by private enterprise. Since then rate of production has accelerated and the corporation completed 1000 houses in 1971, 1284 in 1972, 868 in 1973, 653 in 1974, 844 in 1975 and 1402 in 1976, when the total for the period since designation was 7850 by the corporation, 1812 by local authorities, and 2967 by private enterprise.

An aim in building new towns is to synchronize the provision of houses with employment, which is governed largely by the industrial intake. In Telford from 1970 to 1972 the provision of housing was ahead of industrial intake and employment, due largely to the recession in the manufacturing industry in the West Midlands in this period, so that the corporation had a number of vacant houses available for letting. In the spring of 1972, however, an improvement took place in industrial intake and employment, and continued into 1974, so that the demand for houses slightly exceeded the supply.

A contributory influence in this improvement was the provision of standard factories, which proved attractive to several industries, although the standard factory programme has been reduced since 1974 because of difficulties with government finance and authorizations. Factory building has taken place mainly in the Halesfield and Tweedale industrial estates. Recent industrial progress in Telford is a rewarding experience for the development corporation.

Housing and Residential Areas

Madeley district in the south, the first part of the new town to be built, was largely completed in 1973. It consists of the residential estates of Sutton Hill and Woodside and the smaller one surrounding the district centre. Both Sutton Hill and Woodside are planned on the principle of a major encircling road enclosing pedestrian residential areas fed by branch roads, and with a network of footways. The footways are the main thoroughfares to which the houses are related, either facing them or conveniently accessible from them. The majority of the houses in Sutton Hill are 2-storeyed in terrace rows of from 3 to 6 dwellings, varied with detached and semi-detached houses and with 3-storeyed structures of flats and maisonettes as in Severn Walk.

In Woodside there is considerable variety of layout. In one part there are a series of parallel straight culs-de sac with T terminations with main footpaths between, which run off from a main spine footpath, and grouped between the footpaths are blocks of dwellings pyramidal on plan with the bases towards the roads.

A good variety of architectural effect is achieved in the two neighbourhoods,

Figure 34.2 Housing and pedestrian walkways, Sutton Hill.

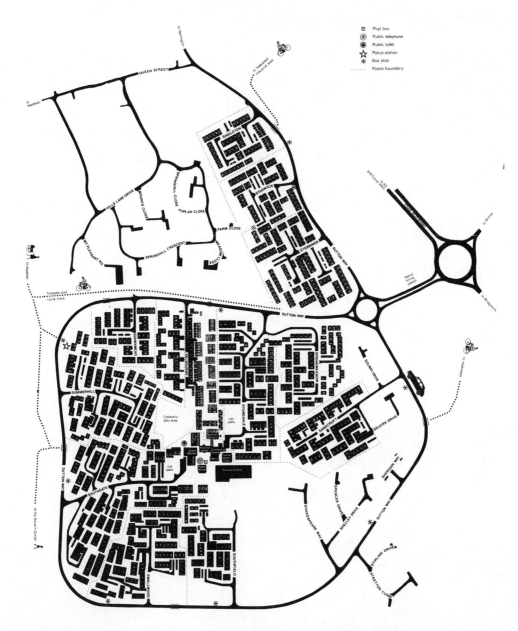

Figure 34.3 Sutton Hill estate plan.

obtained partly by the layout of the houses, partly by the use of different facing materials for the elevations (brick, timber, variously painted tiles and cedar shingles), and partly by the varied roofing where low pitched roofs mingle with mono-pitched roofs, butterfly roofs and flat roofs as in Severn Walk. Considerable attention has been given to landscaping and in the residential districts a large number of trees have been planted.

District and Local Centres

The first district centre to be completed was Madeley in the south, the first phase having been built in 1969 and the second and final phase in 1971. The centre is pedestrian with 2 squares, each faced on 3 sides with shops, about 20 in all, including 3 supermarkets. Russell Square, the first to be built, has on the north side a pedestrian bridge reached by a spiral ramp. On this upper level are the district centre library and the office of the Department of Employment above the shops. The square and trees on the south side make a very pleasant architectural composition. On the north is an open area called The Green, in which is situated the Madeley War Memorial, moved from its old location at a road junction. The upper level pedestrian way leads westwards and is lined on the south side by flats and maisonnettes which overlook The Green. Service roads are on the south and east sides and give access to a car park in the north-east.

Sutton Hill and Woodside in the Madeley district were the first 2 local centres to be completed (in 1968 and 1969). The Sutton Hill centre consists of a pedestrian square round which buildings are grouped, with shops and a supermarket on the west side, a public house to the south, and a multi-purpose building to the east, including a clinic with a doctor's and a dentist's surgery, community centre, library, and a pastoral centre which projects into the square with two octagonal shaped forms. In the north-west corner is a children's play centre and beyond is an extensive play area. In the centre of the square is a seating space partly enclosed by brick edged shrub beds.

Figure 34.4 View of Russell Square, Madeley district.

City Centre

The main centre to serve the whole area of Telford with an ultimate population in the region of 150 000 was started in March 1972, and the first phase was completed in October 1974. It consists of a central pedestrian mall, east–west, with 2 straight branches north and south. North and south are car parks, and at the east end is the bus station. At the west end is a large Carrefour hypermarket, at the east end a large Sainsbury supermarket and between them facing the malls are 15 shops for food, dress, shoes, furniture and stationery. The whole area is enclosed and air conditioned. The continuation of this centre will involve development north and south, and, in addition to further shops, there will be an arts centre, theatre, county library, cinema, swimming pools and many other services of a recreational character which a modern city of this size requires, although the provision of each will necessarily be commensurate with demand and financial resources. An item of particular interest on which the success of the centre, in attracting custom from the outlying parts of Telford and from areas further afield, will partly depend is the possibility of a railway station at Hollinswood nearby, and it will be a good thing for Telford and the surrounding areas if one is provided. An important basis for the success of any large centre is access by public transport and this does not mean only by road where traffic too often becomes congested.

The second phase of the town centre was begun in 1976 and is expected to be completed by the end of 1978.

An attractive feature adjacent to the centre is the town park of 450 acres (182 ha) which stretches southwards towards Madeley and the Severn Gorge and includes a large and beautiful lake.

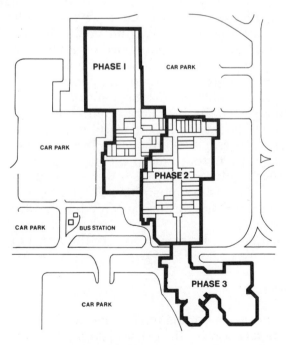

Figure 34.5 Town centre plan.

Industry and Industrial Areas

At the time of designation of Telford in October 1968, there was considerable existing industry. Here in the early years of the eighteenth century with the iron smelting industry and the use of coal for the purpose was one of the beginnings of the industrial revolution. After a considerable period of prosperity, greatly assisted by the Severn as a transport route, there was a decline in the iron industry here in the nineteenth century, but this was accompanied by a fairly large-scale development of the clay industries. In the twentieth century the southern part of the area suffered further gradual decline. The position for the manufacturing industries in 1968 was that, for the whole area, employment was about 18 000. A task of the development corporation has been not only to introduce new industry but to maintain and revive existing industry. In the 1970 report of the corporation, the Chairman, Sir Frank Price, said that, 'at this stage the Corporation's own industry still forms only a small part of the total, which suggests that a great deal of additional employment could be provided if existing industry can be encouraged to expand, and if the historic decline in the local economy can be halted and reversed.' This is a laudable aim. From 1968 to 1972 steady progress was made, hampered a little in the latter part of the period by the slight depression in the West Midlands, but, as previously recorded (see the section on Building the Town), early in 1972 considerable improvement occurred and the industrial intake and factory building began to make encouraging progress. The building by the corporation of standard factories contributed considerably to this progress, and as a result there is a programme of providing annually 350 000 sq. feet (31 500 m²) of speculative factories to meet increasing demand.

Up to 1972 the principal factory building had taken place in Tweedale a little north-east of Madeley centre, and the much larger industrial estate of Halesfield to the east. This will be extended by a land reclamation scheme involving the removal of the former Kemberton Colliery spoil heaps. Also in 1973 the site at Stafford Park was being prepared for factory building, which commenced the following year.

By 1977 160 firms were in operation in 310 new factories on the Tweedale and Halesfield and Stafford Park estates employing about 4950. The factories in these estates are spaciously sited to allow room for expansion which is a good economic provision, because as remarked in the 1971 Report of the development corporation, 'the general pattern appears to be for the firm to start by renting more floor space than it actually needs, to expand its employment over the early years to a point at which the floor space is intensively used, and then to extend its floor-space'.

The appearance of both industrial estates is generally pleasing. The buildings are low with variously shaped roofs demonstrating different designs for admitting light. Office blocks in front of the factories are also of varied design and are mostly restrained in character.

Another large industrial site, Horton Wood, to the north of the town, was being developed in 1977.

Social Aspect

Where there is a large nucleus of population in a new town the social problems result in some measure from the reactions of the existing population and the mixing of the old and new. In the case of Telford the existing population was as much as 68 000—about

21 000 in Dawley and the remainder in Wellington and Oakengates. The early intake of population has been mainly in the south at Madeley, a little north of the Severn Gorge, an area that had suffered gradual decline during the present century. The reactions of the existing population, as far as can be ascertained from conversation, vary, but if any broad conclusion can be reached it is that the attitude of the older sections of the population is 'why don't they leave us alone', whereas many of the younger welcome the development as a revival and as giving new life to a decaying area. One of the tasks of the development corporation is to soften the effects of change among those who are adverse to it.

Perhaps the most notable provision in the social field made at Telford so far is the Court Centre at Madeley, which is a combined comprehensive school and a public recreational centre mainly for indoor and outdoor sport, but not very much for cultural activities, which may be provided later at Madeley Court (see the next section). It was opened in August 1971 and has been much used by the public. The playing fields and open land surrounding the premises extend for 56 acres (23 ha). The administration is in the hands of the Telford Trust, which comprises ten members with representatives from various sports and other bodies including the development corporation, the Shropshire County Council and the Dawley UDC. The experiment indicates that there are advantages in the combined school and adult centres, but experience suggests also some reservations.

Historical and Cultural Interests of the Area

The southern part of the site could justly claim to be the cradle of the industrial revolution. It is rich in its early relics, mainly along the north bank of the Severn Gorge from Coalbrookdale in the west to Ironbridge on to Coalport in the east. A furnace for smelting iron ore with charcoal as fuel was in existence at Coalbrookdale in 1638. In 1708 Abraham Darby came here from Bristol and founded the Coalbrookdale Company, and in the following year began using coke for the smelting of iron ores, thus leading the way to the rapid expansion in the use of iron for industry. Many of the first uses of iron for various industrial purposes can be found in this area and the surrounding region, including the first metal railway (1767), and the first iron bridge built in 1779, a remarkable structure of 100 feet (30 m) clear span, and the first of several iron bridges in the vicinity. The first cast-iron columns and beams used in building are found mainly in this region.

The Coalbrookdale Company still operates on the site, employing some 500 workers, having become in 1929 a member of the Allied Ironfounders group. Part of its premises is devoted to the preservation of many of the early remains of the iron industry, including the eighteenth-century furnace, cast-iron columns, beams and rails, and an old locomotive, while an excellently-arranged museum displays a large number of smaller iron objects made during the past 200 years.

A little east of Coalbrookdale near Blists Hill is the sole surviving length of the old Coalport Canal built by Telford, while a little farther east were the works of Coalport China, one of the oldest and most famous of all English pottery firms and the originator in England of such famous designs as the Willow Pattern and the Indian Tree.

The Severn Gorge from Buildwas to Coalport is of considerable beauty, and the industrial and urban development that took place in the eighteenth and early nineteenth centuries is now wedded to the landscape, often with quite felicitous results. The urban settlement at Ironbridge is in parts on fairly steeply sloping ground rising from the Severn and includes the attractive, well-proportioned late Georgian houses that are very pleasingly grouped.

The desire to preserve these unique relics of the beginnings of the industrial revolution was strongly felt by the development corporation, and as a result of its efforts the Ironbridge Gorge Museum Trust was formed with the purpose of securing, 'the preservation, restoration, improvement, enhancement and maintenance of features and objects of historical, domestic and industrial interest in the area'.

The Coalbrookdale museum was transformed to public ownership in 1970 and is now under the direction of the Ironbridge Gorge Museum Trust. Nearly two miles (3 km) east at Blists Hill a major open air museum occupying 200 acres (81 ha) has been created. Here is the surviving length of the Coalport Canal, terminating in the incline (the longest and steepest of canal inclines) which has been restored, the Blists Hill Iron Works founded in 1832, the tar tunnel, and remains of the clay and tile works. It is proposed to assemble on the site many of the industrial relics now scattered in the region. It is also proposed to build a 2-mile (3 km) narrow gauge railway on the alignment of the old Coalport branch which will enable visitors to park north of the Gorge area and gain access to the museum by train.

Thus with these 2 museums of Coalbrookdale and Blists Hill near the Severn Gorge, along the southern boundary of Telford, is formed one of the most important centres of industrial archaeology in Great Britain and probably in Europe. With appropriate restoration and the continual augmentation of its collection of industrial relics, and with its becoming more widely known, it will increasingly attract tourists of all ages from various parts of the world. This itself will also attract certain types of industry and it may be necessary for the development corporation to provide adequate hotel accommodation in the vicinity.

One other item of historic interest in the region is the distinctive Elizabethan manor house of Madeley Court, which was for a time the home of Abraham Darby, and which in the draft master plan for Dawley was mentioned as a building that might be acquired for a cultural centre. It was announced in the Report of the development corporation for 1973 that the completion of the tenth year of its existence will be marked by the restoration (in conjunction with the Historic Buildings Council) of Madeley Court, and this is now taking place. It will be used presumably as a cultural centre in accordance with the first expressed intention.

Reference

34.1.   See *Town and Country Planning*, **30**, October 1961.

35   Redditch

Designated on 10 April 1964, Redditch is the second new town intended to relieve congestion in the West Midlands conurbation in the process of rehousing a high proportion of the population, the first being Dawley, subsequently Telford, designated a year earlier.

The population of the designated area of 7200 acres (2914 ha) was about 32 000 and it was proposed to provide for an intake, mainly from Birmingham, of 33 000 in 15 years which, with allowance for natural growth, means a target population of about 70 000 by 1982. Provision is made in the plan for a further growth by natural increase, possibly to approximately 90 000 by about the end of the century.

The site is roughly square in shape, and consists of the northern half of the district of Redditch, and a small part to the east in the Stratford district. The existing town of Redditch lies to the north-west of the site, and from its centre, which will form the nucleus of that of the new town, to the centre of Birmingham is only 14 miles (23 km). More significantly, from the northern boundary of the new town to the southern boundary of Birmingham is only 4 miles (6 km). This, we understand, is to be part of the Birmingham green belt. The statement made on behalf of the Minister at the inquiry into the draft order on the question of this green belt separating Birmingham and Redditch is 'that the Minister fully appreciates the need for a green belt separating the town from Birmingham and, whilst he cannot determine its precise boundaries until housing needs in the area have been finally settled, he intends to ensure that Birmingham and any new town at Redditch shall be kept separate by a green belt most firmly held'. Commenting on this, Sir Hugh Wilson and Lewis Womersley, who prepared the master plan, ask if it is necessary, with an eventual population of 90 000, to consider whether the town will grow beyond that limit. If it is necessary then they think it is 'imperative that further growth should not take place to the north or east, since the proposed Birmingham green belt must not be encroached upon further in these directions if it is to be "firmly held"'. They consider that if further expansion should take place southward along the ridge of high ground, such is the flexibility of the new town plan and its transport system, that it could be accepted without concern for its effect on Redditch. What is important is that every effort must be made to preserve the green belt between Birmingham and Redditch, otherwise the latter will become a part of the West Midlands conurbation.

The River Arrow flows through the site from north to south, a little east of centre, to join the River Avon further south. The land east of the river, which was little built on and where much of the new development has taken place, is fairly flat or gently undulating. West of the river the site is more sharply undulating with a fairly high ridge, rising in places to over 500 feet (150 m), which runs north–south. On a projecting plateau at the northern end is the old town of Redditch and some of the scattered building is southward along this ridge. In parts the area is well wooded, and here and there rather beautiful, especially on the hilly ground to the west, where the corporation offices are situated.

The area is well served with roads. The A441 from Birmingham to Evesham runs north–south through the centre of Redditch, and is linked on the south by the A448 with the A435 which runs along the eastern boundary of the site. The B4101 traverses its northern boundary. The district is not well served by British Rail. There was once a loop from Barnt Green to Evesham on the Birmingham–Cheltenham–Bristol main line, but the section from Redditch to Evesham was closed and the track destroyed. Thus only the branch to Redditch is left. The passenger service operates, however, only for morning and evening business trains. With the expansion of the town, this service should be improved, especially as it would provide a needed link with the fast electric main line trains to London and the North-West. It would be better than a road link. We understand that there is a prospect of a good service to Birmingham now that Redditch is growing rapidly.

Outline Plan

Transport has been a guiding factor in determining the character of the plan. Whereas the first group of new towns was planned with considerable dependence on the private car, with an inadequate public transport system, there is here a change of emphasis from private to public transport. The essential framework of the plan is a ring road which is in sections exclusively for public transport linking the residential with the industrial areas and with the town centre, with a cross-link through the centre. The authors of this plan liken this concept 'to a necklace, the beads of varying shape and size representing the districts, and the string the public transport system'. Each residential district, or neighbourhood, is grouped round a local centre which forms a major bus stop and shopping area. A few other social facilities would be grouped round these centres.

The existing road system is adapted for the needs of the new town. The line of the A441 is partly altered in its course, swinging east of the town centre; at this point a new road links with the A435 on the eastern boundary; and south of this another new road runs eastward from the A448 across the centre of the site. A road box is thus formed near the middle of the town from which 5 roads radiate. District distributor roads are linked with these primary roads, and encircle the various residential and industrial areas, and from these access roads feed into the districts. To complete the transport system are footpaths which traverse the whole town and run through the residential areas, giving access to the houses and linking with the stops on the bus route.

The residential districts are sited in relation to the bus route and the houses are grouped so that few are more distant than a $\frac{1}{3}$ of a mile (0.5 km) or 7 or 8 minutes' walk away from a bus stop. One district centre, which is typical, has a major bus stop, a few shops, a primary school, a hall, health facilities, a library, and a pub, and near another centre and bus stop is a church.

The average housing densities are 50 persons to the acre (123 per ha), varying from 75 persons to the acre (185 per ha) near the district centres to 25 persons (62 per ha)

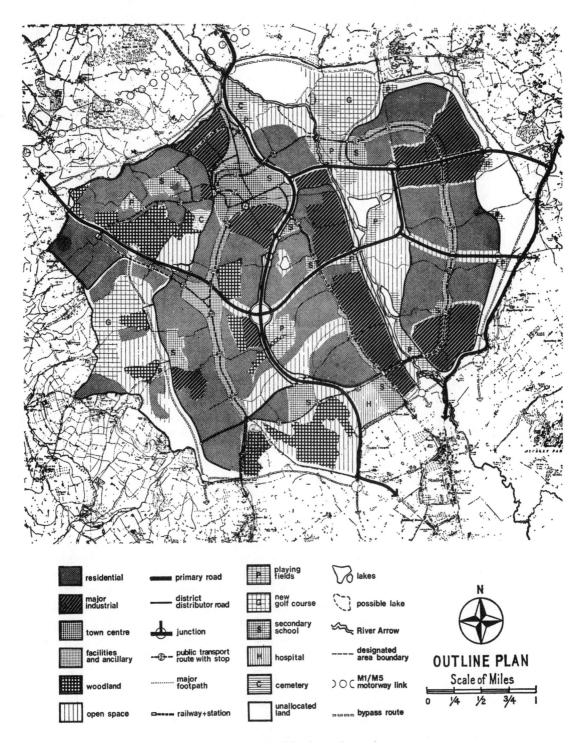

Figure 35.1 Redditch outline plan.

towards the outskirts which means, on the basis of 3.5 persons per house, net housing densities of 7 to 21 per acre (17 to 52 per ha). It is proposed to accommodate about 60 000 persons—about 17 143 dwellings—in about 1200 acres (486 ha). This should make possible at least 80% houses with gardens, with perhaps 20% flats and maisonettes. Provision is made for accommodating at least one car per dwelling, with some additional space for visitors' cars. In the layout of the residential areas there is maximum separation of pedestrians and vehicles.

The existing industries in Redditch show some diversification, the principal ones being the manufacture of miscellaneous metal goods, engineering and electrical goods, vehicles, construction and distributive trades, while several other varied industries give employment to a fair proportion of the population. This diversification, which is good in any area, will no doubt continue. The principal industrial sites in the plan are in the centre, along the west bank of the River Arrow where several factories already exist, and in the north-east and south-east, while several smaller sites are grouped on the western side.

There is a generous provision of open space, the principal areas being along the east bank of the river, where there are several lakes capable of attractive development as water-gardens; and many wooded areas among the hills to the south and west. Some of the open space is being utilized as playing fields and golf courses.

In the interim report the planners discussed the alternatives of the redevelopment and expansion of the existing centre at Redditch or the development of a new centre in a position nearer to the geographical centre. Finding a satisfactory site for a new centre was attended with difficulties, while there was also the disadvantage of a town with two centres, the old and the new, in competition with each other, and it is doubtful if this would be socially or economically satisfactory. It has, therefore, been wisely decided to develop and expand the existing centre. The one disadvantage of this is that it is well to the north-west of the site and not in the geographical centre, so that it is nearly $2\frac{1}{4}$ miles (4 km) from some parts of the eastern and southern districts. Against this, it is easily and conveniently reached from any part of the town by the road transport system, and it contains the railway station.

One of the disadvantages of grafting a new town on to one of considerable size, in which the existing centre is the nucleus of the new one, is that instead of starting from scratch and building an efficient centre for modern needs, the existing pattern inevitably effects some control, as only a part can be rebuilt and changed. Still, this marriage of the old and new often proves to be a stimulus to ingenious planning, and the result is sometimes excellent. Such may prove to be the case with the Redditch centre. Some of the existing features are so good as to prompt a desire to preserve them, and combine them with the new development. Such appears partly to be the intention, for the planners remarked that 'Church Green with St Stephen's Church forms the visual climax of Redditch, and it should be developed as a very significant open space of the new town centre'. In preserving certain features of the old there is also the aim to secure the maximum separation of pedestrians and vehicles, which has become a conspicuous feature of the planning of town centres.

The provision of facilities in the centre is visualized as falling into the four main categories of shopping and service trades, civic, educational and recreational. In the last category the aim is to provide a sports centre with swimming pool and ice rink, a bowling alley, a dance hall, cinemas, and a theatre.

The consultants had a difficult task in providing a satisfactory plan for a new town on a site with an existing town and scattered development, yet they have produced an imaginative and coherent solution of the problem presented. The plan, in its transport systems, has marked similarities to that of Runcorn, and both are very successful in linking the various parts of the town in a social and physical unity. They are more successful in this respect than the first generation of new towns, and a major contribution to this is in the emphasis given to an efficient public transport system.

A public inquiry was held on the master plan in July and August 1967 and was then submitted to the Minister of Housing and Local Government. In June 1968 the plan was approved with a request for minor amendments.

Possible Revisions of the Master Plan

The outline or master plan is kept in constant review by the development corporation, and experience has prompted several revisions. In its reports for 1970 and 1971 the corporation stated that in the designated area there was a shortage of land for housing and industry, the former being due partly to the higher proportion of housing land than was originally envisaged and a marked resistance to high density development. In the 1971 report it was stated that, 'the incoming population want houses with more garden space and certainly not flats nor high-rise/high-density dwellings', and, 'the high density of the earlier housing in Redditch has been criticised'. Also the education authority of the region appears to require playing fields adjacent to the schools, rather than outside the residential areas as envisaged in the master plan. Another point made in the 1970 report was that more people were using their cars for going to work than was anticipated, thus creating a need for larger car parks, but whether this is an economical or wise use of land is very much open to doubt. Meeting such a need lies partly in the sphere of better public transport.

In the report of the corporation for 1973 the possibility of the expansion of Redditch was discussed, and it was stated that, 'following the report of the West Midlands Planning Authorities Conference that the population of the town could be increased to a possible 150 000 by 2010, a Joint Working Party with Worcestershire and Warwickshire is expected to report upon the expansion areas by the early summer', and the request was made to the Secretary of State for the Environment, 'to reach very early decisions on the scale and areas for expansion in order to reduce the uncertainty which must be caused in the areas'. The assumption was made by the chairman of the corporation that 'the Secretary for the Environment will endorse the view of the West Midlands Planning Authorities Conference that the best method to handle the further development would be through extensions of the designated area'.

In the original plan the target population was about 70 000 by 1982, with provision for further growth by natural increase, possibly to 90 000 by the end of the century.

To contemplate an increase to double the originally planned size is to upset entirely the conception and structure of the town and is to disregard the spirit attending the new towns policy, where limitation of size with a surrounding green belt was an essential condition, so that the open country can be enjoyed and the community spirit fostered. Also in the particular case of Redditch, which is separated from the Birmingham conurbation by a belt of country only 4 miles (6 km) wide, the undesirability of a very large urban development must be apparent.

This is a repetition of what is happening with other new towns and represents a disregard of the principles on which they were planned. Development to take additional population should not be by blind urban expansion, so that it ultimately joins neighbouring conurbations, but by starting other new towns further west towards the Welsh border, as is discussed in the chapter on Newtown and Mid-Wales. Fortunately, on 5 April 1977 the Secretary of State announced that there were no grounds for the expansion of Redditch.

Building the Town

The circumstances that there were already 300 factories in the designated area of Redditch, and that in 1966 about 1750 persons travelled here to work from the Birmingham conurbation indicates that the first need in building the town was to provide houses. Constructional work began in July 1966 for a housing estate extending the residential district of Greenlands south-east of the existing town, and the first houses were completed in the following year. Shortly afterwards a start was made with other residential districts, and between 1969 and 1972 most of the large residential district of Woodrow in the south was built. A little later Matchborough, Lodge Park and Winyates were built. Some indication of progress is provided by the figures for completion of houses. In the first few years when so much site clearance and other preparatory work had to be done the completion of houses was necessarily small. However, by the end of 1969, 1029 houses had been built by the development corporation, 143 by the local authority, and 563 by private developers. In the following year the rate of building was accelerated, and 1039 houses were completed by the development corporation, with a little over 100 each by the local authority and private developers. There was, however, a considerable decline to 517 in 1971 and only 268 in 1972, but in these years the good totals were reached by private developers of 482 and 561, partly in collaboration with the development corporation. In 1973 the corporation completed 391, in 1974, 558, in 1975, 524 and in 1976, 932. And thus, since designation to the end of 1976, 9800 houses have been built at Redditch of which 5072 were by the corporation, 961 by the local authority, and 3767 by private developers.

The 300 factories in Redditch at the time of designation were very varied; large and small, modern and old and some almost decaying. In addition to attracting new industry to the town the corporation has had to relocate many of the existing industries and to provide the necessary premises. This has meant altogether a big programme of demolition, of site preparation and building, which has been conducted rapidly and generally a little in advance of the housing.

Residential Districts

The planning of each residential district—Greenlands, Woodrow, Matchborough, Winyates—has been actuated by similar principles. The large district of Woodrow can be taken as an example. It is roughly an equilateral triangular shape with the apex at the north. There is a boundary road and one loop road of a similar shape within the area, and branch roads from the periphery and loop roads spread into the area. Spread is the word, because each main branch has several sub-branches like a tree. Sometimes the branches are fairly straight, sometimes curved. Within this layout there is a fair variety of housing: some, mainly for letting, are rows of terrace houses, from 5 to 11 in a row, with garages either grouped, or placed at the ends of gardens—one to each house; some houses, mainly for sale, are detached or semi-detached with attached garages.

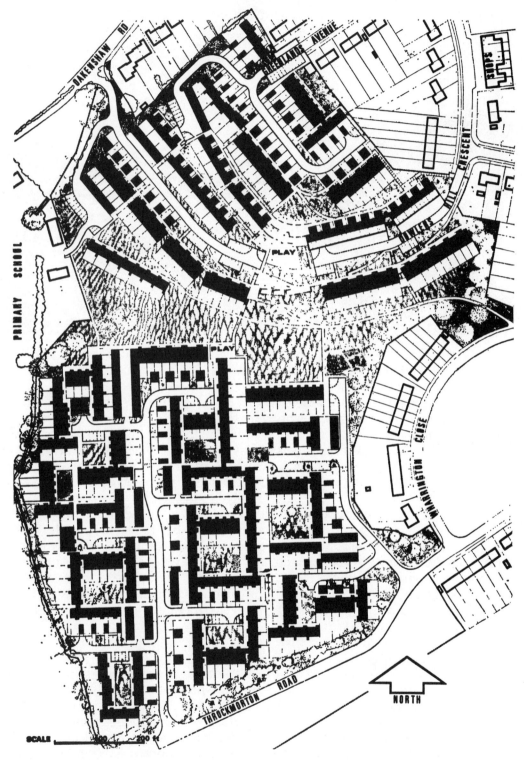

Figure 35.2 Plan of housing layout of Greenlands neighbourhood.

Figure 35.3 Matchborough residential district. View of pedestrian route between houses.

Sometimes these are linked in series. There is a footpath system throughout the area which often runs along the fronts of the houses, with road access at the rear, on the Radburn principle. Here and there are pedestrian squares graced with trees and shrubs, and occasionally serving as children's playgrounds. The houses are planned mainly for families of 4 to 6 with 2, 3 and 4 bedrooms. They are usually 2-storey. Some at Greenlands are the split level type which received a housing medal in 1970.

There is a tendency in this type of development for the houses to be rather closely packed resulting in a higher density than is acceptable to many people. This is particularly the case with the rows of terrace houses built for letting. The long pedestrian way called Woodrow Walk running west from the centre, between long rows of terrace houses separated by only 30 feet (9 m), gives the impression of somewhat monotonous close building. Such effects of closeness and lack of space may have prompted the resistance to high density development to which the corporation referred in its 1970–71 reports.

District Centres

All the district centres so far planned are pedestrian precincts which border the public transport route. That at Woodrow forms an east termination to the long straight pedestrian spine of Woodrow Walk. Walking along this one passes beneath a bridge formed by a 3-storey building, containing library and meeting rooms, into a square flanked on 3 sides by shops; and continuing one passes beneath another bridge into a second square again flanked by shops, including a supermarket, and then under a third bridge with maisonettes with balconies over to the road and bus stop. On the corner is a public house. It is all closely built and intimate.

The layout of Winyates centre—although following similar principles—is a little different, and although closely packed and intimate is a little more open to the sky, which is an advantage. Approaching from the bus stop there is a garden with a small play area on the right and a site for a health centre, with a public house on the left. Then beyond is a short pedestrian way flanked by shops. In one corner is a site for a library adjacent to an old people's home, and a health centre is located adjacent to the bus stop. At the rear of the shops on either side are the service areas and car parks. Old farm buildings located on the opposite side of the bus route have been converted into workshops for artists and craftsmen. There is a good sprinkling of trees which contribute to making this a delightful small centre.

Town Centre

In the description of the outline plan it was stated that it was wisely decided to develop and expand the existing centre instead of finding a site elsewhere, although this was attended with the disadvantage of its not being in the geographical centre. The advantages for the course decided are very strong and are made apparent in the original planning proposals of the consultants from which it is illuminating to quote. The most obvious site for the central area, they argue, 'is that occupied by the existing centre of Redditch on the plateau at the end of the northern spur of the ridge. The image of Redditch is that of a ridge town with its centre on a hill; the plateau with the existing centre and the church spire forms a landmark for the surrounding countryside and for much of the town. It is important in any new town to exploit the qualities of the site; in Redditch this should be done not only by respecting its fine woodland character but also by taking advantage of the dominant site available for the centre, a site which seems to be inevitable from every point of view. It is the established focus for the existing town and the hinterland and its development would do much to ensure integration of new and old. The fact that the location will be geographically off-centre in the designated area is no disadvantage since it is well related to the town road system and to the town and country bus services and it contains the railway station. Any growth of the town to the south should be related to the bus routes and primary roads and thus have good access to the centre'.

The integration of a new centre with an existing one that served a population of 32 000 and which has many features worth preserving is a far more difficult exercise in planning than starting from scratch and building an entirely new centre. Among the buildings that it is desirable to preserve, in addition to the central church and its attractive garden, are the row of shops nearby, the hospital, two other churches, a cinema and theatre.

As it is intended to make the new centre very largely pedestrian and to eliminate any major transport route through the middle, it was necessary to replan the roads and incorporate a ring road round the whole centre comprehending both old and new. On the west side of this ring road is a public transport centre (called transport interchange) which includes railway and bus stations, a taxi rank and a car park. The public transport route passes along the southern boundary of the centre to the bus station and then through the old centre in the northern part, and this presumably is one of the sections of the route exclusively for buses. The road system in the centre is similar in

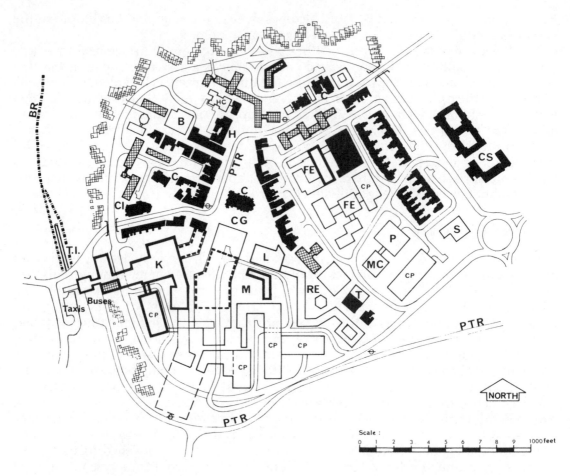

Figure 35.4 Town centre plan.

principle to that of the residential districts with branches feeding inwards from the periphery road to the various areas.

The new part of the centre is to the south, and the part completed by 1973 consists of a large covered air-conditioned shopping area on the first floor, called the Kingfisher centre (35.1), with a multi-storey car park adjacent, from which one can pass by means of a bridge to the shopping area. At one end of the shopping area is the bus station. On the east side of the Kingfisher centre is a large paved area with trees, and beyond this is the open market called Royal Square, within the L-shaped block of shops with balconies, and a food hall sponsored by the UDC. The second phase, opened in 1976, comprises Worcester Square, the covered main town centre with ornamental palm trees, and air conditioned pedestrian malls linking the square with the other new shops. Nearby is the library with the old and new centres on either side of it, while to the east is the College of Further Education and the adjoining site for its extension. By 1976 with the first two phases completed it could be seen that here is a happy integration of old and new.

Industry and Industrial Areas

As previously mentioned there were 300 factories of various sizes and conditions in Redditch at the time of designation. It has been necessary to relocate and rebuild many of these. This task was greatly assisted by the acquisition by the development corporation of the area to the north-west of the town centre of 25 acres (10 ha), on which stood the Enfield works. A part of this was leased to the former owners, part was used for the relocation of some existing industry and part for the introduction of new industry; and it was here that a start was made with the last mentioned by the corporation building a new factory of 60 000 sq. feet (5400 m²) and leasing it to a Redditch company.

The bulk of the manufacturing industry in Redditch (employing nearly 13 000) at the time of designation was engineering or industry based on metals, in common with much of the industry in the West Midlands. Part of the policy of the development corporation is to attract industries of a different type, so as to secure diversification and therefore make employment less vulnerable to periodic economic depressions. As much of the new industry comes from the region of the Birmingham conurbation, this is not easy, and a large number of inquiries come from firms engaged in metals-based industries. Some measure of assistance in this wise objective could, of course, be given by the Department of Industry, but whether this is always as forthcoming as the corporation would wish is a matter for speculation.

As a glance at the outline plan will show, the industrial areas are mainly along the west bank of the River Arrow, to the north-west and south of the town centre, and

Figure 35.5 Part of Washford industrial estate.

beyond the River Arrow to the east and south-east. The first estates to be developed have been the Enfield estate, as already mentioned, and the Washford estate in the south-east. The former is very simply planned with the large factory of Enfield Industrial Engineers in the centre and the other smaller factories grouped round it.

The Washford estate is a triangular site and consists of over 76 factories of various sizes, about 6 fairly large and the rest medium sized and small. What is valuable is that they are fairly spaciously sited and many have space for expansion.

Further employment areas have been developed at Park Farm, west of the River Arrow, and Moons Moat in the north-east.

The corporation has actively followed a policy of building speculative 'advance' factories and will by 1980 have provided 2 119 720 sq. feet (192 000 m²) of floor space using this method.

The dispersal of factories has the two-fold advantage of providing work close to the employees' homes and balancing the peak traffic flows on the road system.

Social Aspect

When a family moves to a new town, which is initially a strange place, the settling in is much facilitated by welcoming with information and assistance. The development corporation has realized this from the start, and in 1966 it established a working party for community and amenity facilities, which included representatives of both county and district councils. One of the purposes has been to provide meeting rooms in the districts, community centres and the provision of dual facilities at schools.

In January 1969, a meeting was held for the first hundred new families at which local councillors and representatives of voluntary organizations were present. Following this a mobile meeting room was provided at Woodrow in advance of the permanent meeting rooms in each district, and this proved to be very useful. Permanent meeting rooms were provided in Woodrow in April 1970, and these have been followed by similar rooms in Matchborough. Their management is under one of the social development officers of the corporation who works in collaboration with an advisory committee of the local voluntary organizations. More recently it has been new town policy to incorporate the meeting facilities with the primary schools for more efficient use and management of amenities. In the spring of 1971 the Redditch Council of Social Service was established. Like other local councils of social service, some of its functions are to coordinate and assist the work of voluntary associations in the region, to set up new organizations, and to assist generally in the social work of the town. Among the activities of the Redditch CSS has been the establishment of a club for physically handicapped young people and a social workers' luncheon club (35.2).

When a married couple move to a house in Redditch, they can visit the local meeting room and are there informed about shopping and transport and recreational facilities, and of the numerous voluntary associations. It would be surprising if there were not among these associations one or two subjects that would attract them. There is nothing like joining a voluntary association and mixing with people of similar interests as an initial way of joining in the social life of a town. It is also a matter of routine for a member of the social development staff of the corporation to visit people who acquire a house in Redditch, whether renting or buying it, to inform them of the amenities and social activities of the town and to present them with a brochure listing them.

At the time of designation in 1964 there were some 200 clubs and societies in

Redditch and this number has considerably increased since. The main difficulties with such organizations is the lack of suitable premises. These could to some extent be provided by a multi-purpose central building with a multi-purpose hall and several meeting rooms. The need for a central hall is mentioned in the report of the development corporation for 1966, and it is pointed out that there is nowhere in Redditch a purpose-built hall for concerts, theatrical performances and the like, and it must therefore be a relatively early task of the corporation to encourage the provision of such facilities. It was announced in the report for 1969 that the Redditch Council had decided, 'to build a major entertainments complex which will use the old Palace Theatre', and, 'the Corporation has therefore decided to offer the theatre, when refurbished, to the town'. It was added that, 'this will provide a centre for multi-purposes community use until the full project, envisaged by the council, is realised'. The Palace Theatre was restored and adapted to needs and opened in 1971.

References

35.1   During the Second World War, Redditch adopted *H.M.S. Kingfisher*. The Temperance Hall—used for a time as a British Restaurant—was named after the ship. This hall was demolished to make room for the new centre, and its name was used for this shopping hall.

35.2   Most local 'councils of social service' have changed their name to 'councils of voluntary service'.

36 Cwmbran

In the valley that stretches for about 8 miles (13 km) almost due north from Newport to Pontypool in Monmouthshire, some industry has gradually been established which includes iron and steel works, brickworks, and some that has spread from the Midlands, including the manufacture of nylon yarn, motor vehicle components, glass, dairy machines, valves, brake linings and biscuits. The region attracted industrialists, partly owing to the good road, sea and railway communications and to the availability of water, gas and electricity supplies, and of suitable sites. Up to about 1955 most of the workers in these industries lived in the surrounding towns and villages, often having to travel more than 5 miles (8 km) to their place of work. The necessity of building housing estates for these workers had frequently been considered.

Approximately halfway between Newport and Pontypool lie the villages of Cwmbran and Pontnewydd which in 1947 together had a population of about 13 000. It was here that it was decided in 1949 to build a new town with a maximum population of 35 000 to provide housing accommodation for the workers in the industries in the valley, and the designation order was made on 4 November 1949. The explanatory memorandum issued by the Ministry of Town and Country Planning, with the draft designation order, stated: 'it is expected that employment will eventually be found for about 7500 persons in the valley in the immediate vicinity of Cwmbran. In addition there will be employment for about 4500 at the recently erected nylon works at Mamhilad and in the Royal Ordnance Factory at Glascoed, both of which are within a reasonable distance of the proposed new town. At present a large percentage of the additional labour required for the factories has to be drawn from other districts. It is clear that if homes near their work are to be provided for those employed at the factories in the vicinity of Cwmbran, there must be a large expansion of population in the district.' In 1962 the development corporation agreed with the Ministry of Housing and Local Government that the town should be planned for an increased population of 45 000. There will then probably be a subsequent slower growth to about 55 000.

Although most of the local authorities in the region welcomed the establishment of a new town there were some criticisms of the exact site, and the principal alternative proposed was that it should be further to the north-east, which, although removing it a little from the main concentration of industry in the valley, would bring it nearer to the nylon factory at Mamhilad and the ordnance factory at Glascoed. Mamhilad lies $2\frac{1}{2}$ miles (4 km) north-north-east of Pontypool and about 6 miles (10 km) north of Cwmbran, while Glascoed lies about 5 miles (8 km) north-north-east of Cwmbran. The reasons against this alternative given in the explanatory memorandum were that 'the nylon works were deliberately established in open country for the benefit of the manufacturing processes, and there are obvious objections to the placing of any large scale development close to the ROF'. It was also pointed out that a situation to the north-east would involve encroaching on valuable agricultural land. These reasons are not entirely convincing.

In principle it cannot be said that the situation of Cwmbran for a new town is ideal. Four miles (6 km) to the south is a town of 113 000 and 4 miles (6 km) to the north is another of 38 330 and it is putting a handicap on the provision of shopping, social and recreational facilities in a new town to place it in such close proximity to established competition. Still, the industries are, for the most part, there, the workers should have houses within convenient distance of their work, and it is difficult to think of a better alternative in the region. The clear demarcation of Cwmbran by means of a green belt should be regarded as imperative, and a continuous urban sprawl between Newport and Pontypool should be avoided at all costs. The problem as seen by the planning consultants was 'to provide more houses near the work rather than to provide more jobs'. Reference is also made to the view of the Board of Trade that no additional large-scale employment is needed at Cwmbran.

The designated area consists of 3160 acres (1279 ha) in the Afon Llwyd valley lying within the borough of Torfaen. The site is an attractive one with contours varying from 125 feet (38 m) at the southern extremity of the valley, rising to about 220 feet (66 m) at the northern end near Pontnewydd. Hills to the east and west rise to 400 feet (120 m) on the hill of St Dials near the west-centre of the site, to nearly 600 feet (180 m) to the north-west and 300 feet (90 m) to the east. Two railways formerly ran south–north through the site, the Monmouthshire Eastern Valley Line and the Hereford–Newport main line with 3 stations in the area, Llantarnam Junction, Cwmbran and Upper Pontnewydd but these were short-sightedly closed a few years after the town was designated. The Newport–Abergavenny trunk road, the A4042, skirts the eastern boundary of the area, while the Llantarnam Road, the A4051 runs through its centre. The Afon Llwyd courses through the middle of the valley, while the disused Monmouthshire Canal follows a roughly similar but straight course.

Outline Plan

In February 1950 Anthony Minoprio, Hugh G.C. Spencely and Peter W. Macfarlane were appointed to make a survey of the area and to prepare an outline plan. This was submitted to the Minister of Town and Country Planning in the following November. It was the subject of a public inquiry in July of the following summer when only three persons submitted objections. It was approved by the Minister in December 1951.

The existing industries are situated mainly between the 2 railway lines in the valley along the north–south length of the site, while a tongue of the industrial region projects westwards. The industrial area thus occupies the centre of the town, and the town centre is planned in the middle of it, with an area for service industry nearby. Seven residential neighbourhoods were originally provided grouped round the town centre and industries. In the north is Pontnewydd, planned for a population of 6680, the new part being mainly to the west; in the east Croes-y-Ceiliog (5050) and Llanyr-Avon (originally Croes-y-Ceiliog South) (5000); in the south are Oakfield (4175) and Coedeva (5450) with St Dials (4300) nearer the centre; while in the west is Greenmeadow (3640). Each neighbourhood has a small shopping centre and primary school

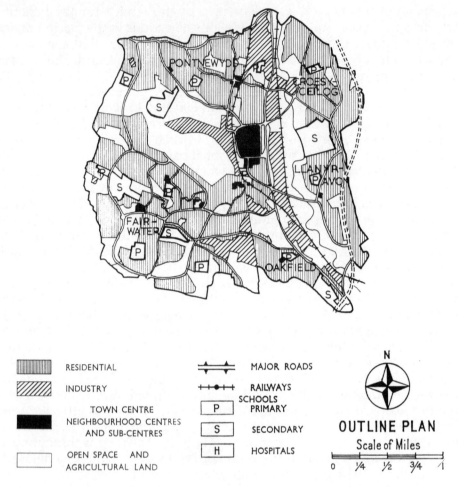

RESIDENTIAL

INDUSTRY

TOWN CENTRE

NEIGHBOURHOOD CENTRES
AND SUB-CENTRES

OPEN SPACE AND
AGRICULTURAL LAND

MAJOR ROADS

RAILWAYS

SCHOOLS

| P | PRIMARY |

| S | SECONDARY |

| H | HOSPITALS |

N

OUTLINE PLAN

Scale of Miles

0　¼　½　¾　1

Figure 36.1 Cwmbran outline plan.

nearby while in addition Pontnewydd has its old shopping centre and St Dials has the shopping centre of Old Cwmbran. Three secondary modern schools have been provided in the north-west, south-west and south-east, and a fourth in the east near the centre forms part of a campus with a grammar school and technical school. Some of these have since been changed to comprehensive schools. Strips of open space are generously provided in the town. One wide strip is between Llan-yr-Avon and the industrial area and the railway, and there is an extensive stretch of open space to the west of the town within the designated area.

It will be seen that the neighbourhoods average about 5000 population, and are thus approximately similar in size and conception to the neighbourhoods of Crawley, with one primary school and shopping centre in each. They make a logical plan, and being grouped on all sides of the town centre all residential districts are within 2 miles (3 km) of it. Among the reasons given by the consultants for planning neighbourhoods of this size was that experience has shown that such a population 'can maintain a local shopping centre of 20 shops, with a bank and post office, a junior and infant school, and certain community buildings such as a hall, a clinic, and branch library'. As in all properly planned residential neighbourhoods main roads do not go through but between them.

One particularly important part of a plan of a new town situated only at short distances from existing towns to the north and south is that it should be surrounded by a clearly defined green belt of adequate width. With Cwmbran a green belt has been allocated over which the development corporation shares planning control with the Monmouthshire County Council. This is about 1 mile (1.6 km) in width to the east and west, but on the north and south where it is most needed it is unfortunately in parts narrower than a mile (1.6 km). The north suburbs of Newport press closely on the green belt, while in the north building is continuous south of Pontypool to within one-third of a mile (0.5 km) of the boundary of the new town. This all too narrow green belt should be regarded as sacred.

When the target population was raised in 1962 to 45 000 provision was made to accommodate the addition mainly in the south-western area which was replanned for the purpose, with Fairwater as the main neighbourhood, and Greenmeadow and Coedeva as residential districts each with a food shop. The town is planned in conformity with contemporary trends in which there is a high degree of segregation of pedestrian and vehicular traffic. A system of footpaths radiates from the unit centres, crossing roads by means of underpasses and bridges.

With the additional population there is scope for new employment, a vital factor if the population is to increase as planned; and provision is made, therefore, for the intake of some new industry on 2 sites.

The target population was increased from 35 000 as originally planned and approved in 1951, to 45 900 in 1962 with a probable further increase of 10 000 by natural growth. In 1972 at the request of the Welsh Office a proposal was made by the development corporation for an expansion of the area, primarily to the south-west. A public inquiry was held in 1976.

Building the Town

The building of Cwmbran began in 1952 after the worst of the economic difficulties of the post-war period had been overcome; while there was little opposition to delay the start. Thus by the end of 1954, about 3 years after the outline plan received official approval, over 1000 houses had been built, and for each of the following years up to 1967 between 500 and 700 houses were completed. Then some reduction of output occurred after 1968 to between 150 and 400 a year. By the end of 1976 since designation, 12 394 houses had been built, 8928 by the development corporation, 2140 by the local authority and 1326 by private enterprise.

By 1976 most of the neighbourhoods were completed or were nearing completion. Except for a few constructional operations here and there the town centre presented by 1975 a fairly completed appearance. One of the later additions was Gwent House, an impressive commercial building completed in 1973. A large Woolco store, above a multi-storey car park was opened in 1975, and in 1977 a sizeable building for Sainsbury was opened and one for Marks and Spencer was in the course of construction.

Cwmbran has become the administrative centre of the new county of Gwent. In 1974 Gwent County Council occupied its new headquarters in the neighbourhood of Croes-y-Ceiliog on the east side of the town. Adjacent to this is the new county constabulary headquarters, and to the south-west of the town in Greenmeadow a police training centre was constructed on a 40 acre (16 ha) site. It includes 3 hostel blocks and was completed in 1974. It was built by the development corporation architects for the Home Office.

Housing and Residential Areas

In the consultants' report the view is expressed 'that a high proportion of flats is unlikely to be popular' and it was suggested 'that not more than 10% of the population should be housed in flats in the first neighbourhoods built' and 'that terrace housing following the contours will prove to be the most useful for development on the steep slopes'. This advice seems to have been followed in the types and layout of houses, and probably not more than 10% of flats have been built. In Croes-y-Ceiliog and Llan-yr-Avon, which lie on the hills to the east of the valley, terrace blocks of varied houses generally follow the contours, although occasionally, as the full utilization of the site requires, a road with a row of houses cuts across the contour on a fairly steep hill. The layout for the most part is one of curved roads with squares or triangular formations set back from the roads, and the terrace housing which prevails is sometimes arranged in

Figure 36.2 Rented housing at Coedeva.

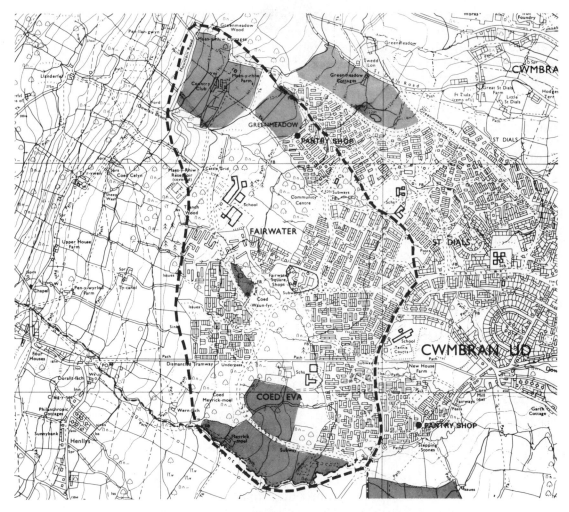

Figure 36.3 Fairwater neighbourhood plan.

echelon fashion. The houses vary considerably; sometimes there is a series with gable ends facing the road, sometimes the series is bound together by long horizontal lines. The roof pitches are generally low, not more than 25 degrees, while a variety of facing materials is used for the houses—brick, roughcast, timber boarding, stone and tiles—often 2 or 3 being used in conjunction.

In some houses the plain wall forming the entrance porch is in rough stone and in some it is in tiles of green Westmorland slate, both of which give a very pleasing effect. Much care has been exercised in the planting of trees to give a promise of verdancy to the neighbourhoods, and such varieties are found as plane, silver birch, mountain ash, wild cherry, hawthorn, ailanthus, maple, copper beech, whitebeam, crab apple, scots pine and silver-leaved box elder. The few flats that are built are usually placed near the neighbourhood or town centres, and these are introduced, it would appear, partly with a view to architectural effect. For example, in the 1957 report it is stated that architectural interest will be added to the main unit centre of Croes-y-Ceiliog by the completion of some 3-storey and 4-storey blocks of flats which are being built immediately adjacent to the shops.

In the later neighbourhoods of Greenmeadow, St Dials, Fairwater and Coedeva, the houses consist mainly of 2-storey terrace blocks variously sited and orientated with roads branching in and linking with garages or car spaces arranged in rows in convenient relation to the houses. Most of the houses have small gardens fenced round, and many are grouped to form pedestrian courts, some of which include collections of stone boulders for children's playgrounds. Variety of architectural effect is obtained by siting, by patterning of different facing materials and by roofing, mostly flat, or low mono-pitched. For example, in Fairwater 2 where the housing looks particularly pleasing, the walls are of brick with dark timber boarding between windows, while the roofs are long, low, mono-pitched, the length of 2 dwellings.

In the centre of the town a 22-storey tower block of flats was completed in 1966. The impetus for building this was probably partly architectural. The development corporation mentions in its 1967 report that the tower block 'identifies the centre of the town and makes a prominent landmark for many miles around'. It also provides (60 m) chimneys for the district heating scheme.

Neighbourhood Centres

At the time of designation there were 3 groups of shops at Pontnewydd, at St Dials, both near railway stations, and at Oakfield. In conformity with the plan shopping centres have been built at Oakfield, Croes-y-Ceiliog, West Pontnewydd and Fairwater. The 6 shops built at Oakfield make a pleasing group. They are single-storey; five are arranged in echelon fashion, with the sixth continuing at the side of the fifth to form a corner; paved arcading with a canopy shelters the shoppers in bad weather, and in front of the shops are lawns with trees, under which seats are arranged. There is a sense of peace and seclusion in this group which is delightful. An attractive looking public house has been built nearby. The provision of canopies and segregation of pedestrians from vehicular traffic are features of the shopping centres.

The shopping centre at West Pontnewydd consists of a row of 8 one-storey shops on the side of an incline so that a raised terrace, approached by steps, runs along the front of the shops. Near this centre are some 3-storey and 4-storey blocks of flats, while a public house with bowling alley was completed in 1960. A tenants' community hall has also been built here together with a county council clinic.

The main shopping centre at Croes-y-Ceilog consists of a row of 6 shops, and a public house, and the sub-unit centre has a row of 4 shops attractively situated with an extensive paved area in front with strips of garden on either side of the adjoining footway which connects with a group of old people's dwellings arranged on three sides of a square.

A very ingeniously planned shopping centre, designed by Gordon Redfern, the corporation's architect, is that at Fairwater. It is situated on a low hill and advantage has been taken of the undulating character of the site. The area is well wooded and part of this character has been retained as an amenity nearby. Round a small central space in which there is a childrens playground, grass and trees, is a 2-level grouping presenting a diagonal formation of buildings to the enclosed space. On the lower level are the shops with windows formed by two sides of a square. On the upper level, which is in the nature of a balcony forming canopies to the shops below, is the access to 3-storey dwellings, some of which are maisonettes. The whole enclosed area is a pedestrian precinct, and service ways are at the rear of the shops. On the immediate periphery is a bus stop, a group medical centre, dental surgery, a County Council child welfare clinic, designed and built by the development corporation, a church, petrol filling station, garages and car parks, and a hard stand for a mobile library. A combined public house and community centre is rather like the one at Hilltop, Hatfield.

The Town Centre

In the original outline plan a layout of the town centre was suggested, which showed a road running through the middle from north to south, but that which has been built

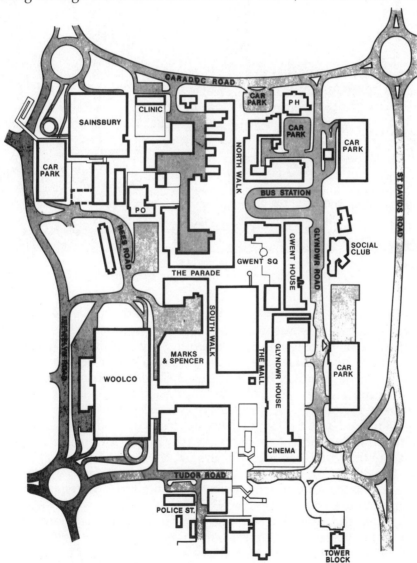

Figure 36.4 Town centre plan.

Figure 36.5 Gwent House in the town centre.

consists of a ring road, on which the main town roads converge, surrounding a pedestrian area with squares and ways between the shops. The main town square called Gwent Square on the east side is surrounded by tall buildings partly with shops on the ground floor and offices above. In 1972 the enclosure of the square was completed by the large complex building called Gwent House which was formally opened by Lady Sharp in January 1973. It comprises offices, a large restaurant and a library. A feature of the building is three large sculptured panels adorning the exterior which depict events in Gwent history. These are the work of Henry and Joyce Collins and were a gift of the Cwmbran Arts Trust. Nearby is the Congress Theatre which is a multi-purpose hall that can be adapted for drama, concerts and conferences. Towards the centre of Gwent Square is a bandstand and on Saturdays the town band plays there, and the adjacent pub puts out tables and coloured umbrellas which give the square a gay continental appearance. Placed in the square for its architectural effect is a tall pole which serves the utilitarian purpose of supporting a spiral stairway that acts as a fire escape from the first floor of Monmouth House. (As mentioned in the section on Building the Town, a large Woolco store above a multi-storey car park was completed in 1975, while a Sainsbury and Marks and Spencer were built in 1977.)

On the west side of the centre is General Rees Square named after the first general manager of the development corporation, Major-General T. W. Rees, who died in October 1959. On its north side is the post office, and in a south-east corner is a spiral ramp encircling a concrete sculpture mounted on a little hill of stone cobbles. The sculpture depicts a family group facing the stresses and strains of growth in a new community expressed as much by seemingly abstract forms as by representation. The work which looks very effective in this setting is by the Welsh sculptor David Horn and was presented to the town in 1965 by the Cwmbran Arts Trust that was formed in the previous year. The spiral ramp leads to the upper level of the Parade which is a two-tier shopping way.

On the east of the centre beyond Glyndwr road are 2 multi-storey car parks, linked with the centre by pedestrian underpasses; one for 450 vehicles completed in 1964 and the other for 600 vehicles, completed a year later. These buildings are attractively designed, the long horizontal hands of vertical concrete bars alternating with plain walls providing in one an effective decorative treatment. Both buildings enhance the general architectural effect of the town centre. Two further multi-storey car parks have been built to the west of the centre inside the periphery road.

In the south-west corner was a site for a college of further education which has now been temporarily 'shelved', while beyond Tudor Road on the south are civic buildings grouped round a civic square. A wide pedestrian way at first floor level with sunken garden and pool leads to the square, crossing Tudor Road. At the south-east corner is the 22-storey tower block of flats which houses the plant for the district heating of the town centre, the first, we believe, for a town centre in the country. In addition to being an example of good planning, this centre of Cwmbran is an achievement of some architectural distinction.

Industrial Areas

As we have said, one of the main purposes of the new town of Cwmbran is to provide homes near the work of those employed in the existing basic industries of the region; these are almost adequate for a population of 35 000, except for service industries situated to the west of the town centre; thus any additional industry could in the early stages be only very limited and should be such as to give added diversification. In the early years application was made by Quality Cleaners Ltd for a site for a factory of 20 000 sq. feet (1800 m²) floor space but apparently, to the regret of the development corporation, the Board of Trade would not issue an industrial development certificate because, 'having regard to the extent of existing industrial development in the area, there shall be no direction of new major industry to the area for the present'. However, a large new bakery for the Monmouthshire Co-operative Bakeries Ltd was built in 1956, and the Cambrian United Dairies Ltd completed their milk distribution centre a little earlier; but these are service industries. Several of the older factories have made considerable extensions to their premises, among them British Nylon Spinners Ltd, Girling Ltd, Guest Keen & Nettlefolds and Alfa Laval Ltd.

The development corporation has felt the need for more diversification of industry so as to avoid unemployment, which would, of course, mean more factories and would involve some modification of the directive of the Board of Trade (since 1970 the Department of Trade and Industry). In its 1957 report the corporation stated that 'the time is approaching when active steps to encourage the establishment of some new lighter industries might be desirable to increase diversity and to balance changing conditions as automation and increased mechanization continue to develop'. Two years later in 1959 the corporation referred to 'some contraction in industry . . . which has resulted in some short-time working, a reduction of overtime work in some industries and in particular the shortage of employment for school leavers', and the corporation refers again to the desirability of introducing new and diversified industries for the area and speaks of consultations, in association with the Cwmbran Urban District Council, with interested parties and organizations. Later in 1971 the GKN factories closed which meant several hundreds being unemployed.

If fairly stable employment is to be secured in the town other and different industries should be introduced. The increase in the size of the town with probably ultimate growth to 55 000 gives validity to this contention. There have occasionally been empty houses waiting for tenants, and it was felt by the development corporation in 1971 that the need to attract more industry to the town, especially in view of the GKN closures was a matter of some urgency. It therefore embarked upon a vigorous campaign to attract industry with some good results; at the same time it went ahead with the development of its 6 industrial estates, Avondale, Grange, Forgehammer, Somerset, Ty Coch and Springvale, the last of which was the 133 acre (54 ha) site of the GKN factories. Among the manufacturing firms that have come to Cwmbran in later years are Atlas Copco Ltd, Perry Tool & Gauge Co Ltd, Eylure (Erida) Ltd, Saunders Valve Co Ltd, Redifon Telecommunications Ltd and Siebe Gorman Ltd, while the Alfa Laval Company, one of Cwmbran's original and major industrial firms, built a large new prestige factory in Ty Coch estate which was completed in 1975. At the time of designation there were 20 factories or industrial plants in Cwmbran employing about 6800. Since designation up to the end of 1976 another 163 factories have been built, mostly smaller units, in which some 3400 have been employed. Since 1975, 43 new factory units have been constructed and have been let. The town now employs almost 17 000 people.

Social Aspect

Social life in a new town might be grouped under the five headings of the more intimate relations of families and friends, the social life of clubs and societies that bring together people of kindred interests, cultural and other classes and similar forms of adult education, the social life attached to churches of various denominations, and the more public social life of inns, hotels, cafés, the streets and parks.

Those responsible for building a new town cannot provide this social life; that must spring from the people themselves; but they can provide the setting and premises whereby this social life can be facilitated and flourish. In providing good houses they meet the requirements of the first category. For the other categories the Cwmbran development corporation has been very much alive to the need of premises for various activities. As in most of the new towns there is a large number of societies and clubs for various pursuits, and it is not perhaps surprising in a town so largely Welsh in character that musical societies are conspicuous.

In providing premises for the various social activities the development corporation has enjoyed the co-operation of the Monmouthshire County Council (since 1974 the Gwent County Council). In building schools in Cwmbran the council has in some instances attached community facilities somewhat on the lines of the Cambridgeshire village college principle. Four 'Community Colleges' forming 'adult wings' to the schools provide a variety of social, recreational and handicraft facilities. This was done firstly at the West Pontnewydd Primary School and then on a bigger scale as a wing of the Coedeva Secondary Modern School at Croes-y-Ceiliog and at the first purpose built comprehensive school in Fairwater. In addition, in response to representations made by the tenants' associations that small meeting halls should be provided to serve needs that cannot be met by the adult wings of schools, meeting halls/community centres have been built at West Pontnewydd, Llanyravon Mill, Hollybush/Coedeva, Fairwater and Greenmeadow III. The functions and classes held at the community colleges have proved very popular and have made a notable contribution to the social life of the town. Several churches have been built and are making their contribution to social life. Among facilities for sport the urban district council built a stadium with a grandstand which was opened in 1967, at Old Cwmbran. It is now a Torfaen Borough Council responsibility, as are the other sports centres. The stadium has the only international running track in Wales and is one of only four in Great Britain. There are also the other usual sports facilities.

In the town centre was an old dilapidated Victorian house, Llantaram Grange, which the development corporation acquired and restored to provide rooms for club meetings on the ground floor and accommodation for the arts club and theatre club on the first floor. Since early 1967 exhibitions of the visual arts have been held in this building with the help of the Welsh Arts Council. An initial disinterested attitude among the public has changed to a constant flow of regular visitors.

The more public activities depend a good deal on buildings for social and recreational purposes as well as public houses and cafés. Houses should have first priority, of course, but there should not be too great a lag in providing those social, cultural and recreational facilities which add so much to the interest and pleasantness of life. In the case of the earlier new towns the lag in providing them during the fifties and early sixties was more the responsibility of the central government than of development corporations.

37 Newtown and Mid-Wales

Mid-Wales is a sparsely populated area which had a larger population a hundred years ago than it has now. During the last century it has consistently declined in population as the result of outward migration. It reached its peak about a hundred years ago in 1871, when the population was about 278 000, compared with that in England and Wales of about 22 712 000, and declined to 204 378 in 1971 compared with 48 594 000 in England and Wales. The birth rate was very little less than in the country as a whole and decline was due mainly to migration. The overall density is roughly one person to 10 acres (4 ha)—the most sparsely populated area in England and Wales. It consists of small towns, villages and hamlets scattered in beautiful hilly country with, however, quite extensive fairly flat areas along the many river valleys, which could accommodate a considerably larger population. In the past, many of the chief industries were based on wool, particularly the flannel industry which flourished in Montgomeryshire. The decline of the woollen industry in the region is probably the main reason for the migration of population. During the present century the main industries have been farming, forestry, a little miscellaneous manufacturing and, of course, service industry (37.1).

All the towns in the area are small. The largest is Aberystwyth with a population in 1971 of 10 680, which has shown a slight increase since 1951. Other towns are Bala (1580), Brecon (6283), Brynmawr (5930), Ffestiniog (5751), Llandrindod Wells (3379), Newtown (6122), Rhayader (4137) and Welshpool (6705) (37.2).

The decline in population of Mid-Wales resulted in the deterioration of social facilities, public services and the area's economy. Mid-Wales became more dependent on central government for funds and found it increasingly difficult to attract new industry. Therefore, in 1957, the former county councils of Cardiganshire, Merioneth, Montgomeryshire, Radnorshire and later Breconshire established the Mid-Wales Industrial Development Association in an attempt to promote industry and thus arrest depopulation and revitalize the economic and social life of the region. It was one of the first regional development bodies in the UK. In 1967, utilizing the existing New Towns legislation, the government established the Mid-Wales Development Corporation. This had similar functions to the Association but had the specific task of undertaking the expansion of Newtown, the major 'growth' town within the Mid-Wales area.

The Mid-Wales Development Corporation was dissolved on 31 March 1977 and the Development Board for Rural Wales was established in its place, as a result of the

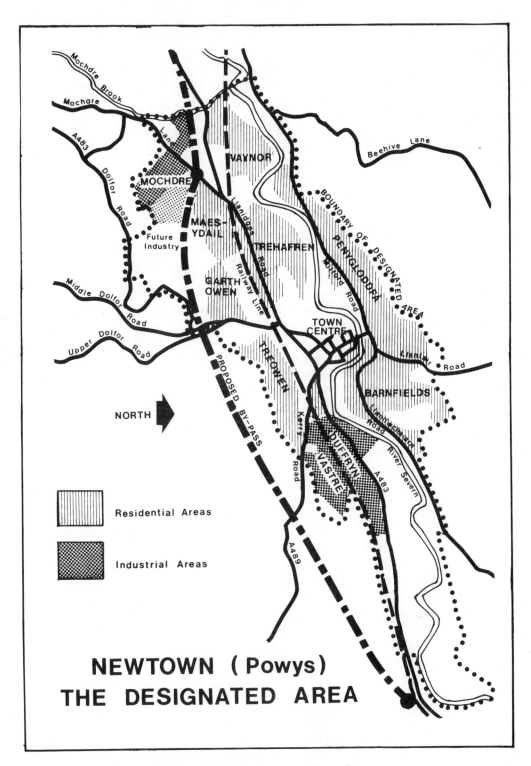

Figure 37.1 Newtown outline plan.

Development of Rural Wales Act 1976. The development board is responsible for Powys and the districts of Ceredigion and Meirionnydd and has taken over the expansion of Newtown.

The designated area of Newtown is 1497 acres (606 ha) and the aim of the plan, which was completed in November 1968, was to enlarge its population by intake from the existing 5500 to about 11 000 by about 1977 and then to reach a population by natural growth of about 13 000 in 1991.

However, with a population for the area of about 7800 in 1977, and taking into account that the population for Great Britain is no longer substantially increasing, it may be doubtful whether the population for Newtown will now reach the originally estimated 13 000 by the end of the century.

Outline Plan

The outline plan was prepared by the Cwmbran Development Corporation acting as agents for the Mid-Wales Development Corporation, and this was submitted to the Secretary of State for Wales in March 1969.

The designated area is long and narrow in shape, being about $3\frac{1}{2}$ miles (6 km) east–west by about one mile (1.6 km) wide in the western part, narrowing to little more than a $\frac{1}{4}$ mile (0.4 km) in the eastern part. The existing town is roughly in the middle of the east–west stretch, and it was proposed to develop this as the centre of the enlarged town, and build new residential districts west and south of the existing town, and a further development of Barnfields to the north of the river. A fairly low density of 10 houses to the acre (25 per ha) was proposed so as to allow for nursery schools, play spaces, allotments, and parking. In planning the residential areas the aim was to provide 'a safe and easy network of footpaths for the use of children on their journey from home to school'.

Although the aim is to preserve the interesting and attractive character of the town centre as much as possible, a fairly large-scale conversion to a pedestrian precinct was proposed. This has unfortunately now been abandoned. However, there are plans for the provision of a loop road to improve the traffic flow in the town centre. Greater use has been made of the river as an amenity, for the flood protection scheme of the former Severn River Authority provides for a retaining wall about a $\frac{1}{4}$ mile (0.4 km) long by the town centre to link with the one near Short Bridge Street, and part of this has become a riverside open space which includes the old Parish Church of St Mary. There are also plans for a new shopping precinct in the Ladywell area of the town.

There were 3 industrial estates in the plan: a long strip running eastward from the centre between the railway and the main road (Duffryn); a smaller one south of the railway (Vastre); and one in the extreme west (Mochdre).

Building the Town

If a contribution to reversing the drift of population away from Mid-Wales was to be made fairly soon it was important to proceed with the building of the town as quickly as possible. The planning proposals had to be finalized, subjected to public comment and be approved by the Secretary of State, while a new sewerage scheme and alleviation of flood risks had to be undertaken. Such operations took time, and the corporation felt there was none to lose and considered that it was unwise to wait for these before starting to build. It therefore undertook a pilot scheme involving the building of three advance factories, one of 30 000 sq. feet (2700 m²) and two of 20 000 sq. feet (1800 m²), and 60 houses. The corporation has continued to build factories and houses as quickly as possible. As a result of this energetic approach, by the end of 1976 the corporation had provided 801 houses, while another 308 were provided by the local authority and private enterprise.

During the same period, 42 factories had been built, including 10 nursery factories, 18 mini-factories and 14 advance factories. The aim has been to synchronize industrial and house building.

Housing and Residential Areas

The first residential area to be built was the Trehafren estate which is situated to the west of the old town between the River Severn and Llanidloes Road. It was built in three phases, the first phase consisting of 59 houses was completed in September 1970. This won a medal and diploma in 1971 for good design in housing awarded by the Welsh Office and the Royal Institute of British Architects. The second phase consisting of 155 houses was completed in 1973, and the third phase consisting of 250 houses was commenced in the autumn of 1972, and completed in 1975.

Figure 37.2 Housing at Trehafren II.

Figure 37.3 Trehafren I, II and III.

The Trehafren residential area is largely a pedestrian precinct with branch roads spreading in from periphery roads. There is one road that runs north from Llanidloes Road to the local centre with a bus pull-in; otherwise the roads branch into parking courts at the rear of the houses which generally, and most satisfactorily, face pedestrian ways. There is provision for a large number of parking spaces, but few garages.

The houses are mostly 2-storey with 2, 3 and 4 bedrooms, and are mainly semi-detached or in rows usually of 3 to 6. They are of very pleasing appearance, the majority with brick facing on the ground floor and ends, with weather-boarding on the first floor either left its natural colour, as in the houses in phase one, or painted white as in phase two. Most of the roofs are the traditional low-pitched, with a few mono-pitched roofs which give variety. The small centre consists of a general purpose shop, a meeting hall, which also serves as a community centre, as well as landscaped open spaces.

The building of the Treowen housing estate to the south of the town was started in 1973. The first phase was completed in 1976 with 145 houses. Here the houses were built in long terraces along the old idea of a Welsh Valley. Phase II of the Treowen estate was started in 1976 and is due for completion in 1978. This estate is for 201 houses. It is an interesting hill site, carefully landscaped retaining existing trees where possible, and houses will mainly be split level and patio style. A new primary school will be opened in September 1977 and work on a meeting hall started in March 1977.

The Maesydail estate, for 190 houses, was started in 1975 and completed in 1977. Houses are built on a court basis, facing inwards, differing from the Trehafren estate where courts are only 3-sided, centred by a car park.

Building commenced on the Vaynor housing estate in 1976 for 186 dwellings. These are similar in design to those at Trehafren and should be ready for occupation in 1978.

Town Centre

The old town which forms the nucleus of the centre of the new town is situated in a loop of the river immediately north of the railway station. It has a wide straight centre street—Broad Street—which terminates at the north end with a bridge over the river, and at the southern end with High Street and Severn Street running transversely. The southern part is more irregular with a main thoroughfare—New Road (A483)—running east–west.

The town centre is now a conservation area. The first two phases of a town centre loop road are completed but approval for the third phase is awaiting Welsh Office approval. Agreement has been reached with the owners for the relocation of the tannery. Again subject to Welsh Office consent, a factory will be provided for it on the Dyffryn industrial estate. The development board is building a new 6350 sq. feet (570 m²) building for Boots in the High Street. In 1975 the Ladywell House office block was completed with a floor space of 48 000 sq. feet (4320 m²).

There are further plans to redevelop the old Ladywell area of the town as a new shopping precinct with a supermarket, 11 shops and car parking space.

Industrial Areas

The industrial estates of the town all lie on the long south side of the designated area. The first to be built was the Dyffryn estate in the south-west which was completed in 1973. It consists of 8 standard factories built in advance for letting, one fairly large factory built especially for a manufacturer of office equipment, and a group of mini-factories. The buildings of this industrial estate with their very slightly pitched roofs sit low on the ground and have an unobtrusive appearance in their valley setting with a background of hills. Two standard factories have been doubled in size and there is space for expansion adjoining the others and the large factory. A special site is reserved for the relocation of the tannery.

Work was started on the Vastre industrial estate in 1973. By 1977 there were 18 mini-factories and four main factories completed with a further two main factories completed in June 1977. Six acres (2.4 ha) remain available for future development on this estate.

At the Mochdre industrial estate a 65 000 sq. feet (5864 m²) unit has been built for Presco Engineering (Staffs) Ltd. Sites have also been developed for service industry, e.g. a tobacco warehouse, a brewery distribution warehouse and an ambulance depot for the county council.

The three industrial estates of Newtown provided about 1000 jobs in December 1976 and on completion will employ 2000.

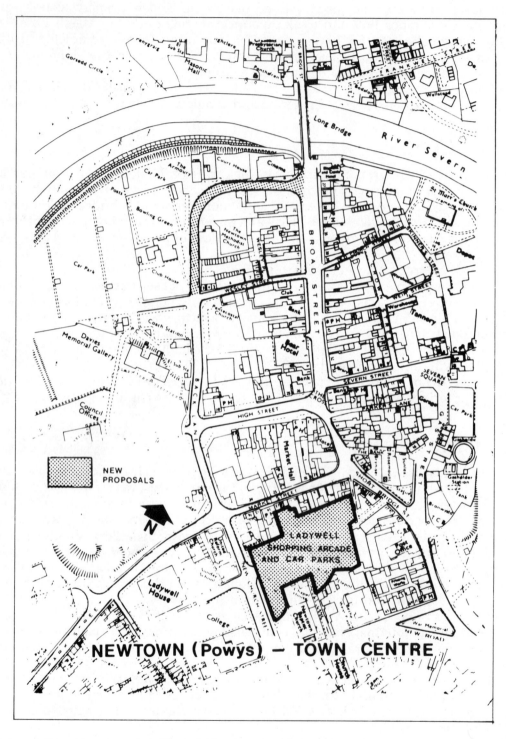

Figure 37.4 Town centre plan.

Figure 37.5 Aerial view of Dyffryn industrial estate (foreground) Vastre industrial estate and Treowen housing.

Social Aspects

Construction of the first phase of a regional sports centre—a swimming pool—is due to commence in 1978. There is a conference room in Ladywell House and exhibitions and dances can be held at the Elephant and Castle hotel which was completed in the sixties; a memorial gallery in the town hall is also used for touring exhibitions. The development corporation, and now the development board, have done their best to help local voluntary organizations to extend their facilities. Projects that have received financial assistance include a learner swimming pool, an evening coffee bar for teenagers and a new 'hut' for the Scouts.

Compared with most, if not all, other new towns which were planned to take overspill, Newtown does not appear rich in recreational and social facilities. However, since designation, emphasis in Newtown has always been on development within a rural area and the view taken by the development corporation and subsequently by the rural development board is that there is not the expectation of facilities on the same scale as in new towns in more densely populated areas where other urban centres are close at hand. (Compare, for example, the short distance of 14 miles (22 km) between Redditch and Birmingham and the much greater one of 32 miles (51 km) between Newtown and Shrewsbury.) At present the town appears to be succeeding and because of its remoteness is attracting people living in the rural hinterland. Further, British Rail has introduced a cheap rail service from Shrewsbury to Newtown because of the popularity of the market and the Pryce Jones department store, which is the largest in Mid-Wales.

There may, however, be a need to reassess these situations in the future should the present successful progress of the town show any degree of decline. But Newtown today is proving to be a thriving town with a community spirit. It is encouraging that depopulation has virtually ceased. Expansion of the town has proved an expensive affair when viewed on a short term basis (over £10 500 000 in capital expenditure) but in the long term it is an investment in growth.

It must be said, however, that in the views of the authors the government commitment to the revitalization of Mid-Wales does not go nearly far enough. It is questionable whether so small a town is, in the long term, socially satisfactory. We believe that the government should be far more imaginative and embark on a much more ambitious programme, designating a group of new towns with target populations in the region of 30 000 to 40 000. This would enable the provision of much more comprehensive facilities for the people and, providing the towns were located in reasonably close proximity, major undertakings such as a sports arena and arts centre could be shared. This, indeed, would be a return to Ebenezer Howard's town cluster idea.

Such a project, though, would involve a rethinking of current government policy and a major commitment to attracting more population to Mid-Wales rather than merely arresting the drift away of the people already living there.

References

37.1   Mid-Wales in this context consists of the 5 former counties of Brecknock, Cardigan, Merioneth, Montgomery and Radnor. The area is now mainly the county of Powys, the southern part of Gwynedd and the northern part of Dyfed.

37.2   The populations are based on the provisional figures given in the Preliminary Report of the Census 1971.

38 East Kilbride

Glasgow and the lower valley of the Clyde comprises one of those large congested areas which exhibit all the reasons for dispersal, and it was no doubt with this in mind that the Secretary of State for Scotland appointed the Clyde Valley Planning Advisory Committee in 1943 to advise on and prepare a plan for the more satisfactory development of the region. As a result the Clyde Valley Plan was published in 1946, and it contained proposals for enlarging certain small towns and building new ones, with the reservation of open country around and between them. One of the sites proposed for a new town was at East Kilbride, and it was provisionally designated by the Secretary of State for Scotland in the autumn of 1946, and after a public inquiry the designation was confirmed on 6 May 1947.

The designated area consists of about 10 250 acres (4150 ha), of which 3500 acres (1416 ha) will be used for the new town and the remainder will form the green belt, and thus East Kilbride and Glenrothes unlike the English new towns have the advantage of the green belt being controlled by the development corporations. A little towards the south-east of the area is the old village of East Kilbride with about 2500 population, situated about 9 miles (14 km) south-east of the centre of Glasgow. The site has been criticized as being too near the city. Between Glasgow and East Kilbride, however, is a range of hills 700 feet (210 m) high, and much of the broader part of the green belt of East Kilbride is on the north side where it is about 2 miles (3 km) wide, while there is a further stretch of open country beyond this. Consequently, there is reason to believe that this stretch of open country, about 3 miles (5 km) wide, will be preserved between Glasgow and the new town. The topography is such as to create a feeling of detachment from the crowded city.

The site of the new town is hilly, a characteristic it shares with those of Glenrothes and Cumbernauld, and this has meant a fair amount of site preparation, levelling and earth moving. The undulating landscape is attractive with pleasant views in many directions.

East Kilbride was originally designed for a population of 45 000. The target was later raised to 50 000, then in 1960, to 70 000 and lastly in the early seventies to 90 000–100 000. When Lord Craigton, Minister of State, visited the town in June 1960, he said that the target population should now be expressed as 70 000, a figure inclusive of the natural increase of the population which will follow the initial build-up to about 55 000 by planned immigration.

Later this was amended to a plan for a population of 70 000 to rise ultimately by natural growth to about 100 000. A report that was prepared by the development corporation in April 1964 to assist the county and burgh councils in assessing their future demands for water supply and drainage facilities in the area stated that: 'The original town plan area and eastern extension area were estimated to accommodate 67 000 persons. Areas to the south of the town with future gross densities of 30 persons per acre (74 per ha) could accommodate 34 200 persons. The area to the north of Lymekilns House and south of the proposed Glasgow ring road could accommodate 9000 persons. Maximum total population that could be accommodated was 110 200 persons. It was recommended that the area to the north of the town and part of the area to the south-west be excluded from the maximum total. A target population for natural expansion is, therefore, suggested at 95 500 for the New Town.'

In May 1963 East Kilbride became a small burgh, and in June the council, composed of 3 councillors from each of 5 wards, was elected. The poll was 70% of the electorate, about double the national percentage for local elections which demonstrated the considerable interest it aroused. The area controlled by the burgh is smaller than the designated area, and excludes the large green belt of agricultural land to the north. In 1967 East Kilbride was raised to large burgh status by Act of Parliament.

Outline Plan

As originally planned the town was divided into 4 neighbourhoods. Mains, which includes the existing village, occupies a triangular site formed by the two main roads through the town, one to the east running north–south and one to the south running approximately west-north-west to east-south-east. Mains neighbourhood was planned for a population of about 11 500. To the east of the north-south road is the neighbourhood of Calderwood with a population of 10 500, and to the south of the

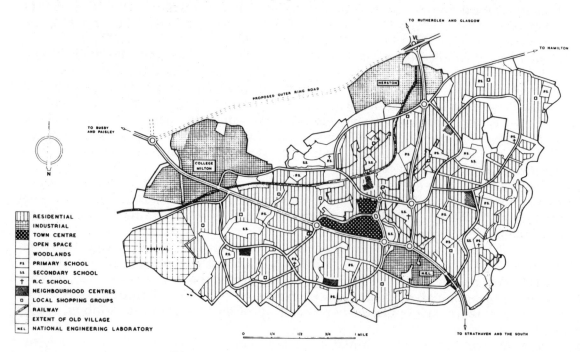

Figure 38.1 East Kilbride—outline plan.

other main road at the east end is The Murray (12 500) divided into east and west and at the west end Westwood (15 500). Each neighbourhood has a principal shopping centre and several smaller groups of food shops: Mains has 4; Calderwood, 1; The Murray, 2; and Westwood, 4. There are 11 primary schools evenly distributed throughout the town, and 6 secondary schools. The town extends about 3 miles (5 km) from east to west, and about 2 miles (3 km) from north to south at its east side, tapering to only about one mile (1.6 km) at its west end. Considering this somewhat awkward shape the town centre is well situated, approximately in the geographical centre, so that no part of any residential area is more than 1½ miles (2 km) away. In the original plan there were 3 industrial areas, Nerston to the north-east, College Milton at the west end, and Birnihill to the south-east. At the west end a large hospital was already in existence.

In 1962 an eastern extension area was planned to accommodate the additional target population. This extension comprised additions to the north-east of Calderwood and a new neighbourhood, St Leonards, to the east and later a further neighbourhood, Greenhills, was added in the south. In 1964 the new industrial site of Kelvin was added in the south-east. Provision is also being made by the town council for extensions to the south-west to accommodate second generation families. These will extend in part beyond the boundary of the existing designated area.

Building the Town

House building started in 1948 in small areas close to the old village, but it was not until 1950 that large contracts began in The Murray immediately south of the town centre. Later, sites in Mains were started, and by 1954 most of the northern part of The Murray, most of the residential district immediately adjacent to the old village in Mains, an area in the eastern part of Westwood, and a small area west of Calderwood were completed. It will be seen, therefore, that the policy was to spread the building widely around the town centre and not to concentrate only on one neighbourhood at a time.

This probably helped the fast rate of building that was achieved which in the years 1953, 1954 and 1955 was about 1000 a year. The rate fell a little to about 750 a year in 1956 and 1957, but rose again to about 1000 a year in 1958, 1959 and 1960, then dropped to about 450 in 1961 rising again to about 750 in 1962 and 1963, and rising sharply in later years to over 1000 a year. From 1964 to 1969 houses built in each year were 1110, 1286, 1355, 1647, 1240 and 1269, a higher rate than was achieved in these years by any other new town in Great Britain. From 1970 onwards there was a considerable decline with 510 in 1970, and then 691 and 511 in 1971 and 1972, to rise a little to 820 in 1973 and 720 in 1974, 940 in 1975, and 1120 in 1976. Altogether by the end of that year from the time of designation 22 925 houses have been built in East Kilbride of which 21 584 were by the development corporation, 258 by the local authority and 1083 by private enterprise.

The decline in the rate of building in the earlier and later years was due mainly to restrictions on capital expenditure. The town as originally planned for 45 000 was mainly completed by 1966, while a considerable part of the north-eastern extension of Calderwood and of St Leonards had been built. At the end of 1976 the population was 76 200.

Progress with the neighbourhood and shopping centres kept in step with the housing, and these have been substantially completed in the four neighbourhoods of

Mains, The Murray, Calderwood and Westwood. In Mains the old village street became the neighbourhood centre where a number of improvements were made.

There was some delay, however, in building the town centre, probably partly because of uncertainty regarding the form it was ultimately to take and the reconsideration of the original plan. This was changed in the early sixties and when the new plan of the pedestrian precinct was adopted progress was much more rapid, so by 1977 the centre was more or less complete.

Industry has more than kept pace with housing; indeed at some stages it seemed to be embarrassingly ahead. In the 1966 report of the corporation it was stated that the 'rate of industrial and commercial growth brought problems, since it outpaced the house building programme. The waiting list lengthened from 1500 to nearly 3000, and the waiting period for all but key workers is now nearly 12 months. With a total of some 7000 additional jobs expected by 31 December 1967, and a maximum of 3000 houses which could be completed by that date, the housing situation is unlikely to improve significantly in the near future.'

The corporation considered whether to refuse new applications for industrial premises, but rightly regarded such a policy as regrettable, and was supported in this by the policies suggested in 'The Scottish Economy 1965–1970—A Plan for Expansion'. There was no repetition of the apprehension regarding industrial intake in the 1967 report.

In the building of East Kilbride industry has apparently always been ahead of housing which represents very healthy progress. It causes embarrassments and presents problems, but that the industrial intake is so successful is a matter for congratulation. The proud position of East Kilbride in 1976 was that industrial companies occupied factory floor area of over 6 000 000 sq. feet (540 000 m²). This success is particularly satisfactory in a country from which until 1971 there had been a heavy migration of population.

Housing and Residential Areas

The development corporation concentrated for the most part on the medium-sized house in the early years of development because the majority coming to the town were young married couples with small children. Later, with an increasing population of teenagers and middle-aged persons, there was a greater need for both larger and smaller houses. The proportions of dwellings of different sizes built up to 1960 were 42% of 4-apartment (3-bedroom), 42% of 3-apartment (2-bedroom), 10% of one- and 2-apartment, and 6% of 5- and 6-apartment (3- or 4-bedroom). A small proportion of houses were built by the corporation for the higher income groups, some by private enterprise for sale, while sites were made available for individually designed private houses.

The provision of a greater proportion of houses for sale by private builders is being encouraged in the new neighbourhood of St Leonards.

A good proportion, some 50% of the dwellings are in 2-storey terrace blocks, about 15% are detached and semi-detached 2-storey houses while about 35% are flats mostly 3-storey and 4-storey blocks, with a few one-storey dwellings for old people, and some 12-storey tower blocks. There are several of the last-mentioned, and the first was completed and opened in October 1966. The corporation apparently discovered that there was a good market for high quality multi-storey flats, 'even,' as it states in its 1966 report, 'at rents three times those charged for ordinary low rise flats'. These multi-storey flats are additional to the normal house construction programme and are available for occupation by people working outside East Kilbride, although local applicants have priority. This means that these flats are available to people working in Glasgow, thus making East Kilbride for such people, a dormitory suburb. In the course of changes of employment it is difficult to avoid this happening, but for the corporation to make such dormitory suburban development possible at the outset is regrettable. As these multi-storey flats are designed for business executives one can be fairly certain that they will be occupied by a good proportion of executives working in Glasgow offices.

The high proportion of flats in East Kilbride, hardly accords with the comments made by Sir Patrick Dollan, the chairman of the development corporation up to 1959, in the Foreword to the corporation's official brochure of 1957 where he says, 'at least 95% of the residents have intimated that they prefer houses with gardens to tenement and flatted homes'. Why in face of this the development corporation have built 36% flats is difficult to understand. The attitude of several people is that if they have to live in flats they may as well stay in Glasgow in closer proximity to the life and amusements of a big city. It may be that in Scotland it is just a little difficult to shake off the tradition of flat building. An explanation given to the authors by a former general manager of the development corporation is that because of the uneconomic rents, 'there is a heavy deficit on all housing' and that they 'build flats considerably cheaper than houses and in consequence the deficit on flats is very much less', while 'to maintain a density of

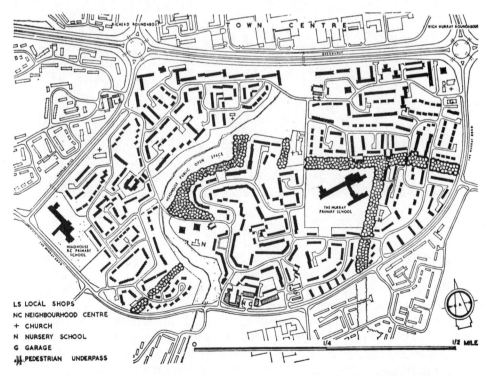

LS LOCAL SHOPS
NC NEIGHBOURHOOD CENTRE
+ CHURCH
N NURSERY SCHOOL
G GARAGE
PEDESTRIAN UNDERPASS

Figure 38.2 Northern part of the Murray neighbourhood immediately south of the town centre.

Figure 38.3 Calderwood housing development.

about 15 dwellings to the acre (37 per ha) it is necessary to build flats. The hilly nature of the sites make it impossible to get 15 houses to the acre (37 per ha).' That it is cheaper to build flats is surely contrary to experience in most other parts of Great Britain where flats above 3 storeys are generally more expensive to erect than 2-storey houses. Further comments on flats and houses are made in the chapter on Glenrothes.

The layout of the residential areas is on the irregular lines of those of most of the new towns, but in East Kilbride this informality seems more pronounced because of the generally hilly character of the site. The areas are divided by curved roads which form islands and into these, culs-de-sac, very varied in character, are introduced. Houses are, for the most part, in terraces. Sometimes semi-detached blocks are arranged in echelon fashion. Rarely do the houses align the roads in a parallel manner; generally the spaces between the house fronts and the road vary; a favourite device is to form a triangular plot of green, the road forming the hypotenuse of the right angled triangle. Occasionally there is a more formal arrangement with terrace or semi-detached houses on two sides of a long rectangle with a grass patch and pedestrian ways in the centre. There is unfortunately a certain dullness in some of the housing units, particularly those which are mainly faced with brown or buff bricks, and this is rather accentuated in the longer terrace blocks. Efforts have been made in a few streets to relieve the monotony with various coloured renderings. Some of the later houses, however, are more attractive in appearance, this being achieved by diversity of wall patterns, such as coloured rendering and brickwork and the introduction of painted timber boarding and hanging tiles. One row in Stephenson Terrace in The Murray is a series of detached houses with gable ends to the front, linked with each other by a bridge which provides space for a room. Of the flats some of the best are the 3-storey blocks in Westwood which are pleasently staggered while having recessed balconies; far better than the projecting exposed balconies of the 3-storey blocks in Park Terrace in West Mains. Houses for the higher-income groups are also of interesting design. Numerous trees have been planted to supplement the few that have been preserved wherever possible, and when the former have grown it will greatly improve the general appearance and give a more varied character to the scene.

One of the most attractively planned neighbourhoods occurs in the north-east of Calderwood, part of the town extension development. As mentioned in the 1964 report of the corporation, 'new layouts for Calderwood XVI, XVIII, XIX and XX have been based on the Radburn principle with pedestrian access to the front of the houses and access for cars at the rear.' The St Leonards neighbourhood was planned on the same principle.

A particularly impressive part of this development occurs in a large scale grouping of various houses on undulating land surrounding a very extensive lawn or 'village green'. Some of the houses are situated on the rising ground surrounding the green which gives the effect somewhat of an amphitheatre. Paved footpaths traverse the area in all directions, there are children's playgrounds near trees in one part, while the lawns present plenty of opportunities for a variety of games. Tree planting is rather sparse and a thicker grouping of trees in parts would enhance the general appearance, especially as the tower blocks of flats loom rather heavily beyond the houses in the immediate surroundings. Still, in spite of minor criticisms, this is one of the best things of its kind in a new town.

Neighbourhood Centres and Sub-Centres

In the neighbourhood shopping centres the pattern is similar to those in many of the other new towns. Shops are arranged either on three sides of a square adjoining the road as in The Murray, or as a straight row of a few shops, or on two sides of a triangle as in Westwood, where a stretch of grass attractively occupies the triangle. In The Murray maisonettes over the shops in 3-storey structures give height and an added sense of enclosure which is agreeable. Perhaps this centre would have been even more successful if there had been a larger pedestrian area in the square, which would have diverted goods vehicles to their rightful place at the backs of the shops where access is provided.

The last of the original four to be built is that at Westwood which is also the first to be planned as a pedestrian precinct. It was completed by 1969. Two rows of shops face each other and between them is a rectangular space divided into a garden with trees and a children's playground. The centres of the 2 neighbourhoods to be built later, St Leonards and Greenhills were completed in 1972 and 1974. They are enclosed shopping precincts.

Town Centre

Not a great deal of progress was made with the town centre in the first 10 years; only 2 blocks of shops, a hotel and a combined post office and telephone exchange had been completed. The delay was partly occasioned by changes of plan. As first planned the centre had a principal street—Princes Street—running through its middle from east to west with a large car park at the western end, and pedestrian shopping ways running off north and south. In the revised plan, adopted in 1960, a much larger area has been allocated to a pedestrian precinct by the conversion of the eastern end of Princes Street. The development corporation was prompted to make this change, which is a decided improvement, by the success of pedestrian shopping centres in some of the new towns in England and in some redeveloped city centres. The centre includes a large covered air conditioned shopping precinct called The Plaza, which has its own multi-storey car park with shops below. This building complex was completed in 1974.

The whole of the shopping centre is surrounded by a ring road, from which roads

Figure 38.4 A view along Righead Gate with the Plaza development on the right and Edinburgh House shopping units on the left.

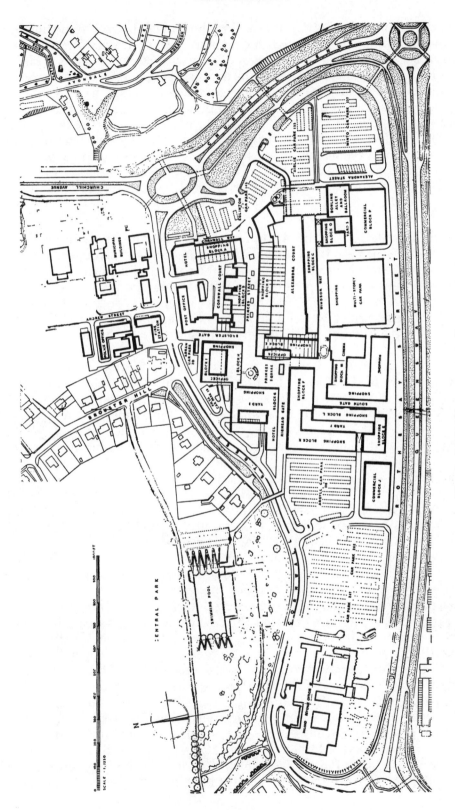

Figure 38.5 Town centre plan.

branch inwards to car parks and service ways at the rear of shops. On the north side of this attractive shopping island, which includes also a hotel, post offices, and some commercial offices,is the civic centre beyond Cornwall Street which is a main dual-carriage bus route. This civic centre contains the district council chambers and offices, the town hall and law courts designed for the council by the architect of the corporation. Nearby it is hoped to build a central library and art gallery and possibly (we would like to say, certainly) a theatre. To the north-west of the shopping island is a 10-acre (4 ha) town-centre park, in which are provided an Olympic length swimming pool, with a very impressive shell concrete roof, a youth centre, and a small boating lake.

Industry

As previously indicated there are 4 industrial areas on the outskirts of the urban development, 3 of which are used for manufacturing industry, Nerston in the north, College Milton in the north-west and Kelvin in the south, while Birnihill, a little to the south-east of the centre, is occupied by the National Engineering Laboratory and the Scottish branches of the Building, Fuel and Road Research Stations. These buildings comprise several rectangular blocks with flat roofs, pleasantly grouped on a spacious site in which an effective general harmony is obtained with the surrounding landscape.

Industry in East Kilbride is perhaps over-weighted with engineering, and it is a question whether there is sufficient balance of other industries and sufficient diversification to ensure in some degree against a vulnerability to depressions.

The policy of the development corporation in seeking new tenants is 'to prefer industrial enterprises which (a) are mainly engaged in manufacturing, which (b) offer employment to skilled male workers and which (c) afford apprenticeship opportunities,' because 'it is these industries which are likely to provide the high density of employment in terms of factory space and the type of occupation required if a proper balance of industry is to be created' (1961 Report). It is this last provision that is especially important if employment in the town is to be kept reasonably stable in comparison with the rest of the country. It is doubtful if the provisions enumerated are adequate for this purpose, which at the stage reached by the late sixties can only be secured by a selection of industries as different as possible from engineering. There are a few food and clothing firms, but they are a very small proportion of the whole, and it would be safer if that proportion were much bigger.

The majority of the bigger factories are devoted to engineering and are occupied by such famous manufacturing firms as Rolls Royce Ltd, making aero-engines; Sunbeam Electric Ltd, electrical engineering; Mavor & Coulson, mining machinery; John Macdonald & Co. (Pneumatic Tools) Ltd; W.D. & J. Bain Ltd, transmission machinery; J. H. Carruthers & Co. Ltd, manufacturers of cranes and pumps; Perma-Sharp, special purpose machinery; Hayward-Tyler Ltd, pumps and general engineering; and Lansing-Bagnall Ltd, materials handling equipment. There are a number of food and clothing manufacturing firms, among the former being Cooper & Co. Stores Ltd, engaged in food processing; Scotbeef Ltd, bacon curing; Kirriemuir Gingerbread (J. T. Urquhart & Co); Kraft Foods Ltd; Schweppes (Home) Ltd, soft drinks; while among the clothing firms are Laird-Portch Fashions Ltd, women's clothing; and Lerose Ltd, knitwear. Among other firms one of the largest is Standard Telephone & Cables Ltd, making microwave equipment. An important latecomer to East Kilbride was the Metal Box Co. Ltd, the large packaging manufacturer who came here in 1974 and also Motorola Electronics. A few firms devoted to printing and drawing office equipment suppliers find a large part of their market in East Kilbride industries. As a means of attracting further industry to the area, the development corporation embarked in 1973 on a large programme of building 86 advance factories with a total area of 400 000 sq. feet (36 000 m^2). These were completed in 1974/75.

Social Aspect

The provision of accommodation for cultural and recreational activities has been slow. Although there have been for some years over 60 social, cultural and recreational organizations, they have not enjoyed adequate facilities, and they have had to depend largely on church and school halls for accommodation. This has not been due to any fault of the development corporation which has done its utmost to secure such accommodation by various means within its limited powers.

In its report for 1960 the corporation refers to its attempts to ensure progress in the provision of community buildings in the new town, and also to the Government's offer to provide one-third of the cost. Little had then been done, but confident hopes were expressed that something definite would materialize. The provision of public amusements has also lagged.

By the end of 1960 Thomson Recreational Enterprises Ltd had provided the Olympia Bowl and Ballroom, consisting of 16 lanes for the Canadian game of 5-pin bowls on the ground floor and on the first floor a ballroom for 1000 dancers. It was not until 1967 that a start was made with building a cinema, largely because of difficulty in interesting the trade in the project. This is in the town centre near the Plaza.

In its report for 1961, the development corporation announced that the Fifth District Council of the County of Lanark, later the Burgh, provided community halls in each of the neighbourhoods. The first was that in The Murray shopping centre. A committee of residents was also formed to find ways and means of providing community premises in the town centre. It seems, therefore, that the many local organizations can look forward to a more comfortable future.

An existing building which gives a note of historical interest to East Kilbride is Hunter House at Long Calderwood, the home of William and John Hunter, the famous physicians and surgeons of the eighteenth century. The property has been conveyed to a trust which maintains it as a memorial, a museum and place of pilgrimage. In 1973 the Hunter Health Centre was opened in the town.

East Kilbride is fulfilling its function well as an overspill town for Glasgow. The majority of the immigrants and much of the industry are from that city. Up to March 1967 the percentage of immigrants from Glasgow was 54%, with 26% from Lanarkshire, 13% from the rest of Scotland and 7% from the rest of the United Kingdom. This last percentage has steadily risen in the last few years, which indicates that East Kilbride is playing a small part in reversing the disastrous drift of population away from Scotland.

By 1976 the population of East Kilbride was about 77 000, and since 1955 the population has increased at an average rate of over 3 300 a year, a rate of expansion at least equal to that of any other new town in Great Britain. In the history of new towns East Kilbride is one of the success stories.

39 Glenrothes

Before the Second World War in the late thirties coal production in Lanarkshire provided nearly half of the total output in Scotland, but in the period immediately following the war this output was markedly falling and some of the seams were becoming exhausted. It was necessary, therefore, to make good this decline by increased production elsewhere, and the National Coal Board decided to expand production in the coalfields of Fife, Clackmannan and the Lothians. In East Fife at this time the annual output of coal averaged about 2 million tons (2 040 000 t), and it was planned to increase this to about 6½ million tons (6 630 000 t). About 6500 miners were then employed in these collieries and with the planned increase in production it was estimated that there would be employment in the area for a further 6500.

To make this plan workable in the best possible way it was necessary to house the miners satisfactorily, with a good home environment, and it was felt that this could best be done by creating a mixed community near but apart from the collieries in the form of a new town. In the Memorandum by the Scottish Secretary of State on the Draft New Town (Glenrothes) Designation Order 1948 it is pointed out that: 'the programme for increased coal production involving the employment of miners on this scale depends for its success on the provision of houses and other facilities for the miners and their families. Past experience has shown that purely mining settlements are basically wrong and prevent healthy community development. In its Report published in 1944 the Scottish Coalfields Committee recommended that miners should, wherever possible, be housed away from the collieries and should have the advantage of living in a mixed community side by side with members of other trades and occupations. This recommendation is now widely accepted and the Secretary of State considers that it should be adopted in providing the housing and other facilities required for the additional mining population in East Fife'. In a reasonably balanced community the proportion of miners to other population was considered to be 1 in 8 or 1 in 9, and on this basis it was proposed that the total population of the new community should be of the order of 30 000.

Although the town should be away from the collieries it was yet considered that it should be within reasonable distance of the main centres of mining. Also it should have a green belt, good road and rail communications, and be well situated for industrial development.

The site chosen was of 5730 acres (2319 ha) immediately north of the East Fife coalfield in the parishes of Markinch, Leslie and Kinglassie and the County of Fife. The River Leven flows west–east through the area, the main railway line from Edinburgh and Kirkcaldy to Aberdeen runs along the eastern boundary, while the A911 road runs east–west through the town north of the river, and the A92 runs south–north a little west of the eastern boundary. As originally conceived, of the 5730 acres (2319 ha), only 1950 acres (789 ha) would form the built-up area of the town; the remainder would form a green belt to continue in agricultural use. Thus Glenrothes, like East Kilbride, but unlike the new towns in England, was to enjoy the advantage of a green belt controlled by the development corporation. The region is one of gentle wooded hills and valleys with the Lomond Hills to the north and Goatmilk Hills to the west, and it can fairly be described as one of the most beautiful of the new town sites.

Since the plan was first prepared in 1951 for a population of 32 000, changes in the manpower estimates in the mining industry prompted a revision of the maximum population. In the report of the development corporation for 1956 reference is made to the changes in population estimates of the Department of Health for Scotland following the re-estimation by the National Coal Board of manpower requirements and 'as a result it had been agreed that a figure of 15 000 should be taken as a safe minimum for the population of the new town', but that it 'was not likely to exceed 18 000'. This was very confusing and frustrating to the development corporation and it meant a considerable modification of the original planning intentions. The position improved however in the following year when the prospects of Glenrothes attracting industry were brightening, and a little later factories began to appear in the northern Queensway industrial estate. Communications and transport facilities would be greatly improved by the construction of the Forth Road Bridge, which would help to make industrialists more favourably disposed towards Glenrothes, and assist in establishing industry in the town. A further change took place in 1959 as a result of the informal approaches made by the development corporation to the City of Glasgow that it should receive overspill from that city. Negotiations were satisfactorily completed and it was agreed that 1800 houses would be made available in Glenrothes for Glasgow overspill. The maximum population not merely returned to about 32 000, but it was possible that because of higher densities than were originally planned the town could accommodate a population of 50 000, especially as the Secretary of State said that 'in the future Glenrothes can make an increasingly significant contribution to the serious problem of Glasgow overspill'. Much depends, of course, on the amount of industry that can be persuaded to go to Glenrothes from Glasgow. In view of the closing of the Rothes colliery announced in 1961 Glenrothes will have to depend for its future to a greater extent on this overspill.

In the White Paper on Central Scotland—a Programme for Development and Growth (1963)—Glenrothes was included as one of the growth points, and in consequence the target population was raised in October 1963 to 55 000. It was expected that after that figure was reached natural growth would raise the population to 70 000. This necessitated a new plan for the town, and in its 1966 report the corporation envisaged an increase by the end of the century to a population in the region of 95 000.

Outline Plan

The burghs of Markinch and Leslie lie 2½ miles (4 km) apart on the A911 just beyond the eastern and western boundaries of the designated area, and between them Glenrothes is being built. The original plan was published in 1952, but the events during the fifties affecting the future of Glenrothes necessitated several changes in planning which

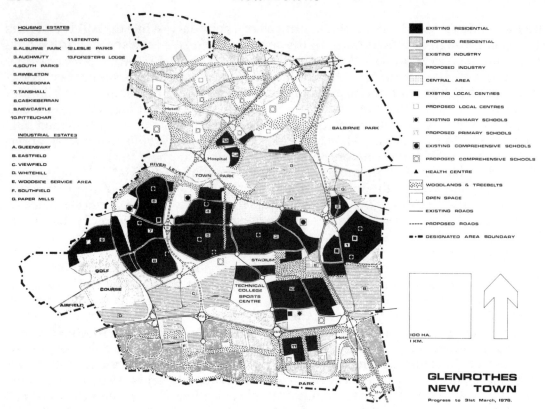

HOUSING ESTATES

1. WOODSIDE   11. STENTON
2. ALBURNE PARK   12. LESLIE PARKS
3. AUCHMUTY   13. FORESTER'S LODGE
4. SOUTH PARKS
5. RIMBLETON
6. MACEDONIA
7. TANSHALL
8. CASKIEBERRAN
9. NEWCASTLE
10. PITTEUCHAR

INDUSTRIAL ESTATES

A. QUEENSWAY
B. EASTFIELD
C. VIEWFIELD
D. WHITEHILL
E. WOODSIDE SERVICE AREA
F. SOUTHFIELD
G. PAPER MILLS

EXISTING RESIDENTIAL
PROPOSED RESIDENTIAL
EXISTING INDUSTRY
PROPOSED INDUSTRY
CENTRAL AREA
EXISTING LOCAL CENTRES
PROPOSED LOCAL CENTRES
EXISTING PRIMARY SCHOOLS
PROPOSED PRIMARY SCHOOLS
EXISTING COMPREHENSIVE SCHOOLS
PROPOSED COMPREHENSIVE SCHOOLS
HEALTH CENTRE
WOODLANDS & TREEBELTS
OPEN SPACE
EXISTING ROADS
PROPOSED ROADS
DESIGNATED AREA BOUNDARY

100 HA.
1 KM.

GLENROTHES
NEW TOWN
Progress to 31st March, 1976.

Figure 39.1 Glenrothes outline plan.

resulted in a revised plan of 1959. In this plan the town is divided into 3 neighbour-hoods grouped round the town centre, to the south-east, west and north. Each neighbourhood was to be sub-divided into precincts, with a primary school and a shopping area as nearly as possible in its centre. The south-east neighbourhood was planned for 3 precincts, Woodside, Auchmuty and Pitteuchar; the western neighbourhood 5: South Parks, Rimbleton, Macedonia, Tanshall and Caskieberran; while the north neighbourhood for 2; Cadham and Pitcairn, with 2 further precincts indicated.

The population of the south-eastern neighbourhood was envisaged as about 10 000 and that of the western neighbourhood about 21 000. In the earlier plan of 1952 this neighbourhood had 3 precincts, but it was replanned at a higher density to include 5. An influencing factor was the need to reserve greater areas of land for industrial development. The neighbourhood is 745 acres (302 ha) and the density proposed for its population of 21 000 was 14.5 dwellings per acre (36 per ha). It was clear from this planning that if building proceeded according to programme the original maximum population would be reached by the completion of the south-eastern and western neighbourhoods, and that building in the northern neighbourhood would all be in excess of that.

Later, further precincts were planned, and in 1974 the town was divided into 5 areas: north, south, east, west and central. Parts of the precincts of South Parks, Rimbleton and Auchmuty became the central area. The east area comprises the precinct of Woodside while the west area is composed of the western halves of South Parks and

Rimbleton, Macedonia, Tanshall, Caskieberran and an additional precinct, Newcastle. Development commenced during 1976 in the northern area a detailed plan for which was prepared and submitted to the Scottish Office in 1973. This plan included two neighbourhood centres. In 1974 a further area with an anticipated 6750 population was planned to the south of Pitteuchar. The neighbourhood centre will service both the southern area and Pitteuchar.

A major paper making firm existed in the River Leven Valley and the Queensway Industrial estate was developed between this and the Town Centre at an early stage. A further large industrial area, Viewfield industrial estate was provided in the south while others are available in the south-east (Eastfield industrial estate) and the south-west (Southfield industrial estate and Whitehill industrial estate).

There is a generous provision of open space, especially in the form of woods, and a woodland belt on the south slopes of the River Leven Valley on the north side of the western neighbourhood.

In view of the increase in the target population to 55 000, possibly by the end of the century to 95 000, a new master plan was prepared and interim proposals were submitted to the Secretary of State for Scotland and the Fife County Council in November 1966. As a result of subsequent consultations these were revised and a formal Master Plan was submitted in 1969. An indication of the spirit in which this new master plan was prepared is given in the 1967 report of the corporation which is worth quoting.

'Over the 15 years since the 1951 outline plan for the town was prepared, dramatic changes have taken place not only in planning theory but in social habits and also through the turn of events. These have rendered obsolete nearly every basis for the original plan. There has been the remarkable increase in the ownership of cars and the consequent need for vehicle/pedestrian segregation and for vast urban motorways and elaborate traffic interchanges; there have also been the failure of Rothes Colliery, the general reduction in working hours, the increase of leisure and the revolution that has taken place in the ways in which people live. The educational system is changing and this is altering the location and sizes of senior schools. Demand for industrial elbow-room has increased. Learning, therefore, from these things and from the chequered history of the town, the corporation, whilst recognizing the uses of computer techniques and statistical analyses, accept that the real challenge to their planning is to maintain flexibility.'

Building the Town

Because of the uncertainty with regard to the number of miners who would require to be housed in Glenrothes and because of the reduction in estimates of this number, the progress in building the town was slow in the early years. Many housing contracts were suspended, and the corporation had continually to ask the Secretary of State for Scotland to authorize more new house building. However, owing to the fillip given by its becoming a reception area for the overspill from Glasgow, the successful attraction of industrial development and later still to the increased target population, more rapid progress has been made. The first few houses were built in 1951, then until 1957 about 300 houses were built a year. In 1958 about 420 were completed, 376 in 1959, 338 in 1960, 290 in 1961, 346 in 1962, 360 in 1963, 378 in 1964, and then a steep rise in 1965 to 760. This higher level was slightly increased in 1966 to 873, and in 1967, 983 were built.

Then from 1968 there was a lower level of output of 528 in that year, 475 in 1969 then a drop to 174 in 1970, to rise again to 404 in 1971 and then to reach a low level of 253, 103 and 132 in the years 1972 to 1974. Then in 1975 it rose to 523 and the total for 1976 was 453. By the end of 1976 since designation 10 247 houses were built in Glenrothes, of which 9484 were by the development corporation, 328 by the local authority and 435 by private enterprise. By 1976 9 residential precincts were completed which are indicated in the section on housing. The process of building has been from the town centre outwards.

The building of the town centre has hardly kept pace with the housing, and industrial buildings at first lagged behind. The corporation in the early years had difficulty in attracting industry to the town. In its report for 1956 it stated that it thought that the elusive first project had been secured, but this had to be deferred because of organizational difficulties of the inquiring company. A year later, however, a start was made with the erection of a creamery for the Scottish Milk Marketing Board, and after that there was a steady flow of industrial firms moving to Glenrothes so that by 1976 93 firms were established in the 5 industrial estates of Queensway, Viewfield, Eastfield, Whitehill, Southfield and 16 in the Woodside Service Industry Site.

Housing and Residential Areas

The first precincts to be built were Woodside and Auchmuty and these were followed by Rimbleton, South Parks, Macedonia, Tanshall, Caskieberran, Newcastle and Pitteuchar. In Auchmuty the high proportion of 491 flats were built, nearly 30%, but in later precincts there were much fewer. In 1975 construction of 450 houses was started in the Stenton precinct in the south of the town.

The reasons given for the early high proportion of flats would doubtless be compactness of urban development and conservation of land. They are hardly an acceptable form of dwelling for so high a proportion, because there is overwhelming evidence to the contrary. Possibly the reason really has its roots in tradition. In Scotland a higher proportion of flats has always been provided than in England, and this can be traced to the stronger continental influence in Scotland. On the continent city defensive walls were maintained much later than in England, and as populations increased, congestion became more acute within the city walls, so vertical extension in the form of high apartment blocks became the custom, whereas in England the growing population was accommodated more by horizontal extension in ever-increasing suburbs. Scotland, so susceptible to French influence, imitated the continental apartment block to a far greater extent than ever obtained in England, and the tradition has not yet died and survives in two of its new towns. Still, it is interesting to note that in its 1960 report the development corporation states that:

'During the course of the year it became evident to the corporation that there was considerable resistance to the letting of flats or maisonettes and as a consequence an urgent review was made of the future programme from the point of view of the proportion of flats and maisonettes to houses in general. Future development in the West Neighbourhood had been proposed on a basis of 20% flats or maisonettes while in the existing Auchmuty Precinct the proportion of flats was 29% with provision for an ultimate figure of 36%.

'After careful study the corporation came to the conclusion that for the time being the proportion of flats and maisonettes should be reduced to 10% in the town as a whole

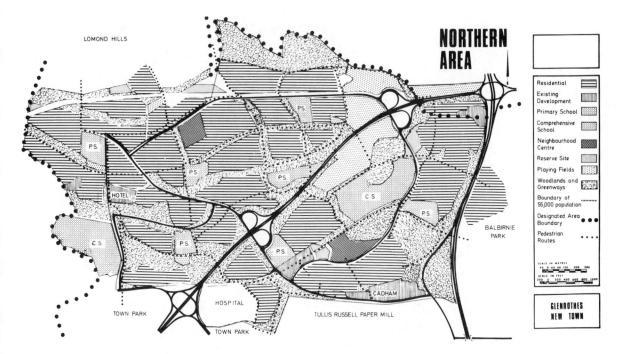

Figure 39.2 Northern area neighbourhood plan.

but that reserve sites should be kept throughout the town for a maximum of $16\frac{2}{3}\%$ in the long run. The effect of this decision in practice has been to release some sites and to reserve others for such appropriate uses as the corporation may decide. It is evident, however, that there will be no need to build further flats for some considerable time as on the basis of the 10% figure, of which mention has been made, a balance of only 272 flats would be required in the whole of the town.'

It would seem that the experience of the corporation has conclusively demonstrated that the great majority of families much prefers a house with a garden to a flat. The corporation is realistic in modifying its plans in this respect, and is thus providing accommodation in accordance not only with the needs but with the wishes of families.

The flats are mainly in 3-storey blocks in rows, and 4-storey Y and star blocks (one of which in Auchmuty received a Saltire award in 1955). These blocks are often effectively sited in relation to the 2-storey houses, and with the undulating land they serve to give variety, especially of height, and it must be admitted that they contribute visually to the residential areas. A certain number of 5-storey blocks of maisonettes have been erected. The corporation looks favourably on this type of dwelling as it stated in its 1958 report that, 'keen interest is being taken in this type of development which may prove one of the best forms of housing, having all the requirements of comfort, land conservation and urban character'. This, however, is hardly borne out by the later, 1960, report. In 1968 a 16-storey block of flats for business executives was built on a site adjoining the Town Centre. This block has a residential caretaker and the dwellings are liked by the tenants.

The numbers of dwellings provided according to size is based on the number of apartments. It was originally 10% 2-apartment, 23.7% 3-apartment, 57.6% 4-apartment

Figure 39.3 Plan of the western precinct of Macedonia.

and 8.1% 5-apartment, but this was later modified for the western neighbourhood to 3% 2-apartment, 40% 3-apartment, 49% 4-apartment, 6% 5-apartment and 2½% over 5-apartment and again in 1976 to one person OAP 6%, 2 person OAP 10%, one person (not OAP) 6%, 4 person 31%, 5 person 40%, 7 person 6.5% and 9 person 0.5%.

Because of the undulating character of the site, and because of the varied types of houses and flats, combined with an irregular grouping, the residential areas are visually attractive. Two examples might be taken in the area near the main shopping centre in Woodside, and another south-east of Auchmuty known as Dovecot Park. In one long rectangular site in Woodside, the two long sides are linked by pedestrian ways and the terrace houses face on to these with gardens backing on to the next pedestrian way, while the houses turn the corner towards one of the roads. Semi-detached houses are irregularly grouped on the plot opposite. The other grouping in The Beeches consists of a row of terrace houses with projecting entrance blocks, running at an angle to the road, abutting a 3-storey block of flats running transversely, while a spacious lawn and flower beds grace the area which is partially enclosed and screened from the road by a row of beeches. This delightful effect is repeated with variations by similar arrangements in other parts.

In the layout at Dovecot Park rows of terrace houses face outwards on an irregularly-shaped island site with a road brought into the centre of the island at the rear of the houses where garages are provided. In some of these central or rear areas are allotments in addition to gardens, while other spaces between the houses are occupied by lawns, and in one area a playground and kick-about spaces enclosed by trees. This planning may be derived in part from the Radburn principle, but it is only a partial adaptation of it as the houses all face on to roads, and it is a question whether there might not have been some improvement in the planning if these had sometimes become footpaths. Nevertheless, in the irregular grouping and the generous intro-duction of trees, the area is a very attractive one.

A more complete adaptation of the Radburn principle was employed in the three western precincts of Madedonia, Tanshall and Caskieberran, the first of which was completed in 1966. The Macedonia precinct with a school in the centre, is encircled by a road, from which roads branch inwards and along these are garages related to the houses. A network of footpaths serves the houses and links with the roads. The houses are mainly in terrace blocks, some sited facing the footpaths with the roads at the rear, and some sited transversely to the footpaths, with frequently a mixture of both. In a few cases there is a double footpath with a lawn between, along which several trees have been preserved or planted. The houses in this precinct are flat-roofed and the whole scheme is very effective.

A good deal of experiment has been conducted with methods of house construction and with various house types. One of the most successful is a series of 3-storey terrace houses with a garage forming part of the ground floor, so planned to save space. Some were completed at Rimbleton in 1966, which are very well designed with well pro-portioned façades.

Residential areas developed later in the mid-seventies are in the northern part of the town at Cadham and Collydean. The layouts of the first two phases of the former are variations on the theme of service roads branching from periphery roads with an independent yet related footway system. The culs-de-sac terminate in circular parking areas, and straight footways, running transversely, are flanked by houses arranged in a symmetrical echelon manner so that the plans of several are rather like a herring-

Figure 39.4 Pittenchar housing precinct.

bone pattern. The gardens are small, but there is a generous provision of public open space between the several rows of houses with children's playgrounds introduced in sections of some.

The first phase of Collydean is a further variation of the same theme. Here a very long main branch service road has several minor branches with T shaped terminations, and again there is an independent, but functionally related footpath system. What both schemes have fortunately avoided is houses facing car parking areas. Planners, fortunately are becoming aware that car parks are among the ugliest features of the urban scene.

Precinct Shopping Centres

Of the shopping centres in each of the precincts, that at Woodside merits special attention because of its very attractive plan and disposition of buildings. It is situated at the corner of Woodside Way and The Beeches. Buildings are grouped on three sides enclosing a paved pedestrian square patterned with flower beds, and furnished with a newspaper and magazine kiosk. On the north side is a long row of shops in 3-storey blocks, with flats above and projecting to form protective arcading for shoppers; at the west end is a shorter row of shops with maisonettes over, and on the south side is a

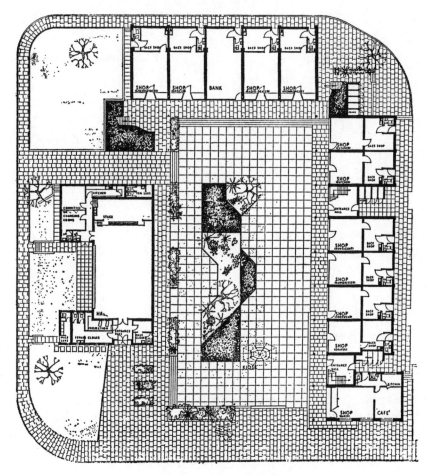

Figure 39.5 Plan of the shopping centre at Woodside with a paved court enclosed in front of the shops and a community hall on the south side.

community hall to seat 240, which has an interesting barrel vault shell concrete roof. The paved courtyard connects with The Beeches by means of a short pedestrian way, and at the rear of the building is a parking area and garages. The buildings are well proportioned, their height is sufficient to give a sense of enclosure, the square is large enough to give an agreeable impression of space, while the flower beds give touches of colour and gaiety. The general effect is very pleasant.

The Town Centre

Encircled by a major town road to which the other town roads radiate, the town centre as planned is a long rectangular shape about ½ mile (0.8 km) east–west by a ¼ mile (0.4 km) north-south, spreading a little wider to the west. The plan has undergone several changes; originally it had a road running through the centre, but now the central part is a long pedestrian way running east–west which opens to a square at the east end. Running off this central way in both directions are smaller ways which link on the

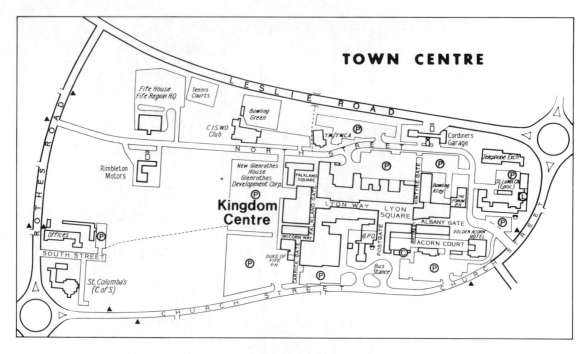

Figure 39.6 Town centre plan.

north side with car parks and a road within the main ring road and on the south side with a bus station and further car parks. Along the principal pedestrian way are shops, 2 departmental stores, one on the south side and one at the east end. A group of civic buildings and offices is sited on the north side of this pedestrian way. They include the regional council offices, police headquarters, central government and development corporation offices, and an exhibition hall. All round these buildings, but within the periphery of the encircling town road, are spaces for car parks and garages. It is a plan that was probably influenced by the Stevenage centre, and it promises to be one of the best. Other buildings already within the centre are a hotel, two restaurants, a post office, four banks, a public house and offices.

The eastern half of the centre is being built first, and a central pedestrian elevated square with a glazed roof was completed in 1967. It was briefly described and illustrated in the second edition of this book (p. 374 and Plate LXIV [a]). Since then, however, it has been completely transformed. The roof was changed from high pitched to a lower flat one, and the whole much lengthened. It accommodates 75 shops, 10 large stores while the whole covered area is heated. This new shopping mall, as it is called, was opened in July 1976. This handsome development with its 1500 car parking space is making the centre a regional shopping focus.

In 1974 the Fife Regional Council decided to locate its headquarters at Glenrothes, which gives, of course, enhanced status to the town. The council purchased the office block previously occupied by the development corporation, which moved in 1976 to part of the tall new block completed in that year.

Industry and Industrial Areas

There are 5 industrial estates for manufacturing industry in Glenrothes: Queensway just north of the town centre with 29 factories early in 1975; Viewfield in the south with 8 factories; Eastfield in the east with 24 factories; Whitehill in the south-west with 41 factories; and Southfield in the south with 10 factories. It will thus be seen that industry is north-east and south of the town centre which is an advantage for morning and evening transport flows. There is also a fairly large area for service industry in Woodside with 16 firms, while 4 are in the town centre. A craft centre at Balbirnie includes silversmiths, leather-workers, furniture designers and makers, a weaver and a stained glass artist.

Glenrothes is probably the chief centre of the electronics industry in Britain, and the large factories in this industry here include Hughes Microelectronics Ltd, Beckham Instruments Ltd, Brand Rex, GEC Telecommunications Ltd, General Instrument Corporation and Burroughs Corporation. Other firms in the electronics industry are expected. Among the other larger factories are those of Anderson Strathclyde, engineering machinery; Intercobra Ltd, making plastic goods and extrusions; Robertson and Ferguson Ltd, engaged in steel fabrications; and Sandusky Ltd, centrificial castings.

Two other fairly large factories are those of Cessna Industrial Products Ltd, making

Figure 39.7 Eastfield industrial estate (foreground); the town (mid-centre); the Lomond Hills in the background.

hydraulic components in the Eastfield Estate, and of Thomas Salter Ltd, toy manufacturers on the Woodside Service Industry Site. Most of the factories have been
established since 1957 when the function of the new town changed. Larger than any of
the new factories, however, are those to the north of the town, Tullis Russell & Co Ltd,
and Fife Paper Mills paper manufacturers, established here in 1809 and 1816. Nearly
2000 are employed in this industry. In addition to the firms mentioned others are
engaged in the manufacture of clothing, rubber coverings and petrol pumps, so it will
be seen that a fair diversification of industry has been secured. In the larger service
industry categories are Union Cold Storage (freezing and packaging) and United Glass
(bottle storage for local distillers).

By 1976, since designation, 145 industrial firms had come to Glenrothes.

Social Aspect

The original purpose of Glenrothes was chiefly to accommodate the miners working in
the colliery to the south of the town, but, as we have noted, it was also the aim that
Glenrothes should be a mixed community so that miners could live with people in
other industries, trades and professions; a proportion of about one miner to 8 others
was the aim. With the closing of the colliery it is no longer a mining town, and instead it
became a general growth area for industry and an overspill town for Glasgow. The
social success of a new town depends very largely on the activities of voluntary
associations and Glenrothes is fortunate in having many of these with a community
association which performs useful co-ordinating functions. The town is also fortunate
in having so soon in its life a very good recreational centre in the north part of the town
centre which though originally provided by the Coal Industry Social Welfare
Organization is for everybody in the town. This centre includes a hall to seat 418, with
adequate stage, club rooms, an old persons' club room and facilities for the many
cultural and recreational organizations of the town. It also has changing rooms for
those using the bowling greens and tennis courts adjacent to the centre. This has been
supplemented at the west of the town adjoining an area reserved for large scale adult
recreation by a town swimming pool and the Institute for Physical and Recreational
Education adjoining the Technical College.

The Glenrothes Art Club which has served to stimulate interest in the arts, was
specially mentioned for its good work in the 1959 and 1960 reports of the development
corporation. Another example of local leisure activity was the building near the
Woodside precinct of club premises for the British Legion largely by voluntary labour.
Unfortunately burnt down soon after, they have now been rebuilt.

With the increasing size of the town there are fresh ambitions for recreation of a
cultural character, especially as it is felt that Glenrothes will gradually become a
regional centre. In 1966 an operatic and musical society was formed, and preparations
are active to set up a local arts guild to co-ordinate and encourage the varied artistic
activities of the town. Also, there is a growing interest in building a theatre as a centre
of dramatic activity of all kinds, an idea that has grown with the years. The only
theatres in Fife are the Byre Theatre at St Andrews which is 25 miles (40 km) away and
Carnegie Hall, Dunfermline, 14 miles (23 km) away. It would be of value if a really good
one emerges at Glenrothes, to serve the region.

In its 1967 report the development corporation states that 'one of the most intransigent problems with which the New Town is faced is the five o'clock executive exit'. 'In

the surrounding County of Fife,' it continues, 'with its cosy villages and little pantiled seaports, there are within easy reach of Glenrothes numerous attractive places in which to set up home. This appeals to many executives who have come to work in the town; yet, socially, there is a need to encourage such people and their families to live within its boundaries'. For that reason the corporation is encouraging private builders to provide houses for executives and has itself built a certain number. This is a problem that is experienced in many other new towns, and it is, of course, an advantage that executives should live, as well as work, in the town as they can make valuable contributions to the social, recreational and cultural life, and many towns have fortunately realized this. So important is this that if private builders are slow or reluctant to provide attractive accommodation for executives, development corporations should not hesitate to do so.

The urban scene of several new towns is enhanced here and there by the introduction of decorative sculptures and Glenrothes is one example. Among the earliest of such works, erected in 1965, is a tall sculpture in the town centre, by Benno Schotz, entitled 'Ex Terra', which shows a mother with children designed in a tree-like form, symbolizing the growth of the town.

In 1968 the Glenrothes Development Corporation appointed David Harding as town artist who works in collaboration with the architect's team. Several interesting works that he has produced occupy various parts of the town, prominent among them is 'Henge' in Pitteuchar Precinct, a circle of concrete decorative slabs reminiscent of primitive stone circles. These slabs are two to three metres high, and the relief sculpture is derived in character from medieval celtic stone crosses and have various symbolic motifs. Another prominent work is 'The Totem', a concrete decorative monolith about three metres high, while several other works are abstracted from such subjects as tree roots, sea horses, mice, human faces and so on, placed at various vantage points. Among the most attractive for children are the groups of hippopotami in the spaces of residential areas, with one group standing in the lake of the town park. These 'hippos' approach life size and each weigh about $1\frac{1}{2}$ tons. It can be imagined how the children like climbing over them.

40 *Cumbernauld*

One of the largest areas of urban congestion, with some of the worst housing conditions in Great Britain, was to be found in Glasgow, which had therefore a very large potential overspill population. In 1946 the Clyde Valley Planning Advisory Committee recommended the enlargement of certain small towns and the building of new ones to relieve this congestion, and one result was that the building of East Kilbride 8 miles (13 km) south-east of Glasgow was begun in 1947. This was originally planned for a maximum population of 45 000, but has since been raised to 70 000, and as the previous population was only 2500 it provides for a substantial migration from Glasgow making available about 18 000 houses. But that would obviously only partially meet the overspill needs. Although the Glasgow City Corporation had built 36 000 houses in the city between the end of the war and 1955, this still left a housing need of at least 100 000, of which, it was estimated, 41 000 were required by families without separate homes. In the 1951 Census it was shown that 48% of dwellings in the city had only 2 rooms or less, while the average gross density in the centre was 400 persons to the acre (988 per ha).

It was estimated in 1952 that sites for about 40 000 houses could be found within the city boundaries, but that the remaining 60 000 would have to be found outside the city. The Clyde Valley Planning Advisory Committee was therefore asked in 1953 to consider and report on the measures to be taken to secure sites outside the city, and in April 1954 the committee recommended that a new town for 50 000 should be built at Cumbernauld to take Glasgow overspill (40.1). The recommendation was accepted by 18 local authorities including Glasgow Corporation and the Dunbarton County Council. In consequence the new town of Cumbernauld was designated on 9 December 1955, in an area of 4150 acres (1680 ha).

Five years later in 1960 the Minister of Housing and Local Government increased the target population to 70 000. By the late sixties it was realized that this population could not be accommodated in the originally designated area if space standards, and acceptable densities were to be secured and as a result an extension of 3638 acres (1472 ha) was designated on 2 April 1973, making a total area of 7788 acres (3152 ha) thus nearly double the original size.

The original site of 4150 acres (1680 ha) is about 14 miles (23 km) north-east of Glasgow within the Strathclyde Region and in the area of the Cumbernauld and Kilsyth District Council. There were 2 villages on the site: Cumbernauld with a population of 1300 and Condorrat with 1200. The site is roughly triangular in shape, about 5 miles (8 km) long from south-west to north-east, and up to 2 miles (3 km) wide.

It lies on the south-east side of the main trunk road from Glasgow to Stirling, the A80, with a small area projecting on the other side of the road at the north-east end, part of the boundary being near the Antonine Wall. The A73 has now been diverted to the west of the town and joins the A80 at the Auchenkilns roundabout. The railway from Glasgow to Stirling passes through the site about $1\frac{1}{4}$ miles (2 km) from the road with which it runs roughly parallel for about $2\frac{1}{2}$ miles (4 km), while another line to Edinburgh runs about $1\frac{1}{4}$ miles (2 km) north of the A80.

Both the road and railway traverse valleys, and between them is a long hill on which the town is being built. Rising to about 480 feet (144 m) and about 220 feet (66 m) above the road, it has a fairly level top; the slopes are steep on the north-west side towards the road, but much gentler on the south-east side towards the railway. There is a small hill a little over 500 feet (150 m) high to the east, another at the north-east end, and a small one by the village of Condorrat at the south-west end. The hilly nature of the area affords extensive views in all directions, but particularly fine to the west and north towards the Kilsyth Hills. There are coal workings west of the A80 and in the vicinity of Condorrat, and fireclay workings in the north-east and south-east of the area, which have some influence on the development of the town, while the nature of the site restricts building to certain areas.

The extension area lies north-west of the originally designated area on the further side of the A80 which will be replaced by a motorway (M80) to run near the boundary of the extension. The Glasgow–Edinburgh railway, with a station at Croy, also runs near this boundary. The character of the country is similar to that of the existing original part of the new town with hills rising to a little over 500 feet (150 m) here and there.

It is questionable whether this is a good site for a new town, and whether a more protected one should have been chosen. Hill towns in southern Italy enjoy a warm sunny climate, but a town in an exposed and windy part of Scotland is very different. Our experience of the climate of Cumbernauld prompted us to refer the subject to the Meteorological Office in Edinburgh, and in the course of the reply it was stated that 'The Forth/Clyde valley is a windy place in general and Cumbernauld lying on an exposed "whale-backed" ridge roughly in the centre of the main gap in the valley must be one of the windiest towns on the mainland of Scotland'. It also seems to have a rather high rainfall (40.2).

Outline Plan

Preliminary planning proposals were published in April 1958, with several outline diagrammatic plans and the First Addendum Report appeared in May 1959 in which several amendments were made followed by a Second Addendum in January 1962. The plan for the extension was published in 1974 and approved in October 1975.

In raising the original maximum population of 50 000 in April 1960 to 70 000 it was calculated that four-fifths would come from Glasgow. The intention was that 50 000 would form the hill town and the remaining 20 000 would occupy surrounding villages. One of the main factors that determines the overall plan, according to the development corporation, is the character of the site and the comparatively small amount that can be used for building which has led to a high-density compact plan. In the original plan for a maximum population of 50 000 only a comparatively small proportion, some 1859 acres ((753 ha) out of 4150 acres (1680 ha), was to be used for the actual town and this included 582 acres (236 ha) of open space. With the increase of the

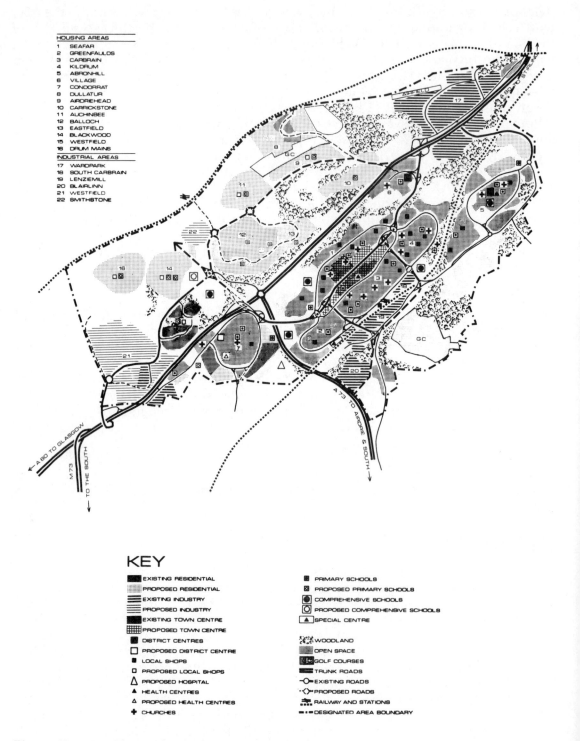

HOUSING AREAS
1 SEAFAR
2 GREENFAULDS
3 CARBRAIN
4 KILDRUM
5 ABRONHILL
6 VILLAGE
7 CONDORRAT
8 DULLATUR
9 AIRDRIEHEAD
10 CARRICKSTONE
11 AUCHINBEE
12 BALLOCH
13 EASTFIELD
14 BLACKWOOD
15 WESTFIELD
16 DRUM MAINS

INDUSTRIAL AREAS
17 WARDPARK
18 SOUTH CARBRAIN
19 LENZIEMILL
20 BLAIRLINN
21 WESTFIELD
22 SMITHSTONE

KEY

EXISTING RESIDENTIAL
PROPOSED RESIDENTIAL
EXISTING INDUSTRY
PROPOSED INDUSTRY
EXISTING TOWN CENTRE
PROPOSED TOWN CENTRE
DISTRICT CENTRES
PROPOSED DISTRICT CENTRE
LOCAL SHOPS
PROPOSED LOCAL SHOPS
PROPOSED HOSPITAL
HEALTH CENTRES
PROPOSED HEALTH CENTRES
CHURCHES

PRIMARY SCHOOLS
PROPOSED PRIMARY SCHOOLS
COMPREHENSIVE SCHOOLS
PROPOSED COMPREHENSIVE SCHOOLS
SPECIAL CENTRE

WOODLAND
OPEN SPACE
GOLF COURSES
TRUNK ROADS
EXISTING ROADS
PROPOSED ROADS
RAILWAY AND STATIONS
DESIGNATED AREA BOUNDARY

Figure 40.1 Cumbernauld outline plan. The area south-east of the A80 is the first part to be designated. That to the north-west of the road is the extension approved in 1975.

maximum population to 70 000 these figures were proportionately increased on the same principles, so that 2783 acres (1127 ha) would be allocated to the town. The remaining 1367 acres (553 ha), which included the existing villages of Cumbernauld and Condorrat, would be reserved for a golf course, a camping and caravan site, wooded areas and a few remaining pieces of farmland all of which merge into the broader green belt lying outside and surrounding the designated area.

The high density plan that evolved arose, for the most part, from a desire to depart from the principles of earlier new town plans with their individual neighbourhoods, each served by its own centre, and to create instead a compact urban integration whose people have to look to the town centre for virtually all their services. The nature of the site and the climatic conditions also played a role in the decision to plan for compactness.

Everything in the plan is directed to securing a compact urban unit of 50 000 to 70 000. The main long hilltop running north-east to south-west is taken as the centre of the town. The road system originally consisted of outer and inner ring roads, fed by radial roads, the inner ring encircling the town centre, but a later modification abandoned the inner ring road and substituted a main spine road to join the A80, south-west and north-east of the town. This spine road passes through the town centre, which is planned on a number of levels, including an upper pedestrian and a lower road level. The road pattern and the conception of the centre seem to be excellent, especially as the latter will secure the much desired segregation of pedestrian and vehicular traffic. This segregation is continued in many parts of the town by a system of footpaths completely separate from the road system. The idea is to have residential areas linked on one side to a main road, giving access for vehicles, and on the other to a pedestrian way leading to the centre. Along the pedestrian ways are the primary schools, churches, halls, public houses, all provided with separate service-road access. It is an adaptation of the Radburn plan discussed in Chapter 20.

As mentioned above, the neighbourhood pattern, which is a feature of all the other new towns, is not adopted. In the preliminary planning proposals certain criticisms of neighbourhood planning are made. It is stated that with the self-contained neighbourhoods in many towns 'the inhabitants are encouraged to look inwards towards the local centre instead of visualizing the town as a whole, to the detriment of the creation of civic pride which should be one of the advantages of a medium sized town'. There is some validity in the criticism, for this thinking of the neighbourhood as one's town rather than that of which it is a part has been experienced, for example, at Crawley; but if neighbourhood and town centre are satisfactorily related the integration of neighbourhood with the town should be constantly apparent to the active members of a community. However, in the case of Cumbernauld, the character of the site is given as one reason for not adopting the neighbourhood system of planning, as it requires 'that the main development should be compact and distances between sections of the town should be short' (40.3) and that major facilities should be concentrated in a central area easily accessible to all the inhabitants.

Shopping is thus concentrated mainly in the centre of the town, but provision is to be made for individual shops for day-to-day needs in the residential areas furthest from the centre, in the ratio of about 1 shop to 300 dwellings, those living in the inner areas of the town being able to use the town centre for all their needs. In the districts of Abronhill and Condorrat which are furthest away from the town centre there are local shopping centres, somewhat on the neighbourhood principle. It is proposed that the shops in the centre should be in a multi-storey structure 'for,' to quote from the Preliminary Planning Proposals (1958, p. 18), 'by taking advantage of the hilly site at Cumbernauld it should be possible to provide a multi-storey centre with pedestrians and vehicles on different levels, with ample car parking facilities within easy walking distance of the shops and a separate system of service roads. The centre should be planned to provide shelter from wind and rain and if possible warmth in the winter. To create a lively, busy atmosphere the spaces between the shops should be restricted in width and related to the height of the buildings, which need not be of more than 2 storeys. It is felt that the scheme should be based on the pedestrian shopping street rather than the market square.'

In the outline plan the two main industrial areas are in the north and south, of similar size. The former borders the trunk road on the north-west side (Wardpark North), while there is a slightly smaller area on the south-east side (Wardpark South). The southern industrial area borders the railway on the south-east side at Lenziemill and Blairlinn, and spreads to the north-west side in the region of Carbrain, Greenyards and the station.

The extension area outline plan, approved with some amendments in 1975, is on similar principles to the original plan, although the distance from the town centre, the lower residential densities and greater space requirements will inevitably lead to a cluster of satellite villages with their own social centres. Additional industrial areas are included, a large one Westfields at the south-west end, and a small one, Smithstone, near the northern boundary. A main loop road of the A80 will form a transport spine of the new area.

Building the Town

The first demand for houses after the designation of the town was for the workers in the large factory of Burroughs Machines Ltd, at Wardpark North in the north-east, erected in 1956–57, which began production in 1958, and 4 years later was employing 2500. Housing, therefore, started at Kildrum, the district nearest to the factory. It was not until 1958 that the first houses were completed. In the first 4 years to the end of 1962, 1734 houses were built, 1677 of these by the development corporation. This was slow progress in view of the needs of the Burroughs factory, but from 1963 onwards output was more rapid. In that year 550 were completed, in 1964 the total rose to 1087, followed by 854 in 1965, 1133 in 1966, 539 in 1967, 898 in 1968, 929 in 1969 and 1081 in 1970. Then in 1971, 1972 and 1973 there was a fall in output to 563, 547 and 567 to rise again in 1974 to 891, 777 in 1975 and 486 in 1976. This fall in output was due partly to economic restriction and partly to consideration regarding the extension to accommodate more residential areas. Altogether since designation 12 766 houses have been built in Cumbernauld of which 12 027 were provided by the development corporation, 91 by the local authority and 648 by private enterprise. By 1976 over 150 factories had been built and over half the town centre with a wide variety of shops was completed and good progress was being made with the remainder.

Housing and Residential Areas

A considerable diversity of housing is being provided, from 2-storey dwellings with and without gardens to tall tower blocks of flats, 11 12-storey and 1 20-storey, which will accommodate about 2.1% of the population of the town. There are also a few 4-storey or 5-storey blocks. The decision to build in this way is partly influenced by the nature of the soil, particularly on the north side of the hill, which may necessitate expensive foundation work for buildings of more than 2 or 3 storeys in height. 'To attain full value from such additional work,' it is asserted, 'it would be desirable to build at considerably greater heights so that the extra cost of foundations is spread over a larger number of dwellings' (Revised Preliminary Planning Proposals 1959, p. 8). A further justification for tall blocks of flats is given in the First Preliminary Proposal (1958, p. 9) where a social survey carried out by the London County Council in connection with high blocks of flats mentions that 'tenants referred to the advantages of being on the upper floors—better atmosphere, greater quiet and privacy and improved outlook'. According to the proposals the 2-storey houses would be built on the gentler slopes of the main hill on the south-east side, and on the flatter land. The tower blocks of flats would be built mainly in the inner areas. Thus the higher densities of about 120 persons an acre (295 per ha) would be nearer the centre, and the lower densities of about 70 an acre (173 per ha) towards the outer areas. It should be noted, however, building tower blocks, or indeed multi-storey flats of any kind was abandoned some years ago as a result of the general rethinking about the social desirability of housing families in high rise buildings. Since 1971, the development corporation has pursued an active policy against the construction of flats as means of obtaining high densities, and the policy in the extension area is to build 2-storey houses with gardens and to give priority to pedestrians in the layout arrangements. Thus, while Cumbernauld is still to be a high density town, the original net density of 26.3 dwellings per

Figure 40.2 General view of town looking south showing housing clustered around town centre on hill top.

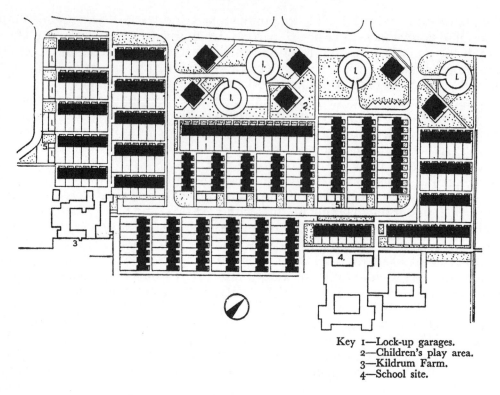

Key 1—Lock-up garages.
2—Children's play area.
3—Kildrum Farm.
4—School site.

Figure 40.3 Housing layout at Kildrum 3.

Figure 40.4 Housing at Park Way in Kildrum.

acre (65 per ha) no longer holds and current estimates show an average of 18.9 dwellings per acre (46.7 per ha).

Most of the houses completed by the end of 1976 are in the areas north-east, north-west, south-west and east of the centre in the Kildrum, Seafar, Londorrat, Carbrain and Abronhill districts, while there is also development at Greenfields in the south-west and Village in the north. The Kildrum area, at the north-east end of the town is just south of Cumbernauld House which has been acquired, with its grounds, as an amenity centre for the new town, the house being at present occupied by the offices of the development corporation. The houses and layout of Kildrum, the first residential area, consist of very varied groupings of 2-storey terrace houses, 4-storey and 5-storey slab blocks of flats, and 5-storey stub blocks. The district is approached by a road running off the A73. South of this road are some rows of terrace houses, all facing one way on to footpaths which run transversely to the roads. On the north side are groups of 4-storey and 5-storey slab blocks arranged to enclose squares of grass or gardens, with one corner of 2-storey terrace houses, similarly grouped. The blocks of flats are designed with the depressing gallery access for which their bright colourful façades hardly make amends. Nearby is a group of 6 5-storey slab blocks, and near these are 39 single-storey patio houses each with a garage, arranged in rows on either side of pedestrian areas with service roads at the back, a slight reminiscence of the Radburn layout. Garages are provided for each dwelling in the tower blocks, arranged in circles with a small break for the entrance.

In the part known as Kildrum 5, blocks of 3- and 4-storey flats are planned in a series of hexagons, with an opening breaking into two sides. This makes a number of enclosures which in a hilltop town in a northern region provides protection from cold winds. An interesting feature is that through these enclosures running under the blocks are footpaths that traverse the whole length of the town from the outskirts to the centre.

One of the most attractive of the housing areas is that at Seafar 2 which received an award of the Saltire Society in 1964. Two-storey houses are situated on the north slope of the hill and are irregularly grouped in the midst of indigenous vegetation of small oak and birch trees and heather with footpaths winding between the houses. The dwellings have plain cement rendered walls, with low mono-pitched roofs, and the living rooms are so orientated as to afford views towards the Campsie Hills in the north, while open to the south to receive the sun. Not far away there is the rather bleak contrast of 3 tower blocks of flats. Generally the housing layouts are made with a view to seclusion from traffic, good orientation and compactness resulting in some very ingenious designs.

Town Centre

Although the planning proposals were made in 1958 the precise and detailed design of the town centre did not take definite shape until 4 years later in 1962. It is an imaginative conception, and could be described as a vast multi-purpose building, one of the largest structures of its kind in the world. It is on 8 levels and the aim is to comprehend in this one vast concrete building all that a modern town needs in its centre. Nearly the whole of the lowest level which steps down on the south-east slope is for vehicular traffic and includes the central spine road running underneath the structure loading docks and parking areas. Above is a series of pedestrian decks

Figure 40.5 View over town centre area looking north. The technical college, medical centre, swimming pool, leisure centre, council offices and Inland Revenue computer centre are all shown.

reached by escalators, lifts, stairs and ramps. This huge construction will contain the complete shopping centre, offices, recreational and cultural facilities and some housing. There are 3 main phases in its construction. The first phase, a central part, completed in 1967, and opened by Princess Margaret, consists of a wide variety of shops, including a supermarket, the largest, we understand, in Scotland, 6 banks, post office, several offices including that of the Scottish branch of the Land Commission for Scotland, a first class hotel called 'The Golden Eagle', a public house and restaurant 'The Kestrel', a health centre, library and public hall. In 1974 the large Woolco Departmental Store was completed, and also the Municipal Office Block for the new Cumbernauld and Kilsyth District Council. On the upper floors on the south side there is a series of penthouses, and on the north a restaurant, function suite and a bowling alley. The second phase which extends both sides of this first central section comprises a long shopping mall leading to a square round which are grouped the leisure centre, sports centre and swimming pool. On the other south-west side is a court and police station, technical college and fire station. The third and fourth phases will include more shops and perhaps a museum. On the north-west side, linked with the completed central part by a pedestrian bridge, is St Mungo's Church and community centre.

The centre being on the summit of a hill, at levels 40 to 80 feet (12 to 24 m) above the ground, extensive views over the surrounding country can be enjoyed in all directions from the many terraces that are provided, although we imagine that more warmth and less wind are common wishes. The immense structure together with the several tower blocks of flats are landmarks for miles around. Seen as a whole from the ground level from other parts of the town this concrete structure appears very different from different points of view. From the north-east it appears as an irregular composition of rectangular masses, with an aesthetic co-ordination that reminds one a little of modern geometric sculpture seemingly irregular yet carefully composed. At a distance from the south-east the long mass is dominated by the series of penthouses at the summit which look very much like five railway coaches held aloft on an irregular grouping of buildings. It is premature to judge of the architectural effect until the centre is completed. It promises much that is unusual and impressive.

In the summer of 1967, Cumbernauld received from the USA the first $25 000 R. S. Reynolds Memorial Award for Community Architecture. The award was made largely for the ingenious conception of the town centre in which multi-level integration has been achieved on a larger scale than elsewhere for the adaptation of the plan to its site, and for the design of its pedestrian and vehicular traffic system (40.4).

Industry

The first industrial building, which as previously mentioned, located the start of the residential areas, was the large factory at Wardpark North in the north-east for Burroughs Machines Ltd. Negotiations with the appropriate government department for the building of this factory were already proceeding at the time of the designation of the new town. The company was granted 72 acres (29 ha) and commenced building its factory in July 1956. The first part was in production in January 1958, and in March of that year 350 persons were employed. Other parts of the factory were completed later and by 1962 about 2500 persons were employed.

The policy of the corporation is to attract diverse industries, and it is itself building standard and nursery factories for letting in addition to the special purpose factories that many larger firms wish to build. Such standard factories have been built at Blairlinn, a little outside the south boundary, 6 at Wardpark South, 2 at Lenziemill and 10 at Gurnhall. These factories are each of 22 000 sq. feet (2037 m²) but can be enlarged by the addition of standard bays to 80 000 sq. feet (7407 m²). A flatted factory was built at Seafar, near the projected town centre, and a group of service workshops at Muirhead. In 1976 there were over 150 industrial concerns occupying factories in Cumbernauld, which included in addition to Burroughs Machines Ltd, Thames Board Mills Ltd, Fort Alloys Ltd and Smith Fullerton & Co. Ltd, an old established Glasgow firm producing marine diesel fuel injection equipment that is transferring completely to Cumbernauld. Several firms from abroad have come here including firms from the United States, Sweden, West Germany and the Netherlands.

Social Aspect

By 1977 Cumbernauld had reached a population of about 45 500, more than half the target population. Despite the climatic drawbacks to which we have referred, there is much in the town that is attractive. The system of footpaths and segregation of vehicular and pedestrian traffic makes life pleasanter, and gives a greater feeling of safety, especially to mothers with young children, than in the older type of town. This segragation is more completely realized than in any of the earlier new towns. The accident record in Cumbernauld is only 22% of the national average.

Organizers of voluntary groups in Cumbernauld appear to be very enterprising. An example is the Cumbernauld Theatre Group. This Group obtained from the corporation in 1962 a lease of part of a group of cottages which it converted by a good deal of work and expense into a small theatre, and has conducted a varied programme of entertainments. A new 220 seat auditorium adjoining the small theatre is nearing completion. Among the sporting activities is a riding school for which farm buildings at Airdriehead were converted, and a canoe club which proposes to exploit the disused Forth/Clyde canal and has leased a 5 mile (8 km) stretch of water in a beautiful setting.

Among other community activities that should be mentioned is the establishment of the Cumbernauld Civic Trust in October 1965, 'to bring all voluntary organizations together in one body and to promote social welfare work in the community'. Representatives of over 50 organizations in the town attended the inaugural meeting. The provision by the corporation of informal tenants' meeting rooms within the residential district has proved to be very popular. There are now 5 of such rooms available for the many voluntary organizations, all naturally heavily booked.

Development in Cumbernauld is progressing with 12 766 houses completed and a population of 45 500 in 1977, and is largely an implementation of the plan proposed for the town. The high densities in the housing areas and the taking of only 820 acres (332 ha) of 4156 (168 ha) for housing, and the high proportion of flats in the early development are regrettable because they do not represent the living conditions that are most acceptable for family life. The second half where the town can spread into the extension area will give lower densities, more 2-storey houses, more space in the residential areas, and more acceptable living conditions.

One virtue of the town, and it is no mean one, is that it has a more complete segregation of vehicles and pedestrians than in any of the earlier new towns.

References and Notes

40.1   The information is based on the Memorandum by the Secretary of State for Scotland on the Draft New Town (Cumbernauld) Designation Order, 1955.

40.2   In an article on Cumbernauld in the *Architectural Review*, December 1967, Patric Nuttgens says, 'The greatest attack on its commercial success is in fact the climate. Rainfall is common and the wind is fierce; by hard luck the winds this year have been the worst in living memory; there is a walking posture known colloquilly as the Cumbernauld lean. This was a fault in the initial planning when the town centre was located in an exposed position; and the original architect for the building perversely accentuated the problem by providing architectural voids all over the place to bring the weather in. This has been corrected where possible, and the next phase is properly enclosed; these difficulties will decrease as more is built'. It is less the fault of planning than of siting. Sir Hugh Wilson, the author of the general plan, was not, as far as we are aware, responsible for the choice of this site, he had to make the best of that which was selected.

40.3   Preliminary Planning Proposals 1958, p. 5.

40.4   The R. S. Reynolds Memorial Award for Community Architecture was established in 1966 and the first 3 awards were made to Stockholm, mainly for the developments in Vallingby and Farsta, Tapiola in Finland, and Cumbernauld. The report of the AIA jury giving the reasons for the awards was given in the AIA Journal of July 1967.

41 *Livingston*

As mentioned in the chapter on Cumbernauld there was in 1955 a need in Glasgow for about 100 000 new dwellings of which 40 000 could be provided within the city, but 60 000 would have to be found outside. Although the new towns of East Kilbride, Glenrothes and Cumbernauld were making a substantial contribution to receive this overspill, it was not enough. To fulfil the housing programme at least another 1000 houses a year would, it was estimated, have to be provided outside Glasgow. It was therefore necessary to find other sites and one selected was in the Livingston district about 13 miles (21 km) west of Edinburgh between Bathgate and Blackburn to the west and Uphall and Mid Calder to the east. The site of 6692 acres (2708 ha) was designated on 17 April 1962. In addition to relieving the congestion in Glasgow and of providing dwellings at acceptable densities in exchange for slums, a new town in this region will revitalize what had largely become a neglected area.

The population proposed for the new town is about 70 000 which for the area designated would allow space for parts of the green belt within the boundary. The designated area is roughly square in shape with a tongue pointing southwards. It lies close to the geographical centre of West Lothian District which, following local government reorganization in 1975, is one of the four districts in the Lothian Region centred on Edinburgh. The site is beautiful, undulating agricultural country with pasture land and scattered woods. It slopes gently from the north to the River Almond which flows through the centre of the site from west to east. On the south side of the river the country is a little flatter and a little beyond the southern boundary are the Pentland Hills. On the fast-flowing River Almond are several small weits, and it can be imagined that the river offers scope for the provision of an interesting water garden. There are large shale heaps, or bings as they are called in Scotland, in various parts of the region which are survivals of the shale workings in this part. There is, however, only one within the site, in the north-west corner, where the commercial extraction for road-making purposes has been undertaken for several years and will eventually leave a cleared site forming part of an industrial estate.

The east–west communications are excellent. The A8 Edinburgh to Glasgow trunk road runs for a little over 4 miles (6 km) along the northern boundary, and the A71 from Edinburgh to Kilmarnock passes through the southern part of the site with a western fork, the A705 to Whitburn and on to Motherwell. The new Glasgow–Edinburgh motorway (M8) traverses the northern part of the town providing a link with the national motorway network.

Two railway lines run through the site in an east–west direction: the Edinburgh–Motherwell–Glasgow main line which passes through the southern tongue with the stations of Mid Calder and West Calder on either side, and the freight line between Edinburgh and Glasgow which traverses the northern part of the site. The communications are much less satisfactory in a north–south direction, although these are better west of the town with the B792 and the A706, yet there is obviously scope for a new north–south road through the town linking more directly with Falkirk, Grangemouth and Bo'ness.

A start for the town was provided by the expanding works of the British Motor Corporation (now British Leyland) at Bathgate which had an initial target of some 5000 employees. Many of the workers in this factory come some distance to work. Provision for them is being made in the small overspill villages of Blackburn, Whitburn and Polbeth but this will not be adequate. Also such a factory attracts linking industries, and it will be appreciated therefore that the industrial area of Livingston would seem to enjoy the prospect of a steady growth in the early days. With the reclamation of land after the shale workings and the removal of deserted buildings the new town should bring new life and grace to a rather neglected region.

Outline Plan

The plan for Livingston represents a return to the system of neighbourhood planning, although in a somewhat disguised form. Although the population proposed in the designation order was 70 000, with 80% coming from Glasgow, the development corporation has since regarded that figure as the target for planned immigration and has made allowances for a further 30 000 by natural increase. The master plan, prepared under the direction of P. G. Daniel, the former chief architect and planning officer of the development corporation, shows how a population of 100 000 could be accommodated in the area. The plan also comprehends the development of the region surrounding the area to the extent of some 120 square miles (311 km²).

The road pattern planned for the town is roughly a rectangular grid having 2 main north–south connectors with the trunk roads and the main town roads forming the rest of the grid. Within the rectangles are the residential units, each with its primary school, whilst those in the more outlying districts have small district shopping centres. A system of footpaths is independent of the major roads and provides access to the centre from various parts of the town.

The average density of the residential areas is about 46 persons to the acre (114 per ha) with the higher densities towards the centre and the lower towards the periphery.

This would mean accommodating approximately 25% of the population in blocks of flats, but the corporation's subsequent policy is to build no more than about 10% of flats overall, the main emphasis being on family houses with small gardens. Four industrial areas are roughly in the four corners of the town, the largest being in the north-east.

The planners have made full use of the scope offered by the river valley in the centre of the site. The town centre is located midway on either side of the river with parkland stretching on either side, and if it is effectively landscaped this centre and its surroundings could be very beautiful. In addition to shops it is proposed to include in the centre: office buildings, a technical college, theatre, churches, a hospital, and a regional sports centre. It is proposed that building would take place from east to west, at the rate of about 1000 houses a year.

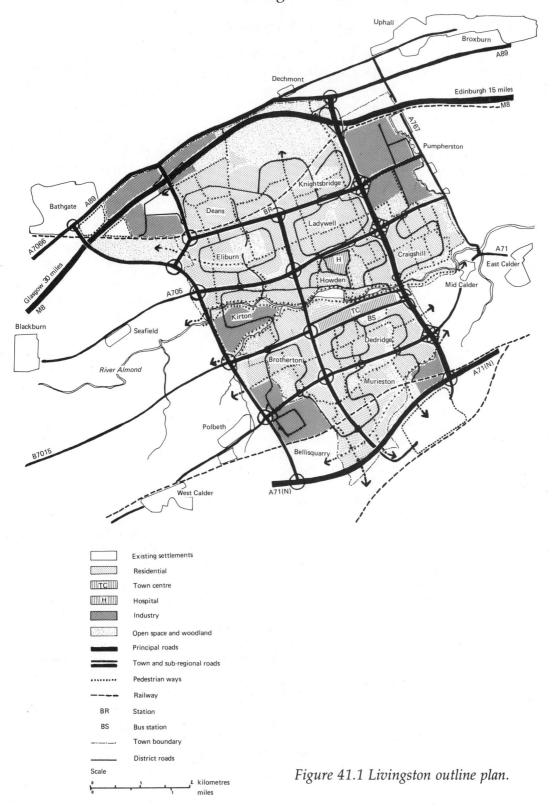

Figure 41.1 Livingston outline plan.

The Region of Greater Livingston

In the draft designation order of 1962 it was recommended that a comprehensive scheme of development for the whole region surrounding Livingston should be prepared so that 'industrial expansion in West Lothian and north-west Midlothian may be co-ordinated and the many problems of agriculture, transport, and social and recreational facilities examined and dealt with as a whole'. Following this, the Secretary of State for Scotland asked the county councils of West Lothian and Midlothian to co-operate 'in the preparation of a regional scheme of development'. The two councils formed a joint planning advisory committee, which included representatives of Livingston New Town, and Sir Robert Matthew and Professor D. J. Robertson were asked to act as consultants. The result is one of the most comprehensive surveys of a region ever published (41.1). The master plan was made with the consciousness of this forthcoming regional survey and plan.

The Lothians Regional Survey and Plan is of significance for planning generally as being the first survey and plan for a region with a new town as a centre and focal point. The terms of reference were:

To carry out a survey and prepare a scheme of development and rehabilitation for the area comprising the parishes of Bathgate, Ecclesmachan, Kirkliston, Livingston, Mid Calder, Kirknewton, Uphall, West Calder and Whitburn within the counties of Midlothian and West Lothian.

The work was divided into two main sections: the social and economic study of the area and the physical survey and plan. The former is by a team of social scientists from Glasgow University working under Professor Robertson, and the latter a survey of the physical possibilities of the area with an advisory plan by Sir Robert Matthew, who was later joined by Professor Percy Johnson-Marshall, with the assistance of a planning research unit drawn from Edinburgh University, and four working parties concerned with rehabilitation, services, roads, and recreation. Later a joint committee on railway services was set up.

The study of the social and economic aspects covers such matters as population, industry and employment, the policy of attracting industry to the peripheral regions of Britain, the regional labour market, the relation of both Glasgow and Edinburgh to the Lothians, and, of course, the present position and future prospects of shopping, transport, and housing in the region with consideration of port facilities in the Firth of Forth, and concludes with a report on 'A Policy for the Lothians'.

The area of the region, which lies immediately west of Edinburgh, is about 133 sq. miles (344 km²), with Livingston, occupying some 10 sq. miles (26 km²), as its centre. It is stated that 'the area will have a better chance of economic growth if it is focused on Livingston which should become "Greater Livingston" with a target population by 1986 of 185 000' in an area of about 35 sq. miles (91 km²). The present population is about 50 000. The target for the whole region is suggested as 230 000 by the same date. The present population is about 87 000. Natural uncrease is likely to ensure continued growth beyond that date. Thus it will be seen that population densities thin out from a centre, for the designated area of Livingston would have 70 000 in 10 sq. miles (26 km²), the immediate surroundings forming the outer part of Greater Livingston would have 115 000 in 25 sq. miles (65 km²), and 45 000 in the outlying areas of nearly 100 sq. miles (260 km²).

The plan suggests that shopping for the region should be centred on Livingston, and that the shopping facilities at Bathgate should not be extended. It is also proposed that consideration should be given to government employment, to inducements of industrial employment, and to social investment. A programme of 1900 houses a year is envisaged for the region, and it is suggested that efforts should be made to build high-quality houses for sale and attract middle-income and professional residents. A communication network to facilitate easy movement between Greater Livingston and Edinburgh is recommended; and this would involve a very much better rail service than there is at present.

The actual site of Livingston is among the most beautiful of new town sites, and its planned centre lies in a valley which should afford some climatic protection, factors which provide many advantages.

After a 10 year period of implementation much of the plan has been realized. However, substantial work remains to be done on the rehabilitation of shale bings but it appears that a more energetic approach will now be possible with the involvement of the recently established Scottish Development Agency. The structure plan for the entire Lothian Region which will include a review of the original Greater Livingston Regional Plan was under preparation in 1977.

Building the Town

The first residential area to be developed was at Deans in the north-west of the town where, between 1964 and 1967, 270 houses were built to accommodate the building labour force that would be needed and for employees of the British Motor Corporation at Bathgate. This and later developments at Deans expanded the original community at Livingston Station, independently from the main pattern of developments from east to west starting with the Craigshill district, which now has 2769 houses.

The original aim was to build 1000 houses per year. From a slow beginning in 1965, by the end of 1968, 2195 houses had been completed, during 1969, 1112 and in 1970, 1019. During 1970, however, a falling off of industrial firms coming to the area resulted in a surplus of houses and the programme was cut. In 1971, 592 houses were completed and in 1972, 277. It takes time to slow down a building programme, but longer to accelerate it again. By 1973 the demand for houses was again high, but only 499 were completed, and in 1974 only 428. However, the situation improved dramatically in 1975 when 905 were built and this continued in 1976 with a total of 1951. Thus by the end of 1976 the total houses provided was 8760, 8480 by the development corporation and 280 by private enterprise.

Similar good progress has been made with the industrial areas. Among the first to be developed were the Houston estate in the north-east and the Deans estate in the north-west.

Housing and Residential Districts

Deans South, the first residential district to be completed, has an excellent layout. The houses are of three main types, two-thirds are 2-storey terrace houses, nearly a quarter single-storey courtyard houses and there are a few flats and maisonettes. The houses are sited mainly in pedestrian areas, and several squares are formed, 3 of

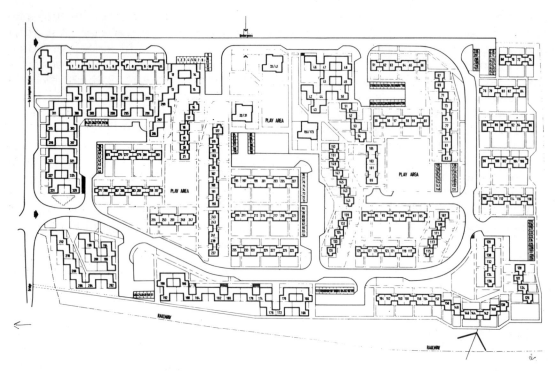

Figure 41.2 Plan of Deans South residential area.

which include play areas. Conveniently related to the houses are rows of garages with road access. There is also provision for car spaces for houses without garages and for visitors' cars. Set among gardens and pedestrian ways the houses are of very pleasant appearance. The terrace blocks have low mono-pitched roofs abutting each other at different levels. The juxtaposition of masses of cement rendering and dark timber boarding between windows is effective.

The single-storey courtyard houses are variously joined and grouped, in some cases with complete courtyards, and in others partially open.

The principle of enclosing residential areas in a periphery road with branch roads inwards and a network of footpaths obtains in the Craigshill district, and is continued with variations in the districts of Howden, Ladywell, Knightsbridge and Dedridge.

Some developments (particularly the southern developments in Howden) consist of a series of courtyards some of which are inward looking and others outward looking. In the former the houses face a square court with gardens backing on to the service roads, all culs-de-sac, occupying a considerable square ahead. This plan gives a fair degree of intimacy and privacy. (In the latter, the roads feed into the squares.)

A later development is the introduction of 'mixer courts' (where the pedestrian and the vehicle may share the same space under carefully designed conditions). Vehicles are slowed down both by physical constraints and psychologically by limiting the driver's view ahead. The first development foreshadowing this approach was in Kirkton, but more advanced versions are now under construction in Deans East and Knightsbridge, and will shortly be followed by others. While these developments lend themselves to the provision of garaging or at least parking within the curtilages of the houses, it is debatable whether they are aesthetically and socially satisfactory in the long term.

Architecturally the evolution of housing in Livingston has, along with other new towns, seen a movement away from the building of flats (such as the industrially built ones at Craigshill) to a predominance of 2-storey houses. In a number of developments mass colour has been used to increase visual interest and the appointment of a town artist has led to the development of mural art in the townscape.

With the development of the town now about half completed, the eastern side is virtually complete, the northern side extending to meet the original community around Deans, and the southern part of the town is also at an advanced stage of development. The western strip will complete conventional development of the town and study has begun to determine the pattern of housing to be adopted in the most central areas. These have been left for development as the final stage of corporation housing.

Thus, as the building of the town progresses, it is the aim of the development corporation to attract professional and management groups with the kind of development that is likely to be acceptable to them.

Local Centres

The policy for shopping in Livingston is to have a large main centre, smaller local centres, and corner shops scattered throughout the residential areas. The size of the local centres is related to their distance from the main centre, those furthest away being the larger, and the nearer being smaller. The first of these centres to be built is that at Craigshill, which is a fairly large district centre as it precedes the construction of the town centre, and until that is partly built it serves many of the shopping needs of the new population.

The Craigshill centre consists of a long central arcade running east–west, with a total of 22 shops aligning both sides, 3 banks and offices, with a supermarket in the centre. The service ways are at the rear of the shops where also are car parks. At the west end is a public house and restaurant. The centre is approached from the east, south and west by pedestrian malls. There are sites for both primary and secondary schools near the centre. Smaller centres have been built at Howden and Ladywell.

Town Centre

The town centre is situated in the Almond Valley, overlooking the river, and is planned to serve a sub-regional catchment population ultimately of more than 200 000. The site extends to about 200 acres (80 ha) and the basic plan is for a linear retail core to run east to west with sites for office, leisure and cultural buildings as well as multi-storey car parks located to the north and south. Those on the northern site will overlook River Gardens and beyond to what is already a mature amenity area, Howden Park. The first phase of the retail core opened in 1976 and comprises 375 000 sq. ft (35 000 m^2) of floor space, including 60 shops and a Woolco store. The shops, other than Woolco, are serviced at roof level, an arrangement which is both visually unobstrusive and lends

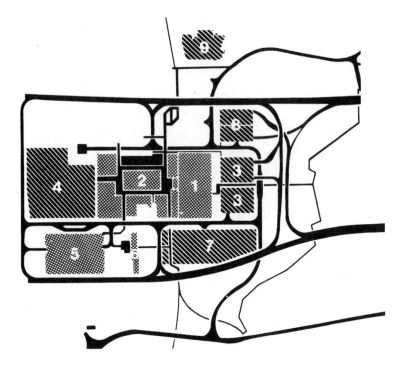

Figure 41.3 Town centre plan. 1. The Woolco store, 2. Ravenseft Properties shopping mall, 3. multi-storey car park, 4. car park, 5. site for bus station, 6. office development, 7. car park, 8. car park, 9. site for sports centre.

greater scale to the retail block than might otherwise have been possible. Internally, two air-conditioned malls link landscaped courtyards onto which shops have their main frontage. To achieve visual harmony, a brown brick theme will be common to all developments in the centre. A regrettable feature of the plan is the number of surface car parks scattered round the centre which would be visually unsightly. Some underground provision or well designed multi-storey structures would be more satisfactory.

Industry and Industrial Areas

The growth and the prosperity of a new town depends on the size and speed of the industrial intake. The development corporation fully realizes this and it has done its utmost, with some measure of success, to attract industry to Livingston. One of the most important measures to achieve this has been the provision of premises in advance for potential incoming industry, and the corporation has done this on a considerable scale from the start. In its report for 1965, it refers to the building of 4 advance factories of 20 000 sq. feet (6096 m²) each, and in its report for 1967 it refers to the building of further advance factories, including one of 40 000 (12 192 m²) and several smaller. It points out in its report for 1972 that experience indicates, 'the wisdom of having factory

*Figure 41.4 Cameron **Ironworks** in the Houston industrial estate.*

premises immediately available and confirms that the building of advance units is necessary for the successful attraction of industry'.

Of the 4 principal industrial areas in Livingston situated in the 4 corners of the square designated area, the largest in the north-east corner, Houston, is the first to be developed. It is immediately north of the first populated area of Craigshill so there is here useful geographical synchronization in the 2 developments. The largest factory on the Houston Estate, and among the first to be built is that of Cameron Iron Works which produces metal forgings for the aircraft industry and ball valves for the gas and oil industries and employs about a thousand. The firms on this estate represent a fair diversification of industry and include engineering, clothing, paper manufacture and related products, building materials and components and food manufacture.

The layout of the factories is spacious with room for expansion in most cases. This is particularly the case with the large factory of Cameron Iron Works which intends to expand and ultimately double the number of employees.

Some factories have been built in the Deans Industrial Estate while there are service industries located in different parts of the estate.

In addition to the 4 main industrial estates there is the Kirkton Campus, 150 acres (61 ha), situated in the west of the town in a triangular area formed by the River Almond to the north and the Killandan Burn, a small stream, in the south which join and form the apex in the east near Livingston village. This site is being developed for science-based industries in collaboration with Edinburgh and Heriot-Watt Universities. Arbrook Ltd, medical suppliers are also established here.

Social Aspect

The development corporation early on established a social relations department, and one of its main purposes is to welcome new residents and provide them with information about the town and its services, to help them to establish contacts with their neighbours and to give them details of the numerous voluntary organizations in the town. The newcomers are asked about their interests and about their willingness to become associated with the work of voluntary organizations.

In the social life of a new town these organizations are vital, and there are generally so many of them and they cover such a wide variety of interests that it is unlikely that there will not be something to win the interest of a newcomer. The difficulty is often in making the first contact, and the development corporation tries to effect the initial liaison. Tenants meeting rooms are provided for this purpose, at first in temporary premises, but in 1971 a purpose-built meeting room was opened in the Ladywell Social Centre and this is being followed by others.

By 1976 there were as many as 250 voluntary organizations covering various general social and sports activities and catering for cultural interests. In 1963 the corporation acquired Howden House and Park situated a little north-east of the town centre overlooking the Almond Valley. It is an eighteenth-century Georgian mansion once the residence of Henry Raeburn, the son of the famous portrait painter. It has been restored and is now used as a community centre, while its outbuildings have been converted for use as a theatre, studio and art gallery which were completed in time for the tenth anniversary celebrations of the founding of the new town held in the summer of 1972. Here during the season, drama, opera, concerts and art exhibitions were

Figure 41.5 Model of Langthorn community complex.

enjoyed. The Livingston Art Guild was formed in 1971 for these activities and the Livingston Art Club has made constant use of the studio.

Suitable premises for social and cultural activities have often been difficult to acquire in new towns, but Livingston seems to have been generally fortunate in this respect. In addition to Howden House, the education authority has made provision for the community use of many of its school buildings. The Craigshill Social Club has itself erected premises for its activities, while the Craigs Farm Centre has converted farm buildings into a community centre. Most of the districts with new populations have acquired their community centres.

A significant contribution to collaboration between the townspeople and local government was the establishment in the spring of 1972 of the Livingston Community Council consisting of 4 representatives of the residents of each of the 6 housing districts. Meetings have been held with representatives of the development corporation and local authorities to further successive community development.

A notable community project is the Lanthorn Complex situated in a linear park in the centre of Dedridge district. 'Lanthorn' is an old Scottish word for lantern indicative of light and warmth. The project is an enterprise of the Scottish Ecumenical Experiment (41.2) in collaboration with the Roman Catholic Church, the Mid-Lothian County Council, the Scottish Education Department, the East Calder District Council and the Livingston Development Corporation.

The complex is designed to serve the local population of 10 000 but if successful it will probably attract people from a wider area. The main building is a 2-storeyed flat-roofed structure. On the ground floor opening from a large entrance hall with adjacent lounge, is a multi-purpose hall, to seat 450, and library. On the first floor are further lounge areas, opening on the south side to a roof terrace. As part of this grouping on the north side is a small shopping courtyard. A separate triangular building to the south consists of a Roman Catholic chapel, and a smaller Protestant chapel, each triangular in shape. The foundation stone for this complex was laid in May 1976.

In 1965 the development corporation moved from its temporary accommodation in Edinburgh to offices that had been built for it at Livingston Village. As if to set a standard of architectural excellence for the town, the building is a very distinctive and felicitous composition of masses in which dark and light contrasting patterning has been employed with very good effect. That this signifies an intention to care for aesthetic values in the town environment is confirmed by the setting up of a committee composed of the corporation and members of the Livingston Arts Guild to provide 'works of sculpture, mural art and special features for the enhancement of the environment'.

References and Notes

41.1 'The Lothians Regional Survey and Plan': 2 vols. HMSO, 1966.
41.2 The participants of the Ecumenical Experiment are the Church of Scotland, the Scottish Episcopal Church, the Congregational Union of Scotland, and the Methodist Church in Scotland.

42 *Irvine*

In both the White Paper on Central Scotland—a Programme for Development and Growth (1963)—and in that which followed on The Scottish Economy 1965–70 (1965), the Irvine region in Ayrshire was regarded as one of growth because of the increase there in recent years of industry and population. In the White Paper of 1963 it was stated that there was considerable scope for further development, and the possibility of a new town here was mentioned. In January 1965 Sir Hugh Wilson and Lewis Womersley, planning consultants, were asked by the Secretary of State for Scotland to prepare 'a report and plan for the area of possible expansion lying to the east of and including the Burghs of Irvine and Kilwinning', which 'should provide for an expansion of population of the order of 55 000'. As the Government wished to make a decision as early as possible, an interim report was requested indicating the proposed land-uses and defining an area of possible designation. This was submitted in May 1965, and was circulated to local authorities concerned. A Draft New Town (Irvine) Designation Order was made in 1966 which covered an area of 13 700 acres (5547 ha). After the inquiry the area was slightly reduced to 12 400 acres (5020 ha) and the confirmation designating the site was made on 9 November 1966. The planning consultants meanwhile continued with their work and their final proposals, which amounted to a master plan, were published in June 1967.

The procedure is interesting as marking a break (for the first time, we believe) with that which obtained for earlier new towns. Formerly a site was selected, a draft designation order was made, objections were heard at an inquiry, and the confirmation was made designating a site with any modifications arising from the inquiry. A development corporation was then appointed who commissioned planning consultants to prepare a master plan for the site given to them. In the procedure at Irvine, the planning consultants were called in at the very beginning to conceive a plan in outline and to define the site in the selected area, and then, after it is designated, continue the project to completion as a master plan.

The situation of the site is excellent for a new town. It extends from a little north of Kilwinning, which it includes, almost to Troon in the south, about $7\frac{1}{2}$ miles (12 km). North of Troon the site extends along the coast for about $3\frac{1}{2}$ miles (6 km) to the mouth of the River Garnock, and from that point eastwards it is about $4\frac{1}{2}$ miles (7 km) wide. It is the largest new town site in Scotland, is fairly flat, and is protected by hills to the north and south. The Royal Burgh of Irvine, separated from the sea by the river mouth and the old harbour, is a little west of centre. From the old Burgh it is about 24 miles (38 km) to the centre of Glasgow in the north-east, 7 miles (11 km) to Kilmarnock in the east, and 9 miles (14 km) due south to Prestwick airport a little beyond the attractive seaside resort of Troon. Ayr lies 2 miles (3 km) beyond Prestwick. There are excellent road and rail communications linking Irvine with surrounding towns. The A78 trunk road runs north–south through Irvine, but this has been re-routed to form a by-pass of the town. A main railway line from Stranraer runs through the site which is joined by a line from Largs in the north at Kilwinning. Three rivers flow through the site, the Garnock in the north-west, the River Annick which winds from the east, and the River Irvine which winds a little further south and joins the Annick a little before it reaches Irvine, and then flows into the wide and marshy Garnock just before it reaches the sea.

Two outline master plans have been produced; the first, already mentioned, by Wilson and Womersley, and the second a revised plan by the Irvine Development Corporation published in January 1971. There are certain important differences in the two plans and for the benefit of students of planning both are illustrated and described.

First Outline Plan

The population of the area at the time of designation was calculated as about 29 000, of which 19 000 were in the Burgh of Irvine, about 8000 in Kilwinning, and the remainder in the villages. On these calculations an intake of about 55 000 would have meant, with some allowance for natural increase, a town of about 90 000. But subsequent investigation found that in 1966 the population was about 34 600 so that it would be necessary to add about 5000 to these figures.

The plan was based on a linear principle of a string of neighbourhoods which runs along the eastern, less developed, part of the site. It is referred to in the plan as a 'necklace, the beads of varying shapes and sizes representing the units of development and the string the public transport system'. The likeness of this description to the basic concept of Redditch by the same consultants will be at once apparent. The difference between the concept for Redditch and that of Irvine, however, is that in the former, the string or necklace makes a figure of 8; in the plan for Irvine the string is unconnected at both ends in the north-west and the south-east, and more beads could be placed on these loose ends if need for expansion in the future arose. A further difference was that the string or communications spine in the Redditch Plan was mainly for public transport (buses), parts being exclusively so; in the Irvine plan it was a multi-purpose route of a certain width developing with the growth of the town. It started with public and private transport together, then another carriageway was to be opened on the route, one exclusively for public transport, and the other for private which, however, permitted the alternative of mixing them in one-way routes. A third development was to be 3 lanes, the centre one for public transport and the outer ones for one-way private transport.

The major stops on this communications spine formed the centres of the residential districts—the beads of various shapes and sizes. These were to be encircled by district distributor roads, from which local distributor roads would branch into the residential areas. They would also be linked with 2 car parks near the centre. A system of footpaths radiate from this centre and also ran along on either side of the transport spine. Grouped round the centre were shops, a pub, church, community and health centres, and library. Primary schools were located in the housing areas, and secondary schools, some 7, were located at various points along the transport spine. There appeared to be 8 residential districts, which would thus have been in the region of

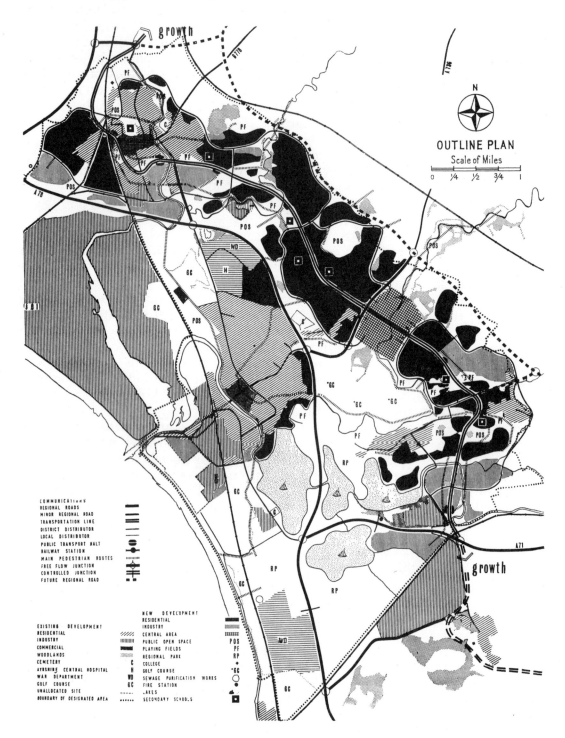

Figure 42.1 Irvine, the first outline plan.

8–10 000 each. Although the old town of Irvine was somewhat outside this development, it involved Kilwinning. Maximum segregation of vehicles and pedestrians was the aim in the residential areas.

The net housing densities were to be from 25 persons (7.6 houses) to 75 persons (21.4 houses) to the acre (62 to 185 persons and 18.7 to 52.8 houses per ha), with the higher densities towards the centres, and the lower towards the fringes. Three kinds of shopping facilities were proposed: corner shops spread in the housing areas, each to serve some 400 families; district shopping centres, and shopping in the central area. Shopping provision of the second kind was to vary according to size and situation of each district, but it was the aim to have more than just a single firm in each trade in each centre. This would not only increase the choice open to the housewife and ensure competition but would also have tended to attract a greater volume of custom than if each trade were represented by only one shop.

The medieval Burgh of Irvine was granted a charter in the thirteenth century by Alexander II and this was confirmed by Robert Bruce. With its harbour it became an important port, for a time the third in Scotland, but now the harbour is comparatively little used. The present burgh was largely built up in the nineteenth century, and some of its better architecture has a classical and Georgian character belonging to the early part of that century. Its situation on undulating ground on the River Irvine, a little east of where the river makes a horseshoe bend, gives it a picturesque character. The planners may have debated whether to make this the centre of the new town, but whether they did or not, they wisely decided to make the burgh a residential district, and preserve much of its character, and place a new centre a little east of it as the largest bead on the string.

So as to preserve the character of the old burgh as much as possible, a few streets and roads were to be changed to pedestrian ways. For example, the High Street running east–west crosses the main road running north–south, and it was proposed to change the west section of the former into a pedestrian way that continued across the river by the railway station and on to the harbour. Other pedestrian ways were planned, one along the river, while some re-arrangement was to be made of the roads.

The site of the town centre was to be about $1\frac{1}{2}$ miles (2 km) east from that of the old town. It was an area of some 220 acres (89 ha) situated in the shallow valley of the River Annick, with woodland areas to the north-east and south-west, both of which, if developed and extended, would be of considerable amenity value and act as breaks to the cold winds. The banks of the river rise in parts a little above the surrounding levels and afford fairly extensive views, which offer features for attractive development. The centre, as planned, was of a multi-storey character somewhat on the lines of that at Cumbernauld, although with better promise in a more protected situation.

The communications spine with the public transport service crossed the centre of the site. Access by private cars was by a one-way system and it was the aim to segregate the various classes of vehicle in the use of the centre: public transport setting down passengers at 3 stops; private cars moving to parking areas; and service and goods vehicles moving to unloading bays. One valuable point was made about parking areas; in siting and arranging them 'it is important that the cars should not be allowed to dominate the centre visually—the pedestrian approach should not be through a vast sea of parked cars, as in the American regional centres'.

The distribution of open space depended partly on needs and partly on the natural features of the site. A large proportion of the 12 440 acres (5034 ha)—some 4360 acres

(1764 ha)—was devoted to open spaces, partly because much is unsuitable for building, partly because the attractive natural features near the coast, properly developed, would contribute to making a regional recreational centre. The principal open space was the regional park, of some 2840 acres (1150 ha), which extended southwards for almost 3 miles (5 km) to the southern tip of the site not far from Troon, and along the $3\frac{1}{2}$ miles (6 km) of coast. There was provision for a good deal of afforestation, partly for wind minimization. At the northern end was to be a large golf course, and there were other golf courses at the southern tip and along the coast. Flowing through the park were the two rivers Annick and Irvine, both of which occasionally flood the surrounding ground. From these rivers 4 lakes were to be created to provide water sports, and there was provision for a yacht club. Playing fields, picnic areas, equestrian sports, and a zoological garden were among the other facilities. Parks and playing fields were spread generously in the other districts of the town, and there was to be a further golf course between the old towns of Irvine and Kilwinning.

This was a very interesting and ingenious plan, with numerous attractive features. It prompts one important doubt: there was no real limitation of size. Although planned for 90 000, made up of the existing 29 000 plus an intake of 55 000 with 6000 for natural growth, it was a linearly planned town with beads on a string, with loose ends north and south to take more beads if necessary. It might have been a long time before the question of other beads arose, but planners must look well ahead. In Scotland, however, where population is nearly stationary or now declining, the danger is not so great, yet if Irvine proved to be as successful as East Kilbride, as it might well be, one could have seen the additional beads linking in the north with Stevenston, Saltcoats, Ardrossan, and on to West Kilbride, and in the south to Dundonald, Symington, and on to Prestwick and Ayr. To which might be replied: 'And why not?' Exactly, except that by such a process it ceases to be a town, a definite community, and becomes instead an urban sprawl over the country. It is very important to complete the analogy of the necklace and link the ends.

Revised Outline Plan

The Irvine Development Corporation was appointed in June 1967, after the planning proposals by Wilson and Womersley had been completed. The corporation was briefed on these, but was free to change the Wilson Plan (as it is referred to in the new plan) if necessary. The corporation found very substantial changes necessary, due partly to changed circumstances and partly to different conceptions of what was the best plan.

In giving further study to the site the planning team of the development corporation realized that more thorough and extensive surveys would be necessary because it was discovered that mining subsidence was more widespread than was at first thought, while it was necessary to relate the proposals to the plans being formulated for land use, road patterns and drainage in the sub-region as a whole. Although the necessary studies were vigorously pursued, it became apparent that the production of a plan based on a thorough and comprehensive survey in a limited time was beyond the capacity of the planning staff. The corporation therefore re-engaged the consultants, Sir Hugh Wilson and Lewis Womersley, to assist in the survey and production of a revised plan, and also to utilize computer techniques developed by Professor Ben-Shachar and Dr Adam Mazor of the Israeli Institute of Urban Studies for cost benefit analyses and other calculations—the first time these techniques had been used in Britain.

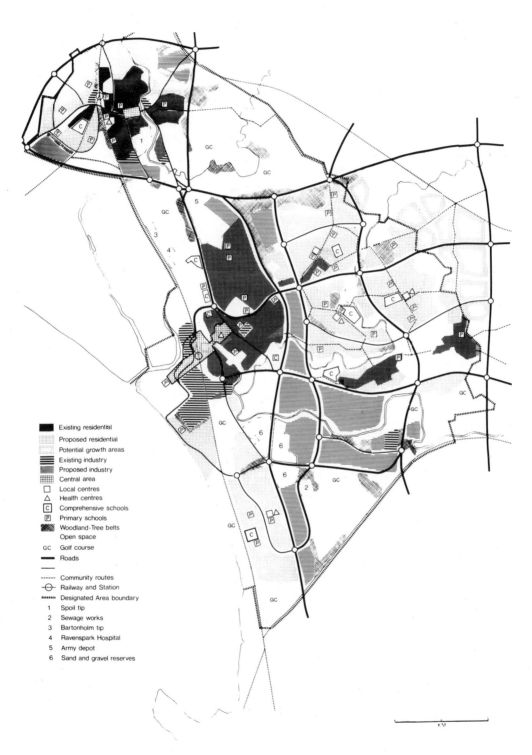

■	Existing residential
	Proposed residential
	Potential growth areas
	Existing industry
	Proposed industry
	Central area
□	Local centres
△	Health centres
C	Comprehensive schools
P	Primary schools
	Woodland-Tree belts
	Open space
GC	Golf course
▬	Roads
----	Community routes
-○-	Railway and Station
▪▪▪▪	Designated Area boundary
1	Spoil tip
2	Sewage works
3	Bartonholm tip
4	Ravenspark Hospital
5	Army depot
6	Sand and gravel reserves

Figure 42.2 Revised outline plan.

Since the original Wilson Plan was published, 2 regional plans for the area were prepared. One was a report by the Clyde Estuary Development Group and the Metra Organization Survey (1969) which recommended a deep water port, iron ore terminal, oil terminal, steel manufacturing complex and oil refinery at Hunterston 10 miles (16 km) north of the area of the new town. Another was a sub-regional plan by the Ayrshire Land–Needs Working Party, published in September 1968, which proposed the expansion of Kilmarnock westwards towards Irvine and of the new town eastwards towards Kilmarnock. Further reference will be made to the proposal.

Seven alternative outline plans were produced by the planning team of the corporation in collaboration with the 2 consultants and one was chosen for further detailing and refinements, and this was published in September 1969. A few amendments were subsequently made and the substantive Irvine New Town Plan was ultimately published in January 1971.

The first outline plan of June 1967 prepared for an intake of about 55 000 which, with the then estimated population of 29 000 meant an increase to 84 000, resulting with natural increase in a town of 90 000. As mentioned, subsequent investigation showed the population in 1966 to be 34 600. In the new plan the proposed maximum population is increased to about 120 000, with a further possible growth to 140 000. With the proposals in the sub-regional plan of the Ayrshire Land–Needs Working Party of an urban expansion of Irvine and Kilmarnock towards each other, a population for the whole area is envisaged as 200 000. This really means a continuous urban area or new town of that size. It is referred to in the plan as a possible city region, and it is stated that there would not be a continuous urban development because of the separation of the river valleys and of the provision of a site for the proposed university about halfway between Kilmarnock and Irvine. It is doubtful, however, if these separations are enough to prevent this continuous urban development, and judging by the regional plan illustrated there is no clear separation of even a kilometre between Irvine and Kilmarnock.

These optimistic regional proposals were based on the planned and hoped-for industrial expansion and of a continued immigration of population to the area. 'The additional people', it is stated, 'would have to come mainly from a redistribution of people within Scotland, partly from natural growth, and immigration from other more crowded areas of Britain, and also, it is hoped, from the attraction back into Scotland of some of the many Scots who have emigrated because of lack of opportunity.' Unfortunately, the emigration from Scotland continues and population is still almost stationary. (The population of Scotland rose from 5 096 415 in 1951 to only 5 179 344 in 1961 and to only 5 227 706 in 1971 and declined to 5 206 200 in 1975 which represents a migration from Scotland during the 24 years of about 365 000).

The first Wilson Plan was based on the linear principle of a string of neighbourhoods along the eastern, less developed part of the site, referred to as a necklace, the beads being the units of development and the string the public transport system. It is similar in conception to the plans for Runcorn and Redditch, except that these make a figure of 8, whereas at Irvine the string is loose at both ends in the north and south so that additional units could be added. The concept of community routes adopted in the new plan is similar perhaps in principle to the transport system of the first Wilson plan, but very different in application. The community routes are planned to utilize existing roads and lanes as public transport routes. Initially these routes will be multi-purpose, but they are ultimately designed for public transport only. There is also a distributor road pattern consisting of a grid of 3 north–south and 4 east–west routes. These are additional to the regional roads—the north–south A78, now constructed, which runs across the western part of the site, and the east–west A71 from the old town of Irvine to Kilmarnock. There is a fairly complete system of pedestrian ways. The industrial areas are distributed throughout the town. There is a main strip running north–south through the centre of the town, with other small areas to the south–east and north–west.

The community routes provide the basis of the plan. Small residential units each of about 89 acres (36 ha) with 1100 dwellings (about 3850 persons) are planned around nodes or small centres on a community route. No house will be more than $\frac{1}{3}$ mile (0.5 km) 5 to 7 minutes' walk away from such a centre. Each centre is planned to have a general shop and primary school, which is a determining factor in the size of the residential unit. There is a series of shopping centres and comprehensive schools conveniently distributed throughout the town in relation to the residential units. The main centre is an extension of the old town of Irvine, westward towards the southern shore of the Carnock and Irvine estuaries. It is planned for a series of functions, and reading from east to west first there is the centre of the existing town, then in succession the new shopping centre, a residential area, a commercial area for offices, the civic centre, and lastly a recreational area near the sea. Just west of the new shopping centre is the railway station. The plan provides for the creation, ultimately, of a comprehensive linear centre from the existing burgh centre to these, thus integrating the old town centre with the new town.

The design and placing of this centre indicates one of the fundamental differences from the first Wilson plan where the main centre was placed $1\frac{1}{2}$ miles (2 km) east from the old town in the shallow valley of the River Annick, as the major point on the communications spine. The consultants debated whether to make the old town of Irvine the basis of a new centre or whether to locate a new centre in the area of major new development. They chose to adopt the latter plan and preserve much of the character of the old town centre, converting a few streets into pedestrian ways.

The authors of the new plan have been influenced in the location of the centre by the prospects of Irvine becoming an important tourist and recreational centre, and much of the plan includes provision for sport and recreation of various kinds. Additional facilities are planned for sailing, fishing, and swimming, there is a generous provision for golf courses, and several new parks are proposed, while a plan for a conference centre a little south of the main centre is included. From the standpoint of a tourist and recreation centre there are, of course, advantages in having the centre on the western edge of the town, near the sea. But from the standpoint of established residents there are distinct advantages of its proposed location in the first Wilson Plan. However, in the new plan people living near the eastern boundary in Springside will be 5 miles (8 km) from the town centre which is a serious disadvantage.

In the revised plan the open space system is based on the river valleys which will form linear parks separating major built-up areas. Eventually they will form a continuous parkway between the peripheral rural lands, the open spaces within urban areas and the central area and foreshore. Six new golf courses are proposed in addition to the four existing.

The respective merits of the Wilson Plan and the new plan prepared by the Irvine Development Corporation in association with the first consultants, necessarily depend on an evaluation of the economic, social and aesthetic aspects, which must be to some extent subjective. From the standpoint of the people living there the first Wilson Plan has more to be said for it, especially if one could eradicate the loose ends of the necklace, pull them round to the west and tie them. The new plan has possibly more economic advantages. It prompts one serious doubt however although this may have been overtaken by the newly emerging regional policies outlined below. In the acquiescence in the regional proposals of future urban expansion of Irvine eastwards and Kilmarnock westwards, the long-term prospect seemed to be a continuous urban mass uniting the 2 with the main centres at either end. Would it not be better to keep Irvine and Kilmarnock as two distinct and separate towns with open country at least 2 miles (3 km) wide between them? Each would then be a distinct entity small enough (about 100 000) to preserve a sense of its own community life, but with related facilities, as in a city region or town cluster, with each town having its own green belt as part of its structure.

Regional Report

Following local government reorganization in 1975, Irvine new town became a part of the Strathclyde Region. The regional council were required by the Secretary of State to prepare a structure plan covering the region and as a first step towards this produced a regional report in 1976. This paints a very different picture from that which was produced by the Ayrshire Land Needs Working Party in 1968. Instead of the prospect of unlimited growth, a decline is seen across the region with particular emphasis being placed upon the loss of population and employment from the central conurbation. The report identifies two key issues, the need to concentrate resources in areas of urban deprivation and the need to combat loss of jobs and high unemployment. The regional council affirm the role of the new towns of Strathclyde (with the exception of Stonehouse), but at a reduced rate consistent with the creation of new jobs and local housing needs. The Secretary of State, in response to the regional report, confirmed his commitment to see Irvine developed to its planned capacity (120 000), but at a rate consistent with the provision of new jobs. The precise effects of these policies have still to be determined, but they will certainly result in an extension of the period of development and will probably see an abandonment of the eventual extension of Irvine eastwards towards Kilmarnock.

Building the Town

The necessity of making further surveys after the publication of the first general plan, and producing a revised outline plan, meant that there would be some inevitable delays in proceeding with the actual work of site clearance and building. The development corporation was anxious to proceed with building as quickly as possible, especially as local authorities in the area and private developers were already building houses, and any restrictions on their activities caused by waiting for the finally adopted plan was not likely to foster good working relations between the 3. By the end of 1968, although the development corporation had not built any houses since the town was designated, local authorities had built about 500 and private developers about 350.

The development corporation therefore selected areas where development could proceed without placing unacceptable constraints on the preparation of the revised outline plan. The first of these for housing was the area of Pennyburn, immediately south-west of Kilwinning, where about 1200 houses were scheduled to be provided by 1977. North-west of this development area, Whitehirst Park, was allocated for private housing where 700 houses were completed in 1977.

Subsequent to the Kilwinning developments, housing estates were developed at Dreghorn, about 2 miles (3 km) due east of the town centre, and at Bourtreehill which is immediately to the north of Dreghorn. A total of 580 houses was built at Dreghorn, 370 for rent and 210 by private developers. By the beginning of 1977, 1460 rental houses had been built in Bourtreehill and two private schemes were due to start. The next area to be developed is Girdle Toll to the north of Bourtreehill. One private scheme was underway in the early part of 1977 and two rental housing contracts were due to start later the same year. Further housing areas to be developed are Lawthorn, to the north of Girdle Toll; Muirhouses, which is to the east of Bourtreehill; and Gailes, which is about two miles (3 km) due south of the centre.

By the end of 1969, the development corporation had completed 290 houses all in Pennyburn, while private developers had built 575. Owing to various difficulties, housing output by the development corporation continued at a low level with annual completions of about 200, with private developers building at an average rate of 180 houses a year. From 1974 to 1977, development corporation completions averaged 690 a year and private developers 170 a year. By early 1977, the development corporation had built 3100 houses for rent and private developers had completed 1200 houses on corporation land.

The first phase of the town centre was opened towards the end of 1975 and the sports and leisure centre was opened in 1976.

The first stage of the restoration and conversion of Trinity Church, which stands immediately adjacent to the new shopping centre, into accommodation for community activities, was almost complete by the beginning of 1977. The conversion, which has been directed by a special Trust formed for the purpose, has been aided by significant grants from the Historic Building Council for Scotland.

Housing and Residential Areas

The first substantial residential district to be completed was Pennyburn, and one of the housing layouts (Pennyburn 1) is illustrated in Figure 42.3 which gives an impression of the corporation's early housing. It occupies a roughly triangular site bounded on the south and north-west by main roads and on the east by the railway from Stranraer to Glasgow, while a branch line runs through its centre. In the south-west of the site is the West Byrehill Industrial Estate, to the south-east are playing fields, and in the north towards the apex of the triangle is some existing housing and a secondary school. The neighbourhood is planned for a population of about 4000. The first 2 sections of the new residential area are west of the branch railway line, and the third and fourth are east of it with the centre between them and a primary school adjacent.

The site of Pennyburn 1 and 2 is a square divided into 16 squares with internal courts on to which the terrace houses face. The courts have lawns, trees and children's play spaces with boulders and log fencing, and there is a network of footpaths throughout the whole layout and within each court, which also has a service road access (but no through road) for vehicles. Garages and parking are at one corner of the squares near the service way entrance so that parking does not intrude into the court area.

The terrace housing is very attractive, some is level, some on sloping ground in

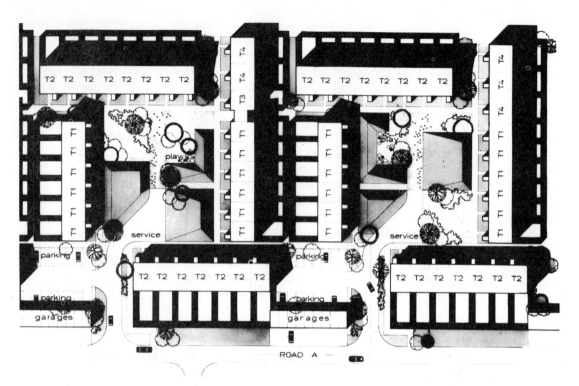

Figure 42.3 Pennyburn I housing layout—2 typical squares.

Figure 42.4 Housing—Pennyburn.

stepped sequence, and much of it is with mono-pitched roofs. The houses are built of no-fines concrete which has good thermal insulating properties. The façades have a strong effective black and white finish, in some cases the dark boarding forming a long wide band for the upper part and white roughcast walls for the lower part, in other cases the wide dark bands of boarding are repeated between the ground and first floor windows, while white boarding faces the ground floor and the entrance porches. For general scenic and architectural effect Pennyburn must rank high among residential areas in new towns.

Pennyburn 3, which was completed early in 1976, consists of approximately 700 houses, with similar external finishes to those used on Pennyburn 1 and 2. It has a wider range of house types, however, including flats and patio housing together with a small group of cottages for the elderly completed early in 1977.

Housing layout design since Pennyburn has undergone some radical changes. It was recognized that in achieving a significant level of segregation of pedestrians and vehicles certain problems arose. This form of development is relatively uneconomic in the use of land and depends upon the pedestrian conforming to the design. It may also require dual-aspect housing, with subsequent loss of privacy.

Layout design in Broomlands and Bourtreehill has been based upon the use of pedestrian and vehicular mixed roads in the immediate area of the houses. The concept acknowledges that in the residential area the pedestrian and the vehicles will inevitably meet, but places the interests of the pedestrian and the dweller before those of the vehicle. At the same time, it demands that adequate provision must be made for the penetration and off-street parking of vehicles within the area. Thus in these areas residential culs-de-sac have been built with groups of 25 or 30 houses (and up to 60 dwellings in later designs) to produce an environment which immediately imposes itself upon the motorist making him conscious of the fact that he intrudes.

Bourtreehill 1 was the first area to be designed using this mix basis and later layouts have been influenced to various degrees. The early designs for Bourtreehill sought to achieve maximum penetration for the private vehicle only, into a car court leading from and beyond the turning circle which limited the penetration of the larger service and commercial vehicles. In the designs for Girdle Toll, which is the next area to be developed after Bourtree hill, a lower ultimate parking standard has been catered for than that used in earlier developments (100% instead of 125%). This has been interpreted to mean a restriction in penetration by the private vehicle. The design for Girdle Toll 3 consists of dwellings grouped around courts with the vehicle excluded from the furthest courtyard and layby parking in other courts. As the road penetrates into the housing courts its effect is reduced by the narrowing of the road.

Local Centres

The local centre of Pennyburn is roughly in the centre of the site and is reached from Pennyburn 1 and 2 by a footbridge over the railway. The centre consists of a mini-Market, two shops, a pub and a primary school, and close by a number of elderly persons' cottages. Cranberrymoss Community Centre was opened in 1976, having been converted from a farmhouse and outbuildings. This provides a large function room, committee rooms, play rooms and craft rooms. It is managed by the local authority, but day to day running is by the residents' community association.

A village centre at Bourtreehill is due to be completed at the beginning of 1978. This

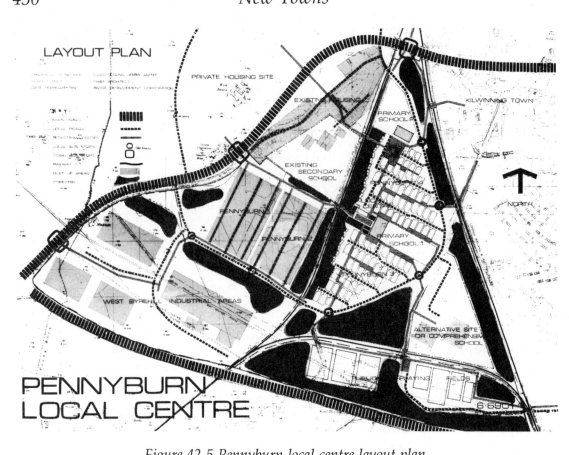

Figure 42.5 Pennyburn local centre layout plan.

consists of a supermarket, twelve shops, a public house, a cafe, a baker, offices, and twenty-four flats. The design for the village centre won an Architectural Design Project Award in 1974. Adjacent to the centre are two churches, Church of Scotland and Roman Catholic, a health centre, and a community centre, which is also to be converted from a farmhouse and outbuildings.

Also within Bourtreehill are two local centres. The first in Bourtreehill 2 was completed in March 1977 and consists of three shops and one public house. The other in Bourtreehill 6 is due for completion in November 1977.

All three centres in Bourtreehill are located adjacent to bus-only community routes, that passing the centre in Bourtreehill 6 having been in operation since 1976.

Town Centre

Phase 1 of the town centre complex, completed in 1975, was developed jointly between Irvine Development Corporation and Ravenseft Properties Limited. The broad provisions of the centre were indicated in the description of the revised outline plan and some idea of the form can be seen from the illustration.

The first phase extends from the old town across the river towards the railway

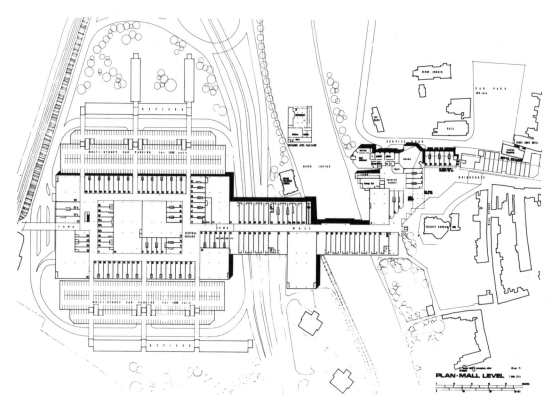

Figure 42.6 Plan of town centre.

station. The second phase will extend to the railway station and it is hoped that it will incorporate a bus station.

The enclosed, 8 m wide, pedestrian mall runs from street level across the river and continues at the same level towards the station, thus forming the main spine of the complex. Servicing by vehicles is at lower level under the mail and shop units, and mechanical services are carried in large ribbed metal box roof ducts running outwards from the main spine duct above the mall.

A multi-storey car park has been provided to the south of the shopping centre with direct pedestrian links to the shops at mall level. Other similar car parks are proposed.

Naturally lighting has been provided to the main pedestrian areas at clear storey level but full advantage has been taken of the view from the River Bridge section north towards the Low Green.

The first phase also includes a spacious, semi-enclosed square suitable for exhibitions or audio-visual presentations.

Two multi-storey office blocks complete the facilities provided under phase 1. One block stands to the north, running parallel to the shopping complex, and the other is built above the main entrance to the shopping centre, enclosing the Bridgegate forecourt. The larger block at Northern Friars Croft is now occupied by the local District Council.

Industrial Areas

The major industrial areas run in a north–south axis contained between the recently completed Irvine Bypass and the north–south distributor road.

The first estates to be opened up by the corporation were at West Byrehill and Nethermains, south and west of Kilwinning. Development has since taken place at North and South Newmoor, Oldhall, Shewalton and Meadowhead Indistrual Estates.

Two basic advance factory types have been evolved by the corporation, one for larger users preferring detached premises, and one for small users from 3200 sq. feet (288 m²) upwards. Each type can be sub-divided to suit demand. The corporation also constructs purpose built premises for known industrialists or leases land from development by the industrialists.

The small advance factory units have been contained in 'super blocks'. Where possible, each pair of 'super blocks' has been positioned to form an enclosed courtyard to contain yard areas, expansion space and parking, with office and canteen facilities looking outwards towards the access roads and site perimeters. Mounding and tree planting has been used about the larger blocks to screen yards and parking with limited use of screen walling.

The development corporation has rendered a service by being able to attract, by 1977, 59 new manufacturing firms to Irvine against a background of rising unemployment in the area. This industrial intake meant the provision of about 2000 new industrial jobs and, as many of these firms hope to expand, there is promise of further industrial employment here in the following few years. At the same time the constructional work of the new town provides considerable employment.

From designation to 1977 the development corporation had completed almost 858 000 sq. feet (80 000 m²) of advanced factory space for rent. In addition, 756 000 sq. feet (70 000 m²) of factory space had been built privately on development corporation land, and a further 929 000 sq. feet (86 000 m²) had been built within the new town on land in other ownership during the same period.

Architectural Distinction

One of the most notable aspects of the new development is the architectural distinctiveness, particularly the work of the development corporation. Admiration was expressed for the appearance of the houses at Pennyburn and a similar scheme at Dreghorn was commended by the Saltire Society in 1972. Interest has been shown on the new housing areas completed at Bourtreehill particularly the integration of vehicular/pedestrian traffic, the bold use of colour and the generous provision of soft landscaping. Both advance factory designs mentioned earlier have received recognition. The smaller block, as provided at Nethermains, gained a Civic Trust Commendation in 1972 and the larger block, as provided at Oldhall, gained a Financial Times Commendation in 1976.

The shopping centre complex and leisure centre completed in 1976 have also attracted wide international interest.

43 *Changes in Planning New Towns*

Thirty-one years have passed since the first new town was designated on 11 November 1946, and in that period 29 new towns have been designated and one de-designated under the New Towns Acts and planned and built by development corporations in Great Britain; while a few more, such as Cramlington and Killingworth, have been developed by other means. Most of the new towns belong either to the first or second periods; the gap of 11 years between is occupied by the solitary designation of Cumbernauld in 1955 (43.1). With changed circumstances and the evolution of planning thought it is inevitable that a few significant changes should have occurred in the physical planning of new towns. These have been noted in the preceding chapters, but a summary and selective emphasis may be useful.

The tendency towards larger new towns has been noted in Chapter 6 (p. 58). The first group (1946–50) was influenced by Abercrombie's indication of about 60 000, but several of these were gradually increased in size and 80 000 to 110 000 became target figures. Later new towns designated between 1961 and 1966 were planned with similar maximum populations. The still later group of five, designated from 1967 to 1970, were much larger with maxima in the region of 200 000 to 250 000 on the scale of small cities as some of them are called. Four of these, in the opinion of many planners, are really town expansions where the addition is about the size of the existing town.

Neighbourhood planning has shown numerous variations, but in principle has been consistently followed with but few exceptions. In the first group some towns (Stevenage, Basildon) have large neighbourhoods of 10 000 to 15 000, occasionally even larger, while others (Crawley, Bracknell, Cwmbran) have small neighbourhoods of 4 000 to 8 000. Significantly in the revised plan of Basildon of 1967 a change was made to small neighbourhoods. In Cumbernauld neighbourhood planning was abandoned, but in the second group of towns, designated between 1961 and 1966, it was again followed, although planners seemed anxious to give it other names like village, residential community, district or area, which are for the most part small, between 4000 and 8000.

One of the principal changes that appeared in planning later new towns has been towards a much greater segregation of pedestrians and vehicular traffic, which is a very big step forward in physical planning. This segregation can be seen in the town centres and neighbourhood centres and in the residential areas. Many of the later new towns have complete systems of pedestrian ways independent of, yet related to, the road systems. In towns of the first period, like Corby, Bracknell and East Kilbride, the town centres were first planned and partly built with the traditional wide through road forming the high street with shops on either side, or through streets were adjacent to the central squares as at Crawley and Harlow. The intermediate town of Cumbernauld was a herald in many ways of town centre planning and of traffic segregation in later towns.

In the towns of the second period each new centre is automatically a pedestrian area encircled by a ring road, from which there are service branch roads to the rear of shops. The first centre to be completely pedestrian was that of Stevenage of the first period, but this was late in coming and was not planned and built until 1960–63, later than the centres of other towns with through roads. Those at Corby, Bracknell and East Kilbride although originally built with main high streets in the old way, have since been converted to pedestrian precincts, while the through roads by the central squares at Harlow and Crawley have been closed to traffic paved over and converted to pedestrian areas. With the town centres of the second period there is a tendency, following the example of Cumbernauld, to make the centres like a vast departmental store. One of the best examples is that at Runcorn where the shopping is on the first floor of a large air-conditioned building, with service access on the ground floor, multi-storey car parks surrounding it and bus stations adjacent (described in Chapter 31). This is a long way from the original town centre of Corby with its traditional wide shopping high street (Corporation Street). In the proposed centre at Milton Keynes, with its wide boulevards, there appears to be some return to older rather *beaux-arts* formal conceptions.

In planning the neighbourhood of the early new towns the road pattern was a major consideration. Houses were variously placed in relation to it; although they were not all aligned along the roads, as in the traditional way, but were variously related to them with varied spaces between the houses and roads and with a generous use of the cul-de-sac. But often roads went through neighbourhoods (see plans for Stevenage, Crawley, Harlow, Peterlee and others), and footpaths sometimes linked culs-de-sac with roads, but there was no footpath system independent of the road system. Too often there was inadequate provision for the footpath crossing of major roads in the urban areas, and in some cases this amounted to serious negligence on the part of the responsible authorities.

With towns of the second period, the residential neighbourhoods are often planned as pedestrian precincts. A neighbourhood is encircled by a distributor road from which roads branch, all culs-de-sac, conveniently related to the houses round which garages are grouped. There is no through road. There is generally a spine footpath on to which the neighbourhood centre faces (with rear road access to the shops), and there are branch footpaths among the houses, some of which open to squares with seats and some accommodate children's playgrounds. This footpath system within each neighbourhood links with others by means of underpasses or overpasses across the distributor roads, so that the whole town has a complete and independent footpath system. Most of the towns of the second period, from Skelmersdale onwards, provide examples of this with many variations on the theme, and examples can be found in some of the later extensions of the new towns, such as the neighbourhood of Wildriding at Bracknell built in 1967–70. This complete footpath system within each town gives a feeling of safety and consequently of repose which is valuable. The only disadvantage of pedestrian precinct planning in residential neighbourhoods is that it tempts planning at higher densities, and some examples show rather close building. A good degree of space is a necessity for a feeling of well-being and too close building may defeat this.

Courtyard planning was introduced more extensively with the development towards more pedestrian areas. This is variously successful. Houses either face inwards towards the courtyard or outwards with rear gardens or patios towards the courtyard. In both the courtyard is often used for several purposes (sometimes called 'mixer courts') such as a garden, children's playground and car parking, but it is doubtful whether the mixing will prove permanently attractive, especially in the type where the car parking is prominent.

One of the best examples of courtyard planning is in Pennyburn at Irvine where terrace houses face inwards and the courtyards have lawns, trees, children's playgrounds with service road access. Car parking is kept to a corner of the square near the access road, and is not visually obtrusive. Pleasantly intimate is the series of small paved courts with houses facing inwards at Laindon in Basildon, which give quiet and seclusion. This is congenial and attractive provided the temptation to high densities is resisted. Space is a very valuable asset.

When the early neighbourhoods of the towns of the first period were planned, a garage was provided for every 5 to 3 houses, because the extent of car ownership was not foreseen in the early fifties. As car ownership gradually increased more garages were provided, and one garage per house became common in many of the towns of the second period. In some cases car-ports are provided by the houses, that is with a roof and one wall, and sometimes in addition to garages hard-standing for additional cars. In several towns the ratio is much less than one garage per house, but car parking spaces makes up the balance to about $1\frac{1}{4}$ or $1\frac{1}{2}$ spaces per house. This is done for reasons of economy but it is regrettable because a large number of parked cars in residential areas is ugly. That is one of the consequences of an inadequacy of garages in the towns of the first period, and residential roads are lined with cars, while central areas have large open car parks.

At Cwmbran, however, the centre is surrounded by well designed multi-storey car parks and the effect is better than open car parks. Underground car parks are still better, as at the new town of North-West Frankfurt, and most economical in the long run as the surface area permits buildings and other developments. Yet many of the centres of later new towns are surrounded by open car parks which will certainly interfere with any pleasing appearance the centres may otherwise have.

Many criticisms have been made of the prominence given to the private car in plans for the new towns in the second period. Ray Thomas, for example, criticized the master plan for Milton Keynes which, he says, is based too much on the assumption of universal car ownership, with its scatter of housing and jobs tied to a grid of highways. He argues for a better public transport system so that at least half of the houses are so located that people need not own cars for daily needs. An example of what could be regarded as an unnecessary and wasteful provision of space is the extension to Newton Aycliffe. Roads were planned to the industrial estate on the assumption that a large number of workers will travel by car, which means not only more extensive provision of road space but of space for car parking round the factories, whereas if they went by buses the number of vehicles required would be about one twentieth, with a great economy of space round the factories (see calculation in Chapter 26). The experiment at Stevenage where transport from one part of the town to the industrial area was changed from private cars to buses, rather than incur the expense of road widening and extensions to accommodate the former, should be widely followed.

A regrettable circumstance of new towns during the fifties was the very poor provision of public transport, and although there were too few garages in residential areas, much of the other p' .nning was on the assumption that a large number of families owned cars. In the seventies it would be a generous estimate that two thirds of the families in new towns owned cars, with perhaps 10% owning two cars. In the former case how are the cars used? With many, as everybody knows, the man takes his car to work, either factory or office, and his wife goes shopping by public transport, returning generally with a heavily loaded basket. Yet in the fifties and sixties public transport in the new towns was very inadequate, Stevenage and Crawley being conspicuous examples. People without cars found it difficult to join in the social activities of the town and could not attend meetings of voluntary societies because of the lack of public transport. If people were making the pioneering effort of living in a half built town they should be supported in that effort by a good subsidized public transport system. Many of the development corporations realized this and would have liked a better public transport system. Under Section 21 (2) of the New Towns Act 1946, a development corporation could be 'authorized by means of an order made by the Minister of Transport to operate trolley vehicle services for the purposes of a new town', but no development corporation, as far as we are aware, took advantage of this provision. Yet it would have helped early settlers in new towns considerably.

In addition rail services could have been developed for the benefit of new towns, but policy seems to have been the reverse of this. There is the legend that when it is decided to build a new town on a branch or loop railway line it is time to close the line. Although a joke there is some truth in it. Shortly after the new town of Telford was designated much of the excellent rail network on the site was scrapped; and it is a common experience that lines running near or through the site of a new town are closed, or used only for freight. When Corby was being built, Corby station on the loop line from Kettering was closed, and when Crawley had grown to the population of 65 000 the railway line from Three Bridges (in Crawley) to East Grinstead and Tunbridge Wells was closed. Now Milton Keynes is beginning to grow there is talk of closing the line to Bedford, but the development corporation is making efforts to keep it open. One gets the impression that the lines mentioned and others must be closed in case there is a wish to use them. The reasons given for closures is well known: they don't pay. But little effort is made to modernize them and run frequent regular services. It is a familiar technique for closure.

It would be a wise policy to encourage a revival in the use and development of railways not only in Great Britain but in Europe (43.2). It has many advantages over road transport. It is much much safer and is segregated from pedestrians, it is faster and more reliable and is not a cause of atmospheric pollution as are petrol fumes. A good rail service for a new town is a great advantage and it is therefore satisfactory to learn of the possibility of new stations being opened in new towns (Telford, Washington, Milton Keynes and Warrington) as part of a possible revival.

Among the leisure activities of people in new towns are the work of voluntary societies and the promotion of music, drama and the visual arts and crafts, yet one of the difficulties in pursuing these activities is the absence or inadequacy of suitable premises. There may be a music or drama group wishing to perform, or there may be a wish for professional concerts and the theatre, but so often in new towns there are no suitable premises. The most that can be obtained is a school hall with its flat floor, which is second rate for such performances.

This lack of premises for meetings for social and cultural activities, and the arts was sometimes a subject of complaint by development corporations. For example Basildon Development Corporation deplored the lack of facilities of this kind in its report of 1954, when it stated that there was no building at all in the area (except schools) of 5000 sq. feet (450 m²) which is the minimum required for such purposes as dances and other entertainments, and the population then was about 30 000. In many of the new towns of the first period with populations of 60 000 there is still in 1977 no good multi-purpose hall in the centre of the town, although the need is strong. Regrettably the hoped for provision became a long story of procrastination. To cite the example of Crawley: although the need for an arts centre has been apparent since 1960, and there have been many discussions between voluntary bodies and the local authority, it has not yet materialized. For a modern town with a population of 75 000 there is no good central meeting hall, no central theatre, no concert hall and no exhibition gallery. Provision for a site for such a centre should have been made in the original plan. An arts centre with some of the facilities mentioned was planned and started in 1973 and site work began, but ceased in 1975 owing to economic restrictions and has not yet (1977) been resumed. Most interested people think the site is in the wrong place, too far from the town centre where there are other much more suitable sites.

The complaint of slowness in assisting with the provision of cultural and recreational facilities continues with the development corporations of later new towns. That of Livingston, for example, in its 1975 report, expresses disappointment 'over the delay in the provision by the authorities concerned of essential recreational and leisure facilities in the newly developed areas of the town'.

One development that is efficacious and economic is the planning of schools so that part is used for adult recreational and cultural purposes in the evenings and weekends. Examples of this can be seen in some of the earlier new towns – Cwmbran among them. One good expression of the idea is at the Stantonbury Campus at Milton Keynes where a theatre for drama and concerts serves three adjacent schools. There are no halls in the schools; instead each uses this central theatre which is also planned for use by adults in evenings and weekends.

Early in 1977 the appraisal of the new towns programme by the Secretary of State for the Environment, Peter Shore, was partly prompted by the lessening increase of population. A main purpose of new towns, however is to accommodate population living in sub-standard and overcrowded conditions. In spite of the slower population growth, the number of households continues to increase and the outward movement of population from the large old cities in the United Kingdom continues unabated. Greater London, for example, has been losing population at the rate of 50–70 000 per annum since the late 1960s. Thus new towns continue to have a purpose and not until environmental and social conditions are sufficiently comparable in the old urban areas to the conditions prevailing outside them will people and firms stop moving out.

This is one reason why the dedesignation of Stonehouse new town in Scotland is such a mistake. Stonehouse was designated in 1973 to receive population from Glasgow of 45 000 with the possibility of natural increase up to 70 000. Instead of creating a new development corporation to build the town, the existing East Kilbride Development Corporation was charged with the task and its title changed to become the East Kilbride and Stonehouse Development Corporation. Stonehouse is only 12 miles (19 km) from East Kilbride itself and East Kilbride was reaching, after 30 years, the end of its period of induced growth. It was good sense, therefore, to use the experience and skills of a practised and successful team to build the new new town than create a new team from scratch.

However, in its first regional report the newly-formed Strathclyde Regional Council came to the view that Stonehouse new town was no longer necessary. Its argument was that the outward movement of population from the Glasgow conurbation should be discouraged and that such economic growth prospects as there were in the region should be directed elsewhere than to Stonehouse. Thus, with many declarations from the Government Minister responsible that the abandoning of Stonehouse new town was not a precedent for cutting back on the new town programme elsewhere in Scotland, it was formally dedesignated by Act of Parliament in the middle of 1977. Simultaneously with the first announcement that Stonehouse was to be dedesignated the Government announced that £120 million was to be made available for a massive renewal project in the East End of Glasgow which would be undertaken by the Scottish Development Agency in partnership with the Strathclyde Regional Council and Glasgow Corporation.

While there is no question that the infusion of substantial public funds into the renewal and rehabilitation of the East End of Glasgow is a good thing (although there is boundless opportunity for the funds to be mis-spent), it will probably not be until the East End project has made substantial inroads into the environmental dereliction and into improving social and housing conditions in the area that there will be any slowing down of the outward movement of population from Glasgow itself. Without Stonehouse new town to go to there will be much more likelihood of people leaving Scotland altogether. Although the industrial site planned for Stonehouse new town is to be retained, it will be much less attractive to firms if it is not part of a planned community with associated facilities of housing, schools, recreation, shopping and all that goes to make up a town.

We are witnessing a major change in the nature of cities whereby they are subject to strong forces of dispersal and disaggregation which cannot be reversed. Such forces are symptoms of increasing prosperity and, above all, an increasing ability by people and firms to buy more space for themselves. If they cannot buy that space in the old urban areas they are bound to seek it elsewhere. The question is: how to channel and direct this change in a beneficial way which gives maximum protection to the countryside, which satisfies the aspirations which people are evincing and which results in attractive and pleasant development both where the people go to and where they have come from. The new town development corporation is so far the best machinery we have devised for accommodating the people and firms once they have left the old urban area. We have yet to use it (although it has been suggested many times that we should) for improving conditions in the old urban areas themselves. Such efficient machinery should be applied in the inner city as much as possible, given the political structures which exist.

The reappraisal by Government in the Spring of 1977 of the future of existing new towns decided that the first (1946–50) and second (1961–66) generation towns should be allowed to continue until their current target populations for induced growth are reached. However, the target populations for the later (third generation 1967–70) new towns, Milton Keynes, Northampton, Peterborough, Telford and Warrington have been reduced to the point where the period of induced growth will continue only to the mid or late 1980s. (See Hansard – 5 April 1977 – 1110–1114). In the meantime we can expect the development corporations of 8 new towns (Stevenage, Harlow, Basildon,

Bracknell, Corby, Skelmersdale, Runcorn and Redditch) to be progressively wound up, within the next five years – 1977–81. (Hansard op. cit. 1110).

It is intended that the Commission for the New Towns, (which so far has taken over the assets of the 4 new towns of Crawley, Hatfield, Hemel Hempstead and Welwyn Garden City), shall no longer have a housing role but will, 'have a vital part to play in securing the orderly wind-up of development corporations and in the management of the very substantial commercial and industrial assets which have been created in our new towns by exchequer funding', as the Department of the Environment press statement discussing the future of the Commission put it in April 1977.

So far as housing assets are concerned, legislation was passed in 1976 providing for the handing over to the local authorities of housing and related assets in those cases where the town had already reached the end of its period of induced growth or 15 years had elapsed since the housing was provided. It has also been proposed by the Government that the unsatisfied demand for housing from the second generation of families in the earlier new towns should be made a local authority responsibility and not that of the particular development corporation.

Whether local authorities will be able to take over the commercial and industrial assets of the Commission is to be considered by the Government where a local authority wishes to take over such assets and has the resources to do so. This issue has been a controversial one for many years. Local authorities have naturally been inclined to think that a development corporation should be wound up as soon as its job seemed to be nearing an end, and as a consequence its assets handed over to the relevant local authority. When the Commission was established there was much local authority opposition because they felt that the new town assets should have been handed over to them. The Government response to this was that the assets were created by and belonged to the nation and, that the local authorities were too small and lacked the relevant experience to manage large estates of commercial and industrial development. Housing was considered suitable for handing over in certain circumstances but not where it would make the local authority too large a landlord of housing in its own area. However, the reorganization of local government with better equipped district councils seems to have modified the Government's attitude in favour of such authorities being perhaps more capable of managing the housing, commercial and industrial assets of a new town (43.3).

Turning to more specific aspects of development in new towns throughout the 31 years since the 1946 New Towns Act, it is significant how ideas and practice have remained unchanged and stood the test of time rather than be subject to major evolutionary change. In housing, for example, with the exception of Cumbernauld, densities have been maintained at a 'suburban' level, with the majority of dwellings being houses with gardens. There has been enormous variety in individual house design and this has in large part been due to the different ideas which development corporations have adopted. They have pioneered many varied forms of new housing systems and forms of construction, but always consistently and predominantly for houses rather than for flats and for low to medium densities. Approaches to housing tenure have inevitably changed – partly as the result of political changes in central government. Richard Crossman, as Minister of Housing and Local Government, argued that the new towns should seek to achieve a 50/50 split between owner-occupied and rented housing by the time they were complete. Thus, from the mid-60s there was an impetus for the development corporations to encourage a larger proportion of houses built for sale. This trend has continued and indeed in the later new towns the proportion of owner-occupied and rented housing has been made an integral part of the forward housing programme from the very beginning, with Peterborough for example having drawn up a programme broadly aiming for 90% rented housing and 10% owner-occupied housing in the early years gradually swinging in the opposite direction to 10% rented and 90% owner-occupied in the years before the end of its period of induced growth.

There is, in fact, little political disagreement on this broad approach to the provision of new housing. However, there is controversy on whether or not the existing rented housing should be sold to sitting tenants. The 1970 Conservative government introduced legislation whereby the tenants of new town houses could purchase them at 20% below their market value provided that did not fall below their economic cost. Some advantage was taken of this opportunity, but the Labour administration of 1974 abandoned it.

Economic and financial problems have, inevitably, affected new town housing. In the period of strict control of building materials in the immediate post-war period when they were in short supply, the quality of housing was not up to the standard of later years. However, the housing cost yardstick (the device used by government to control the capital cost of public subsidy for different house types) has persistently been out-of-date in relation to current construction costs. The result is that in the 1970s development corporations have been hard pressed to maintain the high standards which had been set in the late 1950s and during the 1960s.

The claims that the new towns generally combine functional efficiency with visual attractiveness, and that they are a major contribution to modern urban planning and architecture could be substantiated with voluminous evidence. It must suffice in conclusion to emphasize a few aspects of this excellence.

Aesthetically, good urban design is largely a matter of effective spatial composition, of the relation of buildings, trees, street furniture to the spaces between and surrounding them, often achieved by the disposition of these elements in small or large scale urban enclosures sometimes with glimpses beyond. The centres of many new towns offer some splendid examples: in the formal landscape planning of the great central avenue of Parkway in Welwyn Garden City; in the disposition of trees and buildings on either side of the Boulevard at Crawley with its tall terminal feature; in the central water garden partly enclosed by a block of offices and circular multi-storey car park at Hemel Hempstead; and the east end of the pedestrian square at Basildon with the transition to the smaller lower square with a block of flats and pool with sculpture at its base.

Most of the earlier new towns have lived up to the garden city concept, which has also influenced many of the later ones. Apart from the ideas of Ebenezer Howard the conviction that gardens and verdancy play a conspicuous part in creating the beautiful cities of the world is a determining factor. In addition to bringing the freshness of the country to the dryness of the building scene they provide a decorative element which often enhances an architectural ensemble. This is particularly so with the broad unornamented masses of modern architecture. In many new towns the layout of houses in residential areas enhances the delight in the mingling of buildings with landscape effects, with such elements as irregular areas of lawn sprinkled with trees with various sized enclosures linked by paths and roads, giving the impression of houses disposed in natural settings.

Generally efforts have been made to avoid the monotonous street enclosed by continuous facades of houses, so familiar in the inner suburbs of large cities. Instead diversity has been a constant if difficult aim. In achieving this, as frequently noted, many, many variations on this difficult theme have been employed, especially in the siting of houses so that they often appear at different angles and in unusual groups in relation to roads, paths and surrounding spaces. In contrast to the street between walls, houses are seen much more three dimensionally giving more scope for architectural appreciation. This more marked three dimensional urban effect is a distinctive experience afforded by many new towns.

The British new towns represent one of the finest social, economic and aesthetic achievements of the century, and they have been the admiration of the world (44.3). Each town has attracted thousands of planners, architects and sociologists from all continents.

The work is not yet complete. We still need many more new towns. Many areas of the great cities are still congested and overcrowded, too often with squalid conditions. If urban renewal in these areas is to be done on standards comparable with those in new towns, a further dispersal of at least another million persons is necessary. The way of doing this which has proved to be socially and environmentally successful, as this book has endeavoured to demonstrate, is to continue the programme of new towns.

References and Notes:

43.1 The periods of the new towns are sometimes referred to as the first, second and third generations or Mark I, II and III. Mark I are 1946–50, Mark II 1955–67 and Mark III 1968–71. The last group are expansions of fairly large towns like Peterborough, Northampton and Warrington.

43.2 In November 1973 a meeting of the International Union of Railways discussed its plan for Europe's further trunk rail network which promised considerable development and expansion.

43.3 In most cases a new town is a part of a district council area, but in a few there is identity as at Stevenage, Harlow and Redditch. In Basildon, Bracknell and Crawley the new town is the major part. Welwyn Garden City and Hatfield are combined to make the Welwyn Hatfield District Council. Hemel Hempstead is a little under two thirds of the new district of Dacorum.

43.4 When editing the *Encyclopaedia of Urban Planning*, with contributions from over 40 countries, the experience is remembered of the great admiration expressed by many contributors for British New Towns. It confirmed the belief that they constituted one of the greatest planning achievements of the century.

Appendix 1: Selected Data on the New Towns

Tables reproduced by courtesy of The Town and Country Planning Association

Table 1. Area and population data

	Date of designation	Designated area in acres and in hectares in brackets		Original	Population Proposed[1]	31 Dec 1976
Basildon	4 Jan 1949	7818	(3165)	25,000	103,600 130,000	91,890
Bracknell	17 June 1949	3303	(1337)	5149	55–60,000 55–60,000	45,000
Crawley	9 Jan 1947	5920	(2396)	9100	— 85,000	75,000
Harlow	25 Mar 1947	6395	(2588)	4500	undecided undecided	81,000
Hatfield	20 May 1948	2340	(947)	8500	25,000 29,000	26,000
Hemel Hempstead	4 Feb 1947	5910	(2391)	21,000	65,000 85,000	78,000
Stevenage	11 Nov 1946	6256	(2532)	6700	80,000 100–105,000	74,000
Welwyn Garden City	20 May 1948	4317	(1747)	18,500	42,000 *50,000	41,000
Newton Aycliffe	19 Apr 1947	3103	(1254)	60	undecided 45,000	26,500
Central Lancs.	26 Mar 1970	35,255	(14,267)	234,500	271,000 not estimated	248,000
Corby	1 Apr 1950	4423	(1791)	15,700	not estimated 70,000	53,500
Milton Keynes	23 Jan 1967	22,000	(8900)	40,000	150,000 200,000	77,000
Northampton	14 Feb 1968	19,966	(8080)	133,000	173,000 180,000	158,000
Peterborough	1 Aug 1967	15,940	(6453)	81,000	160,000	109,000

	Date of designation	Designated area in acres and in hectares in brackets		Original	Population Proposed[1]	31 Dec 1976
Peterlee	10 Mar 1948	2799	(1133)	200	28,000 30,000	27,500
Redditch	10 Apr 1964	7180	(2906)	32,000	70,000 90,000	53,200
Runcorn	10 Apr 1964	7234	(2930)	28,500	71,000 100,000	54,600
Skelmersdale	9 Oct 1961	4124	(1669)	10,000	73,300 80,000	41,000
Telford	12 Dec 1968	19,300	(7790)	70,000	135,000 150,000	99,700
Warrington	26 Apr 1968	18,612	(7535)	122,300	160,000 170,000	135,400
Washington	26 July 1964	5610	(2271)	20,000	65,000 80,000	46,000
Cwmbran	4 Nov 1949	3160	(1278)	12,000	55,000 not estimated	45,000
Mid-Wales (Newtown)	18 Dec 1967	1497	(606)	5000	11,500 13,000	7700
Cumbernauld	9 Dec 1955	7788	(3152)	3000	70,000 100,000	45,000
East Kilbride	6 May 1947	10,250	(4148)	2400	82,500 90,000	76,200
Glenrothes	30 June 1948	5765	(2333)	1100	55,000 70,000	33,700
Irvine	9 Nov 1966	12,440	(5022)	34,600	116,000 120,000	52,305
Livingston	17 Apr 1962	6692	(2708)	2000	70,000 100,000	29,000

Sources: Development corporations, Commission for the New Towns and Peter Shore's statement, April 1977.

1 Two figures are given: the first is the population size when planned migration is to stop; the second is the proposed ultimate population for natural increase.

2 Planned migration has already stopped.

Table 2. Financial results for the year ended 31 March 1976 (new towns in Great Britain)

	Profit or loss in year				Net capital advances at 31.3.76 £	Cumulative average rate of interest %
	General Revenue (before tax) £	Ancillaries £	Disposals (before tax) £	Total £		
Aycliffe	− 752,566	—	+ 87,018	− 665,548	30,534,788	9.02
Basildon	− 1,220,394	—	+ 266,795	− 953,599	114,584,593	7.93
Bracknell	+ 1,100,481	—	+ 306,387	+ 1,406,868	51,695,649	7.61
Corby	+ 269,161	—	+ 28,370	+ 297,531	34,877,687	8.34
Cwmbran	+ 231,098	− 49,265	+ 48,927	− 231,436	45,367,278	8.73
Harlow	+ 2,113,852	—	+ 285,230	+ 2,399,082	61,899,677	5.71
Peterlee	− 1,574,674	—	+ 22,800	− 1,551,874	37,872,924	8.59
Stevenage	+ 916,250	—	+ 852,214	+ 1,768,464	63,526,701	6.70
8 England and Wales	+ 621,012	− 49,265	+ 1,897,741	+ 2,469,488	440,359,297	
Crawley	+ 2,719,476	—	+ 1,542,653	+ 5,563,473	91,493,978	5.05
Hatfield	{		+ 267,326	{	{	{
Hemel Hempstead	(shared)		+ 273,502	(shared)	(shared)	(shared)
Welwyn Garden City	}		+ 760,516	}	}	}
	+ 2,719,476	—	+ 2,843,997	+ 5,563,473	91,493,978	
12 England and Wales	+ 3,340,488	49,265	+ 4,741,738	+ 8,032,961	531,853,275	
Central Lancashire	− 3,830,470	− 299,041	+ 79,392	− 4,208,903	48,099,581	13.97
Mid-Wales (Newtown)	− 206,591	—	+ 60,500	− 267,091	11,425,352	12.20
Milton Keynes	− 5,574,903	− 3,477,332	+ 15,933	− 9,068,168	147,240,439	12.38
Northampton	− 1,744,755	− 17,996	+ 4677	− 1,767,428	62,430,734	12.37
Peterborough	− 4,739,760	—	+ 301,276	− 4,438,484	88,689,998	12.60
Redditch	− 1,502,853	+ 6693	+ 25,290	− 1,484,256	71,118,533	10.56
Runcorn	− 1,434,537	− 354,887	+ 63,103	− 1,852,527	79,252,156	10.86
Skelmersdale	− 1,918,655	− 211,593	− 191,124	− 2,321,372	82,015,791	9.67
Telford	− 4,105,899	—	+ 28,360	− 4,134,259	117,257,638	11.30
Warrington	− 3,266,201	− 246,913	+ 105,451	− 3,407,663	55,593,332	12.45
Washington	− 1,342,092	− 18,830	+ 149,677	− 1,211,245	65,053,139	11.35
	− 26,666,716	− 4,633,285	+ 138,605	− 34,161,396	828,176,693	
23 England and Wales	− 26,326,228	− 4,682,550	+ 4,880,343	− 26,128,435	1,360,029,968	
Cumbernauld	+ 656,622	—	+ 223,954	+ 432,668	74,792,970	8.71
East Kilbride & Stonehouse	+ 1,548,093	—	+ 469,680	+ 2,017,773	82,281,947	7.65
Glenrothes	− 296,104	—	+ 58,050	− 238,054	45,505,758	8.40
Irvine	− 806,670	—	+ 12,361	− 819,031	44,520,195	12.46
Livingston	− 1,362,467	—	+ 16,791	− 1,379,258	75,255,440	10.72
5 Scotland	− 1,573,770	—	+ 722,532	− 851,238	322,356,310	
28 Total: Great Britain	− 27,899,998	− 4,682,550	+ 5,602,875	− 26,979,673	1,682,386,278	

Source: Accounts of the Commission for the New Towns and the development corporations (Table prepared by J. N. Kay of the Commission for the New Towns)

Table 3.   New town statistics—a summary

	Added 1976	Total to December 1976
New population	57,937	984,386
Total employment	10,343	915,086
New schools	36	676
New shops	179	4469
New factories (number)	135*	3264
(area sq. ft)	5,769,860*	83,301,442
New offices (area sq. ft)	1,156,720*	10,422,065
Capital expenditure	£298.5m	£2042.3m
Capital expenditure (housing only)	£204.1m	£1260.9m
New dwellings completed:		
Development corporations, etc.	17,633	251,730
Local authorities	4027*	40,539*
Others	61,149	6683

* These figures underestimate totals

Appendix 2: Some 'New Towns' Planned since 1900

Reports of new foundations and projects arrive in mounting volume from all parts of the world, especially developing countries. The following list, though much extended since the earlier editions of this book, is by no means complete. Nor do all the 'communities' named fully comply with this book's definition of 'new towns', with local employment and green belts. But most of them have been planned in advance as 'communities', and have been influenced, directly or indirectly, by the British new towns' initiative, and most have at least a partial element of industrial or other local employment which takes them out of the class of suburban dormitories pure and simple.

The date given for the town plan is often approximate. In many cases, as in Britain, the original target population has been subsequently revised; it usually allows for natural increases. The 'present' population is the most recent estimate available.

Country	Town	Information	Designation date	Target population	Present population
Abu Dhabi	Mina Zaid	Planned oil refining town	1970s		
	Ruwais	Planned industrial town		85,000	
Argentina	Caleta Olivia		1921	15,000	
	General Belgrana	Planned satellite 27 km Buenos Aires	1948	50,000	28,000(1967)
	18 small towns established under Law of Development and Population (1958)				
Australia	Albury-Wodonga		1960s	300,000	
	Bathurst-Orange	Canberra satellite	1960s	240,000	
	Belconnen		1966	120,000	40,000(1974)
	Canberra	Federal capital	1910 1963	100,000 250,000	202,000(1976)
	Dampier	1600 km Perth. Mineral processing	1963	3000	3000(1976)
	Elizabeth	Automobile industry		70,000	50,000(1972)
	Griffin	627 km Sydney. Fruit, rice and wine	1914	30,000	9500(1966)
	Kambalda	620 km Perth. Nickel			5700(1976)
	Karratha	1600 km Perth. Shipping, mineral processing	1968	30,000	9500(1976)
	Koolyanobbing	425 km Perth. Iron ore	1964		350(1976)
	Kununurra	3360 km Perth. Farming	1959	3000– 5000	2000(1976)

Country	Town	Information	Designation date	Target population	Present population
Australia	Kwinana	32 km Perth. Various	1953	40,000	5700(1976)
	Laverton	950 km Perth. Nickel	1974		1548(1976)
	Leeton	612 km Sydney. Food processing	1913		5800(1966)
	Medina	32 km Perth. Petroleum	1952	40,000	13,000(1975)
	Monarto	57 km Adelaide	1975	150,000–200,000	
	Mount Druit			180,000	100,000(1975)
	Mount Isa	Mining	1950s		200,700(1968)
	Murray New Town	52 km Adelaide	1972	100,000	
	Newman	1200 km Perth. Haematite	1970		5000(1976)
	North Pinjarra	85 km Perth. Bauxite	1969		1000(1976)
	Paraburdoo	1650 km Perth. Haematite	1968		2600(1976)
	South Hedland	1600 km Perth. Haematite	1968	40,000	6000(1976)
	Tom Price	1600 km Perth. Haematite	1963		3750(1976)
	Whyalla	285 km Adelaide	1937	53,000	32,000(1972)
	Wickham	1600 km Perth. Landing jetty	1970	11,000	2500(1976)
	Woden	Canberra satellite	1962	90,000	50,000(1976)
	Yallourn	Mining, electricity	1947		4200(1966)

Australia has a number of very small new towns associated mainly with irrigation, hydro-electricity and mining.

Country	Town	Information	Designation date	Target population	Present population
Austria	Lenzing	Textiles	1939		4000(1962)
	Timmelkarn	80 km Salzburg	1943	5000	
	Vienna South	New satellite planned	1965	70,000	
Belgium	Louvain-la-Neuve	University town	1971	50,000	7000(1976)
Belize	Belmopan	Refugee town	1960	30,000	3000(1976)
Botswana	Gaborone	Capital city	1961	88,000	20,000(1972)
	Selebipikwe	160 km Francistown. Copper mining	1968	25,000	17,000(1972)
Brazil	Brasilia	New capital	1957	500,000	544,862(1972)
	Cidas des Motores	32 km Rio de Janeiro. Tractor industry		25,000	176,000(1960)
	Volta Redonda	144 km Rio de Janeiro		100,000	85,000(1966)
Cameroons	Buea	80 km Douala		26,000	16,000(1972)
	Foumbot	24 km Bafoussam	1965	30,000	12,000(1972)
	Kumba	New city. 177 km Douala		170,000	40,000(1972)
	Matomb	Satellite Yaoundé	1965	3000	2000(1972)
	Mbalmayo	Satellite Yaoundé	1965	30,000	16,000(1972)

Country	Town	Information	Designation date	Target population	Present population
Cameroons	Mbanga	Satellite Douala		45,000	17,000(1972)
	Mbouda	314 km Douala		30,000	12,000(1972)
	Obala	40 km Yaoundé	1969	15,000	8500(1972)
	Tiko	32 km Douala		40,000	14,000(1972)
	Victoria	80 km Douala		40,000	25,000(1972)
	Yabassi	93 km Douala		30,000	5000(1972)
	Yagoua	109 km Maroua		32,000	12,000(1972)
Canada	Ajax	30 km Toronto. Industrial	1948	20,000–30,000	
	Bramalea	24 km Toronto. Industrial	1957	125,000	
	Bromont	Tourist centre	1966	1100	1100(1971)
	Candiac	16 km Montreal. Glass, fibre-glass, food	1957	5200	5200(1971)
	Churchill	965 km Winnipeg	1971	5000	2800(1973)
	Churchill Falls	1125 km Montreal. Hydro-electricity	1968	1000	1000(1976)
	Deep River	93 km Pembroke. Atomic energy	1957	20,000	
	Don Mills	Adjoining N.E. Toronto	1946	25,000–30,000	
	Ear Falls	65 km Red Lake. Forestry, mining and tourism	1966	4000	2500(1971)
	Elliot Lake	Uranium mining	1955	29,000	
	Erin Mills	32 km West Toronto	1953	170,000	
	Fermont	222 km Sept-Illes. Iron	1970	5000	5000(1976)
	Fort McMurray	286 km Edmonton. Tar sands mining	1970	9000–15,000	6681(1971)
	Fox Creek	255 km Edmonton. Oil and gas, highway services.	1956		1281(1971)
	Gander	Transit point for trans-Atlantic flights	1952	11,300	9600(1976)
	Gagnon	140 km Sept-Illes. Mining	1958	5000–7000	3800(1972)
	Gold River	N.W. Vancouver. Paper and pulp	1965	6000	
	Grande Cache	145 km Hinton. Coking coal	1966		2525(1971)
	Iroquois	Relocated communities after floods	1955	6500	
	Kanata	West of Ottawa		69,000	4500(1971)
	Kitimat	Aluminium and pulp	1952	50,000	
	Labrador City	S.W. Labrador. Iron ore	1958	8500	8300(1974)
	Lebel-sur-Quévillion	644 km Montreal. Pulp and paper	1964	7000	7000(1971)
	Malvern	North-eastern Toronto	1953	57,000	

Country	Town	Information	Designation date	Target population	Present population
Canada	Meadowvale	40 km Toronto. Commerce and industry	1956	75,000	
	Mill Woods	Adjoining Edmonton	1969	120,000	
	Nacawick	Hydro-electricity and forestry	1964	5000	
	North Pickering	Airport and related activities		150,000–200,000	
	Pinawa	104 km Winnipeg. Nuclear research	1960	7000	completed 1972
	Port-Cartier	65 km Sept-Illes. Clearing centre for iron	1959	6500	completed 1975
	Sackville	25 km Halifax. Population growth point	1967	30,500	
	Saltfleet	S.E. Hamilton, Ontario	1969	70,000	
	Waterloo	1051 km Toronto	1968	65,000	

Canada possesses many small new towns associated mainly with hydro-electricity and mining, e.g. High Level in Alberta, Inuvik in the North West Territories, Mica Creek in British Columbia.

Country	Town	Information	Designation date	Target population	Present population
Chile	Chuquicamata	225 km Antofagusta. Copper mining	1915	2500	27,000(1967)
	Coyhaique	Agricultural centre	1929	5000	13,000(1967)
	El Salvador	Copper mining	1957	3200	3600(1967)
	Huachipata		1950	35,000	
	Puerto Aysen	Service and administration	1926	3000	6400(1967)
Czechoslovakia	Bratislava	4 new towns projected at 10 km intervals	1961	25,000–30,000	
	Havirov	Mining	1952	50,000	
	Poruba			26,000	
	Prague S.W. New Town		1975	130,000	
Denmark	Albertslund	Satellite of Copenhagen	1962	7000	7500(1972)
	By Po Nordal	Engineering industries	1962	16,000	7800(1972)
	Copenhagen	2 satellite towns	1961	250,000 each	
	Hantsholm	19 km Thisted. Fishing	1966	5000	1700(1972)
	Koge Bay	Set of new towns near Copenhagen. Industrial	1963–	150,000	50,000(1972)
Dubai	Jebel Ali	Proposed industrial city			
	Port Rashid	Proposed oil refining port			
Egypt	Halfa-el-Fedida	To rehouse Nubians displaced by Aswan Dam	1969	30,000	

Country	Town	Information	Designation date	Target population	Present population
Finland	Hervanta	8 km Tampere. Light industry	1970	40,000	
	Kivenlahti	20 km Helsinki. Seaside town	1966	40,000	22,000(1976)
	Naantali	16 km Turku	1966	21,000	6857(1972)
	Raisio	8 km Turku	1967	31,000	14,750(1972)
	Rovaniemi	Capital Lapland	1945–1952	20,000	
	Seinajoki	88 km Vaasa	1968	30,500	20,353(1972)
	Tapiola	9 km Helsinki. Offices and service trades	1952	175,000	16,000(1976)
	Unikaupunki	88 km Turku. Car industry	1953	14,000	7469(1972)
France	Ain	6 km Lyons	1971		
	Bobigny	11 km Paris	1970	70,000	40,000(1971)
	Carros-le Neuf	Alpes-Maritimes district		10,000	
	Cergy-Pontoise	25 km Paris	1966	350,000	70,000(1974)
	Creteil	11 km Paris	1967	125,000	50,000(1972)
	La Dame Blanche	Near Paris	1960	25,000	
	Etang de Berre	15 km Marseilles	1971	750,000	50,000(1974)
	Evry	30 km Paris	1967	455,000	200,000(1974)
	Grande Quevilly	Satellite of Rouen	1960	25,000	
	Lille-Est	5 km Lille. University town	1968	100,000–110,000	40,000(1975)
	L'Isle d'Abeau	35 km Lyons. Service industries	1970	250,000	50,000(1975)
	Marne-la-Vallée	10 km Paris	1966	550,000	125,000(1974)
	Melun Cenart	20 km Paris	1965	291,000	75,000(1970)
	Orleans	11 km. New satellite. University town	1962	25,000–30,000	
	Royan	Completely rebuilt	1957		
	Saint Quentin-en-Yvelines	30 km Paris	1967	480,000	90,000(1974)
	Sophia Antipolis	Multi-disciplinary science centre	1969		
	Surville	72 km Paris		47,000	
	Toulouse-le-Mirail	Light industry		100,000	
	Le Vaudreuil	25 km Rouen. Service industries	1967	140,000	15,000(1974)
	Vitrolles	Near Marseilles. Heavy industry			
East Germany	Hellerau	Near Dresden. Industrial suburb	1908	15,000	
	Stalinstadt-on-Oder		1954	30,000	

Country	Town	Information	Designation date	Target population	Present population
West Germany	Amorbach	28 km Würzburg. Timber			4186(1976)
	Chorweiler	Near Cologne	1957		
	Espelkamp	35 km Bielefeld. Mechanical engineering, Plastics	1948	20,000	22,670(1976)
	Geretsried	42 km Munich. Metal and plastics			17,330(1976)
	Heitlingen	9 km Hanover	1961	25,000	
	Hochdal	12 km Düsseldorf. Light industries	1961	30,000–35,000	
	Köln-Nord	Industrial satellite	1960	80,000–100,000	
	Laatzen	10 km Hanover. Mechanical engineering, vehicles	1968	27,500	30,927(1976)
	Limest	12 km Frankfurt	1962	17,000	10,000(1972)
	Marl	Chemicals	1914	100,000	91,930(1976)
	Meckenheim	38 km Cologne. Chemicals		25,000	11,645(1976)
	Neckarsulm	Motor industry	1950	5000	20,112(1976)
	Salzgitter	Steel industry	1938	130,000	117,341(1976)
	Sennestadt	Near Bielefeld. Various industries	1954	35,000	23,000(1972)
	Traunreut	96 km Munich	1950	30,000	12,510(1972)
	Überherrn	Steel and coal	1960	15,000	11,345(1976)
	Waldkraiburg	65 km Munich. Clothing and mechanical engineering			20,140(1976)
	Wolfsburg	Automobile industry	1937	230,000	126,298(1976)
	Wulfen	Heavy industry	1958	50,000	4500(1973)
Ghana	Akosombo	Industrial town	1960	30,000	9000(1963)
	Tema	Volta River Port. Various industries	1956	250,000	70,000(1967)
Greece	Aspra Spitia	104 km Athens. Aluminium industry		6000	
Guinea	Sabende	Bauxite, aluminium		20,000–40,000	10,000(1960)
Hong Kong	Castle Peak	Planned new territories		500,000	
	Qusen Wan-Kwai Ching	New territory town	1973		
	Sha Tin	New territory town	1973	500,000	
	Tsing Yi	New territory town	1973	500,000	
	Tsuen Wan	New territory town	1956	175,000	
	Tuen Min	New territory town	1973	500,000	

Country	Town	Information	Designation date	Target population	Present population
Hungary	Ajka		1951	20,000	
	Dunaujvaros	Formerly Sztalinvaros. Steel industry	1949	25,000–80,000	44,200(1970)
	Kazincbarcika	Chemical industry	1950	40,000	25,844(1970)
	Komlo	Mining	1960	30,000	28,186(1970)
	Leninvaros	Chemicals	1955	40,000	9834(1970)
	Oroszlany	Oil refinery	1952	25,000	18,218(1970)
	Szazhalombatta	Oil refinery	1962	30,000	5974(1970)
	Tatabanga			65,000	
	Tiszapalkonya		1955	40,000	
	Varpalota		1949	25,000	
India	Ashok Nagar	Resettlement town	1964	15,000	
	Barauni	Oil town			
	Bhadravaty		1941	40,000	20,000(1952)
	Bhilai	10 km Durg. Steel and associated industries	1956	200,000	110,000(1967)
	Bhubaneshwar	New capital of Orissa province	1948	500,000	120,000(1967)
	Bilastur	Administrative city			
	Birlangar	Various industries	1956	200,000	110,000(1967)
	Chandigarh	New capital of Punjab	1950/1	500,000	90,000(1968)
	Chittaranjan	Locomotive works		42,000	40,000(1962)
	Dandeli	Industrial town		50,000	14,000(1961)
	Durgapur	268 km Calcutta. Steel	Early 50s	125,000	65,000(1962)
	Faridabad	27 km Delhi. Heavy and light industries	1949	50,000	40,000(1961)
	Gandhi	95 km Kotah	1951	2500	2500(1967)
	Ghandhidam	Port	1950	250,000	12,000(1962)
	Ghandhi Dham		1967	250,000	27,000(1961)
	Ghandinagar	New capital of Gujarat	1967	250,000	
	Jamshedpur	Industrial town	1945		466,000(1969)
	Kalyani	Satellite of Calcutta	1950	60,000	5000(1969)
	Korba	Mining and various industries	1950	90,000	25,000(1967)
	Nangal	80 km Chandigarh. Chemicals		50,000	20,000(1967)
	Nepanagar	515 km Bombay. Paper and pulp	1947	12,000	9000(1967)
	New Calcutta	6 km Calcutta	1965	300,000	
	Nilokheri	Resettlement town	1948	36,000	8000(1961)
	Patialia	Refugee town of Cutch			
	Rajpura	Refugee town of Cutch	1950	16,000	17,000(1961)
	Ranchi	Industrial city			
	Rourekeia	457 km Calcutta. Steel		100,000	90,000(1961)

Country	Town	Information	Designation date	Target population	Present population
India	Sindri			30,000	41,000(1961)
	Ulhasnagar	Resettlement town	1950	200,000	138,000(1969)
Iran	Isfahan	Steel town		300,000	
Iraq	Surchinar	Industry		60,000	38,000(1961)
Ireland	Oranmore	Projected new town. 25 km Galway			
	Shannon	25 km Limerick	1962	16,000	4300(1962)
Israel	Affuleh		1925	20,000	
	Akko			20,000	
	Arrad		1961		
	Ashdod	35 km Tel Aviv Port. Power, various industries	1956	350,000	30,000(1967)
	Ashkelon	Regional centre	1951	40,000–60,000	
	Bet Shean	Regional centre	1951	40,000–60,000	
	Beer Sheva	Regional centre	1951	40,000–60,000	
	Dimona	Minerals	1951	6000–12,000	
	Eilat	Gulf of Aqaba. Port, light industry, tourism		75,000	15,000(1962)
	Hazor	Regional sub-centre	1951	6000–12,000	
	Hedera	Regional sub-centre	1951	6000–12,000	
	Karmiel	Minerals	1964		
	Ma'alot	Regional sub-centre	1951	6000–12,000	
	Mizpe Ramon	Minerals	1951	6000–12,000	
	Netivot	Regional sub-centre	1951	6000–12,000	
	Ofaquim	Regional sub-centre	1951	6000–12,000	
	Qiryat-Gat	Regional sub-centre	1951	6000–12,000	
	Ramla	Regional centre	1951	20,000–40,000	
	Tiberias	Regional centre	1951	40,000–60,000	

Country	Town	Information	Designation date	Target population	Present population
Israel	Yeruham	Minerals	1951	6000–12,000	
	Zefat	Regional centre	1951	40,000–60,000	

Israel founded 1933–1948 200 Kibbutzim (collective settlements) and Mosharei Ovdim (co-operative settlements)

Country	Town	Information	Designation date	Target population	Present population
Italy	Citta Falchera	Near Turin	1952		
	Ivrea	Near Turin	1952		
	Milan	3 new city districts 'Degli Olmi', Forlanini			
	Pontine Marshes	New towns	1930		
	Porto	Administrative and commercial new town. Near Florence.			
	QT8	Projected new town within Milan			
	Villaggio Cardinale Ruffine	Near Palermo, Sicily			
	Zingonia	Near Milan			
Japan	Chiba	35 km Tokyo	1967	340,000	2000(1976)
	Chiba-Tohnanbu	40 km Tokyo. 80% residential	1969	90,000	7000(1976)
	Heijyo	30 km Osaka. 80% residential	1970	75,000	7000(1976)
	Hokusetsu	30 km Osaka. 80% residential	1970	128,000	Nil (1976)
	Kamo-Gakuen	30 km Hiroshima. University	1976	15,000	Nil (1976)
	Kashima	80 km Tokyo. Petrochemicals, chemicals	1967	300,000	159,000(1976)
	Kenkyu-Gakuen	60 km Tokyo. University town	1968	120,000	7000(1976)
	Kita-Kobe	30 km Osaka. 80% residential	1969	75,000	Nil (1976)
	Kohhoku	10 km Yokohama. 80% residential	1969	220,000	15,000(1976)
	Kozouji	20 km Nagoya. 80% residential	1963	81,000	32,000(1976)
	Iwaki	5 km Taira. 80% residential	1976	25,000	Nil (1976)
	Minami Tama	35 km Tokyo. 80% residential	1965	410,000	2000(1976)
	Nagaoka	80% residential	1975	40,000	Nil (1976)
	Ryugasaki	50 km Tokyo. 80% residential	1971	81,000	1000(1976)
	Seishin	40 km Osaka. 60% residential	1970	70,000	Nil (1976)
	Senboku	20 km Osaka. 80% residential	1965	18,000	114,000(1976)
	Senri	15 km Osaka. 80% residential	1964	150,000	128,000(1976)
	Tomakomai	60 km Sapporo. Light metals, paper, cement	1952	300,000	159,000(1976)
	Tsu Kuba	70 km Tokyo. Academic city	1976	120,000	7000(1976)

Country	Town	Information	Designation date	Target population	Present population
Kenya	Broderick Falls		1970	10,000	
	Kakamega	515 km Nairobi. Gold mining and farming	1910	20,000	20,000(1967
	Kisuma	Port on Lake Victoria. Various industries	1910	50,000	30,700(1976
	Mumies	Sugar refining			
	Nairobi	Capital city. Light industry	1960		509,000(1976
	Nakuru	97 km Nairobi. Agricultural and industrial	1904		47,800(1972
	Nyere	168 km Nairobi. Farming	1910	50,000	50,000(1967
	Thika	Satellite	1947		30,000(1970
Korea	An Yang	25 km Seoul. Textiles, manu-facturing industries	1949	106,000	53,000(1967
	Ulsan	48 km Pusan. Chemicals	1962	500,000	113,000(1967
Kuwait		New town proposed south of Kuwait city			
Malaysia	Petaling-Jaya	10 km Kuala Lumpur. Agri-cultural processing	1954		100,000(1976
	Shah Alam	25 km Kuala Lumpur. New state capital of Selangor			

25 new towns proposed for the agricultural hinterlands

Country	Town	Information	Designation date	Target population	Present population
Mexico	Cancun	Recreational resort	1973		18,000(1975
	Ciudad Industrial Bernardino de Sahugan	Motor cars, diesel engines		6000	7000(1958
	Compeche	A series of new population centres in State of Compeche			
	Cuautitlan Ixcalli	Dispersal centre for Mexico City		1,500,000	
	Las Truchas	Port, industrial growth centre			
	Reforma Chiapas	New urban centre for S.E. region			
Morocco	Agadir		1960	54,000	61,192(197

New towns under Lyautey regime from 1913 onwards. (Casablanca, Rabta, Fez, Marakes Meknes, Mohammedia and Kenitra)

Country	Town	Information	Designation date	Target population	Present population
Netherlands	Almere	25 km Amsterdam. On South Flevoland Polder.	1970	125,000– 250,000	First reside Nov. 19
	Bahrendrecht West-Smitshoek	8 km Rotterdam. Growth area	1976	45,000– 60,000	20,000(197
	Bijlmermeer/ Gaasperdam	8 km Amsterdam. Very high density dormitory	1960	100,000	30,000(197

Country	Town	Information	Designation date	Target population	Present population
Netherlands	Capelle a.d. Ijssel/ Rotterdam East/ Zevenhuizen	5 km Rotterdam. Growth area	1960's	80,000– 100,000	41,500(1976)
	Dronten	Service centre for East Flevo-land Polder	1955	Reached	16,500(1976)
	Duiven-Westervoort	8 km Arnhem. Growth area	1976	50,000+	14,500(1976)
	Emmeloord	Service centre for N.E. Polder	1940	Reached	30,000(1976)
	Hoorn	35 km Amsterdam	1960s	45,000	24,500(1976)
	Houten	8 km Utrecht. Major growth centre	1970	50,000	7500(1976)
	Huizen	30 km Amsterdam. Mainly residential	1960s	Nearly reached	25,500(1976)
	Lelystad	Provincial capital of Ijsselmeer Polders	1960	100,000– 150,000	20,000(1976)
	Nieuwegein	8 km Utrecht. Overspill town of Utrecht	1960s	40,000	23,000(1976)
	Pijnacker-Nootdorp	10 km Den Haag. Growth centre	1976	50,000	21,000(1976)
	Purmerend	20 km Amsterdam. Growth centre	1965	80,000– 100,000	32,500(1976)
	Spijkenisse	18 km Rotterdam. Growth centre	1962 & 1976	60,000	32,000(1976)
	Zoetermeer	13 km Den Haag. Light and service industries	1965	150,000	45,500(1976)
New Zealand	Kawerau	205 km Auckland. Pulp and paper industries	1953	11,000	7743(1976)
	Murupara	205 km Auckland. Paper and pulp industries	1955	4500	2961(1976)
	Porirua	18 km Wellington. 70% residential	1949	60,000	56,024(1976)
	Tokoroa	209 km Auckland. Forestry	1948	34,000	18,635(1976)
	Turangi	342 km Auckland. Hydro-electricity	1964		5496(1976)
	Twizel	305 km Christchurch. Hydro-electricity	1967	3000	6000(1976)
Norway	Heimdal	11 km Trondheim	1972	50,000	

Norway possesses many single-industry towns based on extractive industries or hydro-electricity plants. Among these are Ardal (1960, about 2000 pop.), Glomfiord (2000), Hayanger (2500), Notodden (9000), Odda (7500) and Sunndalsora (2500).

Oman	Azaiba	Planned urban development			
	Ruwi	Central business area planned			
Pakistan	Islamabad	New capital	1961	1,000,000	100,000(1976)
	Korangi	Refugee town	1958/9	500,000	160,000(1970)

Country	Town	Information	Designation date	Target population	Present population
Pakistan	Mirpur	Projected new town			
	Nazimabad	Satellite town	1950	80,000	
	Punjab	5 market towns in Thal Development area			
	Solamakad		1960		50,000(1967
Peru	Ventanilla	32 km Lima. Industrial	1961	70,000	
Philippines	Baguio City	257 km Manila	1960		84,500(1972
	Batangas City	112 km Manila. Planned city port			109,000(1972
	Cagayan de Oro	Planned city near Manila			128,000(1972
	Iligan City	Planned city			104,000(1969
	Makati	6 km Manila	1952		265,000(1972
	Mariveles	161 km Manila	1948 and 1970		16,000(1972
	Montalban	25 km Manila	1970	130,000	21,000(1972
Poland	Gydnia		1920		
	Jastrazebie			60,000	
	Nowa Huta	Near Cracow. Steel mill	1949	120,000	170,000(197:
	Nowe Tchy	97 km Katowice	1947	130,000	70,000(19/6
	Plock			120,000	
	Stawola Wola		1937 1950	30,000 extended to 37,000	
	Tainowskie Gory			100,000	
Portugal	Alvabade	Near Lisbon	1950	45,000	
	Sines	Near Lisbon. Harbour	1970s		
Puerto Rico	Cibuco	22 km San Juan. Growth centre	1966	50,000–100,000	
Rhodesia	Kariba	Dam construction town	1955	10,000	
Rumania	Dr. Petru Grozia	Extractive industries	1952	12,000	6000(196
	Gh. Gheorghiu-Dej	Oil and chemical industry	1952	60,000	35,000(196
	Hundedoara	Machinery industries	1952	80,000	101,000(197
	Mortru	Mining	1961	35,000	6300(196
	Pertrila Lonea	Mining and processing	1961	29,000	18,000(196
	Resita	Industrial town	1953	70,000	121,500(197
	Uricani	Mining	1952	13,000	6200(196
	Victoria	Chemical industry	1959	17,000	6700(196

6 further new towns are projected in Rumania. They are: Bicaz, Calan, Cugir, Focsani, Slatir Slobozia.

Country	Town	Information	Designation date	Target population	Present population
Santa Lucia	Castries	Capital. Rebuilt after destruction	1949	32,000	47,000(1976)
Saudi Arabia		Proposed new town 17 km north of Jeddah		33,000	
Singapore	Ang Mo Kio	12 km Singapore City. Retail and light industries	1972	220,000	65,000(1976)
	Bedok	12 km Singapore City. Retail and light industries	1971	210,000	60,000(1976)
	Clementi	11 km Singapore City. 85% industrial, retail	1973	120,000	15,000(1976)
	Jurong	16 km Singapore. Mixed industries	1960	380,000	106,000(1976)
	Nee Soon	18 km Singapore City. Retail and light industries	1974	230,000	Nil
	Queenstown	6 km Singapore City. Retail and light industries	1949	150,000	150,000(1976) completed
	Telok Blangah (formerly Pusir Panjang)	6 km Singapore City. Retail and light industries	1970	70,000	65,000(1976)
	Toa Payoh	7 km Singapore City. Retail and light industries	1960	190,000	190,000(1976) completed
	Woodlands	25 km Singapore City	1971	290,000	30,000(1976)
	Long Range Concept Plan's framework provides for a further 2–3 new towns.				
South Africa	Allanridge	177 km Bloemfontein. Gold mining	1956	25,000	2200(1976)
	Atlantis	50 km Cape Town. Industrial	1972	500,000	700(1976)
	Bontehuitel	Near Cape Town. Industrial			
	Cape Town	Near Cape Town. Dormitory with light industry	1975	250,000	
	Carltonville	Gold mining			
	Cato Ridge	Ferro-Manganese industry, regional abbatoir	1960	32,000	2000(1976)
	Factretron	Industrial village near Cape Town			
	Hammarsdale/ Mpumalanga	Near Durban. Clothing, poultry processing	1962	110,000	24,000(1976)
	Isethebe				
	Mamry	Near Cape Town	1973	25,000	
	Mitchells Plain	21 km Cape Town. Local industry	1973	250,000	4000(1976)
	Newcastle/ Madadeni-Osizweni	Near Johannesburg. Industrial Steel Corporation	1972	635,000	102,000(1976)
	Pinelands	11 km Cape Town. Business centre	1923	12,000	12,000

Country	Town	Information	Designation date	Target population	Present population
South Africa	Richards Bay/ Ezikhaweni	Near Durban. Harbour industries	1971	350,000	
	Sasolburg	80 km Johannesburg. Petrol and chemicals	1951	30,000	22,000(1976)
	Stilfontein	Gold mining	1954	19,500	17,000 (1976)
	Tugela Basin Ulundi	Industrial town	1960		
	Vanderbij Park	Steel industries	1943	243,600	66,000(1976)
	Virginia	137 km Bloemfontein. Gold mining	1954	20,000	14,000(1976)
	Vredenburg Saldanha	160 km Cape Town	1974	1,000,000	24,000(1976)
	Welkom	150 km Bloemfontein	1948	80,000	34,000(1976)
	Westonaria	Gold mining	1938	75,000	28,000(1963)
	Witbank	Near Pretoria	1951		
South Yemen	Little Aden	Oil and other industries	1955		
Spain	El Encin	35 km Madrid	1970	150,000	
	La Cartuja	Near Seville	1970	100,000	
	Las Mercedes	9 km Madrid. Motor industry	1964	15,000	
	Martorell	Proposed new town for Barcelona	1970		
	Puente de Santiago	Near Zaragoza	1970	100,000	
	Riera de Caldas	25 km Barcelona	1970	120,000	
	Rio de San Pedro	25 km Cadiz	1970	150,000	
	Sabadell-Tarrasa	25 km Barcelona	1970	150,000	
	Tres Cantos	18 km Madrid	1975	150,000	Nil (1976)
Sweden	Angered-Bergum		1968	150,000	
	Boliden	Near Skelleftea. Mining			
	Gustavsberg	Near Stockholm. Ceramics	1940		
	Hasselby Strand	Proposed new town			
	Hogdalen			60,000	
	Kortadala	Satellite of Gothenberg	1959		
	Marsta	37 km Stockholm. Building and construction industries	1964	50,000	13,000(1976)
	Oxelosund	97 km Stockholm. Iron, glass, shipping	1959	25,000	6000(1967)
	Sharholmen			60,000	
	Stenungsund	49 km Gothenberg. Power, petrol, chemicals	1964	25,000	6000(1967)
	Taby			18,000	

Country	Town	Information	Designation date	Target population	Present population
Switzerland	Birrfeld	Near Baden	1957	40,000	9400(1967)
	Gland	Near Geneva	1969		
	Le Lignon	Near Geneva		10,000	
	Zürich	2 satellites proposed			
Tanzania	Dodoma	557 km Dar-es-Salaam. New capital city	1975		
	Kibaha	Regional headquarters of coastal region	1974		
	Muleba	Small scale industries	1975		
Taiwan	Linkou New Town	16 km Taipei. Various industries	1967	350,000	
Tunisia	Bizerta	Oil refining town	1961		
	El Borma	Oil refining town	1964		
	Katania		1950		
Uganda	Entebbe				8000(1960)
	Jinja	Hydro-electricity, textiles	1952	80,000	30,000(1962)
	Kampala	Commercial centre	1913		331,000(1976)
	Toror	Mining and cement			
USA	Ahwatukee (Arizona)			42,000	1350(1975)
	Allamuchy Township (New Jersey)			10,500	800(1975)
	Audobon (New York)			28,500	180(1975)
	Baldwin Hills (California)	Radburn-type community	1941	2500	completed
	Battery Park City (N.Y.)			45,000	Nil (1975)
	Beckett N.T. (New Jersey)			60,000	Nil (1975)
	Belcamp (Maryland)			12,000	Nil (1975)
	Blackberry Centre (Illinois)			22,000	Nil (1975)
	Boca del Mar (Florida)			15,000	Nil (1975)
	Butler Farms (Florida)			14,000	Nil (1975)
	Butterfield (Illinois)			26,729	579(1975)
	Calabasas Park (California)			9000	1800(1975)

Country	Town	Information	Designation date	Target population	Present population
USA	California City (California)		1957	720,000	2450(1975)
	Cameron Park (California)		1960	36,000	1500(1975)
	Candle Ridge (Texas)			13,300	Nil (1975)
	Canaveral (Florida)		1960	43,000	
	Cedar Riverside (Minneapolis)	New town-in-town	1968	25,000	4670(1975)
	Century Village	Planned new town	1975	24,000	Nil (1975)
	Christine (Florida)			11,000	400(1975)
	Churchill Estate (Maryland)			9000	285(1975)
	Clear Lake City (Texas)	Oil and other industries	1963	50,000	20,000(1975)
	Clinton Township (New Jersey)			12,275	Nil (1975)
	Colorado City (Colorado)	Near Pueblo	1960s	40,000	902(1975)
	Columbia (Maryland)	32 km Washington	1962	110,000	35,000(1975)
	Coral Springs (Florida)			130,000	18,000(1975)
	Countryside (Florida)			33,600	3400(1975)
	Deltona (Florida)	N.W. Cape Kennedy. 'Space' industry	1963	75,000	13,000(1975)
	Diamond Bar (California)		1960s	70,000	17,000(1975)
	El Dorado Hills (California)		1966	70,000	2200(1975)
	Elk Grove (Illinois)		1960s	65,000	26,000(1975)
	EPCOT (Florida)	Experimental prototype city of tomorrow		15,000	Nil (1975)
	Fairlane (Michigan)			15,000	1367(1975)
	Farmington (Georgia)			20,525	4496(1975)
	Florida Centre (Florida)			50,000	11,000(1975)
	Flower Mound (Texas)	Dallas satellite	1971	57,000	Nil (1975)

Country	Town	Information	Designation date	Target population	Present population
USA	Forest Park (Ohio)			23,000	14,000(1975)
	Fort Lincoln (Washington)	5 km Washington	1972	4600	Nil (1975)
	Foster City (California)	28 km San Francisco	1963	35,000	22,000(1975)
	Fountain Hills (Arizona)			70,000	2500(1975)
	Fox Valley East (Illinois)	Suburban area of Chicago		150,000	80,000(1975)
	Greenbelt (Maryland)		1937	30,000	8000(1962)
	Greenbier (Virginia)			25,000	Nil (1975)
	Greendale (Wisconsin)	6 km Milwaukee	1937	20,000	17,600(1965)
	Greenhills (Ohio)	9 km Cincinnati	1937	10,000	5400(1965)
	Green Run (Virginia)			24,917	12,459(1975)
	Green Valley (Arizona)			18,000	6000(1975)
	Gulf Stream Plantation (Florida)			33,000	Nil (1975)
	Harbison (S. Carolina)	Satellite		25,000	Nil (1975)
	Heartland (Illinois)			35,000	Nil (1975)
	Hawaii Kai (Hawaii)			65,000	25,000(1975)
	Highland Chase (California)	Suburb of Hollywood	1975	30,540	6200(1975)
	Horizon City (Texas)		1960s	100,000	2200(1975)
	Indian Lakes (Virginia)			16,898	1800(1975)
	Irvine Ranch (California)	64 km Los Angeles	1960	300,000	25,583(1975)
	Jonathan (Minnesota)	40 km Minneapolis. Light industry	1967	50,000	2200(1975)
	Joppatowne (Maryland)		1962	16,000	8387(1975)
	Kearny (Arizona)			6000	3300(1975)
	Kings Grant (New Jersey)			20,000	60(1975)

Country	Town	Information	Designation date	Target population	Present population
USA	Kingwood (Texas)			90,000	3200(1975)
	Laguna Hills (California)	Leisure world		25,000	18,000(1975)
	Laguna Niguel (California)	81 km Los Angeles	1972	37,500	13,500(1975)
	Lake Havasu City (Arizona)	247 km Las Vegas. Dam, industrial	1963	50,000	10,000(1975)
	Lake San Marcos (California)			6000	2000(1975)
	Lake St Louis (Missouri)			20,000	2687(1975)
	Lehigh Acres (Florida)		1956	30,000	13,500(1975)
	Liberty Harbour			60,000	Nil (1975)
	Litchfield Park (Arizona)	Various industries	1965	75,000–100,000	3053(1975)
	Lynwood (Illinois)			12,000	1000(1975)
	Madison Township (New Jersey)			17,500	Nil (1975)
	Maili-Kai (Hawaii)			20,000	7000(1975)
	Marco Island (Florida)			34,000	7000(1975)
	Marion Oaks (Florida)			60,000	140(1975)
	Maumelle (Arkansas)	Satellite	1968	60,000	15(1975)
	McCormick Ranch (Arizona)			45,000	1200(1975)
	Miami Lakes (Florida)		1960s	25,000	12,000(1975)
	Mililani Town (Hawaii)			65,000	12,000(1975
	Mission Viego (California)	80 km Los Angeles. Industrial	1960s	80,000	11,000(1970
	Montbello (Colorado)	Adjacent Denver	1966	49,400	17,970(1975
	Montgomery Village (Maryland)		1960s	30,000	15,000(1975
	Mountain Park (Oregon)		1960s	12,000	6800(197
	New Century Town (Illinois)			18,000	12(197

Country	Town	Information	Designation date	Target population	Present population
USA	Northglen (Colorado)		1960s	50,000	35,000(1975)
	Northampton (Maryland)			58,600	6944(1975)
	Oak Openings (Ohio)			50,000	3000(1975)
	Oak Ridge (Tennessee)	Atomic energy	1947	50,000	29,700(1967)
	Orangewood (Florida)			48,500	Nil (1975)
	Oriole-Oakland (Florida)			52,675	12(1975)
	Palm Beach Gardens (Florida)	Electronics	1960	24,500	9331(1975)
	Palm Beach Lakes (Florida)			27,500	1500(1975)
	Palm Coast (Florida)			500,000	1000(1975)
	Park Forest South (Illinois)	Satellite of Chicago	1947	110,000	49,280(1975)
	Pine Island Ridge (Colorado)	Planned new town	1975	15,800	800(1975)
	Plaza del Oro (Texas)			50,000	Nil (1975)
	Port Charlotte (Florida)		1960s	75,000	25,000(1975)
	Port Malabar (Florida)			200,000	7500(1975)
	Port St Lucie (Florida)		1958	220,000	9500(1975)
	Porter Ranch (California)		1960s	32,904	12,355(1975)
	Preston Meadows N. (Texas)			25,000	Nil (1975)
	Prestwick (Indiana)			10,000	Nil (1975)
	Radburn (New Jersey)	Planned community	1928	25,000	
	Radisson (New York)			18,000	10(1975)
	Rancho San Bernado (California)	Petroleum	1963	32,000	26,256(1975)
	Rancho Mission (California)			91,150	30,458(1975)
	Rancho San Diego (California)			15,500	Nil (1975)

Country	Town	Information	Designation date	Target population	Present population
USA	Redwood Shores (California)			17,000	1500(1975)
	Reston (Virginia)	32 km Washington	1963	75,000	23,000(1975)
	Rio Communities (New Mexico)			30,000	2000(1975)
	Rio Rancho Estate (New Mexico)			14,000	5500(1975)
	Rio Verde (Arizona)			8000	120(1975)
	Riverchase (Alabama)			12,000	Nil (1975)
	Riverton (New York)	Satellite of New York	1972	20,000	1000(1975)
	Roosevelt Island (New York)			19,000	Nil (1975)
	Rosement (Virginia)			13,775	Nil (1975)
	Rossmore (California)	Leisure world and Retirement centre	1960s	26,000	17,300(1975)
	St Charles (Maryland)		1970	80,000	7000(1975)
	San Antonio Ranch (Texas)	Satellite	1972	88,000	Nil (1975)
	San Diego California)	New university city	1962	100,000	10,000(1967)
	San Marin (California)			24,000	5680(1975)
	San Ramon Village (California)	Industrial	1969	16,000	14,900(1975)
	Sea Pines Plantation (S. Carolina)			13,000	1500(1975)
	Shenandoah (Georgia)			69,000	Nil (1975)
	Silver Spring Shores (Florida)			105,000	2400(1975)
	Somerset West (Oregon)		1960s	30,000	4500(1975)
	Soul City (N. Carolina)	20% industrial	1972	44,000	100(1975)
	Spring Hill (Florida)		1967	70,000	6000(1975)
	Spring Lake (Florida)		1960s	20,000	350(1975)
	Stansbury (Utah)			40,000	200(1975)

Country	Town	Information	Designation date	Target population	Present population
USA	Sun City (Arizona)			50,000	34,122(1975)
	Sun City Centre (Florida)		1960	100,000	6000(1975)
	Sun Lake Estates (Florida)			45,000	Nil (1975)
	Sunnyside (New York)	Pioneer garden suburb	1924	5000	
	Sun River (Oregon)			25,000	360(1975)
	The Colony (Texas)			57,000	Nil (1975)
	Timber Lake (Tennessee)			250,000	Nil (1975)
	Timber Lake (Virginia)			11,055	337(1975)
	Valencia (California)	48 km Los Angeles	1966	30,000	10,000(1975)
	Wailea (Hawaii)			50,000	
	Waipo (Hawaii)			16,000	400(1975)
	Waikaloa (Hawaii)			30,000	400(1975)
	Waterwood (Texas)			250,000	50(1975)
	Westlake Village (California)		1966	200,000	70,000(1975)
	West Lakeland Venture (Florida)			14,800	Nil (1975)
	Wilkshire Hills (Ohio)		1967	15,000	957(1975)
	Windsor Oaks (Virginia)			10,049	2750(1975)
	Woodlands (Texas)	48 km Houston. Satellite	1972	97,871	22,000(1975)
USSR	There are 1000–2000 new towns in USSR, 400 of which are free-standing. The most important are:				
	Amalyk (Uzbekistan)	Metallurgy industries			41,900(1959)
	Al'met'yevsk (Tatar)	Oil	1950		49,000(1959)
	Angarsk (W. Siberia)	Chemicals and oil	1949		204,000(1970)

Country	Town	Information	Designation date	Target population	Present population
USSR	Apatity (N.W. Region)	Administrative centre			134,000(1967)
	Belovo (W. Siberia)	Coal mining			116,000(1967)
	Berezniki (Urals)	Chemicals			134,000(1967)
	Bratsk (E. Siberia)	Hydro-electricity			122,000(1967)
	Chervonograd (S.W. Region)				
	Dudinka (Krasnoyarsk)	Port town on River Yenesei	1951		16,400(1959)
	Dushanbe (Tadzhikistan)	Capital of Tadzhikistan	1930		33,000(1967)
	Dzerzhinsk (Gorky)	Chemicals			201,000(1967)
	Dzherzhinsk (Ukraine)	Mining and coke			45,000(1959)
	Eletrostal (Moscow Region)	Satellite	1938		204,000(1970)
	Igren' (S.W. Region)	Miscellaneous industries			
	Kapchagay (Kazakhstan)	Electricity			
	Karaganda (Kazakhstan)	Iron ore, coal	1934		565,000(1975)
	Karazhal (Kazakhstan)	Mining			
	Kemerova (W. Siberia)	Engineering, chemicals, food, coal	1918		364,000(1967)
	Kirovsk (Murmansk)	Mining			38,400(1959)
	Kiskniev (Moldavia)	Construction			452,000(1975)
	Kohtle Yarve (Estonia)	Shale mining			29,200(1959)
	Komsomol'sk na Amure (Far East)	Steel and iron	1932		209,000(1963)
	Krovoyrog (Ukraine)	Iron ore	1926		628,000(1975)
	Magnitogorsk (Urals)	Iron and steel engineering	1929		357,000(1967)
	Mingechaur (Azerbaidjan)	Power, engineering	1946		33,000(1959)
	Molodgvardeysk (Donets)	Mining			

Country	Town	Information	Designation date	Target population	Present population
USSR	Naftalan (S. Central Region)	Resort centre			
	Noril'sk (Siberia)	Mining and smelting, rare metals	1953		129,000(1967)
	Novayakakahovka (Ukraine)	Hydro-electricity	1951		19,000(1959)
	Novokuykbyshevsk (Urals)	Oil refining	1952		107,000(1967)
	Novokuznetsk (W. Siberia)	Manufacturing, coal	1931		525,000(1975)
	Novomoskovsk (Donbas)	Lignite mining, chemicals	1931		126,000(1967)
	Novopolotsk (S.W. Region)	Chemicals and oil			80,000(1970)
	Novoshakhtinsk (Donbas)	Coal (Donbas Field)			107,000(1967)
	Novotroitsk (Urals)	'Green belt town'. Iron, steel and building materials	1940		64,000(1970)
	Novovolynsk (Ukraine)	Coal mining, building materials			60,000(1970)
	Nuvringry (Yakutia)	Coal mining	1975		20,000(1976)
	Oktyabrsk (Volga)	Port, building materials	1956		33,800(1959)
	Oktjabrskiy (Bashkiria)	Engineering	1946		68,000(1961)
	Orsk (Urals)	Oil			215,000(1967)
	Propop'yesk (W. Siberia)	Coal			290,000(1975)
	Rustavi (Georgia)	Satellite of Tbilisi	1948		70,000(1961)
	Salavat (Bashkiria)	Petrochemicals	1949		68,000(1961)
	Stavropol (Kuibyshev)	Port, engineering	1955		158,000(1963)
	Sumgait (Azerbaydzhan)	Manufacturing, steel	1939		104,000(1967)
	Tayshet (Irkutsk)	Major steel centre			226,000(1967)
	Temirtau (Kazakhstan)	Manufacturing, steel	1945		150,000(1967)
	Togliatti (Urals)	Hydro-electricity, Automobiles			500,000(1975)
	Volzhskiy (Urals)	Near Volgograd. Electricity			114,000(1967)

Country	Town	Information	Designation date	Target population	Present population
USSR	Vorkuta	241 km north of Arctic Circle. Coal mining	1947		59,000(1961)
	Zaporozhye (Ukraine)	Hydro-electricity	1928		744,000(1975)
	Zelenograd (Central Region)	Scientific centre			127,000(1970)
	Zhukovsky	Moscow region	1956		42,300(1959)
Venezuela	Ciudad Guayana	Heavy industry	1951	500,000	400,000(1975)
	Ciudad Losada	64 km Caracas	1967	400,000	21,000(1972)
	El Tablazo	32 km Maracaibo	1968	300,000	11,000(1972)
Yugoslavia	Banja Laka	Rebuilding of old settlement after earthquake	1969		
	Novi Beograd	Extension of capital	1950	200,000	120,000(1972)
	Novi Tavnik	Mining			
	Ploce	New seaport on Adriatic	1954		
	Skopje	Reconstruction of city after earthquake	1965	350,000	
	Velenje	Coal mining	1955	30,000	
Zambia	Kafue	50 km Lusaka. Textile mills	1967	100,000	20,000(1970)
	Lusaka	Capital	1931		480,000(1976)

Urban development in Zambia is an entirely twentieth century phenomenon. Lusaka and copperbelt towns such as Kitwe, Ndola, Mufulira, Luanshya and Chingola account for 90% of urban population and were all established after 1900.

Appendix 3: Selected Bibliography

The literature of New Towns has in recent years become voluminous. Many of the publications and articles in journals deal with single foundations and projects. The following brief selection is intended as an aid to study of the British experience and its more or less direct influences.

ABERCROMBIE, PATRICK: *Greater London Plan, 1944*. London, 1945. Historically important as first metropolitan plan to work out definite policy of decongestion, renewal and dispersal to new towns.

ARMYTAGE, W. H. G.: *Heavens Below: Utopian Experiments in Britain 1560–1960*. London, 1961. Rich collection of theoretical ideals and projects for action.

ASH, MAURICE: *Regions of Tomorrow: Towards the Open City*. Bath, 1969.

A Guide to the Structure of London. Bath, 1971.

'BARLOW REPORT': *Report and Minutes of Evidence*. Royal Commission on Distribution of Industrial Population. HMSO, London, 1940. Massive assembly of facts on urban concentration. Report proved decisive turning point in British planning policy.

BERESFORD, M.: *New Towns of the Middle Ages*. London, 1967. Brilliant historical study.

BEST, ROBIN H.: *Land for New Towns. A study of land use, densities, and agricultural displacements*. TCPA, London, 1964.

BEST, ROBIN H. and COPPOCK, J. T.: *The Changing Use of Land in Britain*. London, 1962. Expert assessment of amount of land used and likely to be used for urban, agricultural and other purposes.

BIDSTRUP, KNUT: *Ebenezer's Disciple*. Copenhagen, 1971 (Danish text). Claims Howard's influence on Danish planning.

BLOCK, G. D. H.: *The Spread of Towns*. Conservative Research Department, London, 1954.

BUDER, STANLEY: Ebenezer Howard: 'Genesis of the Town Planning Movement', *Journal of American Institute of Planners, November, 1969*.

CENTRE DE RECHERCHE D'URBANISME: *Espace et Loisir dans la Sociéte Française*. Paris, 1967.

Grands Ensembles: Banlieus Nouvelles. Paris, 1967.

Les Pavillonnaires: L'Habitat Pavillonnaire: La Politique Pavillonnaire (3 vols.) Paris, 1966. French text. Illuminating research studies.

CHERRY, G. E.: *Evolution of British Town Planning*. London, 1974.

CONSERVATIVE POLITICAL CENTRE: *Change and Challenge: Next Steps in Town and Country Planning*. London, 1962.

CRANE, JACOB L.: *Urban planning: Illusion and Reality: a New Philosophy for Planned City Building*. New York, 1973.

CREESE, W. L.: *The Search for Environment: The Garden City Movement Before and After*. New Haven, 1966.

CULLINGWORTH, J. D.: *Town and Country Planning In England and Wales*. London, 1964. First-class account of recent developments in legislation, policy and administration, with some controversial views.

CULLINGWORTH, J. D. and KAM, V. A.: *Ownership and Management of Housing in the New Towns*, London, 1968.

Environmental Planning 1939–1969: Vol. 1. Reconstruction and Land use planning: Vol. 2. National Parks and recreation in the countryside. Both 1975. *Vol. 3. New Towns 1977; Vol. 4. Compensation and Betterment 1978.* London, H.M.S.O. These are official histories and give accounts of the part played by government, government departments, and official committees in shaping planning policy and devising its machinery.

DOXIADIS, CONSTANTINE A.: *Confessions of a Criminal.* Athens Centre of Ekistics, 1971.

DUFF, A. C.: *Britain's New Towns: An Experiment in Living.* London, 1961. Brief realistic outline by a former general manager of Stevenage.

ENCYCLOPAEDIA OF URBAN PLANNING. See Whittick, Arnold.

ENVIRONMENT, DEPARTMENT OF (DOE): *Relationship between New Town Master Plans and Structure and Local Plans.* Circular 7/74. HMSO 1974. Guidance to planning authorities whose aims include or will include new towns.

EVANS, HAZEL (Ed.): *New Towns: the British Experience,* TCPA, London, 1972. Informative collection of essays on main aspects, with good select bibliography.

GOLANY, GIDEON: *New Towns Planning and Development: A World-wide Bibliography.* Urban Land Institute, USA, 1973 (4551 entries).

New Town Planning: Principles and Practice. New York, 1976.

GOLANY, GIDEON and WALDEN, DANIEL (Eds.): *The Contemporary New Communities Movement in the United States.* University of Illinois Press, Urban, 1974.

HOWARD, EBENEZER: *Garden Cities of Tomorrow.* London, 1898. Definitive edition, 1946, with editorial preface by F. J. Osborn and introductory essay by Lewis Mumford. Paperback edition, 1965. Translations published in French, German, Japanese and Spanish.

INTERNATIONAL CITY MANAGERS' ASSOCIATION: *New Towns: A New Dimension of Urbanism.* Chicago, 1966

INTERNATIONAL FEDERATION FOR HOUSING AND PLANNING: *Report of Jubilee Congress,* Arnhem, 1963. The Hague, 1964.

LUBOVE, ROY: *Community Planning in the 1920's.* Pittsburgh, 1963. Excellent historical study of the advocacy of Clarence Stein, Lewis Mumford and others in the Regional Association of America.

McALLISTER, G. and E.: *Town and Country Planning,* London, 1941.

MACFADYEN, D.: *Sir Ebenezer Howard and the Garden City Movement,* Manchester, 1933, 1972. A biography of the founder of the movement.

MANDELKER, D. R.: *Green Belts and Urban Growth.* Madison, Wis., 1962.

MARKELIN, ANTERO, and TRIEB, MICHAEL (Ed.): *'Mensch und Stadtgestalt'* with contributions by Gerd Albers, David Cantier, Enrique Ciriani, Michael Corajoud, Gordon Cullen, Marc Emery, Christian Farenholtz, Joachim Franke, Hermann Henselmann, Borja Huidobro, Derk de Jonge, Kevin Lynch, Artero Markelin, Thomas Sieverts, Michael Southworth, Susan Southworth, Michael Trieb, Arnold Whittick and Gary Winkel. Stuttgart 1970.

MATTHEW, SIR ROBERT: *Belfast Regional Survey and Plan.* Government of Northern Ireland, 1962. Proposal for limitation of Belfast and expansion of smaller towns.

MAYER, ALBERT: *The Urgent Future.* New York, 1967. Brilliantly argued and magnificently illustrated statement of case for urban renewal, regional planning and new towns.

MERLIN, PIERRE: *Les Villes Nouvelles,* Paris, 1969. English translation with title, *New Towns,* London 1971. Covers new towns in Britain Scandinavia, Netherlands, France, Poland, Hungary and USA.

MIDLOTHIAN AND W. LOTHIAN PLANNING ADVISORY COMMITTEE: *The Lothian Regional Survey and Plan,* Edinburgh, 1966.

MINISTRY OF HOUSING (G.B.): *The Green Belts,* HMSO, 1962.

The South East Study, 1961–1980, HMSO, 1964.

MINISTRY OF HOUSING AND LOCAL GOVERNMENT: *Bibliography,* No. 65: *New Towns in Great Britain.* London. Kept up to date.

MITCHELL, ELIZABETH: *The Plan that Pleased*. TCPA, London, 1967. Delightful personal record of successful movement for new towns in Scotland.

MUINDROIT, C.: *Villes et Campagnes Britanniques*, Paris, 1967.

MUMFORD, LEWIS: *The Culture of Cities*. New York, 1938. Profound historical survey, containing first academic recognition of importance of Howard's garden city concept. Of world-wide influence.

The City in History. New York, 1961. Carries further historical analysis and philosophic study of urban development from beginnings to modern times. Again endorses Howard's thesis.

The Pentagon of Power. New York, 1972.

MUMFORD, LEWIS and OSBORN, F. J.: *The Letters of Lewis Mumford and Frederic J. Osborn: A Transatlantic Dialogue 1938–1970*. M. R. Hughes (Ed.) Bath, 1971.

NEWMAN, OSCAR: *Defensible Space: Crime Prevention through Urban Design*. USA, 1973. Condemnation of high-rise housing as conducive to crime.

NEW TOWNS, COMMISSION FOR: Reports (annual) for towns taken over, with financial accounts, 1965 to date. HMSO, London.

NEW TOWNS COMMITTEE ('Reith Committee'): *First and Second Interim Reports and Final Report*. London 1946. Compact prescriptions for every aspect of new town construction and organization.

NEW TOWNS DEVELOPMENT CORPORATIONS: Brochures. Most of the corporations publish short illustrated descriptions of their towns.

NORTH-WEST ECONOMIC PLANNING COUNCIL: *Social Planning in New Communities*. 1971.

OSBORN, F. J.: *New Towns After the War*. London, 1918 and 1942. Short restatement of Garden City concept as realized at Letchworth and Welwyn, and argument for national New Towns policy.

Green-Belt Cities. The British Contribution. London 1946. Revaluation of garden city movement, study of experience at Letchworth and Welwyn, and proposals for national policy. New edition, 1969.

'Ebenezer Howard: The Evolution of His Ideas', Town Planning Review. October, 1950. Brief biographical study with personal assessment of character and work.

Bigger Cities or More Cities? Address at IFHP Conference, 1963. (see I.F.H.P.)

Genesis of Welwyn Garden City. TCPA, London, 1970.

PERLOFF, HARVEY S. and SANDBERG, NEIL C.: *New Towns: Why – And for Whom*. New York and London, 1973.

PURDOM, C. B.: *The Building of Satellite Towns*. London 1925 and 1949. Well-documented record of foundation and early development of Letchworth and Welwyn Garden City.

RIBOUD, JACQUES: *Developpement Urbain: Recherche d'un Principe*. Paris, 1965. French text. Well-argued case for regional complexes of new towns in France.

ROBINSON, ALBERT J.: *Economics and New Towns: a Comparative Study of the United States, the United Kingdom, and Australia*. New York, 1975.

ROSNER, R.: *Neue Stadte in England*. Munich, 1962. German text.

SCHAFFER, FRANK: *The New Town Story*. TCPA, London, 1970. Indispensable. A balanced record.

SEELEY, IVOR. H.: *Planned Expansion of Country Towns*. 1968. Practical treatment of problems involved.

SELF, PETER: *Cities in Flood*. London, 1957 and 1961. Excellent study of metropolitan problems and practical possibilities of corrective national policy.

The New Towns Principle and the Urban Region. Berkeley, USA, 1963.

SENIOR, DEREK. (Ed.): *The Regional City: an Anglo-American discussion of Metropolitan Planning*. London, 1967.

SOUTH EAST JOINT PLANNING TEAM: *Strategic Plan for the South East*. HMSO, 1970.

SOUTH EAST REGIONAL ECONOMIC PLANNING COUNCIL: *A Strategy for the South East*. HMSO, 1967.

STEIN, CLARENCE: *Toward New Towns for America*. Liverpool, 1951 and Cambridge, Mass., 1966. Fully illustrated and documented account of Radburn and Greenbelt Towns.

STONE, P. A.: *Housing, Town Development, Land and Costs*. London, 1963. Expert analysis of costs of the alternative of high-density central city housing and partial dispersal to smaller towns.

SUSSMAN, CARL: Planning *the Fourth Migration: The Neglected Vision of the Regional Plane Association of America.*, M.I.T. Press, Boston, 1976.

THOMAS, RAY: *London's New Towns: Self-contained and Balconied Communities*. London, 1969.

Aycliffe to Cumbernauld: Seven New Towns in their Regions, London, 1969.

THOMAS, RAY and CRESSWELL, PETER: *The New Town Idea*. Unit 26 of the Social Sciences Course, Open University, 1973.

TOWN AND COUNTRY PLANNING (monthly journal): New Towns Issues each January up to 1974 and then each February 1975, 76, 77. Specially useful issues: January, 1968: *New Towns Come of Age*, and January, 1974.

TOWN AND COUNTRY PLANNING ASSOCIATION:
London under Stress. TCPA, 1970.

Region in Crisis: Study of Greater London Development Plan. London, 1971.

The New Citizen's Guide to Town and Country Planning. London, 1974. First-class description of the British system, including reorganization of local government and central ministries.

The British New Towns Programme. Evidence to House of Commons Committee dealing freshly with aims and methods. Published in *Town and Country Planning*, January, 1974.

TOWNROE, P.: *Planning Industrial Location*. London, 1976.

UNITED NATIONS: *Human Settlements* (quarterly). New York, 1921 to date. Important reports of seminars on environment.

Planning of Metropolitan Areas and New Towns. New York, 1967. Reports of Symposia of Experts at Stockholm 1961 and Moscow 1964.

UNWIN, RAYMOND: *Town Planning in Practice*. London, 1920 and 1932. Classic study of town-form; visual and social considerations brilliantly integrated. Vastly influential.

URBAN AMERICA INC.: *New Communities*. New York, 1971. Able essays by advocates of new towns.

VIET-JEAN: *Les Villes Nouvelles (New Towns): a Selected Annotated Bibliography* (in French and English). Unesco, 1960. List of 790 books and articles in many countries. Now needs supplementation but of great value. Admirable foreword by Dame Evelyn (Lady) Sharp, then Permanent Secretary of Ministry of Housing and Local Government, concludes: 'The new towns have been a great experiment and are on their way to being a great success. Mistakes have been made and there are many problems still to resolve. But for thousands of families they are providing living conditions among the best in Britain; and for industry they are providing the conditions for efficiency. They will prove a first class investment, in money as well as in health and productivity. They will repay study'.

WIBBERLEY, G. P.: *Agriculture and Urban Growth*. London, 1960. Able and balanced study by Professor of Agriculture well informed about town planning.

WHITTICK, ARNOLD (Ed.): *Encyclopaedia of Urban Planning*. New York and London, 1974.

European Architecture in the Twentieth Century, London, 1974. Includes chapters on new towns and communities.

Index